THE LONGMAN STANDARD HISTORY OF TWENTIETH-CENTURY PHILOSOPHY

D0073825

THE LONGMAN STANDARD HISTORY OF TWENTIETH-CENTURY PHILOSOPHY

DANIEL KOLAK

William Paterson University of New Jersey

GARRETT THOMSON

College of Wooster

PEARSON

Longman

New York   San Francisco   Boston
London   Toronto   Sydney   Tokyo   Singapore   Madrid
Mexico City   Munich   Paris   Cape Town   Hong Kong   Montreal

Publisher: Priscilla McGeehon
Executive Marketing Manager: Ann Stypuloski
Media and Supplements Editor: Kristi Olson
Production Manager: Denise Phillip
Project Coordination, Text Design, and Electronic Page Makeup: WestWords, Inc.
Senior Cover Designer/Manager: Nancy Danahy
Cover Photo: © Getty Inc./The Image Bank. Truck Crossing the Talmadge Bridge,
    Savannah, Georgia, USA. Photographer: Alexandra Michaels
Senior Manufacturing Buyer: Dennis J. Para
Printer and Binder: Courier Corporation
Cover Printer: Courier Corporation

Library of Congress Cataloging-in-Publication Data

Kolak, Daniel.
  The Longman standard history of philosophy / Daniel Kolak, Garrett Thomson.
      p. cm.
  Includes bibliographical references and index.
   ISBN 0-321-23511-8 (volume 6 (comprehensive) : alk. paper)—ISBN 0-321-23513-4
(volume 1 (ancient) : alk. paper)—ISBN 0-321-23512-6 (volume 3 (modern) : alk. paper)—
ISBN 0-321-23510-X (volume 5 (20th century) : alk. paper)
   1. Philosophy—History. I. Title: Standard history of philosophy. II. Thomson, Garrett. III. Title.
  B72.K635 2006
  190—dc22
                                                        2005010370

Please visit our website at http://www.ablongman.com

ISBN 0-321-23510-X

1 2 3 4 5 6 7 8 9 10—CRS—08 07 06 05

◆ CONTENTS ◆

PREFACE

Philosophy may not be the oldest profession but it is the oldest discipline, the source of our views about reality, knowledge, and morality. To understand the revolutionary nature of the evolution of philosophy is to understand ourselves and our world anew. Inspired by the intellectual intimacy that philosophy affords, the mind is broadened and refreshed. In that sense philosophy is always anything but old: awash with new possibilities of inquiry and understanding, the illuminating questions of philosophy liberate us from the blinding obviousness of accepted answers, the blinders of our individual and collective biases.

Though philosophers build upon the work of their predecessors, they continually revise and often overthrow the views of their predecessors—sometimes, even those of their own teachers. One of the most famous examples is the sequence from Socrates to Plato to Aristotle. And yet throughout the evolution of thought that philosophy heralds much remains the same: the call to wonder, to dispute, to question, to liberate, to ponder, to inquire, to understand everything one can about the whole of our being—reality, knowledge, and morality—without becoming ourselves closed off. To behold the whole without being conquered by the wholeness of the vision, that is the sum and substance of the western intellectual tradition made possible by philosophy.

To see new wisdom in the old and old wisdom in the new is to be not just learned but wise. And to not just tolerate such expansive openness but to love it now and then is what it means to be a philosopher, then and now. This book may not make you a philosopher. But it will provide you with everything you need to become one. A big claim and, therefore, a big book: with 28 of the greatest works by 23 of the most important western philosophers of the twentieth century, this volume assembles into one book some of the most profound and edifying ideas in the history of human thought. In addition to the classics of analytical philosophy, this volume contains some of the major works continental thinkers such as those of Husserl, Heidegger, Sartre, Habermas, Foucault and Derrida. It also includes two selections from more recent North American thinkers, Richard Rorty and Charles Taylor.

Suitable for a one-semester introduction to contemporary philosophy, or the history of twentieth century philosophy, this book is a covert assembly with a covert purpose, to bring philosophy to you but even more importantly: to bring you to philosophy.

We have structured the book to make this possible. The volume as a whole is divided into 8 standard divisions: "Part I, the Logical Atomists," "Part II, the Pragmatists," "Part III, the Logical Positivists," "Part IV, the Ordinary Language Philosophers," "Part V, Analytic Philosophers," "Part VI, Phenomenology and Existentialism," "Part VII, Hermeneutics and Post-Modernism," and "Part VIII, Recent North American Thinkers."

Each Part opens with a "Prologue", offering a context for specific philosophers, such as "Prologue to Putnam," or to key schools of thought, such as "Prologue to Existentialism." These are designed to let you in on what has come before, so that you don't enter the conversation in the middle. Individual "Biographical Histories" give pertinent details about the life and times of each philosopher, such as "Russell: A Biographical History." The purpose is to show you that philosophers are neither divine demigods nor depersonalized thinking machines but individual human beings with a penchant for grappling with the perennial big questions. The purpose of the "Philosophical Overviews" to each philosopher is two-fold: first, to show how that philosopher's thinking about reality, knowledge and morality integrate into a coherent view; second, to integrate each particular philosopher into a broader philosophical context.

Each reading selection comes with its own concise introduction designed to quicken your entry into the issues and prepare you for what is to come. The selections themselves have been chosen for their profundity and edited to highlight the central importance, while leaving in the all-important methods, processes, and development of the views expressed therein. Where translations are involved, we have in each case selected the most lucid. The "Study Questions" at the end of each chapter, such as "Study Questions for Wittgenstein's Philosophical Investigations," provide comprehension questions as well as wider discussion questions; these are for you, to test yourself, to see how well you have understood what you have read. "The Philosophical Bridges" at the end of each chapter, such as "The Influence of Russell," summarizes the influence of each thinker on later generations in order that you can appreciate the threads connecting different philosophers and see how philosophy's perennial questions lead to ever more evolving views.

Special thanks to each of the following reviewers, whose comments about one or more of the volumes in the "Longman Standard History of Philosophy" series helped to enhance each book.

Michael L. Anderson, University of Maryland
Marina P. Banchetti-Robino, Florida Atlantic University
David Boersema, Pacific University
Stephen Braude, University of Maryland Baltimore County
Cynthia K. Brown, Catholic University of America
Richard J. Burke, Oakland University
Marina Bykova, North Carolina State University
Jeffrey Carr, Christopher Newport University
James P. Cooney, Montgomery County Community College
Elmer H. Duncan, Baylor University
Christian Early, Eastern Mennonite University
Emma L. Easteppe, Boise State University
James E. Falcouner, Brigham Young University
Chris L. Firestone, Trinity International University
Merigala Gabriel, Georgia Southern University
Bruce Hauptli, Florida International University
Larry Hauser, Alma College
David J. Hilditch, Webster University
Mary Beth Ingham, Loyola Marymount University
Betty Kiehl, Palomar College
John H. Kulten, Jr., University of Missouri

Nelson P. Lande, University of Massachusetts
Dorothea Lotter, Wake Forest University
Charles S. MacKenzie, Reformed Theological Seminary
Thomas J. Martin, University of North Carolina Charlotte
D. A. Masolo, University of Louisville
Leemon B. McHenry, California State University, Northridge
John T. Meadors, Mississippi College
Glenn Melancon, Southeastern Oklahoma State University
Mark Michael, Austin Peay State University
Thomas Osborne, University of Nevada, Las Vegas
Walter Ott, East Tennessee State University
Anna Christina Ribeiro, University of Maryland
Stefanie Rocknak, Hartwick College
George Rudebusch, Northern Arizona University
Ari Santas, Valdosta State University
Candice Shelby, University of Colorado-Denver
Daniel Silber, Florida Southern College
Allan Silverman, Ohio State University
James K. Swindler, Illinois State University
David B. Twetten, Marquette University
Thomas Upton, Gannon University
Barry F. Vaughan, Mesa Community College
Daniel R. White, Florida Atlantic University
David M. Wisdo, Columbus State University
Evelyn Wortsman Deluty, Nassau Community College

We would like to thank the following people for their help. Brandon West of the College of Wooster for his sterling work as a student research assistant. Amy Erickson and Patrice Reeder of the College of Wooster for their unfailing secretarial help. Professors Martin Gunderson, Ron Hustwit, Henry Kreuzman, Adrian Moore, Elizabeth Schiltz, and Philip Turetzsky for their useful comments. Everyone at Longman Publishers for their very professional work, especially Priscilla McGeehon, who has supported the project with tireless energy and enthusiasm. Our wives, Wendy and Helena, for their help and understanding. Finally, we would like to dedicate this volume to our children: Julia, Sophia, Dylan, and Andre Kolak; and to Andrew, Frances, Verena, Susana, and Robert Thomson.

GENERAL INTRODUCTION

During the twentieth century, there were many rapid worldwide social, political, and cultural changes. The century saw two world wars, the rise and fall of Fascism and Communism, as well as the beginning of the end of colonialism, and cultural and economic globalization. It was a time of tremendous technological advances, population growth, and many new social problems. Similarly, during this period, humanity's understanding of itself and the world went through some dramatic developments. This was the century of quantum physics, relativity, molecular biology, chaos theory, and computer science. In the human sciences, the twentieth century saw Sigmund Freud, Jean Piaget, Noam Chomsky, behaviorism, structuralism, and cognitive science. In similar ways, philosophy changed dramatically in the last century.

The story of twentieth century philosophy is in part a tale of the development of two apparently conflicting types of philosophy, the analytic and the continental traditions. In the analytic tradition, there are thinkers such as Bertrand Russell, Ludwig Wittgenstein, the logical positivists, W. V. O. Quine, and Donald Davidson, who have tended to focus on the analysis of language. In the continental tradition, there are thinkers such as Edmund Husserl, Martin Heidegger, Jean-Paul Sartre, Jürgen Habermas, and Michel Foucault, who have tended to study questions related to the human condition and politics. There are many differences of substance, style, and emphasis between the two traditions. However, toward the end of the century, the distinction between the two traditions became blurred to some extent. Analytic philosophers became more interested in social issues and in existential questions. Continental philosophers became more explicitly interested in language and interpretation. Furthermore, there was much more cross-fertilization between the two traditions. So, the twentieth century is in part a story of divergence and, later, convergence.

Another important change in later twentieth-century philosophy is the broadening of philosophical studies. For example, in analytic philosophy, there are thinkers working in diverse areas such as the philosophy of biology, of physics, of law, of economics, and of cognitive science. Analytic philosophy deals with more than just the traditional ethical, metaphysical, and epistemological problems that were the main concerns of previous centuries. As a result, there is also increased specialization and fragmentation.

In addition, philosophers from both traditions have opened their doors to other disciplines and to sociopolitical problems. As a consequence, there are more thinkers working outside and against what might have earlier been considered 'mainstream' philosophy.

1

For example, there are many different kinds of feminist philosophers trying to construct new feminist approaches to all areas of knowledge and society. There are thinkers inspired by an ecological vision of humanity and the world. There are also more philosophers concerned with cross-cultural approaches to philosophy and the philosophies of the different parts of the world, rather than being limited to only Western thought. Note that all the philosophers represented in this volume come from North America, Britain, France, and the countries of central Europe, such as Germany and Austria. For all the reasons cited above, we can no longer contrast analytic and continental philosophy as if this were a mutually exclusive and exhaustive categorization. As a consequence of all this, it is much harder to have a broad overview of the discipline as a whole, and in some ways, philosophy is no longer a single discipline in the way that it was at the beginning of the twentieth century.

General labels, such as 'postmodernism' and 'ordinary language philosophy,' are powerful simplifying tools, useful for a book such as this. They can help us see quickly some similarities between philosophers. At the same time, however, they can mask other similarities and differences. They can prevent us also from approaching the work of each thinker individually and with a fresh outlook. Having said that, we now need to give the briefest and most general overview possible of twentieth century philosophy, leaving the more detailed expositions of each thinker for the Prologues and Philosophical Overviews.

Frege and Husserl

Continental and analytic philosophy both had their sources in the Germany of 1900. Gottlob Frege was a major inspiration of much of the analytic tradition, and Husserl of the continental tradition. Frege, whose work is excerpted in Volume IV, was interested in the philosophy of logic, mathematics, and language, and his work inspired a broadly scientific approach to language and mental states. In contrast, Husserl developed phenomenology, an approach to experience that opposed the encroachment of the natural sciences in the understanding of consciousness. Despite the differences between them, Frege and Husserl, who corresponded with each other, have some views in common. For example, both insist on a distinction between the content of thought and the psychological process of thinking. They separate what thought is about, i.e., its reference, and its content, or sense.

Frege's Legacy

Frege's distinction between sense and reference introduces issues that are important for much analytic philosophy during the twentieth century. We can begin to appreciate why by comparing two groups of technical notions. On the one hand, there are extensional notions, such as 'reference,' 'set,' and 'true' and 'false.' On the other hand, there are intensional concepts such as 'content,' 'meaning,' and 'sense.' The difference and its importance will become apparent after we consider two points.

First, the former group seems much more straightforward than the latter. Consider the extensional notions. For example, the extension of a name is its reference, the object that it names; the reference of 'Henry Jones' is a particular person. The extension of a predicate is the set of things to which that predicate applies: the extension of the predicate 'is red' is simply all red things. In contrast, the intensional concepts seem to involve the existence of nonphysical entities, such as meanings, that do not have clear boundaries of identity and that do not fit well into a scientific conception of reality.

Second, by definition, extensional sentences comply with a fundamental principle of logic and mathematics, namely, the law of substitution, which says that words with the same extension can be substituted for each other in the sentence (without changing whether the sentence as a whole is true). For example, in the sentence 'Venus has no water' we can substitute for 'water,' the term 'H_2O' and for the name 'Venus' any unique description of the planet, such as 'the Evening Star' or 'the hottest planet in the solar system.' In contrast, sentences using intensional notions do not comply with the law of substitution. 'Venus has no water' does not *mean* the same as 'The hottest planet in the solar system has no H_2O.' Furthermore, a person could believe the first without believing the second. Notions such as 'meaning' and 'belief' are intensional.

The distinction raises some fundamental issues that impact on many of the readings. For example, some analytic philosophers argue that the language of science can be defined or constructed using only clear extensional notions, avoiding unclear intensional ones. This is an important aspect of logical positivism (Section III). Others have argued that language more generally can be characterized adequately in purely extensional terms. This claim is important in logical atomism (Section I), and in the works of Quine and Davidson (Section V).

Other broader questions emerge that pertain to the readings in the analytic tradition. Notions such as the *content* of a mental state and the *significance* of a social practice are intensional; they pertain to meaning broadly conceived. In contrast, the concepts of physics are extensional. Now consider the question 'Can the intensional notions of the humanities, psychology, and sociology be reduced to the extensional concepts of physics?' This kind of question strikes close to the heart of many debates, such as the relation between mental states and the brain, the nature of perception and of understanding, and the status of scientific knowledge claims. When put in less technical terms, these disputes are central to many analytic philosophers in this volume, though not all (for example, see Sections II and IV). They are also a concern of some continental thinkers as well.

Husserl's Legacy

Here is a very brief preview of twentieth century continental philosophy; a more detailed explanation of each thinker can be found in the Philosophical Overviews. At the beginning of the century, Husserl rejected any attempt to reduce the intentionality or subjectivity of consciousness to the concepts of natural science. To oppose such a reduction, he tries to define and practice phenomenology, a new method of describing experience and consciousness without making any assumptions regarding what exists. In this method, one describes how something is understood and how it appears to the persons concerned. One characterizes its meaning. Husserl's pupil Heidegger, in *Being and Time* (1927), altered and extended this new method to disclose and describe the meaning of our mode of being. In this process of interpretation, he tried to show how our cares and concerns constitute the world we live in, and how the scientific world model is an abstraction from this lived-in world. In this process of disclosing meaning, Heidegger attempted to show how we can live either authentically or inauthentically, depending on whether one is aware of the temporal meaning of our way of being or not. An inauthentic way of living involves using superficial interpersonal relationships to escape from facing the meaning of one's being and death.

The French philosopher and writer Jean-Paul Sartre can be seen as extending the work of Heidegger. In *Being and Nothingness* (1943), Sartre argued that human existence is defined by free choice, rather than a God-given human nature. We live in bad faith when we try to hide from this existential free choice from ourselves, for example by pretending that we are determined by some human essence. Simone de Beauvoir, Sartre's companion, extended the existentialist analysis to the subjugation of women in her classic feminist work *The Second Sex* (1949). De Beauvoir argues that there are no essential differences between the sexes because even biological differences have a social meaning. She introduces into existentialism the claim that moral choices may depend on social conditions.

Sartre and de Beauvoir were friends with Maurice Merleau-Ponty. In his classic work, *The Phenomenology of Perception* (1945), Merleau-Ponty, who was also a psychologist, tries to refine Husserl's phenomenology and to extend it to include the body, stressing that perception cannot be merely a question of passively receiving sensations or ideas. For instance, it may also include moving one's body to see something from different angles or touching what one is seeing.

In Germany, Hans Georg Gadamer developed some aspects of the thought of Husserl and Heidegger in a different direction by working out a theory of interpretation, called hermeneutics. In *Truth and Method* (1960), Gadamer distinguishes between the human sciences and the humanities on the one hand, and the natural sciences on the other, and argues that many disciplines such as literary criticism, law, theology, and sociology, are interpretive in nature. He tries to uncover the nature of interpretation by revealing the roles that truth, prejudice, and tradition play in hermeneutics.

Another important recent German philosopher is Habermas. Much of his work can be seen as an attempt to provide a basis for and extend the Critical Theory movement. The Critical Theorists, such as Max Horkheimer and Theodore Adorno in the *Dialectic of Enlightenment* (1947), attempt to renew a Marxist-inspired critique of capitalist society and consumer culture by criticizing the Enlightenment notion of reason. Habermas argues that this kind of critique needs to be based on the nature of communication, and by examining the conditions of communicative acts he develops a discourse ethic in works such as *Moral Consciousness and Communicative Action* (1983).

To understand the recent French poststructuralist thinkers, we need to step back. At the beginning of the nineteenth century, G. W. F. Hegel claimed that all understanding must be historically situated. Most of the continental philosophers mentioned so far take this claim very much to heart. However, structuralism, which became a popular movement in France in the 1960s, emphasizes a non-historical and more holistic approach to language by understanding it as a system of signs. The poststructuralist French philosophers Jacques Derrida and Foucault have worked both within and against a structuralist framework to undermine, in various ways, the Enlightenment conceptions of reason and truth. For example, in various books written from 1961–1984, Foucault shows how the exercise of power relations determines the nature of all knowledge claims. He develops a historical analysis of the changing roles of various social institutions, such as the prison and the clinic, and shows how these act as an instrument of power. His analyses are always tied to the specific conditions of the time, thereby avoiding generalized historical narratives such as those of Marxism.

His contemporary, Derrida, is well known for deconstructing the official readings of texts, an idea that has influenced some contemporary literary criticism. Deconstruction involves showing how a text contains elements that contradict its standard interpretation. For Derrida, this process has a philosophical point; he wants to undermine the assumption that there are fixed determinate givens, such as meaning, God, self, truth, and the world, which transcend the changing interplay between signs.

Some Conclusions

Looking back over twentieth century philosophy, we can see some interesting broad patterns. First, compared to earlier periods, there has been a more direct focus on the nature of language and understanding. This was a prime concern of much analytic philosophy. But it has been also of central importance to Husserl, Heidegger, Gadamer, and, more recently, Derrida and Foucault. One reason why philosophers have focused explicitly on language, meaning, and interpretation is that by comprehending understanding itself, we may hope to gain comprehension of many other issues. Language has been seen as pivotal.

Second, the relationship between the natural sciences and the study of human beings has been a continuing central concern. Are the concepts and methods of the natural sciences adequate or applicable to the study of human life? During the birth of science and the modern period (1600–1800), this question was loaded explicitly with theological connotations. In contrast, in the twentieth century, the question was understood in terms of the nature of understanding itself. For this reason, parts of this volume introduce the debate between, on the one hand, scientific naturalistic approaches to language and, on the other, broadly phenomenological and hermeneutical approaches.

A third pattern of the twentieth century is that the nature of skepticism has altered. After 1600, much skepticism was concerned with the nature of perception: how can we claim to know the external world when our knowledge is based on the internal perception of ideas? This question still plagued Bertrand Russell and the early logical positivists. However, Heidegger and the later Wittgenstein attempted to show how this question is itself based on false assumptions and, as a result, there is much more widespread recognition of the public and social nature of knowledge. This, in turn, has given rise to a new breed of skepticism concerning the nature of concepts and interpretation, which seem to be radically underdetermined. This skeptical thesis can be seen in the work of the later Wittgenstein and of Quine, Thomas Kuhn, hermeneutics and poststructuralism, all of which are contained in this book.

Fourthly, there has been the opening up of philosophy, as described earlier, which has resulted in so many '-isms' or schools of thought.

SECTION I

◆ LOGICAL ATOMISM ◆

PROLOGUE

At the beginning of the twentieth century, much British philosophy was largely a form of idealism inspired by the work of G. W. F. Hegel and Francis Bradley. However, the two young Cambridge students, G. E. Moore and Bertrand Russell, rebelled against idealism, and argued in favor of a commonsense philosophy. For instance, Moore argued against the idealist claim that to be is to be perceived, and in favor of the commonsense thesis that we can know that propositions such as 'the earth exists' are true.

Meanwhile, Russell became deeply interested in the philosophical foundations of mathematics. He studied the work of the German philosopher Gottlob Frege (1848–1925), who had made the most significant advances in logic since the time of Aristotle. Frege, who had devised a new logical notation, had undertaken the project of showing rigorously how arithmetic was reducible to logic, a task that Russell was later to try to complete. Frege's mathematical project required him to develop new concepts in the philosophy of language, which we need to review briefly to understand logical atomism. Frege's work was contained in Volume IV of this series.

Regarding language, Frege introduced four important basic concepts. First, he argued for the distinction between sense and reference. This distinction is best explained in terms of 'subject-terms,' which refer to particular things. Subject-terms include ordinary proper names, such as 'John'; referring phrases such as 'the number nine'; and definite descriptions, such as 'the only son of Marina.' Frege argued that knowing the reference of a subject term is not the same as knowing its sense. We can know to whom the name 'John' refers, without knowing that the phrase 'the only son of Marina' refers to the same person. Furthermore, we can understand the sense or meaning of these terms without knowing that they have the same reference. Hence, sense and reference are distinct. According to Frege, the sense of a subject term is what we grasp when we understand it, and it determines what the reference is. For this reason, two names or subject terms with the same sense must have the same reference, even though two names with the same reference need not have the same sense.

Second, Frege argued that the true unit of meaning is the sentence. A word on its own asserts nothing. Only sentences affirm something and express thoughts. This implies that individual words do not have a sense or meaning except in the context of a sentence. They have meaning only in so far as they contribute to the sense of whole sentences. Moreover, the meaning of a sentence is determined by the contribution made by each of the words in the sentence. Its sense is determined by its composition, by the meaning of its parts.

Third, he introduced the idea of concepts or predicates as functions. In so doing, Frege showed us how to think about sentence structure, and how sentences are built up from their parts. Consider a simple subject-predicate sentence, such as 'John is bald.' This sentence consists of two parts: (1) the subject-term 'John,' which, in the context of a sentence, refers to an individual; and (2) the predicate term 'is bald.' This predicate term does not refer to any object, but serves as a function, telling us that the object is of a certain kind, or giving us a principle for grouping things into kinds. In mathematics, a function effects a systematic transformation from one number to another. For example, the function $\sqrt{}$ transforms any number to its square root. According to Frege, a predicate term serves as a function because it transforms the sense of the subject term into the sense of a subject-predicate sentence, and the reference of a subject term into the truth-value of a sentence.

Fourth, Frege introduced the idea of the existential and universal quantifiers. He recognized that not all sentences have a subject-predicate form. For example, 'John exists' and 'Everything is blue' do not. Such sentences must be explained in terms of the quantifiers that bind variables, such as 'x.' The sentence 'John exists' involves the existential quantifier. It has the logical form 'There is an x, and x is identical to John,' or in logical notation, '∃x (x = John).' The sentence 'Everything is blue' involves the universal quantifier. It has the logical form 'For all x, x is blue,' or in logical notation, (x) (Bx). This logical notation allows us to analyze sentences in which the quantifiers have an ambiguous scope, such as 'Everyone loves someone,' and to show how they are composed of their parts.

But what are senses? Frege firmly rejects the claim that they are purely subjective or private psychological ideas, for this would make communication impossible. They are objective features of words and sentences. Frege's distinction between sense and reference seemed to require a Platonic realm of abstract objects, in addition to the existence of material things. Later philosophers, such as Wittgenstein and at one time, Russell, were unhappy with Frege's conception of sense because it seemed to require the existence of strange and unclear entities, such as senses, propositions, or meanings. It is quite different from the much clearer notion of reference. Part of Frege's legacy was that he left philosophical logic with this fundamental problem. Incidentally, Frege also made the suggestion that the sense of a sentence can be understood in terms of its truth-conditions, which became the basis of proposed solutions to the problem.

Briefly, logical atomism can be understood as an attempt to continue with Frege's project of formalizing language, but without the need for Platonic senses. The goal is to explain the meaning of every expression in a language in terms of two concepts. First, the language contains simple or primitive expressions that have a reference. Second, it contains certain logical rules that specify how the references of complex expressions are determined by their structure and the reference of their constituent expressions.

Russell was mentor to one of the greatest philosophers of the twentieth century, Ludwig Wittgenstein, who developed the basic ideas of logical atomism in a direction that is rather different from Russell's. However, both reject Frege's idea that language requires the postulation of abstract entities, senses. They share the idea that language can be formalized, and the conviction that traditional philosophical problems can be resolved in the process.

BERTRAND RUSSELL (1872–1970)

Biographical History

Bertrand Russell had a long, active, and interesting life. His parents died while he was still a child, and he was raised by his grandfather, Lord John Russell. Russell's first important philosophical works were in the philosophy of logic and mathematics. The groundbreaking *The Principles of Mathematics* was published in 1903. He and the mathematician Alfred North Whitehead (1861–1947) collaborated on the three-volume work, *Principia Mathematica* (1910–1913). Their project was to prove that mathematics can be reduced to pure logic, thereby obviating the need for Platonic mathematical abstract objects. Starting with logically primitive concepts stated as axioms, they try to derive rigorously the whole of mathematics. As with Frege, each step in the derivation would be proved logically, with no vague appeal to intuition. Indeed, it is possible to view the entire three volumes as an attempt to write a program—a set of algorithmic procedures—for deductive mathematics.

After the publication of *Principia Mathematica*, Russell's philosophical interests broadened and became less technical. Furthermore, his views on many central philosophical issues changed during his long academic life.

He was a devout atheist and a lifelong opponent of religion. He was also an adamant critic of traditional morality and education, and an outspoken pacifist, which got him fired from his teaching post in England during World War I. He was jailed many times in his life. At the age of 89, he was arrested for protesting against nuclear arms. In 1940, he was prevented from accepting a teaching position at the College of the City of New York because of his liberal views on sex. A prolific writer and a household figure, Russell published over 70 books and hundreds of articles, as well as essays on virtually every topic. He was awarded the Order of Merit in 1949, and in 1950, he won the Nobel Prize for Literature.

Philosophical Overview

Russell's theory of descriptions is famous for apparently solving an old philosophical problem, which is 'How can a meaningful name fail to refer to something?' For example, the name 'Pegasus' refers to a mythical flying horse, but no such horse ever existed. In reply to this question, the philosopher Alexius Meinong postulates nonexisting objects. Russell rejects this idea of nonexisting actual objects, citing Ockham's razor, the principle that one should not postulate entities beyond what is strictly necessary. Instead, Russell tries to solve the problem by revealing the logical structure of sentences, such as 'The present king of France is bald.' This sentence is really a conjunction of three distinct sentences: (1) There is a thing that is the present king of France, (2) There is only one of them, and (3) That thing is bald. Understood in this way, the problem is solved because statement (1) is just false. In other words, what superficially appears to be a proper name becomes on analysis a definite description.

Russell's theory of descriptions is important for three reasons.

1. *First, it provides a solution to the ancient philosophical problem of nonreferring expressions, which had plagued philosophy since the time of Parmenides.*
2. *Second, the theory of descriptions is the basis of Russell's theory of knowledge. How can we think about things with which we are not directly acquainted? To answer this question, Russell distinguishes between knowledge by acquaintance and knowledge by description. He claims that we are*

only ever directly acquainted with particular sense-data and universal. He argues that every proposition that we can understand must be composed of primitive expressions that refer to particulars and universals that we are directly acquainted with. However, knowledge of things that we are not directly acquainted with is possible because we can have knowledge of complex facts described with definite descriptions.

3. *Third, the theory of descriptions is a central part of the program of logical atomism, according to which the world must consist of logical atoms. According to Russell, these logical atoms include particular sense-data, which are referred to or denoted by logically proper names or primitive referring expressions. These primitive expressions alone are guaranteed to refer to some existent particular. In contrast, complex expressions, such as definite descriptions, can fail to refer. In this way alone, we can explain how false propositions are possible, for if a proposition were regarded as a simple name of some fact, then false propositions would be impossible. A proposition can be false because it is a complex.*

In brief, the following picture of language and the world emerges. The only particular things are sense-data, and we can refer to them with primitive or logically proper names. These sense-data have properties and stand in relation to each other, and the corresponding expressions in language are simple concept terms, described as functions by Frege. All other referring expressions that might look like names are really complex definite descriptions, which can fail to refer. This means that all the words that we use to refer to physical objects are complex expressions constructed from simple names that refer to sense-data. In a similar way, the mind itself is a construction from sense-data, and Russell's logical atomism points toward the kind of radical Empiricism found in Hume. It also indicates a way to analyze linguistic meaning formally in terms of simple names and the logical rules that allow us to construct complex expressions and propositions from such elements.

DESCRIPTIONS

The selected reading is Russell's classic piece outlining his theory of descriptions, which comes from his book *An Introduction to Mathematical Philosophy*, published in 1919. In reading this work, it is important to remember why this analysis of names and definite descriptions has philosophical significance. Quite apart from the important points we mentioned earlier in the Philosophical Overview, there is also the following. How do thoughts and sentences hook up with the world? How do we manage to talk and think about or refer to objects? A clear and straightforward reply to this question would be a major conceptual advance that would impact many fields such as psychology and linguistics. Russell thinks that he has a viable answer to these questions because he can show how sentences such as 'Unicorns exist' and 'The present king of France is bald' are false but still meaningful.

To appreciate the importance of this, let us examine Russell's definition of a name: it is a simple symbol that directly designates an individual who (or that) is its meaning. This implies that a name has its meaning independently of all other words by virtue of referring directly to something in the world. It also implies that a simple name cannot fail to refer without being meaningless. The meaning of a simple name is what it refers to.

Russell is convinced that language must contain simple names in order to be able to refer to anything at all. Given this assumption, then, the problem of showing how sentences such as 'The present king of France is bald' can be false but still meaningful becomes theoretically important.

The theory of descriptions solves this theoretical problem. It shows how expressions such as 'the present king of France' can be meaningful and yet fail to refer. Such expressions are not simple names; they are complex descriptions. It can remain true of simple names that if they are meaningful, they must refer to something.

One of the outcomes of Russell's analysis is that ordinary proper names, such as 'Amanda Smith,' are not simple names at all. They do not comply with the definition of a simple name given earlier. Such proper names are shorthand for a group of definite descriptions, and in this way these ordinary proper names such as 'Sherlock Holmes' can fail to refer but still be meaningful.

We dealt in the preceding chapter with the words *all* and *some;* in this chapter we shall consider the word *the* in the singular, and in the next chapter we shall consider the word *the* in the plural. It may be thought excessive to devote two chapters to one word, but to the philosophical mathematician it is a word of very great importance: like Browning's Grammarian with the enclitic $\delta\epsilon$, I would give the doctrine of this word if I were "dead from the waist down" and not merely in a prison.

We have already had occasion to mention "descriptive functions," *i.e.* such expressions as "the father of *x*" or "the sine of *x*." These are to be defined by first defining "descriptions."

A "description" may be of two sorts, definite and indefinite (or ambiguous). An indefinite description is a phrase of the form "a so-and-so," and a definite description is a phrase of the form "the so-and-so" (in the singular). Let us begin with the former.

"Who did you meet?" "I met a man." "That is a very indefinite description." We are therefore not departing from usage in our terminology. Our question is: What do I really assert when I assert "I met a man"? Let us assume, for the moment, that my assertion is true, and that in fact I met Jones. It is clear that what I assert is *not* "I met Jones." I may say "I met a man, but it was not Jones"; in that case, though I lie, I do not contradict myself, as I should do if when I say I met a man I really mean that I met Jones. It is clear also that the person to whom I am speaking can understand what I say, even if he is a foreigner and has never heard of Jones.

But we may go further: not only Jones, but no actual man, enters into my statement. This becomes obvious when the statement is false, since then there is no more reason why Jones should be supposed to enter into the proposition than why anyone else should. Indeed the statement would remain significant, though it could not possibly be true, even if there were no man at all. "I met a unicorn" or "I met a sea-serpent" is a perfectly significant assertion, if we know what it would be to be a unicorn or a sea-serpent, *i.e.* what is the definition of these fabulous monsters. Thus it is only what we may call the *concept* that enters into the proposition. In the case of "unicorn," for example, there is only the concept: there is not also, somewhere among the shades, something unreal which may be called "a unicorn." Therefore, since it is significant (though false) to say "I met a unicorn," it is clear that this proposition, rightly analysed, does not contain a constituent "a unicorn," though it does contain the concept "unicorn."

The question of "unreality," which confronts us at this point, is a very important one. Misled by grammar, the great majority of those logicians who have dealt with this question have dealt with it on mistaken lines. They have regarded grammatical form as a surer guide in analysis than, in fact, it is. And they have not known what differences in grammatical form are important. "I met Jones" and "I met a man" would count traditionally as propositions of the same form, but in actual fact they are of quite different forms: the first names an actual person, Jones; while the second involves a propositional function, and becomes, when made explicit: "The function 'I met *x* and *x* is human' is sometimes true." (It will be remembered that we adopted the convention of using

From *Introduction to Mathematical Philosophy* by Bertrand Russell, Routledge, The Bertrand Russell Peace Foundation, 1938. Reprinted by permission of Taylor & Francis, Ltd.

"sometimes" as not implying more than once.) This proposition is obviously not of the form "I met *x*," which accounts for the existence of the proposition "I met a unicorn" in spite of the fact that there is no such thing as "a unicorn."

For want of the apparatus of propositional functions, many logicians have been driven to the conclusion that there are unreal objects. It is argued, *e.g.* by Meinong, that we can speak about "the golden mountain," "the round square," and so on; we can make true propositions of which these are the subjects; hence they must have some kind of logical being, since otherwise the propositions in which they occur would be meaningless. In such theories, it seems to me, there is a failure of that feeling for reality which ought to be preserved even in the most abstract studies. Logic, I should maintain, must no more admit a unicorn than zoology can; for logic is concerned with the real world just as truly as zoology, though with its more abstract and general features. To say that unicorns have an existence in heraldry, or in literature, or in imagination, is a most pitiful and paltry evasion. What exists in heraldry is not an animal, made of flesh and blood, moving and breathing of its own initiative. What exists is a picture, or a description in words. Similarly, to maintain that Hamlet, for example, exists in his own world, namely, in the world of Shakespeare's imagination, just as truly as (say) Napoleon existed in the ordinary world, is to say something deliberately confusing, or else confused to a degree which is scarcely credible. There is only one world, the "real" world: Shakespeare's imagination is part of it, and the thoughts that he had in writing Hamlet are real. So are the thoughts that we have in reading the play. But it is of the very essence of fiction that only the thoughts, feelings, etc., in Shakespeare and his readers are real, and that there is not, in addition to them, an objective Hamlet. When you have taken account of all the feelings roused by Napoleon in writers and readers of history, you have not touched the actual man; but in the case of Hamlet you have come to the end of him. If no one thought about Hamlet, there would be nothing left of him; if no one had thought about Napoleon, he would have soon seen to it that some one did. The sense of reality is vital in logic, and whoever juggles with it by pretending that Hamlet has another kind of real-

ity is doing a disservice to thought. A robust sense of reality is very necessary in framing a correct analysis of propositions about unicorns, golden mountains, round squares, and other such pseudo-objects.

In obedience to the feeling of reality, we shall insist that, in the analysis of propositions, nothing "unreal" is to be admitted. But, after all, if there *is* nothing unreal, how, it may be asked, *could* we admit anything unreal? The reply is that, in dealing with propositions, we are dealing in the first instance with symbols, and if we attribute significance to groups of symbols which have no significance, we shall fall into the error of admitting unrealities, in the only sense in which this is possible, namely, as objects described. In the proposition "I met a unicorn," the whole four words together make a significant proposition, and the word "unicorn" by itself is significant, in just the same sense as the word "man." But the *two* words "a unicorn" do not form a subordinate group having a meaning of its own. Thus if we falsely attribute meaning to these two words, we find ourselves saddled with "a unicorn," and with the problem how there can be such a thing in a world where there are no unicorns. "A unicorn" is an indefinite description which describes nothing. It is not an indefinite description which describes something unreal. Such a proposition as "*x* is unreal" only has meaning when "*x*" is a description, definite or indefinite; in that case the proposition will be true if "*x*" is a description which describes nothing. But whether the description "*x*" describes something or describes nothing, it is in any case not a constituent of the proposition in which it occurs; like "a unicorn" just now, it is not a subordinate group having a meaning of its own. All this results from the fact that, when "*x*" is a description, "*x* is unreal" or "*x* does not exist" is not nonsense, but is always significant and sometimes true.

We may now proceed to define generally the meaning of propositions which contain ambiguous descriptions. Suppose we wish to make some statement about "a so-and-so," where "so-and-so's" are those objects that have a certain property ϕ, *i.e.* those objects *x* for which the propositional function ϕx is true. (*E.g.* if we take "a man" as our instance of "a so-and-so," ϕx will be "*x* is human.") Let us now wish to assert the property ψ of "a so-and-so," *i.e.* we wish to assert that "a so-and-so" has that property which x has when ψx is true. (*E.g.* in the case of "I met a man," ψx will be "I met x.") Now the proposition that "a so-and-so" has the property ψ is *not* a proposition of the form "ψx." If it were, "a so-and-so" would have to be identical with x for a suitable x; and although (in a sense) this may be true in some cases, it is certainly not true in such a case as "a unicorn." It is just this fact, that the statement that a so-and-so has the property ψ is not of the form ψx, which makes it possible for "a so-and-so" to be, in a certain clearly definable sense, "unreal." The definition is as follows:—

> The statement that "an object having the property ϕ has the property ψ"

means:

> "The joint assertion of ϕx and ψx is not always false."

So far as logic goes, this is the same proposition as might be expressed by "some ϕ's are ψ;'s" but rhetorically there is a difference, because in the one case there is a suggestion of singularity, and in the other case of plurality. This, however, is not the important point. The important point is that, when rightly analysed, propositions verbally about "a so-and-so" are found to contain no constituent represented by this phrase. And that is why such propositions can be significant even when there is no such thing as a so-and-so.

The definition of *existence*, as applied to ambiguous descriptions, results from what was said at the end of the preceding chapter. We say that "men exist" or "a man exists" if the propositional function "x is human" is sometimes true; and generally "a so-and-so" exists if "x is so-and-so" is sometimes true. We may put this in other language. The proposition "Socrates is a man" is no doubt *equivalent* to "Socrates is human," but it is not the very same proposition. The *is* of "Socrates is human" expresses the relation of subject and predicate; the *is* of "Socrates is a man" expresses identity. It is a disgrace to the human race that it has chosen to employ the same word "is" for these two entirely different ideas—a disgrace which a symbolic logical language of course remedies. The identity in "Socrates is a man" is identity between an object named (accepting "Socrates" as a name, subject to qualifications explained later) and an object

ambiguously described. An object ambiguously described will "exist" when at least one such proposition is true, *i.e.* when there is at least one true proposition of the form "x is a so-and-so," where "x" is a name. It is characteristic of ambiguous (as opposed to definite) descriptions that there may be any number of true propositions of the above form—Socrates is a man, Plato is a man, etc. Thus "a man exists" follows from Socrates, or Plato, or anyone else. With definite descriptions, on the other hand, the corresponding form of proposition, namely, "x is the so-and-so" (where "x" is a name), can only be true for one value of x at most. This brings us to the subject of definite descriptions, which are to be defined in a way analogous to that employed for ambiguous descriptions, but rather more complicated.

We come now to the main subject of the present chapter, namely, the definition of the word *the* (in the singular). One very important point about the definition of "a so-and-so" applies equally to "the so-and-so"; the definition to be sought is a definition of propositions in which this phrase occurs, not a definition of the phrase itself in isolation. In the case of "a so-and-so," this is fairly obvious: no one could suppose that "a man" was a definite object, which could be defined by itself. Socrates is a man, Plato is a man, Aristotle is a man, but we cannot infer that "a man" means the same as "Socrates" means and also the same as "Plato" means and also the same as "Aristotle" means, since these three names have different meanings. Nevertheless, when we have enumerated all the men in the world, there is nothing left of which we can say, "This is a man, and not only so, but it is *the* 'a man,' the quintessential entity that is just an indefinite man without being anybody in particular." It is of course quite clear that whatever there is in the world is definite: if it is a man it is one definite man and not any other. Thus there cannot be such an entity as "a man" to be found in the world, as opposed to specific men. And accordingly it is natural that we do not define "a man" itself, but only the propositions in which it occurs.

In the case of "the so-and-so" this is equally true, though at first sight less obvious. We may demonstrate that this must be the case, by a consideration of the difference between a *name* and a *definite description*. Take the proposition, "Scott is the author of *Waverley*." We have here a name, "Scott," and a description, "the author of *Waverley*," which are asserted to apply to the same person. The distinction between a name and all other symbols may be explained as follows:—

A name is a simple symbol whose meaning is something that can only occur as subject, *i.e.* something of the kind that we defined as an "individual" or a "particular." And a "simple" symbol is one which has no parts that are symbols. Thus "Scott" is a simple symbol, because, though it has parts (namely, separate letters), these parts are not symbols. On the other hand, "the author of *Waverley*" is not a simple symbol, because the separate words that compose the phrase are parts which are symbols. If, as may be the case, whatever *seems* to be an "individual" is really capable of further analysis, we shall have to content ourselves with what may be called "relative individuals," which will be terms that, throughout the context in question, are never analysed and never occur otherwise than as subjects. And in that case we shall have correspondingly to content ourselves with "relative names." From the standpoint of our present problem, namely, the definition of descriptions, this problem, whether these are absolute names or only relative names, may be ignored, since it concerns different stages in the hierarchy of "types," whereas we have to compare such couples as "Scott" and "the author of *Waverley*," which both apply to the same object, and do not raise the problem of types. We may, therefore, for the moment, treat names as capable of being absolute; nothing that we shall have to say will depend upon this assumption, but the wording may be a little shortened by it.

We have, then, two things to compare: (1) a *name*, which is a simple symbol, directly designating an individual which is its meaning, and having this meaning in its own right, independently of the meanings of all other words; (2) a *description*, which consists of several words, whose meanings are already fixed, and from which results whatever is to be taken as the "meaning" of the description.

A proposition containing a description is not identical with what that proposition becomes when a name is substituted, even if the name names the same object as the description describes. "Scott is the author of *Waverley*" is obviously a different proposition from "Scott is Scott": the first is a fact in literary history, the second a trivial truism. And if we put anyone other than Scott in place of "the author of

Waverley," our proposition would become false, and would therefore certainly no longer be the same proposition. But, it may be said, our proposition is essentially of the same form as (say) "Scott is Sir Walter," in which two names are said to apply to the same person. The reply is that, if "Scott is Sir Walter" really means "the person named 'Scott' is the person named 'Sir Walter,'" then the names are being used as descriptions: *i.e.* the individual, instead of being named, is being described as the person having that name. This is a way in which names are frequently used in practice, and there will, as a rule, be nothing in the phraseology to show whether they are being used in this way or *as* names. When a name is used directly, merely to indicate what we are speaking about, it is no part of the *fact* asserted, or of the falsehood if our assertion happens to be false: it is merely part of the symbolism by which we express our thought. What we want to express is something which might (for example) be translated into a foreign language; it is something for which the actual words are a vehicle, but of which they are no part. On the other hand, when we make a proposition about "the person called 'Scott,'" the actual name "Scott" enters into what we are asserting, and not merely into the language used in making the assertion. Our proposition will now be a different one if we substitute "the person called 'Sir Walter.'" But so long as we are using names *as* names, whether we say "Scott" or whether we say "Sir Walter" is as irrelevant to what we are asserting as whether we speak English or French. Thus so long as names are used *as* names, "Scott is Sir Walter" is the same trivial proposition as "Scott is Scott." This completes the proof that "Scott is the author of *Waverley*" is not the same proposition as results from substituting a name for "the author of *Waverley*," no matter what name may be substituted.

When we use a variable, and speak of a propositional function, ϕx say, the process of applying general statements about x to particular cases will consist in substituting a name for the letter "x," assuming that ϕ is a function which has individuals for its arguments. Suppose, for example, that ϕx is "always true"; let it be, say, the "law of identity," $x = x$. Then we may substitute for "x" any name we choose, and we shall obtain a true proposition. Assuming for the moment that "Socrates," "Plato," and "Aristotle" are names (a very rash assumption), we can infer from the law of identity that Socrates is Socrates, Plato is Plato, and Aristotle is Aristotle. But we shall commit a fallacy if we attempt to infer, without further premisses, that the author of *Waverley* is the author of *Waverley*. This results from what we have just proved, that, if we substitute a name for "the author of *Waverley*" in a proposition, the proposition we obtain is a different one. That is to say, applying the result to our present case: If "*x*" is a name, "*x* = *x*" is not the same proposition as "the author of *Waverley* is the author of *Waverley*," no matter what name "*x*" may be. Thus from the fact that all propositions of the form "*x* = *x*" are true we cannot infer, without more ado, that the author of *Waverley* is the author of *Waverley*. In fact, propositions of the form "the so-and-so is the so-and-so" are not always true: it is necessary that the so-and-so should *exist* (a term which will be explained shortly). It is false that the present King of France is the present King of France, or that the round square is the round square. When we substitute a description for a name, propositional functions which are "always true" may become false, if the description describes nothing. There is no mystery in this as soon as we realise (what was proved in the preceding paragraph) that when we substitute a description the result is not a value of the propositional function in question.

We are now in a position to define propositions in which a definite description occurs. The only thing that distinguishes "the so-and-so" from "a so-and-so" is the implication of uniqueness. We cannot speak of "*the* inhabitant of London," because inhabiting London is an attribute which is not unique. We cannot speak about "the present King of France," because there is none; but we can speak about "the present King of England." Thus propositions about "the so-and-so" always imply the corresponding propositions about "a so-and-so," with the addendum that there is not more than one so-and-so. Such a proposition as "Scott is the author of Waverley" could not be true if *Waverley* had never been written, or if several people had written it; and no more could any other proposition resulting from a propositional function *x* by the substitution of "the author of *Waverley*" for "*x*." We may say that "the author of *Waverley*" means "the value of *x* for which '*x* wrote *Waverley*' is true."

Thus the proposition "the author of *Waverley* was Scotch," for example, involves:

(1) "*x* wrote *Waverley*" is not always false;
(2) "if *x* and *y* wrote *Waverley*, *x* and *y* are identical" is always true;
(3) "if *x* wrote *Waverley*, *x* was Scotch" is always true.

These three propositions, translated into ordinary language, state:

(1) at least one person wrote *Waverley*;
(2) at most one person wrote *Waverley*;
(3) whoever wrote *Waverley* was Scotch.

All these three are implied by "the author of *Waverley* was Scotch." Conversely, the three together (but no two of them) imply that the author of *Waverley* was Scotch. Hence the three together may be taken as defining what is meant by the proposition "the author of *Waverley* was Scotch."

We may somewhat simplify these three propositions. The first and second together are equivalent to: "There is a term *c* such that '*x* wrote *Waverley*' is true when *x* is *c* and is false when *x* is not *c*." In other words, "There is a term *c* such that '*x* wrote *Waverley*' is always equivalent to '*x* is *c*.'" (Two propositions are "equivalent" when both are true or both are false.) We have here, to begin with, two functions of *x*, "*x* wrote *Waverley*" and "*x* is *c*," and we form a function of *c* by considering the equivalence of these two functions of *x* for all values of *x*; we then proceed to assert that the resulting function of *c* is "sometimes true," *i.e.* that it is true for at least one value of *c*. (It obviously cannot be true for more than one value of *c*.) These two conditions together are defined as giving the meaning of "the author of *Waverley* exists."

We may now define "the term satisfying the function *ϕx* exists." This is the general form of which the above is a particular case. "The author of *Waverley*" is "the term satisfying the function '*x* wrote *Waverley*.'" And "the so-and-so" will always involve reference to some propositional function, namely, that which defines the property that makes a thing a so-and-so. Our definition is as follows:—

"The term satisfying the function *ϕx* exists" means:

"There is a term *c* such that *ϕx* is always equivalent to '*x* is *c*.'"

In order to define "the author of *Waverley* was Scotch," we have still to take account of the third of our three propositions, namely, "Whoever wrote *Waverley* was Scotch." This will be satisfied by merely adding that the *c* in question is to be Scotch. Thus "the author of *Waverley* was Scotch" is:

> *"There is a term c such that (1) 'x wrote* Waverley' *is always equivalent to 'x is c,' (2) c is Scotch."*

And generally: "the term satisfying ϕx satisfies ψx" is defined as meaning:

> *"There is a term c such that (1) ϕx is always equivalent to 'x is c,' (2) ψx is true."*

This is the definition of propositions in which descriptions occur.

It is possible to have much knowledge concerning a term described, *i.e.* to know many propositions concerning "the so-and-so," without actually knowing what the so-and-so is, *i.e.* without knowing any proposition of the form "*x* is the so-and-so," where "*x*" is a name. In a detective story propositions about "the man who did the deed" are accumulated, in the hope that ultimately they will suffice to demonstrate that it was A who did the deed. We may even go so far as to say that, in all such knowledge as can be expressed in words—with the exception of "this" and "that" and a few other words of which the meaning varies on different occasions—no names, in the strict sense, occur, but what seem like names are really descriptions. We may inquire significantly whether Homer existed, which we could not do if "Homer" were a name. The proposition "the so-and-so exists" is significant, whether true or false; but if *a* is the so-and-so (where "*a*" is a name), the words "*a* exists" are meaningless. It is only of descriptions—definite or indefinite—that existence can be significantly asserted; for, if "*a*" is a name, it *must* name something: what does not name anything is not a name, and therefore, if intended to be a name, is a symbol devoid of meaning, whereas a description, like "the present King of France," does not become incapable of occurring significantly merely on the ground that it describes nothing, the reason being that it is a *complex* symbol, of which the meaning is derived from that of its constituent symbols. And so, when we ask whether Homer existed, we are using the word "Homer" as an abbrevi-

ated description: we may replace it by (say) "the author of the *Iliad* and the *Odyssey*." The same considerations apply to almost all uses of what look like proper names.

When descriptions occur in propositions, it is necessary to distinguish what may be called "primary" and "secondary" occurrences. The abstract distinction is as follows. A description has a "primary" occurrence when the proposition in which it occurs results from substituting the description for "*x*" in some propositional function ϕx; a description has a "secondary" occurrence when the result of substituting the description for *x* in ϕx gives only *part* of the proposition concerned. An instance will make this clearer. Consider "the present King of France is bald." Here "the present King of France" has a primary occurrence, and the proposition is false. Every proposition in which a description which describes nothing has a primary occurrence is false. But now consider "the present King of France is not bald." This is ambiguous. If we are first to take "*x* is bald," then substitute "the present King of France" for "*x*," and then deny the result, the occurrence of "the present King of France" is secondary and our proposition is true; but if we are to take "*x* is not bald" and substitute "the present King of France" for "*x*," then "the present King of France" has a primary occurrence and the proposition is false. Confusion of primary and secondary occurrences is a ready source of fallacies where descriptions are concerned.

Descriptions occur in mathematics chiefly in the form of *descriptive functions, i.e.* "the term having the relation R to *y*," or "the R of *y*" as we may say, on the analogy of "the father of *y*" and similar phrases. To say "the father of *y* is rich," for example, is to say that the following propositional function of *c*: "*c* is rich, and '*x* begat *y*' is always equivalent to '*x* is *c*,'" is "sometimes true," *i.e.* is true for at least one value of *c*. It obviously cannot be true for more than one value.

The theory of descriptions, briefly outlined in the present chapter, is of the utmost importance both in logic and in theory of knowledge. But for purposes of mathematics, the more philosophical parts of the theory are not essential, and have therefore been omitted in the above account, which has confined itself to the barest mathematical requisites.

STUDY QUESTIONS: RUSSELL, *DESCRIPTIONS*

1. Why is it not excessive to devote two chapters to one word, according to Russell? What is that word?
2. What is a descriptive function? What is a function? How does his view of functions compare to Frege's?
3. What are the two sorts of descriptions? What is their significance?
4. What does he mean by 'concept'?
5. What is the importance of the question of unreality?
6. What is his disagreement with Meinong?
7. Does Hamlet, according to Russell, exist in his own world? Why? What is the significance of this?
8. What is the importance of the sense of reality in logic?
9. What does it mean to assert of something that it exists?
10. How does he use the Scott (author of *Waverley*) example? What is he trying to show, and why? What is the significance for his overall view?
11. What is a propositional function?
12. What is a definite description? With what is it contrasted, and why?
13. What does he mean by the difference between the primary and secondary occurrence of a description?
14. Is the present king of France bald? Why?

Philosophical Bridges: Russell's Influence

Russell was an extremely prolific writer whose work touched many areas of philosophy during a long period. His most influential compositions were *Principia Mathematica*, which he coauthored with Whitehead in 1910–1913, and his own *The Principles of Mathematics* and *Introduction to Mathematical Philosophy*. These books were groundbreaking in the newly emerging field of mathematical logic. For example, Russell discovered the logical paradox named after him, and put forward the theory of types as a solution. In brief, Russell's work gave a tremendous impetus to mathematical logic and thus to later computational theory.

Russell's pioneering writing in the field of logic set the tone and the direction of much twentieth-century analytical philosophy of language, such as the logical positivists' program (see below). His was one of the first steps toward a purely formal analysis of language and a syntactical theory of thought. Formal and syntactical theories are those that avoid the concept of meaning and that aim to translate language and reasoning into a purely formal machine language. These were the first steps on the long road to artificial intelligence much later in the century.

Russell's theory of definite descriptions is important as a model of how we can solve philosophical problems by uncovering the logical structure of language. In particular, it shows that the superficial grammatical form of a sentence can be quite different from the logical structure of the proposition it expresses. According to Russell, this indicates that philosophical analysis can reveal the logical structure of propositions and can lead to the construction of a logically perfect language. It presents the hope that other philosophical problems can be solved in a similar way. For this reason, it became a model for many analytic philosophers.

The theory of descriptions became an integral part of Russell's Empiricist program of showing how the concepts of objects and of the self are logical constructions out of sense-data. This idea had considerable influence on the early logical positivists. For example, in his work *The Logical Construction of the World* (1928), Rudolf Carnap tries to carry out in detail a program that is akin to Russell's. He tries to show how all scientific and psychological concepts can be constructed from immediate sense experience. In a similar way, Russell had a substantial influence over other British Empiricists of the twentieth century, such as A. J. Ayer, who thought that all of our concepts had to be derived from our immediate experience of sense-data.

Finally, logical atomism was a view shaped jointly by Russell and Wittgenstein. It is difficult to know who influenced whom.

LUDWIG WITTGENSTEIN (1889–1951)

Biographical History, Part I

Ludwig Wittgenstein was born in Vienna to a prominent Jewish family that had converted to Roman Catholicism. After receiving a degree in engineering in Berlin, he moved to England with the idea of going to the University of Manchester to study aeronautical engineering. However, his growing interest in the foundations of mathematics prevailed and, instead, following Frege's advice, he went to Cambridge University to study with Russell. World War I interrupted Wittgenstein's studies, and he left England to serve as an officer in the Austrian army. In the trenches, he began writing what would become his doctoral dissertation, which he completed in an Italian prison camp: *Tractatus Logico-Philosophicus* (1922). It created a revolution in philosophy.

Wittgenstein was convinced that he had successfully answered all of philosophy's main questions, and he abandoned the profession in favor of teaching elementary school in the Austrian Alps. Shunning what he considered the trappings of wealth, Wittgenstein had by then given away his share of the family fortune. When he grew disillusioned with teaching elementary school, he worked as a gardener in a nearby monastery, taking time off to design a house for one of his sisters. Seven years later, in 1929, Wittgenstein returned to Cambridge as a research fellow, where he was awarded a doctorate in philosophy on the basis of the *Tractatus*. However, by this time, he had begun to develop a new vision of philosophy, culminating in his work, the *Philosophical Investigations*, which was to cause a second revolution in philosophy, and which is the subject of Part V of this collection.

Philosophical Overview

In the *Tractatus*, Wittgenstein tries to show how logic and language are possible. Linguistic propositions represent how things are in the world. Like thoughts, they picture facts. Wittgenstein's analysis consists of three layers. At each level, language and the world reflect each other: logic is the structure of language and of the world.

1. *First, there are names, which are simple signs that, in the context of a sentence, refer to logically simple objects. Names have no sense; they only denote the simple objects that they stand for. These simple objects cannot be identified with everyday objects, which are themselves complex. This is because the assertion that something does not exist must involve a complex definite description rather than a simple name. The theory of descriptions shows us that it cannot make sense to say of*

a simple object that it does not exist. As a result, any simple object must exist in all possible worlds. Simple names and their corresponding objects are necessary to explain how language hooks onto the world. Without simple names and the objects they denote, sentences could not have a determinate meaning and analysis could proceed indefinitely. However, just as a name by itself asserts nothing, and is only meaningful in the context of a proposition, so too objects must exist as elements of possible facts. It is essential that objects can exist in different configurations as possible states of affairs. They cannot be thought of as isolated, but rather they must be conceived as the constituents of possible states of affairs. They essentially have a form. In this way, we come to the second level of Wittgenstein's analysis.

2. *Second, language consists of elementary propositions and the world consists of the totality of atomic facts. An elementary proposition consists only of simple names in a certain structure. Similarly, an atomic fact consists only of simple objects in a structure. When an elementary proposition is true, there is corresponding atomic fact. True elementary propositions are pictures of the atomic facts they depict, in virtue of what Wittgenstein calls their 'logical form.' Propositions are pictures of facts because pictures are themselves facts and both have the same logical form. A true elementary proposition and the atomic fact it depicts have their corresponding simple elements in the same logical structure. This point is necessary to account for the fact that false propositions are possible. A proposition cannot name a fact, for otherwise false propositions would be impossible. The sense of an elementary proposition consists in its truth conditions, i.e., the possible state of affairs or combination of objects that would make the proposition true, but whether a proposition is true or not (i.e., its truth-value) depends on the facts or which state of affairs holds. It is only in this way that a false proposition can have sense. What makes a proposition elementary is that its truth or falsity does not depend on the truth or falsity of any other proposition. Similarly, an atomic fact is independent of all other atomic facts. This point brings us to the third level of Wittgenstein's analysis.*

3. *Third, all complex sentences are truth-functional combinations of elementary sentences. Sentences can be combined to form more complex sentences through the logical connectives, such as 'not,' 'and,' 'or,' and 'if . . . then . . .' These connectives define how the truth-value of the whole sentence is a determinate function of the truth-value of the component sentences, and the connectives can be defined in terms of various truth tables. Wittgenstein notes that all the other connectives can be defined in terms of joint denial. He conceives of joint denial as an operation that can be performed successively on any sentence or set of sentences. He uses the sign 'N' for this operation (cf. 5.5). So, for example, 'N(p)' is equivalent to 'not p' and 'NN(p)' is equivalent to 'not not p' or 'p.' 'N(pq)' is equivalent to 'neither p nor q.' Wittgenstein claims that every complex sentence is a result of successive applications of the operation 'N' to sets of elementary sentences.*

In short, Wittgenstein's view is that any language must consist only of truth-functional combinations of elementary sentences, which consist of logically proper names in a logical structure; otherwise, the sense of a sentence would not be determinate. Only in this way, propositions can picture facts. Literally, nothing else can be said. He notes that much of our language does not appear to be a truth-functional combination of elementary sentences. For instance, psychological statements, such as 'A believes that P,' do not appear to be so. Yet, they are, and must be, because nothing else can be said. Much of the rest of the *Tractatus* consists in revealing the surprising implications of his austere view of language for metaphysics and philosophy.

One of these implications is that all logical tautologies, such as 'p entails p,' are senseless. This is because they do not picture any fact. They are compatible with all possibilities. They exclude nothing and, therefore, they do not say anything. A tautology simply shows the sense of the logical connectives, but this is not some fact about the world that can be pictured.

Similarly, the sense of a proposition itself cannot be pictured. The complex sentence 'Proposition "P" says that p' is not a truth-functional combination of elementary propositions. However, a proposition *shows* its sense. Wittgenstein distinguishes what can be shown and what can be said: what can be shown cannot be said. He argues that various philosophical positions consist in what can be shown and cannot be said. In other words, philosophical theories consist of pseudo propositions, which do not picture facts at all. In this way, the *Tractatus* reveals the limits of language. For this reason, it gave much impetus to the antimetaphysical views of the logical positivists. However, at the same time, ironically, it is also a unique brand of mysticism, which claims that certain things can be shown even though they cannot be said.

Surprisingly, these points apply to the *Tractatus* itself. Wittgenstein's own picture theory of meaning implies that it itself is senseless. In other words, the *Tractatus* consists only of pseudo-propositions. It literally says nothing. Wittgenstein embraces this paradoxical implication of his own work. To describe the limits of language requires standing outside language, which is impossible. Therefore, the book ends with a call to silence.

TRACTATUS LOGICO-PHILOSOPHICUS

The *Tractatus* contains seven propositions, numbered 1–7, along with secondary propositions that are observations regarding the first, numbered 1.1, 2.1, etc., each of which is followed by tertiary propositions that are observations of the observations, numbered 1.11, 2.11, and so on. The more secondary propositions such as 4.3 explain and expand the primary ones, such as 4. Likewise, the tertiary ones such as 4.31 explain the secondary ones, such as 4.3. This means that in reading the *Tractatus*, one needs to bear in mind the overall context. Furthermore, Wittgenstein's text consists mainly of brief and cryptic sayings, which are not linked explicitly to each other. Using the Philosophical Overview may help the reader to overcome these difficulties.

In order to help the reader further, we shall explain briefly and informally some of the logic that Wittgenstein uses at 4.24, 4.31, 5.101, and 5.1311 when he expounds his claim that elementary or atomic sentences can be combined using the logical connectives into complex sentences. This brief explanation will make more sense once the reader has reached the relevant passages.

The letters 'p' and 'q' stand for any proposition or assertive sentence such as 'The grass is green.' These are well-formed formulas. In other words, these are admissible symbols. The letters can be combined with the connectives to stand for more complex sentences. For the moment, we shall introduce four basic connectives, which have to be defined informally as follows.

'Not' or '∼'	If 'p' is true then '∼p' is false.
'And' or '&'	'p & q' is true if and only if both 'p' and 'q' are true.
'Or' or '∨'	'p ∨ q' is false if and only if both 'p' and 'q' are false; otherwise, it is true.
'If . . . then . . .' or '⊃'	'p ⊃ q' is false if and only if 'p' is true and 'q' is false; otherwise it is true.

From *Wittgenstein's Tractatus* by Daniel Kolak. Reprinted by permission of The McGraw-Hill Companies.

The connectives combine sentences, and the truth or falsity of the new complex sentences depends entirely on the truth or falsity of its component sentences and on the connectives. We can show how the connectives determine the truth or falsity of the complex sentences with truth tables:

1	2	3	4	5	6
p	q	p & q	p ∨ q	p ⊃ q	p|q
T	T	T	T	T	F
T	F	F	T	F	F
F	T	F	T	T	F
F	F	F	F	T	T

Please ignore column 6 for the moment. The first two vertical columns specify the different true/false possibilities for 'p' and 'q.' The third, fourth, and fifth vertical columns define whether the complex sentences formed by the relevant connective are true or false. For instance, the third column specifies when 'p & q' is true and when it is false in relation to 'p' and 'q' in columns 1 and 2.

With a little study, you should be able to see that the following definitions apply:

'p & q' is equivalent to ~(~p ∨ ~q)
'p ⊃ q' is equivalent to ~p ∨ q

With these explanations, you should be able to understand the truth functions at 5.101. Please note that Wittgenstein uses the sign '.' instead of '&' for 'and.'

At 5.1311, Wittgenstein defines a new connective, which is usually called joint denial and which is represented by '|.' This connective can be defined informally as follows: 'p|q' is true if and only if 'p' and 'q' are both false; otherwise, it is false. In symbols:

'p|q' is equivalent to ~(p & q)

The truth table for this new connective is given in column 6. Wittgenstein uses joint denial because all of the other connectives can be defined in terms of it alone, as follows:

'~p' is equivalent to 'p|p'
'p & q' is equivalent to '(p|p)|(p|q)'
'p ∨ q' is equivalent to '(p|p)|(q|q)'

PREFACE

This book will perhaps be understood only by those who have themselves already thought the thoughts which are expressed in it—or similar thoughts. It is therefore not a text-book. Its purpose would be achieved if there were one person who read it with understanding and to whom it gave pleasure.

The book deals with the problems of philosophy and shows, as I believe, that the method of formulating these problems rests on a misunderstanding of the logic of our language. Its whole meaning might be summed up as follows: What can be said at all can be said clearly; and what we cannot speak thereof we must be silent.

The book will, therefore, draw a limit to thought, or rather—not to thought, but to the expression of thought; for, in order to draw a limit to thought we should have to be able to think both sides of this limit (we should therefore have to be able to think what cannot be thought).

The limit can, therefore, only be drawn in language and what lies on the other side of the limit will be simply nonsense.

How far my efforts agree with those of other philosophers I cannot judge. Indeed what I have here written makes no claim to novelty in points of detail; and therefore I give no sources, because it makes no difference to me whether what I have though has already been thought before me by someone else.

I will only mention that to the great works of Frege and the writings of my friend Bertrand Russell I owe for much of the stimulation of my thoughts.

If this work has a value it consists in two things. First that in it thoughts are expressed, and this value will be the greater the better the thoughts are expressed—the more the nail has been hit on the head, the greater will be its value. Here I am conscious that I have fallen far short of the possible. Simply because my powers are insufficient to cope with the task. May others come and do it better.

On the other hand the *truth* of the thoughts communicated here seems to me unassailable and definitive. I therefore believe that the problems have in essentials been finally solved. And if I am not mistaken in this, then the value of this work secondly consists in the fact that it shows how little has been achieved when these problems have been solved.

1. **The world is all that is the case.**
   1.1 The world is the totality of facts, not of things.
   1.11 The world is determined by the facts, and by these being all the facts.
   1.12 For the totality of facts determines all that is the case and also all that is not the case.
   1.13 The facts in logical space are the world.
   1.2 The world can be broken down into facts.
   1.21 Each one can be the case or not be the case while all else remains the same.

2. **What is the case—a fact—is the existence of elementary facts.**
   2.01 An elementary fact is a combination of objects (items, things).
   2.011 It is essential that such objects can be constituents of an elementary fact.
   2.012 In logic nothing is accidental: if something *can* be a constituent of an elementary fact, it must already include within itself the possibility of that elementary fact.
   2.0121 It would, so to speak, appear as an accident, if it turned out that an elementary fact accommodated something that could already exist on its own.

   Just as we cannot think of spatial objects outside space nor temporal objects outside time, so we cannot think of *any* object outside the possibility of its combining with other things.

   If I can think of an object combining with others into an elementary fact, I cannot think of it without the *possibility* of such combinations.
   2.0122 This thing [the constituting object] is independent [of the elementary fact] to the extent that it can occur in all *possible* elementary facts, but this form of independence is a form of connection with elementary facts and thus ultimately a form of dependence. (Words cannot appear in two different roles: by themselves, and in sentences.)
   2.0123 If I know an object, I also know all the possibilities of its occurrence in elementary facts.
   2.0124 If all objects are given, then thereby are all *possible* elementary facts also given.
   2.013 Everything exists, as it were, in a space of possible elementary facts. I can imagine this space empty, but nothing without this space.
   2.0131 A spatial object must be surrounded by an infinite space. (A point in space is a place for an argument.)

   A spot in the visual field need not be red but it must have some color: it is surrounded by color-space. Notes must have some pitch, tactile objects some degree of hardness, and so on.
   2.014 Objects contain the possibility of all elementary facts.
   2.0141 The possibility of an object being part of an elementary fact is its form.
   2.02 Objects are simple.
   2.0201 Every complex assertion [involving compounds of objects] can be broken down

into an assertion about simple constituents using sentences that describe the complex completely.

2.021 Objects form the substance of the world. That is why they cannot be compound.

2.0211 Were the world without substance, whether one sentence made sense would depend on whether another sentence was true.

2.0212 It would then be impossible to form a picture of the world (true or false).

2.022 Obviously, a world that exists only in thought, however different from the real world, must have something—a form—in common with it.

2.023 This fixed form consists of objects.

2.0231 The substance of the world *can* only determine such a form and not the material properties. Material properties can only be presented by means of sentences—they can only be constituted by the configuration of objects.

2.0232 Roughly speaking, objects are colorless.

2.0233 Two objects of the same logical form—apart from their external properties—are only distinct from one another in that they are different.

2.02331 Either a thing has unique properties, and then we can immediately distinguish it from others using a description as well as refer to it; or, on the other hand, there are several things that have a common set of all their properties, in which case it is impossible to distinguish them.

For if something is distinguished by nothing, I cannot distinguish it—otherwise it would be distinguished.

2.024 Substance is that which exists independently of what is the case.

2.025 It is form and content.

2.0251 Space, time, and color (the state of being colored) are forms of objects.

2.026 Only if objects exist can the world have a fixed form.

2.027 The fixed, the existent, and the object are one.

2.0271 The object is the fixed, the existent; the configuration of objects is the changing, the variable.

2.0272 The configuration of objects forms the elementary fact.

2.03 In an elementary fact the objects hang in one another like the links of a chain.

2.031 In an elementary fact the objects combine with one another in a definite way.

2.032 The definite way in which objects are connected in an elementary fact is the structure of the elementary fact.

2.033 Form is the possibility of structure.

2.034 The structure of a fact consists of the structures of its elementary facts.

2.04 The world is a totality of all existing elementary facts.

2.05 The totality of all existing elementary facts determines which elementary facts do not exist.

2.06 The existence and nonexistence of elementary facts is reality.

(We also call the existence of elementary facts a positive fact, and their nonexistence a negative fact.)

2.061 Elementary facts exist independently of one another.

2.062 From the existence or nonexistence of one elementary fact we cannot infer the existence or nonexistence of any other elementary fact.

2.063 The sum total of reality is the world.

2.1 We make pictures of facts to ourselves.

2.11 Such a picture represents an elementary fact in logical space, the existence and nonexistence of elementary facts.

2.12 Such a picture is a model of reality.

2.13 To the objects correspond, in such a picture, the elements of the picture.

2.131 The picture's elements stand, in the picture, for the objects.

2.14 The picture consists in its elements being combined in a definite way.

2.141 The picture is a fact.

2.15 The definite way in which the picture elements combine represents how things are related.

Let us call this combination of elements the *structure* of the picture, and let us call the possibility of this structure the *form of representation* of the picture.

2.151 The form of representation is the possibility that things combine in the same way as do the pictorial elements.

2.1511 In this way the picture makes contact with, or reaches up to, reality.

2.1512 It lays against reality like a ruler.

2.1513 A picture conceived in this way includes the representing relation, which makes the picture a picture.

2.1514 The representing relation consists of the correlations of picture elements with things.

2.1515 These correlations are the antennae of the picture's elements, which put the picture in touch with reality.

2.16 To be a picture, a fact must have something in common with what it depicts.

2.17 What a picture must have in common with reality to be capable of depicting it the way it does—rightly or wrongly—is its form of representation.

2.171 A picture can represent any reality whose form it has.

A spatial picture, anything spatial; a colored picture, anything colored; etc.

2.172 A picture cannot, however, depict its form of representation; it can only show it.

2.173 A picture represents its subject from the outside (its point of view is its form of representation), and that is how it represents its subject rightly or wrongly.

2.174 A picture cannot place itself outside its form of representation.

2.18 What any such picture, of any form, must have in common with reality to be capable of representing it the way it does—rightly or wrongly—is logical form, that is, the form of reality.

2.181 A picture whose form of representation is logical is a logical picture.

2.182 Every such picture is *also* a logical picture. (Whereas, for example, every picture is not a spatial picture.)

2.19 Logical pictures are depictions of the world.

2.2 A picture must have the logical form of representation in common with what it depicts.

2.201 A picture depicts reality by representing the possible existence and nonexistence of elementary facts.

2.202 Such a picture represents a possible elementary fact in logical space.

2.203 Such a picture contains the possibility of the elementary fact that it represents.

2.21 Such a picture agrees with reality or not; it is right or wrong, true or false.

2.22 Such a picture represents what it represents independently of its truth or falsity, via its representational form.

2.221 What this picture represents is its sense.

2.222 Its truth or falsity consists in the agreement or disagreement of its sense with reality.

2.223 To see whether the picture is true or false we must compare it with reality.

2.224 We cannot see whether the picture is true or false merely by looking at it.

2.225 There is no such picture that is true a priori.

3. A thought is a logical picture of a fact.

3.001 "An elementary fact is thinkable" means: we can form a mental picture of it.

3.01 The totality of all true thoughts is a picture of the world.

3.02 A thought contains the possibility of the facts that it thinks. What is thinkable is also possible.

3.03 Thought cannot be of anything illogical, else we would have to think illogically.

3.031 As the old saying goes: God can create anything so long as it does not contradict the laws of logic. The truth is that we could not even *say* what an illogical world might look like.

3.032 It is as impossible to say something that contradicts logic as it is to draw a figure that contradicts the laws of space or to specify the coordinates of a nonexistent point.

3.04 A thought that was correct a priori would ensure its truth in virtue of its possibility.

3.1 In a sentence the thought expresses itself perceptibly.

3.11 We use a sentence (spoken or written, etc.) as a projection of a possible fact.

The method of projection is our thinking the sense of the sentence.

3.12 The sign with which a thought expresses itself, I will call a sentential sign. And a sentence is a sentential sign conceived in its projective relation to the world.

3.13 The sentence has everything that the projection has, except what is projected.

Therefore, the possibility of what is projected is in the sentence, but not the projection itself.

And so the sentence does not yet contain its sense; what it does contain is the possibility of expressing that sense.

("The content of the sentence" means the content of a sentence that makes sense.)

The sentence contains the [empty, logical] form of its sense, without any content.

3.14 What constitutes a sentence is that its elements, the words, stand in a determinate relation to one another.

A sentential sign is a fact.

3.141 A sentence is not merely a mixture of words. (Just as a musical theme is not merely a mixture of notes.)

A sentence is articulate.

3.142 Only facts can express a sense; a class of names cannot.

3.143 That a sentential sign is a fact is concealed in its usual form of expression, whether written or printed.

For example, in a printed sentence there is no essential difference between the sentence and the word.

3.1431 The essential nature of the sentential sign can be seen very clearly once we think of it as composed not of written signs but of spatial objects (such as tables, chairs, and books).

Then the mutual spatial layout of these objects expresses the sense of the sentence.

3.1432 We must not say, "The complex sign 'aRb' says that *a* stands to *b* in relation R," but, rather, "*That* '*a*' stands to '*b*' in a certain relation says *that aRb*."

3.144 Facts can be described but not named.

(Names are like points, sentences like arrows—they designate.)

3.2 In sentences, thoughts can be expressed such that the objects of the thoughts correspond to the elements of the sentential signs.

3.201 I call these elements "simple signs," and such a sentence "completely analyzed."

3.202 A simple sign used in a sentence I will call a *name*.

3.203 A name signifies an object. The designated object is what the name means. ("A" is the same sign as "A".)

3.21 The configuration of simple signs in the sentential sign corresponds to the configuration of objects in the fact.

3.22 In a sentence a name signifies an object.

3.221 Objects can only be *named*. Signs represent them. I can only speak *about* objects: I *cannot put them into words*. A sentence can only say *how* a thing is, not *what* it is.

3.23 The demand for the possibility of simple signs is the demand that sense be determinate.

3.24 A sentence about a complex stands in an internal relation to a sentence about its constituent part.

A complex can be given only by its description, which either will fit or not fit. A sentence that mentions a complex that does not exist is not meaningless, merely false.

3.25 There is one and only one complete analysis of a sentence.

3.251 A sentence expresses itself clearly and distinctly: a sentence is articulate.

3.26 A name cannot be further analyzed using definitions. It is a primitive sign.

3.261 Every defined sign signifies *via* the signs by which it is defined; the definitions show the way.

3.262 What a sign fails to express gets shown by its application. What a sign conceals, its application declares.

3.263 The meanings of primitive signs can be explained through clarifications. Clarifications are sentences containing the primitive signs. Therefore, they can only be understood when the meanings of these signs is already known.

3.3 Only sentences make sense; only in the context of a sentence does a name signify anything.

3.31 Any part of a sentence that characterizes the sense of the sentence I call an *expression* (a symbol).

(A sentence is itself an expression.)

Expressions are everything essential for the sense of the sentence that sentences can have in common with each other.

An expression characterizes the form and content.

3.318 I conceive a sentence—like Frege and Russell—as a function of the expressions it contains.

3.32 A sign is the perceptible aspect of a symbol.

3.321 Two different symbols can therefore have one and the same sign (written or spoken, etc.) in common—in which case each will signify in a different way.

3.323 In ordinary language it often happens that the same word signifies in two different ways—and therefore belongs to two different symbols—or that two words, which signify in different ways, are apparently applied in the same way in the sentence.

Thus the word "is" appears as a copula, as a sign for identity, and as an expression for existence; "exist" appears as an intransitive verb, like "go"; and "identical" appears as an adjective; we speak of *something*, and also of *something* happening.

(In the sentence, "Green is green"—where the first word is a proper name and the last an adjective—not only do these words have different meanings, they are *different symbols*.)

3.324 This is how the most fundamental confusions can easily arise (philosophy is full of them).

3.325 To avoid such errors we must employ a symbolic language that excludes them, by never applying the same sign in different symbols and by not applying signs in the same way that signify in different ways: a symbolic language, that is to say, that obeys the rules of *logical* grammar—of logical syntax.

(The logical symbolism of Frege and Russell is such a language that, however, still does not exclude all errors.)

3.33 The meaning of a sign should never play a role in logical syntax. It must be possible to formulate logical syntax without mentioning the *meaning* of a sign; it ought *only* to presuppose the description of the expressions.

3.332 No sentence can assert anything about itself, because a sentence cannot be contained in itself (that is the essence of the "theory of types").

3.333 A function cannot be its own argument because the sign for a function already contains the prototype of its argument, and so cannot contain itself.

3.334 All the rules of logical syntax become self-evident once we know how every single sign signifies.

3.4 A sentence determines a place in logical space. The existence of this logical place is guaranteed by the existence of the expressions of which the sentence is composed—by the existence of the meaningful sentence.

3.5 A sentential sign, applied and thought, is a thought.

4. A sentence that makes sense is a thought.

4.001 The totality of sentences is the language.

4.002 Human beings possess the capacity of constructing languages in which every sense can be expressed without our having any idea how and what each word means, just as we speak without knowing how the individual sounds are produced.

Ordinary language is a part of the human organism and no less complicated than it.

It is humanly impossible to gather from it the logic of language.

Language disguises thought, so that from the external form of the clothes one cannot infer the form of the thought beneath, because the external form of the clothes is designed not to reveal the form of the body but for different purposes.

The silent adjustments to understand ordinary language are extremely complicated.

4.003 Most of the statements and questions found in philosophy are not false but nonsensical. We cannot, therefore, answer such questions at all but only show them to be nonsensical. Most questions and statements of the philosophers result from our inability to understand the logic of our language.

(They are of the same variety as the question, "Is the Good more or less identical than the Beautiful?")

No wonder that the deepest problems are actually *not* problems.

4.0031 All philosophy is a "critique of language." (But not at all in Mauthner's sense.) Russell's merit is to have shown that the apparent logical form of a sentence need not be its real form.

4.01 A sentence is a picture of reality.

A sentence is a model of reality as we think it is.

4.011 At first glance a sentence—say as it is laid out on the printed page—does not seem to be a picture of the reality that it is about. But neither does the musical score appear at first glance to be a picture of a musical piece; nor does our phonetic spelling (the letters of the alphabet) seem to be a picture of our spoken language. And yet these symbolisms turn out to be pictures—even in the ordinary sense of the word—of what they represent.

4.02 This we see from the fact that we understand the sense of a sentence without having had it explained to us.

4.021 A sentence is a picture of reality, for if I understand the sentence, I know the fact represented by it. And I understand the sentence without its sense having been explained to me.

4.022 A sentence *shows* its sense.

A sentence *shows* how things are *if* it is true. And it *says* that that is how they are.

4.023 A sentence determines reality to the degree that one only needs to say "yes" or "no" to it, and nothing more, to make it agree with reality.

Reality must therefore be completely described by the sentence.

A sentence is the description of a fact.

Just as a description describes an object by its external properties, so a sentence describes reality by its internal properties.

A sentence constructs a world with the help of a logical scaffolding, so that one can actually see in the sentence all the logical features of reality *if* it is true. One can *draw conclusions* from a false sentence.

4.024 To understand a sentence means to know what is the case if it is true.

(One therefore understands it independently of knowing whether it is true.)

One understands the sentence if one understands its expressions.

4.025 The translation of one language into another is not a process of translating each sentence of one language into a sentence of the other language but only the constituent parts.

(And the dictionary translates not only substantives but also adverbs and conjunctions, etc., and it treats them all alike.)

4.026 The meanings of simple signs (the words) must be explained to us before we can understand them.

By means of sentences we explain ourselves.

4.027 It is essential to sentences that they can communicate a new sense to us.

4.03 A sentence must communicate a new sense with old words.

A sentence communicates a fact to us, therefore it must be *essentially* connected with the fact.

And the connection is that it is its logical picture.

A sentence asserts something only insofar as it is a picture.

4.04 In a sentence there must be exactly as many things distinguishable as there are in the fact that it represents.

They must both possess the same logical (mathematical) multiplicity. (Compare Hertz's *Mechanics* on dynamic models.)

4.041 Naturally, this mathematical multiplicity cannot itself be represented. Yet one cannot miss it in the representation.

4.05 The reality is compared with the sentence.

4.06 Sentences can be true or false only by being pictures of the reality.

4.1 A sentence presents the existence and nonexistence of elementary facts.

4.11 The totality of true sentences is the whole of natural science (or the totality of the natural sciences).

4.111 Philosophy is not one of the natural sciences.

(The word "philosophy" must mean something that stands above and below the natural sciences, not alongside them.)

4.112 The goal of philosophy is the logical clarification of thought.

Philosophy is not a theory but an activity.

A philosophical work consists essentially of clarifications.

The end result of philosophy is not a number of "philosophical sentences" but to make sentences clear.

Philosophy should make clear and sharpen the contrast of thoughts that are otherwise opaque and blurred.

4.1121 Psychology is no more related to philosophy than is any other natural science.

The theory of knowledge is the philosophy of psychology.

Does not my study of symbolism correspond to the study of thought processes that philosophers have held to be so essential to the philosophy of logic? Only they got involved for the most part in inessential psychological investigations, and there is an analogous danger with my method.

4.1122 The Darwinian theory has nothing to do with philosophy, any more than does any hypothesis in the natural sciences.

4.113 Philosophy limits the domain of natural science.

4.114 It must limit the thinkable and thereby the unthinkable.

It must limit the unthinkable from within through the thinkable.

4.1213 Now we understand our feeling that we possess the right logical conception, if only all is right in our symbolism.

4.125 That an internal relation holds between possible facts expresses itself in language by means of the internal relation that holds between the sentences that present them.

4.2 The sense of a sentence is in its agreement and disagreement with the possibilities of the existence and nonexistence of elementary facts.

4.21 The simplest sentence, the elementary sentence, asserts the existence of an elementary fact.

4.211 It is a characteristic of an elementary sentence that no elementary sentence can contradict it.

4.22 An elementary sentence consists of names. It is a connection, a linkage of names.

4.221 Obviously, in analyzing sentences, we must arrive at elementary sentences consisting of names in immediate connection.

This raises the question of how such sentential connections arise.

4.2211 Even if the world is infinitely complex, so that every fact consists of infinitely many elementary facts and every elementary fact consists of infinitely many objects, even so there must be objects and elementary facts.

4.23 A name occurs in a sentence only in the context of an elementary sentence.

4.24 Names are the simplest symbols, and so I indicate them by single letters ("x", "y", "z").

An elementary sentence I write as a function of names in the form "$f(x)$", "$\phi(x,y)$", etc.

Or I indicate it by the letters "p", "q", "r".

4.241 When I use two different signs to signify one and the same object, I indicate this by placing the sign "$=$" between them.

Thus, "$a = b$" means that the sign "b" can be substituted for the sign "a".

(If I use an equation to introduce a new sign "b", saying that this will be a substitute for some already known sign "a", then (like Russell) I write the definition of the equation in the form "$a = b$ Def". A definition is a rule about signs.)

4.25 If the elementary sentence is true, the elementary fact exists; if the elementary sentence is false, the elementary fact does not exist.

4.26 The specification of all true elementary sentences describes the world completely. The world is completely described by the specification of all elementary sentences plus the specification of which ones are true and which false.

4.3 Truth-possibilities of elementary sentences signify the possibilities of the existence and nonexistence of elementary facts.

4.31 We can show truth-possibilities by the following sort of schemata ("T" means "true," "F" means "false"; the columns of T's and F's under the row of elementary sentences symbolize their truth-possibilities perspicuously):

p	q	r		p	q		p
T	T	T		T	T		T
F	T	T		F	T		F
T	F	T		T	F		
T	T	F		F	F		
F	F	T					
F	T	F					
T	F	F					
F	F	F					

4.4 A sentence is an expression of agreement and disagreement with the truth-possibilities of elementary sentences.

4.41 The truth-possibilities of elementary sentences are the conditions of the truth and falsehood of the sentence.

4.46 Among the possible groups of truth-conditions are two limiting cases.

In one case the sentence is true for all the truth-possibilities of the elementary sentences: the truth conditions are *tautological*.

In the second case the sentence is false for all truth-possibilities: the truth-conditions are *self-contradictory*.

In the first case we call the sentence a tautology; in the second case we call it a contradiction.

4.461 A sentence shows what it says; a tautology and a contradiction show that they say nothing.

Because a tautology is true unconditionally, it has no truth-conditions; likewise, on no condition is a contradiction true.

Tautologies and contradictions do not make any sense.

(Like a point with two arrows emerging in opposite directions.)

(For example, in knowing that it is either raining or not raining, I know nothing about the weather.)

4.4611 However, neither are tautologies nor contradictions nonsensical. They belong to the symbolism, just as "0" belongs to the symbolism of arithmetic.

4.462 Tautologies and contradictions are not pictures of the reality. They present no possible facts. For tautologies admit *all* possible facts, and contradictions admit *none*.

In the tautology the conditions of agreement with the world—the presenting relations—cancel each other out, so that in the tautology no aspect of reality can present itself.

4.5 We are in a position now to state the most general form of a sentence—that is, to describe the sentence of any symbolic language whatsoever such that every sense can be expressed by a symbol satisfying the description and every symbol satisfying the description can express a sense, provided that the signification of each name is well chosen.

Clearly, only what is essential to the most general form of a sentence may be included in its description—otherwise, it would not be the most general form.

The existence of a general form of a sentence is proved in that no sentence can be given whose form could not have been foreseen (i.e., constructed). The general form of a sentence is soandso is the case.

4.51 Suppose *all* elementary sentences were given me: then we can simply ask what sentences I can build out of them. And these are *all* the sentences and *that* is how they are bound.

5. A sentence is a truth-function of elementary sentences.

(An elementary sentence is a truth-function of itself.)

5.01 Elementary sentences are the truth-arguments of sentences.

5.1 The truth-functions can be ordered in a series.

This is the foundation for the theory of probability.

5.101 The truth-functions of every number of elementary sentences can be arranged in the following sort of schema:

$(TTTT)(p,q)$ Tautology (if p then p, and if q then q) $[p \supset p . q \supset q]$

$(FTTT)(p,q)$ in words : Not both p and q. $[\sim(p.q)]$

$(TFTT)(p,q)$ " " If q then p. $[q \supset p]$

$(TTFT)(p,q)$ " " If p then q. $[p \supset q]$

(TTTF)(p,q) "   " p or q. [$p \lor q$]

(FFTT)(p,q) "   "   Not q. [$\sim q$]

(FTFT)(p,q) "   "   Not p. [$\sim p$]

(FTTF)(p,q) "   " p or q, but not both.
[$p. \sim q : \lor: q.\sim p$]

(TFFT)(p,q) "   "   If p, then q; and if
q, then p. [$p \equiv q$]

(TFTF)(p,q) "   " p

(TTFF)(p,q) "   " q

(FFFT)(p,q) "   "   Neither p nor q.
[$\sim p.\sim q$ or $p|q$]

(FFTF)(p,q) "   " p and not q. [$p.\sim q$]

(FTFF)(p,q) "   " q and not p. [$q.\sim p$]

(TFFF)(p,q) "   " p and q. [$p.q$]

(FFFF)(p,q) Contradiction (p and not p; and
q and not q.) [$p.\sim p.q.\sim q$]

The truth-possibilities of a sentence's truth-arguments that make the sentence true I shall call its *truth-grounds*.

5.11 If the truth-grounds common to several sentences are also the truth-grounds of some one sentence, then we say that the truth of that sentence follows from the truth-grounds of the others.

5.12 In particular, the truth of a sentence "p" follows from the truth of a sentence "q" if all the truth-grounds of "q" are the truth-grounds "p".

5.13 Whether the truth of one sentence follows from the truth of other sentences can be seen in the structure of the sentences.

5.131 That the truth of one sentence follows from the truth of others is expressed by relations in which the forms of those sentences stand to one another: nor need we set up these relations between them by combining them with one another into a single sentence. These relations are internal and exist simultaneously with, and through, the existence of the sentences.

5.1311 When from $p \lor q$ and $\sim p$ we infer q, the relation between the forms of the sentences "$p \lor q$" and "$\sim p$" is concealed by our method of symbolizing. But if instead of "$p \lor q$" we write "$p|q.|.p|q$" and instead of "$\sim p$" we write "$p|p$", (where $p|q$ = neither p nor q), then the inner connection [the

inference from $(p|q.|.p|q)$ and $(p|p)$ to $(q|q.|.q|q)$] becomes apparent.

5.133 All inference takes place a priori.

5.134 From an elementary sentence no other can be inferred.

5.135 There is no possible way to make an inference from the existence of one fact to the existence of another, entirely different, fact.

5.136 There is no causal linkage to justify any such inference.

5.1361 The future *cannot* be inferred from the present.

Superstition is the belief in causal "linkage."

5.1362 Free will consists in the impossibility of our knowing future actions now. Future actions could only be known if causality were a form of logical inference and had some such *inner* necessity. The connection between knowledge and the known is that of logical necessity.

("A knows that p is the case" makes no sense if p is a tautology.)

5.14 If a sentence follows from another, then the latter says more than the former and the former says less than the latter.

5.141 If p follows from q and q follows from p, then they are one and the same sentence.

5.142 A tautology follows from all propositions: it says nothing.

5.143 A contradiction is that which is common to sentences that *no* sentence has in common with any other. A tautology is that which is common to all sentences that have nothing in common with each other.

Contradiction vanishes, so to speak, outside, and tautology inside, all sentences.

Contradiction is the outer boundary of sentences; tautology is the insubstantial point at their center.

5.153 A sentence is in itself neither probable nor improbable. An event occurs or does not occur, there is no middle course.

5.2 The structures of sentences stand to one another in internal relations.

5.21 We can emphasize these internal relations in our form of expression, by representing one sentence as the result of an operation that produces it out of other sentences (the bases of the operation).

5.22 The operation is the expression of a relation between the structures of its result and of its bases.

5.23 The operation is what has to happen to a sentence to turn it into another one.

5.24 An operation shows itself in a variable; it shows how we can get from one sentence form to another.

It expresses the difference between the forms.

(And the bases themselves are what the bases of an operation and the result have in common.)

5.25 The occurrence of an operation does not characterize the sense of a sentence.

For the operation does not assert anything, only its result does, and this depends on the bases of the operation.

(Operation and function must not be confused with one another.)

5.3 All sentences are the result of truth-operations on the elementary sentences.

The truth operation is the way in which a truth-function arises from elementary sentences.

According to the nature of truth-operations, truth-functions generate further truth functions in the same way that elementary sentences generate their own truth-functions. Every truth-operation creates from truth-functions of elementary sentences another truth-function of elementary sentences, that is, another sentence. The result of every truth-operation on the results of truth-operations on elementary sentences is also the result of one truth-operation on elementary sentences.

Every sentence is the result of truth-operations on elementary sentences.

5.31 The schemata in 4.31 are also meaningful even when "*p*", "*q*", "*r*", etc., are not elementary sentences.

And one can easily see that the sentence in 4.442 expresses a single truth-function of elementary sentences even when "*p*" and "*q*" are truth functions of elementary sentences.

5.32 All truth-functions are results of successive applications of a finite number of truth-operations to elementary sentences.

5.4 It is here that the nonexistence of "logical objects" or "logical constants" (in the sense of Frege and Russell) shows itself.

5.41 For: all results of truth-operations on truth-functions are always identical whenever they are one and the same truth function of elementary sentences.

5.42 That $\vee$, $\supset$, etc., are not relations in the sense of right and left, etc., is obvious.

5.45 If logical primitive signs, then any correct logic must clearly show their relative status and justify their presence [*Dasein*]. The construction of logic *out of* its primitive signs must be clearly shown.

5.46 When we have properly introduced the logical signs, we have introduced the sense of all their combinations at the same time; that is, not only "p $\vee$ q" but "~(p$\vee$~q)" as well, etc., etc. We should then already have introduced the effect of all possible combinations of brackets; and we would thereby have made clear that the proper general primitive signs of logic are not "p $\vee$ q", "($\exists$(x).fx", etc., but rather the most general form of their combinations.

5.452 The introduction of any new device into the symbolism must always be a momentous event. No new symbol may be "innocently" introduced in logic using brackets or in a footnote with a perfectly innocent face.

(Thus in *Principia Mathematica* Russell and Whitehead suddenly present a definition and a fundamental law in words. Why the sudden appearance of words? It requires justification but of course they don't give any because they can't, the whole procedure is forbidden.)

But if at some point there is a need for a new symbol, we must first ask: when will the use of this device now become unavoidable? Its proper place in logic must be clearly shown.

5.47 Clearly, whatever can be said *from the very beginning* about the form of all sentences, must be sayable *all at once*.

All logical operations can be expressed in terms of the elementary sentences themselves. For "*fa*" says the same thing as

"$(\exists x).fx.x = a$".

Where there is complexity, there is argument and function, and where these are present, there are already all the logical constants.

One could say: the sole logical constant is what *all* sentences, by their nature, have in common.

This however is the general form of a sentence.

5.471 The general form of a sentence is the essence of a sentence.

5.4711 The essence of a sentence gives the essence of all description and therefore reveals the essence of the world.

5.473 Logic must take care of itself.

If a sign is *possible*, it is capable of signifying something. Everything that is possible in logic is also permitted. ("Socrates is identical" does not mean anything because there is no such quality as "identical." The sentence is nonsensical because we have not made some arbitrary determination but not because of the symbol being impermissible in itself.)

That is the sense in which we cannot make mistakes in logic.

5.4731 The self-evidence that Russell talked so much about can be completely dispensed with in logic because language itself absolutely forbids all logical mistakes. What makes logic a priori is the impossibility of thinking illogically.

5.4732 We cannot give the wrong sense to a sign.

5.5 Each truth-function is a result of successive applications of the operation

"$(-----T)(\xi,....)$".

This operation negates all the sentences in the right-hand brackets and so I call it the negation of those sentences.

5.501 When the terms of a bracketed expression are sentences—and their order inside the brackets is irrelevant—I indicate this by a sign of the form "$(\bar{\xi})$". "ξ" is a variable whose values are terms of the bracketed expression and the bar over it signifies that it is the representative of all the values inside the brackets.

(E.g., if ξ has three values, P, Q, and R, then

$$(\bar{\xi}) = (P,Q,R).)$$

The values of the variable are prescribed.

The prescription is a description of the sentences having the variable as their representative.

We can distinguish three types of description: 1. Direct enumeration. In this case we substitute for the variable the constants that are its values. 2. Giving a function fx whose values for all values of x are the sentences that are to be described. 3. Giving a formal law, according to which those sentences are constructed, in which case the bracketed expression has as its members all the terms of a formal series.

5.502 Instead of "$(-----T)(\xi,....)$", I can thus write "$N(\bar{\xi})$".

"$N(\bar{\xi})$" is the negation of all the values of the sentence variable ξ.

5.503 It is obviously easy to express using this operation how sentences may and may not be constructed. So it must be possible to express this exactly.

5.51 If ξ has but one value, then $N(\bar{\xi}) = {\sim}p$ (not *p*); if it has two values, then $N(\bar{\xi}) = {\sim}p. {\sim} q$ (neither *p* nor *q*).

5.52 Suppose the value of ξ are all the values of a given function fx for all values of x, then $N(\bar{\xi}) = {\sim}(\exists x).fx$.

5.53 Identity of the object I express by identity of the sign and not by means of a sign of identity. Difference of the objects I express by difference of the signs.

5.5301 That identity is not a relation between objects is obvious. This becomes very clear if, for example, one considers the sentence "$(x){:}fx. \supset .x = a$". This sentence says simply that *only a* satisfies function *f*, not that only objects having a certain relation to *a* satisfy function *f*.

One might then say that *only a* has this relation to *a*, but this would have to be expressed using the identity sign.

5.54 In their general form, sentences occur in other sentences only as bases of truth-operations.

5.541 At first glance, it appears as if there were another way in which one sentence could occur in another.

Especially in certain forms of sentences in psychology, such as "A believes that p is the case" or "A thinks p," etc.

Here it appears superficially as if the sentence p stood in some sort of relation to an object A.

(And these sentences have actually been so taken in modern theory of knowledge [Russell, Moore, etc.].)

5.542 Clearly, however, "A believes that *p*," "A thinks *p*," "A says *p*," are of the form "'*p*' says *p*", and this in no way involves a correlation of fact to object, but rather the correlation of facts by means of the correlation of their objects.

5.5421 This also shows that the soul—the subject, etc.—as conceived in contemporary superficial psychology, does not exist.

For a composite soul would no longer be a soul.

5.5422 The correct explanation of the form of the sentence "A judges that p" must show the impossibility of a judgment being a piece of nonsense. (Russell's theory does not satisfy this condition.)

5.55 The question about all the possible forms of elementary sentences must now be answered a priori.

Elementary sentences consist of names. However, since we cannot specify the number of names having different meanings, we cannot give the composition of elementary sentences.

5.6 *The boundary of my language* is the boundary of my world.

5.61 Logic fills the world: the boundary of logic is also the boundary of the world.

So in logic we cannot say "The world has this in it and this, but not that."

For that would apparently presuppose that some possibilities were thereby being excluded, which cannot possibly be the case, since this would require that logic should extend beyond the boundary of the world; for only then could it have a view from the other side of the boundary.

What we cannot think, that we cannot think: we cannot therefore *say* what we cannot think.

5.62 This thought itself shows how much truth there is in solipsism.

What the solipsist intends to say is absolutely correct. The problem is that the truth cannot speak but only shows itself.

That the world is my world reveals itself in the fact that the boundary of language (the language that I alone understand) is the boundary of my world.

5.621 The world and life are one.

5.63 I am my world. (The microcosm.)

5.631 The thinking, perceiving subject does not exist.

If I were to write a book, *The World as I Found It*, I would also have to include an account of my body in it, and report which parts are subject to my will and which are not, etc. This then would be a method of isolating the subject, or rather of showing that in an important sense there is no subject; that is to say, of it alone in this book mention could *not* be made.

5.632 The subject does not belong to the world but is the boundary of the world.

5.633 Where *in* the world could a metaphysical subject be?

You say this is just like the case with the eye and the visual field. But you do *not* really see the eye.

And there is nothing *in the visual field* to let you infer that it is being seen through an eye.

5.6331 For the form of the visual is clearly not like this:

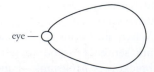

eye —

5.634 This is connected with the fact that no aspect of our experience is a priori.

Everything we see could be other than it is.

Everything we describe could be other than it is.

There is no arrangement of things a priori.

5.64 Here we can see that solipsism thoroughly thought out coincides with pure realism. The *I* in solipsism shrinks to an extensionless point and there remains the reality coordinated with it.

5.641 Thus there really is a sense in which philosophy can speak about the self in a nonpsychological way.

The *I* occurs in philosophy through the fact that the "world is my world."

The philosophical *I* is not the human being, not the human body, nor the human soul with which psychology deals. The philosophical self is the metaphysical subject, the boundary—nowhere in the world.

6. The general form of a truth-function is $[\mathbf{p}, \overline{\boldsymbol{\xi}}, \mathbf{N}(\overline{\boldsymbol{\xi}})]$.

This is the general form of a sentence.

6.001 This says only that every sentence is the result of successive applications of the operation $N'(\overline{\xi})$ to the elementary sentences.

6.002 If we are given the general form of the way in which a sentence is constructed, then we are thereby also given the general form of the way in which by an operation out of one sentence we can create another.

6.1 The sentences of logic are tautologies.

6.11 The sentences of logic therefore say nothing. (They are analytic sentences.)

6.12 The fact that the sentences of logic are tautologies shows the formal—logical—properties of language, of the world.

That its constituent parts connected together *in this way* form a tautology is a characteristic of its constituent parts.

To be able to form a tautology, sentences connected together in a definite way must have definite properties of structure. That they form a tautology when *so* connected shows therefore that they possess these properties of structure.

6.124 The sentences of logic describe the scaffolding of the world, or rather, they present it. They are not *about* anything. They presuppose that names mean something, that elementary sentences make sense [express thoughts]: and that is their connection to the world. Clearly, that some combinations of essentially determinate symbols are tautologies says something about the world. That's the decisive point.

We said that in the symbols that we use, there is something arbitrary, something not. In logic only the latter expresses; but this means that in logic it is not *we* who express, by means of signs, what we want; in logic the nature of inevitably necessary signs *speaks for itself*. Thus in learning the logical syntax of any symbolic language we are *given* all the sentences of logic.

6.127 All sentences in logic are of equal rank, rather than some being essentially primitive from which the others are derived.

Every tautology shows itself that it is a tautology.

6.2 Mathematics is a logical method.

Mathematical sentences are equations and, therefore, pseudo-statements.

6.21 Mathematical sentences express no thoughts.

6.211 In our daily lives we never need mathematical sentences, we use them only to infer from sentences that are not a part of mathematics to other sentences that also are not mathematical.

(In philosophy the question "Why do we really use that word, that sentence?" always leads to valuable insights.)

6.22 The logic of the world that the sentences of logic show to be tautologies, mathematics shows to be equations.

6.23 If two expressions are connected by the sign of equality, this means that they can be substituted for one another. But whether this is the case must be visible in the two expressions themselves.

That two expressions can be substituted for one another characterizes their logical form.

6.24 The way mathematics arrives at its equations is by the method of substitution.

    For equations express the substitutability of two expressions, and we proceed from a number of equations to new ones, replacing expressions by others in accordance with the equations.

6.3 The investigation of logic means the investigation of *all* conformity to *laws*. And outside logic, all is accident.

6.31 The so-called law of induction cannot in any way be a logical law, for obviously it is a meaningful sentence. And therefore it cannot be an a priori law either.

6.32 The law of causality is not a law but the form of a law.

6.321 "Law of causality" is a general name. And just as in mechanics there are, for instance, minimum-laws, such as that of least action, so in physics there are causal laws, laws of the form of causality.

6.3211 People thought that there must be a "law of least action" even before they knew exactly what it was. (Here, as always, a priori certainty turns out to be something purely logical.)

6.33 We do not *believe* a priori in a law of conservation; rather, we *know* a priori the possibility of a logical form.

6.34 All sentences, such as the law of causation, the law of continuity in nature, the law of least expenditure in nature, etc., etc., all these are a priori intuitions of possible forms of sentences in science.

6.341 Newtonian mechanics, for instance, brings the description of the universe into a unified form. Imagine a white surface with irregular black spots. We then say: Whatever kind of picture these make I can always get as near as I like to its description, provided I cover the surface with some sufficiently fine square network and then say of each square that it is either white or black. In this way I bring the description of the surface into a unified form. The form itself is arbitrary because I could have applied with equal success a net with, say, a triangular or hexagonal mesh. It might be that the description would then

have been simpler, that is, we might well have described the surface more accurately with a triangular and coarser, rather than with the finer, square mesh, or vice versa, and so on. To such different networks correspond different systems of describing the world. Mechanics determine a form of description by saying that all sentences in the description of the world must be obtained in a given way from a certain number of already given sentences, the mechanical axioms. It thus provides the bricks for building the edifice of science and says: Whatever building you would erect, you must construct it in some manner with these, and only these, bricks.

    (Just as within the system of numbers we must be able to write down any arbitrary number, so within the system of mechanics we must be able to write down any arbitrary physical sentence.)

6.342 And now we can see the position of logic in relation to mechanics. (We construct the network out of indifferent kinds of figures, such as triangles and hexagons together.) That such a picture can be described by a network of a given form asserts *nothing* about the picture. (For this holds of every picture of this kind.) But *this* does characterize the picture in that it can be described *completely* by a particular net with a *particular* size mesh.

    Likewise, that the world can be described by Newtonian mechanics says nothing about the world, but it does say something, namely, that the world can be described in that particular way. The fact, too, that the world can be described more simply by one system of mechanics rather than by some other says something about the world.

6.343 Mechanics can be seen as an attempt to construct according to a single plan all *true* sentences that we need for the description of the world.

6.3432 Let us not forget that the mechanical description of the world must always be general. There is, for instance, never any mention of *particular* material points in it, but always only of *some points or other.*

6.35 Although the spots in our picture are geometrical figures, geometry can obviously say nothing about their actual form and position. But the network is *purely* geometrical, and all its properties can be given a priori.

Laws, like the law of causation, etc., are of the network and not of what the network describes.

6.36 If there were a law of causality, it might go like this: "There are natural laws."

But clearly, no one can say this: it shows itself.

6.362 What can be described can also happen, and what is excluded by the law of causality cannot be described.

6.363 The process of induction is the process of assuming the *simplest* law that can be reconciled with our experience.

6.3631 However, this process has no logical foundation, only a psychological one.

Clearly, there are no reasons for believing that the simplest course of events will really happen.

6.36311 That the sun will rise tomorrow is a hypothesis, which means that we do not *know* whether the sun will rise.

6.37 Nothing forces one thing to happen because something else has happened. The only kind of necessity is *logical* necessity.

6.371 The entire modern worldview is based on the illusion that the so-called laws of nature can explain natural phenomena.

6.372 People thus treat the laws of nature as if they were unassailable, which is how the ancients treated God and Fate.

And they are right but also wrong, except the ancients were far clearer, in that they recognized a clear endpoint—whereas the moderns make it seem as if *everything* is explained.

6.373 The world exists independently of my will.

6.374 Even if everything we wished for would happen, this would only have been granted, so to say, by fate, for there is no *logical* connection between the will and the world that could guarantee such a thing; and the assumed physical connection itself is not something we can will.

6.375 Just as there is only *logical* necessity, so there is only *logical* impossibility.

6.4 All sentences are of equal value.

6.41 The meaning of the world must lie outside the world. In the world everything is as it is, everything happens as it does happen; there is no value *in* it—if there were any, the value would be worthless.

For a value to be worth something, it must lie outside all happening and outside being this way or that. For all happening and being this way or that is accidental.

The nonaccidental cannot be found in the world, for otherwise this too would then be accidental.

The value of the world lies outside it.

6.42 Likewise, there can be no sentences in ethics. Sentences cannot express anything higher.

6.421 Clearly, ethics cannot be put into words.

Ethics is transcendent.

(Ethics and esthetics are one.)

6.422 As soon as we set up an ethical law having the form "thou shalt . . . ," our first thought is: So then what if I don't do it? But clearly ethics has nothing to do with punishment and reward in the ordinary sense. The question about the consequences of my action must therefore be irrelevant. At least these consequences will not be events. For there must be something right in that formulation of the question. There must be some sort of ethical reward and ethical punishment, but this must lie in the action itself.

6.423 We cannot speak of the will as if it were the ethical subject.

And the will as a phenomenon is only of interest to psychology.

6.43 If good or bad willing changes the world, it only changes the boundaries of the world, not the facts, not the things that can be expressed in language.

6.431 In death, too, the world does not change but only ceases.

6.4311 Death is not an event in life. Death is not lived through.

If by *eternity* we mean not endless temporal duration but timelessness, then to live eternally is to live in the present.

In the same way as our visual field is without boundary, our life is endless.

6.4312 The temporal immortality of the human soul—its eternal survival after death—is not only without guarantee, this assumption could never have the desired effect. Is a riddle solved by the fact that I survive forever? Is eternal life not as enigmatic as our present one? The solution of the riddle of life in space and time lies *outside* of space and time.

(Certainly it does not involve solutions to any of the problems of natural science.)

6.432 *How* the world is is completely indifferent to what is higher. God does not reveal himself *in* the world.

6.4321 The facts all belong to the setting up of the problem, not to its solution.

6.44 It's not *how* the world is that is mystical, but *that* it is.

6.45 To view the world *sub specie aeterni* is the view of it as a—bounded—whole.

The feeling of the world as a bounded whole is the mystical feeling.

6.5 If the answer cannot be put into words, the question, too, cannot be put into words.

The *riddle* does not exist.

If a question can be put at all, then it *can* also be answered.

6.51 Skepticism is *not* irrefutable, only nonsensical, insofar as it tries to raise doubts about what cannot be asked.

For doubt can only exist provided there is a question; a question can exist only provided there is an answer, and this can only be the case provided something *can* be *said*.

6.52 We feel that even if *all possible* scientific questions were answered, the problems of life would still not have been touched at all. To be sure, there would then be no question left, and just this is the answer.

6.521 The vanishing of this problem is the solution to the problem of life.

(Is this not the very reason why people to whom, after long bouts of doubt, the meaning of life became clear, could not then say what this meaning is?)

6.522 The inexpressible indeed exists. This *shows* itself. It is the mystical.

6.53 The right method in philosophy would be to say nothing except what can be said using sentences such as those of natural science—which of course has nothing to do with philosophy—and then, to show those wishing to say something metaphysical that they failed to give any meaning to certain signs in their sentences. Although they would not be satisfied—they would feel you weren't teaching them any philosophy—*this* would be the only right method.

6.54 My sentences are illuminating in the following way: to understand me you must recognize my sentences—once you have climbed out through them, on them, over them—as senseless. (You must, so to speak, throw away the ladder after you have climbed up on it.)

You must climb out through my sentences; then you will see the world correctly.

7. Of what we cannot speak we must be silent.

STUDY QUESTIONS: WITTGENSTEIN, *TRACTATUS*

1. What is the significance of the numbering of the propositions?
2. What makes logic and language possible, according to Wittgenstein?
3. What are sentences pictures of? How are they like thoughts?
4. What is a name?
5. What are elementary sentences?
6. What is an atomic fact?
7. What is the world?
8. What is an object?
9. Space, time, and color are the forms of what?
10. What must a picture have in common with what it depicts?

11. What do logical pictures depict?
12. Where does a thought express itself perceptibly?
13. What is a sentential sign? When and how can we see its essential nature?
14. Can a sentence assert anything about itself? Why?
15. How is a sentence related to its sense?
16. What is the relationship between sentences and facts?
17. What make logic a priori?
18. What is the boundary of my world?
19. Does the subject belong to the world? How is the subject related to the boundary of the world?
20. What is the relationship between *I* (me) and (my) *world*?
21. What do the sentences of logic say?
22. Where is the meaning of the world?
23. Are all sentences of equal value?
24. Can ethics be put into words?
25. How are ethics and aesthetics related?
26. What is mystical about the world?
27. In what way does Wittgenstein think his sentences are illuminating?
28. If you cannot speak about something, what must you do?

Philosophical Bridges: The Influence of the Early Wittgenstein

The philosophers of the Vienna Circle, the logical positivists, hailed the *Tractatus* as a work of genius. One aspect of Wittgenstein's work that seemed especially insightful to them was his analysis of logical claims. According to Wittgenstein, logical claims say nothing because they do not picture any facts. Instead, they articulate or show the logical structure of language. Carnap adapted this idea in his 1934 book, *The Logical Syntax of Language*; he attempted to eradicate the need for Wittgenstein's notion of showing by arguing that the language of science has the capacity to describe its own logical form or syntax.

The positivists tended to see in the *Tractatus* their own ideas in embryonic form and probably misinterpreted Wittgenstein in the process. For instance, Wittgenstein gives us no idea as to what the simple objects in his system are. In the early days of their movement, the positivists tended to assume that these primitive objects would be sense-data and that atomic sentences would be about sense-data.

One of other ways in which the *Tractatus* has had impact on analytic philosophy is its unflinching commitment to the thesis of extensionality, the claim that all true sentences are extensional or referentially transparent (this term is explained in the Introduction to the volume and in the Philosophical Overview of W. V. O. Quine in Section V). The thesis was seen as necessary to avoid postulating the existence of nonmaterial senses or propositions, a claim endorsed later by Carnap and Quine. This thesis was important in later syntactical theories of the mind that try to avoid semantic concepts, such as meaning and content, in explaining mental states.

The most intriguing influence of the early Wittgenstein was that he had on his later self. The *Philosophical Investigations* of 1953 paints a radically different portrait of philosophy than the *Tractatus*, and Wittgenstein develops his new way of thinking in large part by rebutting the assumptions of his earlier work, such as the claims that all sense must determinate and that words can refer independently of their use in a context. Despite the deep differences, there are continuities in Wittgenstein's thought.

BIBLIOGRAPHY

RUSSELL
Primary
The Analysis of Matter, Kegan Paul, 1927
The Analysis of Mind, Allen and Unwin, 1921
Mysticism and Logic and Other Essays, Longman Green and Co., 1918
'On Denoting,' *Mind*, 14, 1908
Our Knowledge of the External World, Allen and Unwin, 1914
'Philosophy of Logical Atomism,' *Monist*, 28, 1918
The Principles of Mathematics, Cambridge University Press, 1903

Secondary
Ayer, A. J., *Bertrand Russell*, University of Chicago Press, 1988
Griffin, N., *Russell's Idealist Apprenticeship*, Oxford University Press, 1991
Hylton, P. W., *Russell, Idealism, and the Emergence of Analytic Philosophy*, Oxford University Press, 1990

Pears, D. F., *Bertrand Russell and the British Tradition in Philosophy*, Fontana, 1967
Sainsbury, Mark, *Russell*, Routledge, 1979

WITTGENSTEIN
Primary
Notebooks 1914–1916, ed. Elizabeth Anscombe, Blackwell, 1961
Tractatus Logico-Philosophicus, ed. Daniel Kolak, *Wittgenstein's Tractatus*, McGraw-Hill, 1998

Secondary
Anscombe, Elizabeth, *An Introduction to Wittgenstein's 'Tractatus,'* Hillary House, 1959
Hacker, P. M. S, *Insight and Illusion*, Clarendon Press, 1986
Mounce, H. G., *Wittgenstein's Tractatus: An Introduction*, Blackwell, 1981
Monk, R., *Wittgenstein: The Duty of Genius*, Jonathan Cape, 1990

SECTION II

◆ PRAGMATISM ◆

PROLOGUE

Charles Peirce (1839–1914) and William James (1842–1910) were the founders of pragmatism. In 1870, Peirce established a discussion group, called 'the Metaphysical Group,' from which pragmatism originated. Peirce argued for a conception of meaning that made it inseparable from experimental evidence; the meaning of a sentence consists in the conditions under which we are warranted in asserting it. At the same time, he claimed that any belief system is fallible and open to revision. He tried to avoid skepticism by claiming that a true theory is one that would be verified in the long run by the scientific community. These claims aim to avoid the false problems that arise from metaphysical theories divorced from common sense.

In 1898, William James coined the term 'pragmatism' to refer to the idea that all differences in belief must be explained in terms of experience or conduct. In his 1907 book, *Pragmatism*, James defines pragmatism as a theory of truth, according to which a theory is true when it permits successful actions, such as prediction, and is coherent with experience. James argues against the correspondence theory of truth, which defines a true sentence as one that corresponds with the facts, and which, therefore, tries to define 'truth' independently of our means of arriving at truths. Selections from the works of Peirce and James are contained in Volume IV of this series.

The philosophy of John Dewey continues with and extends the pragmatist tradition established by Peirce and James. Dewey's work is marked first by his systematic attempt to argue against the classical tradition in philosophy, which identifies the real as the changeless. According to Dewey, the classical tradition generates many metaphysical problems, such as the problems of knowledge and the relationship between mind and body, which can be overcome with pragmatic conceptions of knowledge, truth, and meaning. It is also marked by Dewey's attempts to extend this pragmatic conception to areas such as the philosophy of education, politics, morality, and art.

John Dewey (1859–1952)

Biographical History

John Dewey, who was born in Burlington, Vermont, entered the University of Vermont, where he became interested in philosophy, especially Leibniz, Kant, and Hegel, as well as the evolutionary views of T. H. Huxley. He taught high school for two years in Pennsylvania, but decided to attend graduate school in philosophy at Johns Hopkins University. In only two years, he received his doctoral degree for his dissertation, *The Psychology of Kant.* Six years later, he published a seminal work on Leibniz's critique of Locke, *Leibniz's New Essays Concerning Human Understanding: A Critical Exposition* (1888).

Dewey taught at the University of Michigan for ten years before he became chairman of the Department of Philosophy, Psychology and Education at the University of Chicago, where he designed and ran his Laboratory School. This was an experimental learning environment for children from ages 4 to 15 employing his unorthodox methods of teaching. In 1905, he joined the Philosophy Department at Columbia University, where he remained for the rest of his life. Dewey was a founder of the American Civil Liberties Union. He wrote over 40 books; his major works include *Democracy and Education* (1916), *Human Nature and Conduct* (1922), *Experience and Nature* (1925), *The Quest for Certainty* (1929), and *Logic: The Theory of Inquiry* (1938).

Philosophical Overview

Dewey's main aim is to naturalize philosophy and, in so doing, argue against classical metaphysics that is based on an ontology of independent substances and that results in apparently insoluble philosophical problems, such as skepticism and the mind/body problem. He tries to replace traditional metaphysics with an instrumentalist approach to metaphysics, meaning, and knowledge according to which our experience is the outcome of thoroughly natural interactions and processes. Dewey conceives all phenomena, such as mind, meaning, and knowledge, as natural biological functions of interactions between organisms and a precarious environment of change. We experience real events in relation to ourselves and to each other. The stable elements of the world do not consist in essences and substances, but rather relationships between one process of change and another, such as the correlation between temperature and pressure for a given volume of gas. In this way, Dewey tries to dissolve the philosophical problems concerning the relations between mind and body, subjectivity and objectivity, and the knower and the known.

Mind/Body

Human beings are part of the natural world, and, therefore, cognition is merely an interaction among natural processes. In this way, Dewey argues that the philosophical problem of the mind/body relation is really a scientific concern. Since experience is continuous with nature, the issue is only really how one set of natural events relates to another. The mind is not a substance independent of the body, but rather the natural outcome of biological processes and interactions between an organism and its natural and social environment.

Objective/Subjective

In a similar vein, Dewey also rejects the traditional conception of the subjective/objective distinction, which results in the thesis that nature is purely quantitative and never qualitative. In modern philosophy, objective reality is shorn of all secondary qualities, such as color and other characteristics such as lovely, interesting, and grotesque, which are assigned to the subjective experience of our minds. Dewey rejects this way of distinguishing the subjective and objective by arguing against the concept of independent substances. All such qualities are the result of complex interactions between nature and organisms that are a part of nature. As such, they are neither subjective mental contents nor the properties of independent objects; they are the objective features of natural interactions, which we can experience directly and form part of our access to reality. Experience reveals qualities as real features of the world. It is meaning laden. However, these qualities are not entities or substances, but rather the results of qualitative changes that Dewey calls 'histories.' A history is a process of qualitative change that has a specific outcome. In short, Dewey replaces an ontology of independent substances with that of changing interactions and natural processes, and thereby tries to dissolve the subjective/objective distinction as traditionally conceived.

Knowledge and Meaning

Similarly, Dewey argues that the philosophical problem of knowledge is a misconception. He repudiates the claim that knowledge is a correspondence between a mental image and an object. He tries to replace it with the instrumentalist idea that we have knowledge when we know how to use objects for our practical purposes. Contemplating a mental image could never perform such a role. There is no mental idea of a table beyond the ways in which one can manipulate the table in order to bring about predictable outcomes. In effect, Dewey defines terms such as 'table' operationally in terms of the functions we perform with the object. In other words, Dewey's theory of knowledge is based on an instrumentalist view of meaning, and, as a consequence, knowers are not mere spectators of reality, but rather knowing is essentially an act of participation.

Given this point, Dewey also argues that the philosophical notion of truth as correspondence is misconceived. It should be replaced by the idea of warrant. Whether a belief claim is warranted or not depends on confirmation from a community of appropriate inquirers. Thus, the Cartesian quest for certainty is also misconceived. The claim that one is in a state of certainty at the present moment must itself be false because any such claim depends on future confirmations, and is a matter of degree and is fallible. As a result, warrant is always open to revision. In the *Quest for Certainty*, Dewey argues the search for certainty has wrongly emphasized the theoretical and ideal rather than the practical and useful. It is this intellectual alienation away from practical experience that leads philosophers to overestimate the power of pure reason for comprehending reality, and to underestimate the importance of practice and use.

Dewey rejects the idea of epistemology as a normative philosophical discipline, and he claims that all so-called epistemological problems are really naturalistic or scientific. The logic of enquiry develops from the processes and aims of solving specific problems rather than from preestablished philosophical norms. For instance, science is the activity of predicting and controlling natural phenomena, and, thus, the logic of scientific inquiry is set by these goals. As we shall see, Dewey employs a similar analysis to understand morality.

THE QUEST FOR CERTAINTY

Dewey argues that his version of pragmatism, which he calls instrumentalism, has important educational, moral, and social implications. Some of these implications are discussed in the final chapter of *The Quest for Certainty*, which is excerpted here.

Dewey was convinced that modern society is permeated with false metaphysical modes of thought due to its classical heritage, which assumes separate realms of being, such as Plato's Forms. Furthermore, such classical thought assumes there is a rational world of true timeless being and essences in contrast to the world of becoming. This false metaphysical assumption leads to the dangerous notions of moral absolutes and essences, which stunt human potential. In contrast to the limiting idea of fixed human essences, Dewey claims that character and personality consist of the various habits that result from interactions between individuals and the environment. The mind and self are a changing complex of such habits. Thus, education can use these conditions of character formation to nurture individuals who can function well in society.

In this reading, Dewey rejects the idea of absolute moral norms. He shows how moral demands and goods are constructed socially, in collaboration with others, as part of various social practices, which form part of our democratic or shared way of life. Shared experience requires collaboration and communication. Morality is a way of providing particular solutions to interpersonal problems in a way that unites the individual with his or her social environment and others, which makes possible what Dewey calls 'social intelligence.'

THE CONSTRUCTION OF GOOD

We saw at the outset of our discussion that insecurity generates the quest for certainty. Consequences issue from every experience, and they are the source of our interest in what is present. Absence of arts of regulation diverted the search for security into irrelevant modes of practice, into rite and cult; thought was devoted to discovery of omens rather than of signs of what is to occur. Gradually there was differentiation of two realms, one higher, consisting of the powers which determine human destiny in all important affairs. With this religion was concerned. The other consisted of the prosaic matters in which man relied upon his own skill and his matter-of-fact insight. Philosophy inherited the idea of this division. Meanwhile in Greece many of the arts had attained a state of development which raised them above a merely routine state; there were intimations of measure, order and regularity in materials dealt with which give intimations of underlying rationality. Because of the growth of mathematics, there arose also the ideal of a purely rational knowledge, intrinsically solid and worthy and the means by which the intimations of rationality within changing phenomena could be comprehended within science. For the intellectual class the stay and consolation, the warrant of certainty, provided by religion was hence-forth found in intellectual demonstration of the reality of the objects of an ideal realm.

With the expansion of Christianity, ethico-religious traits came to dominate the purely rational ones. The ultimate authoritative standards for regulation of the dispositions and purposes of the human will were fused with those which satisfied the demands for necessary and universal truth. The authority of ultimate Being, moreover, represented on earth by the Church; that which in its nature transcended intellect was made known by a revelation of which the Church was the interpreter and guardian. The system endured for centuries. While it endured, it provided an integration of belief and conduct for the western world. Unity of thought and practice extended down to every detail of the management of life; efficacy of its operation did not depend upon thought. It was guaranteed by the most powerful and authoritative of all social institutions.

Its seemingly solid foundation was, however, undermined by the conclusions of modern science. They effected, both in themselves and even more in the new interests and activities they generated, a breach between what man is concerned with here and now and the faith concerning ultimate reality which, in determining his ultimate and eternal destiny, had previously given regulation to his present life. The problem of restoring integration and coöperation between man's beliefs about the world in which he lives and his beliefs about the values and purposes that should direct his conduct is the deepest problem of modern life. It is the problem of any philosophy that is not isolated from that life.

The attention which has been given to the fact that in its experimental procedure science has surrendered the separation between knowing and doing has its source in the fact that there is now provided within a limited, specialized and technical field the possibility and earnest, as far as theory is concerned, of effecting the needed integration in the wider field of collective human experience. Philosophy is called upon to be the theory of the practice, through ideas sufficiently definite to be operative in experimental endeavor, by which the integration may be made secure in actual experience. Its central problem is the relation that exists between the beliefs about the nature of things due to natural science to beliefs about values—using that word to designate whatever is taken to have rightful authority in the direction of conduct. A philosophy which should take up this problem is struck first of all by the fact that beliefs about values are pretty much in the position in which beliefs about nature were before the scientific revolution. There is either a basic distrust of the capacity of experience to develop its own regulative standards, and an appeal to what philosophers call eternal values, in order to ensure regulation of belief and action; or there is acceptance of enjoyments actually experienced irrespective of the method or operation by which they are brought into existence. Complete

bifurcation between rationalistic method and an empirical method has its final and most deeply human significance in the ways in which good and bad are thought of and acted for and upon.

As far as technical philosophy reflects this situation, there is division of theories of values into two kinds. On the one hand, goods and evils, in every region of life, as they are concretely experienced, are regarded as characteristic of an inferior order of Being—intrinsically inferior. Just because they are things of human experience, their worth must be estimated by reference to standards and ideals derived from ultimate reality. Their defects and perversion are attributed to the same fact; they are to be corrected and controlled through adoption of methods of conduct derived from loyalty to the requirements of Supreme Being. This philosophic formulation gets actuality and force from the fact that it is a rendering of the beliefs of men in general as far as they have come under the influence of institutional religion. Just as rational conceptions were once superimposed upon observed and temporal phenomena, so eternal values are superimposed upon experienced goods. In one case as in the other, the alternative is supposed to be confusion and lawlessness. Philosophers suppose these eternal values are known by reason; the mass of persons that they are divinely revealed.

Nevertheless, with the expansion of secular interests, temporal values have enormously multiplied; they absorb more and more attention and energy. The sense of transcendent values has become enfeebled; instead of permeating all things in life, it is more and more restricted to special times and acts. The authority of the church to declare and impose divine will and purpose has narrowed. Whatever men say and profess, their tendency in the presence of actual evils is to resort to natural and empirical means to remedy them. But in formal belief, the old doctrine of the inherently disturbed and unworthy character of the goods and standards of ordinary experience persists. This divergence between what men do and what they nominally profess is closely connected with the confusions and conflicts of modern thought.

It is not meant to assert that no attempts have been made to replace the older theory regarding the authority of immutable and transcendent values by conceptions more congruous with the practices of daily life. The contrary is the case. The utilitarian theory, to take one instance, has had great power. The idealistic school is the only one in contemporary philosophies, with the exception of one form of neo-realism, that makes much of the notion of a reality which is all one with ultimate moral and religious values. But this school is also the one most concerned with the conservation of "spiritual" life. Equally significant is the fact that empirical theories retain the notion that thought and judgment are concerned with values that are experienced independently of them. For these theories, emotional satisfactions occupy the same place that sensations hold in traditional empiricism. Values are constituted by liking and enjoyment; to be enjoyed and to be a value are two names for one and the same fact. Since science has extruded values from its objects, these empirical theories do everything possible to emphasize their purely subjective character of value. A psychological theory of desire and liking is supposed to cover the whole ground of the theory of values; in it, immediate feeling is the counterpart of immediate sensation.

I shall not object to this empirical theory as far as it connects the theory of values with concrete experiences of desire and satisfaction. The idea that there is such a connection is the only way known to me by which the pallid remoteness of the rationalistic theory, and the only too glaring presence of the institutional theory of transcendental values can be escaped. The objection is that the theory in question holds down value to objects *antecedently* enjoyed, apart from reference to the method by which they come into existence; it takes enjoyments which are casual because unregulated by intelligent operations to be values in and of themselves. Operational thinking needs to be applied to the judgment of values just as it has now finally been applied in conceptions of physical objects. Experimental empiricism in the field of ideas of good and bad is demanded to meet the conditions of the present situation.

The scientific revolution came about when material of direct and uncontrolled experience was taken as problematic; as supplying material to be transformed by reflective operations into known objects. The contrast between experienced and known objects was found to be a temporal one; namely, one between empirical subject-matters which were had or "given" prior to the acts of experimental variation and redisposition and those which succeeded these acts and issued from them.

The notion of an act whether of sense or thought which supplied a valid measure of thought in immediate knowledge was discredited. Consequences of operations became the important thing. The suggestion almost imperatively follows that escape from the defects of transcendental absolutism is not to be had by setting up as values enjoyments that happen anyhow, but in defining value by enjoyments which are the consequences of intelligent action. Without the intervention of thought, enjoyments are not values but problematic goods, becoming values when they re-issue in a changed form from intelligent behavior. The fundamental trouble with the current empirical theory of values is that it merely formulates and justifies the socially prevailing habit of regarding enjoyments as they are actually experienced as values in and of themselves. It completely side-steps the question of regulation of these enjoyments. This issue involves nothing less than the problem of the directed reconstruction of economic, political and religious institutions.

The formal statement may be given concrete content by pointing to the difference between the enjoyed and the enjoyable, the desired and the desirable, the satis*fying* and the satis*factory*. To say that something is enjoyed is to make a statement about a fact, something already in existence; it is not to judge the value of that fact. There is no difference between such a proposition and one which says that something is sweet or sour, red or black. It is just correct or incorrect and that is the end of the matter. But to call an object a value is to assert that it satisfies or fulfills certain conditions. Function and status in meeting conditions is a different matter from bare existence. The fact that something is desired only raises the *question* of its desirability; it does not settle it. Only a child in the degree of his immaturity thinks to settle the question of desirability by reiterated proclamation: "I want it, I want it, I want it." What is objected to in the current empirical theory of values is not connection of them with desire and enjoyment but failure to distinguish between enjoyments of radically different sorts. There are many common expressions in which the difference of the two kinds is clearly recognized. Take for example the difference between the ideas of "satisfying" and "satisfactory." To say that something satisfies is to report something as an isolated finality. To assert that it is satis*factory* is to define it in its connections and interactions. The fact that it pleases or is immediately congenial poses a problem to judgment. How shall the satisfaction be rated? Is it a value or is it not? Is it something to be prized and cherished, *to be* enjoyed? Not stern moralists alone but everyday experience informs us that finding satisfaction in a thing may be a warning, a summons to be on the lookout for consequences. To declare something satis*factory* is to assert that it meets specifiable conditions. It is, in effect, a judgment that the thing "will do." It involves a prediction; it contemplates a future in which the thing will continue to serve; it *will* do. It asserts a consequence the thing will actively institute; it will *do*. That it is satisfying is the content of a proposition of fact; that it is satisfactory is a judgment, an estimate, an appraisal. It denotes an attitude *to be* taken, that of striving to perpetuate and to make secure.

This element of direction by an idea of value applies to science as well as anywhere else. For in every scientific undertaking, there is passed a constant succession of estimates; such as "it is worth treating these facts as data or evidence; it is advisable to try this experiment; to make that observation; to entertain such and such a hypothesis; to perform this calculation," etc.

The word "taste" has perhaps got too completely associated with arbitrary liking to express the nature of judgments of value. But if the word be used in the sense of an appreciation at once cultivated and active, one may say that the formation of taste is the chief matter wherever values enter in, whether intellectual, esthetic or moral. Relatively immediate judgments, which we call tact or to which we give the name of intuition, do not precede reflective inquiry, but are the funded products of much thoughtful experience. Expertness of taste is at once the result and the reward of constant exercise of thinking. Instead of there being no disputing about tastes, they are the one thing worth disputing about, if by "dispute" is signified discussion involving reflective inquiry. Taste, if we use the word in its best sense, is the outcome of experi-

ence brought cumulatively to bear on the intelligent appreciation of the real worth of likings and enjoyments. There is nothing in which a person so completely reveals himself as in the things which he judges enjoyable and desirable. Such judgments are the sole alternative to the domination of belief by impulse, chance, blind habit and self-interest. The formation of a cultivated and effectively operative good judgment or taste with respect to what is esthetically admirable, intellectually acceptable and morally approvable is the supreme task set to human beings by the incidents of experience.

Propositions about what is or has been liked are of instrumental value in reaching judgments of value, in as far as the conditions and consequences of the thing liked are thought about. In themselves they make no claims; they put forth no demand upon subsequent attitudes and acts; they profess no authority to direct. If one likes a thing he likes it; that *is* a point about which there can be no dispute:—although it is not so easy to state just *what* is liked as is frequently assumed. A judgment about what is *to be* desired and enjoyed is, on the other hand, a claim on future action; it possesses *de jure* and not merely *de facto* quality. It is a matter of frequent experience that likings and enjoyments are of all kinds, and that many are such as reflective judgments condemn. By way of self-justification and "rationalization," an enjoyment creates a tendency to assert that the thing enjoyed is a value. This assertion of validity adds authority to the fact. It is a decision that the object has a right to exist and hence a claim upon action to further its existence.

The analogy between the status of the theory of values and the theory of ideas about natural objects before the rise of experimental inquiry may be carried further. The sensationalistic theory of the origin and test of thought evoked, by way of reaction, the transcendental theory of *a priori* ideas. For it failed utterly to account for objective connection, order and regularity in objects observed. Similarly, any doctrine that identifies the mere fact of being liked with the value of the object liked so fails to give direction to conduct when direction is needed that it automatically calls forth the assertion that there are values eternally in Being that are the standards of all judgments and the obligatory ends of all action. Without the introduction of operational thinking, we oscillate between a theory that, in order to save the objectivity of judgments of values, isolates them from experience and nature, and a theory that, in order to save their concrete and human significance, reduces them to mere statements about our own feelings.

Not even the most devoted adherents of the notion that enjoyment and value are equivalent facts would venture to assert that because we have once liked a thing we should go on liking it; they are compelled to introduce the idea that *some* tastes are to be cultivated. Logically, there is no ground for introducing the idea of cultivation; liking is liking, and one is as good as another. If enjoyments *are* values, the judgment of value cannot regulate the form which liking takes; it cannot regulate its own conditions. Desire and purpose, and hence action, are left without guidance, although the question of regulation of their formation is the supreme problem of practical life. Values (to sum up) may be connected inherently with liking, and yet not with *every* liking but only with those that judgment has approved, after examination of the relation upon which the object liked depends. A casual liking is one that happens without knowledge of how it occurs nor to what effect. The difference between it and one which is sought because of a judgment that it is worth having and is to be striven for, makes just the difference between enjoyments which are accidental and enjoyments that have value and hence a claim upon our attitude and conduct. . . .

When theories of values do not afford intellectual assistance in framing ideas and beliefs about values that are adequate to direct action, the gap must be filled by other means. If intelligent method is lacking, prejudice, the pressure of immediate circumstance, self-interest and class-interest, traditional customs, institutions of accidental historic origin, are *not* lacking, and they tend to take the place of intelligence. Thus we are led to our main proposition: *Judgments about values are judgments about the conditions and the results of experienced objects; judgments about that which should regulate the formation of our desires, affections and enjoyments.* For whatever decides their formation will determine the main course of our conduct, personal and social.

If it sounds strange to hear that we should frame our judgments as to what has value by considering the connections in existence of what we like and enjoy, the reply is not far to seek. As long as we do not engage in this inquiry enjoyments (values if we choose to apply that term) are casual; they are given by "nature," not constructed by art. Like natural objects in their qualitative existence, they at most only supply material for elaboration in rational discourse. A *feeling* of good or excellence is as far removed from goodness in fact as a feeling that objects are intellectually thus and so is removed from their being actually so. To recognize that the truth of natural objects can be reached only by the greatest care in selecting and arranging directed operations, and then to suppose that values can be truly determined by the mere fact of liking seems to leave us in an incredible position. All the serious perplexities of life come back to the genuine difficulty of forming a judgment as to the values of the situation; they come back to a conflict of goods. Only dogmatism can suppose that serious moral conflict is between something clearly bad and something known to be good, and that uncertainty lies wholly in the will of the one choosing. Most conflicts of importance are conflicts between things which are or have been satisfying, not between good and evil. And to suppose that we can make a hierarchical table of values at large once for all, a kind of catalogue in which they are arranged in an order of ascending or descending worth, is to indulge in a gloss on our inability to frame intelligent judgments in the concrete. Or else it is to dignify customary choice and prejudice by a title of honor.

The alternative to definition, classification and systematization of satisfactions just as they happen to occur is judgment of them by means of the relations under which they occur. If we know the conditions under which the act of liking, of desire and enjoyment, takes place, we are in a position to know what are the consequences of that act. The difference between the desired and the desirable, admired and the admirable, becomes effective at just this point. Consider the difference between the proposition "That thing has been eaten," and the judgment "That thing is edible." The former statement involves no knowledge of any relation except the one stated; while we are able to judge of the edibility of anything only when we have a knowledge of its interactions with other things sufficient to enable us to foresee its probable effects when it is taken into the organism and produces effects there.

To assume that anything can be known in isolation from its connections with other things is to identify knowing with merely having some object before perception or in feeling, and is thus to lose the key to the traits that distinguish an object as known. It is futile, even silly, to suppose that some quality that is directly present constitutes the whole of the thing presenting the quality. It does not do so when the quality is that of being hot or fluid or heavy, and it does not when the quality is that of giving pleasure, or being enjoyed. Such qualities are, once more, effects, ends in the sense of closing termini of processes involving causal connections. They are something to be investigated, challenges to inquiry and judgment. The more connections and interactions we ascertain, the more we *know* the object in question. Thinking is search for these connections. Heat experienced as a consequence of directed operations has a meaning quite different from the heat that is casually experienced without knowledge of how it came about. The same is true of enjoyments. Enjoyments that issue from conduct directed by insight into relations have a meaning and a validity due to the way in which they are experienced. Such enjoyments are not repented of; they generate no after-taste of bitterness. Even in the midst of direct enjoyment, there is a sense of validity, of authorization, which intensifies the enjoyment. There is solicitude for perpetuation of the *object* having value which is radically different from mere anxiety to perpetuate the *feeling* of enjoyment.

Such statements as we have been making are, therefore, far from implying that there are values apart from things actually enjoyed as good. To find a thing enjoy*able* is, so to say, a *plus* enjoyment. We saw that it was foolish to treat the scientific object as a rival to or substitute for the perceived object, since the former is intermediate between uncertain and settled situations and those experienced under conditions of greater control. In the same way, judgment of the value of an object to be experienced is instrumental to appreciation of it when it is realized. But the notion that every object that happens to satisfy has an equal claim with every other to be a value is like supposing that every

object of perception has the same cognitive force as every other. There is no knowledge without perception; but objects perceived are *known* only when they are determined as consequences of connective operations. There is no value except where there is satisfaction, but there have to be certain conditions fulfilled to transform a satisfaction into a value.

It is not a dream that it is possible to exercise some degree of regulation of the occurrence of enjoyments which are of value. Realization of the possibility is exemplified, for example, in the technologies and arts of industrial life—that is, up to a definite limit. Men desired heat, light, and speed of transit and of communication beyond what nature provides of itself. These things have been attained not by lauding the enjoyment of these things and preaching their desirability, but by study of the conditions of their manifestation. Knowledge of relations having been obtained, ability to produce followed, and enjoyment ensued as a matter of course. It is, however, an old story that enjoyment of these things as goods is no warrant of their bringing only good in their train. As Plato was given to pointing out, the physician knows how to heal and the orator to persuade, but the ulterior knowledge of whether it is better for a man to be healed or to be persuaded to the orator's opinion remains unsettled. Here there appears the split between what are traditionally and conventionally called the values of the baser arts and the higher values of the truly personal and humane arts.

This distinction between higher and lower types of value is itself something to be looked into. Why should there be a sharp division made between some goods as physical and material and others as ideal and "spiritual"? The question touches the whole dualism of the material and the ideal at its root. To denominate anything "matter" or "material" is not in truth to disparage it. It is, if the designation is correctly applied, a way of indicating that the thing in question is a condition or means of the existence of something else. And disparagement of effective means is practically synonymous with disregard of the things that are termed, in eulogistic fashion, ideal and spiritual. For the latter terms if they have any concrete application at all signify something which is a desirable consummation of conditions, a cherished fulfillment of means. The sharp separation between material and ideal good thus deprives the latter of the underpinning of effective support while it opens the way for treating things which should be employed as means as ends in themselves. For since men cannot after all live without some measure of possession of such matters as health and wealth, the latter things will be viewed as values and ends in isolation unless they are treated as integral constituents of the goods that are deemed supreme and final.

The relations that determine the occurrence of what human beings experience, especially when social connections are taken into account, are indefinitely wider and more complex than those that determine the events termed physical; the latter are the outcome of definite selective operations. This is the reason why we know something about remote objects like the stars better than we know significantly characteristic things about our own bodies and minds. We forget the infinite number of things we do not know about the stars, or rather that what we call a star is itself the product of the elimination, enforced and deliberate, of most of the traits that belong to an actual existence. The amount of knowledge we possess about stars would not seem very great or very important if it were carried over to human beings and exhausted our knowledge of them. It is inevitable that genuine knowledge of man and society should lag far behind physical knowledge.

But this difference is not a ground for making a sharp division between the two, nor does it account for the fact that we make so little use of the experimental method of forming our ideas and beliefs about the concerns of man in his characteristic social relations. For this separation religions and philosophies must admit some responsibility. They have erected a distinction between a narrower scope of relations and a wider and fuller one into a difference of kind, naming one kind material, and the other mental and moral. They have charged themselves gratuitously with the office of diffusing belief in the necessity of the division, and with instilling contempt for the material as something inferior in kind in its intrinsic nature and worth. Formal philosophies undergo evaporation of their technical solid contents; in a thinner and more viable form they find their way into the minds of those who know nothing of their original forms. When these diffuse and, so to say, airy emanations re-crystallize in the popular mind they form a hard deposit of opinion that alters slowly and with great difficulty.

What difference would it actually make in the arts of conduct, personal and social, if the experimental theory were adopted not as a mere theory, but as a part of the working equipment of habitual attitudes on the part of everyone?

Change from forming ideas and judgments of value on the basis of conformity to antecedent objects, to constructing enjoyable objects directed by knowledge of consequences, is a change from looking to the past to looking to the future. I do not for a moment suppose that the experiences of the past, personal and social, are of no importance. For without them we should not be able to frame any ideas whatever of the conditions under which objects are enjoyed nor any estimate of the consequences of esteeming and liking them. But past experiences are significant in giving us intellectual instrumentalities of judging just these points. They are tools, not finalities. Reflection upon what we have liked and have enjoyed is a necessity. But it tells us nothing about the *value* of these things until enjoyments are themselves reflectively controlled, or, until, as they are recalled, we form the best judgment possible about what led us to like this sort of thing and what has issued from the fact that we liked it.

We are not, then, to get away from enjoyments experienced in the past and from recall of them, but from the notion that they are the arbiters of things to be further enjoyed. At present, the arbiter is found in the past, although there are many ways of interpreting what in the past is authoritative. Nominally, the most influential conception doubtless is that of a revelation once had or a perfect life once lived. Reliance upon precedent, upon institutions created in the past, especially in law, upon rules of morals that have come to us through unexamined customs, upon uncriticized tradition, are other forms of dependence. It is not for a moment suggested that we can get away from customs and established institutions. A mere break would doubtless result simply in chaos. But there is no danger of such a break. Mankind is too inertly conservative both by constitution and by education to give the idea of this danger actuality. What there is genuine danger of is that the force of new conditions will produce disruption externally and mechanically: this is an ever present danger. The prospect is increased, not mitigated, by that conservatism which insists upon the adequacy of old standards to meet new conditions. What is needed is intelligent examination of the consequences that are actually effected by inherited institutions and customs, in order that there may be intelligent consideration of the ways in which they are to be intentionally modified in behalf of generation of different consequences.

This is the significant meaning of transfer of experimental method from the technical field of physical experience to the wider field of human life. We trust the method in forming our beliefs about things not directly connected with human life. In effect, we distrust it in moral, political and economic affairs. In the fine arts, there are many signs of a change. In the past, such a change has often been an omen and precursor of changes in other human attitudes. But, generally speaking, the idea of actively adopting experimental method in social affairs, in the matters deemed of most enduring and ultimate worth, strikes most persons as a surrender of all standards and regulative authority. But in principle, experimental method does not signify random and aimless action; it implies direction by ideas and knowledge. The question at issue is a practical one. Are there in existence the ideas and the knowledge that permit experimental method to be effectively used in social interests and affairs?

Where will regulation come from if we surrender familiar and traditionally prized values as our directive standards? Very largely from the findings of the natural sciences. For one of the effects of the separation drawn between knowledge and action is to deprive scientific knowledge of its proper service as a guide of conduct except once more in those technological fields which have been degraded to an inferior rank. Of course, the complexity of the conditions upon which objects of human and liberal value depend is a great obstacle, and it would be too optimistic to say that we have as yet enough knowledge of the scientific type to enable us to regulate our judgments of value very extensively. But we have more knowledge than we try to put to use, and until we try

more systematically we shall not know what are the important gaps in our sciences judged from the point of view of their moral and humane use.

Another great difference to be made by carrying the experimental habit into all matter of practice is that it cuts the roots of what is often called subjectivism, but which is better termed egoism. The subjective attitude is much more widespread than would be inferred from the philosophies which have that label attached. It is as rampant in realistic philosophies as in any others, sometimes even more so, although disguised from those who hold these philosophies under the cover of reverence for and enjoyment of ultimate values. For the implication of placing the standard of thought and knowledge in antecedent existence is that our thought makes no difference in what is significantly real. It then affects only our own attitude toward it.

This constant throwing of emphasis back upon a change made in ourselves instead of one made in the world in which we live seems to me the essence of what is objectionable in "subjectivism." Its taint hangs about even Platonic realism with its insistent evangelical dwelling upon the change made within the mind by contemplation of the realm of essence, and its depreciation of action as transient and all but sordid—a concession to the necessities of organic existence. All the theories which put conversion "of the eye of the soul" in the place of a conversion of natural and social objects that modifies goods actually experienced, is a retreat and escape from existence—and this retraction into self is, once more, the heart of subjective egoisms. The typical example is perhaps the other-worldliness found in religions whose chief concern is with the salvation of the personal soul. But other-worldliness is found as well in estheticism and in all seclusion within ivory towers.

The nature in detail of the revolution that would be wrought by carrying into the region of values the principle now embodied in scientific practice cannot be told; to attempt it would violate the fundamental idea that we know only after we have acted and in consequences of the outcome of action. But it would surely effect a transfer of attention and energy from the subjective to the objective. Men would think of themselves as agents not as ends; ends would be found in experienced enjoyment of the fruits of a transforming activity. In as far as the subjectivity of modern thought represents a discovery of the part played by personal responses, organic and acquired, in the causal production of the qualities and values of objects, it marks the possibility of a decisive gain. It puts us in possession of some of the conditions that control the occurrence of experienced objects, and thereby it supplies us with an instrument of regulation. There is something querulous in the sweeping denial that things as experienced, as perceived and enjoyed, in any way depend upon interaction with human selves. The error of doctrines that have exploited the part played by personal and subjective reactions in determining what is perceived and enjoyed lies either in exaggerating this factor of constitution into the sole condition—as happens in subjective idealism—or else in treating it as a finality instead of, as with all knowledge, an instrument in direction of further action.

A third significant change that would issue from carrying over experimental method from physics to man concerns the import of standards, principles, rules. With the transfer, these, and all tenets and creeds about good and goods, would be recognized to be hypotheses. Instead of being rigidly fixed, they would be treated as intellectual instruments to be tested and confirmed—and altered—through consequences effected by acting upon them. They would lose all pretence of finality—the ulterior source of dogmatism. It is both astonishing and depressing that so much of the energy of mankind has gone into fighting for (with weapons of the flesh as well as of the spirit) the truth of creeds, religious, moral and political, as distinct from what has gone into effort to try creeds by putting them to the test of acting upon them. The change would do away with the intolerance and fanaticism that attend the notion that beliefs and judgments are capable of inherent truth and authority; inherent in the sense of being independent of what they lead to when used as directive principles. The transformation does not imply merely that men are responsible for acting upon what they profess to believe; that is an old doctrine. It goes much further. Any belief as such is tentative, hypothetical; it is not just to be acted upon, but is to be *framed* with

reference to its office as a guide to action. Consequently, it should be the last thing in the world to be picked up casually and then clung to rigidly. When it is apprehended as a tool and only a tool, an instrumentality of direction, the same scrupulous attention will go to its formation as now goes into the making of instruments of precision in technical fields. Men, instead of being proud of accepting and asserting beliefs and "principles" on the ground of loyalty, will be as ashamed of that procedure as they would now be to confess their assent to a scientific theory out of reverence for Newton or Helmholz or whomever, without regard to evidence.

The various modifications that would result from adoption in social and humane subjects of the experimental way of thinking are perhaps summed up in saying that it would place *method and means* upon the level of importance that has, in the past, been imputed exclusively to ends. Means have been regarded as menial, and the useful as the servile. Means have been treated as poor relations to be endured, but not inherently welcome. The very meaning of the word "ideals" is significant of the divorce which has obtained between means and ends. "Ideals" are thought to be remote and inaccessible of attainment; they are too high and fine to be sullied by realization. They serve vaguely to arouse "aspiration," but they do not evoke and direct strivings for embodiment in actual existence. They hover in an indefinite way over the actual scene; they are expiring ghosts of a once significant kingdom of divine reality whose rule penetrated to every detail of life.

It is impossible to form a just estimate of the paralysis of effort that has been produced by indifference to means. Logically, it is truistic that lack of consideration for means signifies that so-called ends are not taken seriously. It is as if one professed devotion to painting pictures conjoined with contempt for canvas, brush and paints; or love of music on condition that no instruments, whether the voice or something external, be used to make sounds. The good workman in the arts is known by his respect for his tools and by his interest in perfecting his technique. The glorification in the arts of ends at the expense of means would be taken to be a sign of complete insincerity or even insanity. Ends separated from means are either sentimental indulgences or if they happen to exist are merely accidental. The ineffectiveness in action of "ideals" is due precisely to the supposition that means and ends are not on exactly the same level with respect to the attention and care they demand.

Practical needs are imminent; with the mass of mankind they are imperative. Moreover, speaking generally, men are formed to act rather than to theorize. Since the ideal ends are so remotely and accidentally connected with immediate and urgent conditions that need attention, after lip service is given to them, men naturally devote themselves to the latter. If a bird in the hand is worth two in a neighboring bush, an actuality in hand is worth, for the direction of conduct, many ideals that are so remote as to be invisible and inaccessible. Men hoist the banner of the ideal, and then march in the direction that concrete conditions suggest and reward.

The present state of industrial life seems to give a fair index of the existing separation of means and ends. Isolation of economics from ideal ends, whether of morals or of organized social life, was proclaimed by Aristotle. Certain things, he said, are conditions of a worthy life, personal and social, but are not constituents of it. The economic life of man, concerned with satisfaction of wants, is of this nature. Men have wants and they must be satisfied. But they are only prerequisites of a good life, not intrinsic elements in it. Most philosophers have not been so frank nor perhaps so logical. But upon the whole, economics has been treated as on a lower level than either morals or politics. Yet the life which men, women and children actually lead, the opportunities open to them, the values they are capable of enjoying, their education, their share in all the things of art and science, are mainly determined by economic conditions. Hence we can hardly expect a moral system which ignores economic conditions to be other than remote and empty.

Industrial life is correspondingly brutalized by failure to equate it as the means by which social and cultural values are realized. That the economic life, thus exiled from the pale of higher values, takes revenge by declaring that it is the only social reality, and by means of the doctrine of materialistic determination of institutions and conduct in all fields, denies to deliberate morals and politics any share of causal regulation, is not surprising.

When economists were told that their subject-matter was merely material, they naturally thought they could be "scientific" only by excluding all reference to distinctively human values. Material wants, efforts to satisfy them, even the scientifically regulated technologies highly developed in industrial activity, are then taken to form a complete and closed field. If any reference to social ends and values is introduced it is by way of an external addition, mainly hortatory. That economic life largely determines the conditions under which mankind has access to concrete values may be recognized or it may not be. In either case, the notion that it is the means to be utilized in order to secure significant values as the common and shared possession of mankind is alien and inoperative. To many persons, the idea that the ends professed by morals are impotent save as they are connected with the working machinery of economic life seems like deflowering the purity of moral values and obligations.

We have noted more than once how modern philosophy has been absorbed in the problem of affecting an adjustment between the conclusions of natural science and the beliefs and values that have authority in the direction of life. The genuine and poignant issue does not reside where philosophers for the most part have placed it. It does not consist in accommodation to each other of two realms, one physical and the other ideal and spiritual, nor in the reconciliation of the "categories" of theoretical and practical reason. It is found in that isolation of executive means and ideal interests which has grown up under the influence of the separation of theory and practice. For this, by nature, involves the separation of the material and the spiritual. Its solution, therefore, can be found only in action wherein the phenomena of material and economic life are equated with the purposes that command the loyalties of affection and purpose, and in which ends and ideals are framed in terms of the possibilities of actually experienced situations. But while the solution cannot be found in "thought" alone, it can be furthered by thinking which is operative—which frames and defines ideas in terms of what may be done, and which uses the conclusions of science as instrumentalities. William James was well within the bounds of moderation when he said that looking forward instead of backward, looking to what the world and life might become instead of to what they have been, is an alteration in the "seat of authority."

It was incidentally remarked earlier in our discussion that the serious defect in the current empirical philosophy of values, the one which identifies them with things actually enjoyed irrespective of the conditions upon which they depend, is that it formulates and in so far consecrates the conditions of our present social experience. Throughout these chapters, primary attention has perforce been given to the methods and statements of philosophic theories. But these statements are technical and specialized in formulation only. In origin, content and import they are reflections of some condition or some phase of concrete human experience. Just as the theory of the separation of theory and practice has a practical origin and a momentous practical consequence, so the empirical theory that values are identical with whatever men actually enjoy, no matter how or what, formulates an aspect, and an undesirable one, of the present social situation. . . .

STUDY QUESTIONS: DEWEY, *THE QUEST FOR CERTAINTY*

1. What generated the quest for certainty, and what were the consequences of that?
2. What is the deepest problem of modern life?
3. What are the most important consequences of the division between rational and empirical methods?
4. Why does operational thinking need to be applied to value judgments?
5. What is the current empirical theory of values? What, according to Dewey, is problematic about it? What is the transcendental absolute theory of values? What is the problem with that theory?
6. What is the difference between 'satisfying' and 'satisfactory'? For what purpose does Dewey make this distinction?
7. What is Dewey's main proposition?
8. How does Dewey characterize knowing? How does this impact on the study of values?
9. What does Dewey say about the division of goods into physical and ideal?
10. What are the benefits of employing the experimental method in the study of humans?
11. What are the main points that Dewey makes concerning industrial life?

Philosophical Bridges: Dewey's Influence

In the first half of the twentieth century, Dewey was perhaps the most influential philosopher in the United States. Today he is best known for three aspects of his pragmatic philosophy.

1. Dewey's attacks on traditional epistemology and metaphysics have undergone recently a revival, having influenced contemporary U.S. philosophers such as Richard Rorty (see Section VIII). Dewey argues systematically against traditional epistemology. He rejects the thesis that knowledge and truth require a correspondence between a mental image and an object. Rather, we have knowledge when we know how to use objects for our practical purposes. Mental images are nothing beyond knowing how to manipulate these objects appropriately. These aspects of Dewey's analysis have inspired recent challenges, such as Rorty's, to theories of knowledge based on representations and correspondence. Furthermore, Dewey's aim is to naturalize philosophy. This means showing that, once they are freed of misconceptions, philosophical problems are scientific.

2. Dewey's alternative philosophical vision is centered on social practices. For example, truth should be replaced by the idea of warrant, which depends on confirmation from a community of appropriate inquirers. In morality, Dewey eschewed the idea of absolute moral standards and instead stressed the collaborative process of constructing the good. In politics, democracy is a way of life that involves social intelligence. This social aspect of Dewey's thought has appealed to recent thinkers such as Rorty, who have seen in it a way to combine pragmatism with the insights of the later Wittgenstein (see Section IV).

3. Dewey's educational philosophy, which emphasizes learning through doing and active problem solving, led to a relatively popular progressive education movement in the United States and beyond, which has had an enormous influence on teaching practices.

BIBLIOGRAPHY

DEWEY
Primary
Democracy and Education, Free Press, 1966
Experience and Nature, Open Court, 1925
Human Nature and Conduct, H. Holt, 1922
Logic: The Theory of Inquiry, H. Holt, 1938
The Quest for Certainty, Minton Balch, 1929

Secondary
Boisvert, R., *Dewey's Metaphysics*, Fordham University Press, 1987

Campbell, J., *Understanding John Dewey*, Open Court, 1995
Hook, Sidney, *John Dewey: An Intellectual Portrait*, Greenwood Press, 1971
Gouinlock, J., *John Dewey's Philosophy of Value*, Humanities Press, 1972
Sleeper, R. W., *The Necessity of Pragmatism*, Yale University Press, 1986

SECTION III

THE LOGICAL POSITIVISTS

PROLOGUE

When Moritz Schlick was appointed to the chair of philosophy in Vienna in 1922, he gathered around him a group of like-minded thinkers who were named the Vienna Circle and, later, the logical positivists. Among those present at their Thursday evening meetings were Schlick, Friedrich Waismann, Herbert Feigl, as well as the mathematicians Hans Hahn and Kurt Gödel and the economist Otto Neurath. The young German philosopher Rudolf Carnap joined the group in 1926. Hans Reichenbach formed a similar group in Berlin, which included Carl Hempel.

For three years from 1926, the Vienna Circle met to study Wittgenstein's *Tractatus*. In 1928, Carnap published his work, *The Logical Structure of the World*. In this work, he audaciously tries to carry out the philosophical program, proposed originally by Russell, of showing how our concepts of the world and the mind are logical constructions out of sense-data. Carnap saw his philosophical program as part of a larger battle for scientific clarity, according to which the contemporary world needs to combat the irrationalist philosophies, such as Heidegger's.

This view influenced the group, which in 1929 issued its pamphlet, *The Scientific Conception of the World: The Vienna Circle*. In this philosophical manifesto, they advocate the principle of verification according to which, to be meaningful, any statement must be verifiable in principle. They welcomed the implication that this rendered all metaphysics meaningless nonsense. Philosophy needed a new and more scientific start, and to put behind it its metaphysical past.

Afterward, logical positivism went through two fundamental changes. First, in 1932, Neurath urged a reformulation of the positivist view. He contended that the sciences rest on physical objects that exist independently of our perceptions rather than being based on sense-data. In other words, he objected to the phenomenalism of Carnap's early work, which conceives of objects as constructions out of sense-data.

Second, the positivists revised the verification principle to meet objections to its early formulations. For example, statements about other galaxies and the distant past cannot be verified for physical reasons. Furthermore, 'All humans are mortal' does not seem to follow from a finite number of observations, and the same point applies to physical laws. For these reasons, the verification principle needed revision.

Meanwhile, two figures entered the scene: Karl Popper (1902–1994) and A. J. Ayer (1910–1989). Popper, who was friends with the members of the Vienna Circle, was not a logical positivist. He argued that universal physical laws could never be derived from a finite set of observational statements. In contrast to the principle of verification, he advocated a principle of falsifiability, according to which scientific claims must be falsifiable to be meaningful. Furthermore, he was skeptical of Carnap's project of constructing a logical syntax to unify the sciences.

In 1932, Ayer was sent by his Oxford teacher, Gilbert Ryle, to Vienna to study logical positivism. During the months that Ayer attended the meetings of the Vienna Circle, the American philosopher Quine was also present. When Ayer returned to Oxford full of enthusiasm, he wrote *Language, Truth and Logic* (1936), which was the first book-length exposition of logical positivism to appear in English.

Meanwhile, the political landscape of Austria was changing: fascism was on the rise. Many members of the Vienna circle were left-wing atheists, and others were Jewish. After Schlick was assassinated in 1936, members of the circle immigrated to the United States and England. The circle was broken and dispersed, but logical positivism continued to exercise an important influence on analytic philosophy until well after the end of World War II.

Rudolf Carnap (1891–1970)

Biographical History

In 1910, Rudolf Carnap went to Jena to study philosophy with Frege. However, in 1917, he was called up to fight for the German army on the Russian front in World War I, after which he returned to his studies, gaining his doctorate in 1919 for a dissertation on the nature of space. Afterward, he was appointed professor at the University of Vienna and became one of the leading spokespersons for the logical positivists. In 1930, he and Reichenbach launched the journal *Erkenntnis*. In 1936, he moved to Chicago. Toward the end of his life, Carnap worked on probability theory.

Philosophical Overview

Roughly speaking, Carnap's thought can be divided into three phases:

1. During the first phase, just prior to joining the Vienna Circle, Carnap composed *The Logical Structure of the World* (1928). In this work, he tries show how our concepts of the world and the mind are logical constructions out of sense-data.

In 1932, Otto Neurath criticized Carnap's program on two grounds. First, in contrast to Carnap's phenomenalism, Neurath claimed that science is based on the existence of physical objects and not sense-data. Therefore, he rejected Carnap's protocol sentences. Protocol sentences are immediately verifiable, logically independent, and incorrigible sentences about sense-data. They were supposed to be the foundations of science. Second, Neurath argued that protocol statements could not be compared with reality, but only with other statements. Thus, truth does not consist in the correspondence of statements to reality, but in their internal coherence as a group. This implied a certain conventionalism. In other words, when two sets of internally coherent sentences are incompatible, which one is accepted is purely a matter of convention.

2. In part, as a consequence of Neurath's criticisms, Carnap wrote *The Logical Syntax of Language* (1934). Carnap argues that philosophy is the discipline that analyzes the language of science. To defend this view, he has to show that philosophy is not itself nonsense. In other words, he has to solve the problem of Wittgenstein's *Tractatus,* according to which the *Tractatus* implies that it itself is meaningless. So, in his own work Carnap tries to show that a language that is rich enough to include arithmetic can also describe its own logical syntax. For this reason, he aims to reconstruct the syntax of scientific language through a program of formalization. To carry out this task, he distinguishes the material and formal modes of speech. In the material mode, we refer to and describe objects with sentences such as 'There are five apples on the table.' In the formal mode, we describe the syntax of a language with sentences such as ' "Five" is a number word.' Carnap uses this distinction to criticize traditional philosophy, which confuses the material and formal modes of speech by producing pseudo propositions, such as 'Five is a number.'

In line with Neurath's critique of his previous work, Carnap abandons his earlier notion of protocol sentences. He argues that the language of science can be completely characterized in terms of its formation and transformation rules, which show under what conditions sentences are derivable from each other. Carnap now thought that meaning rules, linking some expressions to observations, were dispensable. This position has the logical consequence that such formation rules could generate many incompatible, but internally coherent, systems of sentences. Carnap accepted the indeterminism and conventionalism implicit in this position, arguing that the system accepted by the scientific community would be considered true. This point is important for understanding the work of his American pupil, Quine, as we shall see in Section V.

3. This second program was itself put into doubt by the work of the logician Alfred Tarski, who had argued that the project of formalizing artificial languages could not be applied to natural language. This was because the definition of truth for a formal language has to be stated in terms of a meta-language, which to be formalized would require a meta-meta-language and so on. In contrast, a natural language, such as German, is its own meta-language. As a result of Tarski's work, Carnap abandoned the purely syntactical view of language of his 1934 book. He concluded that some semantic concepts were necessary, and that an analysis of language had to rely on some intensional notions. This led to the publication of the main works of his third period, *Introduction to Semantics* (1942) and *Meaning and Necessity* (1946). These works rely on the claim that every linguistic designation refers to both an extension and an intension. Extensional entities are individuals, sets, and truth-values. In contrast, intensional entities are concepts, properties, and propositions. These are referred to respectively by names, predicates, and declarative sentences. Carnap's later view has many similarities to Frege's distinction between sense and reference. In particular, it does not solve the problem that Russell and Wittgenstein had seen with Frege's work, namely, 'What are senses?' The problem now emerging from Carnap's work is 'What are intensional items?' Quine felt that Carnap had gone too far in abandoning the principle of extensionality and postulating the existence of intensional entities.

For this collection, we have selected sections from Carnap's early work, *The Logical Structure of the World.* Although Carnap repudiates many aspects of this work in his later phases, it is a classic statement of logical Empiricism, which brings to fruition some of the ideas of David Hume and Russell. We also include the pamphlet on logical positivism, *The Scientific Conception of the World: The Vienna Circle*, which Carnap coauthored with Hahn and Neurath. For the logical positivist critique of metaphysics, we turn to Ayer.

THE SCIENTIFIC CONCEPTION OF THE WORLD: THE VIENNA CIRCLE

Hans Hahn, Rudolf Carnap, and Otto Neurath

The reading is the famous pamphlet published in 1929 by three members of the logical positivist group to declare their philosophical aims. These include the elimination of metaphysics through the logical clarification of concepts, and the advancement of a unified scientific conception of the world and society. According to this vision, philosophy is not a discipline separate from science. Put simply, logical positivism consists of three claims:

1. The central one is that all meaningful statements are either reducible to observations, or they are mere tautologies, which have no factual content, such as the sentences of mathematics and logic. All other putative statements, such as those of theology and metaphysics, are not true or false propositions at all. They are pseudo-propositions. Strictly speaking, they are nonsense, or merely expressions of attitudes and feelings. Metaphysical views, such as those expressed by Martin Heidegger, are all meaningless.

2. This claim is based on a theory of meaning, expressed by the sentence 'The meaning of a proposition is its method of verification.' Carnap formulated the classic early version of this theory of meaning: elementary propositions or protocol statements describe the experience of sense-data or acts of verification, and all other propositions are logically derivable from these protocol statements, given the resources of logic and the rules of syntax. The parallel with the *Tractatus* should be obvious, but so should the differences; for example, Wittgenstein's philosophy has no protocol statements.

3. The sciences are a unity. If all theoretical propositions can be reduced to protocol statements, then there is only one science. Later, this claim was revised to the idea that the social sciences can be reduced to psychology, which can be reduced to biology, which in turn reduces to physics. Science provides the only theoretically adequate language. Everything that is sayable can be said within it.

PREFACE

At the beginning of 1929 Moritz Schlick received a very tempting call to Bonn. After some vacillation he decided to remain in Vienna. On this occasion, for the first time it became clear to him and us that there is such a thing as the 'Vienna Circle' of the scientific conception of the world, which goes on developing this mode of thought in a collaborative effort. This circle has no rigid organization; it consists of people of an equal and basic scientific attitude; each individual endeavors to fit in, each puts common ties in the foreground, none wishes to disturb the links through idiosyncrasies. In many cases one can deputize for another, the work of one can be carried on by another.

From *Otto Neurath: Empiricism and Sociology* edited by Marie Neurath. Dordrecht, Reidel Publishers, 1973, pp. 299–318. Reprinted with kind permission from Springer Science and Business Media.

The Vienna Circle aims at making contact with those similarly oriented and at influencing those who stand further off. Collaboration in the Ernst Mach Society is the expression of this endeavor; Schlick is the chairman of this society and several members of Schlick's circle belong to the committee.

On 15–16 September 1929, the Ernst Mach Society, with the Society for Empirical Philosophy (Berlin), will hold a conference in Prague, on the epistemology of the exact sciences, in conjunction with the conference of the German Physical Society and the German Association of Mathematicians which will take place there at the same time. Besides technical questions, questions of principle are to be discussed. It was decided that on the occasion of this conference the present pamphlet on the Vienna Circle of the scientific conception of the world was to be published. It is to be handed to Schlick in October 1929 when he returns from his visiting professorship at Stanford University, California, as token of gratitude and joy at his remaining in Vienna. The second part of the pamphlet contains a bibliography compiled in collaboration with those concerned. It is to give a survey of the area of problems in which those who belong to, or are near to, the Vienna Circle are working.

Vienna, August 1929
For the Ernst Mach Society
Hans Hahn
Otto Neurath   Rudolf Carnap

1. THE VIENNA CIRCLE OF THE SCIENTIFIC CONCEPTION OF THE WORLD

1.1 Historical Background

Many assert that metaphysical and theologizing thought is again on the increase today, not only in life but also in science. Is this a general phenomenon or merely a change restricted to certain circles? The assertion itself is easily confirmed if one looks at the topics of university courses and at the titles of philosophic publications. But likewise the opposite spirit of enlightenment and *anti-metaphysical factual research* is growing stronger today, in that it is becoming conscious of its existence and task. In some circles the mode of thought grounded in experience and averse to speculation is stronger than ever, being strengthened precisely by the new opposition that has arisen.

In the research work of all branches of empirical science this *spirit of a scientific conception of the world* is alive. However only a very few leading thinkers give it systematic thought or advocate its principles, and but rarely are they in a position to assemble a circle of like-minded colleagues around them. We find anti-metaphysical endeavors especially in England, where the tradition of the great empiricists is still alive; the investigations of Russell and Whitehead on logic and the analysis of reality have won international significance. In the U.S.A. these endeavors take on the most varied forms; in a certain sense James belongs to this group too. The new Russia definitely is seeking for a scientific world conception, even if partly leaning on older materialistic currents. On the continent of Europe, a concentration of productive work in the direction of a scientific world conception is to be found especially in Berlin (Reichenbach, Petzoldt, Grelling, Dubislav and others) and in Vienna.

That Vienna was specially suitable ground for this development is historically understandable. In the second half of the nineteenth century, liberalism was long the dominant political current. Its world of ideas stems from the enlightenment, from empiricism, utilitarianism and the free trade movement of England. In Vienna's liberal movement, scholars of world renown occupied leading positions. Here an anti-metaphysical spirit was cultivated, for instance, by men like Theodor Gomperz who translated the works of J. S. Mill, Suess, Jodl and others.

Thanks to this spirit of enlightenment, Vienna has been leading in a scientifically oriented people's education. With the collaboration of Victor Adler and Friedrich Jodl, the society for popular education was founded and carried forth; 'popular university courses' and the 'people's college' were set up by the well-known historian Ludo Hartmann whose anti-metaphysical attitude and materialist conception of history expressed itself in all his actions. The same spirit also inspired the movement of the 'Free School' which was the forerunner of today's school reform.

In this liberal atmosphere lived Ernst Mach (born 1838) who was in Vienna as student and as *privat-dozent* (1861–64). He returned to Vienna only at an advanced age when a special chair of the philosophy of the inductive sciences was created for him (1895). He was especially intent on cleansing empirical science, and in the first place, of physics, of metaphysical notions. We recall his critique of absolute space which made him a forerunner of Einstein, his struggle against the metaphysics of the thing-in-itself and of the concept of substance, and his investigations of the construction of scientific concepts from ultimate elements, namely sense data. In some points the development of science has not vindicated his views, for instance in his opposition to atomic theory and in his expectation that physics would be advanced through the physiology of the senses. The essential points of his conception however were of positive use in the further development of science. Mach's chair was later occupied by Ludwig Boltzmann (1902–06) who held decidedly empiricist views.

The activity of the physicists Mach and Boltzmann in a philosophical professorship makes it conceivable that there was a lively dominant interest in the epistemological and logical problems that are linked with the foundations of physics. These problems concerning foundations also led toward a renewal of logic. The path towards these objectives had also been cleared in Vienna from quite a different quarter by Franz Brentano (during 1874–80 professor of philosophy in the theological faculty, and later lecturer in the philosophical faculty). As a Catholic priest Brentano understood scholasticism; he started directly from the scholastic logic and from Leibniz's endeavors to reform logic, while leaving aside Kant and the idealist system-builders. Brentano and his students time and again showed their understanding of men like Bolzano (*Wissenschaftslehre*, 1837) and others who were working toward a rigorous new foundation of logic. In particular Alois Höfler (1853–1922) put this side of Brentano's philosophy in the foreground before a forum in which, through Mach's and Boltzmann's influence, the adherents of the scientific world conception were strongly represented. In the Philosophical Society at the University of Vienna numerous discussions took place under Höfler's direction, concerning questions of the foundation of physics and allied epistemological and logical problems. The Philosophical Society published *Prefaces and Introductions to Classical Works on Mechanics* (1899), as well as the individual papers of Bolzano (edited by Höfler and Hahn, 1914 and 1921). In Brentano's Viennese circle there was the young Alexius von Meinong (1870–82, later professor in Graz), whose theory of objects (1907) has certainly some

affinity to modern theories of concepts and whose pupil Ernst Mally (Graz) also worked in the field of logistics. The early writings of Hans Pichler (1909) also belong to these circles.

Roughly at the same time as Mach, his contemporary and friend Josef Popper-Lynkeus worked in Vienna. Beside his physical and technical achievements we mention his large-scale, if unsystematic philosophical reflections (1899) and his rational economic plan (*A General Peacetime Labour Draft*, 1878). He consciously served the spirit of enlightenment, as is also evident from his book on Voltaire. His rejection of metaphysics was shared by many other Viennese sociologists, for example Rudolf Goldscheid. It is remarkable that in the field of political economy, too, there was in Vienna a strictly scientific method, used by the marginal utility school (Carl Menger, 1871); this method took root in England, France and Scandinavia, but not in Germany. Marxist theory likewise was cultivated and extended with special emphasis in Vienna (Otto Bauer, Rudolf Hilferding, Max Adler and others).

These influences from various sides had the result, especially since 1900, that there was in Vienna a sizeable number of people who frequently and assiduously discussed more general problems in close connection with empirical sciences. Above all these were epistemological and methodological problems of physics, for instance Poincaré's conventionalism, Duhem's conception of the aim and structure of physical theories (his translator was the Viennese Friedrich Adler, a follower of Mach, at that time *privatdozent* in Zürich); also questions about the foundations of mathematics, problems of axiomatics, logistic and the like. The following were the main strands from the history of science and philosophy that came together here, marked by those of their representatives whose works were mainly read and discussed:

1. Positivism and empiricism: Hume, Enlightenment, Comte, J. S. Mill, Richard Avenarius, Mach.
2. Foundations, aims and methods of empirical science (hypotheses in physics, geometry, etc.): Helmholtz, Riemann, Mach, Poincaré, Enriques, Duhem, Boltzmann, Einstein.
3. Logistic and its application to reality: Leibniz, Peano, Frege, Schröder, Russell, Whitehead, Wittgenstein.

4. Axiomatics: Pasch, Peano, Vailati, Pieri, Hilbert.
5. Hedonism and positivist sociology: Epicurus, Hume, Bentham, J. S. Mill, Comte, Feuerbach, Marx, Spencer, Müller-Lyer, Popper-Lynkeus, Carl Menger (the elder).

1.2 The Circle Around Schlick

In 1922 Moritz Schlick was called from Kiel to Vienna. His activities fitted well into the historical development of the Viennese scientific atmosphere. Himself originally a physicist, he awakened to new life the tradition that had been started by Mach and Boltzmann and, in a certain sense, carried on by the anti-metaphysically inclined Adolf Stöhr. (In Vienna successively: Mach, Boltzmann, Stöhr, Schlick; in Prague: Mach, Einstein, Philipp Frank.)

Around Schlick, there gathered in the course of time a circle whose members united various endeavors in the direction of a scientific conception of the world. This concentration produced a fruitful mutual inspiration. Not one of the members is a so-called 'pure' philosopher; all of them have done work in a special field of science. Moreover they come from different branches of science and originally from different philosophic attitudes. But over the years a growing uniformity appeared; this too was a result of the specifically scientific attitude: "What can be said at all, can be said clearly" (Wittgenstein); if there are differences of opinion, it is in the end possible to agree, and therefore agreement is demanded. It became increasingly clearer that a position not only free from metaphysics, but opposed to metaphysics was the common goal of all.

The attitudes toward questions of life also showed a noteworthy agreement, although these questions were not in the foreground of themes discussed within the Circle. For these attitudes are more closely related to the scientific world-conception than it might at first glance appear from a purely theoretical point of view. For instance, endeavors toward a new organization of economic and social relations, toward the unification of mankind, toward a reform of school and education, all show an inner link with the scientific world-conception; it appears that these endeavors are welcomed and regarded with sympathy by the members of the Circle, some of whom indeed actively further them.

The Vienna Circle does not confine itself to collective work as a closed group. It is also trying to make contact with the living movements of the present, so far as they are well disposed toward the scientific world-conception and turn away from metaphysics and theology. The Ernst Mach Society is today the place from which the Circle speaks to a wider public. This society, as stated in its program, wishes to "further and disseminate the scientific world-conception. It will organize lectures and publications about the present position of the scientific world-conception, in order to demonstrate the significance of exact research for the social sciences and the natural sciences. In this way intellectual tools should be formed for modern empiricism, tools that are also needed in forming public and private life." By the choice of its name, the society wishes to describe its basic orientation: science free of metaphysics. This, however, does not mean that the society declares itself in programmatic agreement with the individual doctrines of Mach. The Vienna Circle believes that in collaborating with the Ernst Mach Society it fulfils a demand of the day: we have to fashion intellectual tools for everyday life, for the daily life of the scholar but also for the daily life of all those who in some way join in working at the conscious re-shaping of life. The vitality that shows itself in the efforts for a rational transformation of the social and economic order permeates the movement for a scientific world-conception too. It is typical of the present situation in Vienna that when the Ernst Mach Society was founded in November 1928, Schlick was chosen chairman; round him the common work in the field of the scientific world-conception had concentrated most strongly.

Schlick and Philipp Frank jointly edit the collection of *Monographs on the Scientific World-Conception* [*Schriften zur wissenschaftlichen Weltauffassung*] in which members of the Vienna Circle preponderate.

2. THE SCIENTIFIC WORLD CONCEPTION

The scientific world conception is characterized not so much by these of its own, but rather by its basic attitude, its points of view and direction of research. The goal ahead is *unified* science. The endeavor is to link and harmonize the achievements of individual investigators in their various fields of science. From this aim follows the emphasis on *collective efforts*, and also the emphasis on what can be grasped intersubjectively; from this springs the search for a neutral system of formulas, for a symbolism freed from the slag of historical languages; and also the search for a total system of concepts. Neatness and clarity are striven for, and dark distances and unfathomable depths rejected. In science there are no 'depths'; there is surface everywhere: all experience forms a complex network, which cannot always be surveyed and can often be grasped only in parts. Everything is accessible to man; and man is the measure of all things. Here is an affinity with the Sophists, not with the Platonists; with the Epicureans, not with the Pythagoreans; with all those who stand for earthly being and the here and now. The scientific world-conception knows *no unsolvable riddle*. Clarification of the traditional philosophical problems leads us partly to unmask them as pseudo-problems, and partly to transform them into empirical problems and thereby subject them to the judgment of experimental science. The task of philosophical work lies in this clarification of problems and assertions, not in the propounding of special 'philosophical' pronouncements. The method of this clarification is that of *logical analysis*; of it, Russell says (*Our Knowledge of the External World*, p. 4) that it "has gradually crept into philosophy through the critical scrutiny of mathematics . . . It represents, I believe, the same kind of advance as was introduced into physics by Galileo: the substitution of piecemeal, detailed and verifiable results for large untested generalities recommended only by a certain appeal to imagination."

It is *the method of logical analysis* that essentially distinguishes recent empiricism and positivism from the earlier version that was more biological-psychological in its orientation. If someone asserts "there is a God", "the primary basis of the world is the unconscious", "there is an entelechy which is the leading principle in the living organism", we do not say to him: "what you say is false"; but we ask him: "what do you mean by these statements?" Then it appears that there is a sharp boundary between two kinds of statements. To one belong statements as they are made by empirical science; their meaning can be determined by logical analysis or, more precisely, through reduction to the simplest statements about the empirically given. The other statements, to which belong those cited above, reveal themselves as empty of meaning if one takes them in the way that metaphysicians intend. One can, of course, often reinterpret them as empirical statements; but then they lose the content of feeling which is usually essential to the metaphysician. The metaphysician and the theologian believe, thereby misunderstanding themselves, that their statements say something, or that they denote a state of affairs. Analysis, however, shows that these statements say nothing but merely express a certain mood and spirit. To express such feelings for life can be a significant task. But the proper medium for doing so is art, for instance lyric poetry or music. It is dangerous to choose the linguistic garb of a theory instead: a theoretical content is simulated where none exists. If a metaphysician or theologian wants to retain the usual medium of language, then he must himself realize and bring out clearly that he is giving not description but expression, not theory or communication of knowledge, but poetry or myth. If a mystic asserts that he has experiences that lie above and beyond all concepts, one cannot deny this. But the mystic cannot talk about it, for talking implies capture by concepts and reduction to scientifically classifiable states of affairs.

The scientific world-conception rejects metaphysical philosophy. But how can we explain the wrong paths of metaphysics? This question may be posed from several points of view: psychological, sociological and logical. Research in a psychological direction is still in its early stages; the beginnings of more penetrating explanation may perhaps be seen in the investigations of Freudian psychoanalysis. The state of sociological investigation is similar; we may mention the theory of the 'ideological superstructure'; here the field remains open to worthwhile further research.

More advanced is the clarification of *the logical origins of metaphysical aberration*, especially through the works of Russell and Wittgenstein. In metaphysical theory, and even in the very form of the questions, there are two basic logical mistakes: too narrow a tie to the form of *traditional languages* and a confusion about the logical achievement of thought. Ordinary language for instance uses the same part of speech, the substantive, for things ('apple') as well as as for qualities ('hardness'), relations ('friendship'), and processes ('sleep'); therefore it misleads one into a thing-like conception of functional concepts (hypostasis, substantialization). One can quote countless similar examples of linguistic misleading that have been equally fatal to philosophers.

The second basic error of metaphysics consists in the notion that *thinking* can either lead to knowledge out of its own resources without using any empirical material, or at least arrive at new contents by an inference from given states of affair. Logical investigation, however, leads to the result that all thought and inference consists of nothing but a transition from statements to other statements that contain nothing that was not already in the former (tautological transformation). It is therefore not possible to develop a metaphysic from 'pure thought'.

In such a way logical analysis overcomes not only metaphysics in the proper, classical sense of the word, especially scholastic metaphysics and that of the systems of German idealism, but also the hidden metaphysics of Kantian and modern *apriorism*. The scientific world-conception knows no unconditionally valid knowledge derived from pure reason, no 'synthetic judgments a priori' of the kind that lie at the basis of Kantian epistemology and even more of all pre-and post-Kantian ontology and metaphysics. The judgments of arithmetic, geometry, and certain fundamental principles of physics that Kant took as examples of a priori knowledge will be discussed later. It is precisely in the rejection of the possibility of synthetic knowledge a priori that the basic thesis of modern empiricism lies. The scientific world-conception knows only empirical statements about things of all kinds, and analytic statements of logic and mathematics.

In rejecting overt metaphysics and the concealed variety of apriorism, all adherents of the scientific world-conception are at one. Beyond this, the Vienna Circle maintain the view that the statements of (critical) *realism* and *idealism* about the reality or non-reality of the external world and other minds are of a metaphysical character, because they are open to the same objections as are the statements of the old metaphysics: they are meaningless, because unverifiable and without content. For us, *something is 'real' through being incorporated into the total structure of experience*.

Intuition which is especially emphasized by metaphysicians as a source of knowledge is not rejected as such by the scientific world-conception. However, rational justification has to pursue all intuitive knowledge step by step. The seeker is allowed any method; but what has been found must stand up to testing. The view which attributes to intuition a superior and more penetrating power of knowing, capable of leading beyond the contents of sense experience and not to be confined by the shackles of conceptual thought—this view is rejected.

We have characterized the *scientific world-conception* essentially by *two features. First it is empiricist and positivist:* there is knowledge only from experience, which rests on what is immediately given. This sets the limits for the content of legitimate science. *Second,* the scientific world-conception is marked by application of a certain method, namely *logical analysis*. The aim of scientific effort is to reach the goal, unified science, by applying logical analysis to the empirical material. Since the meaning of every statement of science must be statable by reduction to a statement about the given, likewise the meaning of any concept, whatever branch of science it may belong to, must be statable by stepwise reduction to other concepts, down to the concepts of the lowest level which refer directly to the given. If such an analysis were carried through for all concepts, they would thus be ordered into a reductive system, a 'constitutive system'. Investigations towards such a constitutive system, the 'constitutive theory', thus form the framework within which logical analysis is applied by the scientific world-conception. Such investigations show very soon that traditional Aristotelian scholastic logic is quite inadequate for this purpose. Only modern symbolic logic ('logistic') succeeds in gaining the required precision of concept definitions and of statements, and in formalizing the intuitive process of inference of ordinary thought, that is to bring it into a rigorous automatically controlled form by means of a symbolic mechanism. Investigations into constitutive theory show that the lowest layers of the constitutive system contain concepts of the experience and qualities of the individual psyche; in the layer above are physical objects; from these are constituted other minds and lastly the objects of social science. The arrangement of the concepts of the various branches of science into the constitutive system can already be discerned in outline today, but much remains to be done in detail. With the proof of the possibility and the outline of the shape of the total system of concepts, the relation of all statements to the given and with it the general structure of *unified science* become recognizable too.

A scientific description can contain only the *structure* (form of order) of objects, not their 'essence'. What unites men in language are structural formulas; in them the content of the common knowledge of men presents itself. Subjectively experienced qualities— redness, pleasure—are as such only experiences, not knowledge; physical optics admits only what is in principle understandable by a blind man too.

3. FIELDS OF PROBLEMS

3.1 Foundations of Arithmetic

In the writings and discussions of the Vienna Circle many different problems are treated, stemming from various branches of science. Attempts are made to arrange the various lines of problems systematically and thereby to clarify the situation.

The problems concerning the foundations of arithmetic have become of special historical significance for the development of the scientific world-conception because they gave impulse to the development of a new logic. After the very fruitful developments of mathematics in the 18th and 19th century during which more attention was given to the wealth of new results than to subtle examination of their conceptual foundations, this examination became unavoidable if mathematics were not to lose the traditionally celebrated certainty of its structure. This examination became even more urgent when certain contradictions, the 'paradoxes of set theory', arose. It was soon recognized that these were not just difficulties in a special part of mathematics, but rather they were general logical contradictions, 'antinomies', which pointed to essential mistakes in the foundations of traditional logic. The task of eliminating these contradictions gave a very strong impulse to the further development of logic. Here efforts for *clarification of the concept of number* met with those for an internal *reform of logic*. Since Leibniz and Lambert, the idea had come up again and again to master reality through a greater precision of concepts and inferential processes, and to obtain this precision by

means of a symbolism fashioned after mathematics. After Boole, Venn and others, especially Frege (1884), Schröder (1890) and Peano (1895) worked on this problem. On the basis of these preparatory efforts *Whitehead* and *Russell* (1910) were able to establish a coherent system of logic in symbolic form ('logistic'), not only avoiding the contradictions of traditional logic, but far exceeding that logic in intellectual wealth and practical applicability. From this logical system they derived the concepts of arithmetic and analysis, thereby giving mathematics a secure foundation in logic.

Certain difficulties however remained in this attempt at overcoming the foundation crisis of arithmetic (and set theory) and have so far not found a definitively satisfactory solution. At present three different views confront each other in this field; besides the 'logicism' of Russell and Whitehead, there is Hilbert's 'formalism' which regards arithmetic as a playing with formulas according to certain rules, and Brouwer's 'intuitionism' according to which arithmetic knowledge rests on a not further reducible intuition of duality and unity [*Zwei-einheit*]. The debates are followed with great interest in the Vienna Circle. Where the decision will lead in the end cannot yet be foreseen; in any case, it will also imply a decision about the structure of logic; hence the importance of this problem for the scientific world-conception. Some hold that the three views are not so far apart as it seems. They surmise that essential features of all three will come closer in the course of future development and probably, using the far-reaching ideas of Wittgenstein, will be united in the ultimate solution.

The conception of mathematics as tautological in character, which is based on the investigations of Russell and Wittgenstein, is also held by the Vienna Circle. It is to be noted that this conception is opposed not only to apriorism and intuitionism, but also to the older empiricism (for instance of J. S. Mill), which tried to derive mathematics and logic in an experimental-inductive manner as it were.

Connected with the problems of arithmetic and logic are the investigations into the nature of the *axiomatic method* in general (concepts of completeness, independence, monomorphism, unambiguity and so on) and on the establishment of axiom-systems for certain branches of mathematics.

3.2 Foundations of Physics

Originally the Vienna Circle's strongest interest was in the method of empirical science. Inspired by ideas of Mach, Poincaré, and Duhem, the problems of mastering reality through scientific systems, especially through *systems of hypotheses and axioms,* were discussed. A system of axioms, cut loose from all empirical application, can at first be regarded as a system of implicit definitions; that is to say, the concepts that appear in the axioms are fixed, or as it were defined, not from their content but only from their mutual relations through the axioms. Such a system of axioms attains a meaning for reality only by the addition of further definitions, namely the 'coordinating definitions', which state what objects of reality are to be regarded as members of the system of axioms. The development of empirical science, which is to represent reality by means of as uniform and simple a net of concepts and judgments as possible, can now proceed in one of two ways, as history shows. The changes imposed by new experience can be made either in the axioms or in the coordinating definitions. Here we touch the problem of conventions, particularly treated by Poincaré.

The methodological problem of the application of axiom systems to reality may in principle arise for any branch of science. That these investigations have thus far been fruitful almost solely for physics, however, can be understood from the present stage of historical development of science: in regard to precision and refinement of concepts, physics is far ahead of the other branches of science.

Epistemological analysis of the leading concepts of natural science has freed them more and more from *metaphysical admixtures* which had clung to them from ancient time. In particular, Helmholtz, Mach, Einstein, and others have cleansed the concepts of *space, time, substance, causality, and probability.* The doctrines of absolute space and time have been overcome by the theory of relativity; space and time are no longer absolute containers but only ordering manifolds for elementary processes. Material substance has been dissolved by atomic theory and field theory. Causality was divested of the anthropomorphic character of 'influence' or 'necessary connection' and reduced to a relation among conditions, a functional coordination. Further, in place of the many laws of nature which were considered to be strictly valid, statistical laws have appeared; following the quantum theory there is even doubt whether the concept of strictly causal lawfulness is applicable to phenomena in very small space-time regions. The concept of probability is reduced to the empirically graspable concept of relative frequency.

Through the application of the *axiomatic method* to these problems, the empirical components always separate from the merely conventional ones, the content of statements from definitions. No room remains for a priori synthetic judgments. That knowledge of the world is possible rests not on human reason impressing its form on the material, but on the material being ordered in a certain way. The kind and degree of this order cannot be known beforehand. The world might be ordered much more strictly than it is; but it might equally be ordered much less without jeopardizing the possibility of knowledge. Only step by step can the advancing research of empirical science teach us in what degree the world is regular. The method of induction, the inference from yesterday to tomorrow, from here to there, is of course only valid if regularity exists. But this method does not rest on some a priori presupposition of this regularity. It may be applied wherever it leads to fruitful results, whether or not it be adequately founded; it never yields certainty. However, epistemological reflection demands that an inductive inference should be given significance only insofar as it can be tested empirically. The scientific world-conception will not condemn the success of a piece of research because it has been gathered by means that are inadequate, logically unclear or empirically unfounded. But it will always strive at testing with clarified aids, and demand an indirect or direct reduction to experience.

3.3 Foundations of Geometry

Among the questions about the foundations of physics, the problem of *physical space* has received special significance in recent decades. The investigations of Gauss (1816), Bolyai (1823), Lobatchevski (1835) and others led to *non-Euclidean geometry,* to a realization that the hitherto dominant classical geometric system of Euclid was only one of an infinite set of systems, all of equal logical merit. This raised the question, which of these geometries was that of actual space. Gauss had wanted to resolve this question by measuring the angles of a large triangle. This made *physical geometry* into an empirical science, a branch of physics. The problems were further studied particularly by Riemann (1868), Helmholtz (1868) and Poincaré (1904). Poincaré especially emphasized the link of physical geometry with all other branches of physics: the question concerning the nature of actual space can be answered only in connection with a total system of physics. Einstein then found such a total system, which answered the question in favor of a certain non-Euclidean system.

Through this development, physical geometry became more and more clearly separated from pure *mathematical* geometry. The latter gradually became more and more formalized through further development of logical analysis. First it was arithmetized, that is, interpreted as the theory of a certain number system. Next it was axiomatized, that is, represented by means of system of axioms that conceives the geometrical elements (points, etc.) as undefined objects, and fixes only their mutual relations. Finally geometry was logicized, namely represented as a theory of certain structural relations. Thus geometry became the most important field of application for the axiomatic method and for the general theory of relations. In this way, it gave the strongest impulse to the development of the two methods which in turn became so important for the development of logic itself, and thereby again for the scientific world-conception.

The relations between mathematical and physical geometry naturally led to the problem of the application of axiom systems to reality which, as mentioned, played a big role in the more general investigations about the foundations of physics.

3.4 Problems of the Foundations of Biology and Psychology

Metaphysicians have always been fond of singling out biology as a special field. This came out in the doctrine of a special life force, the theory of *vitalism*. The modern representatives of this theory endeavor to bring it from the unclear, confused form of the past into a conceptually clear formulation. In place of the life force, we have 'dominants' (Reinke, 1899) or 'entelechies' (Driesch, 1905). Since these concepts

do not satisfy the requirement of reducibility to the given, the scientific world-conception rejects them as metaphysical. The same holds true of so-called 'psycho-vitalism' which puts forward an intervention of the soul, a 'role of leadership of the mental in the material'. If, however, one digs out of this metaphysical vitalism the empirically graspable kernel, there remains the thesis that the processes of organic nature proceed according to laws that cannot be reduced to physical laws. A more precise analysis shows that this thesis is equivalent to the assertion that certain fields of reality are not subject to a uniform and pervasive regularity.

It is understandable that the scientific world-conception can show more definite confirmation for its views in those fields which have already achieved conceptual precision than in others: in physics more than in psychology. The linguistic forms which we still use in psychology today have their origin in certain ancient metaphysical notions of the soul. The formation of concepts in psychology is made difficult by these defects of language: metaphysical burdens and logical incongruities. Moreover there are certain factual difficulties. The result is that hitherto most of the concepts used in psychology are inadequately defined; of some, it is not known whether they have meaning or only simulate meaning through usage. So, in this field nearly everything in the way of epistemological analysis still remains to be done; of course, analysis here is more difficult than in physics. The attempt of behaviorist psychology to grasp the psychic through the behavior of bodies, which is at a level accessible to perception, is, in its principled attitude, close to the scientific world-conception.

3.5 Foundations of the Social Sciences

As we have specially considered with respect to physics and mathematics, every branch of science is led to recognize that, sooner or later in its development, it must conduct an epistemological examination of its foundations, a logical analysis of its concepts. So too with the social sciences, and in the first place with history and economics. For about a hundred years, a process of elimination of metaphysical admixtures has been operating in these fields. Of course the purification has not yet reached the same degree as in physics; on the other hand, the task of cleansing is less urgent perhaps. For it seems that even in the heyday of metaphysics and theology, the metaphysical strain was not particularly strong here; maybe this is because the concepts in this field, such as war and peace, import and export, are closer to direct perception than concepts like atom and ether. It is not too difficult to drop concepts like 'folk spirit' and instead to choose, as our object, groups of individuals of a certain kind. Scholars from the most diverse trends, such as Quesnay, Adam Smith, Ricardo, Comte, Marx, Menger, Walras, Müller-Lyer, have worked in the sense of the empiricist, anti-metaphysical attitude. The object of history and economics are people, things and their arrangement.

4. RETROSPECT AND PROSPECT

The modern scientific world-conception has developed from work on the problems just mentioned. We have seen how in physics, the endeavors to gain tangible results, at first even with inadequate or still insufficiently clarified scientific tools, found itself forced more and more into methodological investigations. Out of this developed the method of forming hypotheses and, further, the axiomatic method and logical analysis; thereby concept formation gained greater clarity and strength. The same methodological problems were met also in the development of foundations research in physical geometry, mathematical geometry and arithmetic, as we have seen. It is mainly from all these sources that the problems arise with which representatives of the scientific world-conception particularly concern themselves at present. Of course it is still clearly noticeable from which of the various problem areas the individual members of the Vienna Circle come. This often results in differences in lines of interests and points of view, which in turn lead to differences in conception. But it is characteristic that an endeavor toward precise formulation, application of an exact logical language and symbolism, and accurate differentiation between the theoretical content of a thesis and its mere attendant notions, diminish the separation. Step by step the common fund of conceptions is increased, forming the nucleus of a scientific world-conception around which the outer layers gather with stronger subjective divergence.

Looking back we now see clearly what is the *essence of the new scientific world-conception* in contrast with traditional philosophy. No special 'philosophic assertions' are established, assertions are merely clarified; and at that assertions of empirical science, as we have seen when we discussed the various problem areas. Some representatives of the scientific world-conception no longer want to use the term 'philosophy' for their work at all, so as to emphasize the contrast with the philosophy of (metaphysical) systems even more strongly. Whichever term way be used to describe such investigations, this much is certain: *there is no such thing as philosophy as a basic or universal science alongside or above the various fields of the one empirical science*; there is no way to genuine knowledge other than the way of experience; there is no realm of ideas that stands over or beyond experience. Nevertheless the work of 'philosophic' or 'foundational' investigations remains important in accord with the scientific world-conception. For the logical clarification of scientific concepts, statements and methods liberates one from inhibiting prejudices. Logical and epistemological analysis does not wish to set barriers to scientific enquiry; on the contrary, analysis provides science with as complete a range of formal possibilities as is possible, from which to select what best fits each empirical finding (example: non-Euclidean geometries and the theory of relativity).

The representatives of the scientific world-conception resolutely stand on the ground of simple human experience. They confidently approach the task of removing the metaphysical and theological debris of millennia. Or, as some have it: returning, after a metaphysical interlude, to a unified picture of this world which had, in a sense, been at the basis of magical beliefs, free from theology, in the earliest times.

The increase of metaphysical and theologizing leanings which shows itself today in many associations and sects, in books and journals, in talks and university lectures, seems to be based on the fierce social and economic struggles of the present: one group of combatants, holding fast to traditional social forms, cultivates traditional attitudes of metaphysics and theology whose content has long since been superseded; while the other group, especially in central Europe, faces modern times, rejects these views and takes its stand on the ground of empirical science. This development is connected with that of the modern process of production, which is becoming ever more rigorously mechanized and leaves ever less room for metaphysical ideas. It is also connected with the disappointment of broad masses of people with the attitude of those who preach traditional metaphysical and theological doctrines. So it is that in many countries the masses now reject these doctrines much more consciously then ever before, and along with their socialist attitudes tend to lean towards a down-to-earth empiricist view. In previous times, *materialism* was the expression of this view; meanwhile, however, modern empiricism has shed a number of inadequacies and has taken a strong shape in the *scientific world-conception*.

Thus, the scientific world-conception is close to the life of the present. Certainly it is threatened with hard struggles and hostility. Nevertheless there are many who do not despair but, in view of the present sociological situation, look forward with hope to the course of events to come. Of course not every single adherent of the scientific world-conception will be a fighter. Some, glad of solitude, will lead a withdrawn existence on the icy slopes of logic; some may even disdain mingling with the masses and regret the 'trivialized' form that these matters inevitably take on spreading. However, their achievements too will take a place among the historic developments. We witness the spirit of the scientific world-conception penetrating in growing measure the forms of personal and public life, in education, upbringing, architecture, and the shaping of economic and social life according to rational principles. *The scientific world-conception serves life, and life receives it.*

APPENDIX

1. *Members of the Vienna Circle*
   Gustav Bergmann
   Rudolf Carnap
   Herbert Feigl
   Philipp Frank
   Kurt Gödel
   Hans Hahn
   Viktor Kraft
   Karl Menger
   Marcel Natkin
   Otto Neurath
   Olga Hahn-Neurath
   Theodor Radakovic
   Moritz Schlick
   Friedrich Waismann

2. *Those Sympathetic to the Vienna Circle*
   Walter Dubislav
   Josef Frank
   Kurt Grelling
   Hasso Härlen
   E. Kaila
   Heinrich Loewy
   F. P. Ramsey
   Hans Reichenbach
   Kurt Reidemeister
   Edgar Zilsel

3. *Leading Representatives of the Scientific World-Conception*
   Albert Einstein
   Bertrand Russell
   Ludwig Wittgenstein

STUDY QUESTIONS: CARNAP ET AL., *THE SCIENTIFIC CONCEPTION OF THE WORLD: THE VIENNA CIRCLE*

1. What is the purpose of the Vienna Circle? Are the roles of the members unique or interchangeable?
2. How do its members view metaphysics?
3. What made Ernst Mach a forerunner of Einstein?
4. What is their view of Kantian things-in-themselves?
5. What sort of science is the goal of the scientific world-conception?
6. What distinguishes their form of Empiricism and positivism from their earlier versions?
7. What are the two main features of their scientific world-conception?
8. Can a scientific description contain the essence of an object? What does it contain?
9. Why are the foundations of mathematics important for philosophy as they conceive it?

10. Why are the foundations of geometry important?
11. Why are the foundations of physics important?
12. Are the foundations of biology, psychology, and the social sciences equally important?
13. What is their view of logicism?
14. What is the role of the axiomatic method?
15. What does the scientific world-conception serve?

THE LOGICAL STRUCTURE OF THE WORLD

Published in 1928, this classic early work by Carnap is sometimes referred to as the *Aufbau*. Carnap's main aim is to show how we construct our concepts of the material world and our psychological concepts from our experience of sense-data. He tries to do this by demonstrating how statements about material objects and about mental states can be derived from or reduced to propositions about sense-data. In Part 1, Carnap explains carefully the aims and tools of this project, including the key idea that if his project is successful, then there will be only one domain of objects and hence only one science. He also outlines the plan of his work, and explains in what sense the constructed system would be axiomatic.

Part II contains some preliminary discussions. Carnap tries to establish the conclusion that science deals only with the description of structural features of objects. These structural features are relational and formal. These two points are important. First, the relational features of sense-data do not pertain to the purely subjective aspect of experience. Second, by claiming that the relevant features are formal, Carnap means that they can be defined in terms of set theory and extensional logic.

PART ONE

INTRODUCTION: OBJECTIVE AND PLAN OF THE INVESTIGATION

A

The Objective

The supreme maxim in scientific philosophizing is this: Wherever possible, logical constructions are to be substituted for inferred entities.

Russell

1. The Aim: A Constructional System of Concepts

The present investigations aim to establish a "constructional system", that is, an epistemic-logical system of objects or concepts. The word "object" is here always used in its widest sense, namely, for any-thing about which a statement can be made. Thus, among objects we count not only things, but also properties and classes, relations in extension and intension, states and events, what is actual as well as what is not.

Unlike other conceptual systems, a constructional system undertakes more than the division of concepts into various kinds and the investigation of the differences and mutual relations between these kinds. In addition, it attempts a step-by-step derivation or "construction" of all concepts from certain fundamental concepts, so that a genealogy of concepts results in which each one has its definite place. It is the main thesis of construction theory that all concepts can in this way be derived from a few fundamental concepts, and it is in this respect that it differs from most other ontologies.

Abridgement reprinted by permission of Open Court Publishing Company, a division of Carus Publishing Company, Peru, IL from *The Logical Structure of the World* by Rudolph Carnap, translated by Rolf George, 1967.

In order to indicate more clearly the nature of our objective, the "constructional system", some important concepts of construction theory should first be explained. An object (or concept) is said to be *reducible* to one or more other objects if all statements about it can be transformed into statements about these other objects. . . .

If *a* is reducible to *b*, and *b* to *c*, then *a* is reducible to *c*. Thus, reducibility is transitive.

According to the explanation given above, if an object *a* is reducible to objects *b*, *c*, then all statements about *a* can be transformed into statements about *b* and *c*. To reduce *a* to *b*, *c* or to *construct a* out of *b*, *c* means to produce a general rule that indicates for each individual case how a statement about *a* must be transformed in order to yield a statement about *b*, *c*. This rule of translation we call a *construction rule* or *constructional definition* (it has the form of a definition; cf. § 38).

By a *constructional system* we mean a step-by-step ordering of objects in such a way that the objects of each level are constructed from those of the lower levels. Because of the transitivity of reducibility, all objects of the constructional system are thus indirectly constructed from objects of the first level. These *basic objects* form the *basis* of the system.

> **EXAMPLE** A constructional system of arithmetical concepts can be established by deriving or "constructing" step-by-step (through chains of definitions) all arithmetical concepts from the fundamental concepts of natural number and immediate successor.

A theory is *axiomatized* when all statements of the theory are arranged in the form of a deductive system whose basis is formed by the axioms, and when all concepts of the theory are arranged in the form of a constructional system whose basis is formed by the fundamental concepts. So far, much more attention has been paid to the first task, namely, the deduction of statements from axioms, than to the methodology of the systematic construction of concepts. The latter is to be our present concern and is to be applied to the conceptual system of unified science. Only if we succeed in producing such a unified system of all concepts will it be possible to overcome the separation of unified science into unrelated special sciences.

Even though the subjective origin of all knowledge lies in the contents of experiences and their connections, it is still possible, as the constructional system will show, to advance to an intersubjective, objective world, which can be conceptually comprehended and which is identical for all observers.

3. The Method: The Analysis of Reality with the Aid of the Theory of Relations

The present investigations, as far as their method is concerned, are characterized by the fact that they attempt to bring to bear upon one another two branches of science that have so far been treated separately. Both branches have been developed independently to a considerable extent, but in our opinion they can make further progress only if they are conjoined. Logistics (symbolic logic) has been advanced by Russell and Whitehead to a point where it provides a *theory of relations* which allows almost all problems of the pure theory of ordering to be treated without great difficulty. On the other hand, the reduction of "reality" to the "given" has in recent times been considered an important task and has been partially accomplished, for example, by Avenarius, Mach, Poincaré, Külpe, and especially by Ziehen and Driesch (to mention only a few names). The present study is an attempt *to apply the theory of relations to the task of analyzing reality.* This is done in order to formulate the logical requirements which must be fulfilled by a constructional system of concepts, to bring into clearer focus the basis of the system, and to demonstrate by actually producing such a system (though part of it is only an outline) that it can be constructed on the indicated basis and within the indicated logical framework.

4. The Unity of the Object Domain

If a constructional system of concepts or objects (it can be taken in either sense; cf. § 5) is possible in the manner indicated, then it follows that the objects do not come from several unrelated areas, but that *there is only one domain of objects and therefore only one science.* We can, of course, still differentiate various types of objects if they belong to different levels of the constructional system, or, in case they are on the same level, if their form of construction is different. Later on (III A), we shall show that the objects on higher levels are not constructed by mere summation, but that they are *logical complexes.* The object *state,* for example, will have to be constructed in this constructional system out of psychological processes, but it should by no means be thought of as a sum of psychological processes. We shall distinguish between a *whole* and a *logical complex*. The whole is composed of its elements; they are its parts. An independent logical complex does not have this relation to its elements, but rather, it is characterized by the fact that all statements about it can be transformed into statements about its elements.

5. *Concept and Object*

Since we always use the word "object" in its widest sense (§ 1), it follows that to every concept there belongs one and only one object: "its object" (not to be confused with the objects that fall *under* the concept). In opposition to the customary theory of concepts, it seems to us that the generality of a concept is relative, so that the borderline between general and individual concepts can be shifted, depending on the point of view (cf. § 158). Thus, we will say that even general concepts have their "objects". It makes no logical difference whether a given sign denotes the concept or the object, or whether a sentence holds for objects or concepts. There is at most a psychological difference, namely, a difference in mental imagery. Actually, we have here not two conceptions, but only two different interpretative modes of speech. Thus, in construction theory we sometimes speak of constructed objects, sometimes of constructed concepts, without differentiating.

These two parallel languages which deal with concepts and with objects and still say the same thing are actually the languages of realism and idealism. Does thinking "create" the objects, as the Neo-Kantian Marburg school teaches, or does thinking "merely apprehend" them, as realism asserts? Construction theory employs a neutral language and maintains that objects are neither "created" nor "apprehended" but *constructed*. In wish to emphasize from the beginning that the phrase "to construct" is always meant in a completely neutral sense. From the point of view of construction theory, the controversy between "creation" and "apprehension" is an idle linguistic dispute.

We can actually go even further (without here giving any reasons) and state boldly that the object and its concept are one and the same. This identification does not amount to a reification of the concept, but, on the contrary, is a "functionalization" of the object.

B

The Plan of the Investigation

6. *The Preliminary Discussions* (Part II)

The second part will be preparatory to the construction theory itself. Thus, the arguments given there do not presuppose the basic assumption of construction theory, namely, the possibility of a unified constructional system, but merely seek to clarify the scientific, or perhaps more exactly, the ontological situation as it exists today.

In the first chapter (A) of Part II, the very important concept of a *structure* (in the sense of the purely formal aspects of a relation extension) will be explained, and its fundamental importance for science will be shown. It will be demonstrated that it is in principle possible to characterize all objects through merely structural properties (i.e., certain formal-logical properties of relation extensions or complexes of relation extensions) and thus to transform all scientific statements into purely structural statements.

In the second chapter (B), the most important *types of objects*, namely the physical, the psychological, and the cultural will be briefly discussed as to their characteristics, differences, and mutual relations. We will speak, not from the point of view and in the language of construction theory, but from the traditional viewpoint and in the (realistic) language of the empirical sciences. This discussion will give us, in a sense, a synopsis of the material which will be used in the formulation of the constructional system. This leads to a nonformal requirement which must be fulfilled, namely, the assignment of definite positions within the system for all the indicated objects.

7. *The Formal Problems of the Constructional System* (Part III)

The presentation of construction theory will begin with Part III. In the first chapter (A), the concept of construction will be discussed in more detail; in particular, it will be shown how it differs from composition by the summation of parts. It will be shown that the construction of an object must be given in the logical form of a definition: every object to be constructed will be introduced through its constructional definition either as a class or as a relation extension. Thus, in each step within the constructional system, one of these two forms will be produced. They are the *ascension forms* of the constructional system. Other are not required.

In the second chapter (B), we shall undertake logical and factual investigations concerning the *object forms* and the *system form* of the constructional system. By the object form of a constructed object is meant the series of constructional steps which lead to it from the basic objects. We shall show in a general way how the object form can be established from the information found in the empirical sciences about this object, especially about its indicators. By "system form" is meant the form of the system as a whole, i.e., the arrangement of the various steps in the system and the objects which are constructed by these steps. From the various logically and factually possible system forms, we shall select that one which best represents the epistemic relations of the objects to one another.

In the third chapter (C), we shall treat of the problem of the *basis* of the constructional system, i.e., of basic objects of two essentially different kinds, namely, the *basic elements* and the *basic relations*, where the latter expression refers to the order which is initially established between the basic elements. We choose as basic elements of the system "my experiences" (more precisely, entities which initially have neither names nor properties, and which can be called terms of relations only after certain constructions have been carried out). Thus, we choose a system form with an "autopsychological basis". It will then be shown how it is possible to envisage these basic elements as unanalyzable units and nevertheless to construct those objects which are later on called the "properties" or "constituents" of these experiences through a procedure which is actually synthetic, but takes on the linguistic forms of an analysis. (We shall call this procedure "quasi analysis".)

The actual basic concepts of the constructional system, i.e., those concepts to which all other concepts of science are to be reduced, are not the basic elements, but the basic relations. This corresponds to a fundamental assumption of construction theory, namely, that *a system of relations is primary relative to its members*. We will choose the basic relations after certain nonformal considerations. These considerations will already prepare the lower levels of the system by dealing with the question as to how and in what sequence the objects of the lower levels can be constructed, and what basic relations are required for the purpose. As it turns out, a very small number of basic relations, perhaps even only one, suffices.

In the fourth chapter (D), we shall discuss why and in what manner the constructions in the system outline (which constitutes Part IV) are given in four languages: namely, in the language of logistics, which is the proper language of the system, and in three translations which are to facilitate both the understanding of the individual constructions and the investigation into whether these constructions fulfill certain formal requirements. These three translations are: paraphrase of the constructional definitions in word language, the transformation of each definition into a statement indicating a state of affairs in realistic language, and the transformation of each definition into a rule of operation on the basis of certain fictions which serve as an aid to intuition ("language of fictitious constructive operations").

8. *The Outline of a Constructional System* (Part IV)

In Part IV, some of the results of the preceding investigations are applied in practice; an outline of a constructional system is attempted. The lower levels of the system are given in great detail (Chapter A) by representing the individual constructions in symbolic form and translating them into three auxiliary languages (cf. § 7). We give this part in such great detail, not because its content is absolutely secure, but in order to give a very clear example of the point of the whole investigation and, in addition, to do some spade work on the problem of achieving a reasonable formulation of the lower levels. Using only one basic relation, we shall construct in this part, among other things, the sense qualities, the sense modalities, the visual sense, the spatial order of the visual field, the qualitative order of the color solid, and a preliminary time order.

In the second chapter (B), the constructions are given only in the word language, and no longer with the previous precision, but the individual steps are still clearly described. Here, the space-time world and the visual things in it, including "my body", as one of these visual things, the other senses (besides vision), and the other "autopsychological" entities, components, and states are constructed. The visual world is supplemented by the other senses until it becomes the sensory world, and this world is contrasted with the world of physics, which is no longer concerned with sensory qualities.

In the third chapter (C), constructions are given in rough outline and only to the extent necessary to show that they can be carried out. In particular, we shall indicate the construction of the "heteropsychological" on the basis of "other persons" (as physical things) with the aid of the expression relation; the construction of the "world of the other person" and the "intersubjective world". Finally, the construction of cultural objects and values is also briefly indicated.

9. *The Clarification of Some Philosophical Problems* (Part V)

In Part V, we shall consider some of the traditional philosophical problems and show how construction theory can be used in order to clarify the problem situations to the extent to which they are part of (rational) science. The problems which are treated there are to serve only as examples of the method, and we shall not discuss them in great detail.

To begin with (Chapter A), some problems of essence are discussed, especially the problems of identity, of psychophysical dualism, of intentionality, and of causality.

In Chapter B, we shall try to clarify the problem of psychophysical parallelism.

Subsequently (C, D), the problem of reality is discussed. It is shown that construction theory is the common basis of the various philosophical positions which attempt an answer to this problem, namely, realism, idealism, and phenomenalism; it will also be shown that these positions differ from one another only where they go beyond construction theory; that is, in the field of metaphysics.

In the last chapter (E), the aims and limits of science are discussed, and their clear separation from metaphysics is demanded.

PART TWO

PRELIMINARY DISCUSSIONS

A

The Form of Scientific Statements

10. Property Description and Relation Description

In the following, we shall maintain and seek to establish the thesis that *science deals only with the description of structural properties of objects*. At the outset we shall define the concept of a structure. Afterward, in order to establish the thesis, we shall undertake an investigation concerning the possibility and meaning of structural descriptions. However, an actual proof for the thesis can be given only by demonstrating the possibility of a constructional system which is formal, but which nevertheless contains (in principle, if not in practice) all objects. We shall attempt this demonstration by formulating a constructional system in outline (Part IV).

In order to develop the concept of a structure, which is fundamental for construction theory, we make a distinction between two types of description of the objects of any domain; these we call property description and relation description. A *property description* indicates the properties which the individual objects of a given domain have, while a *relation description* indicates the relations which hold between these objects, but does not make any assertion about the objects as individuals. Thus, a property description makes individual or, in a sense, absolute, assertions while a relation description makes relative assertions.

Examples   A property description looks something like this: the domain is formed by objects *a*, *b*, *c*; *a*, *b*, *c* are persons. *a* is 20 years old and tall; *b* 21 years old, short, and thin; *c* is fat. A relation description looks something like this: the domain is formed by objects *a*, *b*, *c*; *a* is father of *b*, *b* the mother of *c*, *c* is the son of *b*, *a* is 60 years older than *c*.

No matter how many different forms both of the two types of description may assume, they are nevertheless fundamentally different from one another.

We place such strong emphasis upon the difference between these two types of description because we shall maintain that they are not of equal value.

Relation descriptions form the starting-point of the whole constructional system and hence constitute the basis of unified science. Furthermore, it is the goal of each scientific theory to become, as far as its content is concerned, a pure relation description. It can, of course, take on the linguistic form of a property description; this will sometimes even be an advantage; but it differs from a genuine property description in the fact that it can be transformed, if necessary, without loss into a relation description. In science, any property description either plays the role of a relation description except that it is in more convenient form, or else, if transformation is not yet possible, it indicates the provisional character of the theory in question.

11. The Concept of Structure

There is a certain type of relation description which we shall call *structure description*. Unlike relation descriptions, these not only leave the properties of the individual elements of the range unmentioned, they do not even specify the relations themselves which hold between these elements. In a structure description, only the *structure* of the relation is indicated, i.e., the totality of its formal properties. (A more precise definition of structure will be given later.) By formal properties of a relation, we mean those that can be formulated without reference to the meaning of the relation and the type of objects between which it holds. They are the subject of the theory of relations. The formal properties of relations can be defined exclusively with the aid of logistic symbols, i.e., ultimately with the aid of the few fundamental symbols which form the basis of logistics (symbolic logic). (Thus these symbols do not specifically belong to the theory of relations, but form the basis for the entire system of logic—propositional logic, the theory of propositional functions (concepts), the theory of classes, and the theory of relations.)

16. All Scientific Statements are Structure Statements

It becomes clear from the preceding investigations about structural definite descriptions that each object name which appears in a scientific statement can in principle (if enough information is available) be replaced by a structural definite description of the object, together with an indication of the object domain to which the description refers. This holds, not only for the names of individual objects, but also for general names, that is, for names of concepts, classes, relations (as we have seen in the example of § 14, for the relation of road connections and so forth). Thus, each scientific statement can in principle be transformed into a statement which contains only structural properties and the indication of one or more object domains. Now, the fundamental thesis of construction theory (cf. § 4), which we will attempt to demonstrate in the following investigation, asserts that fundamentally there is only one object domain and that each scientific statement is about the objects in this domain. Thus, it becomes unnecessary to indicate for each statement the object domain, and the result is that *each scientific statement can in principle be so transformed that it is nothing but a structure statement.* But this transformation is not only possible, it is imperative. For science wants to speak about what is objective, and whatever does not belong to the structure but to the material (i.e., anything that can be pointed out in a concrete ostensive definition) is, in the final analysis, subjective. One can easily see that physics is almost altogether desubjectivized, since almost all physical concepts have been transformed into purely structural concepts.

> To begin with, all mathematical concepts are reducible to concepts which stem from the theory of relations: four-dimensional tensor and vector fields are structural schemata; the network of world lines with the relations of coincidence and local time order is a structural schema in which only two relations are still named; and even these are uniquely determined through the character of the schema.

From the point of view of construction theory, this state of affairs is to be described in the following way. The series of experiences is different for each subject. If we want to achieve, in spite of this, agreement in the names for the entities which are constructed on the basis of these experiences, then this cannot be done by reference to the completely divergent content, but only through the formal description of the structure of these entities. However, it is still a problem how, through the application of uniform formal construction rules, entities result which have a structure which is the same for all subjects, even though they are based on such immensely different series of experiences. This is the problem of intersubjective reality. We shall return to it later. Let it suffice for the moment to say that, *for science, it is possible and at the same time necessary to restrict itself to structure statements.* This is what we asserted in our thesis. It is nevertheless evident from what has been said in § 10 that scientific statements may have the linguistic form of a material relation description or even the form of a property description.

B

Survey Of the Object Types and Their Relations

17. The Significance of Object Types for Construction Theory

In the present chapter (II, B), we do not undertake any new investigations, but merely give a survey of the different independent object types according to their familiar characteristic properties. We shall also discuss those relations between these types which have given rise to metaphysical problems (as, for example, the psychophysical relation), or are important for the logical-epistemic relation between the object types and therefore also for the problems of construction (as, for example, the expression relation).

The problem of object types and their mutual relations is of great importance for construction theory since its aim is a system of objects. The various differences and relations which can be indicated, and especially the differences between the various "object spheres", must some-how be reflected in the system that we are about to develop. This is an especially important test for our form of construction theory, since we subscribe to the thesis that the concepts of all objects can be derived from a single common basis.

When, later on, we give a presentation of construction theory, we shall not presuppose any of the factual results and problems of the present chapter, but will undertake the entire construction from the very beginning. There are only a few stages in the development of the system where we shall pay any attention to some of these facts. They will become the most important test when we judge our final result. On the other hand, the theory will lead to the conclusion that the *problems* which are discussed in the present chapter do not even occur in the newly developed system of objects; the obscurity and confusion which is the source of these problems did not arise because the facts themselves are complicated but because of certain traditional conceptual mistakes, which must be explained historically rather than by reference to the facts in question. (Objections against the assertions of this chapter should therefore be postponed until these assertions are later on employed in the formulation of the system.)

18. The Physical and Psychological Objects

The concepts of the physical and the psychological are here to be taken in their customary sense, and therefore we will not give any explicit explanation, much less a definition, especially since both of them are in certain respects vague and, moreover, "logically impure" concepts (§ 29).

As examples of physical objects, we consider their most important type, namely, *physical bodies.* These are characterized especially by the fact that, at a given time, they occupy a given space (i.e., an extended piece of space). Thus, place, shape, size, and position belong to the determining characteristics of any physical body. Furthermore, at least one sensory quality belongs to these determining characteristics, e.g., color, weight, temperature, etc.

Since we take the word "object" here always in its widest sense (i.e., as something about which a statement can be made), we make no distinction between events and objects. To the *psychological objects* belong, to begin with, the acts of consciousness: perceptions, representations, feelings, thoughts, acts of will, and so on. We count among them also unconscious processes to the extent to which they can be considered analogous to acts of consciousness, for example, unconscious representations.

The psychological objects have in common with the physical ones that they can be temporally determined. In other respects, a sharp distinction must be drawn between the two types. A psychological object does not have color or any other sensory quality and, furthermore, no spatial determination. Outside of these negative characteristics, psychological objects have the positive characteristic that each of them belongs to some individual subject.

19. Psychophysical Relation, Expression Relation, and Designation Relation

The *psychophysical relation* holds between a psychological process and the "corresponding" or "parallel" process of the central nervous system. The theory which is advanced most frequently holds that all psychological objects belong to the domain of this relation, while the converse domain is formed by only a very small segment of the physical objects, namely, the processes in the nervous system of the living animal (or, perhaps, only the human) body.

Through voice, facial expressions, and other gestures, we can understand "what goes on within" a person. Thus, physical processes allow us to draw conclusions concerning psychological ones. The relation between a gesture, etc., and the psychological process we call the *expression relation*. To its domain belong almost all motions of the body and its members, in particular also the involuntary ones. To its converse domain belong part of the psychological objects, especially the emotions.

21. Problems of Correlation and Essence of the Aforementioned Relations

... Brain physiology, psychology, and psychopathology concern themselves with the correlation problem of the psychophysical relations. They attempt to ascertain what kind of physiological process in the central nervous system corresponds to a given psychological process, and vice versa. Very little has been done to solve this problem. The technical difficulties of such an investigation are patent; on the other hand, it is certainly not the case that there are fundamental obstacles, i.e., absolute limits to our knowledge of these matters. There has not been much research into the expression relation, even though it is very important for practical life, since our understanding of other persons depends upon it. However, we possess and utilize this knowledge, not in a theoretically explicit manner, but only intuitively ("empathy"). This is the reason why there is no satisfactory solution of the correlation problem of this relation. On the other hand, there are today promising beginnings to theories of physiognomics, graphology, and characterology. The correlation problem of the vast and variegated designation relation can hardly be resolved within a single theoretical system. In spite of the immense extension of the designation relation (written signs, signals, badges, etc.), there are fewer difficulties to be expected in this case than with the other discussed relations; at least, there will be no fundamental difficulties.

Thus we see that the correlation problems of the indicated relations will have to be solved within certain special sciences, and that no fundamental difficulties stand in the way of these solutions. On the other hand, the *essence problems* of these relations are a different matter. Since we are here concerned not with the *ascertainment*, but with the *interpretation* of facts, these questions cannot be empirically answered. Thus, their treatment is not among the tasks of the special sciences.

If, in connection with correlation problems, we encounter several competing hypotheses, between which we cannot decide, we can at least indicate which empirical data would be required to decide in favor of one hypothesis or another. On the other hand, no decisions have been made between various fundamentally opposed answers to essence problems, and apparently it is impossible to make such decisions: a depressing aspect for the impartial observer, since, even with the boldest hopes for future progress in knowledge, he cannot expect to find out which empirical or other sort of knowledge could bring about such a decision.

The question about the essence of the expression relation has received different, diverging, and even in part contradicting answers. The expressive act has sometimes been interpreted as the effect of the psychological facts that are expressed (thus, the problem has been pushed back to the essence problem of the causal relation), or else as its cause, or the two have been identified with one another. Occasionally, the expressed emotion is said to "inhere" in a special, unanalyzable way in the physical expression. Thus, the most divergent essential relations have been envisaged. The problem of the designation relation is somewhat simpler, since the connection between sign and signified object always contains a conventional component; that is, it is somehow brought about voluntarily. Only rarely has a special essential relation of "symbolizing" been assumed.

22. The Psychophysical Problem as the Central Problem of Metaphysics

The essence problem of the psychophysical relation can be called simply the psychophysical problem. Among the traditional problems of philosophy, it is the one which is most closely connected with the psychophysical relation, and, in addition, it has gradually become the main problem of metaphysics.

The question is this: provided that to all or some types of psychological processes there correspond simultaneous processes in the central nervous system, what connects the processes in question with one another? Very little has been done toward a solution of the correlation problem of the psychophysical relation, but, even if this problem were solved (i.e., if we could infer the characteristics of a brain process from the characteristics of a psychological process, and vice versa), nothing would have been achieved to further the solution of the essence problem (i.e., the "psychophysical problem"). For this problem is not concerned with the correlation, but with the essential relation; that is, with that which "essentially" or "fundamentally" leads from one process to the other or which brings forth both from a common root.

The attempted solutions and also their irreconcilable divergences are well known. The theories of occasionalism and of preëstablished harmony have perhaps only historical interest. Thus, there still remain, in the main, three hypotheses: mutual influence, parallelism, and identity in the sense of the two-aspect theory. The hypothesis of *mutual influence* assumes an essential relation between the two terms (i.e., a causal efficacy in both directions). The hypothesis of *parallelism* (in the narrowest sense, i.e., excluding the identity theory) denies the existence of an essential relation and assumes that there is only a functional correlation between the two types of objects (types of processes). Finally, the *identity theory* does not even admit that there are two types of objects, but assumes that the psychological and the physical are the two "aspects" ("the outer" and "the inner") of the same fundamental process. The counterarguments which are brought forth against each of these hypotheses by its adversaries seem to be conclusive: science generally assumes an uninterrupted causal nexus of all spatial processes; but this is not consistent with psychophysical mutual influence. On the other hand, one cannot see how a merely functional correlation, that is, a logical and not a real relation, can result in an experience which corresponds to the stimuli that impinge upon the senses. And the identity of two such different types of objects as the psychological and the physical remains an empty word as long as we are not told what is meant by the figurative expression "fundamental process" and "inner and outer aspects." (We do not wish to say anything against parallelism or the hypothesis of mutual influence as long as they are merely used heuristically, as working hypotheses for psychology. We are here concerned with metaphysical opinions.)

Three contradicting and equally unsatisfactory answers and no possibility of finding or even imagining an empirical fact that could here make the difference: a more hopeless situation can hardly be imagined. It could lead us to wonder whether the questions concerning problems of essence, especially the psychophysical problem, are not perhaps posed in a fallacious way. Construction theory will in fact lead to the conclusion that this is so. Once the constructional forms of the objects and the object types are found and their logical locations in the constructional system are known, and if furthermore the correlation problem of one of the above relations has been resolved, then we have found everything (rational) science can say about that relation. An additional question concerning the "essence" of the relation would lack any sense. It cannot even be formulated in scientific terms. The discussions of Part V will show this in more detail (§ 157 ff.).

23. The Cultural Objects

For philosophy, the most important types of objects, outside of the physical and the psychological ones, are the *cultural* (historical, sociological) *objects*. They belong in the object domain of the cultural sciences. Among the cultural objects, we count individual incidents and large scale occurrences, sociological groups, institutions, movements in all areas of culture, and also properties and relations of such processes and entities.

The philosophy of the nineteenth century did not pay sufficient attention to the fact that the cultural objects form an autonomous type. The reason for this is that epistemological and logical investigations tended to confine their attention predominately to physics and psychology as paradigmatic subject matter areas. Only the more recent history of philosophy (since Dilthey) has called attention to the methodological and object-theoretical peculiarity of the area of the cultural sciences.

The cultural objects have in common with the psychological ones the fact that they, too, are subject bound; their "bearers" are always the persons of a certain group. But, in contrast to the psychological objects, their bearers may change: a state or a custom can persist even though the bearing subjects perish and others take their place. Moreover, the cultural objects are not composed of psychological (much less physical) objects. They are of a completely different object type; the cultural objects belong to other object spheres (in a sense to be explained later on, § 29) than the physical and the psychological objects. This means that no cultural object may be meaningfully inserted into a proposition about a physical or a psychological object.

Later on, in the context of construction theory, we shall show in what way the assertion of the unity of the entire domain of objects of knowledge refers to the derivation ("construction") of all objects starting from one and the same basis, and that the assertion that the various spheres of objects are different means that there are different constructional levels and forms. Thus the two apparently opposing positions are reconciled (cf. § 41).

24. The Manifestations and Documentations of Cultural Objects

I wish to discuss here only the two most important relations between cultural and other objects, since knowledge of cultural objects, and thus their construction, depends entirely upon these relations. We call these two relations "manifestation" and "documentation".

A cultural object, which exists during a certain time, does not have to be actual (i.e., manifested) at all points during this span. The psychological processes in which it appears or "manifests" itself, we shall call its (psychological) manifestation. The relation of the (psychological) manifestation of a cultural object to the object itself, we shall call the manifestation relation (more precisely: the psychological-cultural or, more briefly, the psychological manifestation relation).

EXAMPLE This relation holds, for example, between the present resolve of a man to lift his hat before another man, and the custom of hat-lifting. This custom does not exist merely during those moments in which somebody somewhere manifests it, but also during the times in between, as long as there are any persons who have the psychological disposition to react to certain impressions by greeting somebody through lifting their hats. During the times in between, the custom is "latent".

A physical object can also be the manifestation of a cultural one. Thus, the custom of hat-lifting manifests itself, for example, in the appropriate bodily motions of a certain man. But closer scrutiny shows that, even here, the psychological manifestation relation is fundamental. Thus we shall always mean the latter when we simply speak of the manifestation relation.

We call documentations of a cultural object those permanent physical objects in which the cultural life is, as it were, solidified: products, artifacts, and documents of a culture.

EXAMPLES The documentations or representations of an art style consist of the buildings, paintings, statues, etc. which belong to this style. The documentation of the present railroad system consists of all stationary and rolling material and the written documents of the railroad business.

It is the task of the cultural sciences to deal with the correlation problems of the manifestation and documentation relation. These sciences have to ascertain in which acts (in the physical and psychological sense) the individual cultural objects become overt and manifest themselves. In so doing they form, as it were, definitions for all the names of cultural objects. On the other hand, the documentation relation is of special importance for the cultural sciences, because the research into no longer existing cultural objects (and these, after all, form the larger part of the domain) rests almost exclusively upon conclusions drawn from documentation, namely, from written records, illustrations, things that have been built or formed, etc. But these conclusions presuppose that the documentation correlation (that is, the answer to the correlation problem of the documentation relation) is known. Thus, for the cultural sciences, the tasks of providing definitions, and of finding criteria for the recognition of their objects will be fulfilled by resolving these two correlation problems.

As with the relations which we considered earlier (§ § 21, 22), here, too, examination of the correlation problems is part of the task of the special sciences. The study of the essence problems, on the other hand, belongs to metaphysics. I do not wish to discuss at this time the attempted solutions of the essence problems (e.g., emanation theory, incarnation theory, psychologistic and materialistic interpretation). Here we find a situation very similar to that which held for the earlier essence problems: a struggle between divergent opinions, where there seems to be no possibility that a decision can be made through empirically obtained information.

PART FOUR

OUTLINE OF A CONSTRUCTIONAL SYSTEM

A

The Lower Levels: Autopsychological Objects

106. About Form, Content, and Purpose of this Outline

In the following, we shall give a tentative version of the lower levels of the constructional system (Chapter A); the higher levels, we shall merely suggest (Chapter B and C). By and large, Chapter A comprehends the autopsychological objects; Chapter B, the physical objects; and Chapter C, the heteropsychological and cultural objects.

The constructional forms which we shall apply correspond to the results of the preceding investigations (Part III); according to III, A, we use class and relation extension as ascension forms; according to III, B, we use a system form with autopsychological basis; according to III, C, 1, we use as basic elements the elementary experiences; and, according to III, C, 2, we use recollection of similarity as the only basic relation;

the object forms of the lower levels correspond to the derivations in III, C, 2, and III, D.

The statements or theorems of a constructional system are divided into two different types (the following are given as examples for theorems: Th. 1–6 in § § 108, 110, 114, 117, 118). The first type of theorem can be deduced from the definitions alone (presupposing the axioms of logic, without which no deduction is possible at all). These we call *analytic* theorems. The second type of theorem, on the other hand, indicates the relations between constructed objects which can be ascertained only through experience. We call them *empirical* theorems. If an analytic theorem is transformed into a statement about the basic relation(s), a tautology results; if an empirical theorem is thus transformed, it indicates empirical, formal properties of the basic relation(s). Expressed in the realistic language, this mans that the analytic theorems are tautological statements about concepts (these statements are not necessarily trivial, since the tautology may become apparent only after the transformation, as is the case with mathematical theorems); the empirical theorems express an empirically ascertained state of affairs.

REFERENCES In Kantian terminology, the analytic theorems are analytic judgments a priori; the empirical theorems are synthetic judgments a posteriori. It is the contention of construction theory that there are no such things as the "synthetic judgments a priori" which are essential for Kant's approach to epistemological problems.

As concerns the content of our constructional system, let us emphasize again that it is only a tentative example. The content depends upon the material findings of the empirical sciences; for the lower levels in particular, upon the findings of the phenomenology of perception, and psychology. The results of these sciences are themselves subject to debate; since a constructional system is merely the translation of such findings, its complete material correctness cannot be guaranteed. *The actual purpose of our exposition of construction theory is to pose the problem of a constructional system, and to carry out a logical investigation of the method which will lead to such a system; the formulation of the system is not itself part of the actual purpose.* We have nevertheless formulated some levels of the system and have indicated further levels. We have done this mostly to illustrate the problem, rather than to attempt a beginning of its solution.

107. The Logical and Mathematical Objects

Even before the introduction of the basic relation(s), we must construct the *logical objects,* or objects of pure logistics. Once the basic concepts of any object domain are introduced, e.g., the basic relation(s) of the constructional system, pure logistics is transformed into applied logistics; this holds in particular for the theory of relations. It is not necessary here to give an explicit account of the system of pure logistics.

> **REFERENCES** A complete version of this system has been given by Russell and Whitehead [Princ. Math.], including the mathematical objects. Cf. the bibliography about logistics in § 3 and the explanation of logistic symbols in § 97.

The following basic concepts are required: incompatibility of two statements and validity of a propositional function for all arguments. Then the further connectives for two statements and negation are constructed as the first logical objects from the basic concepts; also, identity and existence. Then classes and relations extensions with their respective connectives are introduced, and finally all objects of the general theory of relations. (Cf. § 25 for the independence of logical objects from psychological and physical objects.)

Mathematics forms a branch of logistics (i.e., it does not require any new basic concepts). It is not necessary here to give an account of the formation of the system of mathematical objects; let us merely recall its main levels.

On the basis of the logical objects, we construct at first the arithmetical objects: cardinal numbers (cf. § 40); then the general relation numbers (or "structures," cf. § 11), which are less frequently employed in mathematics; as a special type of the latter, we then construct the ordinal numbers. For each type of number, we construct its connectives; furthermore, the (general) series, the rational numbers, the real numbers, the vectors, etc.

Geometrical objects, too, are purely logical objects, i.e., they can be constructed within the system of logistics with the indicated basic concepts. By "geometry" we mean here purely mathematical, abstract geometry which is not concerned with space in the ordinary sense of the word, but concerned with certain multidimensional ordered structures which are also called "space", or, more precisely, "abstract space". Intuitive, phenomenally spatial objects form a special object domain; they belong to the real objects and can be constructed only later, after the introduction of the basic relation(s) of the constructional system (§ 125).

It is important to notice that the logical and mathematical objects are not actually objects in the sense of real objects (objects of the empirical sciences). *Logic (including mathematics) consists solely of conventions* concerning the use of symbols, *and of tautologies* on the basis of these conventions. Thus, the symbols of logic (and mathematics) do not designate objects, but merely serve as symbolic fixations of these conventions. Objects in the sense of real objects (including quasi objects) are only the basic relation(s) and the objects constructed therefrom. All signs which have a definite meaning are called *constants* and are thus distinguished from the *variables* (§ 28). The *logical constants* are signs for logical objects; the *nonlogical constants* are signs for real objects (concepts of an object domain).

124. Various Possibilities for the Construction of Physical Space

The following constructional step, namely, the transition from the two-dimensional order of the visual field to the three-dimensional order of the space of visual things is one of the most important steps in the constructional system. Various attempts were made to solve the problem of executing this construction; we shall here mention the most important ones and shall give reasons why we deviate from them.

> **REFERENCES** Russell ([External W.], [Const. Matter], [Sense-Data]) constructs visual things as classes of their aspects, in fact, not merely as classes of the real, experienced aspects, but as classes of *possible aspects.* This method is tenable if, as with Russell, these aspects are taken as basic elements. We have begun our structure several levels further down; thus, in order to be able to follow the same route as Russell, we will first of all have to construct

the aspects from our basic elements, namely, the elementary experiences. However, this is probably impossible for aspects which "have not been seen", or at least, it would offer very considerable difficulties. Hence, it is more advantageous for us to use a different method, namely, to construct the entire visual world at once, rather than the individual visual things. Russell's method has the advantage of greater logical simplicity. The advantage of our method lies, first of all, in the fact that we have used the autopsychological basis, which Russell himself considers a desirable goal (cf. § 64), secondly, in the circumstance that unperceived points and states of a thing are, in our system, not inferred, but constructed. This procedure, too, Russell considers desirable. (Cf. the motto preceding § 1; § 3; [Sense-Data] 157 f., 159). It must be admitted, however, that our kind of construction of physical points and of the physical space is by no means a fully satisfactory solution.

Reasons similar to those just mentioned have induced us to avoid the procedure which Whitehead ([Space], [Nat. Knowledge], [Nature]) has followed. Whitehead constructs space and time only *after* the things, as the structure of the relations which become apparent in the behavior of things to one another. He emphasizes especially that we experience, not spatial or temporal points, but extensions; from these, we must construct the points according to the method of "extensive abstraction". Unquestionably, this procedure has great advantages in method and content; however, we cannot follow it since the problem of constructing the three-dimensional things or four-dimensional events from the position relations in the sensory field, especially the visual field, offer unsurmounted difficulties. (Whitehead fails to indicate a solution to this problem.)

It is still a question whether it is appropriate, or perhaps even necessary, to construct visual space before the construction of the visual things and their physical space. Psychologically, the three-dimensional, metric, non-Euclidean (namely, spherical), visual space forms an intermediate step between the two-dimensional order of the visual field and the three-dimensional Euclidean order of the outside world. However, it is probably appropriate for the constructional system to omit this step. For the introduction of this step does not bring about a formal simplification of construction, and the objects which are found on this intermediate level cannot be described as "real". According to our earlier considerations, such a simplifying deviation from the psychological order of the process of cognition is permissible for the constructional system.

125. The Space-Time World

The points of n-dimensional, real-number space, we call *world points*; they are n-tuples of numbers which serve as subjects of the following assignment.

To some world points, we shall assign colors (later on, also, quality classes or classes of quality classes from other sense modalities); that is to say, we shall establish a one-many relation between world points and colors such that requirements 1–12 (§ 126) are fulfilled as far as possible.

126. The Assignment of Colors to World Points

The assignment of colors to the world points and the subsequent constructions which are connected with this are carried out in such a way that the following desiderata are satisfied as far as possible. They cannot be precisely satisfied because of (in realistic language) hallucinations, disturbances of the eye and the intervening medium, deformations and disintegration of bodies, etc. In § 127, we shall indicate in realistic language the empirical states of affairs on which these individual desiderata or rules of construction rest.

1. There is a series of prominent world points which we call the *points of view*. They form a continuous curve in such a way that each of the $n - 1$ space coördinates is a single-valued, continuous function of the time coördinate.

2. The straight lines which proceed from a given point of view and which form, with the negative direction of time, the angle γ we call the *lines of view*.

3. γ is constant and is very nearly equal to a right angle. Thus, if a point of view has the time coördinate t_1, then we can take as its lines of view the straight lines of its space class (cross section $t = t_1$) which proceed from this point.

4. A one-to-one correspondence is established between elementary experiences and some of the points of view in such a way that an experience which is later in time (Rs_{po}, cf. § 120) corresponds to a point of view with a larger time coördinate.

5. If possible, we assign to each visual sensation (§ 116) of an elementary experience a line of view of the corresponding point of view in such a way that (a) to sensations with proximate visual field places (Proxpl, § 117) we assign lines of view which form only a small angle with one another, and vice versa; and that (b) the pairs of lines of view which are assigned to the visual sensations of two definite places in different elementary experiences all form the same angle, and conversely.

6. The color of a visual sensation is assigned to a world point of the corresponding line of view. Points which are occupied in this way are called "world points seen from the given point of view" or, in short, *seen color spots*. For the choice of position of these points on their lines of view, cf. 11.

7. Furthermore, taking into consideration the requirements 8–10, we shall assign one color each to certain other world points. These world points are called *unseen color spots*. Among the points of each of the bundles of lines of view (according to 3, this means with very near approximation: among the points of each of the space classes), they form at most a two-dimensional area, usually connected surfaces.

8. An unseen color spot may not be located on a line of view between a point of view and a seen color spot.

9. The assignment of colors to unseen color spots according to 7 is carried out in such a way that, as far a possible, each seen color spot belongs to a *world line*. A world line is a continuous curve or curve segment such that precisely one world point belongs to each value of the time coördinate within a given interval; the world point may be either a seen or an unseen color spot. Within the interval, each space coördinate of the segment is a single-valued, continuous function of the time coördinate.

10. According to 7, we have to assign a color to the unseen color spots. Taking into account the colors of seen color spots, we make a preliminary choice of these colors in such a way that the color of the points of a world line, considered as a function of time, shows a rate of change which is as small as possible, i.e., if possible, remains constant.

127. Formulation of the Above Points in Realistic Language

To facilitate understanding, let us here indicate, in realistic language, the states of affairs which lie at the bottom of the indicated requirements which determine the assignment of colors to the world points.

1. The particular point in the interior of the head from which the world seems to be seen has as its world line a continuous curve in the space-time world. (The construction does not have to concern itself with binocular vision, since the determination of depth has a sufficient and more precise foundation elsewhere.)

2. The optical medium between the eye and the seen things can generally be considered homogeneous. Under this assumption, the light rays which impinge upon the eye form straight lines which enclose the angle arc tg c with the negative direction of time (c designates the speed of light).

3. The speed of light, c, is constant and very large. Thus, the light rays are very nearly the straight lines of a momentary space.

4. Each visual perception is based upon an act of seeing from one of the points of view.

5. a. Visual field places that lie next to one another always depict only points of the outside world whose lines of view form a small angle at the eye;

b. A given pair of visual field places always has the same visual angle.

6. We conclude, from a visual sensation, that a point of the outside world which lies on the corresponding line of view has the color of the visual sensation.

7. At any given time, there are many points of the outside world which have a color, but are not seen at that time. These visible, but unseen (by me), world points are, for the most part, points on the surfaces of bodies.

8. A visible, colored point of the outside world which is not seen by me at a given time cannot at that time be located in front of a seen point.

9. We must assume, if there are no reasons to the contrary, that a point of the outside world which has once been seen existed previously and will exist afterward. Its locations form a continuous world line.

10. We shall assume, if there is no reason to the contrary, that each point of the outside world retains at the other times the same or as similar as possible a color as that with which it was seen at one time.

128. *The Visual Things*

If, in a bundle of world lines which have been constructed according to the given requirements (§ § 126, 127), the proximity relations remain at least approximately the same during a protracted stretch (of time), then the class of the corresponding world points is called a *visual thing*.

The class of world points of a thing which are seen from a given point of view is called the "seen part" of the thing in the elementary experience to which the point of view corresponds. Since a point of view and the points which are seen from it are very nearly simultaneous, we can, in first approximation, take the seen part of a thing as a subclass of a state of the thing.

The class of those visual sensations of an elementary experience which correspond to the seen points of a given thing are called the *aspect* of the thing in that experience. Accordingly, the "seen parts" of the thing, that is, roughly speaking, parts of states of the thing, corresponds to aspects of the thing.

129. *"My Body"*

There is a certain visual thing B which fulfills the conditions listed below. These conditions and even an appropriate part of them form a constructional definite description of it; this visual thing is called *my body*.

1. Each state of B is very close to the corresponding point of view.
2. B, as all other visual things, forms an open surface when seen from a point of view. However, in contrast to all other visual things, every total state of B also forms an open surface.
3. The world lines of B or connected areas of them are correlated with the qualities (or classes of qualities) of a certain sense class in such a way that, upon contact with the world line of another visual thing or of another part of B, another quality, called a tactile quality, occurs simultaneously in the experience in question; the so-constructed sense class is called the *tactile sense*.
4. In a similar way, certain motions of B are correlated with the qualities of another sense class; the sense class so described is called *kinesthetic sense*.

5. On the basis of B, it will later on be possible to give a constructional description of the remaining sense classes (§ 131).

The given constructional determinations are founded upon the following empirical states of affairs (in realistic language):

1. My body is always in the vicinity of my eye.
2. The surface of a body can never all be seen at the same time; thus, any part of the surface of a body which is seen at one time can never be a closed surface. However, in the case of some bodies, the entire surface is visible; thus, the visible surface is a closed surface. On the other hand, in the case of my body, even the visible surface is an open surface, since some parts of its surface, for example, the eye and the back, are not visible.
3. The places of the surface of my body correspond to the qualities (or location signs) of the tactile sense in such a way that we experience a tactile sensation of a certain quality if a corresponding part of the skin is touched by another body or by another part of my body.
4. The qualities of kinesthetic sensations correspond to certain types of motions of my body.
5. The other senses are connected in a definite way with certain parts of my body, namely, with the sense organs.

130. *The Tactile-Visual Things*

Earlier, we have assigned colors, i.e., classes of classes of visual qualities, to some world points. We shall now do the same in a somewhat different way with quality classes of the tactile sense, or rather, with classes of such classes, namely those which coincide in their location sign. Earlier, we discussed seen and unseen color spots; in like fashion, we now distinguish touch points. The position of the touched touch points can be determined more precisely than those of the seen color spots. For these touch points touch the corresponding part of my body; hence, if we assume the spatial position of my body as already determined, we do not have to determine any distance or dimension of depth in this case. In most cases, the touch points are also color spots, either seen or unseen. This allows us in many cases to determine more precisely the position of the world lines of the color spots. Sometimes the touch points are not color spots; in these cases, they determine new world lines. In some cases, it takes these world lines of mere touch points, together with the world lines of color spots, in order to form the closed surface of a *tactile-visual thing*. For example, this is the case for the most important tactile-visual thing, namely, for my body. A large part of the surface of my body consists of world lines to which no color spots, but only touch points, correspond. Thus, my body becomes a completely closed thing only by taking into account the qualities of the tactile sense.

131. Definite Description of the Remaining Senses

After my body has been constructed as a complete thing, namely, as a tactile-visual thing, we can, if necessary, give definite descriptions of various of its parts according to their shape or mutual position, since all spatial shape and position relations can be expressed with the aid of the already constructed space coördinates. Thus, the sense organs, which, for subsequent constructions, are the most important parts of my body, can be constructionally described. The events taking place in these organs are correlated in a certain way with certain senses. This enables us to give definite descriptions of the individual senses. For example, after spatial determinations have enabled us to distinguish ear, nose, tongue, etc., from the other parts of the body, hearing, smelling, tasting, etc., can be characterized, for example, by the fact that the quality classes of the sense classes do not, as a rule, occur if the corresponding organ is blocked off from its surroundings in a certain way.

In the case of the senses of pain, warmth, and cold, the organ, namely, the skin, coincides with that of the tactile sense of which we have given a definite description above (§ 129). The constructional definite description of these senses is possible in various ways, for example, through correlation with the stimuli in question. . . .

Thus, in one way or another, we will finally be able to distinguish, or construct, all the individual sense classes. As we have mentioned earlier (§ § 76, 85), we count among the sense classes also the domain of emotions. According to the explanation of the construction of sense classes which we have given above (§ 85), it also holds that, if there are psychological objects (for example, volitions) outside of, and irreducible to, sensations and emotions, then

the various types of such entities each form one sense class. . . .

After definite descriptions of the individual senses have been given, it is possible to construct the various components of the qualities which are represented in the quality classes. By a "component" we understand, for example, pitch of a tone, loudness of a tone, timbre; hue, saturation, brightness.

132. The Domain of the Autopsychological

Earlier, we divided the elementary experiences into individual constituents, namely sensations, and also into general constituents, namely qualities (§ § 93, 116). In the constructions given so far, these constituents have been divided into main areas (sense classes) and have been analyzed into components (especially qualities in the narrower sense, intensity, location sign). Within their main areas, they have been assigned a qualitative and in part also a spatial order. Initially, the elementary experiences were brought into a preliminary time order (Rs$_{po}$, § 120); then, with the aid of the time coördinate of the point of view in the visual world (§ 126), they were placed into a complete time sequence.

The thus-ordered elementary experiences themselves, their constituents and components, and the more complex entities which are to be constructed from these, form the domain of objects of which I am conscious, or *my consciousness*. This domain forms the foundation of the domain of the *autopsychological*. The latter results, if we introduce, in addition, the "unconscious" objects. The construction of unconscious objects on the basis of conscious objects is analogous to that of unseen color spots on the basis of seen color spots (§ 126). There we made a certain assignment to world points, i.e., to coördinate quadruples; here we make an assignment only to time points, i.e., to the individual values of the time coördinate. Through the earlier construction of the seen, namely, through the mediation of the points of view, elementary experiences are assigned to certain time points. Now we assign quality classes, as well as components of qualities and more complex structures formed from them, to intermediate time points as well, even though no point of view and no elementary experience corresponds to them. The methodological tenets of construction theory require that all of these "unconscious" entities should be constructed from previously constructed, i.e., "conscious" objects. It is possible, however, that the unconscious entities are formed from the constituents of experiences and their components in a different way from the conscious entities.

We cannot here give a detailed description of the constructional object forms. The construction (or cognitive synthesis) of the physical world is very nearly completed in prescientific thought. On the other hand, the construction of the autopsychological domain—setting aside certain insignificant beginnings—takes place only in science, indeed, in a science which stands in a very early state of development, namely psychology. Thus, it is understandable that the construction is far from complete. . . .

We speak of "physical things" and their "states". In a similar way, it is customary to envisage the autopsychological entities which correspond to an individual time point—be it an elementary experience with its (quasi) constituents, or an experience supplemented by subconscious entities, or subconscious entities alone—as "states" of a persisting bearer, of a psychological thing, as it were. From the analogy of this cognitive synthesis to that of the physical things, it follows that this bearer, which we do not commonly call "psychological thing", but *the self* or *my mind*, must be constructed as *a class of autopsychological states*. It is of especial importance in this connection to keep in mind that a class is not the collection of its elements (§ 37), but a quasi object which allows us to make statements about that which the elements have in common.

133. *The Assignment of Other Sense Qualities*

So far, we have assigned only the qualities of the visual sense and of the tactile sense to certain world points (§ § 126, 130). Since individual descriptions of the remaining senses are now also available (§ 131), we can proceed to assign their qualities or classes of their qualities to world points. Taking into account the cognitive synthesis as it actually occurs, the constructional system will not undertake this assignment with all qualities, but only with those where the assignment can be carried out in an appropriate way. This means that, for example, the assignment to individual world points of a (visual) world line does not result in too many changes of the assigned qualities in the

course of time. For example, for the qualities of the sense of taste, an assignment is possible; if we assign the quality "sweet" to a certain state of a certain piece of sugar, then the assignment to "tasted points" can be extended to "untasted points" of the world lines (in analogy to the seen and unseen points, § 126). This procedure will not often lead to contradictions through the assignment of different taste qualities to points of the same world line.

However, there is no clear boundary line between assignable and nonassignable sense qualities. Let us consider, for example, the emotions and perhaps also the volitions. . . . We consider the volitions as an independent quality domain, i.e., as a "sense" only for the sake of argument, without wishing to prejudge the necessity, or even possibility, of such a step. . . .

We do not frequently assign qualities of emotions or volitions as properties to things in the outside world. This is due to the scientific orientation of our thinking, which affects us in this way, even outside of science, in daily life. We must assume, however, that to decline this assignment is only the result of a process of abstraction and does not hold from the outset. In the uncritical conception of a child, the apple does not only taste "sourish", but also "delicious" or even "like more". This seems to mean that, not only a taste quality, but also an emotion quality and even a volition quality is assigned to it. In a similar way, a woods is "melancholy", a letter "painful", a dress "arrogant". . . . (It must be carefully noted that these objects are not meant as subjects on the basis of empathy, but as objects with the properties in question.) It must be admitted that these assignments are completely justified, for, just as we may call sugar "sweet", since it produces a taste sensation of an appropriate quality, a melody may be called "gay", a letter "painful", an act "outrageous", since these objects produce the appropriate emotions. Furthermore, an apple looks "begging for a bite", a face looks "pushing for a punch", a noise is "to run away from", since these objects cause volitions of the appropriate kind. The assignment of qualities of emotion and volition is generally dropped as conceptual thinking develops. The reason for this perhaps does not lie so much in pronounced temporal variations of these qualities in the same thing, rather, these assignments are given up because of contradictions which result later on (when the intersubjective world is constructed) between the assignments which are made by the various subjects. This would seem to justify the assumption that emotions (and volitions, if they are an independent domain) actually stand on the same level as sensations (in the narrower, customary sense). Nevertheless, they are not included among the qualities which are assigned to the outside world; they are envisaged as belonging in a certain way to the "inward" man. The only reason for this seems to be that these qualities, even if assigned to the same object, show a higher degree of variation between several subjects than the sensations in the narrower sense. However, the rejection of these qualities for the construction of perceptual things by no means holds throughout; above, we have mentioned the thinking of the child, and similar remarks can frequently be made about the world of poetry.

That we are here concerned only with differences in degree becomes obvious through the fact that, in the course of scientific development, the qualities of taste and of odor are eventually no longer assigned, and the same holds finally even for the qualities of the tactile and the visual sense. This rejection is a necessary consequence of the insight that the assignment, even of the qualities of these sense modalities varies from subject to subject and thus cannot be carried out in a unique and consistent way. In other words, the conceptual formation (and thus also the construction which follows it) of the perceptual world has only provisional validity. In the progress of knowledge (and of construction) it must give way to the strictly unambiguous but completely quality-free world of physics (cf. § 136.)

134. Perceptual Things

Almost without exception, it is points of the tactile-visual things to which the qualities of the remaining senses are assigned in the indicated way. After this assignment we call these things *perceptual things*. The entire space-time world, with the assignment of sense qualities to the individual world points, we call the perceptual world.

Earlier we were able to use spatial relations of shape and position to furnish definite descriptions of the individual parts of my body, taken as *visual* things (§ 131); now we can produce such descriptions on a large scale for individual objects as kinds of objects taken as *perceptual* things.

135. Completion of the Perceptual World through Analogy

Assume that, for large parts of two space-time regions, the assignment of sense qualities is completely or very nearly identical, while the remaining area of one of the space-time regions shows assignments for points where no qualities of the sense in question are assigned to the corresponding points of the other area. In this case, we undertake analogous assignments in the latter area.

The remaining area may be part of the larger region in a temporal or in a spatial sense. Depending upon which of the two is the case, the application of the construction procedure of *assignment by analogy* would seem to be quite different in the two cases. In the first case, the import of the procedure can be intuitively formulated in the following way (in realistic language): if a temporally large part of a known process is repeated in equal or similar ways while it remains unobserved for the remainder of the time, then we assume (if there are no reasons to the contrary) that, during the time when no observations are made, the second process continues in a way analogous to the first, or, more briefly, the processes are subject to mutual analogy. In the second case, i.e., in the case of completion in a spatial direction, the import of the procedure can be formulated thus (in realistic language): if a spatial part of a previously perceived thing is perceived again in the same or in similar ways, while the remaining spatial area remains unobserved, then we assume (if there are no reasons to the contrary) that the unobserved spatial part contains part of a thing which is analogous to the corresponding part of the first thing; or, more briefly, the things are subject to mutual analogy.

Both ways of applying this procedure have occurred earlier when we were concerned with supplementing the seen color spots with unseen color spots so as to arrive at world lines (the first kind in § 126, rules 10, 11, c, d; the second kind in rule 11, c, d), similarly, in the supplementation of touched touch points through untouched touch points (§ 130).

In a sense, the first kind of application of the assignment by analogy can be envisaged as the application of a *postulate of causality*, the second as the application of a *postulate of substance*, or, to put it the other way around, *the two categories of causality and substance amount to the application of the same analogy construction to different coördinates*.

Even if we consider the color spots alone, the application of this procedure brings the assignments very considerably closer to completion. Further supplementations result from the mutual support of the various senses. Through such supplementations, new things and regularities become known, or old ones become better known; with the aid of this information, further supplementations become possible. Thus, we find mutual advancement between the recognition of general laws which hold for things and processes on one hand, and the supplementation of the assignment of qualities to points in the perceptual world on the other.

136. The World of Physics

The perceptual world is constructed through the assignment of sense qualities; from it we must distinguish the *world of physics*, where physical-state magnitudes are assigned to the points of the four-dimensional number space. This construction has the purpose of formulating a domain which is determined through *mathematically expressible laws*. They are to be mathematically expressible in order to allow us to *calculate* certain elements from those other elements which determine them. Furthermore, the necessity of constructing the world of physics rests on the circumstance that only this world, but not the perceptual world (cf. § 132, conclusion), can be made intersubjective in an unequivocal, consistent manner (§ § 146–149).

It is not antecedently obvious that physics, if it wants to establish a domain of thoroughgoing regularity, has to eliminate all qualities and replace them by numbers. The opposition (which Goethe, for example, maintained against Newton in the polemical part of his *Farbenlehre*) asserts that one has to remain within the domain of the sense qualities and that one must ascertain the regularities which hold between them. This would mean that we would have to find the regularities in the domain which we called the perceptual world. Of course, laws like the natural laws of physics do not hold in this domain. One can show, however, that there must be regularities of some sort if the construction of a world of physics, which is

governed by regularities, is to be possible at all. However, the regularities within the perceptual world are of a much more complicated nature than the laws of physics. At the moment, we cannot concern ourselves with these problems. There is a much more simple way to arrive at a domain of thoroughgoing regularity and calculability, and that is to construct the world of physics as a pure world of numbers.

The construction of the physical world, aside from the regularity to which it is to lead, is essentially determined through a special relation which holds between it and the perceptual world; this relation we want to call *physicoqualitative correlation*. To begin with, the world points of physics are in a one-to-one correspondence to the world points of the perceptual world. (Nevertheless, the metric of the physical world can be different from that of the perceptual world; for example, it could be the non-Euclidean metric which is required by the general theory of relativity.) Then there exists a one-many relation between the qualities and the state magnitudes in such a way that, if there is an assignment of physical-state magnitudes of any (purely numerical) structure to a physical point in its neighborhood, then the quality which is correlated with this structure is always assigned to the correlated world point of the perceptual world or, at least, it can be assigned without contradiction. However, in the opposite direction, the correlation is not unique; the assignment of a quality to a world point in the perceptual world does not determine which structure of state magnitudes is to be assigned to the neighborhood of the corresponding physical world point of the world of physics; the assignment of this quality merely determines a class to which this structure must belong. It is clear that the physico-qualitative correlation cannot be free from the imprecision which attaches to the perceptual world generally.

137. Biological Objects; Man

After the world of physics has been constructed, it is possible to give a definite description of each individual event and each thing that belongs to the world. This can be accomplished through indication of place and time or through the relation to other events and things or through properties based on the assignments. We have already assumed earlier that definite descriptions of the individual sense organs of my body are given (§ 131); it is now also possible to give a constructional definite description of all the other parts and events of my body; furthermore, all other individual physical things, their parts, and events in connection with them. Accordingly, these physical things can be placed into classes or into entire systems of classes of various levels according to the properties in which they agree. In this way we obtain, for example, the inorganic and organic substances, furthermore, the inorganic and organic individual objects as well as the entire system of organisms, of plants, and of animals, as well as the system of artifacts. In such a way, the entire domain of physical objects is constructable. . . .

One can show empirically that "my body", a thing which we constructed at first as a visual thing (§ 129) and which we have then, through further assignments, placed in the perceptual world, belongs to the organisms. The class of *men* is constructed as a class of the biological classification of organisms, to which my body belongs. A constructional definite description of this class is given by indicating the degree to which its elements are to agree with my body in size, figure, motions, and other events. Outside of the thing which is called "my body", there are "other men" (as physical things) who belong to this class. This class forms an object type which is of especial importance for the constructional system. Starting from it, we shall construct the heteropsychological domain (§ 140) and thus all higher objects.

138. *The Expression Relation*

The construction of my body, its parts, its motions, and the other events which are connected with it, has already been discussed (§ § 129, 131, 137). It is rela-tively unimportant whether we here mean by "my body" the mere tactile-visual thing, to which we originally gave this name, or the corresponding physical thing, because the events which we need for further constructions can be satisfactorily identified through tactile and visual qualities.

For the subsequent construction of the heteropsychological (§ 140), the *expression relation* is of fundamental importance. As pointed out earlier (§ 19), by this is meant the relation between expressive motions, i.e., facial expressions, gestures, bodily motions, even organic processes, on the one hand, and the simultaneous psychological events which are "expressed" through them, on the other. This explanation is not meant to be the constructional definition of the expression relation, since it would clearly be circular. It is really meant to refer to already known facts in order to provide a clearer understanding of the word. The construction of the expression relation, on the other hand, consists in the following: to a class of autopsychological events which frequently occur simultaneously with certain recognizable physical events of my body, we correlate the class of these physical events as "expression".

The construction of the heteropsychological could also be based upon the *psychophysical relation* (§ § 19, 21), instead of the expression relation, if only this relation were somewhat better known. In this case, the relation would have to be constructed in the following way: to a class of autopsychological events which frequently occur simultaneously with certain physical events of my central nervous system, the class of these physical events is "psychophysically" correlated.

STUDY QUESTIONS: CARNAP, *THE LOGICAL STRUCTURE OF THE WORLD*

1. What is a constructional system?
2. What is an axiomatized theory?
3. How does Carnap's project relate to the unity of the sciences?
4. What does Carnap mean by 'structure'?
5. What is an 'autopsychological basis'?
6. What does Carnap mean by the thesis that science deals only with the description of structural properties of objects? Why is this thesis so important to his project?
7. What does Carnap mean by the 'expression relation'?
8. What is the psychophysical problem? What does Carnap say about it?
9. What does Carnap claim about logical and mathematical objects?
10. How does Russell construct visual things? How does Carnap's proposal differ?

11. According to Carnap, what is the problem with Whitehead's proposal?
12. How does Carnap assign colors to world points?
13. How does Carnap define a visual thing? What is the seen part of such a thing?
14. How does Carnap define 'my body'?
15. How does Carnap define or construct the autopsychological?
16. How does Carnap construct the world of physics?

Philosophical Bridges: The Influence of Carnap

One cannot understand the influence of Carnap's work without appreciating the huge impact that logical positivism had in general on Anglo-Saxon philosophy and beyond. After the positivists fled prewar Germany in the 1930s, they continued their work in the United States and England, where their ideas had a tremendous influence. The logical positivists gave the philosophy of the time a new direction and program: they led it away from the metaphysical extravagance of the previous generation, and this promised a fruitful interaction with the sciences.

The spirit of logical positivism dominated much analytic philosophy even after the influence of the specific view itself had waned. For example, materialism became a popular theory of mind after the 1960s in the United States in part because of Carnap, who was a major spokesperson for the positivist movement in the United States. There was a greatly increased interest in the philosophy of science, which resulted in many significant works on causation, confirmation, induction, and probability, such as the famous works of Karl Hempel and Popper. Similarly, logic became an important field for the sake of clarifying scientific methodology and as part of the study of the structure of language, as well as in its own right. For instance, there is the work of Tarski in defining 'truth' for artificial languages.

The specific influence of Carnap is harder to explain because of the important differences between his early, middle, and later work. For example, the work of his middle period is influential mainly because of the principle of conventionality. The later work *Meaning and Necessity* is influential partly because it is a pioneering work in modal logic (the logic of necessity and possibility), but also because it reintroduces Frege's notion of sense to the philosophy of language.

A. J. Ayer (1910–1989)

Biographical History

A. J. Ayer studied in Oxford under the direction of Gilbert Ryle. In 1932, Ryle advised Ayer to visit the Vienna Circle, and Ayer returned to England an enthusiastic supporter of logical positivism. His *Language, Truth and Logic* (1936) was an influential and popular exposition of logical positivism, the first book-length study to be published in English. In the 1930s, Ayer taught at the University of London and, during the Second World War, he worked in military intelligence. In 1959, he was appointed the Wykeham Professor of Logic at the University of Oxford. Ayer was a well-known public figure in Britain.

Philosophical Overview

Ayer conceived his work in logical positivism as a continuation of the British Empiricist tradition represented by Locke, Hume, John Stuart Mill, and Russell. Four main features characterize this logical positivist philosophy. First, all meaningful propositions are either analytic or empirical claims. Metaphysics is meaningless since it consists in neither. Second, statements about physical objects are reducible to sentences about actual and possible sense-data. Third, the propositions of mathematics and logic are analytic, and all necessity is logical necessity; there is no natural or causal necessity. Fourth, all ethical claims are expressions of attitudes and, as such, are neither true nor false statements.

Later in life, Ayer still subscribed to these theses, except that he modified the second. In *Language, Truth and Logic*, he rejected the idea that there are incorrigible statements about sense-data because such statements would consist solely in demonstratives, such as 'this,' which would be meaningless to others. In order for statements about sense-data to be comprehensible to others, they must be open to doubt and cannot be incorrigible. In *The Foundations of Empirical Knowledge* (1955), Ayer concedes that there might be incorrigible statements about sense-data. Later still, in the *Central Questions of Philosophy* (1973), Ayer turns toward a form of realism, according to which we directly perceive physical objects that are postulated on the basis of the coherence and consistency of our percepts.

LANGUAGE, TRUTH AND LOGIC

This work is the first book-length work in English expressing logical positivist views. In this excerpt, which is the first chapter of the book, Ayer argues that metaphysics should be criticized on the grounds that the statements that purport to describe a transcendent reality are really meaningless. However, this criticism requires some criterion to test meaningfulness, and Ayer proposes verifiability as the appropriate criterion. However, the verification criterion for meaningfulness needs to be stated clearly and with care. For this reason, Ayer distinguishes verifiable in practice and in theory, and strong and weak versions of the principle of verification.

Finally, Ayer claims that a genuine factual proposition is such that some experiential propositions can be deduced from it in conjunction with other premises (but the experiential proposition should not be deducible from those other premises alone). He defines an experiential proposition as one that records an actual or possible observation.

Ayer then proceeds to show what kinds of metaphysical assertions the principle of verifiability rules out as meaningless. As part of this discussion, Ayer makes a famous claim about Heidegger, namely, that he bases his metaphysics on the assumption that 'nothing' is a name that is used to denote something mysterious. Finally, Ayer claims that metaphysics may have aesthetic and moral value even when the relevant sentences are literally meaningless.

CHAPTER 1

THE ELIMINATION OF METAPHYSICS

The traditional disputes of philosophers are, for the most part, as unwarranted as they are unfruitful. The surest way to end them is to establish beyond question what should be the purpose and method of a philosophical enquiry. And this is by no means so difficult a task as the history of philosophy would lead one to suppose. For if there are any questions which science leaves it to philosophy to answer, a straightforward process of elimination must lead to their discovery.

We may begin by criticising the metaphysical thesis that philosophy affords us knowledge of a reality transcending the world of science and common sense. Later on, when we come to define metaphysics and account for its existence, we shall find that it is possible to be a metaphysician without believing in a transcendent reality; for we shall see that many metaphysical utterances are due to the commission of logical errors, rather than to a conscious desire on the part of their authors to go beyond the limits of experience. But it is convenient for us to take the case of those who believe that it is possible to have knowledge of a transcendent reality as a starting-point for our discussion. The arguments which we use to refute them will subsequently be found to apply to the whole of metaphysics.

One way of attacking a metaphysician who claimed to have knowledge of a reality which transcended the phenomenal world would be to enquire from what premises his propositions were deduced. Must he not begin, as other men do, with the evidence of his senses? And if so, what valid process of reasoning can possibly lead him to the conception of a transcendent reality? Surely from empirical premises nothing whatsoever concerning the properties, or even the existence, of anything super-empirical can legitimately be inferred. But this objection would be met by denial on the part of the metaphysician that his assertions were ultimately based on the evidence of his senses. He would say that he was endowed with a faculty of intellectual intuition which enabled him to know facts that could not be known through sense-experience. And even if it could be shown that he was relying on empirical premises, and that his venture

into a non-empirical world was therefore logically unjustified, it would not follow that the assertions which he made concerning this non-empirical world could not be true. For the fact that a conclusion does not follow from its putative premise is not sufficient to show that it is false. Consequently one cannot overthrow a system of transcendent metaphysics merely by criticising the way in which it comes into being. What is required is rather a criticism of the nature of the actual statements which comprise it. And this the line of argument which we shall, in fact, pursue. For we shall maintain that no statement which refers to a "reality" transcending the limits of all possible sense-experience can possibly have any literal significance; from which it must follow that the labours of those who have striven to describe such a reality have all been devoted to the production of nonsense. . . .

The criterion which we use to test the genuineness of apparent statements of fact is the criterion of verifiability. We say that a sentence is factually significant to any given person, if, and only if, he knows how to verify the proposition which it purports to express—that is, if he knows what observations would lead him, under certain conditions, to accept the proposition as being true, or reject it as being false. If, on the other hand, the putative proposition is of such a character that the assumption of its truth, or falsehood, is consistent with any assumption whatsoever concerning the nature of his future experience, then, as far as he is concerned, it is, if not a tautology, a mere pseudo-proposition. The sentence expressing it may be emotionally significant to him; but it is not literally significant. And with regard to questions the procedure is the same. We enquire in every case what observations would lead us to answer the question, one way or the other; and, if none can be discovered, we must conclude that the sentence under consideration does not, as far as we are concerned, express a genuine question, however strongly its grammatical appearance may suggest that it does.

As the adoption of this procedure is an essential factor in the argument of this book, it needs to be examined in detail.

In the first place, it is necessary to draw a distinction between practical verifiability, and verifiability

From "The Elimination of Metaphysics" from *Language, Truth and Logic,* by A.J. Ayer. Reprinted by permission of Dover Publications.

in principle. Plainly we all understand, in many cases believe, propositions which we have not in fact taken steps to verify. Many of these are propositions which we could verify if we took enough trouble. But there remain a number of significant propositions, concerning matters of fact, which we could not verify even if we chose; simply because we lack the practical means of placing ourselves in the situation where the relevant observations could be made. A simple and familiar example of such a proposition is the proposition that there are mountains on the farther side of the moon. No rocket has yet been invented which would enable me to go and look at the farther side of the moon, so that I am unable to decide the matter by actual observation. But I do know what observations would decide it for me, if, as is theoretically conceivable, I were once in a position to make them. And therefore I say that the proposition is verifiable in principle, if not in practice, and is accordingly significant. On the other hand, such a metaphysical pseudo-proposition as "the Absolute enters into, but is itself incapable of, evolution and progress," is not even in principle verifiable. For one cannot conceive of an observation which would enable one to determine whether the Absolute did, or did not, enter into evolution and progress. Of course it is possible that the author of such a remark is using English words in a way in which they are not commonly used by English-speaking people, and that he does, in fact, intend to assert something which could be empirically verified. But until he makes us understand how the proposition that he wishes to express would be verified, he fails to communicate anything to us. And if he admits, as I think the author of the remark in question would have admitted, that his words were not intended to express either a tautology or a proposition which was capable, at least in principle, of being verified, then it follows that he has made an utterance which has no literal significance even for himself.

A further distinction which we must make is the distinction between the "strong" and the "weak" sense of the term "verifiable." A proposition is said to be verifiable, in the strong sense of the term, if, and only if, its truth could be conclusively established in experience. But it is verifiable, in the weak sense, if it is possible for experience to render it probable. In which sense are we using the term when we say that a putative proposition is genuine only if it is verifiable?

It seems to me that if we adopt conclusive verifiability as our criterion of significance, as some positivists have proposed, our argument will prove too much. Consider, for example, the case of general propositions of law—such propositions, namely, as "arsenic is poisonous"; "all men are mortal"; "a body tends to expand when it is heated." It is of the very nature of these propositions that their truth cannot be established with certainty by any finite series of observations. But if it is recognised that such general propositions of law are designed to cover an infinite number of cases, then it must be admitted that they cannot, even in principle, be verified conclusively. And then, if we adopt conclusive verifiability as our criterion of significance, we are logically obliged to treat these general propositions of law in the same fashion as we treat the statements of the metaphysician.

In face of this difficulty, some positivists have adopted the heroic course of saying that these general propositions are indeed pieces of nonsense, albeit an essentially important type of nonsense. But here the introduction of the term "important" is simply an attempt to hedge. It serves only to mark the authors' recognition that their view is somewhat too paradoxical, without in any way removing the paradox. Besides, the difficulty is not confined to the case of general propositions of law, though it is there revealed most plainly. It is hardly less obvious in the case of propositions about the remote past. For it must surely be admitted that, however strong the evidence in favour of historical statements may be, their truth can never become more than highly probable. And to maintain that they also constituted an important, or unimportant, type of nonsense would be unplausible, to say the very least. Indeed, it will be our contention that no proposition, other than a tautology, can possibly be anything more than a probable hypothesis. And if this is correct, the principle that a sentence can be factually significant only if it expresses what is conclusively verifiable is self-stultifying as a criterion of significance. For it leads to the conclusion that it is impossible to make a significant statement of fact at all.

Nor can we accept the suggestion that a sentence should be allowed to be factually significant if, and only if, it expresses something which is definitely confutable by experience. Those who adopt this course assume that, although no finite series of observations is ever sufficient to establish the truth of a hypothesis beyond all possibility of doubt, there are crucial cases in which a single observation, or series of observations, can definitely confute it. But, as we shall show later on, this assumption is false. A hypothesis cannot be conclusively confuted any more than it can be conclusively verified. For when we take the occurrence of certain observations as proof that a given hypothesis is false, we presuppose the existence of certain conditions. And though, in any given case, it may be extremely improbable that this assumption is false, it is not logically impossible. We shall see that there need be no self-contradiction in holding that some of the relevant circumstances are other than we have taken them to be, and consequently that the hypothesis has not really broken down. And if it is not the case that any hypothesis can be definitely confuted, we cannot hold that the genuineness of a proposition depends on the possibility of its definite confutation.

Accordingly, we fall back on the weaker sense of verification. We say that the question that must be asked about any putative statement of fact is not, Would any observations make its truth or falsehood logically certain? but simply, Would any observations be relevant to the determination of its truth or falsehood? And it is only if a negative answer is given to this second question that we conclude that the statement under consideration is nonsensical.

To make our position clearer, we may formulate it in another way. Let us call a proposition which records an actual or possible observation an experiential proposition. Then we may say that it is the mark of a genuine factual proposition, not that it should be equivalent to an experiential proposition, or any finite number of experiential propositions, but simply that some experiential propositions can be deduced from it in conjunction with certain other premises without being deducible from those other premises alone.

This criterion seems liberal enough. In contrast to the principle of conclusive verifiability, it clearly does not deny significance to general propositions or to propositions about the past. Let us see what kinds of assertion it rules out.

A good example of the kind of utterance that is condemned by our criterion as being not even false but nonsensical would be the assertion that the world of sense-experience was altogether unreal. It must, of course, be admitted that our senses do sometimes deceive us. We may, as the result of having certain sensations, expect certain other sensations to be obtainable which are, in fact, not obtainable. But, in all such cases, it is further sense-experience that informs us of the mistakes that arise out of sense-experience. We say that the senses sometimes deceive us, just because the expectations to which our sense-experiences give rise do not always accord with what we subsequently experience. That is, we rely on our senses to substantiate or confute the judgments which are based on our sensations. And therefore the fact that our perceptual judgements are sometimes found to be erroneous has not the slightest tendency to show that the world of sense-experience is unreal. And, indeed, it is plain that no conceivable observation, or series of observations, could have any tendency to show that the world revealed to us by sense-experience was unreal. Consequently, anyone who condemns the sensible world as a world of mere appearance, as opposed to reality, is saying something which, according to our criterion of significance, is literally nonsensical.

An example of a controversy which the application of our criterion obliges us to condemn as fictitious is provided by those who dispute concerning the number of substances that there are in the world. For it is admitted both by monists, who maintain that reality is one substance, and by pluralists, who maintain that reality is many, that it is impossible to imagine any empirical situation which would be relevant to the solution of their dispute. But if we are told that no possible observation could give any probability either to the assertion that reality was one substance or to the assertion that it was many, then we must conclude that neither assertion is significant. We shall see later on that there are genuine logical and empirical questions involved in the dispute between monists and pluralists. But the metaphysical question concerning "substance" is ruled out by our criterion as spurious.

A similar treatment must be accorded to the controversy between realists and idealists, in its metaphysical aspect. A simple illustration, which I have made use of in a similar argument elsewhere, will help to demonstrate this. Let us suppose that a picture is discovered and the suggestion made that it was painted by Goya. There is a definite procedure for dealing with such a question. The experts examine the picture to see in what way it resembles the accredited works of Goya, and to see if it bears any marks which are characteristic of a forgery; they look up contemporary records for evidence of the existence of such a picture, and so on. In the end, they may still disagree, but each one knows what empirical evidence would go to confirm or discredit his opinion. Suppose, now, that these men have studied philosophy, and some of them proceed to maintain that this picture is a set of ideas in the perceiver's mind, or in God's mind, others that it is objectively real. What possible experience could any of them have which would be relevant to the solution of this dispute one way or the other? In the ordinary sense of the term "real," in which it is opposed to "illusory," the reality of the picture is not in doubt. The disputants have satisfied themselves that the picture is real, in this sense, by obtaining a correlated series of sensations of sight and sensations of touch. Is there any similar process by which they could discover whether the picture was real, in the sense in which the term "real" is opposed to "ideal"? Clearly there is none. But, if that is so, the problem is fictitious according to our criterion. This does not mean that the realist-idealist controversy may be dismissed without further ado. For it can legitimately be regarded as a dispute concerning the analysis of existential propositions, and so as involving a logical problem which, as we shall see, can be definitively solved. What we have just shown is that the question at issue between idealists and realists becomes fictitious when, as is often the case, it is given a metaphysical interpretation.

There is no need for us to give further examples of the operation of our criterion of significance. For our object is merely to show that philosophy, as a genuine branch of knowledge, must be distinguished from metaphysics. We are not now concerned with the historical question how much of what has traditionally passed for philosophy is actually metaphysical. We shall, however, point out later on that the majority of the "great philosophers" of the past were not essentially metaphysicians, and thus reassure those who would otherwise be prevented from adopting our criterion by considerations of piety.

As to the validity of the verification principle, in the form in which we have stated it, a demonstration will be given in the course of this book. For it will be shown that all propositions which have factual content are empirical hypotheses; and that the function of an empirical hypothesis is to provide a rule for the anticipation of experience. And this means that every empirical hypothesis must be relevant to some actual, or possible, experience, so that a statement which is not relevant to any experience is not an empirical hypothesis, and accordingly has no factual content. But this is precisely what the principle of verifiability asserts.

It should be mentioned here that the fact that the utterances of the metaphysician are nonsensical does not follow simply from the fact that they are devoid of factual content. It follows from that fact, together with the fact that they are not *a priori* propositions. And in assuming that they are not *a priori* propositions, we are once again anticipating the conclusions of a later chapter in this book. For it will be shown there that *a priori* propositions, which have always been attractive to philosophers on account of their certainty, owe this certainty to the fact that they are tautologies. We may accordingly define a metaphysical sentence as a sentence which purports to express a genuine proposition, but does, in fact, express neither a tautology nor an empirical hypothesis. And as tautologies and empirical hypotheses form the entire class of significant propositions, we are justified in concluding that all metaphysical assertions are nonsensical. Our next task is to show how they come to be made.

The use of the term "substance," to which we have already referred, provides us with a good example of the way in which metaphysics mostly comes to be written. It happens to be the case that we cannot, in our language, refer to the sensible properties of a thing without introducing a word or phrase which appears to stand for the thing itself as opposed to anything which may be said about it. And, as a result of this, those who are infected by the primitive superstition that to every name a single real entity must correspond assume that it is necessary to distinguish logically between the thing itself and any, or all, of its sensible properties. And so they employ the term "substance" to refer to the thing itself. But from the fact that we happen to employ a single word to refer to a thing, and make that word the grammatical subject of the sentences in which we refer to the sensible appearances of the thing, it does not by any means follow that the thing itself is a "simple entity," or that it cannot be defined in terms of the totality of its appearances. It is true that in talking of "its" appearances we appear to distinguish the thing from the appearances, but that is simply an accident of linguistic usage. Logical analysis shows that what makes these "appearances" the "appearances of" the same thing is not their relationship to an entity other than themselves, but their relationship to one another. The metaphysician fails to see this because he is misled by a superficial grammatical feature of his language.

A simpler and clearer instance of the way in which a consideration of grammar leads to metaphysics is the case of the metaphysical concept of Being. The origin of our temptation to raise questions about Being, which no conceivable experience would enable us to answer, lies in the fact that, in our language, sentences which express existential propositions and sentences which express attributive propositions may be of the same grammatical form. For instance, the sentences "Martyrs exist" and "Martyrs suffer" both consist of a noun followed by an intransitive verb, and the fact that they have grammatically the same appearance leads one to assume that they are of the same logical type. It is seen that in the proposition "Martyrs suffer," the members of a certain species are credited with a certain attribute, and it is sometimes assumed that the same thing is true of such a proposition as "Martyrs exist." If this were actually the case, it would, indeed, be as legitimate to speculate about the Being of martyrs as it is to speculate about their suffering. But, as Kant pointed out, existence is not an attribute. For, when we ascribe an attribute to a thing, we covertly assert that it exists: so that if existence were itself an attribute, it would follow that all positive existential propositions were tautologies, and all negative existential propositions self-contradictory; and this is not the case. So that those who raise questions about Being which are based on the assumption that existence is an attribute are guilty of following grammar beyond the boundaries of sense.

A similar mistake has been made in connection with such propositions as "Unicorns are fictitious." Here again the fact that there is a superficial grammatical resemblance between the English sentences "Dogs are faithful" and "Unicorns are fictitious," and between the corresponding sentences in other languages, creates the assumption that they are of the same logical type. Dogs must exist in order to have the property of being faithful, and so it is held that unless unicorns in some way existed they could not have the property of being fictitious. But, as it is plainly self-contradictory to say that fictitious objects exist, the device is adopted of saying that they are real in some non-empirical sense—that they have a mode of real being which is different from the mode of being of existent things. But since there is no way of testing whether an object is real in this sense, as there is for testing whether it is real in the ordinary sense, the assertion that fictitious objects have a special non-empirical mode of real being is devoid of all literal significance. It comes to be made as a result of the assumption that being fictitious is an attribute. And this is a fallacy of the same order as the fallacy of supposing that existence is an attribute, and it can be exposed in the same way.

In general, the postulation of real non-existent entities results from the superstition, just now referred to, that, to every word or phrase that can be the grammatical subject of a sentence, there must somewhere be a real entity corresponding. For as there is no place in the empirical world for many of these "entities," a special non-empirical world is invoked to house them. To this error must be attributed, not only the utterances of a Heidegger, who bases his metaphysics on the assumption that "Nothing" is a name which is used to denote something peculiarly mysterious, but also the prevalence of such problems as those concerning the reality of propositions and universals whose senselessness, though less obvious, is no less complete.

These few examples afford a sufficient indication of the way in which most metaphysical assertions come to be formulated. They show how easy it is to write sentences which are literally non-sensical without seeing that they are nonsensical. And thus we see that the view that a number of the traditional "problems of philosophy" are metaphysical, and consequently fictitious, does not involve any incredible assumptions about the psychology of philosophers.

Among those who recognise that if philosophy is to be accounted a genuine branch of knowledge it must be defined in such a way as to distinguish it from metaphysics, it is fashionable to speak of the metaphysician as a kind of misplaced poet. As his statements have no literal meaning, they are not subject to any criteria of truth or falsehood: but they may still serve to express, or arouse, emotion, and thus be subject to ethical or aesthetic standards. And it is suggested that they may have considerable value, as means of moral inspiration, or even as works of art. In this way, an attempt is made to compensate the metaphysician for his extrusion from philosophy.

I am afraid that this compensation is hardly in accordance with his deserts. The view that the metaphysician is to be reckoned among the poets appears to rest on the assumption that both talk nonsense. But this assumption is false. In the vast majority of cases the sentences which are produced by poets do have literal meaning. The difference between the man who uses language scientifically and the man who uses it emotively is not that the one produces sentences which are incapable of arousing emotion, and the other sentences which have no sense, but that the one is primarily concerned with the expression of true propositions, the other with the creation of a work of art. Thus, if a work of science contains true and important propositions, its value as a work of science will hardly be diminished by the fact that they are inelegantly expressed. And similarly, a work of art is not necessarily the worse for the fact that all the propositions comprising it are literally false. But to say that many literary works are largely composed of falsehoods, is not to say that they are composed of pseudo-propositions. It is, in fact, very rare for a literary artist to produce sentences which have no literal meaning. And where this does occur, the sentences are carefully chosen for their rhythm and balance. If the author writes nonsense, it is because he considers it most suitable for bringing about the effects for which his writing is designed.

The metaphysician, on the other hand, does not intend to write nonsense. He lapses into it through being deceived by grammar, or through committing errors of reasoning, such as that which leads to the view that the sensible world is unreal. But it is not the mark of a poet simply to make mistakes of this sort. There are some, indeed, who would see in the fact that the metaphysician's utterances are senseless a reason against the view that they have aesthetic value. And, without going so far as this, we may safely say that it does not constitute a reason for it.

It is true, however that although the greater part of metaphysics is merely the embodiment of humdrum errors, there remain a number of metaphysical passages which are the work of genuine mystical feeling; and they may more plausibly be held to have moral or aesthetic value. But, as far as we are concerned, the distinction between the kind of metaphysics that is produced by a philosopher who has been duped by grammar, and the kind that is produced by a mystic who is trying to express the inexpressible, is of no great importance: what is important to us is to realise that even the utterances of the metaphysician who is attempting to expound a vision are literally senseless; so that henceforth we may pursue our philosophical researches with as little regard for them as for the more inglorious kind of metaphysics which comes from a failure to understand the workings of our language.

STUDY QUESTIONS: AYER, LANGUAGE, TRUTH AND LOGIC

1. What is the criterion of verifiability?
2. What does it mean to say that a sentence is 'factually significant'?
3. What is sense experience? What is an observation?
4. How does Ayer distinguish between practical verifiability and verifiability in principle? What is the significance of the distinction?
5. What is the difference between the 'strong' and 'weak' sense of the term 'verifiable'?
6. What is the difference between unimportant and important nonsense? Who relies on this distinction, and why?
7. Can any proposition be known to be so with absolute certainty, or only as highly probable?
8. What does he make of the disagreements between realists and idealists?
9. What is the example of the painting by Goya supposed to show?
10. What is his view of the term 'substance'?
11. How does the grammar of our language mislead us?
12. How does he regard Heidegger's philosophy?

13. Why is a metaphysician a misplaced poet, according to Ayer?
14. What role does a proper analysis of language play?

Philosophical Bridges: Ayer's Influence

Ayer was a popular spokesperson of logical positivism, especially influential in Britain, where it was considered more or less as a continuation of the Empiricist tradition of Hume and Mill. Ayer's works after the publication of *Language, Truth and Logic* were also in this tradition. Consequently, in Britain, much of the focus of the debate around logical positivism was on the idea of sense-data and on theories of perception.

Logical positivism also created the space and the need for emotive and prescriptive theories of ethical claims, such as those of C. L. Stevenson and R. M. Hare. Ayer himself argues that, since ethical claims are not verifiable, they cannot be true or false statements at all but rather must be either expressions of emotion or else imperatives. Stevenson in the United States and Hare in the UK amplified these ideas into full-blown theories about ethics. In turn, these theories generated interest in the nondescriptive uses of language more generally. It was in this context that J. L. Austin in Oxford developed his theory of speech acts, while Wittgenstein was working on his ideas about language usage found in the *Philosophical Investigations*.

BIBLIOGRAPHY

GENERAL

Achinson, Peter, and Barker, Stephen, *The Legacy of Logical Positivism*, Johns Hopkins University Press, 1969

Giere, Ronald, and Richardson, Alan, *Origins of Logical Positivism*, University of Minnesota Press, 1996

Hanfling, Oswald, *Logical Positivism*, Columbia University Press, 1981

CARNAP

Primary

The Logical Structure of the World, University of California Press, 1967

The Logical Syntax of Language, Routledge and Kegan Paul, 1937

Meaning and Necessity, University of Chicago Press, 1947

Secondary

Coffa, J. A., *The Semantic Tradition from Kant to Carnap*, Cambridge University Press, 1991

Richardson, Alan, *Carnap's Construction of the World*, Cambridge University Press, 1998

AYER

Primary

Central Questions of Philosophy, Weldenfield, 1973

The Concept of a Person and Other Essays, St. Martin's Press, 1963

Language, Truth and Logic, Dover Publications, 1946

The Problem of Knowledge, Pelican Books, 1956

Secondary

Forster, John, *Ayer*, Routledge, 1985

Gower, Barry, ed., *Logical Positivism in Perspective: Essays on* Language Truth and Logic, Croom Helm, 1987

MacDonald, Graham, and Wright, Crispin, eds., *Fact, Science and Morality: Essays on Ayer's* Language Truth and Logic, Blackwell, 1987

SECTION IV

THE ORDINARY LANGUAGE PHILOSOPHERS

PROLOGUE

In 1929, when Wittgenstein returned to Cambridge, he was already unhappy with his earlier work, the *Tractatus*. He also repudiated logical positivism, the movement that his own work had helped encourage. He began to examine the way that language is actually used in ordinary everyday contexts and how philosophical problems and puzzles are created by the misuse of these ordinary words. His book, *The Philosophical Investigations*, published in 1953, changed the face of much philosophical thought.

Meanwhile, Gilbert Ryle, in Oxford, who was influenced by Wittgenstein, began thinking in a similar direction. Ryle and his former students, Austin and Peter Strawson, developed what is called ordinary language philosophy. A chapter from Ryle's *The Concept of Mind* (1949) is contained in this volume and is described in Ryle's Philosophical Overview. However, the work of J. L. Austin (1911–1960) has not been included, and we shall describe it briefly now as important background material to the ordinary language movement.

In *Sense and Sensibilia* (1962), Austin attacks the two central theses of classical Empiricism, namely, that we can only directly perceive our own sense-data and that propositions about sense-data form the incorrigible foundation of our claims to know objects. In *How to Do Things with Words* (1962), Austin presents a speech-act theory of language, which is fundamentally opposed to logical atomism. In earlier papers, Austin had attacked the descriptive fallacy, the fallacious idea that language can only be used to describe, by drawing a distinction between constative and performative utterances. Performative utterances, such as 'I hereby promise' and 'I hereby name this ship,' are not true or false descriptions of reality. Instead, by making such utterances (in the appropriate circumstances), one performs the action in question, such as promising or naming a ship. In his later work, *How to Do Things with Words*, Austin extends his earlier analysis by showing how language, even descriptive language, consists in various speech acts. He distinguishes three types of speech acts. The locutionary act is that of uttering a particular sentence with a certain sense and reference. The illocutionary act is the action we intentionally carry out in performing a locutionary act; for example, illocutionary acts include promising, stating, commanding, and questioning. Perlocutionary acts consist in trying to bring about an effect by performing an illocutionary act, such as convincing, deterring, persuading, and misleading. In effect, Austin invented a new approach to the philosophy of language, sometimes called pragmatics, with the intention of shifting the focus of philosophical analysis away from abstract propositions toward contextualized utterances. Finally, Austin has been influential because of his way of practicing philosophy, which he called 'linguistic phenomenology,' an examination of 'what we should say when.' He employed a meticulous examination of how words are used in their various ordinary everyday contexts to criticize philosophical positions and gain philosophical insights.

LUDWIG WITTGENSTEIN

Biographical History, Part II

In 1929, Wittgenstein returned to Cambridge as a research fellow at Trinity College, after many years away from academia. In 1939, he was appointed to the chair of philosophy at Cambridge. During this period, he filled many notebooks with philosophical reflections, some of which he circulated among his students, but he did not allow any of his works to be published during his lifetime. At the beginning of World War II, he volunteered as a hospital orderly in London. After the war, he returned to Cambridge again, but, after two years, he resigned his position and went to live in seclusion in Ireland, where he continued to write and where he completed the manuscript, *The Philosophical Investigations*, which was published posthumously in 1953. Subsequently, many of Wittgenstein's notebooks were edited and published. The most important of these include *The Blue and Brown Books* (1958), *Zettel* (1967), *On Certainty* (1969), *Remarks on the Foundations of Mathematics* (1978), and *Remarks on the Philosophy of Psychology* (1980).

Philosophical Overview

One of the revolutionary aspects of Wittgenstein's later work is his new conception of philosophy, which is roughly as follows. In general, Wittgenstein conceives the aim of philosophy not in terms of providing theories but rather as trying to dissolve philosophical problems, which arise because of 'the bewitchment of our intelligence' by language. Philosophy unties knots in our understanding, and is like the treatment of an illness. This treatment consists in passing from a disguised to a patent piece of nonsense by showing how the words used in philosophy, such as 'private,' 'external,' and 'real,' have a rule-guided ordinary usage. The claims of standard philosophical theories are senseless, and they arise because language has 'gone on holiday.' In other words, philosophical theories use ordinary words in a way that disregards the grammatical rules and criteria inherent in their ordinary use. In contrast to these *theories*, the *practice* of philosophy is a therapy that makes this misuse plain. In his later works, such as *The Philosophical Investigations*, Wittgenstein practices philosophy in this manner.

PHILOSOPHICAL INVESTIGATIONS

The sections of the *Investigations* that we have selected contain at least six important and interrelated themes.

Naming

Wittgenstein begins with a repudiation of his earlier view of language. He starts by rejecting the thesis that words must name things. Words should be compared to tools rather than labels. Even when we do use a word like a label, the connection between the word and the thing named is a practice, which is only possible given certain background conditions, such as our conventions about pointing. One of the misconceptions that causes the idea that words are labels is the view that we learn language through ostensive definition, by associating words with things. Many words are not learned in this way, and, even when they are, once again, this is only possible because of background conditions and practices. If I point to a red ball, and say 'red,' you have to know what aspect of the object I am referring to. Wittgenstein advises that, instead of asking for the meaning of a word, in many cases, we should look to its use.

Family Resemblances

Some philosophers assume that general words, such as 'game,' must refer to all things that have a set of qualities in common. All games must have certain common features. Wittgenstein rejects this assumption by showing how games can constitute a family resemblance with a network of overlapping similarities rather than one set of shared characteristics. This shows how understanding what an 'X' is does not require knowing a rule that specifies the necessary and sufficient conditions for being X. In this way, philosophy does not have to consist in giving definitions that delineate essences. This reinforces Wittgenstein's claim that the meaning of a word should be thought of as its use. Furthermore, it challenges the idea of the *Tractatus* that sense must be exact. However, Wittgenstein's ultimate aim is that 'meaning as use' itself constitutes a family resemblance.

Language Games

This last point emerges from Wittgenstein's notion of a language game. Language games can be primitive forms of language; the use of specific parts of language, such as promising; and the use of language as a part of an activity, such as moving slabs. The point of the notion of language games is not to provide a new theory of language, but rather to give an analogy to emphasize that we should look at the many ways language is used in context without assuming that these uses must have a common essence. The main point of the analogy is to reveal the idea that the use of language, like that of a tool, is itself a family resemblance consisting of many varied activities.

Rule Following

Wittgenstein's next idea is that rules do not determine their own application. Because of this, rules do not determine practice, but rather indeterminately guide it within a given context of shared practices or a form of life. For this reason, he compares rules to signposts. Wittgenstein brings out this point by claiming that there is no single correct way of following even a mathematical rule such as '+2,' where the correctness is established by the rule alone (186). This is an analogy for our use of language, especially general terms. In other words, the idea of carrying on or proceeding in the same way (for example, in a classification) cannot be predetermined by a rule alone. Ultimately, the point is that 'the same X,' and correctness and incorrectness, cannot be defined in following rules alone. Likewise, justification does not terminate in rules, but rather in terms of shared practices. This, however, does not mean that our practices are arbitrary.

These parts of the *Investigations* are aimed at his own earlier calculus theory of language. More profoundly, they lead to the claim that the dichotomy between a Sophist and a Platonic view of understanding is based on a false assumption, which is that there can be no notion of correctness and incorrectness without rules. We do not have to accept the Platonic idea of necessary and universal rules in order to avoid Sophist-like subjectivism.

Understanding

Wittgenstein claims that we should not think that using a word meaningfully consists in employing it with an accompanying mental state, namely, understanding. It merely consists in using it appropriately. The accompanying mental understanding is redundant.

Private Languages

The so-called private language argument is a refutation of the claim that there can be a purely and essentially private language that refers to private sensations. This claim is a basic assumption of Descartes' Skepticism and of Empiricist theories of understanding, such as Locke's. It also undermines the Empiricist claim that we can only ever perceive our own ideas. Descartes' method of doubt and Locke's Empiricism require an essentially private language, one that obtains its meaning directly by referring to the privately felt quality of sensations, or to their introspective feel, without relying on external causal factors.

In brief, Wittgenstein argues against the possibility of an essentially private language (EPL). He imagines a person who uses the letter 'S' to refer to a sensation. When the same sensation occurs again, the person intends to use 'S' to refer to it. Wittgenstein's argument against the possibility of an EPL is as follows:

1. *Meaningful word usage requires the possibility of error.*
2. *In an EPL, there is no possibility of a distinction between 'X appears to be right' and <u>X is right</u>.*
3. *Therefore, a meaningful EPL is impossible.*

The first premise claims that meaning requires that the mistaken employment of a word is possible, such as calling a dog 'a cat.' The second states that in an essentially private language, there is no possibility of such misapplication of words because, in the private realm, there is no possible distinction between how things are and how they seem. If I have a sensation that seems to me to be S, then, in the essentially private realm, nothing possibly can count as my being mistaken. Wittgenstein says, 'Whatever is going to seem right to me is right. And that only means that here we can't talk about 'right" (258).

Ultimately, this argument undermines the very idea of essentially private ideas as objects, because if an essentially private language is impossible, then the essentially private identification of sensations and mental states is also impossible. This claim has some important general implications.

a. *The content of mental states can be identified only in terms of their public behavioral criteria. Wittgenstein reinforces this idea later by claiming that concepts such as 'pain' only make sense against a background of shared behavior.*

b. *It attacks the conception of ideas as mental items and the view that words name such items. This, in turn, also undermines the claim that we can only perceive such items or ideas, a claim that leads to skepticism about our knowledge of the external world. This means that Descartes, Locke, George Berkeley, and Hume mistakenly draw a distinction between the private inner realm and the external world.*

c. *Language is public use. However, according to Wittgenstein, even to assert this is misleading, because the claim 'Sensations are private' is not false, but rather senseless. A similar point applies to 'Language is public.'*

In the above ways, Wittgenstein tries to dissolve the mind-body problem, rather than provide a theory that solves the problem.

PREFACE

The thoughts which I publish in what follows are the precipitate of philosophical investigations which have occupied me for the last sixteen years. They concern many subjects: the concepts of meaning, of understanding, of a proposition, of logic, the foundations of mathematics, states of consciousness, and other things. I have written down all these thoughts as *remarks*, short paragraphs, of which there is sometimes a fairly long chain about the same subject, while I sometimes make a sudden change, jumping from one topic to another.—It was my intention at first to bring all this together in a book whose form I pictured differently at different times. But the essential thing was that the thoughts should proceed from one subject to another in a natural order and without breaks.

After several unsuccessful attempts to weld my results together into such a whole, I realized that I should never succeed. The best that I could write would never be more than philosophical remarks; my thoughts were soon crippled if I tried to force them on in any single direction against their natural inclination.—And this was, of course, connected with the very nature of the investigation. For this compels us to travel over a wide field of thought crisscross in every direction.—The philosophical remarks in this book are, as it were, a number of sketches of landscapes which were made in the course of these long and involved journeyings.

The same or almost the same points were always being approached afresh from different directions, and new sketches made. Very many of these were badly drawn or uncharacteristic, marked by all the defects of a weak draughtsman. And when they were rejected a number of tolerable ones were left, which now had to be arranged and sometimes cut down, so that if you looked at them you could get a picture of the landscape. Thus this book is really only an album.

Up to a short time ago I had really given up the idea of publishing my work in my lifetime. It used, indeed, to be revived from time to time: mainly because I was obliged to learn that my results (which I had communicated in lectures, typescripts and discussions), variously misunderstood, more or less mangled or watered down, were in circulation. This stung my vanity and I had difficulty in quieting it.

Four years ago I had occasion to re-read my first book (the *Tractatus Logico-Philosophicus*) and to explain its ideas to someone. It suddenly seemed to me that I should publish those old thoughts and the new ones together: that the latter could be seen in the right light only by contrast with and against the background of my old way of thinking.

For since beginning to occupy myself with philosophy again, sixteen years ago, I have been forced to recognize grave mistakes in what I wrote in that first book. I was helped to realize these mistakes—to a degree which I myself am hardly able to estimate—by the criticism with my ideas encountered from Frank Ramsey, which whom I discussed them in innumerable conversations during the last two years of his life. Even more than to this—always certain and forcible—criticism I am indebted to that which a teacher of this university, Mr. P. Sraffa, for many

From *Philosophical Investigations* by Ludwig Wittgenstein, translated by E. Anscombe. Reprinted by permission of Blackwell Publishing.

years unceasingly practiced on my thoughts. I am indebted to *this* stimulus for the most consequential ideas of this book.

For more than one reason what I publish here will have points of contact with what other people are writing to-day.—If my remarks do not bear a stamp which marks them as mine,—I do not wish to lay any further claim to them as my property.

I make them public with doubtful feelings. It is not impossible that it should fall to the lot of this work, in its poverty and in the darkness of this time, to bring light into one brain or another—but, of course, it is not likely.

I should not like my writing to spare other people the trouble of thinking. But, if possible, to stimulate someone to thoughts of his own.

I should have liked to produce a good book. This has not come about, but the time is past in which I could improve it.

Cambridge,
January 1945.

1. "When they (my elders) named some object, and accordingly moved towards something, I saw this and I grasped that the thing was called by the sound they uttered when they meant to point it out. Their intention was shewn by their bodily movements, as it were the natural language of all peoples: the expression of the face, the play of the eyes, the movement of other parts of the body, and the tone of voice which expresses our state of mind in seeking, having, rejecting, or avoiding something. Thus, as I heard words repeatedly used in their proper places in various sentences, I gradually learnt to understand what objects they signified; and after I had trained my mouth to form these signs, I used them to express my own desires."

(Augustine, *Confessions*, I. 8.)

These words, it seems to me, give us particular picture of the essence of human language. It is this: the individual words in language name objects—sentences are combinations of such names.—In this picture of language we find the roots of the following idea: Every word has a meaning. This meaning is correlated with the word. It is the object for which the word stands.

Augustine does not speak of there being any difference between kinds of word. If you describe the learning of language in this way you are, I believe, thinking primarily of nouns like "table," "chair", "bread", and of people's names, and only secondarily of the names of certain actions and properties; and of the remaining kinds of word as something in that will take care of itself.

Now think of the following use of language: I send someone shopping. I give him a slip marked "five red apples". He takes the slip to the shopkeeper, who opens the drawer marked "apples"; then he looks up the word "red" in a table and finds a colour sample opposite it; then he says the series of cardinal numbers—I assume that he knows them by heart—up to the word "five" and for each number he takes an apple of the same colour as the sample out of the drawer.—It is in this and similar ways that one operates with words.—"But how does he know where and how he is to look up the word 'red' and what he is to do with the word 'five'?"—Well, I assume that he *acts* as I have described. Explanations come to an end somewhere.—But what is the meaning of the word "five"?—No such thing was in question here, only how the word "five" is used.

2. That philosophical concept of meaning has its place in a primitive idea of the way language functions. But one can also say that it is the idea of a language more primitive than ours.

Let us imagine a language for which the description given by Augustine is right. The language is meant to serve for communication between a builder A and an assistant B. A is building with building stones: there are blocks, pillars, slabs and beams. B has to pass the stones, and that in the order in which A needs them. For this purpose they use a language consisting of the words "block", "pillar", "slab", "beam". A calls them out;—B brings the stone which he has learnt to bring at such-and-such a call.—Conceive this as a complete primitive language.

3. Augustine, we might say, does describe a system of communication; only not everything that we call language is this system. And one has to say this in many cases where the question arises "Is this an appropriate description or not?" The answer is: "Yes, it is appropriate, but only for this narrowly circumscribed region, not for the whole of what you were claiming to describe."

It is as if someone were to say: "A game consists in moving objects about on a surface according to certain rules . . ."—and we replied: You seem to be thinking of board games, but there are others. You can make your definition correct by expressly restricting it to those games.

5. If we look at the example in §1, we may perhaps get an inkling how much this general notion of the meaning of a word surrounds the working of language with a haze which makes clear vision impossible. It disperses the fog to study the phenomena of language in primitive kinds of application in which one can command a clear view of the aim and functioning of the words.

A child uses such primitive forms of language when it learns to talk. Here the teaching of language is not explanation, but training.

6. We could imagine that the language of §2 was the *whole* language of A and B; even the whole language of a tribe. The children are brought up to perform *these* actions, to use *these* words as they do so, and to react in *this* way to the words of others.

An important part of the training will consist in the teacher's pointing to the objects, directing the child's attention to them, and at the same time uttering a word; for instance, the word "slab" as he points to that shape. (I do not want to call this "ostensive definition", because the child cannot as yet *ask* what the name is. I will call it "ostensive teaching of words".— I say that it will form an important part of the training, because it is so with human beings; not because it could not be imagined otherwise.) This ostensive teaching of words can be said to establish an association between the world and the thing. But what does this mean? Well, it may mean various things; but one very likely thinks first of all that a picture of the object comes before the child's mind when it hears the word. But now, if this does happen—is it the purpose of the word?—Yes, it *may* be the purpose.—I can imagine such a use of words (of series of sounds). (Uttering a word is like striking a note on the keyboard of the imagination.) But in the language of §2 it is *not* the purpose of the words to evoke images. (It may, of course, be discovered that that helps to attain the actual purpose.)

But if the ostensive teaching has this effect,—am I to say that it effects an understanding of the word? Don't you understand the call "Slab!" if you act upon it in a such-and-such a way?—Doubtless the ostensive teaching helped to bring this about; but only together with a particular training. With different

training the same ostensive teaching of these words would have effected a quite different understanding.

"I set the brake up by connecting up rod and lever."—Yes, given the whole of the rest of the mechanism. Only in conjunction with that is it a brake-lever, and separated from its support it is not even a lever; it may be anything, or nothing.

8. Let us now look at an expansion of language (2). Besides the four words "block", "pillar", etc., let it contain a series of words used as the shopkeeper in (1) used the numerals (it can be the series of letters of the alphabet); further, let there be two words, which may as well be "there" and "this" (because this roughly indicates this purpose), that are used in connexion with a pointing gesture; and finally a number of colour samples. A gives an order like: "d—slab—there". At the same time he shews the assistant a colour sample, and when he says "there" he points to a place on the building site. From the stock of slabs B takes one for each letter of the alphabet up to "d", of the same colour as the sample, and brings them to the place indicated by A.—On other occasions A gives the order "this—there". At "this" he points to a building stone. And so on.

11. Think of the tools in a tool-box: there is a hammer, pliers, a saw, a screw-driver, a rule, a glue-pot, glue, nails and screws.—The functions of words are as diverse as the functions of these objects. (And in both cases there are similarities.)

Of course, what confuses is the uniform appearance of words when we hear them spoken or meet them in script and print. For their *application* is not presented to us so clearly. Especially when we are doing philosophy!

13. When we say: "Every word in language signifies something" we have so far said *nothing whatever*; unless we have explained exactly *what* distinction we wish to make. (It might be, of course, that we wanted to distinguish the words of language (8) from words 'without meaning' such as occur in Lewis Carroll's poems, or words like "Lilliburlero" in songs.)

14. Imagine someone's saying: "*All* tools serve to modify something. Thus the hammer modifies the position of nail, the saw the shape of the board, and so on."—And what is modified by the rule, the glue-pot, the nails?—"Our knowledge of a thing's length, the temperature of the glue, and the solidity of the box."—Would anything be gained by this assimilation of expressions?—

15. The word "to signify" is perhaps used in the most straightforward way when the object signified is marked with the sign. Suppose that the tools A uses in building bear certain marks. When A shews his assistant such a mark, he brings the tool that has that mark on it.

It is in this and more or less similar ways that a name means and is given to a thing.—It will often prove useful in philosophy to say to ourselves: naming something is like attaching a label to a thing.

17. It will be possible to say: In language (8) we have different *kinds of word*. For the functions of the word "slab" and the word "block" are more alike than those of "slab" and "d". But how we group words into kinds will depend on the aim of the classification,—and on our own inclination.

Think of the different points of view from which one can classify tools or chess-men.

18. Do not be troubled by the fact that languages (2) and (8) consist only of orders. If you want to say that this shews them to be incomplete, ask yourself whether our language is complete;—whether it was so before the symbolism of chemistry and the notation of the infinitesimal calculus were incorporated in it; for these are, so to speak, suburbs of our language. (And how many houses or streets does it take before a town begins to be a town?) Our language can be seen as an ancient city: a maze of little streets and squares, of old and new houses, and of houses with additions from various periods; and this surrounded by a multitude of new boroughs with straight regular streets and uniform houses.

19. It is easy to imagine a language consisting only of orders and reports in battle.—Or a language consisting only of questions and expressions for answering yes and no. And innumerable others.—And to imagine a language means to imagine a form of life.

23. But how many kinds of sentence are there? Say assertion, question, and command?—There are *countless* kinds: countless different kinds of use of what we call "symbols", "words", "sentences". And this multiplicity is not something fixed, given once for all; but new types of language, new language-games, as we may say, come into existence, and others become obsolete and get forgotten. (We can get a *rough picture* of this form the changes in mathematics.)

Here the term "language-*game*" is meant to bring into prominence the fact that the *speaking* of language is part of an activity, or of a form of life.

Review the multiplicity of language-games in the following examples, and in others:

Giving orders, and obeying them—
Describing the appearance of an object, or giving
    its measurements—
Constructing an object from a description (a
    drawing)—
Reporting an event—
Speculating about an event—
Forming and testing a hypothesis—
Presenting the result of an experiment in tables
    and diagrams—
Making up a story; and reading it—
Play-acting—
Singing catches—
Guessing riddles—
Making a joke; telling it—
Solving a problem in practical arithmetic—
Translating from one language into another—
Asking, thanking, cursing, greeting, praying.

—It is interesting to compare the multiplicity of the tools in language and of the ways they are used, the multiplicity of kinds of word and sentence, with what logicians have said about the structure of language. (Including the author of the *Tractatus Logico-Philosophicus*.)

28. Now one can ostensively define a proper name, the name of a colour, the name of a material, a numeral, the name of a point of the compass and so on. The definition of the number two, "That is called 'two'"—pointing to two nuts—is perfectly exact.—But how can two be defined like that? The person one gives the definition to doesn't know what one wants to call "two"; he will suppose that "two" is the name given to *this* group of nuts!—He *may* suppose this; but perhaps he does not. He might make the opposite mistake; when I want to assign a name to this group of nuts, he might understand it as a numeral. And he might equally well take the name of a person, of which I give an ostensive definition, as that of a colour, of a race, or even of a point of the compass. That is to say: an ostensive definition can be variously interpreted in every case.

38. But what, for example, is the word "this" the mean of in language-game (8) or the word "that" in the ostensive definition "that is called. . . ."?—If you do not want to produce confusion you will do best not to call these words names at all.—Yet, strange to say, the word "this" has been called the only *genuine* name; so that anything else we call a name was one only in an inexact, approximate sense.

This queer conception springs from a tendency to sublime the logic of our language—as one might put it. The proper answer to its is: we call very different things "names"; the word "name" is used to characterize many different kinds of use of a word, related to one another in many different ways;—but the kind of use that "this" has is not among them.

It is quite true that, in giving an ostensive definition for instance, we often point to the object named and say the name. And similarly, in giving an ostensive definition for instance, we say the word "this" while pointing to a thing. And also the word "this" and a name often occupy the same position in a sentence. But it is precisely characteristic of a name that it is defined by means of the demonstrative expression. "That is N" (or "That is called 'N'"). But do we also give the definitions: "That is called 'this'", or "This is called 'this'"?

This is connected with the conception of naming as, so to speak, an occult process. Naming appears as a *queer* connexion of a word with an object.—And you really get such a queer connexion when the philosopher tries to bring out *the* relation between name and thing by starting at an object in from of him and repeating a name or even the word "this" innumerable times. For philosophical problems arise when language *goes on holiday*. And *here* we may indeed fancy naming to be some remarkable act of mind, as it were a baptism of an object. And we can also say the word "this" *to* the object, as it were *address* the object as "this"—a queer use of this word, which doubtless only occurs in doing philosophy.

43. For a *large* class of cases—though not for all—in which we employ the word "meaning" it can be defined thus: the meaning of a word is its use in the language. . . .

And the *meaning* of a name is sometimes explained by pointing to its *bearer*.

65. Here we come up against the great question that lies behind all these considerations.—For someone might object against me: "You take the easy way out! You talk about all sorts of language-games, but have nowhere said what the essence of a language-game, and hence of language, is: what is common to all these activities, and what makes them into language or parts of language. So you let yourself off the very part of the investigation that once gave you yourself most headache, the part about the *general form of propositions* and of language." . . .

And this is true—Instead of producing something common to all that we call language, I am saying that these phenomena have no one thing in common which makes us use the same word for all,—but that they are *related* to one another in many different ways. And it is because of this relationship, or these relationships, that we call them all "language". I will try to explain this.

66. Consider for example the proceedings that we call "games". I mean board-games, card-games, ball-games, Olympic games, and so on. What is common to them all?—Don't say: "There *must* be something common, or they would not be called 'games'"—but *look and see* whether there is anything common to all.—For if you look at them you will not see something that is common to *all*, but similarities, relationships, and a whole series of them at that. To repeat: don't think, but look!—Look for example at board-games, with their multifarious relationships. Now pass to card-games; here you find many correspondences with the first group, but many common features drop out, and others appear. When we pass next to ball-games, much that is common is retained, but much is lost.—Are they all 'amusing'? Compare chess with noughts and crosses. Or is there always winning and losing, or competition between players? Think of patience. In ball games there is winning and losing; but when a child throws his ball at the wall and catches it again, this feature has disappeared. Look at the parts played by skill and luck; and at the difference between skill in chees and skill in tennis. Think now of games like ring-a-ring-a-roses; here is the element of amusement, but how many other characteristic features have disappeared! And we can go through the many, many other groups of games in the same way; can see how similarities crop up and disappear.

And the result of this examination is: we see a complicated network of similarities overlapping and criss-crossing: sometimes overall similarities, sometimes similarities of detail.

67. I can think of no better expression to characterize these similarities than "family resemblances"; for the various resemblances between members of a family: build, features, colour of eyes, gait, temperament, etc. etc. overlap and criss-cross in the same way.—And I shall say: 'games' form a family.

And for instance the kinds of number form a family in the same way. Why do we call something a "number"? Well, perhaps because it has a—direct—relationship with several things that have hitherto been called number, and this can be said to give it an indirect relationship to other things we call the same name. And we extend our concept of number as in spinning a thread we twist fibre on fibre. And the strength of the thread does not reside in the fact that some one fibre runs through its hole length, but in the overlapping of many fibres.

But if someone wished so say: "There is something common to all these construction—namely the disjunction of all their common properties"—I should reply: Now you are only playing with words. One might as well say: "Something runs through the whole thread—namely the continuous overlapping of those fibres".

84. I said that the application of a word is not everywhere bounded by rules. But what does a game look like that is everywhere bounded by rules? whose rules never let a doubt creep in, but stop up all the cracks where it might?—Can't we imagine a rule determining the application of a rule, and a doubt which *it* removes—and so on?

85. A rule stands there like a sign-post.—Does the sign-post leave no doubt open about the way I have to go? Does it shew which direction I am to take when I have passed it; whether along the road or the footpath

or cross-country? But where is it said which way I am to follow it; whether in the direction of its finger or (e.g.) in the opposite one?—And if there were, not a single sign-post, but a chain of adjacent ones or of chalk marks on the ground—is there only *one* way of interpreting them? . . .

87. The sign-post is in order—if, under normal circumstances, it fulfils its purpose.

88. If I tell someone "Stand roughly here"—may not this explanation work perfectly? And cannot every other one fail too?

But isn't it an inexact explanation?—Yes; why shouldn't we call it "inexact"? Only let us understand what "inexact" means. For it does not mean "unusable". And let us consider what we call an "exact" explanation in contrast with this one. Perhaps something like drawing a chalk line round an area? Here it strikes us at once that the line has breadth. So a colour-edge would be more exact. But has this exactness still got a function here: isn't the engine idling? And remember too that we have not yet defined what is to count as overstepping this exact boundary; how, with what instruments, it is to be established. And so on.

We understand what it means to set a pocket watch to the exact time or to regulate it to be exact. But what if it were asked: is this exactness ideal exactness, or how nearly does it approach the ideal?—Of course, we can speak of measurements of time in which there is a different, and as we should say a greater, exactness than in the measurement of time by a pocket-watch; in which the words "to set the clock to the exact time" have a different, though related meaning, and 'to tell the time' is a different process and so on.—Now, if I tell someone: "You should come to dinner more punctually; you know it begins at one o'clock exactly"—is there really no question of *exactness* here? because it is possible to say: "Think of the determination of time in the laboratory or the observatory; *there* you see what 'exactness' means"?

"Inexact" is really a reproach, and "exact" is praise. And that is to say that what is inexact attains its goal less perfectly than what is more exact. Thus the point here is what we call "the goal". Am I inexact when I do not give our distance from the sun to the nearest foot, or tell a joiner the width of a table to the nearest thousandth of an inch?

No *single* ideal of exactness has been laid down; we do not know what we should be supposed to imagine under this head—unless you yourself lay down what is to be so called. But you will find it difficult to hit upon such a convention; at least any that satisfies you.

90. We feel as if we had to *penetrate* phenomena: our investigation, however, is directed not towards phenomena, but, as one might say, towards the '*possibilities*' of phenomena. We remind ourselves, that is to say, of the *kind of statement* that we make about phenomena. Thus Augustine recalls to mind the different statements that are made about the duration, past present or future, of events. (These are, of course, not *philosophical* statements about time, the past, the present and the future.)

98. On the one hand it is clear that every sentence in our language is in order as it is'. That is to say, we are not *striving after* an ideal, as if our ordinary vague sentences had not yet got a quite unexceptionable sense, and a perfect language awaited construction by us.—On the other hand it seems clear that where there is sense there must be perfect order.—So there must be perfect order even in the vaguest sentence.

99. The sense of a sentence—one would like to say—may, of course, leave this or that open, but the sentence must nevertheless have *a* definite sense. An indefinite sense—that would really not be a sense *at all*.—This is like: An indefinite boundary is not really a boundary at all. Here one thinks perhaps: if I say "I have locked the man up fast in the room—there is only one door left open"—then I simply haven't locked him in at all; his being locked in is a sham. One would be inclined to say here: "You haven't done anything at all". An enclosure with a hole in it is as good as *none*.—But is that true?

102. The strict and clear rules of the logical structure of propositions appear to us as something in the background—hidden in the medium of the understanding. I already see them (even though through a medium): for I understand the propositional sign, I use it to say something.

103. The ideal, as we think of it, is unshakable. You can never get outside it; you must always turn back. There is no outside; outside you cannot breathe.—Where does this idea come from? It is like a pair of glasses on our nose through which we see whatever we look at. It never occurs to us to take them off.

109. It was true to say that our considerations could not be scientific ones. It was not of any possible interest to us to find out empirically 'that, contrary to our preconceived ideas, it is possible to think such-and-such'—whatever that may mean. (The conception of thought as a gaseous medium.) And we may not advance any kind of theory. There must not be anything hypothetical in our considerations. We must do away with all *explanation*, and description alone must take its place. And this description gets its light, that is to say its purpose, from the philosophical problems. These are, of course, not empirical problems; they are solved, rather, by looking into the workings of our language, and that in such a way as to make us recognize those workings: *in despite of* an urge to misunderstand them. The problems are solved, not by giving new information, but by arranging what we have always known. Philosophy is a battle against the bewitchment of our intelligence by means of language.

115. A *picture* held us captive. And we could not get outside it, for it lay in our language and language seemed to repeat it to us inexorably.

116. When philosophers use a word—"knowledge", "being", "object", "I", "proposition", "name"—and try to grasp the *essence* of the thing, one must always ask oneself: is the word ever actually used in this way in the language-game which is its original home?—

What *we* do is to bring words back from their metaphysical to their everyday use.

119. The results of philosophy are the uncovering of one or another piece of plain nonsense and of bumps that the understanding has got by running its head up against the limits of language. These bumps make us see the value of the discovery.

123. A philosophical problem has the form: "I don't know my way about".

124. Philosophy may in no way interfere with the actual use of language; it can in the end only describe it.

For it cannot give it any foundation either.

It leaves everything as it is.

It also leaves mathematics as it is, and no mathematical discovery can advance it. A "leading problem of mathematical logic" is for us a problem of mathematics like any other.

125. It is the business of philosophy, not to resolve a contradiction by means of a mathematical or logico-mathematical discovery, but to make it possible for us to get a clear view of the state of mathematics that troubles us: the state of affairs *before* the contradiction is resolved. (And this does not mean that one is sidestepping a difficulty.)

The fundamental fact here is that we lay down rules, a technique, for a game, and that then when we follow the rules, things do not turn out as we had assumed. That we are therefore as it were entangled in our own rules.

This entanglement in our rules is what we want to understand (i.e. get a clear view of).

It throws light on our concept of *meaning* something. For in those cases things turn out otherwise than we had meant, foreseen. That is just what we say when, for example, a contradiction appears: "I didn't mean it like that."

The civil status of a contradiction, or its status in civil life: there is the philosophical problem.

126. Philosophy simply puts everything before us, and neither explains nor deduces anything.— Since everything lies open to view there is nothing to explain. For what is hidden, for example, is of no interest to us.

One might also give the name "philosophy" to what is possible *before* all new discoveries and inventions.

127. The work of the philosopher consists in assembling reminders for a particular purpose.

128. If one tried to advance *theses* in philosophy, it would never be possible to debate them, because everyone would agree to them.

149. If one says that knowing the ABC is a state of the mind. one is thinking of a state of a mental apparatus (perhaps of the brain) by means of which we explain the *manifestations* of that knowledge. Such a state is called a disposition. But there are objections to speaking of a state of the mind here, inasmuch as there ought to be two different criteria for such a state: a knowledge of the construction of the apparatus, quite apart from what it does. (Nothing would be more confusing here than to use the words "conscious" and "unconscious" for the contrast between states of consciousness and dispositions. For this pair of terms covers up a grammatical difference.)

150. The grammar of the word "knows" is evidently closely related to that of "can", "is able to". But also closely related to that of "understands". ('Mastery' of a technique,)

151. But there is also *this* use of the word "to know": we say "Now I know!"—and similarly "Now I can do it!" and "Now I understand!"

185. Let us return to our example (143). Now—judged by the usual criteria—the pupil has mastered the series of natural numbers. Next we teach him to write down other series of cardinal numbers and get him to the point of writing down series of the form

$$o, n, 2n, 3n, etc.$$

at an order of the form "+n"; so at the order "+1" he writes down the series of natural numbers.—Let us suppose we have done exercises and given him tests up to 1000.

Now we get the pupil to continue a series (say +2) beyond 1000—and he writes 1000, 1004, 1008, 1012.

We say to him: "Look what you've done!"—He doesn't understand. We say: "You were meant to add *two*: look how you began the series!"—He answers: "Yes, isn't it right? I thought that was how I was *meant* to do it."—Or suppose he pointed to the series and said: "But I went on in the same way."—It would now be no use to say: "But can't you see. . . . ?"—and repeat the old examples and explanations.—In such a case we might say, perhaps: It comes natural to this person to understand our order with our explanations as *we* should understand the order: "Add 2 up to 1000, 4 up to 2000, 6 up to 3000 and so on."

Such a case would present similarities with one in which a person naturally reacted to the gesture of pointing with the hand by looking in the direction of the line from finger-tip to wrist, not from wrist to finger-tip.

186. "What you are saying, then, comes to this: a new insight—intuition—is needed at every step to carry out the order '+n' correctly."—To carry it out correctly! How is it decided what is the right step to take at any particular stage?—"The right step is the one that accords with the order—as it was *meant*."—So when you gave the order +2 you meant that he was to write 1002 after 1000—and did you also mean that he should write 1868 after 1866, and 100036 after 100034, and so on—an infinite number of such propositions?—"No: what I meant was, that he should write the next but one number after *every* number that he wrote; and from this all those propositions follow in turn."—But that is just what is in question: what, at any state, does follow from that sentences. Or, again, what, at any stage we are to call "being in accord" with that sentence (and with the *mean*-ing you then put into the sentence—whatever that may have consisted in). It would almost be more correct to say, not that an institution was needed in every stage, but that a new decision was needed at every stage.

187. "But I already knew, at the time when I gave the order, that he ought to write 1002 after 1000."—Certainly; and you can also say you *meant* it then; only you should not let yourself be misled by the grammar of the words "know" and "mean". For you don't want to say that you thought of the step from 1000 to 1002 at that time—and even if you did think of this step, still you did not think of other ones. When you said "I already knew at the time. . . . ." that meant something like: "If I had then been asked what number should be written after 1000, I should have replied '1002'." And that I don't doubt. This assumption is rather of the same kind as: "If he had fallen into the water then, I should have jumped in after him".—Now, what was wrong with your idea?

188. Here I should first of all like to say: your idea was that that act of meaning the order had in its own way already traversed all those steps: that when you meant it your mind as it were flew ahead and took all the steps before you physically arrived at this or that one.

Thus you were inclined to use such expressions as: "The steps are *really* already taken, even before I take them in writing or orally or in thought." And it seemed as if they were in some *unique* way predeter-

mined, anticipated—as only the act of meaning can anticipate reality.

198. "But how can a rule shew me what I have to do at *this* point? Whatever I do is, on some interpretation, in accord with the rule."—That is not what we ought to say, but rather: any interpretation still hangs in the air along with what it interprets, and cannot give it any support. Interpretations by themselves do not determine meaning.

"Then can whatever I do be brought into accord with the rule?"—Let me ask this: what has the expression of a rule—say a sign-post—got to do with my actions? What sort of connexion is there here?—Well, perhaps this one: I have been trained to react to this sign in a particular way, and now I do so react to it.

But that is only to give a causal connexion; to tell how it has come about that we now go by the sign-post; not what this going-by-the-sign really consists in. On the contrary; I have further indicated that a person goes by a sign-post only in so far as there exists a regular use of sign-posts, a custom.

199. Is what we call "obeying a rule" something that it would be possible for only *one* man to do, and to do only *once* in his life?—This is of course a note on the grammar of the expression "to obey a rule".

It is not possible that there should have been only one occasion on which someone obeyed a rule. It is not possible that there should have been only one occasion on which a report was made, an order given or understood; and so on.—To obey a rule, to make a report, to give an order, to play a game of chess, are *customs* (uses, institutions).

To understand a sentence means to understand a language. To understand a language means to be master of a technique.

201. This was our paradox: no course of action could be determined by a rule, because every course of action can be made out to accord with the rule. The answer was: if everything can be made out to accord with the rule, then it can also be made out to conflict with it. And so there would be neither accord not conflict here.

It can be seen that there is a misunderstanding here from the mere fact that in the course of our argument we give one interpretation after another; as if each one contented us at least for a moment, until we thought of yet another standing behind it. What this shews is that there is a way of grasping rule which is *not* an *interpretation*, but which is exhibited in what we call "obeying the rule" and "going against it" in actual cases.

Hence there is an inclination to say: every action according to the rule is an interpretation. But we ought to restrict the term "interpretation" to the substitution of one expression of the rule for another.

202. And hence also 'obeying a rule' is a practice. And to *think* one is obeying a rule is not to obey a rule. Hence it is not possible to obey a rule 'privately': otherwise thinking one was obeying a rule would be the same thing as obeying it.

206. Following a rule is analogous to obeying an order. We are trained to do so; we react to an order in a particular way. But what if one person reacts in one way and another in another to the order and the training? Which one is right?

Suppose you came as an explorer into an unknown country with a language quite strange to you. In what circumstances would you say that the people there gave orders, understood them, obeyed them, rebelled against them, and so on?

The common behaviour of mankind is the system of reference by means of which we interpret an unknown language.

214. If you have to have an intuition in order to develop the series 1 2 3 4 . . . you must also have one in order to develop the series 2 2 2 2. . . .

215. But isn't *the same* at least the same?

We seem to have an infallible paradigm of identity in the identity of a thing with itself. I feel like saying: "Here at any rate there can't be a variety of interpretations. If you are seeing a thing you are seeing identity too."

Then are two things the same when they are what *one* thing is? And how am I to apply what the *one* thing shews me to the case of two things?

216. "A thing is identical with itself."—There is no finer example of a useless proposition, which yet is connected with a certain play of the imagination. It is as if in imagination we put a thing into its own shape and saw that it fitted.

We might also say: "Every thing fits into itself." Or again: "Everything fits into its own shape." At the same time we look at a thing and imagine that there was a blank left for it, and that now it fits into it exactly.

Does this spot 'fit' into its white surrounding?— *But that is just how it would look* if there had at first been a hole in its place and it then fitted into the hole. But when we say "it fits" we are not simply describing this appearance; not simply this *situation*.

"Every coloured patch fits exactly into its surrounding" is a rather specialized form of the law of identity.

217. "How am I able to obey a rule?"—if this is not a question about causes, then it is about the justification for my following the rule in the way I do.

If I have exhausted the justifications I have reached bedrock, and my spade is turned. Then I am inclined to say: "This is simply what I do."

(Remember that we sometimes demand definitions for the sake not of their content, but of their form. Our requirement is an architectural one; the definition a kind of ornamental coping that supports nothing.)

218. Whence comes the idea that the beginning of a series is a visible section of rails invisibly laid to infinity? Well, we might imagine rails instead of a rule. And infinitely long rails correspond to the unlimited application of a rule.

219. "All the steps are really already taken" means: I no longer have any choice. The rule, once stamped with a particular meaning, traces the lines along which it is to be followed through the whole of space.—But if something of this sort really were the case, how would it help?

No; my description only made sense if it was to be understood symbolically.—I should have said: *This is how it strikes me*.

When I obey a rule, I do not choose.

I obey the rule *blindly*.

224. The word "agreement" and the word "rule" are *related* to one another, they are cousins. If I teach anyone the use of the one word, he learns the use of the other with it.

225. The use of the word "rule" and the use of the word "same" are interwoven. (As are the use of "proposition" and the use of "true".)

241. "So you are saying that human agreement decides what is true and what is false?"—It is what human beings *say* that is true and false; and they agree in the *language* they use. That is not agreement in options but in form of life.

242. If language is to be a means of communication there must be agreement not only in definitions but also (queer as this may sound) in judgments. This seems to abolish logic, but does not do so.—It is one thing to describe methods of measurement, and another to obtain and state results of measurement. But what we call "measuring" is partly determined by a certain constancy in results of measurement.

243. A human being can encourage himself, give himself orders, obey, blame and punish himself; he can ask himself a question and answer it. We could even imagine human beings who spoke only in monologue; who accompanied their activities by talking to themselves.—An explorer who watched them and listened to their talk might succeed in translating their language into ours. (This would enable him to predict these people's actions correctly, for he also hears them making resolutions and decisions.)

But could we also imagine a language in which a person could write down or give vocal expression to his inner experiences—his feelings, moods, and the rest—for his private use?—Well, can't we do so in our ordinary language?—But that is not what I mean. The individual words of this language are to refer to what can only be known to the person speaking; to his immediate private sensations. So anther person cannot understand the language.

244. How do words *refer* to sensations?—There doesn't seem to be any problem here; don't we talk about sensations every day, and give them names? But how is the connexion between the name and the thing named set up? This question is the same as: how does a human being learn the meaning of the names of sensations?—of the word "pain" for example. Here is one possibility; words are connected with the primitive, the natural, expressions of the sensation and used in their place. A child has hurt himself and he cries; and then adults talk to him and teach him exclamations and, later, sentences. They teach the child new pain-behaviour.

"So you are saying that the word 'pain' really means crying?"—On the contrary: the verbal expression of pain replaces crying and does not describe it.

245. For how can I go so far as to try to use language to get between pain and its expression?

248. The proposition "Sensations are private" is comparable to: "One plays patience by oneself".

249. Are we perhaps over-hasty in our assumption that the smile of an unweaned infant is not a pretence?—And on what experience is our assumption based?

(Lying is a language-game that needs to be learned like any other one.)

250. Why can't a dog simulate pain? Is he too honest? Could one teach a dog to simulate pain? Perhaps it is possible to teach him to howl on particular occasions as if he were in pain, even when he is not. But the surroundings which are necessary for this behaviour to be real simulation are missing.

252. "This body has extension." To this we might reply: "Nonsense!"—but are inclined to reply "Of course!"—Why is this?

253. "Another person can't have my pains."— Which are *my* pains? What counts as a criterion of identity here? Consider what makes it possible in the case of physical objects to speak of "two exactly the same", for example, to say "This chair is not the one you saw here yesterday, but is exactly the same as it".

In so far as it makes *sense* to say that my pain is the same as his, it is also possible for us both to have the same pain. (And it would also be imaginable for two people to feel pain in the same—not just the corresponding—place. That might be the case with Siamese twins, for instance).

I have seen a person in a discussion on this subject strike himself on the breast and say: "But surely another person can't have THIS pain!"—The answer to this is that one does not define a criterion of identity by emphatic stressing of the word "this". Rather, what the emphasis does is to suggest the case in which we are conversant with such a criterion of identity, but have to be reminded of it.

255. The philosopher's treatment of a question is like the treatment of an illness.

256. Now, what about the language which describes my inner experiences and which only I myself can understand? *How* do I use words to stand for my sensations?—As we ordinarily do? Then are my words for sensations tied up with my natural expressions of sensation? In that case my language is not a 'private' one. Someone else might understand it as well as I.—But suppose I didn't have any natural expression for the sensation, but only had the sensation? And now I simply *associate* names with sensations and use these names in descriptions.—

257. "What would it be like if human beings shewed no outward signs of pain (did not groan, grimace, etc.)? Then it would be impossible to teach a child the use of the word 'tooth-ache'."—Well, let's assume the child is a genius and itself invents a name for the sensation!—But then, of course, he couldn't make himself understood when he used the word.—So does he understand the name, without being able to explain its meaning to anyone?—But what does it mean to say that he has 'named his pain'?—How has he done this naming of pain?! And whatever he did, what was its purpose?—When one says "He gave a name to his sensation" one forgets that a great deal of stage-setting in the language is presupposed if the mere act of naming is to make sense. And when we speak of someone's having given a name to pain, what is presupposed is the existence of the grammar of the word "pain"; it shews the post where the new word is stationed.

258. Let us imagine the following case. I want to keep a diary about the recurrence of a certain sensation. To this end I associate it with the sign "S" and write this sign in a calendar for every day on which I have the sensation.—I will remark first of all that a definition of the sign cannot be formulated.—But still I can give myself a kind of ostensive definition.—How? Can I point to the sensation? Not in the ordinary sense. But I speak, or write the sign down, and at the same time I concentrate my attention on the sensation—and so, as it were, point to it inwardly.—But what is this ceremony for? for that is all it seems to be! A definition surely serves to establish the meaning of a sign.—Well, that is done precisely by the concentrating of my attention; for in this way I impress on myself the connexion between the sign and the sensation.—But "I impress it on myself" can only mean: this process brings it about that I remember the connexion *right* in the future. But in the present case I have no criterion of correctness. One would like to say: whatever is going to seem right to me is right. And that only means that here we can't talk about 'right'.

259. Are the rules of the private language *impressions* of rules?—The balance on which impressions are weighed is not the *impression* of a balance.

260. "Well, I *believe* that this is the sensation S again."—Perhaps you *believe* that you believe it!

Then did the man who made the entry in the calendar make a note of *nothing whatever*?—Don't consider it a matter of course that a person is making a note of something when he makes a mark—say in a calendar. For a note has a function, and this "S" so far has none.

(One can talk to oneself.—If a person speaks when no one else is present, does that mean he is speaking to himself?)

261. What reason have we for calling "S" the sign for a *sensation*? For "sensation" is a word of our common language, not of one intelligible to me alone. So the use of this word stands in need of a justification which everybody understands.—And it would not help either to say that it need not be a *sensation*; that when he writes "S," he has *something*—and that is all that can be said. "Has" and "something" also belong to our common language.—So in the end when one is doing philosophy one gets to the point where one would like just to emit an inarticulate sound.—But such a sound is an expression only as it occurs in a particular language-game, which should now be described.

265. Let us imagine a table (something like a dictionary) that exists only in our imagination. A dictionary can be used to justify the translation of a word X by a word Y. But are we also to call it a justification if such a table is to be looked up only in the imagination?—"Well, yes; then it is a subjective justification."—But justification consists in appealing to something independent.—"But surely I can appeal from one memory to another. For example, I don't know if I have remembered the time of departure of a train right and to check I call to mind how a page of the time-table looked. Isn't it the same here?"—No; for this process has got to produce a memory which is actually *correct*. If the mental image of the time-table could not itself be *tested* for correctness, how could it confirm the correctness of the first memory? (As if someone were to buy several copies of the morning paper to assure himself that what it said was true.)

Looking up a table in the imagination is no more looking up a table than the image of the result of an imagined experiment is the result of an experiment.

268. Why can't my right hand give my left hand money?—My right hand can put it into my left hand. My right hand can write a deed of gift and my left hand a receipt—But the further practical consequences would not be those of a gift. When the left hand has taken the money from the right, etc., we shall ask; "Well, and what of it?" And the same could be asked if a person had given himself a private definition of a word; I mean, if he has said the word to himself and at the same time has directed his attention to a sensation.

269. Let us remember that there are certain criteria in a man's behaviour for the fact that he does not understand a word: that it means nothing to him, that he can do nothing with it. And criteria for his 'thinking he understands', attaching some meaning to the word, but not the right one. And lastly, criteria for his understanding the word right. In the second case one might speak of a subjective understanding. And sounds which no one else understands but which I 'appear to understand' might be called a "private language".

271. "Imagine a person whose memory could not retain *what* the word 'pain' meant—so that he constantly called different things by the name—but nevertheless used the word in a way fitting in with the usual symptoms and presuppositions of pain"—in short he uses it as we all do. Here I should like to say: a wheel that can be turned though nothing else moves with it, is not part of the mechanism.

274. Of course, saying that the word "red" "refers to" instead of "means" something private does not help us in the least to grasp its function; but it is the more psychologically apt expression for a particular experience in doing philosophy. It is as if when I uttered the word I cast a sidelong glance at the private sensation, as it were in order to say to myself: I know all right what I mean by it.

275. Look at the blue of the sky and say to yourself "How blue the sky is!"—When you do it spontaneously—without philosophical intentions—the idea never crosses your mind that this impression of colour belongs only to *you*. And you have no hesitation in exclaiming that to someone else. And if you point at anything as you say the words you point at the sky. I am saying: you have not the feeling of

pointing-into-yourself, which often accompanies 'naming the sensation' when one is thinking about 'private language'. Nor do you think that really you ought not to point to the colour with your hand, but with your attention. (Consider what it means "to point to something with the attention".)

278. "I know how the colour green looks to *me*"—surely that makes sense!—Certainly: what use of the proposition are you thinking of?

279. Imagine someone saying: "But I know how tall I am!" and laying his hand on top of his head to prove it.

292. Don't always think that you read off what you say from the facts; that you portray these in words according to rules. For even so you would have to apply the rule in the particular case without guidance.

293. If I say of myself that it is only from my own case that I know what the word "pain" means—must I not say the same of other people too? And how can I generalize the *one* case so irresponsibly?

Now someone tells me that *he* knows what pain is only from his own case!—Suppose everyone had a box with something in it: we call it a "beetle". No one can look into anyone else's box, and everyone says he knows what a beetle is only by looking at *his* beetle.—Here it would be quite possible for everyone to have something different in his box. One might even imagine such a thing constantly changing.—But suppose the word "beetle" had a use in these people's language?—If so it would not be used as the name of a thing. The thing in the box has no place in the language-game at all; not even as a *something*: for the box might even be empty.—No, one can 'divide through' by the thing in the box; it cancels out, whatever it is.

That is to say: if we construe the grammar of the expression of sensation on the model of 'object and designation' the object drops out of consideration as irrelevant.

295. "I know . . . . only from my *own* case"—what kind of proposition is this meant to be at all? An experiential one? No.—A grammatical one?

Suppose everyone does say about himself that he knows what pain is only from his own pain.—Not that people really say that, or are even prepared to say it. But *if* everybody said it—it might be a kind of exclamation. And even if it gives no information, still it is a picture, and why should we not want to call up such a picture? Imagine an allegorical painting take the place of those words.

When we look into ourselves as we do philosophy, we often get to see just such a picture. A full-blown pictorial representation of our grammar. Not facts; but as it were illustrated turns of speech.

296. "Yes, but is *something* there all the same accompanying my cry of pain. And it is on account of that that I utter it. And this something is what is important—and frightful."—Only whom are we informing of this? And on what occasion?

297. Of course, if water boils in a pot, steam comes out of the pot and also pictured steam comes out of the pictured pot. But what if one insisted on saying that there must also be something boiling in the picture of the pot?

298. The very fact that we should so much like to say: "*This* is the important thing"—while we point privately to the sensation—is enough to shew how much we are inclined to say something which gives no information.

304. "But you will surely admit that there is a difference between pain-behaviour accompanied by pain and pain-behaviour without any pain?"—Admit it? What greater difference could there be?—"And yet you again and again reach the conclusion that the sensation itself is a *nothing*."—Not at all. It is not a *something*, but not a *nothing* either! The conclusion was only that a nothing would serve just as well as a something about which nothing could be said. We have only rejected the grammar which tries to force itself on us here.

The paradox disappears only if we make a radical break with the ideal that language always functions in one way, always serves the same purpose: to convey thoughts—which may be about houses, pains, good and evil, or anything else you please.

305. "But you surely cannot deny that, for example, in remembering, an inner process takes place."—What gives the impression that we want to deny anything? When one says "Still, an inner process does take place here"—one wants to go on: "After all, you *see* it." And it is this inner process that one means by the word "remembering."—The impression that we wanted to deny something arises from our setting our faces against the picture of the 'inner process'. What

we deny is that the picture of the inner process gives us the correct idea of the use of the word "to remember". We say that this picture with its ramifications stands in the way of our seeing the use of the word as it is.

306. Why should I deny that there is a mental process? But "There has just taken place in me the mental process of remembering . . . ." means nothing more than: "I have just remembered . . . .". To deny the mental process would mean to deny the remembering, to deny that anyone ever remembers anything.

307. "Are you not really a behaviourist in disguise? Aren't you at bottom really saying that everything except human behaviour is fiction?"

308. How does the philosophical problem about mental processes and states and about behaviourism arise?—The first step is the one that altogether escapes notice. We talk of processes and states and leave their nature undecided. Sometime perhaps we shall know more about them—we think. But that is just what commits us to a particular way of looking at the matter. For we have a definite concept of what it means to learn to know a process better. (The decisive movement in the conjuring trick has been made, and it was the very one that we thought quite innocent.)—And now the analogy which was to make us understand our thoughts falls to pieces. So we have to deny the yet uncomprehended process in the yet unexplored medium. And now it looks as if we had denied mental processes. And naturally we don't want to deny them.

309. What is your aim in philosophy?—To shew the fly the way out of the fly-bottle.

311. "What difference could be greater?"—In the case of pain I believe that I can give myself a private exhibition of the difference. But I can give anyone an exhibition of the difference between a broken and an unbroken tooth.—But for the private exhibition you don't have to give yourself actual pain; it is enough to *imagine* it—for instance, you screw up your face a bit. And do you know that what you are giving yourself this exhibition of is pain and not, for example, a facial expression? And how do you know what you are to give yourself an exhibition of before you do it? This *private* exhibition is an illusion.

353. Asking whether and how a proposition can be verified is only a particular way of asking "How

d'you mean?" The answer is contribution to the grammar of the proposition.

381. How do I know that this colour is red?—It would be an answer to say: "I have learnt English".

384. You learned the *concept* 'pain' when you learned language.

412. The feeling of an unbridgeable gulf between consciousness and brain-process: how does it come about that this does not come into the considerations of our ordinary life? This idea of a difference in kind is accompanied by slight giddiness,—which occurs when we are performing a piece of logical sleight-of-hand (The same giddiness attacks us when we think of certain theorems in set theory.) When does this feeling occur in the present case? It is when I, for example, turn my attention in a particular way on to my own consciousness, and, astonished, say to myself: THIS is supposed to be produced by a process in the brain!—as it were clutching my forehead.—But what can it mean to speak of "turning my attention on to my own consciousness"? This is surely the queerest thing there could be! It was a particular act of gazing that I called doing this. I stared fixedly in front of me—but *not* at any particular point or object. My eyes were wide open, the brows not contracted (as they mostly are when I am interested in a particular object). No such interest preceded this gazing. My glance was vacant; or again *like* that of someone admiring the illumination of the sky and drinking in the light.

Now bear in mind that the proposition which I uttered as a paradox (THIS is produced by a brain-process!) has nothing paradoxical about it. I could have said it in the course of an experiment whose purpose was to shew that an effect of light which I see is produced by stimulation of a particular part of the brain.—But I did not utter the sentence in the surroundings in which it would have had an everyday and unparadoxical sense. And my attention was not such as would have accorded with making an experiment. (If it had been, my look would have been intent, not vacant.)

414. You think that after all you must be weaving a piece of cloth: because you are sitting at a loom—even if it is empty—and going through the motions of weaving.

415. What we are supplying are really remarks on the natural history of human beings; we are not contributing curiosities however, but observations which no one has doubted, but which have escaped remark only because they are always before our eyes.

416. "Human beings agree in saying that they see, hear, feel, and so on (even though some are blind and some are deaf). So they are their own witnesses that they have *consciousness*."—But how strange this is! Whom do I really inform, if I say "I have consciousness"? What is the purpose of saying this to myself, and how can another person understand me?—Now, expressions like "I see", "I hear", "I am conscious" really have their uses. I tell a doctor "Now I am hearing with this ear again", or I tell someone who believes I am in a faint "I am conscious again", and so on.

431. "There is a gulf between an order and its execution. It has to be filled by the act of understanding."

"Only in the act of understanding is it meant that we are to do THIS. The *order*—why, that is nothing but sounds, ink-marks.—"

432. Every sign *by itself* seems dead. *What* gives it life?—In use it is *alive*. Is life breathed into it there?—Or is the *use* its life?

445. It is in language that an expectation and its fulfillment make contact.

464. My aim is: to teach you to pass from a piece of disguised nonsense to something that is patent nonsense.

485. Justification by experience comes to an end. If it did not it would not be justification.

580. An 'inner process' stands in need of outward criteria.

593. A main cause of philosophical disease—a one-sided diet: one nourishes one's thinking with only one kind of example.

599. In philosophy we do not draw conclusions. "But it must be like this!" is not a philosophical proposition. Philosophy only states what everyone admits.

STUDY QUESTIONS: WITTGENSTEIN, *PHILOSOPHICAL INVESTIGATIONS*

1. Must words name things? Why? Is this what Wittgenstein thought in the *Tractatus*?
2. Are words more like tools or labels? What is the significance of this?
3. What is usually more important, according to Wittgenstein: the meaning of a word or its use?
4. What does he mean by family resemblance?
5. What is his view of games?
6. What is a language game? What is the main point of the analogy between language and games?
7. What is the assumption behind the dichotomy between a Sophist and Platonic view of understanding?
8. What is the private language argument? What does it try to refute? How does it compare with Descartes' Skepticism? With Locke's empirical theory of understanding?
9. Is it possible to have a private language? Why?
10. What should be the aim of philosophy, according to Wittgenstein?
11. Why does Wittgenstein quote Augustine? What does he think the passage shows? What does he think of Augustine's view?
12. What is the point of the Lewis Carroll analogy?
13. Do all games have any particular thing in common? How is this related to his notion of family resemblances?
14. When Wittgenstein says, 'Don't think, but look!' what is he trying to get you to do, exactly?
15. How is a rule like a signpost?
16. What does he mean by 'bumps' in understanding?
17. What does it mean to understand a sentence?
18. Are language games innate? Or learned?

Philosophical Bridges: The Influence of the Later Wittgenstein

While many philosophers were following the agenda established by logical positivism, Wittgenstein was brewing a view of understanding that would transform philosophy. There was a whole generation of philosophers affected directly by his later work, such as F. Waismann, Elizabeth Anscombe, Georg Von Wright, Anthony Kenny, John Wisdom, Peter Hacker, Peter Winch, and O. K. Bouwsma, to name only a few.

There are four primary ways in which the later Wittgenstein's work has been very influential on the course of philosophy. First, he developed a new style of thinking that tries to dissolve philosophical problems rather than creating theories that answer or solve them. It regards philosophy as conceptual therapy. The therapist's cure is to help the patient to examine how the relevant parts of language function ordinarily in a variety of specific contexts. The aim is to enable him or her to see that the problem or puzzle, like the theories that try to solve it, involves a misuse of language.

Second, in the philosophy of the language, Wittgenstein tries to undermine the assumption that words derive their meaning by referring independently of context and practice, whether this reference is to private ideas, essences, or Platonic Forms. In contrast, he emphasizes how words are used in a variety of ways in different contexts and language games, and in so doing he stresses the social nature of language.

Third, in the philosophy of mind, Wittgenstein's influence primarily has been to remove some of the motivation that had held thinkers in the grasp of Descartes' introspectivism i.e., the view that mental states are defined in essentially private terms by how they feel to the person having them. In contrast, Wittgenstein insists on the need for outer, behavioral criteria, and he challenges the assumption that there are private mental entities such as ideas, sensations, and beliefs.

Fourth, in epistemology, Wittgenstein challenges the assumption that knowledge requires certainty, and, in the process, he tries to undermine the tendency toward solipsism and skepticism. As with the philosophy of mind, he confronts the assumption that we know the contents of our own minds better than we know external objects. He questions the whole basis of such an inner versus external distinction. Partly as a result of Wittgenstein's work, the idealism of earlier years and the sense-data-based theories of perception that tended to dominate philosophy are rarely discussed as live issues today.

The cumulative effect of Wittgenstein's impact on philosophy has been to put more distance between contemporary philosophy and some of the assumptions in the works of Descartes and Locke on the one hand, and Plato on the other.

GILBERT RYLE (1900–1976)

Biographical History

Gilbert Ryle spent his whole academic career at the University of Oxford. He was appointed lecturer in philosophy at Christ Church College in 1924, where he remained until the Second World War, during which time he worked in military intelligence. After the war, Ryle was appointed professor of metaphysics and fellow of Magdalen College, retiring in 1967. Ryle was editor of the journal *Mind* from 1948 to 1971. His classic work, *The Concept of Mind*, was published in 1949, and a collection of essays, *Dilemmas*, appeared in 1954.

Philosophical Overview

In a 1931 article titled 'Systematically Misleading Expressions,' Ryle characterizes the task of philosophy as to detect how mistaken theories arise from linguistic idioms. The syntactical or grammatical form of an expression does not always fit that of the facts it is supposed to depict, and this may give rise to misunderstanding. As an example, he contrasts 'Mr. Pickwick is a fiction' and 'Mr. Menzies is a statesman.' Grammatically, they are similar, but this does not mean that the first sentence describes a person. Ryle applies a similar type of analysis to metaphysics. For example, with a sentence such as 'Punctuality is a virtue,' we may assume that 'punctuality' is a name that refers to an abstract object. Similarly, in the sentence 'The idea of taking a holiday just occurred to me,' it appears that the phrase 'the idea of taking a holiday' picks out a mental entity, an idea. Metaphysically minded philosophers might be tempted to conclude that abstract objects and mental entities exist. As a remedy to this, Ryle advocates that philosophers should reframe or analyze sentences to remove their systematically misleading nature, much in the way that Russell's theory of descriptions does. The point is that *The Concept of Mind* can be regarded as a continuation of this view of the role of philosophy.

THE CONCEPT OF MIND

The Concept of Mind (1949) is a classic work of ordinary language philosophy in which Ryle tries to undermine Descartes' dualism and the Empiricist assumption that our mental lives consist in the having of private ideas.

In this selected first chapter, Ryle argues against the myth of the ghost in the machine. He compares this myth to the claim that a university is some entity over and above a set of buildings. Such a claim constitutes a category mistake. In other words, Ryle argues that it is a mistake to claim that the mind and mental processes are entities distinct from the body and our behavior. Ryle analyzes mental terms, such as 'think,' 'imagine,' and 'to have in mind,' in order to show in detail how these words mislead us systematically into conceiving the mind as a Cartesian 'ghost in a machine.' For example, like Austin and Wittgenstein, Ryle argues that it is a mistake to apply verbs such as 'see' and 'perceive' to sensations. Consequently, the concept of sense-data and the early Empiricist notion of ideas as objects of perception are both mistaken.

Ryle's thesis is that to talk about a person's mental states is not to refer to the properties of a distinct mind, but rather to refer to dispositions and abilities to behave in certain ways. For example, Ryle argues that the difference between seeing and not seeing should not be characterized as the presence or absence of a private inner mental process. 'Seeing' is an achievement-word that marks success in a task, rather than a process-word. It is more like 'winning a race' than 'running a race.' However, Ryle is aware of the problems of this kind of behavioristic thesis. For example, there are many occasions when a person does not express his or her thoughts. Nevertheless, he insists that we should not conceive of, for example, imagining as contemplating private mental images. To imagine Mt. Everest is simply to think about how the mountain might appear. To imagine a unicorn does not consist in having a private picture in one's mind, but rather in thinking about how unicorns look.

CHAPTER 1

DESCARTES' MYTH

(1) The Official Doctrine

There is a doctrine about the nature and place of minds which is so prevalent among theorists and even among laymen that it deserves to be described as the official theory. Most philosophers, psychologists and religious teachers subscribe, with minor reservations, to its main articles and, although they admit certain theoretical difficulties in it, they tend to assume that these can be overcome without serious modifications being made to the architecture of the theory. It will be argued here that the central principles of the doctrine are unsound and conflict with the whole body of what we know about minds when we are not speculating about them.

The official doctrine, which hails chiefly from Descartes, is something like this. With the doubtful exceptions of idiots and infants in arms every human being has both a body and a mind. Some would prefer to say that every human being is both a body and a mind. His body and his mind are ordinarily harnessed together, but after the death of the body his mind may continue to exist and function.

Human bodies are in space and are subject to the mechanical laws which govern all other bodies in space. Bodily processes and states can be inspected by external observers. So a man's bodily life is as much a public affair as are the lives of animals and reptiles and even as the careers of trees, crystals and planets.

But minds are not in space, nor are their operations subject to mechanical laws. The workings of one mind are not witnessable by other observers; its career is private. Only I can take direct cognisance of the states and processes of my own mind. A person therefore lives through two collateral histories, one consisting of what happens in and to his body, the other consisting of what happens in and to his mind. The first is public, the second private. The events in the first history are events in the physical world, those in the second are events in the mental world.

It has been disputed whether a person does or can directly monitor all or only some of the episodes of his own private history; but, according to the official doctrine, of at least some of these episodes he has direct and unchallengeable cognisance. In consciousness, self-consciousness and introspection he is directly and authentically apprised of the present states and operations of his mind. He may have great or small uncertainties about concurrent and adjacent episodes in the physical world, but he can have none about at least part of what is momentarily occupying his mind.

It is customary to express this bifurcation of his two lives and of his two worlds by saying that the things and events which belong to the physical world, including his own body, are external, while the workings of his own mind are internal. This antithesis of outer and inner is of course meant to be construed as a metaphor, since minds, not being in space, could not be described as being spatially inside anything else, or as having things going on spatially inside themselves. But relapses from this good intention are common and theorists are found speculating how stimuli, the physical sources of which are yards or miles outside a person's skin, can generate mental responses inside his skull, or how decisions framed inside his cranium can set going movements of his extremities.

Even when 'inner' and 'outer' are construed as metaphors, the problem how a person's mind and body influence one another is notoriously charged with theoretical difficulties. What the mind wills, the legs, arms and the tongue execute; what affects the ear and the eye has something to do with what the mind perceives; grimaces and smiles betray the mind's moods and bodily castigations lead, it is hoped, to moral improvement. But the actual transactions between the episodes of the private history and those of the public history remain mysterious, since by definition they can belong to neither series. They could not be reported among the happenings described in a person's autobiography of his inner life, but nor could they be reported among those described in some one else's biography of that person's overt career. They can be inspected neither by introspection nor by laboratory experiment. They are theoretical shuttlecocks which are forever being bandied from the physiologist back to the psychologist and from the psychologist back to the physiologist.

Underlying this partly metaphorical representation of the bifurcation of a person's two lives there is a seemingly more profound and philosophical assumption. It is assumed that there are two different kinds of existence or status. What exists or happens may have the status of physical existence, or it may have the status of mental existence. Somewhat as the faces of coins are either heads or tails, or somewhat as living creatures are either male or female, so, it is supposed, some existing is physical existing, other existing is mental existing. It is a necessary feature of what has physical existence that it is in space and time, it is a necessary feature of what has mental existence that it is in time but not in space. What has physical existence is composed of matter, or else is a function of matter; what has mental existence consists of consciousness, or else is a function of consciousness.

There is thus a polar opposition between mind and matter, an opposition which is often brought out as follows. Material objects are situated in a common field, known as 'space', and what happens to one body in one part of space is mechanically connected with what happens to other bodies in other parts of space. But mental happenings occur in insulated fields, known as 'minds', and there is, apart maybe from telepathy, no direct causal connection between what happens in one mind and what happens in another. Only through the medium of the public physical world can the mind of one person make a difference to the mind of another. The mind is its own place and in his inner life each of us lives the life of a ghostly Robinson Crusoe. People can see, hear and jolt one another's bodies, but they are irremediably blind and deaf to the workings of one another's minds and inoperative upon them.

What sort of knowledge can be secured of the workings of a mind? On the one side, according to the official theory, a person has direct knowledge of the best imaginable kind of the workings of his own mind. Mental states and processes are (or are normally) conscious states and processes, and the consciousness which irradiates them can engender no illusions and leaves the door open for no doubts. A person's present thinkings, feelings and willings, his perceivings, rememberings and imaginings are intrinsically 'phosphorescent'; their existence and their nature are inevitably betrayed to their owner. The inner life is a stream of consciousness of such a sort that it would be absurd to suggest that the mind whose life is that stream might be unaware of what is passing down it.

True, the evidence adduced recently by Freud seems to show that there exist channels tributary to this stream, which run hidden from their owner. People are actuated by impulses the existence of which they vigorously disavow; some of their thoughts differ from the thoughts which they acknowledge; and some of the actions which they think they will to perform they do not really will. They are thoroughly gulled by some of their own hypocrisies and they successfully ignore facts about their mental lives which on the official theory ought to be patent to them. Holders of the official theory tend, however, to maintain that anyhow in normal circumstances a person must be directly and authentically seized of the present state and workings of his own mind.

Besides being currently supplied with these alleged immediate data of consciousness, a person is also generally supposed to be able to exercise from time to time a special kind of perception, namely inner perception, or introspection. He can take a (non-optical) 'look' at what is passing in his mind. Not only can he view and scrutinize a flower through his sense of sight and listen to and discriminate the notes of a bell through his sense of hearing; he can also reflectively or introspectively watch, without any bodily organ of sense, the current episodes of his inner life. This self-observation is also commonly supposed to be immune from illusion, confusion or doubt. A mind's reports of its own affairs have a certainty superior to the best that is possessed by its reports of matters in the physical world. Sense-perceptions can, but consciousness and introspection cannot, be mistaken or confused.

On the other side, one person has no direct access of any sort to the events of the inner life of another. He cannot do better than make problematic inferences from the observed behaviour of the other person's body to the states of mind which, by analogy from his own conduct, he supposes to be signalised by that behaviour. Direct access to the workings of a mind is the privilege of that mind itself; in default of such privileged access, the workings of one mind are inevitably occult to everyone else. For the supposed arguments from bodily movements similar to their own to mental workings similar to their own would lack any possibility of observational corroboration. Not unnaturally, therefore, an adherent of the official theory finds it difficult to resist this consequence of his premises, that he has no good reason to believe that there do exist minds other than his own. Even if he prefers to believe that to other human bodies there are harnessed minds not unlike his own, he cannot claim to be able to discover their individual characteristics, or the particular things that they undergo and do. Absolute solitude is on this showing the ineluctable destiny of the soul. Only our bodies can meet.

As a necessary corollary of this general scheme there is implicitly prescribed a special way of construing our ordinary concepts of mental powers and operations. The verbs, nouns and adjectives, with which in ordinary life we describe the wits, characters and higher-grade performances of the people with whom we have do, are required to be construed as signifying special episodes in their secret histories, or else as signifying tendencies for such episodes to occur. When someone is described as knowing, believing or guessing something, as hoping, dreading, intending or shirking something, as designing this or being amused at that, these verbs are supposed to denote the occurrence of specific modifications in his (to us) occult stream of consciousness. Only his own privileged access to this stream in direct awareness and introspection could provide authentic testimony that these mental-conduct verbs were correctly or incorrectly applied. The onlooker, be he teacher, critic, biographer or friend, can never assure himself that his comments have any vestige of truth. Yet it was just because we do in fact all know how to make such comments, make them with general correctness and correct them when they turn out to be confused or mistaken, that philosophers found it necessary to construct their theories of the nature and place of minds. Finding mental-conduct concepts being regularly and effectively used, they properly sought to fix their logical geography. But the logical geography officially recommended would entail that there could be no regular or effective use of these mental-conduct concepts in our descriptions of, and prescriptions for, other people's minds.

(2) The Absurdity of the Official Doctrine

Such in outline is the official theory. I shall often speak of it, with deliberate abusiveness, as 'the dogma of the Ghost in the Machine'. I hope to prove that it is entirely false, and false not in detail but in principle. It is not merely an assemblage of particular mistakes. It is one big mistake and a mistake of a special kind. It is, namely, a category-mistake. It represents the facts of mental life as if they belonged to one logical type or category (or range of types or categories), when they actually belong to another. The dogma is therefore a philosopher's myth. In attempting to explode the myth I shall probably be taken to be denying well-known facts about the mental life of human beings, and my plea that I aim at doing nothing more than rectify the logic of mental-conduct concepts will probably be disallowed as mere subterfuge.

I must first indicate what is meant by the phrase 'Category-mistake'. This I do in a series of illustrations.

A foreigner visiting Oxford or Cambridge for the first time is shown a number of colleges, libraries, playing fields, museums, scientific departments and administrative offices. He then asks 'But where is the University? I have seen where the members of the Colleges live, where the Registrar works, where the scientists experiment and the rest. But I have not yet seen the University in which reside and work the members of your University.' It has then to be explained to him that the University is not another collateral institution, some ulterior counterpart to the colleges, laboratories and offices which he has seen. The University is just the way in which all that he has already seen is organized. When they are seen and when their co-ordination is understood, the University has been seen. His mistake lay in his innocent assumption that it was correct to speak of Christ Church, the Bodleian Library, the Ashmolean Museum *and* the University, to speak, that is, as if 'the University' stood for an extra member of the class of which these other units are members. He was mistakenly allocating the University to the same category as that to which the other institutions belong.

The same mistake would be made by a child witnessing the march-past of a division, who, having had pointed out to him such and such battalions, batteries, squadrons, etc., asked when the division was going to appear. He would be supposing that a division was a counterpart to the units already seen, partly similar to them and partly unlike them. He would be shown his mistake by being told that in watching the battalions, batteries and squadrons marching past he had been watching the division marching past. The march-past was not a parade of battalions, batteries, squadrons *and* a division; it was a parade of the battalions, batteries and squadrons *of* a division.

One more illustration. A foreigner watching his first game of cricket learns what are the functions of the bowlers, the batsmen, the fielders, the umpires and the scorers. He then says 'But there is no one left on the field to contribute the famous element of team-spirit. I see who does the bowling, the batting and the wicket-keeping; but I do not see whose role it is to exercise *esprit de corps*.' Once more, it would have to be explained that he was looking for the wrong type of thing. Team-spirit is not another cricketing-operation supplementary to all of the other special tasks. It is, roughly, the keenness with which each of the special tasks is performed, and performing a task keenly is not performing two tasks. Certainly exhibiting team-spirit is not the same thing as bowling or catching, but nor is it a third thing such that we can say that the bowler first bowls *and* then exhibits team-spirit or that a fielder is at a given moment *either* catching *or* displaying *esprit de corps*.

These illustrations of category-mistakes have a common feature which must be noticed. The mistakes were made by people who did not know how to wield the concepts *University*, *division* and *team-spirit*. Their puzzles arose from inability to use certain items in the English vocabulary.

The theoretically interesting category-mistakes are those made by people who are perfectly competent to apply concepts, at least in the situations with which they are familiar, but are still liable in their abstract thinking to allocate those concepts to logical types to which they do not belong. An instance of a mistake of this sort would be the following story. A student of politics has learned the main differences between the British, the French and the American Constitutions, and has learned also the differences and connections between the Cabinet, Parliament, the various Ministries, the Judicature and the Church of England. But he still becomes embarrassed when asked questions about the connections between the Church of England, the Home Office and the British Constitution. For while the Church and the Home Office are institutions, the British Constitution is not another institution in the same sense of that noun. So inter-institutional relations which can be asserted or denied to hold between the Church and the Home Office cannot be asserted or denied to hold between either of them and the British Constitution. 'The British Constitution' is not a term of the same logical type as 'the Home Office' and 'the Church of England'. In a partially similar way, John Doe may be a relative, a friend, an enemy or a stranger to Richard Roe; but he cannot be any of these things to the Average Taxpayer. He knows how to talk sense in certain sorts of discussions about the Average Taxpayer, but he is baffled to say why he could not come across him in the street as he can come across Richard Roe.

It is pertinent to our main subject to notice that, so long as the student of politics continues to think of the British Constitution as a counterpart to the other institutions, he will tend to describe it as a mysteriously occult institution; and so long as John Doe continues to think of Average Taxpayer as a fellow-citizen, he will tend to think of him as an elusive insubstantial man, a ghost who is everywhere yet nowhere.

My destructive purpose is to show that a family of radical category-mistakes is the source of the double-life theory. The representation of a person as a ghost mysteriously ensconced in a machine derives from this argument. Because, as it true, a person's thinking, feeling and purposive doing cannot be described solely in the idioms of physics, chemistry and physiology, therefore they must be described in counterpart idioms. As the human body is a complex organised unit, so the human mind must be another complex organized unit, though one made of a different sort of stuff and with a different sort of structure. Or, again, as the human body, like any other parcel of matter, is a field of causes and effects, so the mind must be another field of causes and effects, though not (Heaven be praised) mechanical causes and effects.

(3) The Origin of the Category-mistake

One of the chief intellectual origins of what I have yet to prove to be the Cartesian category-mistake seems to be this. When Galileo showed that his methods of scientific discovery were competent to provide a mechanical theory which should cover every occupant of space, Descartes found in himself two conflicting motives. As a man of scientific genius he could not but endorse the claims of mechanics, yet as a religious and moral man he could not accept, as Hobbes accepted, the discouraging rider to those claims, namely that human nature differs only in degree of complexity from clockwork. The mental could not be just a variety of the mechanical.

He and subsequent philosophers naturally but erroneously availed themselves of the following escape-route. Since mental-conduct words are not to be construed as signifying the occurrence of mechanical processes, they must be construed as signifying the occurrence of non-mechanical processes; since mechanical laws explain movements in space as the effects of other movements in space, other laws must explain some of the non-spatial workings of minds as the effects of other non-spatial workings of minds. The difference between the human behaviours which we describe as intelligent and those which we describe as unintelligent must be a difference in their causation; so, while some movements of human tongues and limbs are the effects of mechanical causes, others must be the effects of non-mechanical causes, i.e. some issue from movements of particles of matter, others from workings of the mind.

The differences between the physical and the mental were thus represented as differences inside the common framework of the categories of 'thing', 'stuff', 'attribute', 'state', 'process', 'change', 'cause' and 'effect'. Minds are things, but different sorts of things from bodies; mental processes are causes and effects, but different sorts of causes and effects from bodily movements. And so on. Somewhat as the foreigner expected the University to be an extra edifice, rather like a college but also considerably different, so the repudiators of mechanism represented minds as extra centres of causal processes, rather like machine but also considerably different from them. Their theory was a para-mechanical hypothesis.

That this assumption was at the heart of the doctrine is shown by the fact that there was from the beginning felt to be a major theoretical difficulty in explaining how minds can influence and be influenced by bodies. How can a mental process, such as willing, cause spatial movements like the movements of the tongue? How can a physical change in the optic nerve have among its effects a mind's perception of a flash of light? This notorious crux by itself shows the logical mould into which Descartes pressed his theory of the mind. It was the self-same mould into which he and Galileo set their mechanics. Still unwittingly adhering to the grammar of mechanics, he tried to avert disaster by describing minds in what was merely an obverse vocabulary. The workings of minds had to be described by the mere negatives of the specific descriptions given to bodies; they are not in space, they are not motions, they are not modifications of matter, they are not accessible to public observation. Minds are not bits of clockwork, they are just bits of not-clockwork.

As thus represented, minds are not merely ghosts harnessed to machines, they are themselves just spectral machines. Though the human body is an engine, it is not quite an ordinary engine, since some of its workings are governed by another engine inside it—this interior governor-engine being one of a very special sort. It is invisible, inaudible and it has no size or weight. It cannot be taken to bits and the laws it obeys are not those known to ordinary engineers. Nothing is known of how it governs the bodily engine.

A second major crux points the same moral. Since, according to the doctrine, minds belong to the same category as bodies and since bodies are rigidly governed by mechanical laws, it seemed to many theorists to follow that minds must be similarly governed by rigid non-mechanical laws. The physical world is a deterministic system, so the mental world must be a deterministic system. Bodies cannot help the modifications that they undergo, so minds cannot help pursuing the careers fixed for them. *Responsibility, choice, merit* and *demerit* are therefore inapplicable concepts—unless the compromise solution is adopted of saying that the laws governing mental processes, unlike those governing physical processes, have the congenial attribute of being only rather rigid. The problem of the Freedom of the Will was the problem how to reconcile the hypothesis that minds are to be described in terms drawn from the categories of mechanics with the knowledge that higher-grade human conduct is not of a piece with the behaviour of machines.

It is an historical curiosity that it was not noticed that the entire argument was broken-backed. Theorists correctly assumed that any sane man could already recognise the differences between, say, rational and non-rational utterances or between purposive and automatic behaviour. Else there would have been nothing requiring to be salved from mechanism. Yet the explanation given presupposed that one person could in principle never recognise the difference between the rational and the irrational utterances issuing from other human bodies, since he could never get access to the postulated immaterial causes of some of their utterances. Save for the doubtful exception of himself, he could never tell the difference between a man and a Robot. It would have to be conceded, for example, that, for all that we can tell, the inner lives of persons who are classed as idiots or lunatics are as rational as those of anyone else. Perhaps only their overt behaviour is disappointing; that is to say, perhaps 'idiots' are not really idiotic, or 'lunatics' lunatic. Perhaps, too, some of those who are classed as sane are really idiots. According to the theory, external observers could never know how the overt behaviour of others is correlated with their mental powers and processes and so they could never know or even plausibly conjecture whether their applications of mental-conduct concepts to these other people were correct or incorrect. It would then be hazardous or impossible for a man to claim sanity or logical consistency even for himself, since he would be debarred from comparing his own performances with those of others. In short, our characterisations of persons and their performances as intelligent, prudent and virtuous or as stupid, hypocritical and cowardly could never have been made, so the problem of providing a special causal hypothesis to serve as the basis of such diagnoses would never have arisen. The question, 'How do persons differ from machines?' arose just because everyone already knew how to apply mental-conduct concepts before the new causal hypothesis was introduced. This causal hypothesis could not therefore to be the source of the criteria used in those applications. Nor, of course, has the causal hypothesis in any degree improved our handling of those criteria. We still distinguish good from bad arithmetic, politic from impolitic conduct and fertile from infertile imaginations in the ways in which Descartes himself distinguished them before and after he speculated how the applicability of these criteria was compatible with the principle of mechanical causation.

He had mistaken the logic of his problem. Instead of asking by what criteria intelligent behaviour is actually distinguished from non-intelligent behaviour, he asked 'Given that the principle of mechanical causation does not tell us the difference, what other causal principle will tell it us?' He realised that the problem was not one of mechanics and assumed that it must therefore be one of some counterpart to mechanics. Not unnaturally psychology is often cast for just this role.

When two terms belong to the same category, it is proper to construct conjunctive propositions embodying them. Thus a purchaser may say that he bought a left-hand glove and a right-hand glove, but not that he bought a left-hand glove, a right-hand glove and a pair of gloves. 'She came home in a flood of tears and a sedan-chair' is a well-known joke based on the absurdity of conjoining terms of different types. It would have been equally ridiculous to con-

struct the disjunction 'She came home either in a flood of tears or else in a sedan-chair'. Now the dogma of the Ghost in the Machine does just this. It maintains that there exist both bodies and minds; that there occur physical processes and mental processes; that there are mechanical causes of corporeal movements and mental causes of corporeal movements. I shall argue that these and other analogous conjunctions are absurd; but, it must be noticed, the argument will not show that either of the illegitimately conjoined propositions is absurd in itself. I am not, for example, denying that there occur mental processes. Doing long division is a mental process and so is making a joke. But I am saying that the phrase 'there occur mental processes' does not mean the same sort of thing as 'there occur physical processes', and, therefore, that it makes no sense to conjoin or disjoin the two.

If my argument is successful, there will follow some interesting consequences. First, the hallowed contrast between Mind and Matter will be dissipated, but dissipated not by either of the equally hallowed absorptions of Mind by Matter or of Matter by Mind, but in quite a different way. For the seeming contrast of the two will be shown to be as illegitimate as would be the contrast of 'she came home in a flood of tears' and 'she came home in a sedan-chair'. The belief that there is a polar opposition between Mind and Matter is the belief that they are terms of the same logical type.

It will also follow that both Idealism and Materialism are answers to an improper question. The 'reduction' of the material world to mental states and processes, as well as the 'reduction' of mental states and processes to physical states and processes, presuppose the legitimacy of the disjunction 'Either there exist minds or there exist bodies (but not both)'. It would be like saying, 'Either she bought a left-hand and a right-hand glove or she bought a pair of gloves (but not both)'.

It is perfectly proper to say, in one logical tone of voice, that there exist minds and to say, in another logical tone of voice, that there exist bodies. But these expressions do not indicate two different species of existence, for 'existence' is not a generic word like 'coloured' or 'sexed'. They indicate two different senses of 'exist', somewhat as 'rising' has different senses in 'the tide is rising', 'hopes are rising', and 'the average age of death is rising'. A man would be thought to be making a poor joke who said that three things are now rising, namely the tide, hopes and the average age of death. It would be just as good or bad a joke to say that there exist prime numbers and Wednesdays and public opinions and navies; or that there exist both minds and bodies. In the succeeding chapters I try to prove that the official theory does rest on a batch of category-mistakes by showing that logically absurd corollaries follow from it. The exhibition of these absurdities will have the constructive effect of bringing out part of the correct logic of mental-conduct concepts.

(4) Historical Note

It would not be true to say that the official theory derives solely from Descartes' theories, or even from a more widespread anxiety about the implications of seventeenth century mechanics. Scholastic and Reformation theology had schooled the intellects of the scientists as well as of the laymen, philosophers and clerics of that age. Stoic-Augustinian theories of the will were embedded in the Calvinist doctrines of sin and grace; Platonic and Aristotelian theories of the intellect shaped the orthodox doctrines of the immortality of the soul. Descartes was reformulating already prevalent theological doctrines of the soul in the new syntax of Galileo. The theologian's privacy of conscience became the philosopher's privacy of consciousness, and what had been the bogy of Predestination reappeared as the bogy of Determinism.

It would also not be true to say that the two-worlds myth did no theoretical good. Myths often do a lot of theoretical good, while they are still new. One benefit bestowed by the para-mechanical myth was that it partly superannuated the then prevalent para-political myth. Minds and their Faculties had previously been described by analogies with political superiors and political subordinates. The idioms used were those of ruling, obeying, collaborating and rebelling. They survived and still survive in many ethical and some epistemological discussions. As, in physics, the new myth of occult Forces was a scientific improvement on the old myth of Final Causes, so, in anthropological and psychological theory, the new myth of hidden operations, impulses and agencies was an improvement on the old myth of dictations, deferences and disobediences.

STUDY QUESTIONS: RYLE, *THE CONCEPT OF MIND*

1. What is the official theory? By what other names does Ryle call it?
2. What are the differences between mental and physical existence, according to this theory?
3. Why can introspection not be mistaken, according to the official theory?
4. What examples does Ryle give of a category mistake? Why do these count as category mistakes?
5. How does Ryle use the example of the British Constitution?
6. According to Ryle, how did Descartes make a category mistake following the work of Galileo?
7. In Section 3, Ryle describes two major cruxes (points) in Descartes' theory. What are they?
8. How does the question 'How do persons differ from machines?' become a part of Descartes' theory?
9. What is the test by which we can judge whether two terms belong to the same logical category?
10. Why are idealism and materialism both answers to an improper question, according to Ryle? What implications does this point have for reduction?
11. Ryle claims that existence is not a generic word like 'colored.' What does this mean? What is the alternative, and to what does Ryle compare it?

Philosophical Bridges: Ryle's Influence

Ryle's *The Concept of Mind* was one of the most discussed philosophical works in the United States and especially Britain until the early 1960s. First, this was because the work struck at the heart of the British Empiricist tradition by denying the existence of sensations and other mental items, such as ideas and sense-data. Many philosophers, especially those from the previous generation, assumed that physical objects should be understood as constructions from sense-data, in much the way that Russell had argued. In sharp contrast, Ryle urged that this conception of sense-data was a mistake resulting from the effect of misleading expressions. Ryle's argument inspired many philosophers to rethink perception. The claim that we can perceive only our own ideas directly was replaced by the assertion that we can perceive material objects directly.

Second, Ryle's willingness to deny that mental objects exist spurred other thinkers to consider seriously materialism. Especially in Australia, philosophers such as J. C. C. Smart and David Armstrong argued for a materialistic identity theory during the 1950s and 1960s. The identity theory holds that mental states are identical to brain states.

Bibliography

RYLE
Primary
Collected Papers, 2 vols., Hutchinson, 1971
The Concept of Mind, Hutchinson, 1949
Dilemmas, Cambridge University Press, 1954

Secondary
Lyons, William, *Gilbert Ryle: An Introduction to His Philosophy,* Harvester Press, 1980
Wood, O., and Pitcher, G., eds., *Ryle,* Macmillan, 1970

WITTGENSTEIN
Primary
The Blue and Brown Books, Blackwell, 1958
Philosophical Grammar, Blackwell, 1974
Philosophical Investigations, Blackwell, 1958
Remarks on the Foundations of Mathematics, Blackwell, 1978
Remarks on the Philosophy of Psychology, Blackwell, 1980

Secondary
Baker, G. P., and Hacker, P., *An Analytic Commentary on the Philosophical Investigations,* 4 vols., Blackwell, 1980–1996
Hacker, P., *Insight and Illusion,* Clarendon Press, 1972
Hallet, Garth, *A Companion to Wittgenstein's 'Philosophical Investigations,'* Cornell University Press, 1977
Hanfling, O., *Wittgenstein's Later Philosophy,* MacMillan, 1989
Kenny, A., *Wittgenstein,* Penguin, 1973
McGinn, Marie, *Routledge Philosophy Guidebook to Wittgenstein and the Philosophical Investigations,* Routledge, 1997
Sluga, Hans, and Stern, David, *The Cambridge Companion to Wittgenstein,* Cambridge University Press, 1996

SECTION V

◆ ANALYTIC PHILOSOPHY ◆

PROLOGUE

In the 1950s, much analytic philosophy in the United States was in part motivated by the desire to rethink logical positivism, and more generally Empiricism, but within the general tradition as defined broadly by the works of Frege, Russell, and Carnap. For instance, in his famous paper 'Two Dogmas of Empiricism' (1951), Quine argues against logical positivism, while retaining the extensional view of language inherent in logical atomism. Quine rejects the postulation of intensional items as proposed by Frege and also by Carnap in his later works. Quine also argues that the reductionist program of the early logical positivists fails. As a consequence, he constructs a theory of language that eschews all intensional notions, such as concepts, senses, meanings, and propositions. Such notions cannot be reduced; therefore, they must be eliminated.

In a similar vein, Goodman's famous piece called 'The New Riddle of Induction' (1955) can be seen as challenging logical positivism in the philosophy of science. In order to be able to reason inductively, we must be able to distinguish causal laws from accidental generalizations, and Goodman invents a fundamentally new and deep problem for traditional ways of upholding this distinction. In other words, he presents a skeptical challenge.

In his 1962 book *The Structure of Scientific Revolutions*, Thomas Kuhn provides a radical critique of logical positivism. He presents a historical account of science that opposes the idea of uniform scientific progress and a nonhistorical Empiricist methodology of science. Kuhn's work may be considered as a watershed because, by the 1960s, analytic philosophy was becoming less dominated by the Empiricism inherent in logical positivism.

For example, in this respect the work of Donald Davidson is very different from that of Quine, despite the similarities. In his 1967 article 'Truth and Meaning,' Davidson argues that the intensional notion of meaning can be salvaged even within the extensional framework proposed by Quine. Meaning can be understood in terms of the truth conditions of sentences, which can be provided by an extensional truth theory for a language. Davidson's theory of meaning is best understood in the context of his equally influential, nonreductionist form of materialism in the philosophy of mind, anomalous monism, which is outlined in his 1971 article 'Mental Events.'

By the 1960s, there was another change. Analytic philosophy was becoming less focused exclusively on problems concerning science, knowledge, and language. For instance, John Rawls' book *A Theory of Justice* (1971) sparked a new concern for political theory. In a similar vein, there was more interest in ethical theory, applied ethics, and philosophy of the social sciences.

The work of Hilary Putnam represents another change that occurred in the 1970s. In the previous decade, Putnam had argued for a scientific view of philosophy, but in the 1970s, he was willing to consider philosophy in a broader perspective, including social, moral, and religious issues. In the paper 'Why There Isn't a Ready-made World,' he argues against a metaphysical realism that he thinks is inherent in much contemporary materialism. Analytic philosophers are increasingly willing to turn their critical attention to what Putnam calls scientism.

W. V. O. QUINE (1908–2000)

Biographical History

Willard Van Orman Quine, who was born in Akron, Ohio, studied mathematics and philosophy at Oberlin College. In 1930, he went to graduate school at Harvard, where he wrote a dissertation on the mathematical logic of *Principia Mathematica*, which was subsequently published as *A System of Logic*. He received his doctorate in philosophy after only two years.

Afterward, Quine was awarded a traveling scholarship and he studied in Vienna, where he met Moritz Schlick, Hans Reichenbach, and Rudolf Carnap. He also studied logic with the great Polish logicians, Tarski and Jan Lukasiewicz. In 1936, Quine returned to the United States and became an instructor at Harvard. When the United States entered World War II, he joined the navy and ended up working for radio intelligence in Washington. After the war, Quine returned to Harvard, where he became a full professor in 1948 until his retirement 30 years later. During his academic career, Quine had written many books and articles. His books include *From a Logical Point of View* (1953), *Word and Object* (1960), *Ways of Paradox* (1966), *The Roots of Reference* (1967), and *Ontological Relativity* (1969).

Philosophical Overview

Quine's main philosophical aim is to explain naturalistically, or factually in scientific terms, how our theories of the world arise from sense perception. This constitutes a revised and radical form of Empiricism, which substitutes Carnap's early notion of reduction with one of naturalististic explanation, inspired by pragmatism and Hume. To provide background to Quine's thought, let us briefly review four aspects of his philosophy.

Stimulus Meaning

All theories are based on sensory input. This input should be conceived of in strictly behaviorist terms in the following way. The stimulus meaning of a sentence for a speaker at a particular time can be defined behaviorally in terms of the sensory stimuli a person would need in order to agree with or assent to the sentence. If a person assents to sentence S given stimulus A, then A is part of the stimulus meaning of S for that speaker at that time. Thus, in the case of observation statements, meaning and evidence are identical. According to Quine, observation statements form the basis of all scientific theories. By explaining these observation statements in the way he does, Quine is advocating behaviorism, according to which all intensional language, such as 'believes' and 'desires,' should be eliminated from psychology and science (see below).

Holism and the Indeterminacy of Meaning

Holism means that single theoretical sentences do not have evidential support on their own in relation to observations, but only together as a theory. Since the meaning of a statement solely depends on what would count as evidence for its truth, Quine also accepts a holistic conception of meaning. Additionally, theories are underdetermined by sensory inputs. In other words, the same sensory inputs could generate many different incompatible theories. Thus, meaning is underdetermined too. This, in turn, implies the indeterminacy of translation: one could have two incompatible translation manuals for a given language, both of which are compatible with the speech dispositions of a linguistic community. Because of holism and indeterminacy, the notion of *the* meaning of a sentence is mistaken.

Ontological Relativity

Every theory has an ontological commitment, a claim about what there is or what kinds of things exist. As a consequence of the indeterminacy of evidence and meaning, Quine argues that opposing ontological stances, such as phenomenalism and physicalism, can be underdetermined. He calls this view ontological relativity. What can be said to exist is always relative to a theory, and there can be competing alternative ontological theories, encased in conflicting conceptual schemes, which are observational underdetermined.

Extensionality

According to Quine, the language in which scientific theories are constructed should be purely extensional. The structure of this language is defined solely in terms of the quantifiers and truth functions basic to Frege's logic. This is called the thesis of extensionality. An extensional sentence permits substitution of terms with identical reference. Because he endorses the thesis of extensionality, Quine tries to explain stimulus meaning in strictly behaviorist terms, as mentioned above. The thesis also commits Quine to the program of showing how intensional (or nonextensional) phrases can be eliminated from language. This is called the regimentation of language into the canonical idiom. According to Quine, this program has three advantages. First, the theory of language itself will appeal purely to clear extensional notions, such as 'reference' and 'truth conditions,' and not to unclear intensional notions, such as 'meaning,' 'analytic,' and 'sense.' This point feeds back into the claim that meaning is indeterminate. Second, the corresponding ontology will not require so-called intensional entities, such as propositions, meanings, concepts, and propositional attitudes, such as beliefs and desires. To support this point, Quine argues that such proposed 'intensional entities' do not have acceptable principles of identity or individuation. They cannot be identified and individuated. This point also shows why Quine is opposed to traditional empiricism, which is idea based. As traditionally conceived, ideas are intensional items. Third, in this way, Quine argues for the unity of science, the claim that the psychological and social sciences are unified with the physical sciences.

TWO DOGMAS OF EMPIRICISM

In 'Two Dogmas of Empiricism' (1951), Quine argues that traditional Empiricism, mostly recently exemplified by logical positivism, is based on two dogmas, which have the same root: the failure to recognize the holism of meaning.

The first dogma of Empiricism is the analytic-synthetic distinction. After reviewing various ways to make this distinction, Quine claims that 'a boundary between analytic and synthetic statements simply has not been drawn.' That such a distinction can be made is the first dogma of Empiricism. Quine replaces it with the idea that beliefs can be more or less open to revision. What we call analytic truths are simply those beliefs that we are least prone to revise in the face of evidence. Nevertheless, given sufficient relevant evidence, any belief can be revised. This is a form of Empiricism that is even more radical than Hume's.

At root, Quine is against the analytic-synthetic distinction because the relevant notions of synonymy and meaning cannot be defined clearly, or rather extensionally. 'Analyticity' fails to reach the standards of clarity required by extensionality. Any attempt to draw the distinction requires the intensional concepts of synonymy and meaning, and remains within the circle of intensional concepts.

The second dogma of Empiricism is a form of reductionism. According to the empiricist version of reductionism, every meaningful statement can be translated into a statement about immediate experience. Quine claims that such a reduction is impossible because single statements do not have a unique set of confirming and disconfirming experiences. Only theories as a whole can be confirmed or falsified with observations, and even if there is an observation that apparently disconfirms a theory, adjustments can be made to the theory to preserve it. According to Quine, the two dogmas amount to the same thing: the holism of meaning. Because of this holism, the analytic-synthetic distinction and the Empiricist reduction are impossible.

Modern empiricism has been conditioned in large part by two dogmas. One is a belief in some fundamental cleavage between truths which are *analytic*, or grounded in meanings independently of matters of fact, and truths which are *synthetic*, or grounded in fact. The other dogma is *reductionism*: the belief that each meaningful statement is equivalent to some logical construct upon terms which refer to immediate experience. Both dogmas, I shall argue, are ill-founded. One effect of abandoning them is, as we shall see, a blurring of the supposed boundary between speculative metaphysics and natural science. Another effect is a shift toward pragmatism.

1. BACKGROUND FOR ANALYTICITY

Kant's cleavage between analytic and synthetic truths was foreshadowed in Hume's distinction between relations of ideas and matters of fact, and in Leibniz's distinction between truths of reason and truths of fact. Leibniz spoke of the truths of reason as true in all possible worlds. Picturesqueness aside, this is to say that the truths of reason are those which could not possibly be false. In the same vein we hear analytic statements defined as statements whose denials are self-contradictory. But this definition has small explanatory value; for the notion of self-contradictoriness, in the quite broad sense needed for this definition of analyticity, stands in exactly the same need of clarification as does the notion of analyticity itself. The two notions are the two sides of a single dubious coin.

Kant conceived of an analytic statement as one that attributes to its subject no more than is already conceptually contained in the subject. This formulation has two shortcomings: it limits itself to statements of subject-predicate form, and it appeals to a notion of containment which is left at a metaphorical level. But Kant's intent, evident more from the use he makes of the notion of analyticity than from his definition of it, can be restated thus: a statement is analytic when it is true by virtue of meanings and independently of fact. Pursuing this line, let us examine the concept of *meaning* which is presupposed.

Meaning, let us remember, is not to be identified with naming. Frege's example of 'Evening Star' and 'Morning Star', and Russell's of 'Scott' and 'the author of *Waverley*', illustrate that terms can name the same thing but differ in meaning. The distinction between meaning and naming is no less important at the level of abstract terms. The terms '9' and 'the number of the planets' name one and the same abstract entity but presumably must be regarded as unlike in meaning; for astronomical observation was needed, and not mere reflection on meanings, to determine the sameness of the entity in question.

The above examples consist of singular terms, concrete and abstract. With general terms, or predicates, the situation is somewhat different but parallel. Whereas a singular term purports to name an entity, abstract or concrete, a general term does not; but a general term is *true of* an entity, or of each of many, or of none. The class of all entities of which a general term is true is called the *extension* of the term. Now paralleling the contrast between the meaning of a singular term and the entity named, we must distinguish equally between the meaning of a general term and its extension. The general terms 'creature with a heart' and 'creature with kidneys', for example, are perhaps alike in extension but unlike in meaning.

Confusion of meaning with extension, in the case of general terms, is less common than confusion of meaning with naming in the case of singular terms. It is indeed a commonplace in philosophy to oppose intension (or meaning) to extension, or, in a variant vocabulary, connotation to denotation.

The Aristotelian notion of essence was the forerunner, no doubt, of the modern notion of intension or meaning. For Aristotle it was essential in men to be rational, accidental to be two-legged. But there is an important difference between this attitude and the doctrine of meaning. From the latter point of view it may indeed be conceded (if only for the sake of argument) that rationality is involved in the meaning of the word 'man' while two-leggedness is not; but two-leggedness may at the same time be viewed as involved in the meaning of 'biped' while rationality is not. Thus from the point of view of the doctrine of meaning it makes no sense to say of the actual individual, who is at once a man and a biped, that his rationality is essential and his two-leggedness accidental or vice versa. Things had essences, for Aristotle, but only linguistic forms have meanings. Meaning is what essence becomes when it is divorced from the object of reference and wedded to the word.

For the theory of meaning a conspicuous question is the nature of its objects: what sort of things are meanings? A felt need for meant entities may derive from an earlier failure to appreciate that meaning and reference are distinct. Once the theory of meaning is sharply separated from the theory of reference, it is a short step to recognizing as the primary business of the theory of meaning simply the synonymy of linguistic forms and the analyticity of statements; meanings themselves, as obscure intermediary entities, may well be abandoned.

The problem of analyticity then confronts us anew. Statements which are analytic by general philosophical acclaim are not, indeed, far to seek. They fall into two classes. Those of the first class, which may be called *logically true*, are typified by:

(1) No unmarried man is married.

The relevant feature of this example is that it not merely is true as it stands, but remains true under any and all reinterpretations of 'man' and 'married'. If we suppose a prior inventory of *logical* particles, comprising 'no', 'un-', 'not', 'if', 'then', 'and', etc., then in general a logical truth is a statement which is true and remains true under all reinterpretations of its components other than the logical particles.

But there is also a second class of analytic statements, typified by:

(2) No bachelor is married.

The characteristic of such a statement is that it can be turned into a logical truth by putting synonyms for synonyms; thus (2) can be turned into (1) by putting 'unmarried man' for its synonym 'bachelor'. We still lack a proper characterization of this second class of analytic statements, and therewith of analyticity generally, inasmuch as we have had in the above description to lean on a notion of "synonymy" which is no less in need of clarification than analyticity itself.

In recent years Carnap has tended to explain analyticity by appeal to what he calls state-descriptions. A state-description is any exhaustive assignment of truth values to the atomic, or noncompound, statements of the language. All other statements of the language are, Carnap assumes, built up of their component clauses by means of the familiar logical devices, in such a way that the truth value of any complex statement is fixed for each state-description by specifiable logical laws. A statement is then explained as analytic when it comes out true under every state description. This account is an adaptation of Leibniz's "true in all possible worlds." But note that this version of analyticity serves its purpose only if the atomic statements of the language are, unlike 'John is a bachelor' and 'John is married', mutually independent. Otherwise there would be a state-description which assigned truth to 'John is a bachelor' and to 'John is married', and consequently 'No bachelors are married' would turn out synthetic rather than analytic under the proposed criterion. Thus the criterion of analyticity in terms of state-descriptions serves only for languages devoid of extralogical synonym-pairs, such as 'bachelor' and 'unmarried man'—synonym-pairs of the type which give rise to the "second class" of analytic statements. The criterion in terms of state-descriptions is a reconstruction at best of logical truth, not of analyticity.

I do not mean to suggest that Carnap is under any illusions on this point. His simplified model language with its state-descriptions is aimed primarily not at the general problem of analyticity but at another purpose, the clarification of probability and induction. Our problem, however, is analyticity; and here the major difficulty lies not in the first class of analytic statements, the logical truths, but rather in the second class, which depends on the notion of synonymy.

2. DEFINITION

There are those who find it soothing to say that the analytic statements of the second class reduce to those of the first class, the logical truths, by *definition;* 'bachelor', for example, is *defined* as 'unmarried man'. But how de we find that 'bachelor' is defined as 'unmarried man'? Who defined it thus, and when? Are we to appeal to the nearest dictionary, and accept the lexicographer's formulation as law? Clearly this would be to put the cart before the horse. The lexicographer is an empirical scientist, whose business is the recording of antecedent facts; and if he glosses 'bachelor' as 'unmarried man' it is because of his belief that there is a relation of synonymy between those forms, implicit in general or preferred usage prior to his own work. The notion of synonymy presupposed here has still to be clarified, presumably in terms relating to linguistic behavior. Certainly the "definition" which is the lexicographer's report of an observed synonymy cannot be taken as the ground of the synonymy.

Definition is not, indeed, an activity exclusively of philologists. Philosophers and scientists frequently have occasion to "define" a recondite term by paraphrasing it into terms of a more familiar vocabulary. But ordinarily such a definition, like the philologist's, is pure lexicography, affirming a relation of synonymy antecedent to the exposition in hand.

Just what it means to affirm synonymy, just what the interconnections may be which are necessary and sufficient in order that two linguistic forms be properly describable as synonymous, is far from clear; but, whatever these interconnections may be, ordinarily they are grounded in usage. Definitions reporting selected instances of synonymy come then as reports upon usage.

There is also, however, a variant type of definitional activity which does not limit itself to the reporting of preëxisting synonymies. I have in mind what Carnap calls *explication*—an activity to which philosophers are given, and scientists also in their more philosophical moments. In explication the purpose is not merely to paraphrase the definiendum into an outright synonym, but actually to improve upon the definiendum by refining or supplementing its meaning. But even explication, though not merely reporting a preëxisting synonymy between definiendum and definiens, does rest nevertheless on *other* preexisting synonymies. The matter may be viewed as follows. Any word worth explicating has some contexts which, as wholes, are clear and precise enough to be useful; and the purpose of explication is to preserve the usage of these favored contexts while sharpening the usage of other contexts. In order that a given definition be suitable for purposes of explication, therefore, what is required is not that the definiendum in its antecedent usage be synonymous with the definiens, but just that each of these favored contexts of the definiendum, taken as a whole in its antecedent usage, be synonymous with the corresponding context of the definiens.

Two alternative definientia may be equally appropriate for the purposes of a given task of explication and yet not be synonymous with each other; for they may serve interchangeably within the favored contexts but diverge elsewhere. By cleaving to one of these definientia rather than the other, a definition of explicative kind generates, by fiat, a relation of synonymy between definiendum and definiens which did not hold before. But such a definition still owes its explicative function, as seen, to preexisting synonymies.

There does, however, remain still an extreme sort of definition which does not hark back to prior synonymies at all: namely, the explicitly conventional introduction of novel notations for purposes of sheer abbreviation. Here the definiendum becomes synonymous with the definiens simply because it has been created expressly for the purpose of being synonymous with the definiens. Here we have a really transparent case of synonymy created by definition; would that all species of synonymy were as intelligible. For the rest, definition rests on synonymy rather than explaining it.

The word 'definition' has come to have a dangerously reassuring sound, owing no doubt to its frequent occurrence in logical and mathematical writings. We shall do well to digress now into a brief appraisal of the role of definition in formal work.

In logical and mathematical systems either of two mutually antagonistic types of economy may be striven for, and each has its peculiar practical utility. On the one hand we may seek economy of practical expression—ease and brevity in the statement of multifarious relations. This sort of economy calls usually for distinctive concise notations for a wealth of concepts. Second, however, and oppositely, we may seek economy in grammar and vocabulary; we may try to find a minimum of basic concepts such that, once a distinctive notation has been appropriated to each of them, it becomes possible to express any desired further concept by mere combination and iteration of our basic notations. This second sort of economy is impractical in one way, since a poverty in basic idioms tends to a necessary lengthening of discourse. But it is practical in another way: it greatly simplifies theoretical discourse *about* the language, through minimizing the terms and the forms of construction wherein the language consists.

Both sorts of economy, though prima facie incompatible, are valuable in their separate ways. The custom has consequently arisen of combining both sorts of economy by forging in effect two languages, the one a part of the other. The inclusive language, though redundant in grammar and vocabulary, is economical in message lengths, while the part, called primitive notation, is economical in grammar and vocabulary. Whole and part are correlated by rules of translation whereby each idiom not in primitive notation is equated to some complex built up of primitive notation. These rules of translation are the so-called *definitions* which appear in formalized systems. They are best viewed not as adjuncts to one language but as correlations between two languages, the one a part of the other.

But these correlations are not arbitrary. They are supposed to show how the primitive notations can accomplish all purposes, save brevity and convenience, of the redundant language. Hence the definiendum and its definiens may be expected, in each case, to be related in one or another of the three ways lately noted. The definiens may be a faithful paraphrase of the definiendum into the narrower notation, preserving a direct synonymy as of antecedent usage; or the definiens may, in the spirit of explication, improve upon the antecedent usage of the definiendum; or finally, the definiendum may be a newly created notation, newly endowed with meaning here and now.

In formal and informal work alike, thus, we find that definition—except in the extreme case of the explicitly conventional introduction of new notations—hinges on prior relations of synonymy. Recognizing then that the notion of definition does not hold the key to synonymy and analyticity, let us look further into synonymy and say no more of definition.

3. INTERCHANGEABILITY

A natural suggestion, deserving close examination, is that the synonymy of two linguistic forms consists simply in their interchangeability in all contexts without change of truth value—interchangeability, in Leibniz's phrase, *salva veritate*. Note that synonyms so conceived need not even be free from vagueness, as long as the vaguenesses match.

But it is not quite true that the synonyms 'bachelor' and 'unmarried man' are everywhere interchangeable *salva veritate*. Truths which become false under substitution of 'unmarried man' for 'bachelor' are easily constructed with the help of 'bachelor of arts' or 'bachelor's buttons'; also with the help of quotation, thus:

'Bachelor' has less than ten letters.

Such counterinstances can, however, perhaps be set aside by treating the phrases 'bachelor of arts' and 'bachelor's buttons' and the quotation "bachelor" each as a single indivisible word and then stipulating that the interchangeability *salva veritate* which is to be the touchstone of synonymy is not supposed to apply to fragmentary occurrences inside of a word. This account of synonymy, supposing it acceptable on other counts, has indeed the drawback of appealing to a prior conception of "word" which can be counted on to present difficulties of formulation in its turn. Nevertheless some progress might be claimed in having reduced the problem of synonymy to a problem of word-hood. Let us pursue this line a bit, taking "word" for granted.

The question remains whether interchangeability *salva veritate* (apart from occurrences within words) is a strong enough condition for synonymy, or whether, on the contrary, some heteronymous expressions might be thus interchangeable. Now let us be clear that we are not concerned here with synonymy in the sense of complete identity in psychological associations or poetic quality; indeed no two expressions are synonymous in such a sense. We are concerned only with what may be called *cognitive* synonymy. Just what this is cannot be said without successfully finishing the present study; but we know something about it from the need which arose for it in connection with analyticity in §1. The sort of synonymy needed there was merely such that any analytic statement could be turned into a logical truth by putting synonyms for synonyms. Turning the tables and assuming analyticity, indeed, we could explain cognitive synonymy of terms as follows (keeping to the familiar example): to say that 'bachelor' and 'unmarried man' are cognitively synonymous is to say no more nor less than that the statement:

(3) All and only bachelors are unmarried men

is analytic.

What we need is an account of cognitive synonymy not presupposing analyticity—if we are to explain analyticity conversely with help of cognitive synonymy as undertaken in §1. And indeed such an independent account of cognitive synonymy is at present up for consideration, namely, interchangeability *salva veritate* everywhere except within words. The question before us, to resume the thread at last, is whether such interchangeability is a sufficient condition for cognitive synonymy. We can quickly assure ourselves that it is, by examples of the following sort. The statement:

(4) Necessarily all and only bachelors are bachelors

is evidently true, even supposing 'necessarily' so narrowly construed as to be truly applicable only to analytic statements. Then, if 'bachelor' and 'unmarried man' are interchangeable *salva veritate*, the result:

(5) Necessarily all and only bachelors are unmarried men

of putting 'unmarried man' for an occurrence of 'bachelor' in (4) must, like (4), be true. But to say that (5) is true is to say that (3) is analytic, and hence that 'bachelor' and 'unmarried man' are cognitively synonymous.

Let us see what there is about the above argument that gives it its air of hocus-pocus. The condition of interchangeability *salva veritate* varies in its force with variations in the richness of the language at hand. The above argument supposes we are working with a language rich enough to contain the adverb 'necessarily', this adverb being so construed as to yield truth when and only when applied to an analytic statement. But can we condone a language which contains such an adverb? Does the adverb really make sense? To suppose that it does is to suppose that we have already made satisfactory sense of 'analytic'. Then what are we so hard at work on right now?

Our argument is not flatly circular, but something like it. It has the form, figuratively speaking, of a closed curve in space.

Interchangeability *salva veritate* is meaningless until relativized to a language whose extent is specified in relevant respects. Suppose now we consider a language containing just the following materials. There is an indefinitely large stock of one-place predicates (for example, 'F' where 'Fx' means that x is a man) and many-place predicates (for example, 'G' where 'Gxy' means that x loves y), mostly having to do with extralogical subject matter. The rest of the language is logical. The atomic sentences consist each of a predicate followed by one or more variables 'x', 'y', etc.; and the complex sentences are built up of the atomic ones by truth functions ('not', 'and', 'or', etc.) and quantification. In effect such a language enjoys the benefits also of descriptions and indeed singular terms generally, these being contextually definable in known ways. Even abstract singular terms naming classes, classes of classes, etc., are contextually definable in case the assumed stock of predicates includes the two-place predicate of class membership. Such a language can be adequate to classical mathematics and indeed to scientific discourse generally, except in so far as the latter involves debatable devices such as contrary-to-fact conditionals or modal adverbs like 'necessarily'. Now a language of this type is extensional, in this sense: any two predicates which

agree extensionally (that is, are true of the same objects) are interchangeable *salva veritate*.

In an extensional language, therefore, interchangeability *salva veritate* is no assurance of cognitive synonymy of the desired type. That 'bachelor' and 'unmarried man' are interchangeable *salva veritate* in an extensional language assures us of no more than that (3) is true. There is no assurance here that the extensional agreement of 'bachelor' and 'unmarried man' rests on meaning rather than merely on accidental matters of fact, as does the extensional agreement of 'creature with a heart' and 'creature with kidneys'.

For most purposes extensional agreement is the nearest approximation to synonymy we need care about. But the fact remains that extensional agreement falls far short of cognitive synonymy of the type required for explaining analyticity in the manner of §1. The type of cognitive synonymy required there is such as to equate the synonymy of 'bachelor' and 'unmarried man' with the analyticity of (3), not merely with the truth of (3).

So we must recognize that interchangeability *salva veritate*, if construed in relation to an extensional language, is not a sufficient condition of cognitive synonymy in the sense needed for deriving analyticity in the manner of §1. If a language contains an intensional adverb 'necessarily' in the sense lately noted, or other particles to the same effect, then interchangeability *salva veritate* in such a language does afford a sufficient condition of cognitive synonymy; but such a language is intelligible only in so far as the notion of analyticity is already understood in advance.

The effort to explain cognitive synonymy first, for the sake of deriving analyticity from it afterward as in §1, is perhaps the wrong approach. Instead we might try explaining analyticity somehow without appeal to cognitive synonymy. Afterward we could doubtless derive cognitive synonymy from analyticity satisfactorily enough if desired. We have seen that cognitive synonymy of 'bachelor' and 'unmarried man' can be explained as analyticity of (3). The same explanation works for any pair of one-place predicates, of course, and it can be extended in obvious fashion to many-place predicates. Other syntactical categories can also be accommodated in fairly parallel fashion. Singular terms may be said to be cognitively synonymous when the statement of identity formed by putting '=' between them is analytic. Statements may be said simply to be cognitively synonymous when their biconditional (the result of joining them by 'if and only if') is analytic. If we care to lump all categories into a single formulation, at the expense of assuming again the notion of "word" which was appealed to early in this section, we can describe any two linguistic forms as cognitively synonymous when the two forms are interchangeable (apart from occurrences within "words") *salva* (no longer *veritate* but) *analyticitate*. Certain technical questions arise, indeed, over cases of ambiguity or homonymy; let us not pause for them, however, for we are already digressing. Let us rather turn our backs on the problem of synonymy and address ourselves anew to that of analyticity.

4. SEMANTICAL RULES

Analyticity at first seemed most naturally definable by appeal to a realm of meanings. On refinement, the appeal to meanings gave way to an appeal to synonymy or definition. But definition turned out to be a will-o'-the-wisp, and synonymy turned out to be best understood only by dint of a prior appeal to analyticity itself. So we are back at the problem of analyticity.

I do not know whether the statement 'Everything green is extended' is analytic. Now does my indecision over this example really betray an incomplete understanding, an incomplete grasp of the "meanings", of 'green' and 'extended'? I think not. The trouble is not with 'green' or 'extended', but with 'analytic'.

It is often hinted that the difficulty in separating analytic statements from synthetic ones in ordinary language is due to the vagueness of ordinary language and that the distinction is clear when we have a precise artificial language with explicit "semantical rules." This, however, as I shall now attempt to show, is a confusion.

The notion of analyticity about which we are worrying is a purported relation between statements and languages: a statement S is said to be *analytic for* a language L, and the problem is to make sense of this relation generally, that is, for variable 'S' and 'L'.

The gravity of this problem is not perceptibly less for artificial languages than for natural ones. The problem of making sense of the idiom 'S is analytic for L', with variable 'S' and 'L', retains its stubbornness even if we limit the range of the variable 'L' to artificial languages. Let me now try to make this point evident.

For artificial languages and semantical rules we look naturally to the writings of Carnap. His semantical rules take various forms, and to make my point I shall have to distinguish certain of the forms. Let us suppose, to begin with, an artificial language L_0 whose semantical rules have the form explicitly of a specification, by recursion or otherwise, of all the analytic statements of L_0. The rules tell us that such and such statements, and only those, are the analytic statements of L_0. Now here the difficulty is simply that the rules contain the word 'analytic', which we do not understand! We understand what expressions the rules attribute analyticity to, but we do not understand what the rules attribute to those expressions. In short, before we can understand a rule which begins 'A statement S is analytic for language L_0 if and only if . . .', we must understand the general relative term 'analytic for'; we must understand 'S is analytic for L' where 'S' and 'L' are variables.

Alternatively we may, indeed, view the so-called rule as a conventional definition of a new simple symbol 'analytic-for-L_0', which might better be written untendentiously as 'K' so as not to seem to throw light on the interesting word 'analytic'. Obviously any number of classes K, M, N, etc. of statements of L_0 can be specified for various purposes or for no purpose; what does it mean to say that K, as against M, N, etc., is the class of the "analytic" statements of L_0?

By saying what statements are analytic for L_0 we explain 'analytic-for-L_0' but not 'analytic', not 'analytic for'. We do not begin to explain the idiom 'S is analytic for L' with variable 'S' and 'L', even if we are content to limit the range of 'L' to the realm of artificial languages.

Actually we do know enough about the intended significance of 'analytic' to know that analytic statements are supposed to be true. Let us then turn to a second form of semantical rule, which says not that such and such statements are analytic but simply that such and such statements are included among the truths. Such a rule is not subject to the criticism of containing the un-understood word 'analytic'; and we may grant for the sake of argument that there is no difficulty over the broader term 'true'. A semantical rule of this second type, a rule of truth, is not supposed to specify all the truths of the language; it merely stipulates, recursively or otherwise, a certain multitude of statements which, along with others unspecified, are to count as true. Such a rule may be conceded to be quite clear. Derivatively, afterward, analyticity can be demarcated thus: a statement is analytic if it is (not merely true but) true according to the semantical rule.

Still there is really no progress. Instead of appealing to an unexplained word 'analytic', we are now appealing to an unexplained phrase 'semantical rule'. Not every true statement which says that the statements of some class are true can count as a semantical rule—otherwise *all* truths would be "analytic" in the sense of being true according to semantical rules. Semantical rules are distinguishable, apparently, only by the fact of appearing on a page under the heading 'Semantical Rules'; and this heading is itself then meaningless.

We can say indeed that a statement is *analytic-for-L_0* if and only if it is true according to such and such specifically appended "semantical rules," but then we find ourselves back at essentially the same case which was originally discussed: 'S is analytic-for-L_0 if and only if. . . .' Once we seek to explain 'S is analytic for L' generally for variable 'L' (even allowing limitation of 'L' to artificial languages), the explanation 'true according to the semantical rules of L' is unavailing; for the relative term 'semantical rule of' is as much in need of clarification, at least, as 'analytic for'.

It may be instructive to compare the notion of semantical rule with that of postulate. Relative to a given set of postulates, it is easy to say what a postulate is: it is a member of the set. Relative to a given set of semantical rules, it is equally easy to say what a semantical rule is. But given simply a notation, mathematical or otherwise, and indeed as thoroughly understood a notation as you please in point of the translations or truth conditions of its statements, who can say which of its true statements rank as postulates? Obviously the question is meaningless—as meaningless as asking which points in Ohio are start-

ing points. Any finite (or effectively specifiable infinite) selection of statements (preferably true ones, perhaps) is as much *a* set of postulates as any other. The word 'postulate' is significant only relative to an act of inquiry; we apply the word to a set of statements just in so far as we happen, for the year or the moment, to be thinking of those statements in relation to the statements which can be reached from them by some set of transformations to which we have seen fit to direct our attention. Now the notion of semantical rule is as sensible and meaningful as that of postulate, if conceived in a similarly relative spirit—relative, this time, to one or another particular enterprise of schooling unconversant persons in sufficient conditions for truth of statements of some natural or artificial language L. But from this point of view no one signalization of a subclass of the truths of L is intrinsically more a semantical rule than another; and, if 'analytic' means 'true by semantical rules', no one truth of L is analytic to the exclusion of another.

It might conceivably be protested that an artificial language L (unlike a natural one) is a language in the ordinary sense *plus* a set of explicit semantical rules—the whole constituting, let us say, an ordered pair; and that the semantical rules of L then are specifiable simply as the second component of the pair L. But, by the same token and more simply, we might construe an artificial language L outright as an ordered pair whose second component is the class of its analytic statements; and then the analytic statements of L become specifiable simply as the statements in the second component of L. Or better still, we might just stop tugging at our bootstraps altogether.

Not all the explanations of analyticity known to Carnap and his readers have been covered explicitly in the above considerations, but the extension to other forms is not hard to see. Just one additional factor should be mentioned which sometimes enters: sometimes the semantical rules are in effect rules of translation into ordinary language, in which case the analytic statements of the artificial language are in effect recognized as such from the analyticity of their specified translations in ordinary language. Here certainly there can be no thought of an illumination of the problem of analyticity from the side of the artificial language.

From the point of view of the problem of analyticity the notion of an artificial language with semantical rules is a *feu follet par excellence*. Semantical rules determining the analytic statements of an artificial language are of interest only in so far as we already understand the notion of analyticity; they are of no help in gaining this understanding.

Appeal to hypothetical languages of an artificially simple kind could conceivably be useful in clarifying analyticity, if the mental or behavioral or cultural factors relevant to analyticity—whatever they may be—were somehow sketched into the simplified model. But a model which takes analyticity merely as an irreducible character is unlikely to throw light on the problem of explicating analyticity.

It is obvious that truth in general depends on both language and extralinguistic fact. The statement 'Brutus killed Caesar' would be false if the world had been different in certain ways, but it would also be false if the word 'killed' happened rather to have the sense of 'begat'. Thus one is tempted to suppose in general that the truth of a statement is somehow analyzable into a linguistic component and a factual component. Given this supposition, it next seems reasonable that in some statements the factual component should be null; and these are the analytic statements. But, for all it's a priori reasonableness, a boundary between analytic and synthetic statements simply has not been drawn. That there is such a distinction to be drawn at all is an unempirical dogma of empiricists, a metaphysical article of faith.

5. THE VERIFICATION THEORY AND REDUCTIONISM

In the course of these somber reflections we have taken a dim view first of the notion of meaning, then of the notion of cognitive synonymy, and finally of the notion of analyticity. But what, it may be asked, of the verification theory of meaning? This phrase has established itself so firmly as a catchword of empiricism that we should be very unscientific indeed not to look beneath it for a possible key to the problem of meaning and the associated problems.

The verification theory of meaning, which has been conspicuous in the literature from Peirce onward, is that the meaning of a statement is the method of empirically confirming or infirming it. An analytic statement is that limiting case which is confirmed no matter what.

As urged in §1, we can as well pass over the question of meanings as entities and move straight to sameness of meaning, or synonymy. Then what the verification theory says is that statements are synonymous if and only if they are alike in point of method of empirical confirmation or infirmation.

This is an account of cognitive synonymy not of linguistic forms generally, but of statements. However, from the concept of synonymy of statements we could derive the concept of synonymy for other linguistic forms, by considerations somewhat similar to those at the end of §3. Assuming the notion of "word," indeed, we could explain any two forms as synonymous when the putting of the one form for an occurrence of the other in any statement (apart from occurrences within "words") yields a synonymous statement. Finally, given the concept of synonymy thus for linguistic forms generally, we could define analyticity in terms of synonymy and logical truth as in §1. For that matter, we could define analyticity more simply in terms of just synonymy of statements together with logical truth; it is not necessary to appeal to synonymy of linguistic forms other than statements. For a statement may be described as analytic simply when it is synonymous with a logically true statement.

So, if the verification theory can be accepted as an adequate account of statement synonymy, the notion of analyticity is saved after all. However, let us reflect. Statement synonymy is said to be likeness of method of empirical confirmation or infirmation. Just what are these methods which are to be compared for likeness? What, in other words, is the nature of the relation between a statement and the experiences which contribute to or detract from its confirmation?

The most naïve view of the relation is that it is one of direct report. This is *radical reductionism*. Every meaningful statement is held to be translatable into a statement (true or false) about immediate experience. Radical reductionism, in one form or another, well antedates the verification theory of meaning explicitly so called. Thus Locke and Hume held that every idea must either originate directly in sense experience or else be compounded of ideas thus originating; and taking a hint from Tooke we might rephrase this doctrine in semantical jargon by saying that a term, to be significant at all, must be either a name of a sense datum or a compound of such names or an abbreviation of such a compound. So stated, the doctrine remains ambiguous as between sense data as sensory events and sense data as sensory qualities; and it remains vague as to the admissible ways of compounding. Moreover, the doctrine is unnecessarily and intolerably restrictive in the term-by-term critique which it imposes. More reasonably, and without yet exceeding the limits of what I have called radical reductionism, we may take full statements as our significant units—thus demanding that our statements as wholes be translatable into sense-datum language, but not that they be translatable term by term.

This emendation would unquestionably have been welcome to Locke and Hume and Tooke, but historically it had to await an important reorientation in semantics—the reorientation whereby the primary vehicle of meaning came to be seen no longer in the term but in the statement. This reorientation, explicit in Frege ([1], §60), underlies Russell's concept of incomplete symbols defined in use; also it is implicit in the verification theory of meaning, since the objects of verification are statements.

Radical reductionism, conceived now with statements as units, set itself the task of specifying a sense-datum language and showing how to translate the rest of significant discourse, statement by statement, into it. Carnap embarked on this project in the *Aufbau*.

The language which Carnap adopted as his starting point was not a sense-datum language in the narrowest conceivable sense, for it included also the notations of logic, up through higher set theory. In effect it included the whole language of pure mathematics. The ontology implicit in it (that is, the range of values of its variables) embraced not only sensory events but classes, classes of classes, and so on. Empiricists there are who would boggle at such prodigality. Carnap's starting point is very parsimonious, however, in its extralogical or sensory part. In a series of constructions in which he exploits the resources of modern logic with much ingenuity, Carnap succeeds in defining a wide array of important additional sensory concepts which, but for his constructions, one would not have dreamed were definable on so slender a basis. He was the first empiricist who, not content with asserting the reducibility of science to terms of immediate experience, took serious steps toward carrying out the reduction.

If Carnap's starting point is satisfactory, still his constructions were, as he himself stressed, only a fragment of the full program. The construction of even the simplest statements about the physical world was left in a sketchy state. Carnap's suggestions on this subject were, despite their sketchiness, very suggestive. He explained spatio-temporal point-instants as quadruples of real numbers and envisaged assignment of sense qualities to point-instants according to certain canons. Roughly summarized, the plan was that qualities should be assigned to point-instants in such a way as to achieve the laziest world compatible with our experience. The principle of least action was to be our guide in constructing a world from experience.

Carnap did not seem to recognize, however, that his treatment of physical objects fell short of reduction not merely through sketchiness, but in principle. Statements of the form 'Quality q is at point-instant $x;y;z;t$' were, according to his canons, to be apportioned truth values in such a way as to maximize and minimize certain over-all features, and with growth of experience the truth values were to be progressively revised in the same spirit. I think this is a good schematization (deliberately oversimplified, to be sure) of what science really does; but it provides no indication, not even the sketchiest, of how a statement of the form 'Quality q is at $x;y;z;t$' could ever be translated into Carnap's initial language of sense data and logic. The connective 'is at' remains an added undefined connective; the canons counsel us in its use but not in its elimination.

Carnap seems to have appreciated this point afterward; for in his later writings he abandoned all notion of the translatability of statements about the physical world into statements about immediate experience. Reductionism in its radical form has long since ceased to figure in Carnap's philosophy.

But the dogma of reductionism has, in a subtler and more tenuous form, continued to influence the thought of empiricists. The notion lingers that to each statement, or each synthetic statement, there is associated a unique range of possible sensory events such that the occurrence of any of them would add to the likelihood of truth of the statement, and that there is associated also another unique range of possible sensory events whose occurrence would detract from that likelihood. This notion is of course implicit in the verification theory of meaning.

The dogma of reductionism survives in the supposition that each statement, taken in isolation from its fellows, can admit of confirmation or infirmation at all. My countersuggestion, issuing essentially from Carnap's doctrine of the physical world in the *Aufbau,* is that our statements about the external world face the tribunal of sense experience not individually but only as a corporate body.

The dogma of reductionism, even in its attenuated form, is intimately connected with the other dogma—that there is a cleavage between the analytic and the synthetic. We have found ourselves led, indeed, from the latter problem to the former through the verification theory of meaning. More directly, the one dogma clearly supports the other in this way: as long as it is taken to be significant in general to speak of the confirmation and infirmation of a statement, it seems significant to speak also of a limiting kind of statement which is vacuously confirmed, *ipso facto,* come what may; and such a statement is analytic.

The two dogmas are, indeed, at root identical. We lately reflected that in general the truth of statements does obviously depend both upon language and upon extralinguistic fact; and we noted that this obvious circumstance carries in its train, not logically but all too naturally, a feeling that the truth of a statement is somehow analyzable into a linguistic component and a factual component. The factual component must, if we are empiricists, boil down to a range of confirmatory experiences. In the extreme case where the linguistic component is all that matters, a true statement is analytic. But I hope we are now impressed with how stubbornly the distinction between analytic and synthetic has resisted any straightforward drawing. I am impressed also, apart from prefabricated examples of black and white balls in an urn, with how baffling the problem has always been of arriving at any explicit theory of the empirical confirmation of a synthetic statement. My present suggestion is that it is nonsense, and the root of much nonsense, to speak of a linguistic component and a factual component in the truth of any individual statement. Taken collectively, science has its double

dependence upon language and experience; but this duality is not significantly traceable into the statements of science taken one by one.

The idea of defining a symbol in use was, as remarked, an advance over the impossible term-by-term empiricism of Locke and Hume. The statement, rather than the term, came with Frege to be recognized as the unit accountable to an empiricist critique. But what I am now urging is that even in taking the statement as unit we have drawn our grid too finely. The unit of empirical significance is the whole of science.

6. EMPIRICISM WITHOUT THE DOGMAS

The totality of our so-called knowledge or beliefs, from the most casual matters of geography and history to the profoundest laws of atomic physics or even of pure mathematics and logic, is a man-made fabric which impinges on experience only along the edges. Or, to change the figure, total science is like a field of force whose boundary conditions are experience. A conflict with experience at the periphery occasions readjustments in the interior of the field. Truth values have to be redistributed over some of our statements. Reëvaluation of some statements entails reëvaluation of others, because of their logical interconnections—the logical laws being in turn simply certain further statements of the system, certain further elements of the field. Having reëvaluated one statement we must reëvaluate some others, which may be statements logically connected with the first or may be the statements of logical connections themselves. But the total field is so underdetermined by its boundary conditions, experience, that there is much latitude of choice as to what statements to reëvaluate in the light of any single contrary experience. No particular experiences are linked with any particular statements in the interior of the field, except indirectly through considerations of equilibrium affecting the field as a whole.

If this view is right, it is misleading to speak of the empirical content of an individual statement—especially if it is a statement at all remote from the experiential periphery of the field. Furthermore it becomes folly to seek a boundary between synthetic statements, which hold contingently on experience, and analytic statements, which hold come what may. Any statement can be held true come what may, if we make drastic enough adjustments elsewhere in the system. Even a statement very close to the periphery can be held true in the face of recalcitrant experience by pleading hallucination or by amending certain statements of the kind called logical laws. Conversely, by the same token, no statement is immune to revision. Revision even of the logical law of the excluded middle has been proposed as a means of simplifying quantum mechanics; and what difference is there in principle between such a shift and the shift whereby Kepler superseded Ptolemy, or Einstein Newton, or Darwin Aristotle?

For vividness I have been speaking in terms of varying distances from a sensory periphery. Let me try now to clarify this notion without metaphor. Certain statements, though *about* physical objects and not sense experience, seem peculiarly germane to sense experience—and in a selective way: some statements to some experiences, others to others. Such statements, especially germane to particular experiences, I picture as near the periphery. But in this relation of "germaneness" I envisage nothing more than a loose association reflecting the relative likelihood, in practice, of our choosing one statement rather than another for revision in the event of recalcitrant experience. For example, we can imagine recalcitrant experiences to which we would surely be inclined to accommodate our system by reëvaluating just the statement that there are brick houses on Elm Street, together with related statements on the same topic. We can imagine other recalcitrant experiences to which we would be inclined to accommodate our system by reëvaluating just the statement that there are no centaurs, along with kindred statements. A recalcitrant experience can, I have urged, be accommodated by any of various alternative reëvaluations in various alternative quarters of the total system, but, in the cases which we are now imagining, our natural tendency to disturb the total system as little as possible would lead us to focus our revisions upon these specific statements concerning brick houses or centaurs. These statements are felt, therefore, to have a sharper empirical reference than highly theoretical statements of physics or logic or ontology. The latter statements may be thought of as relatively centrally located within the total network, meaning merely that little preferential connection with any particular sense data obtrudes itself.

As an empiricist I continue to think of the conceptual scheme of science as a tool, ultimately, for predicting future experience in the light of past experience. Physical objects are conceptually imported into the situation as convenient intermediaries—not by definition in terms of experience, but simply as irreducible posits comparable, epistemologically, to the gods of Homer. For my part I do, qua lay physicist, believe in physical objects and not in Homer's gods; and I consider it a scientific error to believe otherwise. But in point of epistemological footing the physical objects and the gods differ only in degree and not in kind. Both sorts of entities enter our conception only as cultural posits. The myth of physical objects is epistemologically superior to most in that it has proved more efficacious than other myths as a device for working a manageable structure into the flux of experience.

Positing does not stop with macroscopic physical objects. Objects at the atomic level are posited to make the laws of macroscopic objects, and ultimately the laws of experience, simpler and more manageable; and we need not expect or demand full definition of atomic and subatomic entities in terms of macroscopic ones, any more than definition of macroscopic things in terms of sense data. Science is a continuation of common sense, and it continues the common-sense expedient of swelling ontology to simplify theory.

Physical objects, small and large, are not the only posits. Forces are another example; and indeed we are told nowadays that the boundary between energy and matter is obsolete. Moreover, the abstract entities which are the substance of mathematics—ultimately classes and classes of classes and so on up—are another posit in the same spirit. Epistemologically these are myths on the same footing with physical objects and gods, neither better nor worse except for differences in the degree to which they expedite our dealings with sense experiences.

The over-all algebra of rational and irrational numbers is underdetermined by the algebra of rational numbers, but is smoother and more convenient; and it includes the algebra of rational numbers as a jagged or gerrymandered part. Total science, mathematical and natural and human, is similarly but more extremely underdetermined by experience. The edge of the system must be kept squared with experience; the rest, with all its elaborate myths or fictions, has as its objective the simplicity of laws.

Ontological questions, under this view, are on a par with questions of natural science. Consider the question whether to countenance classes as entities. This, as I have argued elsewhere, is the question whether to quantify with respect to variables which take classes as values. Now Carnap [6] has maintained that this is a question not of matters of fact but of choosing a convenient language form, a convenient conceptual scheme or framework for science. With this I agree, but only on the proviso that the same be conceded regarding scientific hypotheses generally. Carnap ([6], p. 32n) has recognized that he is able to preserve a double standard for ontological questions and scientific hypotheses only by assuming an absolute distinction between the analytic and the synthetic; and I need not say again that this is a distinction which I reject.

The issue over there being classes seems more a question of convenient conceptual scheme; the issue over there being centaurs, or brick houses on Elm Street seems more a question of fact. But I have been urging that this difference is only one of degree, and that it turns upon our vaguely pragmatic inclination to adjust one strand of the fabric of science rather than another in accommodating some particular recalcitrant experience. Conservatism figures in such choices, and so does the quest for simplicity.

Carnap, Lewis, and others take a pragmatic stand on the question of choosing between language forms, scientific frameworks; but their pragmatism leaves off at the imagined boundary between the analytic and the synthetic. In repudiating such a boundary I espouse a more thorough pragmatism. Each man is given a scientific heritage plus a continuing barrage of sensory stimulation; and the considerations which guide him in warping his scientific heritage to fit his continuing sensory promptings are, where rational, pragmatic.

STUDY QUESTIONS: QUINE, *TWO DOGMAS OF EMPIRICISM*

1. Does Quine argue for or against logical positivism?
2. Is he for or against the extensional view of language of the logical atomists?
3. Are theories overdetermined or underdetermined by sensory data? What does this mean? What is its significance?
4. What is an intensional relation? Does his theory accept or reject such relations?
5. What is the analytic-synthetic distinction? What does Quine think of it? Why?
6. What are the two dogmas of Empiricism?
7. Can any belief, according to Quine, be revised? Why? What is the significance of this?
8. Can synonymy be clearly defined? Can meaning? Why? What use does Quine make of this?
9. What does it mean to assert that a language is extensional?
10. How are Kant's, Hume's, and Leibniz's views of the difference between analytic and synthetic truths related?
11. What are the two shortcomings of Kant's view?
12. How does Quine use Frege's example of morning star and evening star?
13. Of what was the Aristotelian notion of essence the forerunner?
14. What is Carnap's notion of 'explication,' and how does Quine employ it?
15. What do the terms 'definiens' and 'definiendum' mean?
16. What is interchangeability *salva veritate*?
17. What does he mean by 'cognitive synonymy'?
18. What is the dogma of reductionism?

ON THE REASONS FOR INDETERMINACY OF TRANSLATION

In this short article, Quine discusses the real point of the 'gavagai' example from his 1960 book *Word and Object*, where he discusses the indeterminacy of meaning, one of the central claims of Quine's philosophy. 'Gavagai' is a word used by a tribe in the presence of rabbits. Echoing themes from the previous reading, 'Two Dogmas of Empiricism,' in this article Quine argues that the meaning and the translation of such a word are radically underdetermined. This does *not* mean that we could not know for certain how to translate this term. It is not a question of lack of knowledge. The point is rather that the meaning of the term itself is radically indeterminate. In the reading, Quine explains why this is so.

My *gavagai* example has figured too centrally in discussions of the indeterminacy of translation. Readers see the example as the ground of the doctrine, and hope by resolving the example to cast doubt on the doctrine. The real ground of the doctrine is very different, broader and deeper.

Let us put translation aside for a while and think about physical theory. Naturally it is underdetermined by past evidence; a future observation can conflict with it. Naturally it is underdetermined by past and future evidence combined, since some observable event that conflicts with it can happen to go unobserved. Moreover many people will agree, far beyond all this, that physical theory is underdetermined even by all *possible* observations. Not to make a mystery of this mode of possibility, what I mean is the following. Consider all the observation sentences of the language: all the occasion sentences that are suited for use in reporting observable events in the external world. Apply dates and positions to them in all combinations, without regard to whether observers were at the place and time. Some of these place-timed sentences will be true and the others false, by virtue simply of the observable though unobserved past and future events in the world. Now my point about physical theory is that physical theory is underdetermined even by all these truths. Theory can still vary though all possible observations be fixed. Physical theories can be at odds with each other and yet compatible with all possible data even in the broadest sense. In a word, they can be logically incompatible and empirically equivalent. This is a point on which I expect wide agreement, if only because the observational criteria of theoretical terms are commonly so flexible and fragmentary. People who agree on this general point need not agree as to how much of physical theory is empirically unfixed in this strong sense; some will acknowledge such slack only in the highest and most speculative reaches of physical theory, while others see it as extending even to common-sense traits of macroscopic bodies.

Now let us turn to the radical translation of a radically foreign physicist's theory. As always in radical translation, the starting point is the equating of observation sentences of the two languages by an inductive equating of stimulus meanings. In order afterward to construe the foreigner's theoretical sentences we have to project analytical hypotheses, whose ultimate justification is substantially just that the implied observation sentences match up. But now the same old empirical slack, the old indeterminacy between physical theories, recurs in second intension. Insofar as the truth of a physical theory is

"Reasons for the Indeterminacy of Translation" by W. V. O. Quine from *The Journal of Philosophy*, Vol. 67, No. 6, 1970. Reprinted by permission of The Journal of Philosophy and Douglas B. Quine for the W. V. Quine Estate.

underdetermined by observables, the translation of the foreigner's physical theory is underdetermined by translation of his observation sentences. If our physical theory can vary though all possible observations be fixed, then our translation of his physical theory can vary though our translations of all possible observation reports on his part be fixed. Our translation of his observation sentences no more fixes our translation of his physical theory than our own possible observations fix our own physical theory.

The indeterminacy of translation is not just an instance of the empirically underdetermined character of physics. The point is not just that linguistics, being a part of behavioral science and hence ultimately of physics, shares the empirically underdetermined character of physics. On the contrary, the indeterminacy of translation is additional. Where physical theories A and B are both compatible with all possible data, we might adopt A for ourselves and still remain free to translate the foreigner either as believing A or as believing B.

Such choice between A and B in translation could be guided by simplicity. By imputing B to the foreigner we might come out with shorter and more direct translations, and with less in the way of elaborate contextual paraphrases, than by imputing A to him. That is one possibility. A second possibility is that both choices, A and B, require forbiddingly circuitous and cumbersome translation rules. In this case we might regard the foreigner as holding neither A nor B; we might attribute to him rather some false physical theory which we can refute, or some obscure one which we despair of penetrating, or we might even regard him as holding no coherent physical theory at all. But we can imagine also, third, the possibility that A and B are both reasonably attributable. It might turn out that with just moderate circuitousness of translation at certain points—different points—A and B could be imputed about equally well. In this event no basis for a choice can be gained by exposing the foreigner to new physical data and noting his verbal response, since the theories A and B fit all possible observations equally well. No basis can be gained by interrogation in a theoretical vein, since the interrogation would take place in the foreigner's language and so could itself be interpreted according to either plan. In this event our

choice would be determined simply by the accident of hitting upon one of the two systems of translation first.

The metaphor of the black box, often so useful, can be misleading here. The problem is not one of hidden facts, such as might be uncovered by learning more about the brain physiology of thought processes. To expect a distinctive physical mechanism behind every genuinely distinct mental state is one thing: to expect a distinctive mechanism for every purported distinction that can be phrased in traditional mentalistic language is another. The question whether, in the situation last described, the foreigner *really* believes A or believes rather B, is a question whose very significance I would put in doubt. This is what I am getting at in arguing the indeterminacy of translation.

My argument in these pages has been and will remain directed to you who already agree that there can be logically incompatible and empirically equivalent physical theories A and B. What degree of indeterminacy of translation you must then recognize, granted the force of my argument, will depend on the amount of empirical slack that you are willing to acknowledge in physics. If you were one of those who saw physics as empirically underdetermined only in its highest theoretical reaches, then by the argument at hand I can claim your concurrence in the indeterminacy of translation only of highly theoretical physics. For my own part, I think the empirical slack in physics extends to ordinary traits of ordinary bodies and hence that the indeterminacy of translation likewise affects that level of discourse. But it is important, for those who would not go so far, to note the graduation of liabilities.

Gavagai, whose troubles I shall now review, lay at an extreme of the scale. It was an observation sentence. Its stimulus meaning was inductively well established, we supposed, coinciding with that of 'Rabbit'. Where indeterminacy threatened was in trying to settle upon the divided reference of *gavagai* as a term: whether rabbits or rabbit stages or undetached rabbit parts. Readers have responded with suggestions of how, with help of screens or other devices, we might hope to give the native informant an inkling of the desired distinctions and so settle the reference.

Ingenuity in this vein proves unrewarding because of vagueness of purpose. The purpose cannot be to drive a wedge between stimulus meanings of observation sentences, thereby linking *Gavagai* rather to 'Rabbit' than to 'Rabbit stage' or 'Undetached rabbit part'; for the stimulus meanings of all these sentences are incontestably identical. They comprise the stimulations that would make people think a rabbit was present. The purpose can only be to settle what *gavagai* denotes for the native as a term. But the whole notion of terms and their denotation is bound up with our own grammatical analysis of the sentences of our own language. It can be projected on the native language only as we settle what to count in the native language as analogues of our pronouns, identity, plurals, and related apparatus; and I urged in *Word and Object* that there would be some freedom of choice on this score. Once such choices are settled, on the other hand, however arbitrarily, the question whether the *gavagai* are rabbits or stages or parts can be settled too, by interrogation.

The most to hope for from the screens and kindred aids, then, is an indirect hint as to which of various analytical hypotheses regarding pronouns, identity, plurals, etc. might in the end work out most naturally. When this kind of hint is available, should we say that the supposed multiplicity of choices was not in fact open after all? Or should we say that the choice is open but that we have found a practical consideration that will help us in choosing? The issue is palpably unreal, and the doctrine of the indeterminacy of translation depends in no way upon it.

The *gavagai* example was at best an example only of the inscrutability of terms, not of the indeterminacy of translation of sentences. As sentence, *Gavagai* had a translation that was unique to within stimulus synonymy; for the occasion sentences 'Rabbit', 'Rabbit stage', and 'Undetached rabbit part' are stimulus-synonymous and holophrastically interchangeable. The *gavagai* example had only this indirect bearing on indeterminacy of translation of sentences: one could imagine with some plausibility that some lengthy nonobservational sentences containing *gavagai* could be found which would go into English in materially different ways according as *gavagai* was equated with one or another of the terms 'rabbit', 'rabbit stage', etc. This whole effort was aimed not at proof but at helping the reader to reconcile the indeterminacy of translation imaginatively with the concrete reality of radical translation. The argument for the indeterminacy is another thing, as seen earlier in this paper.

Over the inscrutability of terms itself there is little room for debate. A clear example from real life was seen in connection with the Japanese classifiers. This example makes it pretty clear, moreover, that the inscrutability of terms need not always bring indeterminacy of sentence translation in its train, however the case may be in particular with *gavagai*. Again the questions raised by deferred ostension (*op. cit.*), e.g., as between expressions and their Gödel numbers, are strictly a matter of inscrutability of terms. This, not the indeterminacy of translation, is the substance of ontological relativity.

There are two ways of pressing the doctrine of indeterminacy of translation to maximize its scope. I can press from above and press from below, playing both ends against the middle. At the upper end there is the argument, early in the present paper, which is meant to persuade anyone to recognize the indeterminacy of translation of such portions of natural science as he is willing to regard as underdetermined by all possible observations. If I can get people to see this empirical slack as affecting not just highly theoretical physics but fairly common-sense talk of bodies, then I can get them to concede indeterminacy of translation of fairly common-sense talk of bodies. This I call pressing from above.

By pressing from below I mean pressing whatever arguments for indeterminacy of translation can be based on the inscrutability of terms. I suppose Harman's example regarding natural numbers comes under this head, theoretical though it is. It is that the sentence '3 ∈ 5' goes into a true sentence of set theory under von Neumann's way of construing natural numbers, but goes into a false one under Zermelo's way. But a limitation of this example, as Harman recognizes, is that '3 ∈ 5' rates as nonsense apart from set-theoretic explications of natural number.

In these pages I prefer not to speculate on how much better one might do from below, or from above either. My purpose here is to separate the issues and identify the arguments; and this may be managed most effectively by leaving the reader to consider what more might be proved.

STUDY QUESTIONS: QUINE ON *THE REASONS FOR THE INDETERMINACY OF TRANSLATION*

1. How is physical theory underdetermined? What does this mean?
2. What is the starting point in radical translation?
3. How does Quine use the claim that physical theory is underdetermined to make a similar point about translation?
4. How does Quine argue that we might adopt theory A for ourselves and yet remain free to translate a foreigner as believing A or B, when A and B are both compatible with all data?
5. Why is the black box analogy misleading?
6. What are the threatened indeterminacies that Quine mentions with regard to his 'gavagai' example?
7. What was the point of the 'gavagai' example?

Philosophical Bridges: Quine's Influence

Quine's 'Two Dogmas of Empiricism' is one of the most discussed pieces of twentieth-century philosophy. In general, Quine's work introduces several new themes into philosophy. For instance, holistic conceptions of science and language were relatively unpopular at the time he first expounded them. They subsequently became influential. Quine also introduced the problems related to radical interpretation and the resulting ideas of the indeterminacy of translation and ontological relativity.

Quine's work gave new impetus to the idea of the underdetermination of theory by data. According to this idea, it is possible to have two theories that explain all empirical data equally well. In such a case, the two theories are underdetermined. Quine embraces this possibility and extends it from evidence to semantics. Meaning or translation is also radically underdetermined. Philosophers have found this an intriguing and significant point, which has generated much debate.

These comparatively new ideas eroded the optimistic assumption of the logical positivists that the reductions that their program needed could be carried out successfully. What makes Quine's position novel and influential is that he tries to show how the thesis of extensionality can be maintained even when reductionism cannot. Quine does this in two ways. First, he argues for an eliminativist position i.e., that all intensional notions, such as meaning and belief, would be eliminated from a description of the world in order to keep that description properly scientific and extensional. Second, he draws on pragmatist conceptions and naturalistic explanations of aspects of our discourse that do not fit into the extensionalist model. Both aspects of Quine's overall strategy have been very influential. For example, in *From Folk Psychology to Cognitive Science*, Stephen Stich supports an eliminativist theory of mind, which he uses in later works to argue for a form of pragmatism. One can find a similar strategy in Rorty's *Philosophy and the Mirror of Nature*. Eliminativist theories of mind reject the employment of intensional concepts, such as meaning and content, in characterizing psychological states.

One of the main influences of Quine was to provoke the work of Donald Davidson. Davidson, who agreed with many of Quine's assumptions such as the rejection of Fregean senses and his holism, took Quine's thought as proposing a challenge: how to explain the concept of understanding a sentence in extensional terms. Davidson tried to meet this challenge by arguing that knowing an extensional truth theory of a language would be sufficient for understanding it. The resulting theory has been very influential in recent philosophy of language.

NELSON GOODMAN (1906–1998)

Biographical History

Nelson Goodman was born in Boston and he studied at Harvard, where he studied for his Ph.D. while running an art gallery. He was a research fellow at Harvard's Center for Cognitive Studies from 1962 to 1963, and he was appointed professor of philosophy at Harvard in 1968. His first book, *The Structure of Appearances*, published in 1951, offers a constructionist and structural system that is an alternative to the one provided by Carnap in the *Logical Structure of the World. Fact, Fiction and Forecast* was published in 1955. As well as writing in the philosophy of science, Goodman has authored several works in aesthetics, such *Language of Art* (1968) and *Ways of Worldmaking* (1978). He was also a founder of Project Zero, an educational research program for the study of thinking and artistic creativity in children.

Philosophical Overview

There are two general aspects of Goodman's work that are especially relevant to the selected reading. First, in *The Structure of Appearances*, Goodman outlines his nominalist system. A nominalist rejects the existence of any abstract objects, such as sets, universals, and properties, and accepts the existence only of particular individual objects. Accordingly, Goodman tries to show how all reference to sets and predicates can be replaced by sentences that quantify over individuals only. Goodman also argues that no system of classification is determined by the way the world is.

Second, in the first chapter of *Fact, Fiction and Forecast*, Goodman analyzes some of the problems concerning dispositions and counterfactual propositions. Counterfactuals are statements of a hypothetical or 'if then' form that describe what could have happened but didn't, such as 'If Hitler had not been born then World War II would not have occurred' and 'If you would have heated the butter to 150 degrees then it would have melted.' How can such assertions ever be warranted? It looks as though at least some can be warranted on the basis of natural causal laws. For example, if we know the relevant causal laws and if we know the mass of a body and the force of air resistance and gravity, then we can calculate its acceleration given the force of its propulsion. Natural causal laws can underwrite counterfactuals. The problem then becomes, 'How can we distinguish natural law–like regularities from those that are not?' This question leads us straight into the new riddle of induction.

THE NEW RIDDLE OF INDUCTION

Hume proposed and formulated the original problem of induction, which is roughly 'How can inductive inferences from past regularities to the prediction of a future event be warranted?' In the selected reading from his book *Fact, Fiction and Forecast*, Goodman advances the new riddle.

Consider emeralds that have all been observed as green prior to 1 January 2010. Goodman constructs a new predicate, 'grue,' which he defines as follows: something is grue if and only if it is green up to a certain time (say, 1/1/2010) and blue thereafter. It appears that all of our evidence supports the claim that emeralds are grue. You might think, 'What reason is there for supposing that emeralds will change color on 1/1/2010?' But if one thought that emeralds are grue, then their becoming blue on that date would not constitute a change of color. One might be tempted to claim that 'green' and 'blue' are somehow more basic predicates than 'grue and 'bleen' (X is bleen if and only if it is blue up to a certain date and green thereafter). However, this suggestion is not clear in part because 'blue' and 'green' can be defined in terms of 'grue' and 'bleen': X is green if and only if it is grue up to 1/1/2010 and it is bleen thereafter. Thus the question remains: do our past observations of emeralds support the claim that all emeralds are grue?

Goodman's riddle raises important conceptual issues. For example, do our concepts mark similarities and distinctions that really exist in the world, or are they merely our way of classifying the world? As a matter of interest, the term 'gruebleen' first appeared in James Joyce's novel *Finnegan's Wake*.

1. THE OLD PROBLEM OF INDUCTION

At the close of the preceding lecture, I said that today I should examine how matters stand with respect to the problem of induction. In a word, I think they stand ill. But the real difficulties that confront us today are not the traditional ones. What is commonly thought of as the Problem of Induction has been solved, or dissolved; and we face new problems that are not as yet very widely understood. To approach them, I shall have to run as quickly as possible over some very familiar ground.

The problem of the validity of judgments about future or unknown cases arises, as Hume pointed out, because such judgments are neither reports of experience nor logical consequences of it. Predictions, of course, pertain to what has not yet been observed. And they cannot be logically inferred from what has been observed; for what *has* happened imposes no logical restrictions on what *will* happen. Although Hume's dictum that there are no necessary connections of matters of fact has been challenged at times, it has withstood all attacks. Indeed, I should be inclined not merely to agree that there are no necessary connections of matters of fact, but to ask whether there are any necessary connections at all—but that is another story.

Hume's answer to the question how predictions are related to past experience is refreshingly non-cosmic. When an event of one kind frequently follows upon an event of another kind in experience, a habit is formed that leads the mind, when confronted with a new event of the first kind, to pass to the idea of an event of the second kind. The idea of necessary connection arises from the felt impulse of the mind in making this transition.

Now if we strip this account of all extraneous features, the central point is that to the question "Why one prediction rather than another?", Hume answers that the elect prediction is one that accords with a past regularity, because this regularity has established a habit. Thus among alternative statements about a future moment, one statement is distinguished by its consonance with habit and thus with regularities observed in the past. Prediction according to any other alternative is errant.

How satisfactory is this answer? The heaviest criticism has taken the righteous position that Hume's account at best pertains only to the source of predictions, not their legitimacy; that he sets forth the circumstances under which we make given predictions—and in this sense explains why we make them—but leaves untouched the question of our

From *Fact, Fiction and Forecast* by Nelson Goodman, Bobs-Merrill, 1965. Reprinted by permission of Pearson Education.

license for making them. To trace origins, runs the old complaint, is not to establish validity: the real question is not why a prediction is in fact made but how it can be justified. Since this seems to point to the awkward conclusion that the greatest of modern philosophers completely missed the point of his own problem, the idea has developed that he did not really take his solution very seriously, but regarded the main problem as unsolved and perhaps as insoluble. Thus we come to speak of 'Hume's problem' as though he propounded it as a question without answer.

All this seems to me quite wrong. I think Hume grasped the central question and considered his answer to be passably effective. And I think his answer is reasonable and relevant, even if it is not entirely satisfactory. I shall explain presently. At the moment, I merely want to record a protest against the prevalent notion that the problem of justifying induction, when it is so sharply dissociated from the problem of describing how induction takes place, can fairly be called Hume's problem.

I suppose that the problem of justifying induction has called forth as much fruitless discussion as has any halfway respectable problem of modern philosophy. The typical writer begins by insisting that some way of justifying predictions must be found; proceeds to argue that for this purpose we need some resounding universal law of the Uniformity of Nature, and then inquires how this universal principle itself can be justified. At this point, if he is tired, he concludes that the principle must be accepted as an indispensable assumption; or if he is energetic and ingenious, he goes on to devise some subtle justification for it. Such an invention, however, seldom satisfies anyone else; and the easier course of accepting an unsubstantiated and even dubious assumption much more sweeping than any actual predictions we make seems an odd and expensive way of justifying them.

2. DISSOLUTION OF THE OLD PROBLEM

Understandably, then, more critical thinkers have suspected that there might be something awry with the problem we are trying to solve. Come to think of it, what precisely would constitute the justification we seek? If the problem is to explain how we know that

certain predictions will turn out to be correct, the sufficient answer is that we don't know any such thing. If the problem is to *find* some way of distinguishing antecedently between true and false predictions, we are asking for prevision rather than for philosophical explanation. Nor does it help matters much to say that we are merely trying to show that or why certain predictions are *probable*. Often it is said that while we cannot tell in advance whether a prediction concerning a given throw of a die is true, we can decide whether the prediction is a probable one. But if this means determining how the prediction is related to actual frequency distributions of future throws of the die, surely there is no way of knowing or proving this in advance. On the other hand, if the judgment that the prediction is probable has nothing to do with subsequent occurrences, then the question remains in what sense a probable prediction is any better justified than an improbable one.

Now obviously the genuine problem cannot be one of attaining unattainable knowledge or of accounting for knowledge that we do not in fact have. A better understanding of our problem can be gained by looking for a moment at what is involved in justifying non-inductive inferences. How do we justify a *deduction?* Plainly, by showing that it conforms to the general rules of deductive inference. An argument that so conforms is justified or valid, even if its conclusion happens to be false. An argument that violates a rule is fallacious even if its conclusion happens to be true. To justify a deductive conclusion therefore requires no knowledge of the facts it pertains to. Moreover, when a deductive argument has been shown to conform to the rules of logical inference, we usually consider it justified without going on to ask what justifies the rules. Analogously, the basic task in justifying an inductive inference is to show that it conforms to the general rules of induction. Once we have recognized this, we have gone a long way towards clarifying our problem.

Yet, of course, the rules themselves must eventually be justified. The validity of a deduction depends not upon conformity to any purely arbitrary rules we may contrive, but upon conformity to valid rules. When we speak of *the* rules of inference we mean the valid rules—or better, *some* valid rules, since there may be alternative sets of equally valid rules. But how is the validity of rules to be determined? Here again we encounter philosophers who insist that these rules follow from some self-evident axiom, and others who try to show that the rules are grounded in the very nature of the human mind. I think the answer lies much nearer the surface. Principles of deductive inference are justified by their conformity with accepted deductive practice. Their validity depends upon accordance with the particular deductive inferences we actually make and sanction. If a rule yields inacceptable inferences, we drop it as invalid. Justification of general rules thus derives from judgments rejecting or accepting particular deductive inferences.

This looks flagrantly circular. I have said that deductive inferences are justified by their conformity to valid general rules, and that general rules are justified by their conformity to valid inferences. But this circle is a virtuous one. The point is that rules and particular inferences alike are justified by being brought into agreement with each other. *A rule is amended if it yields an inference we are unwilling to accept; an inference is rejected if it violates a rule we are unwilling to amend.* The process of justification is the delicate one of making mutual adjustments between rules and accepted inferences; and in the agreement achieved lies the only justification needed for either.

All this applies equally well to induction. An inductive inference, too, is justified by conformity to general rules, and a general rule by conformity to accepted inductive inferences. Predictions are justified if they conform to valid canons of induction; and the canons are valid if they accurately codify accepted inductive practice.

A result of such analysis is that we can stop plaguing ourselves with certain spurious questions about induction. We no longer demand an explanation for guarantees that we do not have, or seek keys to knowledge that we cannot obtain. It dawns upon us that the traditional smug insistence upon a hard-and-fast line between justifying induction and describing ordinary inductive practice distorts the problem. And we owe belated apologies to Hume. For in dealing with the question how normally accepted inductive judgments are made, he was in fact dealing with the question of inductive validity. The validity

of a prediction consisted for him in its arising from habit, and thus in its exemplifying some past regularity. His answer was incomplete and perhaps not entirely correct; but it was not beside the point. The problem of induction is not a problem of demonstration but a problem of defining the difference between valid and invalid predictions.

This clears the air but leaves a lot to be done. As principles of *deductive* inference, we have the familiar and highly developed laws of logic; but there are available no such precisely stated and well-recognized principles of inductive inference. Mill's canons hardly rank with Aristotle's rules of the syllogism, let alone with *Principia Mathematica*. Elaborate and valuable treatises on probability usually leave certain fundamental questions untouched. Only in very recent years has there been any explicit and systematic work upon what I call the constructive task of confirmation theory.

3. THE CONSTRUCTIVE TASK OF CONFIRMATION THEORY

The task of formulating rules that define the difference between valid and invalid inductive inferences is much like the task of defining any term with an established usage. If we set out to define the term "tree", we try to compose out of already understood words an expression that will apply to the familiar objects that standard usage calls trees, and that will not apply to objects that standard usage refuses to call trees. A proposal that plainly violates either condition is rejected; while a definition that meets these tests may be adopted and used to decide cases that are not already settled by actual usage. Thus the interplay we observed between rules of induction and particular inductive inferences is simply an instance of this characteristic dual adjustment between definition and usage, whereby the usage informs the definition, which in turn guides extension of the usage.

Of course this adjustment is a more complex matter than I have indicated. Sometimes, in the interest of convenience or theoretical utility, we deliberately permit a definition to run counter to clear mandates of common usage. We accept a definition of "fish" that excludes whales. Similarly we may decide to deny the term "valid induction" to some inductive inferences that are commonly considered valid, or apply the term to others not usually so considered. A definition may modify as well as extend ordinary usage.

Some pioneer work on the problem of defining confirmation or valid induction has been done by Professor Hempel. Let me remind you briefly of a few of his results. Just as deductive logic is concerned primarily with a relation between statements— namely the consequence relation—that is independent of their truth or falsity, so inductive logic as Hempel conceives it is concerned primarily with a comparable relation of confirmation between statements. Thus the problem is to define the relation that obtains between any statement S_1 and another S_2 if and only if S_1 may properly be said to confirm S_2 in any degree.

With the question so stated, the first step seems obvious. Does not induction proceed in just the opposite direction from deduction? Surely the evidence-statements that inductively support a general hypothesis are consequences of it. That a given piece of copper conducts electricity follows from and confirms the statement that all copper conducts electricity. Since the consequence relation is already well defined by deductive logic, will we not be on firm ground in saying that confirmation embraces the converse relation? The laws of deduction in reverse will then be among the laws of induction.

Let's see where this leads us. We naturally assume further that whatever confirms a given statement confirms also whatever follows from that statement. But if we combine this assumption with our proposed principle, we get the embarrassing result that every statement confirms every other. Surprising as it may be that such innocent beginnings lead to such an intolerable conclusion, the proof is very easy. Start with any statement S_1. It is a consequence of, and so by our present criterion confirms, the conjunction of S_1 and any statement whatsoever—call it S_2. But the confirmed conjunction, $S_1 \cdot S_2$, of course has S_2 as a consequence. Thus every statement confirms all statements.

The fault lies in careless formulation of our first proposal. While the statements that confirm a general hypothesis are consequences of it, not all its consequences confirm it. This may not be immediately evi-

dent; for indeed we do in some sense furnish support for a statement when we establish one of its consequences. We settle one of the questions about it. Consider the heterogeneous conjunction:

8497 is a prime number and the other side of the moon is flat and Elizabeth the First was crowned on a Tuesday.

To show that any one of the three component statements is true is to support the conjunction by reducing the net undetermined claim. But support of this kind is not confirmation; for establishment of one component endows the whole statement with no credibility that is transmitted to other component statements. Confirmation of a hypothesis occurs only when an instance imparts to the hypothesis some credibility that is conveyed to other instances. Appraisal of hypotheses, indeed, is incidental to prediction, to the judgment of new cases on the basis of old ones.

Our formula thus needs tightening. This is readily accomplished, as Hempel points out, if we observe that a hypothesis is genuinely confirmed only by those of its consequences that are instances of it in the strict sense of being derivable from it by instantiation. In other words, a singular statement confirms the hypothesis secured by generalizing from the singular statement—where generalizing means replacing the argument-constants in the singular statement by variables, and prefixing universal quantifiers governing these variables. The predicate constants remain fixed. Less technically, the hypothesis says of all things what the evidence statement says of one thing (or of one pair or other n-ad of things). This obviously covers the confirmation of the conductivity of all copper by the conductivity of a given piece; and it excludes confirmation of our heterogeneous conjunction by any of its components. And, when taken together with the principle that what confirms a statement confirms all its consequences, this criterion does not yield the untoward conclusion that every statement confirms every other.

New difficulties promptly appear from other directions, however. One is the infamous paradox of the ravens. The statement that a given object, say this piece of paper, is neither black nor a raven confirms the hypothesis that all non-black things are non-ravens. But this hypothesis is logically equivalent to the hypothesis that all ravens are black. Hence we arrive at the unexpected conclusion that the statement that a given object is neither black nor a raven confirms the hypothesis that all ravens are black. The prospect of being able to investigate ornithological theories without going out in the rain is so attractive that we know there must be a catch in it. The trouble this time, however, lies not in faulty definition, but in tacit and illicit reference to evidence not stated in our example. Taken by itself, the statement that the given object is neither black nor a raven confirms the hypothesis that everything that is not a raven is not black as well as the hypothesis that everything that is not black is not a raven. We tend to ignore the former hypothesis because we know it to be false from abundant other evidence—from all the familiar things that are not ravens but are black. But we are required to assume that no such evidence is available. Under this circumstance, even a much stronger hypothesis is also obviously confirmed: that nothing is either black or a raven. In the light of this confirmation of the hypothesis that there are no ravens, it is no longer surprising that under the artificial restrictions of the example, the hypothesis that all ravens are black is also confirmed. And the prospects for indoor ornithology vanish when we notice that under these same conditions, the contrary hypothesis that no ravens are black is equally well confirmed.

On the other hand, our definition does err in not forcing us to take into account all the *stated* evidence. The unhappy results are readily illustrated. If two compatible evidence statements confirm two hypotheses, then naturally the conjunction of the evidence statements should confirm the conjunction of the hypotheses. Suppose our evidence consists of the statements E_1 saying that a given thing b is black, and E_2 saying that a second thing c is not black. By our present definition, E_1 confirms the hypothesis that everything is black, and E_2 the hypothesis that everything is non-black. The conjunction of these perfectly compatible evidence statements will then confirm the self-contradictory hypothesis that everything is both black and non-black. Simple as this anomaly is, it requires drastic modification of our definition. What given evidence confirms is not what we

arrive at by generalizing from separate items of it, but—roughly speaking—what we arrive at by generalizing from the total stated evidence. The central idea for an improved definition is that, within certain limitations, what is asserted to be true for the narrow universe of the evidence statements is confirmed for the whole universe of discourse. Thus if our evidence is E_1 and E_2, neither the hypothesis that all things are black nor the hypothesis that all things are non-black is confirmed; for neither is true for the evidence-universe consisting of b and c. Of course, much more careful formulation is needed, since some statements that are true of the evidence-universe—such as that there is only one black thing—are obviously not confirmed for the whole universe. These matters are taken care of by the studied formal definition that Hempel develops on this basis; but we cannot and need not go into further detail here.

No one supposes that the task of confirmation-theory has been completed. But the few steps I have reviewed—chosen partly for their bearing on what is to follow—show how things move along once the problem of definition displaces the problem of justification. Important and long-unnoticed questions are brought to light and answered; and we are encouraged to expect that the many remaining questions will in time yield to similar treatment.

But our satisfaction is shortlived. New and serious trouble begins to appear.

4. THE NEW RIDDLE OF INDUCTION

Confirmation of a hypothesis by an instance depends rather heavily upon features of the hypothesis other than its syntactical form. That a given piece of copper conducts electricity increases the credibility of statements asserting that other pieces of copper conduct electricity, and thus confirms the hypothesis that all copper conducts electricity. But the fact that a given man now in this room is a third son does not increase the credibility of statements asserting that other men now in this room are third sons, and so does not confirm the hypothesis that all men now in this room are third sons. Yet in both cases our hypothesis is a generalization of the evidence statement. The difference is that in the former case the hypothesis is a *lawlike* statement; while in the latter case, the hypothesis is a merely contingent or accidental generality. Only a statement that is *lawlike*—regardless of its truth or falsity or its scientific importance—is capable of receiving confirmation from an instance of it; accidental statements are not. Plainly, then, we must look for a way of distinguishing lawlike from accidental statements.

So long as what seems to be needed is merely a way of excluding a few odd and unwanted cases that are inadvertently admitted by our definition of confirmation, the problem may not seem very hard or very pressing. We fully expect that minor defects will be found in our definition and that the necessary refinements will have to be worked out patiently one after another. But some further examples will show that our present difficulty is of a much graver kind.

Suppose that all emeralds examined before a certain time *t* are green. At time *t*, then, our observations support the hypothesis that all emeralds are green; and this is in accord with our definition of confirmation. Our evidence statements assert that emerald *a* is green, that emerald *b* is green, and so on; and each confirms the general hypothesis that all emeralds are green. So far, so good.

Now let me introduce another predicate less familiar than "green". It is the predicate "grue" and it applies to all things examined before *t* just in case they are green but to other things just in case they are blue. Then at time *t* we have, for each evidence statement asserting that a given emerald is green, a parallel evidence statement asserting that that emerald is grue. And the statements that emerald *a* is grue, that emerald *b* is grue, and so on, will each confirm the general hypothesis that all emeralds are grue. Thus according to our definition, the prediction that all emeralds subsequently examined will be green and the prediction that all will be grue are alike confirmed by evidence statements describing the same observations. But if an emerald subsequently examined is grue, it is blue and hence not green. Thus although we are well aware which of the two incompatible predictions is genuinely confirmed, they are equally well confirmed according to our present definition. Moreover, it is clear that if we simply choose an appropriate predicate, then on the basis of these same observations we shall have equal confirmation, by our definition, for any prediction whatever about other

emeralds—or indeed about anything else. As in our earlier example, only the predictions subsumed under lawlike hypotheses are genuinely confirmed; but we have no criterion as yet for determining lawlikeness. And now we see that without some such criterion, our definition not merely includes a few unwanted cases, but is so completely ineffectual that it virtually excludes nothing. We are left once again with the intolerable result that anything confirms anything. This difficulty cannot be set aside as an annoying detail to be taken care of in due course. It has to be met before our definition will work at all.

Nevertheless, the difficulty is often slighted because on the surface there seem to be easy ways of dealing with it. Sometimes, for example, the problem is thought to be much like the paradox of the ravens. We are here again, it is pointed out, making tacit and illegitimate use of information outside the stated evidence: the information, for example, that different samples of one material are usually alike in conductivity, and the information that different men in a lecture audience are usually not alike in the number of their older brothers. But while it is true that such information is being smuggled in, this does not by itself settle the matter as it settles the matter of the ravens. There the point was that when the smuggled information is forthrightly declared, its effect upon the confirmation of the hypothesis in question is immediately and properly registered by the definition we are using. On the other hand, if to our initial evidence we add statements concerning the conductivity of pieces of other materials or concerning the number of older brothers of members of other lecture audiences, this will not in the least affect the confirmation, according to our definition, of the hypothesis concerning copper or of that concerning other lecture audiences. Since our definition is insensitive to the bearing upon hypotheses of evidence so related to them, even when the evidence is fully declared, the difficulty about accidental hypotheses cannot be explained away on the ground that such evidence is being surreptitiously taken into account.

A more promising suggestion is to explain the matter in terms of the effect of this other evidence not directly upon the hypothesis in question but *indirectly* through other hypotheses that *are* confirmed, according to our definition, by such evidence.

Our information about other materials does by our definition confirm such hypotheses as that all pieces of iron conduct electricity, that no pieces of rubber do, and so on; and these hypotheses, the explanation runs, impart to the hypothesis that all pieces of copper conduct electricity (and also to the hypothesis that none do) the character of lawlikeness—that is, amenability to confirmation by direct positive instances when found. On the other hand, our information about other lecture audiences *disconfirms* many hypotheses to the effect that all the men in one audience are third sons, or that none are; and this strips any character of lawlikeness from the hypothesis that all (or the hypothesis that none) of the men in *this* audience are third sons. But clearly if this course is to be followed, the circumstances under which hypotheses are thus related to one another will have to be precisely articulated.

The problem, then, is to define the relevant way in which such hypotheses must be alike. Evidence for the hypothesis that all iron conducts electricity enhances the lawlikeness of the hypothesis that all zirconium conducts electricity, but does not similarly affect the hypothesis that all the objects on my desk conduct electricity. Wherein lies the difference? The first two hypotheses fall under the broader hypothesis—call it "H"—that every class of things of the same material is uniform in conductivity; the first and third fall only under some such hypothesis as—call it "K"—that every class of things that are either all of the same material or all on a desk is uniform in conductivity. Clearly the important difference here is that evidence for a statement affirming that one of the classes covered by H has the property in question increases the credibility of any statement affirming that another such class has this property; while nothing of the sort holds true with respect to K. But this is only to say that H is lawlike and K is not. We are faced anew with the very problem we are trying to solve: the problem of distinguishing between lawlike and accidental hypotheses.

The most popular way of attacking the problem takes its cue from the fact that accidental hypotheses seem typically to involve some spatial or temporal restriction, or reference to some particular individual. They seem to concern the people in some particular room, or the objects on some particular person's desk; while lawlike hypotheses characteristically concern all ravens or all pieces of copper whatsoever. Complete generality is thus very often supposed to be a sufficient condition of lawlikeness; but to define this complete generality is by no means easy. Merely to require that the hypothesis contain no term naming, describing, or indicating a particular thing or location will obviously not be enough. The troublesome hypothesis that all emeralds are grue contains no such term; and where such a term does occur, as in hypotheses about men in *this room*, it can be suppressed in favor of some predicate (short or long, new or old) that contains no such term but applies only to exactly the same things. One might think, then, of excluding not only hypotheses that actually contain terms for specific individuals but also all hypotheses that are equivalent to others that do contain such terms. But, as we have just seen, to exclude only hypotheses of which *all* equivalents contain such terms is to exclude nothing. On the other hand, to exclude all hypotheses that have *some* equivalent containing such a term is to exclude everything; for even the hypothesis

All grass is green

has as an equivalent

All grass in London or elsewhere is green.

The next step, therefore, has been to consider ruling out predicates of certain kinds. A syntactically universal hypothesis is lawlike, the proposal runs, if its predicates are 'purely qualitative' or 'non-positional'. This will obviously accomplish nothing if a purely qualitative predicate is then conceived either as one that is equivalent to some expression free of terms for specific individuals, or as one that is equivalent to no expression that contains such a term; for this only raises again the difficulties just pointed out. The claim appears to be rather that at least in the case of a simple enough predicate we can readily determine by direct inspection of its meaning whether or not it is purely qualitative. But even aside from obscurities in the notion of 'the meaning' of a predicate, this claim seems to me wrong. I simply do not know how to tell whether a predicate is qualitative or positional, except perhaps by completely begging the question at issue and asking whether the predicate is 'well-behaved'—that is, whether simple syntactically universal hypotheses applying it are lawlike.

This statement will not go unprotested. "Consider", it will be argued, "the predicates 'blue' and 'green' and the predicate 'grue' introduced earlier, and also the predicate 'bleen' that applies to emeralds examined before time t just in case they are blue and to other emeralds just in case they are green. Surely it is clear", the argument runs, "that the first two are purely qualitative and the second two are not; for the meaning of each of the latter two plainly involves reference to a specific temporal position." To this I reply that indeed I do recognize the first two as well-behaved predicates admissible in lawlike hypotheses, and the second two as ill-behaved predicates. But the argument that the former but not the latter are purely qualitative seems to me quite unsound. True enough, if we start with "blue" and "green", then "grue" and "bleen" will be explained in terms of "blue" and "green" and a temporal term. But equally truly, if we start with "grue" and "bleen", then "blue" and "green" will be explained in terms of "grue" and "bleen" and a temporal term; "green", for example, applies to emeralds examined before time t just in case they are grue, and to other emeralds just in case they are bleen. Thus qualitativeness is an entirely relative matter and does not by itself establish any dichotomy of predicates. This relativity seems to be completely overlooked by those who contend that the qualitative character of a predicate is a criterion for its good behavior.

Of course, one may ask why we need worry about such unfamiliar predicates as "grue" or about accidental hypotheses in general, since we are unlikely to use them in making predictions. If our definition works for such hypotheses as are normally employed, isn't that all we need? In a sense, yes; but only in the sense that we need no definition, no theory of induction, and no philosophy of knowledge at all. We get along well enough without them in daily life and in scientific research. But if we seek a theory at all, we cannot excuse gross anomalies resulting from a proposed theory by pleading that we can avoid them in practice. The odd cases we have been considering are clinically pure cases that, though seldom encountered in practice, nevertheless display to best advantage the symptoms of a widespread and destructive malady.

We have so far neither any answer nor any promising clue to an answer to the question what distinguishes lawlike or confirmable hypotheses from accidental or nonconfirmable ones; and what may at first have seemed a minor technical difficulty has taken on the stature of a major obstacle to the development of a satisfactory theory of confirmation. It is this problem that I call the new riddle of induction.

5. THE PERVASIVE PROBLEM OF PROJECTION

At the beginning of this lecture, I expressed the opinion that the problem of induction is still unsolved, but that the difficulties that face us today are not the old ones; and I have tried to outline the changes that have taken place. The problem of justifying induction has been displaced by the problem of defining confirmation, and our work upon this has left us with the residual problem of distinguishing between confirmable and non-confirmable hypotheses. One might say roughly that the first question was "Why does a positive instance of a hypothesis give any grounds for predicting further instances?"; that the newer question was "What is a positive instance of a hypothesis?"; and that the crucial remaining question is "What hypotheses are confirmed by their positive instances?"

The vast amount of effort expended on the problem of induction in modern times has thus altered our afflictions but hardly relieved them. The original difficulty about induction arose from the recognition that anything may follow upon anything. Then, in attempting to define confirmation in terms of the converse of the consequence relation, we found ourselves with the distressingly similar difficulty that our definition would make any statement confirm any other. And now, after modifying our definition drastically, we still get the old devastating result that any statement will confirm any statement. Until we find a way of exercising some control over the hypotheses to be admitted, our definition makes no distinction whatsoever between valid and invalid inductive inferences.

The real inadequacy of Hume's account lay not in his descriptive approach but in the imprecision of his description. Regularities in experience, according to him, give rise to habits of expectation; and thus it is predictions conforming to past regularities that are normal or valid. But Hume overlooks the fact that some regularities do and some do not establish such habits; that predictions based on some regularities are valid while predictions based on other regularities are not. Every word you have heard me say has occurred prior to the final sentence of this lecture; but that does not, I hope, create any expectation that every word you will hear me say will be prior to that sentence. Again, consider our case of emeralds. All those examined before time *t* are green; and this leads us to expect, and confirms the prediction, that the next one will be green. But also, all those examined are grue; and this does not lead us to expect, and does not confirm the prediction, that the next one will be grue. Regularity in greenness confirms the prediction of further cases; regularity in grueness does not. To say that valid predictions are those based on past regularities, without being able to say *which* regularities, is thus quite pointless. Regularities are where you find them, and you can find them anywhere. As we have seen, Hume's failure to recognize and deal with this problem has been shared even by his most recent successors.

As a result, what we have in current confirmation theory is a definition that is adequate for certain cases that so far can be described only as those for which it is adequate. The theory works where it works. A hypothesis is confirmed by statements related to it in the prescribed way provided it is so confirmed. This is a good deal like having a theory that tells us that the area of a plane figure is one-half the base times the altitude, without telling us for what figures this holds. We must somehow find a way of distinguishing law-like hypotheses, to which our definition of confirmation applies, from accidental hypotheses, to which it does not.

Today I have been speaking solely of the problem of induction, but what has been said applies equally to the more general problem of projection. As pointed out earlier, the problem of prediction from past to future cases is but a narrower version of the problem of projecting from any set of cases to others. We saw that a whole cluster of troublesome problems concerning dispositions and possibility can be reduced to this problem of projection. That is why the new riddle of induction, which is more broadly the problem of distinguishing between projectible and non-projectible hypotheses, is as important as it is exasperating.

Our failures teach us, I think, that lawlike or projective hypotheses cannot be distinguished on any merely syntactical grounds or even on the ground that these hypotheses are somehow purely general in meaning. Our only hope lies in re-examining the problem once more and looking for some new approach. This will be my course in the final lecture.

STUDY QUESTIONS: GOODMAN, *THE NEW RIDDLE OF INDUCTION*

1. What is Hume's problem of induction?
2. How does Hume explain our capacity of make inductive inferences?
3. Why does Goodman ask the question 'How do we justify a *deduction*?'
4. Why is the circularity concerning the justification of deduction virtuous? How does the same point apply to induction?
5. What does Goodman mean when he says that the laws of induction will include the laws of deduction in reverse?
6. What is the infamous paradox of the ravens?
7. The fact that a given man in a room is a third son does not support the hypothesis that the other men in the room are also third sons. Yet the fact that a piece of copper conducts electricity does support the hypothesis that all copper conducts electricity. Why is this?
8. How does Goodman define the predicate 'is grue'? What is his purpose in using this predicate? What does the grue example show us that we need?
9. What is the problem with the supposition that accidental hypotheses involve a spatial or temporal restriction or reference to some particular?
10. Why does Goodman introduce the predicate 'is bleen' in addition to 'is grue'? How does he define 'bleen'?

11. In what way was Hume's descriptive approach imprecise? What does Hume overlook?
12. Lawlike hypothesis cannot be distinguished on merely syntactical grounds. What does this mean? How does Goodman support this conclusion?

Philosophical Bridges: Goodman's Influence

Goodman's riddle of induction has generated an enormous amount of discussion. Goodman himself offers a nominalist solution to the problem called the 'entrenchment solution,' based on the idea that certain predicates are more entrenched than others, meaning that they have been used longer and more often in formulating hypotheses that predict well. The claim 'All emeralds are grue' conflicts with the assertion that all emeralds are green. However, evidence to date supports both claims equally. Nevertheless, the predicate 'green' is better entrenched than the predicate 'grue,' and, for this reason, Goodman claims that the grue hypothesis is unprojectible. Other writers have disputed Goodman's own solution and proposed different diagnoses of the problem. There is an excellent collection of articles on the grue problem edited by D. F. Stalker, cited in the Bibliography.

THOMAS KUHN (1922–1996)

Biographical History

Thomas Kuhn, who was born in Cincinnati, Ohio, studied physics at Harvard University, from where he received his Ph.D. in 1949. By this time, he had grown interested in the history and philosophy of science, which he subsequently taught at Berkeley, Princeton, and MIT. In 1962, he published *The Structure of Scientific Revolutions;* his other works include *The Copernican Revolution* (1957) and *The Essential Tension* (1977).

Philosophical Overview

Kuhn argues systematically for a historical conception of science that opposes the idea of uniform scientific progress advocated by the logical positivists. The argument consists in a contrast between normal science and scientific revolutions. According to Kuhn, normally scientists work within a paradigm, which is a set of theoretical assumptions, concepts, and commitments that define the problems, methods, and solutions of scientific investigation. Normal science consists in puzzle solving, or in showing how experimental results and theoretical work fit into the accepted paradigm. In normal science, the paradigm is beyond challenge, and the scientific community's research program consists in interpreting results in terms of it. It defines a worldview.

A paradigm breaks down when the anomalies between it and specific scientific results are too significant for the scientific community to reconcile the two. There occurs a scientific revolution, which consists in the old paradigm being replaced by a new one that is able to explain the new evidence. For example, Einstein's theories of relativity replaced Newton's paradigm. Such paradigm shifts do not consist in new facts coming to light; rather, they consist in a dramatic conceptual change, during which the methods, problems, and language of science alter. After a transitional period, the new paradigm becomes accepted and scientific practices revert back to the stage of normal science.

According to Kuhn, the old and new paradigms are incommensurable for two reasons. First, all paradigms leave some problems unresolved. However, two paradigms will leave different problems unsolved. Therefore, any debate between two paradigms must involve answering the question 'Which of the problems are the most significant?' and any answer to this question involves appeal to the relevant paradigm. Second, observation and theory cannot be sharply distinguished; observations of the facts are always theoretically laden because the only access to facts is through concepts. In this sense, Kuhn challenges the concepts of a theory-neutral world and data. Conflicts between scientific paradigms cannot be settled by appeal to such neutral evidence. This does not necessarily mean that science is irrational and purely subjective. In effect, Kuhn argues for a third alternative, namely, that conflicts between paradigms must be resolved by the informed judgments and the commitments of the scientific community.

THE STRUCTURE OF SCIENTIFIC REVOLUTIONS

Ironically, Thomas Kuhn's work *The Structure of Scientific Revolutions* (1962) was commissioned for the logical positivist *International Encyclopedia of Unified Science*. This is ironic because Kuhn's book challenges the logical positivist view of science and, in particular, scientific progress, and it has been influential in bringing about the demise of logical positivism.

The reading is selected from Chapters 9 and 10 of Kuhn's book. In these chapters, Kuhn introduces two central concepts: paradigm shift and incommensurability. First, Kuhn argues that major scientific revolutions involve a paradigm shift. This means that the background concepts, methods, and assumptions that are normally taken for granted change. For example, the change from Newton's classical physics to Einstein's theories of relativity is a paradigm shift. It is a conceptual change; Einstein's special relativity involves conceptions of mass, space, and time that are radically different from those of Newton's theory. In Einstein's theory, the mass of a body depends on its velocity; likewise for its spatial extension and for duration. In Newton's theory, mass, length, and temporal duration do not depend on velocity.

Second, Kuhn argues that in such shifts, the old and new paradigms can be incommensurable. They cannot be compared in terms of some neutral ground. As a consequence of incommensurability, Kuhn contends that it is misconceived to regard science as a progressive accumulation of knowledge. Such a view of science ignores the point that scientific revolutions involve changes in the meaning of key terms, and it is incompatible with the incommensurability of paradigms. Kuhn also argues against the idea that scientific progress consists in only discoveries. Such a view neglects the conceptual and methodological changes that are part of a scientific revolution. Discovery and conceptual invention cannot be sharply separated.

The reading also presents one of the main arguments in favor of incommensurability, which is that all observations require and involve theoretical concepts. There is no sharp distinction between observation and theory. Thus, there can be no appeal to theory-neutral observations to settle disputes between competing paradigms.

CHAPTER IX

THE NATURE AND NECESSITY OF SCIENTIFIC REVOLUTIONS

What are scientific revolutions, and what is their function in scientific development? Much of the answer to these questions has been anticipated in earlier sections. In particular, the preceding discussion has indicated that scientific revolutions are here taken to be those non-cumulative developmental episodes in which an older paradigm is replaced in whole or in part by an incompatible new one. There is more to be said, however, and an essential part of it can be introduced by asking one further question. Why should a change of paradigm be called a revolution? In the face of the vast and essential differences between political and scientific development, what parallelism can justify the metaphor that finds revolutions in both?

One aspect of the parallelism must already be apparent. Political revolutions are inaugurated by a growing sense, often restricted to a segment of the political community, that existing institutions have ceased adequately to meet the problems posed by an environment that they have in part created. In much the same way, scientific revolutions are inaugurated by a growing sense, again often restricted to a narrow subdivision of the scientific community, that an existing paradigm has ceased to function adequately in the exploration of an aspect of nature to which that paradigm itself had previously led the way. In both political and scientific development the sense of malfunction that can lead to crisis is prerequisite to revolution. . . .

This genetic aspect of the parallel between political and scientific development should no longer be open to doubt. The parallel has, however, a second and more profound aspect upon which the significance of the first depends. Political revolutions aim to change political institutions in ways that those institutions themselves prohibit. Their success therefore necessitates the partial relinquishment of one set of institutions in favor of another, and in the interim, society is not fully governed by institutions at all. Initially it is crisis alone that attenuates the role of political institutions as we have already seen it attenuate the role of paradigms. In increasing numbers individuals become increasingly estranged from political life and behave more and more eccentrically within it. Then, as the crisis deepens, many of these individuals commit themselves to some concrete proposal for the reconstruction of society in a new institutional framework. At that point the society is divided into competing camps or parties, one seeking to defend the old institutional constellation, the others seeking to institute some new one. And, once that polarization has occurred, *political recourse fails*. . . .

The remainder of this essay aims to demonstrate that the historical study of paradigm change reveals very similar characteristics in the evolution of the sciences. Like the choice between competing political institutions, that between competing paradigms proves to be a choice between incompatible modes of community life. Because it has that character, the choice is not and cannot be determined merely by the evaluative procedures characteristic of normal science, for these depend in part upon a particular paradigm, and that paradigm is at issue. When paradigms enter, as they must, into a debate about paradigm choice, their role is necessarily circular. Each group uses its own paradigm to argue in that paradigm's defense.

The resulting circularity does not, of course, make the arguments wrong or even ineffectual. The man who premises a paradigm when arguing in its defense can nonetheless provide a clear exhibit of what scientific practice will be like for those who adopt the new view of nature. That exhibit can be immensely persuasive, often compellingly so. Yet, whatever its force, the status of the circular argument is only that of persuasion. It cannot be made logically or even probabilistically compelling for those who refuse to step into the circle. The premises and values shared by the two parties to a debate over paradigms are not sufficiently extensive for that. As in political revolutions, so in paradigm choice—there is no standard higher than the assent of the relevant community. To discover how scientific revolutions are effected, we shall therefore have to examine not only the impact of nature and of logic, but also the techniques of persuasive argumentation effective within the quite special groups that constitute the community of scientists.

From *The Structure of Scientific Revolutions*, *2E* by Thomas S. Kuhn, 1970. Reprinted by permission of University of Chicago Press as publisher.

To discover why this issue of paradigm choice can never be unequivocally settled by logic and experiment alone, we must shortly examine the nature of the differences that separate the proponents of a traditional paradigm from their revolutionary successors. . . .

Are there intrinsic reasons why the assimilation of either a new sort of phenomenon or a new scientific theory must demand the rejection of an older paradigm?

First notice that if there are such reasons, they do not derive from the logical structure of scientific knowledge. In principle, a new phenomenon might emerge without reflecting destructively upon any part of past scientific practice. Though discovering life on the moon would today be destructive of existing paradigms (these tell us things about the moon that seem incompatible with life's existence there), discovering life in some less well-known part of the galaxy would not. By the same token, a new theory does not have to conflict with any of its predecessors. It might deal exclusively with phenomena not previously known, as the quantum theory deals (but, significantly, not exclusively) with subatomic phenomena unknown before the twentieth century. Or again, the new theory might be simply a higher level theory than those known before, one that linked together a whole group of lower level theories without substantially changing any. Today, the theory of energy conservation provides just such links between dynamics, chemistry, electricity, optics, thermal theory, and so on. Still other compatible relationships between old and new theories can be conceived. Any and all of them might be exemplified by the historical process through which science has developed. If they were, scientific development would be genuinely cumulative. New sorts of phenomena would simply disclose order in an aspect of nature where none had been seen before. In the evolution of science new knowledge would replace ignorance rather than replace knowledge of another and incompatible sort. . . .

Nevertheless, despite the immense plausibility of that ideal image, there is increasing reason to wonder whether it can possibly be an image of *science*. After the pre-paradigm period the assimilation of all new theories and of almost all new sorts of phenomena has in fact demanded the destruction of a prior paradigm and a consequent conflict between competing schools of scientific thought. Cumulative acquisition of unanticipated novelties proves to be an almost non-existent exception to the rule of scientific development. The man who takes historic fact seriously must suspect that science does not tend toward the ideal that our image of its cumulativeness has suggested. . . .

Paradigms provide all phenomena except anomalies with a theory-determined place in the scientist's field of vision.

But if new theories are called forth to resolve anomalies in the relation of an existing theory to nature, then the successful new theory must somewhere permit predictions that are different from those derived from its predecessor. That difference could not occur if the two were logically compatible. In the process of being assimilated, the second must displace the first. Even a theory like energy conservation, which today seems a logical superstructure that relates to nature only through independently established theories, did not develop historically without paradigm destruction. Instead, it emerged from a crisis in which an essential ingredient was the incompatibility between Newtonian dynamics and some recently formulated consequences of the caloric theory of heat. Only after the caloric theory had been rejected could energy conservation become part of science. And only after it had been part of science for some time could it come to seem a theory of a logically higher type, one not in conflict with its predecessors. It is hard to see how new theories could arise without these destructive changes in beliefs about nature. Though logical inclusiveness remains a permissible view of the relation between successive scientific theories, it is a historical implausibility.

A century ago it would, I think, have been possible to let the case for the necessity of revolutions rest at this point. But today, unfortunately, that cannot be done because the view of the subject developed above cannot be maintained if the most prevalent contemporary interpretation of the nature and function of scientific theory is accepted. That interpretation, closely associated with early logical positivism and not categorically rejected by its successors, would restrict the range and meaning of an accepted theory so that it could not possibly conflict with any later theory that made predictions about some of the same natural phenomena. The best-known and the strongest case for this restricted conception of a scientific theory emerges in discussions of the relation between contemporary Einsteinian dynamics and the older dynamical equations that descend from Newton's *Principia*. From the viewpoint of this essay these two theories are fundamentally incompatible in the sense illustrated by the relation of Copernican to Ptolemaic astronomy: Einstein's theory can be accepted only with the recognition that Newton's was wrong. Today this remains a minority view. We must therefore examine the most prevalent objections to it.

The gist of these objections can be developed as follows. Relativistic dynamics cannot have shown Newtonian dynamics to be wrong, for Newtonian dynamics is still used with great success by most engineers and, in selected applications, by many physicists. Furthermore, the propriety of this use of the older theory can be proved from the very theory that has, in other applications, replaced it. Einstein's theory can be used to show that predictions from Newton's equations will be as good as our measuring instruments in all applications that satisfy a small number of restrictive conditions. For example, if Newtonian theory is to provide a good approximate solution, the relative velocities of the bodies considered must be small compared with the velocity of light. Subject to this condition and a few others, Newtonian theory seems to be derivable from Einsteinian, of which it is therefore a special case.

But, the objection continues, no theory can possibly conflict with one of its special cases. If Einsteinian science seems to make Newtonian dynamics wrong, that is only because some Newtonians were so incautious as to claim that Newtonian theory yielded entirely precise results or that it was valid at very high relative velocities. Since they could not have had any evidence for such claims, they betrayed the standards of science when they made them. In so far as Newtonian theory was ever a truly scientific theory supported by valid evidence, it still is. Only extravagant claims for the theory—claims that were never properly parts of science—can have been shown by Einstein to be wrong. Purged of these merely human extravagances, Newtonian theory has never been challenged and cannot be.

Some variant of this argument is quite sufficient to make any theory ever used by a significant group of competent scientists immune to attack. The much-maligned phlogiston theory, for example, gave order to a large number of physical and chemical phenomena. It explained why bodies burned—they were rich in phlogiston—and why metals had so many more properties in common than did their ores. The metals were all compounded from different elementary earths combined with phlogiston, and the latter, common to all metals, produced common properties. In addition, the phlogiston theory accounted for a number of reactions in which acids were formed by the combustion of substances like carbon and sulphur. Also, it explained the decrease of volume when combustion occurs in a confined volume of air—the phlogiston released by combustion "spoils" the elasticity of the air that absorbed it, just as fire "spoils" the elasticity of a steel spring. If these were the only phenomena that the phlogiston theorists had claimed for their theory, that theory could never have been challenged. A similar argument will suffice for any theory that has ever been successfully applied to any range of phenomena at all.

But to save theories in this way, their range of application must be restricted to those phenomena and to that precision of observation with which the experimental evidence in hand already deals. Carried just a step further (and the step can scarcely be avoided once the first is taken), such a limitation prohibits the scientist from claiming to speak "scientifically" about any phenomenon not already observed. Even in its present form the restriction forbids the scientist to rely upon a theory in his own research whenever that research enters an area or seeks a degree of precision for which past practice with the theory offers no precedent. These prohibitions are logically unexceptionable. But the result of accepting them would be the end of the research through which science may develop further.

By now that point too is virtually a tautology. Without commitment to a paradigm there could be no normal science. Furthermore, that commitment must extend to areas and to degrees of precision for which there is no full precedent. If it did not, the paradigm could provide no puzzles that had not already been solved. Besides, it is not only normal science that depends upon commitment to a paradigm. If existing theory binds the scientist only with respect to existing applications, then there can be no surprises, anomalies, or crises. But these are just the signposts that point the way to extraordinary science. If positivistic restrictions on the range of a theory's legitimate applicability are taken literally, the mechanism that tells the scientific community what problems may lead to fundamental change must cease to function. And when that occurs, the community will inevitably return to something much like its pre-paradigm state, a condition in which all members practice science but in which their gross product scarcely resembles science at all. Is it really any wonder that the price of significant scientific advance is a commitment that runs the risk of being wrong?

More important, there is a revealing logical lacuna in the positivist's argument, one that will reintroduce us immediately to the nature of revolutionary change. Can Newtonian dynamics really be *derived* from relativistic dynamics? What would such a derivation look like? Imagine a set of statements, E_1, $E_2, \ldots , E_n$, which together embody the laws of relativity theory. These statements contain variables and parameters representing spatial position, time, rest mass, etc. From them, together with the apparatus of logic and mathematics, is deducible a whole set of further statements including some that can be checked by observation. To prove the adequacy of Newtonian dynamics as a special case, we must add to the E_i's additional statements, like $(v/c)^2 \ll 1$, restricting the range of the parameters and variables. This enlarged set of statements is then manipulated to yield a new set, $N_1, N_2, \ldots , N_m$, which is identical in form with Newton's laws of motion, the law of gravity, and so on. Apparently Newtonian dynamics has been derived from Einsteinian, subject to a few limiting conditions. . . .

Yet the derivation is spurious, at least to this point. Though the N_i's are a special case of the laws of relativistic mechanics, they are not Newton's Laws. Or at least they are not unless those laws are reinterpreted in a way that would have been impossible until after Einstein's work. The variables and parameters that in the Einsteinian E_i's represented spatial position, time, mass, etc., still occur in the N_i's; and they there still represent Einsteinian space, time, and mass. But the physical referents of these Einsteinian concepts are by no means identical with those of the Newtonian concepts that bear the same name. (Newtonian mass is conserved; Einsteinian is convertible with energy. Only at low relative velocities may the two be measured in the same way, and even then they must not be conceived to be the same.) Unless we change the definitions of the variables in the N_i's, the

statements we have derived are not Newtonian. If we do change them, we cannot properly be said to have *derived* Newton's Laws, at least not in any sense of "derive" now generally recognized. Our argument has, of course, explained why Newton's Laws ever seemed to work. In doing so it has justified, say, an automobile driver in acting as though he lived in a Newtonian universe. An argument of the same type is used to justify teaching earth-centered astronomy to surveyors. But the argument has still not done what it purported to do. It has not, that is, shown Newton's Laws to be a limiting case of Einstein's. For in the passage to the limit it is not only the forms of the laws that have changed. Simultaneously we have had to alter the fundamental structural elements of which the universe to which they apply is composed.

This need to change the meaning of established and familiar concepts is central to the revolutionary impact of Einstein's theory. Though subtler than the changes from geocentrism to heliocentrism, from phlogiston to oxygen, or from corpuscles to waves, the resulting conceptual transformation is no less decisively destructive of a previously established paradigm. We may even come to see it as a prototype for revolutionary reorientations in the sciences. Just because it did not involve the introduction of additional objects or concepts, the transition from Newtonian to Einsteinian mechanics illustrates with particular clarity the scientific revolution as a displacement of the conceptual network through which scientists view the world.

Let us, therefore, now take it for granted that the differences between successive paradigms are both necessary and irreconcilable. Can we then say more explicitly what sorts of differences these are? The most apparent type has already been illustrated repeatedly. Successive paradigms tell us different things about the population of the universe and about that population's behavior. They differ, that is, about such questions as the existence of subatomic particles, the materiality of light, and the conservation of heat or of energy. These are the substantive differences between successive paradigms, and they require no further illustration. But paradigms differ in more than substance, for they are directed not only to nature but also back upon the science that produced them. They are the source of the methods, problem-field, and standards of solution accepted by any mature scientific community at any given time. As a result, the reception of a new paradigm often necessitates a redefinition of the corresponding science. Some old problems may be relegated to another science or declared entirely "unscientific." Others that were previously non-existent or trivial may, with a new paradigm, become the very archetypes of significant scientific achievement. And as the problems change, so, often, does the standard that distinguishes a real scientific solution from a mere metaphysical speculation, word game, or mathematical play. The normal-scientific tradition that emerges from a scientific revolution is not only incompatible but often actually incommensurable with that which has gone before. . . .

Previously, we had principally examined the paradigm's role as a vehicle for scientific theory. In that role it functions by telling the scientist about the entities that nature does and does not contain and about the ways in which those entities behave. That information provides a map whose details are elucidated by mature scientific research. And since nature is too complex and varied to be explored at random, that map is as essential as observation and experiment to science's continuing development. Through the theories they embody, paradigms prove to be constitutive of the research activity. They are also, however, constitutive of science in other respects, and that is now the point. In particular, our most recent examples show that paradigms provide scientists not only with a map but also with some of the directions essential for map-making. In learning a paradigm the scientist acquires theory, methods, and standards together, usually in an inextricable mixture. Therefore, when paradigms change, there are usually significant shifts in the criteria determining the legitimacy both of problems and of proposed solutions.

That observation returns us to the point from which this section began, for it provides our first explicit indication of why the choice between competing paradigms regularly raises questions that cannot be resolved by the criteria of normal science. To the extent, as significant as it is incomplete, that two scientific schools disagree about what is a problem and what a solution, they will inevitably talk through each other when debating the relative merits of their respective paradigms. In the partially circular arguments that regularly result, each paradigm will be shown to satisfy more or less the criteria that it dictates for itself and to fall short of a few of those dictated by its opponent. There are other reasons, too, for the incompleteness of logical contact that consistently characterizes paradigm debates. For example, since no paradigm ever solves all the problems it defines and since no two paradigms leave all the same problems unsolved, paradigm debates always involve the question: Which problems is it more significant to have solved? Like the issue of competing standards, that question of values can be answered only in terms of criteria that lie outside of normal science altogether, and it is that recourse to external criteria that most obviously makes paradigm debates revolutionary. Something even more fundamental than standards and values is, however, also at stake. I have so far argued only that paradigms are constitutive of science. Now I wish to display a sense in which they are constitutive of nature as well.

CHAPTER X

REVOLUTIONS AS CHANGES OF WORLD VIEW

Examining the record of past research from the vantage of contemporary historiography, the historian of science may be tempted to exclaim that when paradigms change, the world itself changes with them. Led by a new paradigm, scientists adopt new instruments and look in new places. Even more important, during revolutions scientists see new and different things when looking with familiar instruments in places they have looked before. It is rather as if the professional community had been suddenly transported to another planet where familiar objects are seen in a different light and are joined by unfamiliar ones as well. Of course, nothing of quite that sort does occur: there is no geographical transplantation; outside the laboratory everyday affairs usually continue as before. Nevertheless, paradigm changes do cause scientists to see the world of their research-engagement differently. In so far as their only recourse to that world is through what they see and do, we may want to say that after a revolution scientists are responding to a different world.

It is as elementary prototypes for these transformations of the scientist's world that the familiar demonstrations of a switch in visual gestalt prove so suggestive. What were ducks in the scientist's world before the revolution are rabbits afterwards. The man who first saw the exterior of the box from above later sees its interior from below. Transformations like these, though usually more gradual and almost always irreversible, are common concomitants of scientific training. Looking at a contour map, the student sees lines on paper, the cartographer a picture of a terrain. Looking at a bubble-chamber photograph, the student sees confused and broken lines, the physicist a record of familiar subnuclear events. Only after a number of such transformations of vision does the student become an inhabitant of the scientist's world, seeing what the scientist sees and responding as the scientist does. The world that the student then enters is not, however, fixed once and for all by the nature of the environment, on the one hand, and of science, on the other. Rather, it is determined jointly by the environment and the particular normal-scientific tradition that the student has been trained to pursue. Therefore, at times of revolution, when the normal-scientific tradition changes, the scientist's perception of his environment must be reeducated—in some familiar situations he must learn to see a new gestalt. After he has done so the world of his research will seem, here and there, incommensurable with the one he had inhabited before. That is another reason why schools guided by different paradigms are always slightly at cross-purposes.

In their most usual form, of course, gestalt experiments illustrate only the nature of perceptual transformations. They tell us nothing about the role of paradigms or of previously assimilated experience in the process of perception. But on that point there is a rich body of psychological literature, much of it stemming from the pioneering work of the Hanover Institute. An experimental subject who puts on goggles fitted with inverting lenses initially sees the entire world upside down. At the start his perceptual apparatus functions as it had been trained to function in the absence of the goggles, and the result is extreme disorientation, an acute personal crisis. But after the subject has begun to learn to deal with his new world, his entire visual field flips over, usually after an intervening period in which vision is simply confused. Thereafter, objects are again seen as they had been before the goggles were put on. The assimilation of a previously anomalous visual field has reacted upon and changed the field itself. Literally as well as metaphorically, the man accustomed to inverting lenses has undergone a revolutionary transformation of vision. . . .

In recent years several of those concerned with the history of science have found the sorts of experiments described above immensely suggestive. N. R. Hanson, in particular, has used gestalt demonstrations to elaborate some of the same consequences of scientific belief that concern me here. Other colleagues have repeatedly noted that history of science would make better and more coherent sense if one could suppose that scientists occasionally experienced shifts of perception like those described above. Yet, though psychological experiments are suggestive, they cannot, in the nature of the case, be more than that. They do display characteristics of perception that *could* be central to scientific development, but they do not demonstrate that the careful and controlled observation exercised by the research scientist at all partakes of those characteristics. . . .

Let us then return to the data and ask what sorts of transformations in the scientist's world the historian who believes in such changes can discover. Sir William Herschel's discovery of Uranus provides a first example and one that closely parallels the anomalous card experiment. On at least seventeen different occasions between 1690 and 1781, a number of astronomers, including several of Europe's most eminent observers, had seen a star in positions that we now suppose must have been occupied at the time by Uranus. One of the best observers in this group had actually seen the star on four successive nights in 1769 without noting the motion that could have suggested another identification. Herschel, when he first observed the same object twelve years later, did so with a much improved telescope of his own manufacture. As a result, he was able to notice an apparent disk-size that was at least unusual for stars. Something was awry, and he therefore postponed identification pending further scrutiny. That scrutiny disclosed Uranus' motion among the stars, and Herschel therefore announced that he had seen a new comet! Only several months later, after fruitless attempts to fit the observed motion to a cometary orbit, did Lexell suggest that the orbit was probably planetary. When that suggestion was accepted, there were several fewer stars and one more planet in the world of the professional astronomer. A celestial body that had been observed off and on for almost a century was seen differently after 1781 because, like an anomalous playing card, it could no longer be fitted to the perceptual categories (star or comet) provided by the paradigm that had previously prevailed.

The shift of vision that enabled astronomers to see Uranus, the planet, does not, however, seem to have affected only the perception of that previously observed object. Its consequences were more far-reaching. Probably, though the evidence is equivocal, the minor paradigm change forced by Herschel helped to prepare astronomers for the rapid discovery, after 1801, of the numerous minor planets or asteroids. Because of their small size, these did not display the anomalous magnification that had alerted Herschel. Nevertheless, astronomers prepared to find additional planets were able, with standard instruments, to identify twenty of them in the first fifty years of the nineteenth century. The history of astronomy provides many other examples of paradigm-induced changes in scientific perception, some of them even less equivocal. Can it conceivably be an accident, for example, that Western astronomers first saw change in the previously immutable heavens during the half-century after Copernicus' new paradigm was first proposed? The Chinese, whose cosmological beliefs did not preclude celestial change, had recorded the appearance of many new stars in the heavens at a much earlier date. Also, even without the aid of a telescope, the Chinese had systematically recorded the appearance of sunspots centuries before these were seen by Galileo and his contemporaries. Nor were sunspots and a new star the only examples of celestial change to emerge in the heavens of Western astronomy immediately after Copernicus. Using traditional instruments, some as simple as a piece of thread, late sixteenth-century astronomers repeatedly discovered that comets wandered at will through the space previously reserved for the immutable planets and stars. The very ease and rapidity with which astronomers saw new things when looking at old objects with old instruments may make us wish to say that, after Copernicus, astronomers lived in a different world. In any case, their research responded as though that were the case.

Shifts of this sort are not restricted to astronomy and electricity. We have already remarked some of the similar transformations of vision that can be drawn from the history of chemistry. Lavoisier, we said, saw oxygen where Priestley had seen dephlogisticated air and where others had seen nothing at all. In learning to see oxygen, however, Lavoisier also had to change his view of many other more familiar substances. He had, for example, to see a compound ore where Priestley and his contemporaries had seen an elementary earth, and there were other such changes besides. At the very least, as a result of discovering oxygen, Lavoisier saw nature differently. And in the absence of some recourse to that hypothetical fixed nature that he "saw differently," the principle of economy will urge us to say that after discovering oxygen Lavoisier worked in a different world. . . .

Do we, however, really need to describe what separates Galileo from Aristotle, or Lavoisier from Priestley, as a transformation of vision? Did these men really *see* different things when *looking* at the same sorts of objects? Is there any legitimate sense in which we can say that they pursued their research in different worlds? Those questions can no longer be postponed, for there is obviously another and far more usual way to describe all of the historical examples outlined above. Many readers will surely want to say that what changes with a paradigm is only the scientist's interpretation of observations that themselves are fixed once and for all by the nature of the environment and of the perceptual apparatus. On this view, Priestley and Lavoisier both saw oxygen, but they interpreted their observations differently; Aristotle and Galileo both saw pendulums, but they differed in their interpretations of what they both had seen.

Let me say at once that this very usual view of what occurs when scientists change their minds about fundamental matters can be neither all wrong nor a mere mistake. Rather it is an essential part of a philosophical paradigm initiated by Descartes and developed at the same time as Newtonian dynamics. That paradigm has served both science and philosophy well. Its exploitation, like that of dynamics itself, has been fruitful of a fundamental understanding that perhaps could not have been achieved in another way. But as the example of Newtonian dynamics also indicates, even the most striking past success provides no guarantee that crisis can be indefinitely postponed. Today research in parts of philosophy, psychology, linguistics, and even art history, all converge to suggest that the traditional paradigm is somehow askew. That failure to fit is also made increasingly apparent by the historical study of science to which most of our attention is necessarily directed here.

None of these crisis-promoting subjects has yet produced a viable alternate to the traditional epistemological paradigm, but they do begin to suggest what some of that paradigm's characteristics will be. I am, for example, acutely aware of the difficulties created by saying that when Aristotle and Galileo looked at swinging stones, the first saw constrained fall, the second a pendulum. The same difficulties are presented in an even more fundamental form by the opening sentences of this section: though the world does not change with a change of paradigm, the scientist afterward works in a different world. Nevertheless, I am convinced that we must learn to make sense of statements that at least resemble these. What occurs during a scientific revolution is not fully reducible to a reinterpretation of individual and stable data. In the first place, the data are not unequivocally stable. A pendulum is not a falling stone, nor is oxygen dephlogisticated air. Consequently, the data that scientists collect from these diverse objects are, as we shall shortly see, themselves different. More important, the process by which either the individual or the community makes the transition from constrained fall to the pendulum or from dephlogisticated air to oxygen is not one that resembles interpretation. How could it do so in the absence of fixed data for the scientist to interpret? Rather than being an interpreter, the scientist who embraces a new paradigm is like the man wearing inverting lenses. Confronting the same constellation of objects as before and knowing that he does so, he nevertheless finds them transformed through and through in many of their details.

None of these remarks is intended to indicate that scientists do not characteristically interpret observations and data. On the contrary, Galileo interpreted observations on the pendulum, Aristotle observations on falling stones, Musschenbroek observations on a charge-filled bottle, and Franklin observations on a condenser. But each of these interpretations presupposed a paradigm. They were parts of normal science, an enterprise that, as we have already seen, aims to refine, extend, and articulate a paradigm that is already in existence. Section III provided many examples in which interpretation played a central role. Those examples typify the overwhelming majority of research. In each of them the scientist, by virtue of an accepted paradigm, knew what a datum was, what instruments might be used to retrieve it, and what concepts were relevant to its interpretation. Given a paradigm, interpretation of data is central to the enterprise that explores it.

But that interpretive enterprise—and this was the burden of the paragraph before last—can only articulate a paradigm, not correct it. Paradigms are not corrigible by normal science at all. Instead, as we have already seen, normal science ultimately leads only to the recognition of anomalies and to crises. And these are terminated, not by deliberation and interpretation, but by a relatively sudden and unstructured event like the gesalt switch. Scientists then often speak of the "scales falling from the eyes" or of the "lightning flash" that "inundates" a previously obscure puzzle, enabling its components to be seen in a new way that for the first time permits its solution. On other occasions the relevant illumination comes in sleep. No ordinary sense of the term 'interpretation' fits these flashes of intuition through which a new paradigm is born. Though such intuitions depend upon the experience, both anomalous and congruent, gained with the old paradigm, they are not logically or piecemeal linked to particular items of that experience as an interpretation would be. Instead, they gather up large portions of that experience and transform them to the rather different bundle of experience that will thereafter be linked piecemeal to the new paradigm but not to the old. . . .

It is, of course, by no means clear that we need be so concerned with "immediate experience"—that is, with the perceptual features that a paradigm so highlights that they surrender their regularities almost upon inspection. Those features must obviously change with the scientist's commitments to paradigms, but they are far from what we ordinarily have in mind when we speak of the raw data or the brute experience from which scientific research is reputed to proceed. Perhaps immediate experience should be set aside as fluid, and we should discuss instead the concrete operations and measurements that the scientist performs in his laboratory. Or perhaps the analysis should be carried further still from the immediately given. It might, for example, be conducted in terms of some neutral observation-language, perhaps one designed to conform to the retinal imprints that mediate what the scientist sees. Only in one of these ways can we hope to retrieve a realm in which experience is again stable once and for all—in which the pendulum and constrained fall are not different perceptions but rather different interpretations of the unequivocal data provided by observation of a swinging stone.

But is sensory experience fixed and neutral? Are theories simply man-made interpretations of given data? The epistemological viewpoint that has most often guided Western philosophy for three centuries dictates an immediate and unequivocal, Yes! In the absence of a developed alternative, I find it impossible to relinquish entirely that viewpoint. Yet it no longer functions effectively, and the attempts to make it do so through the introduction of a neutral language of observations now seem to me hopeless.

The operations and measurements that a scientist undertakes in the laboratory are not "the given" of experience but rather "the collected with difficulty." They are not what the scientist sees—at least not before his research is well advanced and his attention focused. Rather, they are concrete indices to the content of more elementary perceptions, and as such they are selected for the close scrutiny of normal research only because they promise opportunity for the fruitful elaboration of an accepted paradigm. Far more clearly than the immediate experience from which they in part derive, operations and measurements are paradigm-determined. Science does not deal in all possible laboratory manipulations. Instead, it selects those relevant to the juxtaposition of a paradigm with the immediate experience that that paradigm has partially determined. As a result, scientists with different paradigms engage in different concrete laboratory manipulations. The measurements to be performed on a pendulum are not the ones relevant to a case of constrained fall. Nor are the operations relevant for the elucidation of oxygen's properties uniformly the same as those required when investigating the characteristics of dephlogisticated air. . . .

The duck-rabbit shows that two men with the same retinal impressions can see different things; the inverting lenses show that two men with different retinal impressions can see the same thing. Psychology supplies a great deal of other evidence to the same effect, and the doubts that derive from it are readily reinforced by the history of attempts to exhibit an actual language of observation. No current attempt to achieve that end has yet come close to a generally applicable language of pure percepts. And those attempts that come closest share one characteristic that strongly reinforces several of this essay's main theses. From the start they presuppose a paradigm, taken either from a current scientific theory or from some fraction of everyday discourse, and they then try to eliminate from it all non-logical and non-perceptual terms. In a few realms of discourse this effort has been carried very far and with fascinating results. There can be no question that efforts of this sort are worth pursuing. But their result is a language that—like those employed in the sciences—embodies a host of expectations about nature and fails to function the moment these expectations are violated. Nelson Goodman makes exactly this point in describing the aims of his *Structure of Appearance:* "It is fortunate that nothing more [than phenomena known to exist] is in question; for the notion of 'possible' cases, of cases that do not exist but might have existed, is far from clear." No language thus restricted to reporting a world fully known in advance can produce mere neutral and objective reports on "the given." Philosophical investigation has not yet provided even a hint of what a language able to do that would be like.

All of this may seem more reasonable if we again remember that neither scientists nor laymen learn to see the world piecemeal or item by item. Except when all the conceptual and manipulative categories are prepared in advance—e.g., for the discovery of an additional transuranic element or for catching sight of a new house—both scientists and laymen sort out whole areas together from the flux of experience. The child who transfers the word 'mama' from all humans to all females and then to his mother is not just learning what 'mama' means or who his mother is. Simultaneously he is learning some of the differences between males and females as well as something about the ways in which all but one female will behave toward him. His reactions, expectations, and beliefs—indeed, much of his perceived world—change accordingly. By the same token, the Copernicans who denied its traditional title 'planet' to the sun were not only learning what 'planet' meant or what the sun was. Instead, they were changing the meaning of 'planet' so that it could continue to make useful distinctions in a world where all celestial bodies, not just the sun, were seen differently from the way they had been seen before. The same point could be made about any of our earlier examples. To see oxygen instead of dephlogisticated air, the condenser instead of the Leyden jar, or the pendulum instead of constrained fall, was only one part of an integrated shift in the scientist's vision of a great many related chemical, electrical, or dynamical phenomena. Paradigms determine large areas of experience at the same time.

It is, however, only after experience has been thus determined that the search for an operational definition or a pure observation-language can begin. The scientist or philosopher who asks what measurements or retinal imprints make the pendulum what it is must already be able to recognize a pendulum when he sees one. If he saw constrained fall instead, his question could not even be asked. And if he saw a pendulum, but saw it in the same way he saw a tuning fork or an oscillating balance, his question could not be answered. At least it could not be answered in the same way, because it would not be the same question. Therefore, though they are always legitimate and are occasionally extraordinarily fruitful, questions about retinal imprints or about the consequences of particular laboratory manipulations presuppose a world already perceptually and conceptually subdivided in a certain way. In a sense such questions are parts of normal science, for they depend upon the existence of a paradigm and they receive different answers as a result of paradigm change.

To conclude this section, let us henceforth neglect retinal impressions and again restrict attention to the laboratory operations that provide the scientist with concrete though fragmentary indices to what he has already seen. One way in which such laboratory operations change with paradigms has already been observed repeatedly. After a scientific revolution many old measurements and manipulations become irrelevant and are replaced by others instead. One does not apply all the same tests to oxygen as to dephlogisticated air. But changes of this sort are never total. Whatever he may then see, the scientist after a revolution is still looking at the same world. Furthermore, though he may previously have employed them differently, much of his language and most of his laboratory instruments are still the same as they were before. As a result, postrevolutionary science invariably includes many of the same manipulations, performed with the same instruments and described in the same terms, as its prerevolutionary predecessor. If these enduring manipulations have been changed at all, the change must lie either in their relation to the paradigm or in their concrete results.

STUDY QUESTIONS: KUHN, *THE STRUCTURE OF SCIENTIFIC REVOLUTIONS*

1. What is a scientific revolution? In what respects can it be compared to a political revolution?
2. What does Kuhn mean by 'normal science'?
3. What is a 'paradigm'? What point does Kuhn make about the choice of a paradigm?
4. How does Kuhn argue against the cumulative view of scientific progress?
5. What point is Kuhn making when he compares Einstein's theory of relativity with Newton's physics?
6. How does Kuhn argue that Newton's laws of motion cannot be derived from Einstein's theory? Why does he want to show that this derivation is spurious?
7. Why are the new and old paradigms incommensurable? What does this mean?
8. How does Kuhn support the claim that 'after a revolution scientists are responding to a different world'?
9. What was the point of Kuhn's use of the inverted lenses example?
10. How did Herschel discover Uranus? How does Kuhn use this example?

11. What was the point concerning Chinese astronomers?
12. What conclusion does Kuhn draw from the comparison of Lavoisier and Priestley?
13. What conclusion would Kuhn draw from the claim that no observation can be theory neutral?
14. How does Kuhn argue that two people with the same retinal impressions can see different things?
15. How is the claim that we do not learn to see the world piecemeal or item by item relevant to Kuhn's argument?
16. How do questions depend on a paradigm?

Philosophical Bridges: Kuhn's Influence

Kuhn's work unsettled the assumption that physics is straightforwardly objective. Because physics had been taken as the model of objective knowledge by many thinkers since the days of Newton, Kuhn's arguments struck a deep nerve. In the short term, they derailed the logical positivist program. In the longer term, Kuhn's arguments have led philosophers to question more deeply what 'the objectivity of science' really means and what the authority of science consists in. Also, Kuhn's arguments have opened the way for more radical postmodern and feminist critiques of scientism and of traditional views of scientific methodology.

The center of the stage is held by Kuhn's claim that rival scientific paradigms are incommensurable. By this he apparently means that rival paradigms cannot be assessed comparatively in terms of a neutral set of facts. Whether one can derive a stronger notion of incommensurability from Kuhn's arguments is contested. In any case, incommensurability in the natural sciences would seem to imply incommensurability in all other areas of knowledge. For this reason, there is much at stake in discussions on this aspect of Kuhn's work.

Kuhn's thesis concerning incommensurability is premised on the failure of the observation/theory distinction. This distinction fails because of the Kantian point that any perception requires concepts. Any observation will presuppose a theory, and, consequently, there are no theory-neutral observations that can be appealed to settle scientific disputes.

These two central theses of Kuhn's work have challenged many aspects of traditional views of science. For example, Carnap, Karl Popper, and Hans Reichenbach were all scientific realists who claimed that science aims at true descriptions of the real world. Incommensurability threatens realism. The lack of a clear observation/theory distinction also pressurizes foundationalism, the view that scientific theories can be justified in terms of some observational foundations. It also begs for a new definition of scientific progress.

Debate about Kuhn's thesis dominated the philosophy of science from the 1960s to the 1980s. Kuhn's work transformed the field. Earlier purely theoretical discussions of the ideal scientific methodology seemed too removed from historical and actual practice to yield any understanding. Kuhn's work was also very influential outside of the philosophy of the natural sciences. It transformed the discussion of the methodology of social sciences and injected new energy into the sociology of science. Kuhn's phrase 'paradigm shift' became popular outside of philosophy and outside of academia.

DONALD DAVIDSON (1917–2003)

Biographical History

Donald Davidson, who was born in Springfield, Massachusetts, studied at Harvard under the supervision of Quine. After receiving his M.A. in 1941, he joined the navy until the end of World War II, after which he returned to Harvard, completing his Ph.D. on Plato in 1949. After that, he taught at various American universities, including Stanford, Princeton, Chicago, and, from 1981 to 2003, Berkeley. Davidson has published many very influential articles, some of which have been collected in five volumes: *Inquiries into Truth and Interpretation* (1984), *Essays on Actions and Events* (1980), *Subjective, Intersubjective, Objective* (2001), *Problems of Rationality* (2004) and *Language, Truth and History* (2005).

Philosophical Overview

Two aspects of Davidson's work have been especially influential: his theory of meaning and his philosophy of mind. The two classic Davidson articles in these areas are 'Truth and Meaning' (1967) and 'Mental Events' (1971).

Theory of Meaning

Davidson's theory of meaning can be seen as a reply to Quine's challenge regarding meaning, within a broadly Quinean framework. Quine's challenge is that we must eliminate intensional notions, such as meaning, from our theory of language. In reply, Davidson develops a theory in which understanding the meaning of a language is analyzed in terms of knowing an extensional truth theory for that language. A truth theory (or T-theory) for a language specifies the truth-conditions for all the sentences of that language. It does not achieve this by listing those conditions for an infinite number of sentences, which would be impossible. The idea is that if one knows the rules that determine how individual words can be used, then we can derive the truth-conditions for any of the potentially infinite sentences one might construct using those rules. The T-theory formalizes this idea. Given the theory, one can generate logically the truth-conditions for a potential infinite number of sentences from a formalized knowledge of a finite number of words.

Davidson claims that to know the meaning of a sentence of a language, it is sufficient to know the T-theory of the language. This strategy employs Frege's idea that knowing the sense of a sentence consists in knowing its truth-conditions, while remaining faithful to both Quine's holism and his thesis of extensionality (see below).

Davidson applies his T-theory concept to elucidate the idea of interpretation. Suppose we encounter a community with a language that we have never heard before. We must learn to interpret their linguistic behavior, apparently knowing nothing about them. How are we to do this? We must see which sentences members of the community assent to, or think true, on the basis of which sensory evidence, and, from this, interpret their utterances, building bit by bit a T-theory for their language. In this task, a difficulty arises because of the interdependence of desire and belief, neither of which can be directly observed. Running toward shelter in the rain can be interpreted as evidence for the belief that rain will make one wet, but only given the desire to keep dry. Davidson argues that we may solve this difficulty only by assuming that the members of the community, by and large, have true and reasonable beliefs and are rational in their inferences and decisions. This he calls 'the Principle of Charity.'

Davidson employs the Principle of Charity to argue against both Skepticism and conceptual relativism. The principle shows that interpretation requires that most of our beliefs are true and, therefore, that global Skepticism is false. Furthermore, it rules out the idea that people might have mutually incomprehensible beliefs.

Philosophy of Mind and Action

Davidson has been influential also for his philosophy of mind and action. Actions are events. Events are particular occurrences that happen at a definite time, and, thus, event A and B are the same event if and only if they occur at the same time at the same place. An action is an event caused by the reasons that a person had for performing the action, which are mental states such as desires and beliefs. Davidson distinguishes between an action and its descriptions. For example, 'Brutus stabbed Caesar to death' and 'Caesar was murdered' are different descriptions of the same event. On the basis of this distinction, Davidson argues against the claim that reasons for action cannot be causes. Some philosophers claim that they cannot because causes and effects must be logically distinct, whereas reasons and actions are not logically distinct. Davidson rejects such reasoning on the grounds that the logical connection between an action and the agent's reasons applies to different descriptions of two events and not to the events themselves.

TRUTH AND MEANING

In this article, Davidson elaborates his theory of meaning, the importance of which was explained in the Philosophical Overview. The idea of a truth theory for a language seems bewilderingly simple, because we can state the truth-conditions for the sentence 'S' as follows:

T: 'S' is true in L if and only if p.

An example of such a T-sentence would be:

T1: '"Snow is white" is true in English if and only if snow is white.'

This type of truth-specifying sentence, invented by the Polish logician Tarski, is called a T-sentence.

Davidson's theory has to navigate between two extremes. In the case of T, we cannot assume that the first sentence, 'S,' has the same meaning as 'p,' as we did in the case of T1, because that assumes the notion of meaning, which we are trying to explain. On the other hand, we do not want 'p' in the case of 'T' to be just any true sentence.

In the reading, Davidson explains his main strategy. This is to specify the notion of 'truth' for a given language by listing all the T-sentences, which state the truth-conditions for each of the sentences of that language. However, a theory of meaning must show how it is possible to generate and understand an indefinite number of sentences given a finite stock of words. Consequently, a truth-theory for a language should not simply list the

From *Synthese,* 17 by Donald Davidson, D. Reidel Publishing Co., 1967, pp. 304-323. Reprinted with kind permission of Springer Science and Business Media and Marcia Cavell.

truth-conditions of each of its sentences directly, because this would not explain the compositional nature of language. As Frege argued, understanding a sentence requires knowing how its component parts contribute to the overall sense of the sentence as a whole. As a consequence, we need a truth-theory that shows how the component parts of any sentence contribute to the truth-conditions for any sentence in that language. Such a theory would entail all the T-sentences for the language in the way that a formal system entails its theorems. Thus, the truth-theory of a language must be extensional.

The T-theory for a language consists of three elements. Consider a very simple artificial language called L, which consists solely of subject-predicate sentences.

A. The List

We can list the subject-terms and predicates and what they refer to and are satisfied by. This would effectively indicate all the particular language-world relations for L. For example, suppose our language has only two subject terms and two predicate terms. The list might be as follows:

1. 'John' in L refers to John.
2. 'Mary' in L refers to Mary.
3. 'is bald' in L is satisfied by bald things.
4. 'is hairy' in L is satisfied by hairy things.

B. The Syntax

The syntax of any language gives the rules for generating well-formed sentences. In the case of L, the syntax is very simple: given any name (say, 'John') and any predicate expression (say, 'is bald'), then we can form a sentence only by placing the name before the predicate expression: 'John is bald.'

C. Satisfaction

Given this, we can introduce a technical term: 'satisfaction.' A predicate term is satisfied when the individual referred to by a name belongs to the relevant class. A general definition of truth for L would be 'Any sentence of L will be true if and only if the predicate term is satisfied by what the name refers to.' More specifically, a sentence is true in L if and only if 'John is bald' and John is bald, or 'Mary is bald' and Mary is bald, or 'John is hairy' and John is hairy, or 'Mary is hairy' and Mary is hairy.

This is merely a list. However, when formally stated, a T-theory will entail all the relevant T sentences for L, just as the axioms and rules of formation and inference will entail all the theorems in a formalized theory in logic and mathematics. To see the power of this idea, we need to enrich L. First, we can make a much longer list of subject and predicate terms, similar to those in 1–4 above. Second, we can make the syntax of L richer. We can introduce the logical connectives, such as 'and' and 'not'; the existential and universal quantifiers; and other elements, such as adverbs, tenses, and so on. In each case, the syntactical elements need to be introduced by specifying the relevant rules. In this way, we have added the essential possibility of generating an indefinite number of sentences from a finite number of words.

The important point is that anyone who knows both the rules for the syntax of L and the relevant list, such as 1–4 above, will thereby know the truth-conditions for all the sentences of L. In other words, knowing the truth-theory for L is sufficient for knowing all the truth-conditions of L. According to Davidson, this is sufficient for understanding L. In this manner, we can explain understanding a language without recourse to intensional entities, such as meaning and sense.

However, there is an important qualification. The truth-theory is supposed to generate T-sentences of L in the same way that theorems can be logically derived from axioms and rules. For this reason, each new element must be introduced in an extensional form. This means that the logical form of the sentences of L must be extensionally transparent. This requirement sets us the task or program of transforming or reparsing the messy, and sometimes intensional, sentences of a natural language into extensional sentences with a clear logical form. In this way, Davidson inherits Quine's notion of the regimentation of language into the canonical idiom. Like Quine, Davidson regards this task as philosophically necessary in any case, because it will reveal the logical form of English statements, in much the same way as Russell's theory of descriptions did.

It is conceded by most philosophers of language, and recently by some linguists, that a satisfactory theory of meaning must give an account of how the meanings of sentences depend upon the meanings of words. Unless such an account could be supplied for a particular language, it is argued, there would be no explaining the fact that we can learn the language: no explaining the fact that, on mastering a finite vocabulary and a finitely stated set of rules, we are prepared to produce and to understand any of a potential infinitude of sentences. I do not dispute these vague claims, in which I sense more than a kernel of truth. Instead I want to ask what it is for a theory to give an account of the kind adumbrated.

One proposal is to begin by assigning some entity as meaning to each word (or other significant syntactical feature) of the sentence; thus we might assign Theaetetus to 'Theaetetus' and the property of flying to 'flies' in the sentence 'Theaetetus flies'. The problem then arises how the meaning of the sentence is generated from these meanings. Viewing concatenation as a significant piece of syntax, we may assign to it the relation of participating in or instantiating; however, it is obvious that we have here the start of an infinite regress. Frege sought to avoid the regress by saying that the entities corresponding to predicates (for example) are 'unsaturated' or 'incomplete' in contrast to the entities that correspond to names, but this doctrine seems to label a difficulty rather than solve it.

The point will emerge if we think for a moment of complex singular terms, to which Frege's theory applies along with sentences. Consider the expression 'the father of Annette'; how does the meaning of the whole depend on the meaning of the parts? The answer would seem to be that the meaning of 'the father of' is such that when this expression is prefixed to a singular term the result refers to the father of the person to whom the singular term refers. What part is played, in this account, by the unsaturated or incomplete entity for which 'the father of' stands? All we can think to say is that this entity 'yields' or 'gives' the father of x as value when the argument is x, or perhaps that this entity maps people on to their fathers. It may not be clear whether the entity for which 'the father of' is said to stand performs any genuine explanatory function as long as we stick to individual expressions; so think instead of the infinite class of expressions formed by writing 'the father of' zero or more times in front of 'Annette'. It is easy to supply a theory that tells, for an arbitrary one of these singular terms, what it refers to: if the term is 'Annette' it refers to Annette, while if the term is complex, consisting of 'the father of' prefixed to a singular term t, then it refers to the father of the person to whom t refers. It is obvious that no entity corresponding to 'the father of' is, or needs to be, mentioned in stating this theory.

It would be inappropriate to complain that this little theory *uses* the words 'the father of' in giving the reference of expressions containing those words. For the task was to give the meaning of all expressions in a certain infinite set on the basis of the meaning of the parts; it was not in the bargain also to give the meanings of the atomic parts. On the other hand, it is now evident that a satisfactory theory of the meanings of complex expressions may not require entities as meanings of all the parts. It behoves us then to rephrase our demand on a satisfactory theory of meaning so as not to suggest that individual words must have meanings at all, in any sense that transcends the fact that they have a systematic effect on the meanings of the sentences in which they occur. Actually, for the case at hand we can do better still in stating the criterion of success: what we wanted, and what we got, is a theory that entails every sentence of the form 't refers to x' where 't' is replaced by a structural description of a singular term, and 'x' is replaced by that term itself. Further, our theory accomplishes this without appeal to any semantical concepts beyond the basic 'refers to'. Finally, the theory clearly suggests an effective procedure for determining, for any singular term in its universe, what that term refers to.

A theory with such evident merits deserves wider application. The device proposed by Frege to this end has a brilliant simplicity: count predicates as a special case of functional expressions, and sentences as a special case of complex singular terms. Now, however, a difficulty looms if we want to continue in our present (implicit) course of identifying the meaning of a singular term with its reference. The difficulty follows upon making two reasonable assumptions: that logically equivalent singular terms have the same reference, and that a singular term does not change its reference if a contained singular term is replaced by another with the same reference. But now suppose that 'R' and 'S' abbreviate any two sentences alike in truth value. Then the following four sentences have the same reference:

(1) R
(2) $\hat{x}(x = x \,.\, R) = \hat{x}(x = x)$
(3) $\hat{x}(x = x \,.\, S) = \hat{x}(x = x)$
(4) S

For (1) and (2) are logically equivalent, as are (3) and (4), while (3) differs from (2) only in containing the singular term '$\hat{x}(x = x \,.\, S)$' where (2) contains '$\hat{x}(x = x \,.\, R)$' and these refer to the same thing if S and R are alike in truth value. Hence any two sentences have the same reference if they have the same truth value. And if the meaning of a sentence is what it refers to, all sentences alike in truth value must be synonymous—an intolerable result.

Apparently we must abandon the present approach as leading to a theory of meaning. This is the natural point at which to turn for help to the distinction between meaning and reference. The trouble, we are told, is that questions of reference are, in general, settled by extra-linguistic facts, questions of meaning not, and the facts can conflate the references of expressions that are not synonymous. If we want a theory that gives the meaning (as distinct from reference) of each sentence, we must start with the meaning (as distinct from reference) of the parts.

Up to here we have been following in Frege's footsteps; thanks to him, the path is well known and even well worn. But now, I would like to suggest, we have reached an impasse: the switch from reference to meaning leads to no useful account of how the meanings of sentences depend upon the meanings of the words (or other structural features) that compose them. Ask, for example, for the meaning of 'Theaetetus flies'. A Fregean answer might go something like this: given the meaning of 'Theaetetus' as argument, the meaning of 'flies' yields the meaning of 'Theaetetus flies' as value. The vacuity of this answer is obvious. We wanted to know what the meaning of 'Theaetetus flies' is; it is no progress to be told that it is the meaning of 'Theaetetus flies'. This much we knew before any theory was in sight. In the bogus account just given, talk of the structure of the sentence and of the meanings of words was idle, for it played no role in producing the given description of the meaning of the sentence.

The contrast here between a real and pretended account will be plainer still if we ask for a theory, analogous to the miniature theory of reference of singular terms just sketched, but different in dealing with meanings in place of references. What analogy demands is a theory that has as consequences all sentences of the form 's means m' where 's' is replaced by a structural description of a sentence and 'm' is replaced by a singular term that refers to the meaning of that sentence; a theory, moreover, that provides an effective method for arriving at the meaning of an arbitrary sentence structurally described. Clearly some more articulate way of referring to meanings than any we have seen is essential if these criteria are to be met. Meanings as entities, or the related concept of synonymy, allow us to formulate the following rule relating sentences and their parts: sentences are synonymous whose corresponding parts are synonymous ('corresponding' here needs spelling out of course). And meanings as entities may, in theories such as Frege's, do duty, on occasion, as references, thus losing their status as entities distinct from references. Paradoxically, the one thing meanings do not seem to do is oil the wheels of a theory of meaning—at least as long as we require of such a theory that it non-trivially give the meaning of every sentence in the language. My objection to meanings in the theory of meaning is not that they are abstract or that their identity conditions are obscure, but that they have no demonstrated use.

This is the place to scotch another hopeful thought. Suppose we have a satisfactory theory of syntax for our language, consisting of an effective method of telling, for an arbitrary expression, whether or not it is independently meaningful (i.e. a sentence), and assume as usual that this involves viewing each sentence as composed, in allowable ways, out of elements drawn from a fixed finite stock of atomic syntactical elements (roughly, words). The hopeful thought is that syntax, so conceived, will yield semantics when a dictionary giving the meaning of each syntactic atom is added. Hopes will be dashed, however, if semantics is to comprise a theory of meaning in our sense, for knowledge of the structural characteristics that make for meaningfulness in a sentence, plus knowledge of the meanings of the ultimate parts, does not add up to knowledge of what a sentence means. The point is easily illustrated by belief sentences. Their syntax is relatively unproblematic. Yet, adding a dictionary does not touch the standard semantic problem, which is that we cannot account for even as much as the truth conditions of such sentences on the basis of what we know of the meanings of the words in them. The situation is not radically altered by refining the dictionary to indicate which meaning or meanings an ambiguous expression bears in each of its possible contexts; the problem of belief sentences persists after ambiguities are resolved.

The fact that recursive syntax with dictionary added is not necessarily recursive semantics has been obscured in some recent writing on linguistics by the intrusion of semantic criteria into the discussion of purportedly syntactic theories. The matter would boil down to a harmless difference over terminology if the semantic criteria were clear; but they are not. While there is agreement that it is the central task of semantics to give the semantic interpretation (the meaning) of every sentence in the language, nowhere in the linguistic literature will one find, so far as I know, a straightforward account of how a theory performs this task, or how to tell when it has been accomplished. The contrast with syntax is striking. The main job of a modest syntax is to characterize *meaningfulness* (or sentencehood). We may have as much confidence in the correctness of such a characterization as we have in the representativeness of our sample and our ability to say when particular expressions are meaningful (sentences). What clear and analogous task and test exist for semantics?

We decided a while back not to assume that parts of sentences have meanings except in the ontologically neutral sense of making a systematic contribution to the meaning of the sentences in which they occur. Since postulating meanings has netted nothing, let us return to that insight. One direction in which it points is a certain holistic view of meaning. If sentences depend for their meaning on their structure, and we understand the meaning of each item in the structure only as an abstraction from the totality of sentences in which it features, then we can give the meaning of any sentence (or word) only by giving the meaning of every sentence (and word) in the language. Frege said that only in the context of a sentence does a word have meaning; in the same vein he might have added that only in the context of the language does a sentence (and therefore a word) have meaning.

This degree of holism was already implicit in the suggestion that an adequate theory of meaning must entail *all* sentences of the form 's means m'. But now, having found no more help in meanings of sentences than in meanings of words, let us ask whether we can get rid of the troublesome singular terms supposed to replace 'm' and to refer to meanings. In a way, nothing could be easier: just write 's means that p', and imagine 'p' replaced by a sentence. Sentences, as we have seen, cannot name meanings, and sentences with 'that' prefixed are not names at all, unless we decide so. It looks as though we are in trouble on another count, however, for it is reasonable to expect that in wrestling with the logic of the apparently non-extensional 'means that' we will encounter problems as hard as, or perhaps identical with, the problems our theory is out to solve.

The only way I know to deal with this difficulty is simple, and radical. Anxiety that we are enmeshed in the intensional springs from using the words 'means that' as filling between description of sentence and sentence, but it may be that the success of our venture depends not on the filling but on what it fills. The theory will have done its work if it provides, for every sentence s in the language under study, a matching sentence (to replace 'p') that, in some way yet to be made clear, 'gives the meaning' of s. One obvious candidate for matching sentence is just s itself, if the object language is contained in the metalanguage; otherwise a translation of s in the metalanguage. As a final bold step, let us try treating the position occupied by 'p' extensionally: to implement this, sweep away the obscure 'means that', provide the sentence that replaces 'p' with a proper sentential connective, and supply the description that replaces 's' with its own predicate. The plausible result is

(T) s is T if and only if p.

What we require of a theory of meaning for a language L is that without appeal to any (further) semantical notions it place enough restrictions on the predicate 'is T' to entail all sentences got from schema T when 's' is replaced by a structural description of a sentence of L and 'p' by that sentence.

Any two predicates satisfying this condition have the same extension, so if the metalanguage is rich enough, nothing stands in the way of putting what I am calling a theory of meaning into the form of an explicit definition of a predicate 'is T'. But whether explicitly defined or recursively characterized, it is clear that the sentences to which the predicate 'is T' applies will be just the true sentences of L, for the condition we have placed on satisfactory theories of meaning is in essence Tarski's Convention T that tests the adequacy of a formal semantical definition of truth.

The path to this point has been tortuous, but the conclusion may be stated simply: a theory of meaning for a language L shows 'how the meanings of sentences depend upon the meanings of words' if it contains a (recursive) definition of truth-in-L. And, so

far at least, we have no other idea how to turn the trick. It is worth emphasizing that the concept of truth played no ostensible role in stating our original problem. That problem, upon refinement, led to the view that an adequate theory of meaning must characterize a predicate meeting certain conditions. It was in the nature of a discovery that such a predicate would apply exactly to the true sentences. I hope that what I am saying may be described in part as defending the philosophical importance of Tarski's semantical concept of truth. But my defence is only distantly related, if at all, to the question whether the concept Tarski has shown how to define is the (or a) philosophically interesting conception of truth, or the question whether Tarski has cast any light on the ordinary use of such words as 'true' and 'truth'. It is a misfortune that dust from futile and confused battles over these questions has prevented those with a theoretical interest in language—philosophers, logicians, psychologists, and linguists alike—from seeing in the semantical concept of truth (under whatever name) the sophisticated and powerful foundation of a competent theory of meaning.

There is no need to suppress, of course, the obvious connection between a definition of truth of the kind Tarski has shown how to construct, and the concept of meaning. It is this: the definition works by giving necessary and sufficient conditions for the truth of every sentence, and to give truth conditions is a way of giving the meaning of a sentence. To know the semantic concept of truth for a language is to know what it is for a sentence—any sentence—to be true, and this amounts, in one good sense we can give to the phrase, to understanding the language. This at any rate is my excuse for a feature of the present discussion that is apt to shock old hands; my freewheeling use of the word 'meaning', for what I call a theory of meaning has after all turned out to make no use of meanings, whether of sentences or of words. Indeed, since a Tarski-type truth definition supplies all we have asked so far of a theory of meaning, it is clear that such a theory falls comfortably within what Quine terms the 'theory of reference' as distinguished from what he terms the 'theory of meaning'. So much to the good for what I call a theory of meaning, and so much, perhaps, against my so calling it.

A theory of meaning (in my mildly perverse sense) is an empirical theory, and its ambition is to account for the workings of a natural language. Like any theory, it may be tested by comparing some of its consequences with the facts. In the present case this is easy, for the theory has been characterized as issuing in an infinite flood of sentences each giving the truth conditions of a sentence; we only need to ask, in sample cases, whether what the theory avers to be the truth conditions for a sentence really are. A typical test case might involve deciding whether the sentence 'Snow is white' *is* true if and only if snow is white. Not all cases will be so simple (for reasons to be sketched), but it is evident that this sort of test does not invite counting noses. A sharp conception of what constitutes a theory in this domain furnishes an exciting context for raising deep questions about when a theory of language is correct and how it is to be tried. But the difficulties are theoretical, not practical. In application, the trouble is to get a theory that comes close to working; anyone can tell whether it is right. One can see why this is so. The theory reveals nothing new about the conditions under which an individual sentence is true; it does not make those conditions any clearer than the sentence itself does. The work of the theory is in relating the known truth conditions of each sentence to those aspects ('words') of the sentence that recur in other sentences, and can be assigned identical roles in other sentences. Empirical power in such a theory depends on success in recovering the structure of a very complicated ability—the ability to speak and understand a language. We can tell easily enough when particular pronouncements of the theory comport with our understanding of the language; this is consistent with a feeble insight into the design of the machinery of our linguistic accomplishments.

The remarks of the last paragraph apply directly only to the special case where it is assumed that the language for which truth is being characterized is part of the language used and understood by the characterizer. Under these circumstances, the framer of a theory will as a matter of course avail himself when he can of the built-in convenience of a metalanguage with a sentence guaranteed equivalent to each sentence in the object language. Still, this fact ought not to con us into thinking a theory any more correct that entails '"Snow is white" is true if and only if snow is white' than one that entails instead:

(S) 'Snow is white' is true if and only if grass is green,

provided, of course, we are as sure of the truth of (S) as we are of that of its more celebrated predecessor. Yet (S) may not encourage the same confidence that a theory that entails it deserves to be called a theory of meaning.

The threatened failure of nerve may be counteracted as follows. The grotesqueness of (S) is in itself nothing against a theory of which it is a consequence, provided the theory gives the correct results for every sentence (on the basis of its structure, there being no other way). It is not easy to see how (S) could be party to such an enterprise, but if it were—if, that is, (S) followed from a characterization of the predicate 'is true' that led to the invariable pairing of truths with truths and falsehoods with falsehoods—then there would not, I think, be anything essential to the idea of meaning that remained to be captured.

What appears to the right of the biconditional in sentences of the form 's is true if and only if p' when such sentences are consequences of a theory of truth plays its role in determining the meaning of s not by pretending synonymy but by adding one more brushstroke to the picture which, taken as a whole, tells what there is to know of the meaning of s; this stroke is added by virtue of the fact that the sentence that replaces 'p' is true if and only if s is.

It may help to reflect that (S) is acceptable, if it is, because we are independently sure of the truth of 'Snow is white' and 'Grass is green'; but in cases where we are unsure of the truth of a sentence, we can have confidence in a characterization of the truth predicate only if it pairs that sentence with one we have good reason to believe equivalent. It would be ill advised for someone who had any doubts about the colour of snow or grass to accept a theory that yielded (S), even if his doubts were of equal degree, unless he thought the colour of the one was tied to the colour of the other. Omniscience can obviously afford more bizarre theories of meaning than ignorance; but then, omniscience has less need of communication.

It must be possible, of course, for the speaker of one language to construct a theory of meaning for the speaker of another, though in this case the empirical test of the correctness of the theory will no longer be trivial. As before, the aim of theory will be an infinite correlation of sentences alike in truth. But this time the theory-builder must not be assumed to have direct insight into likely equivalences between his own tongue and the alien. What he must do is find out, however he can, what sentences the alien holds true in his own tongue (or better, to what degree he holds them true). The linguist then will attempt to construct a characterization of truth-for-the-alien which yields, so far as possible, a mapping of sentences held true (or false) by the alien on to sentences held true (or false) by the linguist. Supposing no perfect fit is found, the residue of sentences held true translated by sentences held false (and vice versa) is the margin for error (foreign or domestic). Charity in interpreting the words and thoughts of others is unavoidable in another direction as well: just as we must maximize agreement, or risk not making sense of what the alien is talking about, so we must maximize the self-consistency we attribute to him, on pain of not understanding *him*. No single principle of optimum charity emerges; the constraints therefore determine no single theory. In a theory of radical translation (as Quine calls it) there is no completely disentangling questions of what the alien means from questions of what he believes. We do not know what someone means unless we know what he believes; we do not know what someone believes unless we know what he means. In radical interpretation we are able to break into this circle, if only incompletely, because we can sometimes tell that a person accedes to a sentence we do not understand.

In the past few pages I have been asking how a theory of meaning that takes the form of a truth definition can be empirically tested, and have blithely ignored the prior question whether there is any serious chance such a theory can be given for a natural language. What are the prospects for a formal semantical theory of a natural language? Very poor, according to Tarski; and I believe most logicians, philosophers of language, and linguists agree. Let me do what I can to dispel the pessimism. What I can in a general and programmatic way, of course, for here the proof of the pudding will certainly be in the proof of the right theorems.

Tarski concludes the first section of his classic essay on the concept of truth in formalized languages with the following remarks, which he italicizes:

... The very possibility of a consistent use of the expression 'true sentence' which is in harmony with the laws of logic and the spirit of everyday language seems to be very questionable, and consequently the same doubt attaches to the possibility of constructing a correct definition of this expression. (165)

Late in the same essay, he returns to the subject:

... the concept of truth (as well as other semantical concepts) when applied to colloquial language in conjunction with the normal laws of logic leads inevitably to confusions and contradictions. Whoever wishes, in spite of all difficulties, to pursue the semantics of colloquial language with the help of exact methods will be driven first to undertake the thankless task of a reform of this language. He will find it necessary to define its structure, to overcome the ambiguity of the terms which occur in it, and finally to split the language into a series of languages of greater and greater extent, each of which stands in the same relation to the next in which a formalized language stands to its metalanguage. It may, however be doubted whether the language of everyday life, after being 'rationalized' in this way, would still preserve its naturalness and whether it would not rather take on the characteristic features of the formalized languages. (267)

Two themes emerge: that the universal character of natural languages leads to contradiction (the semantic paradoxes), and that natural languages are too confused and amorphous to permit the direct application of formal methods. The first point deserves a serious answer, and I wish I had one. As it is, I will say only why I think we are justified in carrying on without having disinfected this particular source of conceptual anxiety. The semantic paradoxes arise when the range of the quantifiers in the object language is too generous in certain ways. But it is not really clear how unfair to Urdu or to Wendish it would be to view the range of their quantifiers as insufficient to yield an explicit definition of 'true-in-

Urdu' or 'true-in-Wendish'. Or, to put the matter in another, if not more serious way, there may in the nature of the case always be something we grasp in understanding the language of another (the concept of truth) that we cannot communicate to him. In any case, most of the problems of general philosophical interest arise within a fragment of the relevant natural language that may be conceived as containing very little set theory. Of course these comments do not meet the claim that natural languages are universal. But it seems to me that this claim, now that we know such universality leads to paradox, is suspect.

Tarski's second point is that we would have to reform a natural language out of all recognition before we could apply formal semantical methods. If this is true, it is fatal to my project, for the task of a theory of meaning as I conceive it is not to change, improve, or reform a language, but to describe and understand it. Let us look at the positive side. Tarski has shown the way to giving a theory for interpreted formal languages of various kinds; pick one as much like English as possible. Since this new language has been explained in English and contains much English we not only may, but I think must, view it as part of English for those who understand it. For this fragment of English we have, *ex hypothesi*, a theory of the required sort. Not only that, but in interpreting this adjunct of English in old English we necessarily gave hints connecting old and new. Wherever there are sentences of old English with the same truth conditions as sentences in the adjunct we may extend the theory to cover them. Much of what is called for is to mechanize as far as possible what we now do by art when we put ordinary English into one or another canonical notation. The point is not that canonical notation is better than the rough original idiom, but rather that if we know what idiom the canonical notation is canonical *for*, we have as good a theory for the idiom as for its kept companion.

Philosophers have long been at the hard work of applying theory to ordinary language by the device of matching sentences in the vernacular with sentences for which they have a theory. Frege's massive contribution was to show how 'all', 'some', 'every', 'each', 'none', and associated pronouns, in some of their uses, could be named; for the first time, it was possible to dream of a formal semantics for a

significant part of a natural language. This dream came true in a sharp way with the work of Tarski. It would be a shame to miss the fact that as a result of these two magnificent achievements, Frege's and Tarski's, we have gained a deep insight into the structure of our mother tongues. Philosophers of a logical bent have tended to start where the theory was and work out towards the complications of natural language. Contemporary linguists, with an aim that cannot easily be seen to be different, start with the ordinary and work toward a general theory. If either party is successful, there must be a meeting. Recent work by Chomsky and others is doing much to bring the complexities of natural languages within the scope of serious theory. To give an example: suppose success in giving the truth conditions for some significant range of sentences in the active voice. Then with a formal procedure for transforming each such sentence into a corresponding sentence in the passive voice, the theory of truth could be extended in an obvious way to this new set of sentences.

One problem touched on in passing by Tarski does not, at least in all its manifestations, have to be solved to get ahead with theory: the existence in natural languages of 'ambiguous terms'. As long as ambiguity does not affect grammatical form, and can be translated, ambiguity for ambiguity, into the metalanguage, a truth definition will not tell us any lies. The chief trouble, for systematic semantics, with the phrase 'believes that' in English lies not in its vagueness, ambiguity, or unsuitability for incorporation in a serious science: let our metalanguage be English, and all *these* problems will be carried without loss or gain into the metalanguage. But the central problem of the logical grammar of 'believes that' will remain to haunt us.

The example is suited to illustrating another, and related, point, for the discussion of belief sentences has been plagued by failure to observe a fundamental distinction between tasks: uncovering the logical grammar or form of sentences (which is in the province of a theory of meaning as I construe it), and the analysis of individual words or expressions (which are treated as primitive by the theory). Thus Carnap, in the first edition of *Meaning and Necessity*, suggested we render 'John believes that the earth is round' as 'John responds affirmatively to "the earth is round" as an English sentence'. He gave this up when Mates pointed out that John might respond affirmatively to one sentence and not to another no matter how close in meaning. But there is a confusion here from the start. The semantic structure of a belief sentence, according to this idea of Carnap's, is given by a three-place predicate with places reserved for expressions referring to a person, a sentence, and a language. It is a different sort of problem entirely to attempt an analysis of this predicate, perhaps along behaviouristic lines. Not least among the merits of Tarski's conception of a theory of truth is that the purity of method it demands of us follows from the formulation of the problem itself, not from the self-imposed restraint of some adventitious philosophical puritanism.

I think it is hard to exaggerate the advantages to philosophy of language of bearing in mind this distinction between questions of logical form or grammar, and the analysis of individual concepts. Another example may help advertise the point.

If we suppose questions of logical grammar settled, sentences like 'Bardot is good' raise no special problems for a truth definition. The deep differences between descriptive and evaluative (emotive, expressive, etc.) terms do not show here. Even if we hold there is some important sense in which moral or evaluative sentences do not have a truth value (for example, because they cannot be verified), we ought not to boggle at '"Bardot is good" is true if and only if Bardot is good'; in a theory of truth, this consequence should follow with the rest, keeping track, as must be done, of the semantic location of such sentences in the language as a whole—of their relation to generalizations, their role in such compound sentences as 'Bardot is good and Bardot is foolish', and so on. What is special to evaluative words is simply not touched: the mystery is transferred from the word 'good' in the object language to its translation in the metalanguage.

But 'good' as it features in 'Bardot is a good actress' is another matter. The problem is not that the translation of this sentence is not in the metalanguage—let us suppose it is. The problem is to frame a truth definition such that '"Bardot is a good actress" is true if and only if Bardot is a good actress'—and all other sentences like it—are consequences. Obviously 'good actress' does not mean 'good and an actress'. We might think of taking 'is a good actress' as an unanalysed predicate. This would obliterate all connection between 'is a good actress' and 'is a good mother', and it would give us no excuse to think of 'good', in these uses, as a word or semantic element. But worse, it would bar us from framing a truth definition at all, for there is no end to the predicates we would have to treat as logically simple (and hence accommodate in separate clauses in the definition of satisfaction): 'is a good companion to dogs', 'is a good 28-years old conversationalist', and so forth. The problem is not peculiar to the case: it is the problem of attributive adjectives generally.

It is consistent with the attitude taken here to deem it usually a strategic error to undertake philosophical analysis of words or expressions which is not preceded by or at any rate accompanied by the attempt to get the logical grammar straight. For how can we have any confidence in our analyses of words like 'right', 'ought', 'can', and 'obliged', or the phrases we use to talk of actions, events, and causes, when we do not know what (logical, semantical) parts of speech we have to deal with? I would say much the same about studies of the 'logic' of these and other words, and the sentences containing them. Whether the effort and ingenuity that have gone into the study of deontic logics, modal logics, imperative and erotetic logics have been largely futile or not cannot be known until we have acceptable semantic analyses of the sentences such systems purport to treat. Philosophers and logicians sometimes talk or work as if they were free to choose between, say, the truth-functional conditional and others, or free to introduce non-truth-functional sentential operators like 'Let it be the case that' or 'It ought to be the case that'. But in fact the decision is crucial. When we depart from idioms we can accommodate in a truth definition, we lapse into (or create) language for which we have no coherent semantical account—that is, no account at all of how such talk can be integrated into the language as a whole.

To return to our main theme: we have recognized that a theory of the kind proposed leaves the whole matter of what individual words mean exactly where it was. Even when the metalanguage is different from the object language, the theory exerts no pressure for improvement, clarification, or analysis of individual words, except when, by accident of vocabulary, straightforward translation fails. Just as synonymy, as between expressions, goes generally untreated, so also synonymy of sentences, and analyticity. Even such sentences as 'A vixen is a female fox' bear no special tag unless it is our pleasure to provide it. A truth definition does not distinguish between analytic sentences and others, except for sentences that owe their truth to the presence alone of the constants that give the theory its grip on structure: the theory entails not only that these sentences are true but that they will remain true under all significant rewritings of their non-logical parts. A notion of logical truth thus given limited application, related notions of logical equivalence and entailment will tag along. It is hard to imagine how a theory of meaning could fail to read a logic into its object language to this degree; and to the extent that it does, our intuitions of logical truth, equivalence, and entailment may be called upon in constructing and testing the theory.

I turn now to one more, and very large, fly in the ointment: the fact that the same sentence may at one time or in one mouth be true and at another time or in another mouth be false. Both logicians and those critical of formal methods here seem largely (though by no means universally) agreed that formal semantics and logic are incompetent to deal with the disturbances caused by demonstratives. Logicians have often reacted by downgrading natural language and trying to show how to get along without demonstratives; their critics react by downgrading logic and formal semantics. None of this can make me happy: clearly demonstratives cannot be eliminated from a natural language without loss or radical change, so there is no choice but to accommodate theory to them.

No logical errors result if we simply treat demonstratives as constants; neither do any problems arise for giving a semantic truth definition. '"I am wise" is true if and only if I am wise', with its bland ignoring of the demonstrative element in 'I' comes off the assembly line along with '"Socrates is wise" is true if and only if Socrates is wise' with its bland indifference to the demonstrative element in 'is wise' (the tense).

What suffers in this treatment of demonstratives is not the definition of a truth predicate, but the plausibility of the claim that what has been defined is truth. For this claim is acceptable only if the speaker and circumstances of utterance of each sentence mentioned in the definition is matched by the speaker and circumstances of utterance of the truth definition itself. It could also be fairly pointed out

that part of understanding demonstratives is knowing the rules by which they adjust their reference to circumstance; assimilating demonstratives to constant terms obliterates this feature. These complaints can be met, I think, though only by a fairly far-reaching revision in the theory of truth. I shall barely suggest how this could be done, but bare suggestion is all that is needed: the idea is technically trivial, and in line with work being done on the logic of the tenses.

We could take truth to be a property, not of sentences, but of utterances, or speech acts, or ordered triples of sentences, times, and persons; but it is simplest just to view truth as a relation between a sentence, a person, and a time. Under such treatment, ordinary logic as now read applies as usual, but only to sets of sentences relativized to the same speaker and time; further logical relations between sentences spoken at different times and by different speakers may be articulated by new axioms. Such is not my concern. The theory of meaning undergoes a systematic but not puzzling change; corresponding to each expression with a demonstrative element there must in the theory be a phrase that relates the truth conditions of sentences in which the expression occurs to changing times and speakers. Thus the theory will entail sentences like the following:

'I am tired' is true as (potentially) spoken by p at t if and only if p is tired at t.
'That book was stolen' is true as (potentially) spoken by p at t if and only if the book demonstrated by p at t is stolen prior to t.

Plainly, this course does not show how to eliminate demonstratives; for example, there is no suggestion that 'the book demonstrated by the speaker' can be substituted ubiquitously for 'that book' *salva veritate*. The fact that demonstratives are amenable to formal treatment ought greatly to improve hopes for a serious semantics of natural language, for it is likely that many outstanding puzzles, such as the analysis of quotations or sentences about propositional attitudes, can be solved if we recognize a concealed demonstrative construction.

Now that we have relativized truth to times and speakers, it is appropriate to glance back at the problem of empirically testing a theory of meaning for an alien tongue. The essence of the method was, it will be remembered, to correlate held-true sentences with held-true sentences by way of a truth definition, and within the bounds of intelligible error. Now the picture must be elaborated to allow for the fact that sentences are true, and held true, only relative to a speaker and a time. Sentences with demonstratives obviously yield a very sensitive test of the correctness of a theory of meaning, and constitute the most direct link between language and the recurrent macroscopic objects of human interest and attention.

In this paper I have assumed that the speakers of a language can effectively determine the meaning or meanings of an arbitrary expression (if it has a meaning), and that it is the central task of a theory of meaning to show how this is possible. I have argued that a characterization of a truth predicate describes the required kind of structure, and provides a clear and testable criterion of an adequate semantics for a natural language. No doubt there are other reasonable demands that may be put on a theory of meaning. But a theory that does no more than define truth for a language comes far closer to constituting a complete theory of meaning than superficial analysis might suggest; so, at least, I have urged.

Since I think there is no alternative, I have taken an optimistic and programmatic view of the possibilities for a formal characterization of a truth predicate for a natural language. But it must be allowed that a staggering list of difficulties and conundrums remains. To name a few: we do not know the logical form of counterfactual or subjunctive sentences; nor of sentences about probabilities and about causal relations; we have no good idea what the logical role of adverbs is, nor the role of attributive adjectives; we have no theory for mass terms like 'fire', 'water', and 'snow', nor for sentences about belief, perception, and intention, nor for verbs of action that imply purpose. And finally, there are all the sentences that seem not to have truth values at all: the imperatives, optatives, interrogatives and a host more. A comprehensive theory of meaning for a natural language must cope successfully with each of these problems.

STUDY QUESTIONS: DAVIDSON, *TRUTH AND MEANING*

1. What is the condition that a satisfactory theory of meaning should meet?
2. What were the main points of Davidson's discussion of the expression 'the father of Annette'?
3. What was the device of 'brilliant simplicity' proposed by Frege?
4. What is the limitation of Frege's account? How does the example of the sentence 'Theaetetus flies' illustrate that point?
5. What does Davidson say about the idea of meanings as entities?
6. For what reason does Davidson claim that only in the context of a language does a sentence have meaning?
7. How does Davidson sweep away the problem concerning 'means that'? What is that problem?
8. How does a theory of meaning for language L relate to a recursive definition of truth-in-L?
9. What does Davidson mean when he affirms that a theory of meaning (in his sense of the term) is an empirical theory?
10. What is the work of such a theory of meaning?
11. How does Davidson deal with the objection that a theory of meaning would generate sentences such as '"Snow is white" is true if and only if grass is green'?
12. What is radical interpretation? What does it require?
13. What are the two points that Tarski might urge regarding the prospects of a formal semantic theory for a natural language?
14. How does Davidson respond to the claim that a natural language would have to be reformed out of all recognition in order for a formal semantic theory to be applied to it?
15. Why does Davidson urge the distinction between questions of logical form and the analysis of individual concepts? How does he illustrate the need for this distinction?

16. What is the large fly in the ointment? Why is this a problem? How does Davidson propose to circumvent this problem?

MENTAL EVENTS

In this reading, Davidson argues for the mild token materialist thesis that every particular, or token, mental event is identical to a particular physical event. In other words, the same event can be described both physically and mentally. Davidson's ingenious argument for this thesis is as follows:

1. *Mental events can cause physical events.*
2. *When one event causes another, their causal interaction can be described in terms of causal laws.*
3. *There are no psychological-physical causal laws.*
4. *Therefore, mental events are physical events.*

In other words, token mental events must also be token physical events because the mental can affect the physical.

As the reading explains, the important premise is the third. Davidson argues for a position called the anomalism of the mental, according to which there are no psychological-physical causal laws because mental states and events are open to interpretation, but not strict scientific laws. He argues for the anomalism of the mental on the basis of the holism of the mental. Mental states cannot occur in isolation; their identity depends on their interconnections with other mental states. Furthermore, mental states are subject to norms that permit them to be interpreted and that specify ways in which they can be rational or irrational. This last point is linked to the Principle of Charity, which was mentioned earlier in the Philosophical Overview. On the basis of the anomalism of the mental, Davidson argues for a nonreductive form of materialism.

Mental events such as perceivings, rememberings, decisions, and actions resist capture in the nomological net of physical theory. How can this fact be reconciled with the causal role of mental events in the physical world? Reconciling freedom with causal determinism is a special case of the problem if we suppose that causal determinism entails capture in, and freedom requires escape from, the nomological net. But the broader issue can remain alive even for someone who believes a correct analysis of free action reveals no conflict with determinism. *Autonomy* (freedom, self-rule) may or may not clash with determinism; *anomaly* (failure to fall under a law) is, it would seem, another matter.

I start from the assumption that both the causal dependence, and the anomalousness, of mental events are undeniable facts. My aim is therefore to explain, in the face of apparent difficulties, how this can be. I am in sympathy with Kant when he says,

> it is as impossible for the subtlest philosophy as for the commonest reasoning to argue freedom away. Philosophy must therefore assume that no true contradiction will be found between freedom and natural necessity in the same human actions, for it cannot give up the idea of nature any more than that of freedom. Hence even if we should never be able to conceive how freedom is possible, at least

---

"Mental Events" from *Essays on Actions and Events* by Donald Davidson. Reprinted by permission of Marcia Cavell.

this apparent contradiction must be convincingly eradicated. For if the thought of freedom contradicts itself or nature . . . it would have to be surrendered in competition with natural necessity.

Generalize human actions to mental events, substitute anomaly for freedom, and this is a description of my problem. And of course the connection is closer, since Kant believed freedom entails anomaly.

Now let my try to formulate a little more carefully the 'apparent contradiction' about mental events that I want to discuss and finally dissipate. It may be seen as stemming from three principles.

The first principle asserts that at least some mental events interact causally with physical events. (We could call this the Principle of Causal Interaction.) Thus for example if someone sank the *Bismarck*, then various mental events such as perceivings, notings, calculations, judgements, decisions, intentional actions, and changes of belief played a causal role in the sinking of the *Bismarck*. In particular, I would urge that the fact that someone sank the *Bismarck* entails that he moved his body in a way that was caused by mental events of certain sorts, and that this bodily movement in turn caused the *Bismarck* to sink. Perception illustrates how causality may run from the physical to the mental: if a man perceives that a ship is approaching, then a ship approaching must have caused him to come to believe that a ship is approaching. (Nothing depends on accepting these as examples of causal interaction.)

Though perception and action provide the most obvious cases where mental and physical events interact causally, I think reasons could be given for the view that all mental events ultimately, perhaps through causal relations with other mental events, have causal intercourse with physical events. But if there are mental events that have no physical events as causes or effects, the argument will not touch them.

The second principle is that where there is causality, there must be a law: events related as cause and effect fall under strict deterministic laws. (We may term this the Principle of the Nomological Character of Causality.) This principle, like the first, will be treated here as an assumption, though I shall say something by way of interpretation.

The third principle is that there are no strict deterministic laws on the basis of which mental events can be predicted and explained (the Anomalism of the Mental).

The paradox I wish to discuss arises for someone who is inclined to accept these three assumptions or principles, and who thinks they are inconsistent with one another. The inconsistency is not, of course, formal unless more premises are added. Nevertheless it is natural to reason that the first two principles, that of causal interaction and that of the nomological character of causality, together imply that at least some mental events can be predicted and explained on the basis of laws, while the principle of the anomalism of the mental denies this. Many philosophers have accepted, with or without argument, the view that the three principles do lead to a contradiction. It seems to me, however, that all three principles are true, so that what must be done is to explain away the appearance of contradiction; essentially the Kantian line.

The rest of this paper falls into three parts. The first part describes a version of the identity theory of the mental and the physical that shows how the three principles may be reconciled. The second part argues that there cannot be strict psychophysical laws; this is not quite the principle of the anomalism of the mental, but on reasonable assumptions entails it. The last part tries to show that from the fact that there can be no strict psychophysical laws, and our other two principles, we can infer the truth of a version of the identity theory, that is, a theory that identifies at least some mental events with physical events. It is clear that this 'proof' of the identity theory will be at best conditional, since two of its premises are unsupported, and the argument for the third may be found less than conclusive. But even someone unpersuaded of the truth of the premises may be interested to learn how they can be reconciled and that they serve to establish a version of the identity theory of the mental. Finally, if the argument is a good one, it should lay to rest the view, common to many friends and some foes of identity theories, that support for such theories can come only from the discovery of psychophysical laws.

I

The three principles will be shown consistent with one another by describing a view of the mental and the physical that contains no inner contradiction and that entails the three principles. According to this view, mental events are identical with physical events. Events are taken to be unrepeatable, dated individuals such as the particular eruption of a volcano, the (first) birth or death of a person, the playing of the 1968 World Series, or the historic utterance of the words, 'You may fire when ready, Gridley.' We can easily frame identity statements about individual events; examples (true or false) might be:

The death of Scott = the death of the author of *Waverley*;

The assassination of the Archduke Ferdinand = the event that started the First World War;

The eruption of Vesuvius in A.D. 79 = the cause of the destruction of Pompeii.

The theory under discussion is silent about processes, states, and attributes if these differ from individual events.

What does it mean to say that an event is mental or physical? One natural answer is that an event is physical if it is describable in a purely physical vocabulary, mental if describable in mental terms. But if this is taken to suggest that an event is physical, say, if some physical predicate is true of it, then there is the following difficulty. Assume that the predicate '*x* took place at Noosa Heads' belongs to the physical vocabulary; then so also must the predicate '*x* did not take place at Noosa Heads' belong to the physical vocabulary. But the predicate '*x* did or did not take place at Noosa Heads' is true of every event, whether mental or physical. We might rule out predicates that are tautologically true of every event, but this will not help since every event is truly describable either by '*x* took place at Noosa Heads' or by '*x* did not take place at Noosa Heads.' A different approach is needed.

We may call those verbs mental that express propositional attitudes like believing, intending, desiring, hoping, knowing, perceiving, noticing, remembering, and so on. Such verbs are characterized by the fact that they sometimes feature in sentences with subjects that refer to persons, and are completed by embedded sentences in which the usual rules of substitution appear to break down. This criterion is not precise, since I do not want to include these verbs when they occur in contexts that are fully extensional ('He knows Paris,' 'He perceives the moon' may be cases), nor exclude them whenever they are not followed by embedded sentences. An alternative characterization of the desired class of mental verbs might be that they are psychological verbs as used when they create apparently nonextensional contexts.

Let us call a description of the form 'the event that is M' or an open sentence of the form 'event *x* is M' a *mental description* or a *mental open sentence* if and only if the expression that replaces 'M' contains at least one mental verb essentially. (Essentially, so as to rule out cases where the description or open sentence is logically equivalent to one or not containing mental vocabulary.) Now we may say that an event is mental if and only if it has a mental description, or (the description operator not being primitive) if there is a mental open sentence true of that event alone. Physical events are those picked out by descriptions or open sentences that contain only the physical vocabulary essentially. It is less important to characterize a physical vocabulary because relative to the mental it is, so to speak, recessive in determining whether a description is mental or physical. (There will be some comments presently on the nature of a physical vocabulary, but these comments will fall far short of providing a criterion.)

On the proposed test of the mental, the distinguishing feature of the mental is not that it is private, subjective, or immaterial, but that it exhibits what Brentano called intentionality. Thus intentional actions are clearly included in the realm of the mental along with thoughts, hopes, and regrets (or the events tied to these). What may seem doubtful is whether the criterion will include events that have often been considered paradigmatic of the mental. Is it obvious, for example, that feeling a pain or seeing an after-image will count as mental? Sentences that report such events seem free from taint of nonextensionality, and the same should be true of reports of raw feels, sense data, and other uninterpreted sensations, if there are any.

However, the criterion actually covers not only the havings of pains and after-images, but much more besides. Take some event one would intuitively accept as physical, let's say the collision of two stars in distant space. There must be a purely physical predicate '*Px*' true of this collision, and of others, but true of only this one at the time it occurred. This particular time, though, may be pinpointed as the same time that Jones notices that a pencil starts to roll across his desk. The distant stellar collision is thus *the* event *x* such that *Px* and *x* is simultaneous with Jones's noticing that a pencil starts to roll across his desk. The collision has now been picked out by a mental description and must be counted as a mental event.

This strategy will probably work to show every event to be mental; we have obviously failed to capture the intuitive concept of the mental. It would be instructive to try to mend this trouble, but it is not necessary for present purposes. We can afford Spinozistic extravagance with the mental since accidental inclusions can only strengthen the hypothesis that all mental events are identical with physical events. What would matter would be failure to include bona fide mental events, but of this there seems to be no danger.

I want to describe, and presently to argue for, a version of the identity theory that denies that there can be strict laws connecting the mental and the physical. The very possibility of such a theory is easily obscured by the way in which identity theories are commonly defended and attacked. Charles Taylor, for example, agrees with protagonists of identity theories that the sole 'ground' for accepting such theories is the supposition that correlations or laws can be established linking events described as mental with events described as physical. He says, 'It is easy to see why this is so: unless a given mental event is invariably accompanied by a given, say, brain process, there is no ground for even mooting a general identity between the two.' Taylor goes on (correctly, I think) to allow that there may be identity without correlating laws, but my present interest is in noticing the invitation to confusion in the statement just quoted. What can 'a given mental event' mean here? Not a particular, dated, event, for it would not make sense to speak of an individual event being 'invariably accompanied' by another. Taylor is evidently thinking of event of a given *kind*. But if the only identities are of kinds of events, the identity theory presupposes correlating laws.

One finds the same tendency to build laws into the statements of the identity theory in these typical remarks:

> When I say that a sensation is a brain process or that lightning is an electrical discharge, I am using 'is' in the sense of strict identity . . . there are not two things: a flash of lightning and an electrical discharge. There is one thing, a flash of lightning, which is described scientifically as an electrical discharge to the earth from a cloud of ionized water molecules.

The last sentence of this quotation is perhaps to be understood as saying that for every lightning flash there exists an electrical discharge to the earth from a cloud of ionized water molecules with which it is identical. Here we have an honest ontology of individual events and can make literal sense of identity. We can also see how there could be identities without correlating laws. It is possible, however, to have an ontology of events with the conditions of individuation specified in such a way that any identity implies a correlating law. Kim, for example, suggests that Fa and Gb 'describe or refer to the same event' if and only if $a = b$ and the property of being $F =$ the property of being G. The identity of the properties in turn entails that $(x)(Fx \leftrightarrow Gx)$. No wonder Kim says:

> If pain is identical with brain state B, there must be a concomitance between occurrences of pain and occurrences of brain state B. . . . Thus, a necessary condition of the pain-brain state B identity is that the two expressions 'being in pain' and 'being in brain state B' have the same extension. . . . There is no conceivable observation that would confirm or refute the identity but not the associated correlation.

It may make the situation clearer to give a fourfold classification of theories of the relation between mental and physical events that emphasizes the independence of claims about laws and claims of identity. On the one hand there are those who assert, and those who deny, the existence of psychophysical laws; on the other hand there are those who say mental events are identical with physical and those who deny this. Theories are thus divided into four sorts: *nomological monism*, which affirms that there are correlating laws and that the events correlated are one (materialists belong in this category); *nomological dualism*, which comprises various forms of parallelism, interactionism, and epiphenomenalism; *anomalous dualism*, which combines ontological dualism with the general failure of laws correlating the mental and the physical (Cartesianism). And finally there is *anomalous monism*, which classifies the position I wish to occupy.

Anomalous monism resembles materialism in its claim that all events are physical, but rejects the thesis, usually considered essential to materialism, that mental phenomena can be given purely physical explanations. Anomalous monism shows an ontological bias only in that it allows the possibility that not all events are mental, while insisting that all events are physical. Such a bland monism, unbuttressed by correlating laws or conceptual economies, does not seem to merit the term 'reductionism'; in any case it is not apt to inspire the nothing-but reflex ('Conceiving the *Art of the Fugue* was nothing but a complex neural event', and so forth).

Although the position I describe denies there are psychophysical laws, it is consistent with the view that mental characteristics are in some sense dependent, or supervenient, on physical characteristics. Such supervenience might be taken to mean that there cannot be two events alike in all physical respects but differing in some mental respect, or that an object cannot alter in some mental respect without altering in some physical respect. Dependence or supervenience of this kind does not entail reducibility through law or definition: if it did, we could reduce moral properties to descriptive, and this there is good reason to *believe* cannot be done; and we might be able to reduce truth in a formal system to syntactical properties, and this we *know* cannot in general be done.

This last example is in useful analogy with the sort of lawless monism under consideration. Think of the physical vocabulary as the entire vocabulary of some language L with resources adequate to express a certain amount of mathematics, and its own syntax. L' is L augmented with the truth predicate 'true-in-L', which is 'mental'. In L (and hence L') it is possible to pick out, with a definite description or open sentence, each sentence in the extension of the truth predicate, but if L is consistent there exists no predicate of syntax (of the 'physical' vocabulary), no matter how complex, that applies to all and only the true sentence of L. There can be no 'psychophysical law' in the form of a biconditional, '(x) (x is true-in-L if and only if x is φ)' where 'φ' is replaced by a 'physical' predicate (a predicate of L). Similarly, we can pick out each mental event using the physical vocabulary alone, but no purely physical predicate, no matter how complex, has, as a matter of law, the same extension as a mental predicate.

It should now be evident how anomalous monism reconciles the three original principles. Causality and identity are relations between individual events no matter how described. But laws are linguistic; and so events can instantiate laws, and hence be explained or predicted in the light of laws, only as those events are described in one or another way. The principle of causal interaction deals with events in extension and is therefore blind to the mental-physical dichotomy. The principle of the anomalism of the mental concerns events described as mental, for events are mental only as described. The principle of the nomological character of causality must be read carefully: it says that when events are related as cause and effect, they have descriptions that instantiate a law. It does not say that every true singular statement of causality instantiates a law.

II

The analogy just bruited, between the place of the mental amid the physical, and the place of the semantical in a world of syntax, should not be strained. Tarski proved that a consistent language cannot (under some natural assumptions) contain an open sentence 'Fx' true of all and only the true sentences of that language. If our analogy were pressed, then we would expect a proof that there can be no physical open sentence 'Px' true of all and only the events having some mental property. In fact, however, nothing I can say about the irreducibility of the mental deserves to be called a proof; and the kind of irreducibility is different. For if anomalous monism is correct, not only can every mental event be uniquely singled out using only physical concepts, but since the number of events that falls under each mental predicate may, for all we know, be finite, there may well exist a physical open sentence coextensive with each mental predicate, though to construct it might involve the tedium of a lengthy and uninstructive alternation. Indeed, even if finitude is not assumed, there seems no compelling reason to deny that there could be coextensive predicates, one mental and one physical.

The thesis is rather that the mental is nomologically irreducible: there may be *true* general statements relating the mental and the physical, statements that have the logical form of a law; but they are not *lawlike* (in a strong sense to be described). If by absurdly remote chance we were to stumble on a nonstochastic true psychophysical generalization, we would have no reason to believe it more than roughly true.

Do we, by declaring that there are no (strict) psychophysical laws, poach on the empirical preserves of science—a form of *hubris* against which philosophers are often warned? Of course, to judge a statement lawlike or illegal is not to decide its truth outright; relative to the acceptance of a general statement on the basis of instances, ruling it lawlike must be a priori. But such relative apriorism does not in itself justify philosophy, for in general the grounds for deciding to trust a statement on the basis of its instances will in turn be governed by theoretical and empirical concerns not to be distinguished from those of science. If the case of supposed laws linking the mental and the physical is different, it can only be because to allow the possibility of such laws would amount to changing the subject. By changing the subject I mean here: deciding not to accept the criterion of the mental in terms of the vocabulary of the propositional attitudes. This short answer cannot prevent further ramifications of the problem, however, for there is no clear line between changing the subject and changing what one says on an old subject, which is to admit, in the present context at least, that there is no clear line between philosophy and science. Where there are no fixed boundaries only the timid never risk trespass.

It will sharpen our appreciation of the anomological character of mental-physical generalizations to consider a related matter, the failure of definitional behaviourism. Why are we willing (as I assume we are) to abandon the attempt to give explicit definitions of mental concepts in terms of behavioural ones? Not, surely, just because all actual tries are conspicuously inadequate. Rather it is because we are persuaded, as we are in the case of so many other forms of definitional reductionism (naturalism in ethics, instrumentalism and operationalism in the sciences, the causal theory of meaning, phenomenalism, and so on—the catalogue of philosophy's defeats), that there is system in the failures. Suppose we try to say, not using any mental concepts, what it is for a man to believe there is life on Mars. One line we could take is this: when a certain sound is produced in the man's presence ('Is there life on Mars?') he produces another ('Yes'). But of course this shows he believes there is life on Mars only if he understands English, his production of the sound was intentional, and was a response to the sounds as meaning something in English; and so on. For each discovered deficiency, we add a new proviso. Yet no matter how we patch and fit the non-mental condi-

tions, we always find the need for an additional condition (provided he *notices, understands,* etc.) that is mental in character.

A striking feature of attempts at definitional reduction is how little seems to hinge on the question of synonymy between definiens and definiendum. Of course, by imagining counterexamples we do discredit claims of synonymy. But the pattern of failure prompts a stronger conclusion: if we were to find an open sentence couched in behavioural terms and exactly coextensive with some mental predicate, nothing could reasonably persuade us that we had found it. We know too much about thought and behaviour to trust exact and universal statements linking them. Beliefs and desires issue in behaviour only as modified and mediated by further beliefs and desires, attitudes and attendings, without limit. Clearly this holism of the mental realm is a clue both to the autonomy and to the anomalous character of the mental.

These remarks apropos definitional behaviourism provide at best hints of why we should not expect nomological connections between the mental and the physical. The central case invites further consideration.

Lawlike statements are general statements that support counter-factual and subjunctive claims, and are supported by their instances. There is (in my view) no non-question-begging criterion of the lawlike, which is not to say there are no reasons in particular cases for a judgement. Lawlikeness is a matter of degree, which is not to deny that there may be cases beyond debate. And within limits set by the conditions of communication, there is room for much variation between individuals in the pattern of statements to which various degrees of nomologicality are assigned. In all these respects nomologicality is much like analyticity, as one might expect since both are linked to meaning.

'All emeralds are green' is lawlike in that its instances confirm it, but 'all emeralds are grue' is not, for 'grue' means 'observed before time *t* and green, otherwise blue', and if our observations were all made before *t* and uniformly revealed green emeralds, this would not be a reason to expect other emeralds to be blue. Nelson Goodman has suggested that this shows that some predicates, 'grue' for example, are unsuited to laws (and thus a criterion of suitable predicates could lead to a criterion of the lawlike). But it seems to me the anomalous character of 'All emeralds are grue' shows only that the predicates 'is an emerald' and 'is grue' are not suited to one another: grueness is not an inductive property of emeralds. Grueness *is* however an inductive property of entities of other sorts, for instance of emerires. (Something is an emerire if it is examined before *t* and is an emerald, and otherwise is a sapphire.) Not only is 'All emerires are grue' entailed by the conjunction of a lawlike statements 'All emeralds are green' and 'All sapphires are blue,' but there is no reason, as far as I can see, to reject the deliverance of intuition, that it is itself lawlike. Nomological statements bring together predicates that we know a priori are made for each other—know, that is, independently of knowing whether the evidence supports a connection between them. 'Blue', 'red', and 'green' are made for emeralds, sapphires, and roses; 'grue', 'bleen', and 'gred' are made for sapphalds, emerires, and emeroses.

The direction in which the discussion seems headed is this: mental and physical predicates are not made for one another. In point of lawlikeness, psychophysical statements are more like 'All emeralds are grue' than like 'All emeralds are green.'

Before this claim is plausible, it must be seriously modified. The fact that emeralds examined before *t* are grue not only is no reason to believe all emeralds are grue; it is not even a reason (if we know the time) to believe *any* unobserved emeralds are grue. But if an event of a certain mental sort has usually been accompanied by an event of a certain physical sort, this often is a good reason to expect other cases to follow suit roughly in proportion. The generalizations that embody such practical wisdom are assumed to be only roughly true, or they are explicitly stated in probabilistic terms, or they are insulated from counterexample by generous escape clauses. Their importance lies mainly in the support they lend singular causal claims and related explanations of particular events. The support derives from the fact that such a generalization, however crude and vague, may provide good reason to believe that underlying the particular case there is a regularity that could be formulated sharply and without caveat.

In our daily traffic with events and actions that must be foreseen or understood, we perforce make use of the sketchy summary generalization, for we do not know a more accurate law, or if we do, we lack a description of the particular events in which we are interested that would show the relevance of the law. But there is an important distinction to be made within

the category of the rude rule of thumb. On the one hand, there are generalizations whose positive instances give us reason to believe the generalization itself could be improved by adding further provisos and conditions stated in the same general vocabulary as the original generalization. Such a generalization points to the form and vocabulary of the finished law: we may say that it is a *homonomic* generalization. On the other hand there are generalizations which when instantiated may give us reason to believe there is a precise law at work, but one that can be stated only by shifting to a different vocabulary. We may call such generalizations *heteronomic*.

I suppose most of our practical lore (and science) is heteronomic. This is because a law can hope to be precise, explicit, and as exceptionless as possible only if it draws its concepts from a comprehensive closed theory. This ideal theory may or may not be deterministic, but it is if any true theory is. Within the physical sciences we do find homonomic generalizations, generalizations such that if the evidence supports them, we then have reason to believe they may be sharpened indefinitely by drawing upon further physical concepts: there is a theoretical asymptote of perfect coherence with all the evidence, perfect predictability (under the terms of the system), total explanation (again under the terms of the system). Or perhaps the ultimate theory is probabilistic, and the asymptote is less than perfection; but in that case there will be no better to be had.

Confidence that a statement is homonomic, correctible within its own conceptual domain, demands that it draw its concepts from a theory with strong constitutive elements. Here is the simplest possible illustration; if the lesson carries, it will be obvious that the simplification could be mended.

The measurement of length, weight, temperature, or time depends (among many other things, of course) on the existence in each case of a two-place relation that is transitive and asymmetric: warmer than, later than, heavier than, and so forth. Let us take the relation *longer than* as our example. The law or postulate of transitivity is this:

$$(L) \quad L(x, y) \text{ and } L(y, z) \rightarrow L(x, z)$$

Unless this law (or some sophisticated variant) holds, we cannot easily make sense of the concept of length. There will be no way of assigning numbers to register even so much as ranking in length, let alone the more powerful demands of measurement on a ratio scale. And this remark goes not only for any three items directly involved in an intransitivity: it is easy to show (given a few more assumptions essential to measurement of length) that there is no consistent assignment of a ranking to any item unless (L) holds in full generality.

Clearly (L) alone cannot exhaust the import of 'longer than'—otherwise it would not differ from 'warmer than' or 'later than'. We must suppose there is some empirical content, however difficult to formulate in the available vocabulary, that distinguishes 'longer than' from the other two-place transitive predicates of measurement and on the basis of which we may assert that one thing is longer than another. Imagine this empirical content to be partly given by the predicate 'O(x, y)'. So we have this 'meaning postulate':

$$(M)\ O(x, y) \rightarrow L(x, y)$$

that partly interprets (L). But now (L) and (M) together yield an empirical theory of great strength, for together they entail that there do not exist three objects a, b, and c such that $O(a, b)$, $O(b, c)$, and $O(c, a)$. Yet what is to prevent this happening if 'O(x, y)' is a predicate we can ever, with confidence, apply? Suppose we *think* we observe an intransitive triad; what do we say? We could count (L) false, but then we would have no application for the concept of length. We could say (M) gives a wrong test for length; but then it is unclear what we thought was the *content* of the idea of one thing being longer than another. Or we could say that the objects under observation are not, as the theory requires, *rigid* objects. It is a mistake to think we are forced to accept some one of these answers. Concepts such as that of length are sustained in equilibrium by a number of conceptual pressures, and theories of fundamental measurement are distorted if we force the decision, among such principles as (L) and (M): analytic or synthetic. It is better to say the whole set of axioms, laws, or postulates for the measurement of length is partly constitutive of the idea of a system of macroscopic, rigid, physical objects. I suggest that the existence of lawlike statements in physical science depends upon the existence of constitutive (or synthetic a priori) laws like those of the measurement of length within the same conceptual domain.

Just as we cannot intelligibly assign a length to any object unless a comprehensive theory holds of objects of that sort, we cannot intelligibly attribute any propositional attitude to an agent except within the framework of a viable theory of his beliefs, desires, intentions, and decisions.

There is no assigning beliefs to a person one by one on the basis of his verbal behaviour, his choices, or other local signs no matter how plain and evident, for we make sense of particular beliefs only as they cohere with other beliefs, with preferences, with intentions, hopes, fears, expectations, and the rest. It is not merely, as with the measurement of length, that each case tests a theory and depends upon it, but that the content of a propositional attitude derives from its place in the pattern.

Crediting people with a large degree of consistency cannot be counted mere charity: it is unavoidable if we are to be in a position to accuse them meaningfully of error and some degree of irrationality. Global confusion, like universal mistake, is unthinkable, not because imagination boggles, but because too much confusion leaves nothing to be confused about and massive error erodes the background of true belief against which alone failure can be construed. To appreciate the limits to the kind and amount of blunder and bad thinking we can intelligibly pin on others is to see once more the inseparability of the question what concepts a person commands and the question what he does with those concepts in the way of belief, desire, and intention. To the extent that we fail to discover a coherent and plausible pattern in the attitudes and actions of others we simply forego the chance of treating them as persons.

The problem is not bypassed but given centre stage by appeal to explicit speech behaviour. For we could not begin to decode a man's sayings if we could not make out his attitudes towards his sentences, such as holding, wishing, or wanting them to be true. Beginning from these attitudes, we must work out a theory of what he means, thus simultaneously giving content to his attitudes and to his words. In our need to make him make sense, we will try for a theory that finds him consistent, a believer of truths, and a lover of the good (all by our own lights, it goes without saying). Life being what it is, there will be no simple theory that fully meets these demands. Many theories will effect a more or less acceptable compromise, and between these theories there may be no objective grounds for choice.

The heteronomic character of general statements linking the mental and the physical traces back to this central role of translation in the description of all propositional attitudes, and to the indeterminacy of translation. There are no strict psychophysical laws because of the disparate commitments of the mental and physical schemes. It is a feature of physical reality that physical change can be explained by laws that connect it with other changes and conditions physically described. It is a feature of the mental that the attribution of mental phenomena must be responsible to the background of reasons, beliefs, and intentions of the individual. There cannot be tight connections between the realms if each is to retain allegiance to its proper source of evidence. The nomological irreducibility of the mental does not derive merely from the seamless nature of the world of thought, preference, and intention, for such interdependence is common to physical theory, and is compatible with there being a single right way of interpreting a man's attitudes without relativization to a scheme of translation. Nor is the irreducibility due simply to the possibility of many equally eligible schemes, for this is compatible with an arbitrary choice of one scheme relative to which assignments of mental traits are made. The point is rather that when we use the concepts of belief, desire, and the rest, we must stand prepared, as the evidence accumulates, to adjust our theory in the light of considerations of overall cogency: the constitutive ideal of rationality partly controls each phase in the evolution of what must be an evolving theory. An arbitrary choice of translation scheme would preclude such opportunistic tempering of theory; put differently, a right arbitrary choice of a translation manual would be of a manual acceptable in the light of all possible evidence; and this is a choice we cannot make. We must conclude, I think, that nomological slack between the mental and the physical is essential as long as we conceive of man as a rational animal.

III

The gist of the foregoing discussion, as well as its conclusion, will be familiar. That there is a categorial difference between the mental and the physical is a commonplace. It may seem odd that I say nothing of the supposed privacy of the mental, or the special authority an agent has with respect to his own propositional attitudes, but this appearance of novelty would fade if we were to investigate in more detail the grounds for accepting a scheme of translation. The step from the categorial difference between the mental and the physical to the impossibility of strict laws relating them is less common, but certainly not new. If there is a surprise, then, it will be to find the lawlessness of the mental serving to help establish the identity of the mental with that paradigm of the lawlike, the physical.

The reasoning is this. We are assuming, under the Principle of the Causal Dependence of the Mental, that some mental events at least are causes or effects of physical events; the argument applies only to these. A second Principle (of the Nomological Character of Causality) says that each true singular causal statement is backed by a strict law connecting events of kinds to which events mentioned as cause and effect belong. Where there are rough, but homonomic, laws, there are laws drawing on concepts from the same conceptual domain and upon which there is no improving in point of precision and comprehensiveness. We urged in the last section that such laws occur in the physical sciences. Physical theory promises to provide a comprehensive closed system guaranteed to yield a standardized, unique description of every physical event couched in a vocabulary amenable to law.

It is not plausible that mental concepts alone can provide such a framework, simply because the mental does not, by our first principle, constitute a closed system. Too much happens to affect the mental that is not itself a systematic part of the mental. But if we combine this observation with the conclusion that no psychophysical statement is, or can be built into, a strict law, we have the Principle of the Anomalism of the Mental: there are no strict laws at all on the basis of which we can predict and explain mental phenomena.

The demonstration of identity follows easily. Suppose m, a mental event, caused p, a physical event; then, under some description m and p instantiate a strict law. This law can only be physical, according to the previous paragraph. But if m falls under a physical law, it has a physical description; which is to say it is a physical event. An analogous argument works when a physical event causes a mental event.

So every mental event that is causally related to a physical event is a physical event. In order to establish anomalous monism in full generality it would be sufficient to show that every mental event is cause or effect of some physical event; I shall not attempt this.

If one event causes another, there is a strict law which those events instantiate when properly described. But it is possible (and typical) to know of the singular causal relation without knowing the law or the relevant descriptions. Knowledge requires reasons, but these are available in the form of rough heteronomic generalizations, which are lawlike in that instances make it reasonable to expect other instances to follow suit without being lawlike in the sense of being indefinitely refinable. Applying these facts to knowledge of identities, we see that it is possible to know that a mental event is identical with some physical event without knowing which one (in the sense of being able to give it a unique physical description that brings it under a relevant law). Even if someone knew the entire physical history of the world, and every mental event were identical with a physical, it would not follow that he could predict or explain a single mental event (so described, of course).

Two features of mental events in their relation to the physical—causal dependence and nomological independence—combine, then, to dissolve what has often seemed a paradox, the efficacy of thought and purpose in the material world, and their freedom from law. When we portray events as perceivings, rememberings, decisions and actions, we necessarily locate them amid physical happenings through the relation of cause and effect; but as long as we do not change the idiom that same mode of portrayal insulates mental events from the strict laws that can in principle be called upon to explain and predict physical phenomena.

Mental events as a class cannot be explained by physical science; particular mental events can when we know particular identities. But the explanations of mental events in which we are typically interested relate them to other mental events and conditions. We explain a man's free actions, for example, by appeal to his desires, habits, knowledge and perceptions. Such accounts of intentional behaviour operate in a conceptual framework removed from the direct reach of physical law by describing both cause and effect, reason and action, as aspects of a portrait of a human agent. The anomalism of the mental is thus a necessary condition for viewing action as autonomous. I conclude with a second passage from Kant:

> It is an indispensable problem of speculative philosophy to show that its illusion respecting the contradiction rests on this, that we think of man in a different sense and relation when we call him free, and when we regard him as subject to the laws of nature. . . . It must therefore show that not only can both of these very well co-exist, but that both must be thought *as necessarily united* in the same subject. . . .

STUDY QUESTIONS: DAVIDSON, *MENTAL EVENTS*

1. What does Davidson mean by the anomalism of the mental?
2. What are the two assumptions from which he starts his paper?
3. What is the apparent contradiction that Davidson wishes to resolve?
4. What are the three principles that give rise to this apparent contradiction?
5. How does Davidson resolve the apparent contradiction?
6. How does Davidson characterize a mental event?
7. What are the four theories of the relation between mental and physical events?
8. What is anomalous monism?
9. The mental is nomologically irreducible. What does that mean?
10. How does this relate to definitional behaviorism?
11. How does Davidson employ the example of 'grue'?
12. What are 'homonomic' and 'heteronomic' generalizations?
13. 'There are no strict psychophysical laws because of the disparate commitments of the mental and physical schemes.' What does this mean? What are these commitments?
14. What is Davidson's argument for the thesis that mental events are physical events?

Philosophical Bridges: The Influence of Davidson

Davidson's thought has been one of the most influential in analytic philosophy in the second half of the twentieth century. His theory of meaning has been seen as preserving some of the benefits of the logical positivist tradition as reinterpreted by Quine while avoiding some of the problems. For instance, on the one hand, like the works of the logical positivists and Quine, Davidson's theory complies with the condition that a linguistic theory should aim to be extensional. It is a scientific view of language. On the other hand, Davidson's theory does not require eliminating all nonextensional notions from our linguistic theory, and it is not tied to the radical Empiricism found in Quine. Rather, it is tied to a theory of interpretation that requires some apparently reasonable assumptions about rationality.

One of the perceived benefits of Davidson's theory of meaning was that it pointed toward a new research program in the philosophy of language. The logical form of language had to be laid bare in order to construct the extensional T-theory of the language. For example, Davidson led the way by showing how statements concerning events and actions should be understood in order to make plain their logical form. This analysis of action statements in terms of an ontology of events was seen as an indication that Davidson's program would be fruitful in other areas too. In the philosophy of mind, Davidson's anomalous monism has also been influential because it has been seen as a relatively sophisticated way to combine a materialist ontology with a nonreductive understanding of the mind.

JOHN RAWLS (1921–2002)

Biographical History

John Rawls was born in Baltimore. He studied for a B.A. degree (1943) and Ph.D. (1950) at Princeton University. He served in the armed forces from 1943 to 1945. He taught at Princeton from 1950 to 1952 and at Cornell University from 1953 to 1959, and was professor at MIT from 1960 to 1962. In 1962, he joined the Harvard Philosophy Department and was appointed the Conant University Professor at Harvard in 1979. His 1971 book *A Theory of Justice*, which advocates a liberal position regarding equality and individual rights, became a classic of political philosophy during his lifetime. His other books include *Political Liberalism* (1993), *Collected Papers* (1999), *Lectures on the History of Moral Philosophy* (2000), and *Justice as Fairness: A Restatement* (2001).

Philosophical Overview

In his classic work *A Theory of Justice*, John Rawls defends a liberal vision of the good society by constructing a theory of justice as fairness. Rawls' theory is liberal in part because he accepts that society must be built around value pluralism and the notion of liberty. Because of this, the state should not impose a specific conception of the good life and people should be free to follow their own values within the limits prescribed by a theory of fairness.

Rawls argues that the principles of social justice are those that would be agreed on by a group of rational, self-interested persons placed behind a veil of ignorance. Behind this veil, the persons would have no knowledge of their personal circumstances, for example of their social position and of their skills and abilities. Rawls argues that from behind the veil of ignorance, persons would choose rationally to adopt certain principles, the implementation of which would constitute a fair and just society.

Rawls' theory of social justice is anti-utilitarian. According to utilitarianism, the right action is the one that maximizes overall utility impartially considered, and utility is the only thing of noninstrumental value. This means that justice and rights have only instrumental value and that the liberty and welfare of one person can be sacrificed justifiably for the greater good. In contrast, Rawls' theory implies that social justice has primacy over utility because no individual may be sacrificed for society's greater good. Instead, Rawls understands justice in basically Kantian terms; we are free, rational agents. The principles of justice reflect this aspect of our nature.

Here are three observations. First, Rawls' theory is one of *social* justice because it defines the principles that should regulate the institutions of a society. It does not evaluate particular actions or the character state of individuals. It is not a moral theory. Second, even though Rawls' derivation of the rules of a just society is contractual, the duty to comply with these rules is not based on the hypothetical social contract. It is rather based on the idea that these rules agree with our reflective moral judgments. Third, Rawls' concept of 'reflective equilibrium' encourages the possibility of adjustments to the theory. Such equilibrium is found in reflection when there is no longer any need to adjust our ethical theory to fit our specific moral judgments, and no need to adapt or revise our moral judgments to fit the theory. It is the point of balance between these two processes.

In his later work *Political Liberalism*, Rawls discusses how a liberal state might accommodate the values of different cultures within one nation through the ideas of an overlapping consensus and of public reason.

A THEORY OF JUSTICE

This reading consists in selections from the central parts of Rawls' book. In this reading, Rawls argues that the principles of social justice are those that would be agreed on by a group of rational, self-interested persons placed behind a veil of ignorance. Behind this veil, one would have no knowledge of one's personal circumstances, for instance of one's social position and of one's skills and abilities. Rawls assumes that the people behind the veil of ignorance want to advance their own ends and that they are not concerned with those of others.

From this position of relative ignorance, which Rawls calls the original position, it is rational to choose to live in a society based on two principles of justice because the people do not have knowledge of their own particular circumstances that would lead them to adopt principles that favor one specific group or set of values or conception of the good life over any other.

The two principles that they would choose are as follows.

From *Theory of Justice* by John Rawls, 1971. Reprinted by permission of Oxford University Press.

1. *First Principle: Each person is to have an equal right to the most extensive total system of equal basic liberties compatible with a similar system of liberty for all.*

2. *Second Principle: Social and economic inequalities are to be arranged so that they are both: a) to the greatest benefit of the least advantaged, consistent with the just savings principle, and b) attached to offices and positions open to all under conditions of fair equality of opportunity.* (Rawls, A Theory of Justice, p. 302)

Part (a) of the second principle is known as the 'difference principle' according to which, in the original position, it is rational to adopt a maximin strategy that maximizes the situation of the worst off in a society.

The two principles are ordered. In other words, the inequalities outlined by the second principle are permitted only given the equality of liberty of the first principle. In short, in a just society, citizens have equal liberty, and all other goods are distributed in a way that maximizes the expectations of the least well off.

According to Rawls, the two principles determine what is to count as a fair or just distribution of benefits and costs among the members of society. They attempt to capture the essence of justice, namely, that there be no 'arbitrary distinctions between persons in the assigning of basic rights and duties' (Rawls, *Theory*, p. 5). Furthermore, the two principles resolve the problem of value pluralism. People have different ends and values that often conflict. A just resolution of such conflicts requires that no single set of values have priority over the others; according to Rawls, the state must not attempt to impose a particular ideal of the good life. For this reason, Rawls rejects the idea that the just society must realize the good life of the community as a whole. Instead, it should allow its individual members to pursue their own conception of the good, within limits. The two principles of justice do this by determining the just distribution of primary social goods, such as rights, liberties, powers, income, and wealth, that are needed for the pursuit of the good.

1. THE ROLE OF JUSTICE

Justice is the first virtue of social institutions, as truth is of systems of thought. A theory however elegant and economical must be rejected or revised if it is untrue; likewise laws and institutions no matter how efficient and well-arranged must be reformed or abolished if they are unjust. Each person possesses an inviolability founded on justice that even the welfare of society as a whole cannot override. For this reason justice denies that the loss of freedom for some is made right by a greater good shared by others. It does not allow that the sacrifices imposed on a few are outweighed by the larger sum of advantages enjoyed by many. Therefore in a just society the liberties of equal citizenship are taken as settled; the rights secured by justice are not subject to political bargaining or to the calculus of social interests. The only thing that permits us to acquiesce in an erroneous theory is the lack of a better one; analo-

gously, an injustice is tolerable only when it is necessary to avoid an even greater injustice. Being first virtues of human activities, truth and justice are uncompromising.

These propositions seem to express our intuitive conviction of the primacy of justice. No doubt they are expressed too strongly. In any event I wish to inquire whether these contentions or others similar to them are sound, and if so how they can be accounted for. To this end it is necessary to work out a theory of justice in the light of which these assertions can be interpreted and assessed. I shall begin by considering the role of the principles of justice. Let us assume, to fix ideas, that a society is a more or less self-sufficient association of persons who in their relations to one another recognize certain rules of conduct as binding and who for the most part act in accordance with them. Suppose further that these rules specify a system of cooperation designed to advance the good of those taking part in it. Then, although a society is a cooperative venture for mutual advantage, it is typically marked by a conflict as well as by an identity of interests. There is an identity of interests since social cooperation makes possible a better life for all than any would have if each were to live solely by his own efforts. There is a conflict of interests since persons are not indifferent as to how the greater benefits produced by their collaboration are distributed, for in order to pursue their ends they each prefer a larger to a lesser share. A set of principles is required for choosing among the various social arrangements which determine this division of advantages and for underwriting an agreement on the proper distributive shares. These principles are the principles of social justice: they provide a way of assigning rights and duties in the basic institutions of society and they define the appropriate distribution of the benefits and burdens of social cooperation.

Now let us say that a society is well-ordered when it is not only designed to advance the good of its members but when it is also effectively regulated by a public conception of justice. That is, it is a society in which (1) everyone accepts and knows that the others accept the same principles of justice, and (2) the basic social institutions generally satisfy and are generally known to satisfy these principles. In this case while men may put forth excessive demands on one another, they nevertheless acknowledge a common point of view from which their claims may be adjudicated. If men's inclination to self-interest makes their vigilance against one another necessary, their public sense of justice makes their secure association together possible. Among individuals with disparate aims and purposes a shared conception of justice establishes the bonds of civic friendship; the general desire for justice limits the pursuit of other ends. One may think of a public conception of justice as constituting the fundamental charter of a well-ordered human association.

3. THE MAIN IDEA OF THE THEORY OF JUSTICE

My aim is to present a conception of justice which generalizes and carries to a higher level of abstraction the familiar theory of the social contract as found, say,

in Locke, Rousseau, and Kant. In order to do this we are not to think of the original contract as one to enter a particular society or to set up a particular form of government. Rather, the guiding idea is that the principles of justice for the basic structure of society are the object of the original agreement. They are the principles that free and rational persons concerned to further their own interests would accept in an initial position of equality as defining the fundamental terms of their association. These principles are to regulate all further agreements; they specify the kinds of social cooperation that can be entered into and the forms of government that can be established. This way of regarding the principles of justice I shall call justice as fairness.

Thus we are to imagine that those who engage in social cooperation choose together, in one joint act, the principles which are to assign basic rights and duties and to determine the division of social benefits. Men are to decide in advance how they are to regulate their claims against one another and what is to be the foundation charter of their society. Just as each person must decide by rational reflection what constitutes his good, that is, the system of ends which it is rational for him to pursue, so a group of persons must decide once and for all what is to count among them as just and unjust. The choice which rational men would make in this hypothetical situation of equal liberty, assuming for the present that this choice problem has a solution, determines the principles of justice.

In justice as fairness the original position of equality corresponds to the state of nature in the traditional theory of the social contract. This original position is not, of course, thought of as an actual historical state of affairs, much less as a primitive condition of culture. It is understood as a purely hypothetical situation characterized so as to lead to a certain conception of justice. Among the essential features of this situation is that no one knows his place in society, his class position or social status, nor does any one know his fortune in the distribution of natural assets and abilities, his intelligence, strength, and the like. I shall even assume that the parties do not know their conceptions of the good or their special psychological propensities. The principles of justice are chosen behind a veil of ignorance. This ensures that no one is advantaged or disadvantaged in the choice of principles by the outcome of natural chance or the contingency of social circumstances. Since all are similarly situated and no one is able to design principles to favor his particular condition, the principles of justice are the result of a fair agreement or bargain. For given the circumstances of the original position, the symmetry of everyone's relations to each other, this initial situation is fair between individuals as moral persons, that is, as rational beings with their own ends and capable, I shall assume, of a sense of justice. The original position is, one might say, the appropriate initial status quo, and thus the fundamental agreements reached in it are fair. This explains the propriety of the name "justice as fairness": it conveys the idea that the principles of justice are agreed to in an initial situation that is fair. The name does not mean that the concepts of justice and fairness are the same, any more than the phrase "poetry as metaphor" means that the concepts of poetry and metaphor are the same.

Justice as fairness begins, as I have said, with one of the most general of all choices which persons might make together, namely, with the choice of the first principles of a conception of justice which is to regulate all subsequent criticism and reform of institutions. Then, having chosen a conception of justice, we can suppose that they are to choose a constitution and a legislature to enact laws, and so on, all in accordance with the principles of justice initially agreed upon. Our social situation is just if it is such that by this sequence of hypothetical agreements we would have contracted into the general system of rules which defines it. Moreover, assuming that the original position does determine a set of principles (that is, that a particular conception of justice would be chosen), it will then be true that whenever social institutions satisfy these principles those engaged in them can say to one another that they are cooperating on terms to which they would agree if they were free and equal persons whose relations with respect to one another were fair. They could all view their arrangements as meeting the stipulations which they would acknowledge in an initial situation that embodies widely accepted and reasonable constraints on the choice of principles. The general recognition of this fact would provide the basis for a public acceptance of the corresponding principles of justice. No society can, of course, be a scheme of cooperation which men enter voluntarily in a literal sense; each person finds

himself placed at birth in some particular position in some particular society, and the nature of this position materially affects his life prospects. Yet a society satisfying the principles of justice as fairness comes as close as a society can to being a voluntary scheme, for it meets the principles which free and equal persons would assent to under circumstances that are fair. In this sense its members are autonomous and the obligations they recognize self-imposed.

One feature of justice as fairness is to think of the parties in the initial situation as rational and mutually disinterested. This does not mean that the parties are egoists, that is, individuals with only certain kinds of interests, say in wealth, prestige, and domination. But they are conceived as not taking an interest in one another's interests. They are to presume that even their spiritual aims may be opposed, in the way that the aims of those of different religions may be opposed. Moreover, the concept of rationality must be interpreted as far as possible in the narrow sense, standard in economic theory, of taking the most effective means to given ends.

In working out the conception of justice as fairness one main task clearly is to determine which principles of justice would be chosen in the original position. To do this we must describe this situation in some detail and formulate with care the problem of choice which it presents. These matters I shall take up in the immediately succeeding chapters. It may be observed, however, that once the principles of justice are thought of as arising from an original agreement in a situation of equality, it is an open question whether the principle of utility would be acknowledged. Offhand it hardly seems likely that persons who view themselves as equals, entitled to press their claims upon one another, would agree to a principle which may require lesser life prospects for some simply for the sake of a greater sum of advantages enjoyed by others. Since each desires to protect his interests, his capacity to advance his conception of the good, no one has a reason to acquiesce in an enduring loss for himself in order to bring about a greater net balance of satisfaction. In the absence of strong and lasting benevolent impulses, a rational man would not accept a basic structure merely because it maximized the algebraic sum of advantages irrespective of its permanent effects on his own basic rights and interests. Thus it seems that the principle of utility is incompatible with the conception of social cooperation among equals for mutual advantage. It appears to be inconsistent with the idea of reciprocity implicit in the notion of a well-ordered society. Or, at any rate, so I shall argue.

I shall maintain instead that the persons in the initial situation would choose two rather different principles: the first requires equality in the assignment of basic rights and duties, while the second holds that social and economic inequalities, for example inequalities of wealth and authority, are just only if they result in compensating benefits for everyone, and in particular for the least advantaged members of society. These principles rule out justifying institutions on the grounds that the hardships of some are offset by a greater good in the aggregate. It may be expedient but it is not just that some should have less in order that others may prosper. But there is no injustice in the greater benefits earned by a few provided that the situation of persons not so fortunate is thereby improved. The intuitive idea is that since everyone's well-being depends upon a scheme of cooperation without which no one could have a satisfactory life, the division of advantages should be such as to draw forth the willing cooperation of everyone taking part in it, including those less well situated. Yet this can be expected only if reasonable terms are proposed. The two principles mentioned seem to be a fair agreement on the basis of which those better endowed, or more fortunate in their social position, neither of which we can be said to deserve, could expect the willing cooperation of others when some workable scheme is a necessary condition of the welfare of all. Once we decide to look for a conception of justice that nullifies the accidents of natural endowment and the contingencies of social circumstance as counters in quest for political and economic advantage, we are led to these principles. They express the result of leaving aside those aspects of the social world that seem arbitrary from a moral point of view.

The problem of the choice of principles, however, is extremely difficult. I do not expect the answer I shall suggest to be convincing to everyone. It is, therefore, worth noting from the outset that justice as fairness, like other contract views, consists of two parts: (1) an interpretation of the initial situation and of the problem of choice posed there, and (2) a set of principles which, it is argued, would be agreed to.

One may accept the first part of the theory (or some variant thereof), but not the other, and conversely. The concept of the initial contractual situation may seem reasonable although the particular principles proposed are rejected. To be sure, I want to maintain that the most appropriate conception of this situation does lead to principles of justice contrary to utilitarianism and perfectionism, and therefore that the contract doctrine provides an alternative to these views. Still, one may dispute this contention even though one grants that the contractarian method is a useful way of studying ethical theories and of setting forth their underlying assumptions.

The merit of the contract terminology is that it conveys the idea that principles of justice may be conceived as principles that would be chosen by rational persons, and that in this way conceptions of justice may be explained and justified. The theory of justice is a part, perhaps the most significant part, of the theory of rational choice. Furthermore, principles of justice deal with conflicting claims upon the advantages won by social cooperation; they apply to the relations among several persons or groups. The word "contract" suggests this plurality as well as the condition that the appropriate division of advantages must be in accordance with principles acceptable to all parties. The condition of publicity for principles of justice is also connoted by the contract phraseology. Thus, if these principles are the outcome of an agreement, citizens have a knowledge of the principles that others follow. It is characteristic of contract theories to stress the public nature of political principles. Finally there is the long tradition of the contract doctrine. Expressing the tie with this line of thought helps to define ideas and accords with natural piety. There are then several advantages in the use of the term "contract." With due precautions taken, it should not be misleading.

A final remark, Justice as fairness is not a complete contract theory. For it is clear that the contractarian idea can be extended to the choice of more or less an entire ethical system, that is, to a system including principles for all the virtues and not only for justice. Now for the most part I shall consider only principles of justice and others closely related to them; I make no attempt to discuss the virtues in a systematic way. Obviously if justice as fairness succeeds reasonably well, a next step would be to study the more general view suggested by the name "rightness as fairness." But even this wider theory fails to embrace all moral relationships, since it would seem to include only our relations with other persons and to leave out of account how we are to conduct ourselves toward animals and the rest of nature.

4. THE ORIGINAL POSITION AND JUSTIFICATION

I have said that the original position is the appropriate initial status quo which insures that the fundamental agreements reached in it are fair. This fact yields the name "justice as fairness." It is clear, then, that I want to say that one conception of justice is more reasonable than another, or justifiable with respect to it, if rational persons in the initial situation would choose its principles over those of the other for the role of justice. Conceptions of justice are to be ranked by their acceptability to persons so circumstanced. Understood in this way the question of justification is settled by working out a problem of deliberation: we have to ascertain which principles it would be rational to adopt given the contractual situation. This connects the theory of justice with the theory of rational choice.

If this view of the problem of justification is to succeed, we must, of course, describe in some detail the nature of this choice problem. A problem of rational decision has a definite answer only if we know the beliefs and interests of the parties, their relations with respect to one another, the alternatives between which they are to choose, the procedure whereby they make up their minds, and so on. As the circumstances are presented in different ways, correspondingly different principles are accepted. The concept of the original position, as I shall refer to it, is that of the most philosophically favored interpretation of this initial choice situation for the purposes of a theory of justice.

But how are we to decide what is the most favored interpretation? I assume, for one thing, that there is a broad measure of agreement that principles of justice should be chosen under certain conditions. To justify a particular description of the initial situation one shows that it incorporates these commonly shared presumptions. One argues from widely accepted but weak premises to more specific conclusions. Each of the presumptions should by itself be natural and plausible; some of them may seem innocuous or even trivial. The aim of the contract approach is to establish that taken together they impose significant bounds on acceptable principles of justice. The ideal outcome would be that these conditions determine a unique set of principles; but I shall be satisfied if they suffice to rank the main traditional conceptions of social justice.

One should not be misled, then, by the somewhat unusual conditions which characterize the original position. The idea here is simply to make vivid to ourselves the restrictions that it seems reasonable to impose on arguments for principles of justice, and therefore on these principles themselves. Thus it seems reasonable and generally acceptable that no one should be advantaged or disadvantaged by natural fortune or social circumstances in the choice of principles. It also seems widely agreed that it should be impossible to tailor principles to the circumstances of one's own case. We should insure further that particular inclinations and aspirations, and persons' conceptions of their good do not affect the principles adopted. The aim is to rule out those principles that it would be rational to propose for acceptance, however little the chance of success, only if one knew certain things that are irrelevant from the standpoint of justice. For example, if a man knew that he was wealthy, he might find it rational to advance the principle that various taxes for welfare measures be counted unjust; if he knew that he was poor, he would most likely propose the contrary principle. To represent the desired restrictions one imagines a situation in which everyone is deprived of this sort of information. One excludes the knowledge of those contingencies which sets men at odds and allows them to be guided by their prejudices. In this manner the veil of ignorance is arrived at in a natural way. This concept should cause no difficulty if we keep in mind the constraints on arguments that it is meant to express. At any time we can enter the original position, so to speak, simply by following a certain procedure, namely, by arguing for principles of justice in accordance with these restrictions.

It seems reasonable to suppose that the parties in the original position are equal. That is, all have the same rights in the procedure for choosing principles; each can make proposals, submit reasons for their acceptance, and so on. Obviously the purpose of these conditions is to represent equality between human beings as moral persons, as creatures having a conception of their good and capable of a sense of justice. The basis of equality is taken to be similarity in these two respects. Systems of ends are not ranked in value; and each man is presumed to have the requisite ability to understand and to act upon whatever principles are adopted. Together with the veil of ignorance, these conditions define the principles of justice as those which rational persons concerned to advance their interests would consent to as equals when none are known to be advantaged or disadvantaged by social and natural contingencies.

There is, however, another side to justifying a particular description of the original position. This is to see if the principles which would be chosen match our considered convictions of justice or extend them in an acceptable way. We can note whether applying these principles would lead us to make the same judgments about the basic structure of society which we now make intuitively and in which we have the greatest confidence; or whether, in cases where our present judgments are in doubt and given with hesitation, these principles offer a resolution which we can affirm on reflection. There are questions which we feel sure must be answered in a certain way. For example, we are confident that religious intolerance and racial discrimination are unjust. We think that we have examined these things with care and have reached what we believe is an impartial judgment not likely to be distorted by an excessive attention to our own interests. These convictions are provisional fixed points which we presume any conception of justice must fit. But we have much less assurance as to what is the correct distribution of wealth and authority. Here we may be looking for a way to remove our doubts. We can check an interpretation of the initial situation, then, by the capacity of its principles to accommodate our firmest convictions and to provide guidance where guidance is needed.

In searching for the most favored description of this situation we work from both ends. We begin by describing it so that it represents generally shared and preferably weak conditions. We then see if these conditions are strong enough to yield a significant set of principles. If not, we look for further premises equally reasonable. But if so, and these principles match our considered convictions of justice, then so far well and good. But presumably there will be discrepancies. In this case we have a choice. We can either modify the account of the initial situation or we can revise our existing judgments, for even the judgments we take provisionally as fixed points are liable to revision. By going back and forth, sometimes altering the conditions of the contractual circumstances, at others withdrawing our judgments and conforming them to principle, I assume that eventually we shall find a description of the initial situation that both expresses reasonable conditions and yields principles which match our considered judgments duly pruned and adjusted. This state of affairs I refer to as reflective equilibrium. It is an equilibrium because at last our principles and judgments coincide; and it is reflective since we know to what principles our judgments conform and the premises of their derivation. At the moment everything is in order. But this equilibrium is not necessarily stable. It is liable to be upset by further examination of the conditions which should be imposed on the contractual situation and by particular cases which may lead us to revise our judgments. Yet for the time being we have done what we can to render coherent and to justify our convictions of social justice. We have reached a conception of the original position.

I shall not, of course, actually work through this process. Still, we may think of the interpretation of the original position that I shall present as the result of such a hypothetical course of reflection. It represents the attempt to accommodate within one scheme both reasonable philosophical conditions on principles as well as our considered judgments of justice. In arriving at the favored interpretation of the initial situation there is no point at which an appeal is made to self-evidence in the traditional sense either of general conceptions or particular convictions. I do not claim for the principles of justice proposed that they are necessary truths or derivable from such truths. A conception of justice cannot be deduced from self-evident premises or conditions on principles; instead, its justification is a matter of the mutual support of many considerations, of everything fitting together into one coherent view.

11. TWO PRINCIPLES OF JUSTICE

I shall now state in a provisional form the two principles of justice that I believe would be chosen in the original position. In this section I wish to make only the most general comments, and therefore the first formulation of these principles is tentative. As we go on I shall run through several formulations and approximate step by step the final statement to be given much later. I believe that doing this allows the exposition to proceed in a natural way.

The first statement of the two principles reads as follows.

> First: each person is to have an equal right to the most extensive basic liberty compatible with a similar liberty for others.
>
> Second: social and economic inequalities are to be arranged so that they are both (a) reasonably expected to be to everyone's advantage, and (b) attached to positions and offices open to all.

There are two ambiguous phrases in the second principle, namely "everyone's advantage" and "equally open to all." Determining their sense more exactly will lead to a second formulation of the principle in § 13. The final version of the two principles is given in § 45; § 39 considers the rendering of the first principle.

By way of general comment, these principles primarily apply, as I have said, to the basic structure of society. They are to govern the assignment of rights and duties and to regulate the distribution of social and economic advantages. As their formulation suggests, these principles presuppose that the social structure can be divided into two more or less distinct parts, the first principle applying to the one, the second to the other. They distinguish between those aspects of the social system that define and secure the equal liberties of citizenship and those that specify and establish social and economic inequalities. The basic liberties of citizens are, roughly speaking, political liberty (the right to vote and to be eligible for public office) together with freedom of speech and assembly; liberty of conscience and freedom of thought; freedom of the person along with the right to hold (personal) property; and freedom from arbitrary arrest and seizure as defined by the concept of the rule of law. These liberties are all required to be equal by the first principle, since citizens of a just society are to have the same basic rights.

The second principle applies, in the first approximation, to the distribution of income and wealth and to the design of organizations that make use of differences in authority and responsibility, or chains of command. While the distribution of wealth and income need not be equal, it must be to everyone's advantage, and at the same time, positions of authority and offices of command must be accessible to all. One applies the second principle by holding positions open, and then, subject to this constraint, arranges social and economic inequalities so that everyone benefits.

These principles are to be arranged in a serial order with the first principle prior to the second. This ordering means that a departure from the institutions of equal liberty required by the first principle cannot be justified by, or compensated for, by greater social and economic advantages. The distribution of wealth and income, and the hierarchies of authority, must be consistent with both the liberties of equal citizenship and equality of opportunity.

It is clear that these principles are rather specific in their content, and their acceptance rests on certain assumptions that I must eventually try to explain and justify. A theory of justice depends upon a theory of society in ways that will become evident as we proceed. For the present, it should be observed that the two principles (and this holds for all formulations) are a special case of a more general conception of justice that can be expressed as follows.

> All social values—liberty and opportunity, income and wealth, and the bases of self-respect—are to be distributed equally unless an unequal distribution of any, or all, of these values is to everyone's advantage.

Injustice, then, is simply inequalities that are not to the benefit of all. Of course, this conception is extremely vague and requires interpretation.

As a first step, suppose that the basic structure of society distributes certain primary goods, that is, things that every rational man is presumed to want. These goods normally have a use whatever a person's rational plan of life. For simplicity, assume that the chief primary goods at the disposition of society are rights and liberties, powers and opportunities, income and wealth. (Later on in Part Three the primary good of self-respect has a central place.) These are the social primary goods. Other primary goods such as health and vigor, intelligence and imagination, are natural goods; although their possession is influenced by the basic structure, they are not so directly under its control. Imagine, then, a hypothetical initial arrangement in which all the social primary goods are equally distributed: everyone has similar rights and duties, and income and wealth are evenly shared. This state of affairs provides a benchmark for judging improvements. If certain inequalities of wealth and organizational powers would make everyone better off than in this hypothetical starting situation, then they accord with the general conception.

Now it is possible, at least theoretically, that by giving up some of their fundamental liberties men are sufficiently compensated by the resulting social and economic gains. The general conception of justice imposes no restrictions on what sort of inequalities are permissible; it only requires that everyone's position be improved. We need not suppose anything so drastic as consenting to a condition of slavery. Imagine instead that men forego certain political rights when the economic returns are significant and their capacity to influence the course of policy by the exercise of these rights would be marginal in any case. It is this kind of exchange which the two principles as stated rule out; being arranged in serial order they do not permit exchanges between basic liberties and economic and social gains. The serial ordering of principles expresses an underlying preference among primary social goods. When this preference is rational so likewise is the choice of these principles in this order.

The fact that the two principles apply to institutions has certain consequences. Several points illustrate this. First of all, the rights and liberties referred to by these principles are those which are defined by the public rules of the basic structure. Whether men are free is determined by the rights and duties established by the major institutions of society. Liberty is a certain pattern of social forms. The first principle simply requires that certain sorts of rules, those defining basic liberties, apply to everyone equally and that they allow the most extensive liberty compatible with a like liberty for all. The only reason for circumscribing the rights defining liberty and making men's freedom less extensive than it might otherwise be is that these equal rights as institutionally defined would interfere with one another.

Another thing to bear in mind is that when principles mention persons, or require that everyone gain from an inequality, the reference is to representative persons holding the various social positions, or offices, or whatever, established by the basic structure. Thus in applying the second principle I assume that it is possible to assign an expectation of well-being to representative individuals holding these positions. This expectation indicates their life prospects as viewed from their social station. In general, the expectations of representative persons depend upon the distribution of rights and duties throughout the basic structure.

Now the second principle insists that each person benefit from permissible inequalities in the basic structure. This means that it must be reasonable for each relevant representative man defined by this structure, when he views it as a going concern, to prefer his prospects with the inequality to his prospects without it. One is not allowed to justify differences in income or organizational powers on the ground that the disadvantages of those in one position are outweighed by the greater advantages of those in another. Much less can infringements of liberty be counterbalanced in this way. Applied to the basic structure, the principle of utility would have us maximize the sum of expectations of representative men (weighted by the number of persons they represent, on the classical view); and this would permit us to compensate for the losses of some by the gains of others. Instead, the two principles require that everyone benefit from economic and social inequalities.

24. THE VEIL OF IGNORANCE

The idea of the original position is to set up a fair procedure so that any principles agreed to will be just. The aim is to use the notion of pure procedural justice as a basis of theory. Somehow we must nullify the effects of specific contingencies which put men at odds and tempt them to exploit social and natural circumstances to their own advantage. Now in order to do this I assume that the parties are situated behind a veil of ignorance. They do not know how the various alternatives will affect their own particular case and they are obliged to evaluate principles solely on the basis of general considerations.

It is assumed, then, that the parties do not know certain kinds of particular facts. First of all, no one knows his place in society, his class position or social status; nor does he know his fortune in the distribution of natural assets and abilities, his intelligence and strength, and the like. Nor, again, does anyone know his conception of the good, the particulars of his rational plan of life, or even the special features of his psychology such as his aversion to risk or liability to optimism or pessimism. More than this, I assume that the parties do not know the particular circumstances of their own society. That is, they do not know its economic or political situation, or the level of civilization and culture it has been able to achieve. The persons in the original position have no information as to which generation they belong. These broader restrictions on knowledge are appropriate in part because questions of social justice arise between generations as well as within them, for example, the question of the appropriate rate of capital saving and of the conservation of natural resources and the environment of nature. There is also, theoretically anyway, the question of a reasonable genetic policy. In these cases too, in order to carry through the idea of the original position, the parties must not know the contingencies that set them in opposition. They must choose principles the consequences of which they are prepared to live with whatever generation they turn out to belong to.

As far as possible, then, the only particular facts which the parties know is that their society is subject to the circumstances of justice and whatever this implies. It is taken for granted, however, that they know the general facts about human society. They understand political affairs and the principles of economic theory; they know the basis of social organization and the laws of human psychology. Indeed, the parties are presumed to know whatever general facts affect the choice of the principles of justice. There are no limitations on general information, that is, on general laws and theories, since conceptions of justice must be adjusted to the characteristics of the systems of social cooperation which they are to regulate, and there is no reason to rule out these facts. It is, for example, a consideration against a conception of justice that in view of the laws of moral psychology, men would not acquire a desire to act upon it even when the institutions of their society satisfied it. For in this case there would be difficulty in securing the stability of social cooperation. It is an important feature of a conception of justice that it should generate its own support. That is, its principles should be such that when they are

embodied in the basic structure of society men tend to acquire the corresponding sense of justice. Given the principles of moral learning, men develop a desire to act in accordance with its principles. In this case a conception of justice is stable. This kind of general information is admissible in the original position.

The notion of the veil of ignorance raises several difficulties. Some may object that the exclusion of nearly all particular information makes it difficult to grasp what is meant by the original position. Thus it may be helpful to observe that one or more persons can at any time enter this position, or perhaps, better, simulate the deliberations of this hypothetical situation, simply by reasoning in accordance with the appropriate restrictions. In arguing for a conception of justice we must be sure that it is among the permitted alternatives and satisfies the stipulated formal constraints. No considerations can be advanced in its favor unless they would be rational ones for us to urge were we to lack the kind of knowledge that is excluded. The evaluation of principles must proceed in terms of the general consequences of their public recognition and universal application, it being assumed that they will be complied with by everyone. To say that a certain conception of justice would be chosen in the original position is equivalent to saying that rational deliberation satisfying certain conditions and restrictions would reach a certain conclusion. If necessary, the argument to this result could be set out more formally. I shall, however, speak throughout in terms of the notion of the original position. It is more economical and suggestive, and brings out certain essential features that otherwise one might easily overlook.

These remarks show that the original position is not to be thought of as a general assembly which includes at one moment everyone who will live at some time; or, much less, as an assembly of everyone who could live at some time. It is not a gathering of all actual or possible persons. To conceive of the original position in either of these ways is to stretch fantasy too far; the conception would cease to be a natural guide to intuition. In any case, it is important that the original position be interpreted so that one can at any time adopt its perspective. It must make no difference when one takes up this viewpoint, or who does so: the restrictions must be such that the same principles are always chosen. The veil of ignorance is a key condition in meeting this requirement. It insures not only that the information available is relevant, but that it is at all times the same.

It may be protested that the condition of the veil of ignorance is irrational. Surely, some may object, principles should be chosen in the light of all the knowledge available. There are various replies to this contention. Here I shall sketch those which emphasize the simplifications that need to be made if one is to have any theory at all. (Those based on the Kantian interpretation of the original position are given later, § 40.) To begin with, it is clear that since the differences among the parties are unknown to them, and everyone is equally rational and similarly situated, each is convinced by the same arguments. Therefore, we can view the choice in the original position from the standpoint of one person selected at random. If anyone after due reflection prefers a conception of justice to another, then they all do, and a unanimous agreement can be reached. We can, to make the circumstances more vivid, imagine that the parties are required to communicate with each other through a referee as intermediary, and that he is to announce which alternatives have been suggested and the reasons offered in their support. He forbids the attempt to form coalitions, and he informs the parties when they have come to an understanding. But such a referee is actually superfluous, assuming that the deliberations of the parties must be similar.

Thus there follows the very important consequence that the parties have no basis for bargaining in the usual sense. No one knows his situation in society nor his natural assets, and therefore no one is in a position to tailor principles to his advantage.

46. FURTHER CASES OF PRIORITY

I now wish to give the final statement of the two principles of justice for institutions. For the sake of completeness, I shall give a full statement including earlier formulations.

First Principle

Each person is to have an equal right to the most extensive total system of equal basic liberties compatible with a similar system of liberty for all.

Second Principle

Social and economic inequalities are to be arranged so that they are both:

a. to the greatest benefit of the least advantaged, consistent with the just savings principle, and
b. attached to offices and positions open to all under conditions of fair equality of opportunity.

First Priority Rule (The Priority of Liberty)

The principles of justice are to be ranked in lexical order and therefore liberty can be restricted only for the sake of liberty. There are two cases:

a. a less extensive liberty must strengthen the total system of liberty shared by all;
b. a less than equal liberty must be acceptable to those with the lesser liberty.

Second Priority Rule (The Priority of Justice over Efficiency and Welfare)

The second principle of justice is lexically prior to the principle of efficiency and to that of maximizing the sum of advantages; and fair opportunity is prior to the difference principle. There are two cases:

a. an inequality of opportunity must enhance the opportunities of those with the lesser opportunity;
b. an excessive rate of saving must on balance mitigate the burden of those bearing this hardship.

General Conception

All social primary goods—liberty and opportunity, income and wealth, and the bases of self-respect—are to be distributed equally unless an unequal distribution of any or all of these goods is to the advantage of the least favored.

By way of comment, these principles and priority rules are no doubt incomplete. Other modifications will surely have to be made, but I shall not further complicate the statement of the principles. It suffices to observe that when we come to nonideal theory, we do not fall back straightway upon the general conception of justice. The lexical ordering of the two principles, and the valuations that this ordering implies, suggest priority rules which seem to be reasonable enough in many cases. By various examples I have tried to illustrate how these rules can be used and to indicate their plausibility. Thus the ranking of the principles of justice in ideal theory reflects back and guides the application of these principles to nonideal situations. It identifies which limitations need to be dealt with first. The drawback of the general conception of justice is that it lacks the definite structure of the two principles in serial order. In more extreme and tangled instances of nonideal theory there may be no alternative to it. At some point the priority of rules for nonideal cases will fail; and indeed, we may be able to find no satisfactory answer at all. But we must try to postpone the day of reckoning as long as possible, and try to arrange society so that it never comes.

STUDY QUESTIONS: RAWLS, *A THEORY OF JUSTICE*

1. What is the first virtue of social institutions?
2. When is a society well-ordered? Is ours?
3. How does he see his own theory in relation to the social contract theories of Locke, Rousseau, and Kant?
4. What does 'justice as fairness' mean? How does it apply?
5. What does he mean by the 'original position'?
6. What is the problem of the choice of principle? What is his solution of it? Does he expect everyone will agree? Why?
7. What is the main merit of the contract terminology?
8. Is 'justice as fairness' a complete contract theory? Why?
9. What is the problem of justification, as he sees it? How does he solve it?
10. What are the two principles of justice that Rawls thinks would be chosen in the original position? Do they apply to institutions as well as individuals?
11. What are the basic liberties of citizens?
12. Must the distribution of wealth and income be equal? Why?
13. How is the theory of justice connected to the theory of rational choice?
14. What is the 'veil of ignorance'? How does it work?
15. What are some of the difficulties raised by the veil of ignorance?
16. Under what condition is the denial of equal liberty defensible?

Philosophical Bridges: Rawls' Influence

Rawls' *A Theory of Justice* is the classic twentieth-century statement of liberal political philosophy. As such, it has provoked a strong reaction and stimulated political philosophy to new levels of dispute. Therefore, the influence of Rawls must include the rival theories, such as Robert Nozick's libertarian conception of justice, developed in *Anarchy State and Utopia*. In contrast to both, Michael Sandel and Alasdair MacIntyre have developed communitarian political visions (e.g., Sandel, *Liberalism and the Limits of Justice*).

From the libertarian side, the most disputed aspect of Rawls' liberalism is the thesis that wealth should be redistributed insofar as it benefits the worst off. Nozick argues that this thesis involves a misunderstanding of property rights, which would be violated by any such redistribution. From the communitarian side, Sandel argues that the notion of a liberal state that is neutral between competing conceptions of the good is impossible. He also contends that Rawls' idea of choice from behind the veil of ignorance requires an impossible conception of a person as no more than an autonomous individual. Such a person would have no historical culture and hence no ends to enable him or her to make choices. From a broader perspective, Rawls' theory can be contrasted with the work of Jürgen Habermas (see Section VII), which it also influenced.

Rawls' work also contains a sustained and influential argument against utilitarianism, which in turn has generated much debate concerning the viability of the utilitarian moral theory. Rawls' appeal to Kant has helped inspire a contemporary revival of Kantian ethics. Furthermore, Rawls has spawned much work concerning contractual theories of morality. For example, John Harsanyi attempts to derive a utilitarian theory from a contractual framework. Finally, Rawls' theory of justice also influenced philosophical theories of the law and the philosophy of economics.

Hilary Putnam (1926–)

Biographical History

Hilary Putnam was born in Chicago in 1926 and lived in France until 1934. He graduated from the University of Pennsylvania and received his Ph.D. in 1951 from the University of California, Los Angeles, where he worked with Hans Reichenbach. He taught at Northwestern, Princeton, and MIT before moving to Harvard, where he was professor of mathematical logic and philosophy. Putnam has published several collections of papers, including three volumes of *Philosophical Papers* and *Realism with a Human Face*. He has also written several books such as *Reason Truth and History*, *Representation and Reality*, *Renewing Philosophy*, and *Pragmatism*. He retired in 2000.

Philosophical Overview

Putnam's thought may be divided into two periods. His earlier works are oriented toward the philosophy of science and mathematics. During this early period, for instance in his 1967 paper, 'The Nature of Mental States,' he argues for machine functionalism, according to which mental states are computational, like the states of a Turing machine. (A Turing machine is an imaginary computer with an indefinitely long storage tape.) He contends that mental states can be realized in different physical systems and thus that their nature depends on organization rather than their composition.

In his paper 'Meaning and Reference' (1973), Putnam argued for a causal theory of reference according to which names and other words refer directly through their causal connections rather than through some Fregean sense. Putnam extended this analysis to so-called natural kind terms, such as 'gold' and 'water.' In order to support this causal view of reference, Putnam also invented the famous Twin Earth thought experiment, which asks us to imagine a twin who lives on an almost identical planet to the earth, except that on that twin planet the liquid called 'water' is not H_2O but rather XYZ. Based on this example, Putnam argues that what we mean by the term 'water' is determined by what the word actually refers to, i.e., by the relevant natural kind. As a consequence, Fregean senses are not necessary for reference, and furthermore, meanings are not internal and mental; they are not in the head. This view is called semantic externalism. Putnam also uses this externalist position to refute a radical form of Skepticism that argues that we have no evidence against the assertion that we are brains in a vat.

Putnam's later works are more oriented toward the reconciliation of values and science. For example, he argues that there can be no fact/value distinction because there can be no interest-free descriptions of facts. He repudiates the machine functionalism that he championed earlier. During this later period, Putnam argues against the idea that science can describe reality as it is independently of the mind. He rejects an absolute conception of reality. At the same time, he also rejects forms of relativism that deny the notion of truth. He attempts to develop a position in between metaphysical realism and relativism, which he calls 'internal realism.'

WHY THERE ISN'T A READY-MADE WORLD

In this reading, Putnam argues against metaphysical realism, the view that there is an absolutely mind-independent, ready-made world. He concentrates on the materialist version of this thesis. The main problem for metaphysical realism is that it requires a definite correspondence between sentences and states of affairs or between words and objects. Putnam argues that there can be no such definite correspondence. This is because there are infinitely many ways to specify such a relation of correspondence, given that we do not have direct access to those mind-independent objects and given that those objects do not have any intrinsic properties or essences. Metaphysical realism requires a definite correspondence, which is impossible.

Putnam examines various responses that the metaphysical realist might make. First, he focuses on the suggestion that the appropriate notion of correspondence can be understood in terms of causality. He tries to rebut this suggestion by showing that the notion of causation cannot be understood in purely physical terms or in purely formal terms because it requires the idea of explanation, which in turn involves ideas such as relevance, which are clearly mind-dependent. He also rejects the idea that causation is a primitive concept, and the claim that causation can be analyzed in terms of counterfactuals. Counterfactuals are hypothetical statements based on what did not happen, such as 'If Hitler had won World War II, then half of Europe would have perished.' Most realist analyses of counterfactuals depend on the primitive notion of the 'similarity of possible worlds,' and Putnam argues that this is not a physical notion.

Second, Putnam asks whether the claim that objects have essential properties might be used to support materialism. He doubts it. Such theories individuate objects in terms of their modal properties (what they must and couldn't be), and modal properties are not physical. For instance, consider the claim that the essence of water is that it is H_2O. According to Putnam, the modal property that it *must* be H_2O is not purely physical. Putnam also shows how his own brand of essentialism, which was mentioned in the Philosophical Overview, depends on the idea of referential intentions. We *intend* the term 'water' to refer to a substance of a particular kind (i.e., to what turns out to be H_2O rather than to XYZ). The concept of such intentions is not a purely physical notion.

Third, Putnam responds to the thesis that reference could be defined physically. The notion of reference could not be explained extensionally by listing cases or instances of reference. Alternatively, the notion of reference might be explained in functional terms, as

Lewis suggests. However, this analysis depends on the notion of causation and, therefore, would take us back to the earlier discussion.

Finally, Putnam suggests an alternative to metaphysical realism, which he calls internal realism. By reflecting on some examples from the history of science, he tries to show that the problems that he has revealed are not specific to a materialist version of metaphysical realism.

Two ideas that have become a part of our philosophical culture stand in a certain amount of conflict. One idea, which was revived by Moore and Russell after having been definitely sunk by Kant and Hegel (or so people thought) is metaphysical realism, and the other is that there are no such things as intrinsic or 'essential' properties. Let me begin by saying a word about each.

What the metaphysical realist holds is that we can think and talk about things as they are, independently of our minds, and that we can do this by virtue of a 'correspondence' relation between the terms in our language and some sorts of mind-independent entities. Moore and Russell held the strange view that *sensibilia* (sense data) are such *mind-independent* entities: a view so dotty, on the face of it, that few analytic philosophers like to be reminded that this is how analytic philosophy started. Today material objects are taken to be paradigm mind-independent entities, and the 'correspondence' is taken to be some sort of causal relation. For example, it is said that what makes it the case that I refer to chairs is that I have causally interacted with them, and that I would not utter the utterances containing the word 'chair' that I do if I did not have causal transactions 'of the appropriate type' with chairs. This complex relationship—being connected with x by a causal chain of the appropriate type—between my word (or way of using the word) and x constitutes the relevant *correspondence* between my word and x. On this view, it is no puzzle that we can refer to physical things, but reference to numbers, sets, moral values, or anything not 'physical' is widely held to be problematic if not actually impossible.

The second doctrine, the doctrine that there are no essential properties, is presaged by Locke's famous rejection of 'substantial forms'. Locke rejected the idea that the terms we use to classify things (e.g.,

'man' or 'water') connote properties which are in any sense the 'real essences' of those things. Whereas the medievals thought that the real essence of water was a so-called substantial form, which exists both in the thing and (*minus* the matter) in our minds, Locke argued that what we have in our minds is a number of conventional marks (e.g., being liquid) which we have put together into a descriptive idea because of certain interests we have, and that any assumption that these marks are the 'real essence' of anything we classify under the idea is unwarranted.

Later empiricists went further and denied there was any place for the notion of an essence at all. Here is a typical way of arguing this case: 'Suppose a piece of clay has been formed into a statue. We are sure the piece of clay would not be what it is (a piece of clay) if it were dissolved, or separated into its chemical elements, or cut into five pieces. We can also say the *statue* would not be what it is (*that* statue) if the clay were squeezed into a ball (or formed into a different statue). But the piece of clay and the statue are *one* thing, not two. What this shows is that it only makes sense to speak of an "essential property" of something *relative to a description*. Relative to the description "that statue", a certain shape is an essential property of the object; relative to the description "that piece of clay", the shape is *not* an essential property (but being clay is). The question "what are the essential properties of the thing *in itself*" is a nonsensical one.'

The denial of essences is also a denial of intrinsic structure: an electron in my body has a certain electrical charge, but on the view just described it is a mistake to think that having that charge is an 'intrinsic' property of the object (except *relative to the description* 'electron') in a way in which the property of being a part of my body is not. In short, it is (or was until recently) commonly thought that

"Why There Isn't a Ready Made World" from *Philosophical Papers, Vol 3, Realism and Reason* by Hilary Putnam, 1983. Reprinted with the permission of Cambridge University Press, publisher.

A thing *is not related to any one of its properties (or relations) any more 'intrinsically' than it is to any of its other properties or relations.*

The problem that the believer in metaphysical realism (or 'transcendental realism' as Kant called it) has always faced involves the notion of 'correspondence'. There are many different ways of putting the signs of a language and the things in a set *S* in correspondence with one another, in fact infinitely many if the set *S* is infinite (and a very large finite number if *S* is a large finite set). Even if the 'correspondence' has to be a reference relation and we specify which *sentences* are to correspond to *states of affairs which actually obtain*, it follows from theorems of model theory that there are still infinitely many ways of *specifying* such a correspondence. How can we pick out any *one* correspondence between our words (or thoughts) and the supposed mind-independent things *if we have no direct access to the mind-independent things?* (German philosophy almost always began with a particular answer to this question—the answer 'we can't'—after Kant.)

One thing is clear: an act of will (or intention) won't work. I can't simply *pick* one particular correspondence *C* and *will* (or stipulate) that *C is to be* the designated correspondence relation, because in order to do that I would need *already* to be able to *think about* the correspondence *C* — and *C*, being a relation to things which are external and mind-independent, is itself something outside the mind, something 'external'! In short, if the mind does not have the ability to grasp external things or forms directly, then no *mental* act can give it the ability to single out a correspondence (or anything else external, for that matter).

But if the denial of intrinsic properties is correct, then no external thing or event is connected to any one relation it may have to other things (including our thoughts) in a way which is special or essential or intrinsic. If the denial of intrinsic properties is right, then it is not more essential to a mental event that it stand in a relation C_1 to any object *x* than it is that it stands in any other relation C_2 to any other object *y*. Nor is it any more essential to a non-mental object that it stand in a relation *C* to any one of my thoughts than it is that it stand in any one of a myriad other relations to any one of my other thoughts. On such a view, no relation *C* is metaphysically singled

out as *the* relation between thoughts and things; reference becomes an 'occult' phenomenon.

The tension or incompatibility between metaphysical realism and the denial of intrinsic properties has not gone unnoticed by modern materialists. And for this reason we now find many materialists employing a metaphysical vocabulary that smacks of the fourteenth century: materialists who talk of 'causal powers', of 'built-in' similarities and dissimilarities between things in nature, even materialists who speak unabashedly of *essences*. In this lecture I want to ask if this modern mixture of materialism and essentialism *is consistent*; and I shall argue that it *isn't*.

WHY I FOCUS ON MATERIALISM

The reason I am going to focus my attack on materialism is that materialism is the only *metaphysical* picture that has contemporary 'clout'. Metaphysics, or the enterprise of describing the 'furniture of the world', the 'things in themselves' apart from our conceptual imposition, has been rejected by many analytic philosophers (though *not*, as I remarked, by Russell), and by all the leading brands of continental philosophy. Today, apart from relics, it is virtually only materialists (or 'physicalists', as they like to call themselves) who continue the traditional enterprise.

It was not always thus. Between the tenth and twelfth centuries the metaphysical community which included the Arabic Averroes and Avicenna, the Jewish Maimonides, and the Angelic Doctor in Paris disagreed on many questions, creation in particular. It was regarded as a hard issue whether the world always existed obeying the same laws (the doctrine ascribed to Aristotle), or was created from preexisting matter (the doctrine ascribed to Plato) or was created *ex nihilo* (the Scriptural doctrine). But the existence of a supersensible Cause of the contingent and moving sensible things was taken to be *demonstrable*. Speculative reason could *know* there was an Uncaused Cause.

When I was seven years old the question 'if God made the world, then who made God?' struck me one evening with vivid force. I remember pacing in circles around a little well for hours while the awful regress played itself out in my mind. If a medieval theologian had been handy, he would have told me that God was self-caused. He might have said God was the *ens necessarium*. I don't know if it would have helped; today philosophers would say that the doctrine of God's 'necessary' existence invokes a notion of 'necessity' which is incoherent or unintelligible.

The issue does, in a covert way, still trouble us. Wallace Matson (1967) ended a philosophic defense of atheism with the words, 'Still, why *is* there something rather than nothing?'. The doctrine that 'you take the universe you get' (a remark Steven Weinberg once made in a discussion) sounds close to saying it's some sort of metaphysical *chance* (we might just as well have *anything*). The idea of a supersensible Cause outside of the universe leads at once to the question that troubled me when I was seven. We don't even have the comfort of thinking of the universe as a kind of *ens necessarium: it* only came into existence a few billion years ago!

This situation was summed up by Kant: Kant held that the whole enterprise of trying to *demonstrate* the existence and nature of a supersensible world by speculation leads only to antinomies. (The universe *must* have a cause; but *that* cause would have to have a cause; but an infinite regress is no explanation and self-causation is impossible . . .) Today, as I remarked, only a few relics would challenge this conclusion, which put an end to rationalism as well as to the medieval synthesis of Greek philosophy with revealed religion.

This decline of medieval philosophy was a long process which overlapped the decline of medieval science (with its substantial forms). Here too Kant summed up the issue for our culture: the medievals (and the rationalists) thought the mind had an intellectual intuition (*intellektuelle Anschauung*), a sort of perception that would enable it to perceive essences, substantial forms, or whatever. But there is no such faculty. 'Nothing is in the mind that was not first in the senses *except the mind itself*', as Kant put it, quoting Leibnitz.

Again, no one but a few relics challenge *this* conclusion. But Kant drew a bold corollary, and this corollary is hotly disputed to the present day.

The corollary depends upon a claim that Kant made. The claim can be illustrated by a famous observation of Wittgenstein's. Referring to the 'duck–rabbit' illusion (the figure that can be seen as either a duck or a rabbit), Wittgenstein remarked that while the physical image is capable of being seen either way, no 'mental image' is capable of being seen either way: the 'mental image' is always unambigu-ously a duck image or a rabbit image (*Philosophical Investigations* II, xi, 194–6). It follows that 'mental images' are really very different from physical images such as line drawings and photographs. We might express this difference by saying the interpretation is *built in* to the 'mental image'; the mental image is a *construction*.

Kant made the same point with respect to *memory.* When I have a memory of an experience this is not, contrary to Hume, *just* an image which 'resembles' the earlier experience. To be a memory the interpretation has to be 'built in': the interpretation that this is a *past* experience of *mine.* Kant (1933, Transcendental Deduction) argues that the notion of the *past* involves causality and that causality involves laws and objects (so, according to Kant, does the assignment of all these experiences to *myself*). Past experiences are not directly available; saying we 'remember' them is saying we have succeeded in constructing a version with causal relations and a continuing self in which they are located.

The corollary Kant drew from all this is that even experiences are in part constructions of the mind: I know what experiences I have and have had partly because I know what *objects* I am seeing and touching and have seen and touched, and partly because I know what *laws* these objects obey. Kant may have been overambitious in thinking he could specify the *a priori* constraints on the construction process; but the idea that all experience involves mental construction, and the idea that the dependence of physical object concepts and experience concepts goes *both* ways, continue to be of great importance in contemporary philosophy (of many varieties).

Since sense data and physical objects are interdependent constructions, in Kant's view, the idea that 'all we know is sense data' is as silly as the idea that we can have knowledge of objects that goes beyond experience. Although Kant does not put it this way, I have suggested elsewhere (Putnam, 1981, ch. 3) that we can view him as rejecting the idea of truth as correspondence (to a mind-independent reality) and as saying that the only sort of truth we can have an idea of, or use for, is *assertibility* (by creatures with our rational natures) *under optimal conditions* (as determined by our sensible natures). Truth becomes a radically epistemic notion.

However, Kant remarks that the *desire* for speculative metaphysics, the desire for a theory of the furniture of the world, is deep in our nature. He thought we should abandon the enterprise of trying to have speculative knowledge of the 'things in themselves' and sublimate the metaphysical impulse in the moral project of trying to make a more perfect world; but he was surely right about the strength of the metaphysical urge.

Contemporary materialism and scientism are a reflection of this urge in two ways. On the one hand, the materialist claims that physics is an approximation to a sketch of the one true theory, the true and complete description of the furniture of the world. (Since he often leaves out quantum mechanics, his picture differs remarkably little from Democritus': it's all atoms swerving in the void.) On the other hand, he meets the epistemological argument against metaphysics by claiming that we don't *need* an intellectual intuition to do *his* sort of metaphysics: his metaphysics, he says, is as open ended, as infinitely revisable and fallible, as science itself. In fact, it *is* science itself! (interpreted as claiming absolute truth, or, rather, claiming *convergence* to absolute truth). The appeal of materialism lies precisely in this, in its claim to be *natural* metaphysics, metaphysics within the bounds of science. That a doctrine which promises to gratify both our ambition (to know the noumena) and our caution (not to be unscientific) should have great appeal is hardly something to be wondered at.

This wide appeal would be reason enough to justify a critique of metaphysical materialism. But a second reason is this: metaphysical materialism has replaced positivism and pragmatism as the dominant contemporary form of scientism. Since scientism is, in my opinion, one of the most dangerous contemporary intellectual tendencies, a critique of its most influential contemporary form is a duty for a philosopher who views his enterprise as more than a purely technical discipline.

CAUSATION

What makes the metaphysical realist a *metaphysical* realist is his belief that there is somewhere 'one true theory' (two theories which are true and complete descriptions of the world would be mere notational variants of each other). In company with a correspondence theory of truth, this belief in one true theory requires a *ready-made* world (an expression suggested in this connection by Nelson Goodman): the world itself has to have a 'built-in' structure since otherwise theories with different structures might correctly 'copy' the world (from different perspectives) and truth would lose its absolute (non-perspectival) character. Moreover, as I already remarked, 'correspondence' between our symbols and something which has no determinate structure is hardly a well-defined notion.

The materialist metaphysician often takes *causal relations* as an example of built-in structure. Events have causes; objects have 'causal powers'. And he proudly proclaims his realism about these, his faith that they are 'in' the world itself, in the metaphysical realist sense. Well, let us grant him that this is so, for the sake of argument: my question for the moment is not whether this sort of realism is justified, but whether it is really compatible with materialism. Is *causation* a physical relation?

In this discussion, I shall follow the materialist in ignoring quantum mechanics since it has *no* generally acceptable interpretation of the kind the realist advocates: the standard (Copenhagen) interpretation makes essential reference to *observers*, and the materialist wants to imagine a physics in which the observer is simply another part of the system, as seen from a God's eye view. Physics is then a theory whose fundamental magnitudes are defined at all points in space and time; a property or relation is physically definable if it is definable in terms of these.

I shall also assume that the fundamental magnitudes are basically the usual ones: if no restraint at all is placed on what counts as a possible 'fundamental magnitude' in future physics, then *reference* or *soul* or *Good* could even be 'fundamental magnitudes' in future physics! I shall not allow the naturalist the escape hatch of letting 'future physics' mean we-know-not-what. Physicalism is only intelligible if 'future physics' is supposed to resemble what *we* call 'physics'. The possibility of natural metaphysics (metaphysics within the bounds of science) is, indeed, not conclusively refuted by showing that present-day materialism cannot be a correct sketch of the one true (metaphysical) theory: but present-day materialism is, as already remarked, the view with clout.

Now if '*A* causes *B*' simply meant 'whenever an *A*-type event happens, then a *B*-type event follows in time', 'causes' would be physically definable. Many attempts have been made to give such a definition of causation—one which would apply to genuine causal laws while not applying to sequences we would regard as coincidental or otherwise non-causal. Few philosophers believe today that this is possible.

But let us assume that 'causes' (in this sense) *is* somehow physically definable. A cause, in the sense this definition tries to capture, is a *sufficient* condition for its effect; whenever the cause occurs, the effect *must* follow (at least in a deterministic world). Following Mill, let us call such a cause a *total cause*. An example of a total cause at time t_0 of a physical event e occurring at a later time t_1 and a point x would be the entire distribution of values of the dynamical variables at time t_0 (inside a sphere S whose center is x and whose radius is sufficiently large so that events outside the sphere S could not influence events at x occurring at t_1 without having to send a signal to x faster than light, which I assume, on the basis of relativity, to be impossible).

Mill pointed out that in ordinary language 'cause' rarely (if ever) means 'total cause'. When I say 'failure to put out the campfire caused the forest fire', I do *not* mean that the campfire's remaining lit during a certain interval was the *total cause* of the forest fire. Many other things—the dryness of the leaves, their proximity to the campfire, the temperature of the day, even the presence of oxygen in the atmosphere—are part of the *total* cause of the forest fire. Mill's point is that we regard certain parts of the total cause as 'background', and refer only to the part of interest as 'the' cause.

Suppose a professor is found stark-naked in a girl's dormitory room at midnight. His being naked in the room at midnight—ε, where ε is so small that he could neither get out of the room or put on his clothes between midnight—ε and midnight without moving faster than light, would be a 'total cause' of his being naked in the girl's room at midnight; but no one would refer to this as the 'cause' of his presence in the room in that state. On the other hand, when it is said that the presence of certain bodies of H_2O in our environment 'causes' us to use the word 'water' as we do, it is certainly *not* meant that the presence of H_2O is the 'total cause'. In its ordinary sense, 'cause' can often be paraphrased by a locution involving *explain;* the presence of H_2O in our environment, our dependence on H_2O

for life, etc., are 'part of' the *explanation* of our having a word which we use as we use the word 'water'. The forest fire is *explained* (given background knowledge) by the campfire's not having been extinguished; but the professor's state at midnight—ε is not what we consider an *explanation* of the state of affairs at midnight.

When it is said that a word refers to x just in case the (use of the) word is connected to x by a 'causal chain of the appropriate type', the notion of 'causal chain' involved is that of an *explanatory* chain. Even if the notion of 'total cause' *were* physically definable, it would not be possible to *use* it either in daily life or in philosophy; the notion the materialist really uses when he employs 'causal chain', etc., in his philosophical explications is the intuitive notion of an *explanation*.

But this notion is certainly not physically definable. To see that it isn't, observe, first, that 'explains' (and 'caused', when it has the force of 'explains why x happened') are abstract notions. Even when we imagine a possible world in which there are non-physical things or properties, we can conceive of these things and properties *causing* things to happen. A disembodied spirit would not have *mass* or *charge*, but (this is a conceptual question of course; I don't mean to suggest there *are* disembodied spirits) it could *cause* something (say, an emotional reaction in another spirit with which it communicated telepathically).

A definition of 'caused' (in this 'explanatory' sense) which was too 'first order', too tied to the particular magnitudes which are the 'fundamental magnitudes' of physics in *our* world, would make it *conceptually impossible* that a disembodied spirit (or an event involving magnitudes which are not 'physical' in *our* world) could be a cause. This is why the suggested Humean definition of *total* cause—A is the (total) cause of B if and only if an A-type event is always followed in time by a B-type event—contained no *specific* physical term (except 'time'): this definition *is* abstract enough to apply to possible worlds different from our own. (Although it fails even so.) Could there be an equally abstract (and more successful) definition of 'cause' in the explanatory sense?

Imagine that Venusians land on Earth and observe a forest fire. One of them says, '*I* know what caused that—the atmosphere of the darned planet is saturated with oxygen.'

What this vignette illustrates is that one man's (or extraterrestrial's) 'background condition' can easily be another man's 'cause'. What is and what is not a 'cause' or an 'explanation' depends on background knowledge and our reason for asking the question.

No purely *formal* relation between events will be sensitive to this relativity of explanatory arguments to background knowledge and interests.

Nelson Goodman has shown that no purely formal criterion can distinguish arguments which are intuitively sound inductive arguments from unsound arguments: for every sound inductive argument there is an unsound one of the very same form. The actual predicates occurring in the argument make the difference, and the distinction between 'projectible' and 'non-projectible' predicates is not a formal one. It is not difficult to show that the same thing is true of *explanations*. If we think of explanation as relation in 'the world', then to define it one would need a predicate which could sort projectible from non-projectible properties; such a predicate could not be purely formal for then it would run afoul of Goodman's result, but it could not involve the particular fundamental magnitudes in *our* world in an essential way for then it would be open to counterexamples in other possible worlds.

'NON-HUMEAN' CAUSATION

Richard Boyd (1980) has suggested that the whole enterprise of *defining* causation was a mistake: physicalists should simply take the notion as a primitive one. He may only mean that to insist on a definition of 'causes' (or anything else) in the standard formalism for mathematics and physics (which contains *names* for only countably many real numbers, etc.) is unreasonable: if so, this would not be an argument against expecting every *physical* property and relation to be definable in an *infinitary extension* of physics, a language which allows *infinitely long* names and sentences. (Indeed, if a property or relation is *not* physically definable even in this liberal sense, what is meant by calling it 'physical'?) But he may have meant that one should literally take 'causes' as an irreducible notion, one whose failure to be physically definable is not due to syntactic accidents, such as the limit on the length of formulas. But can a

philosopher who accepts the existence of an irreducible phenomenon of *causation* call himself a materialist?

'Causes', we have just seen, is often paraphrasable as 'explains'. It rarely or never means 'is the total cause of'. When Boyd, for example, says that a certain micro-structure is a 'causal power' (the micro-structure of sugar is a 'causal power' in Boyd's sense, because it *causally explains* why sugar dissolves in water) he does not mean that the micro-structure in question is the *total cause* of the explained events (sugar will not dissolve in water if the water is *frozen*, for example, or if the water is already saturated with sugar, or if the water-cum-sugar is in an exotic quantum mechanical state). 'Causal powers' are properties that *explain* something, given background conditions and given standards of salience and relevance.

A metaphysical view in which 'causation' and 'causal explanation' are built into the world itself is one in which explanation is wrenched out of what Professor Frederick Will (1974) has called 'the knowledge institution', the inherited tradition which defines for us what is a background condition and what a salient variable parameter, and projected into the structure of reality. Boyd would probably reply that the 'causal structure' of reality *explains* the success of the knowledge institution: our successful explanations simply copy the built-in causal structure.

Be that as it may, salience and relevance are attributes of thought and reasoning, not of nature. To project them into the realist's 'real world', into what Kant called the *noumenal* world, is to mix objective idealism (or, perhaps, medieval Aristoteleanism) and materialism in a totally incoherent way. To say 'materialism is *almost* true: the world is completely describable in the language of physics *plus* the one little added notion that some events intrinsically *explain* other events' would be ridiculous. This would not be a 'near miss' for materialism, but a total failure. If events *intrinsically* explain other events, if there are saliencies, relevancies, standards of what are 'normal' conditions, and so on, built into the world itself independently of minds, then the world is in many ways *like* a mind, or infused with something very much like reason. And if *that* is true, then materialism *cannot* be true. One can try to revive the project of speculative metaphysics, if one wishes: but one should not pass *this* sort of metaphysics off as (future) *physics*.

COUNTERFACTUALS AND 'SIMILARITY'

Suppose I take a match from a new box of matches (in perfect condition), break it, and throw the pieces in the river. After all this, I remark, 'If I had struck that match (instead of breaking it, etc.) it would have lit'. Most of us would say, 'true', or 'probably true'. But what does the statement actually assert?

A first stab at an explication might go as follows: the statement is true if it follows from physical laws (assume these to be given by a list—otherwise there are further problems about 'laws') that if the match is struck (at an average (for me?) angle, with an average amount of force) against that striking surface, then, it ignites. But this doesn't work: even if we describe the match down to the atomic level, and ditto for the striking surface and the angle and force involved, there are still many other relevant variables unmentioned. (Notice the similarity to the problem of 'cause' as 'total cause': the statement 'A caused B', and the statement 'If X had happened, Y would have happened' have simple truth conditions when *all* the 'background conditions'—and all the 'laws'—are specified; but typically they *aren't* specified, and the speaker can't even conceive of *all* of them.) If no oxygen molecules happen to be near the top of the match, or if the entire match-cum-striking-surface-cum-atmosphere system is in a sufficiently strange quantum mechanical state, etc., then the match *won't* ignite (even if struck with that force, at that angle, etc.)

One is tempted to try: 'It follows from the physical laws that if the match is struck against that surface (at the specified force and angle) and everything is *normal* then the match ignites', but this brings the very strange predicate 'normal' into the story. Besides, maybe conditions *weren't* 'normal' (in the sense of 'average') at the time. (In infinitely many respects, conditions are *always* 'abnormal': a truism from statistical theory). Or one is tempted to say: 'It follows from the laws that if the match is struck against that surface (with the specified force and at the specified angle), and *everything else is as it actually was at the time,* then the match must ignite.' But, as Nelson Goodman (1947) pointed out in a celebrated paper on this logical question, *everything* else *couldn't* be as it was at the time if the match were struck. The gravitational fields, the quantum mechanical state, the places where there were oxygen molecules in the air, and infinitely many other things *couldn't have been* 'as they actually were at the time' if the match had been struck.

The reason I mention this is that David Lewis (in 'Causation', *Journal of Philosophy* LXX, 1973) proposed to analyze 'causes' using precisely this sort of contrary-to-fact conditional. The idea is that 'A caused B' can be analyzed as 'if A *had not* happened, B *would not have* happened'.

Actually, this doesn't seem right. (Even if A caused B, there are situations in which it just isn't true that if A hadn't happened, B wouldn't have happened.) But suppose it were right, or that, if it isn't right, contrary-to-fact conditionals can at any rate be used to explicate the notions that we wanted to use the notion of causality to explicate. How are the truth conditions for contrary-to-fact conditionals *themselves* to be explicated?

One famous materialist, John Mackie (1974), thinks contrary-to-fact conditionals aren't true or false. He regards them as ways of indicating what inferences are allowable in one's knowledge situation, rather than as asserting something true or false in the realist sense, independently of one's knowledge situation. 'If I had struck that match it would have lit' indicates that my *knowledge situation* is such that (if I delete the information about what actually happened to the match) an inference from 'the match was struck' to 'the match ignited' would be *warranted*. The contrary-to-fact conditional signals the presence of what Wilfred Sellars calls a 'material rule of inference'. It has *assertibility* conditions, rather than truth conditions in the sense of absolute truth semantics.

Mackie, who follows Lewis in using counterfactuals to analyze 'causes', concludes that *causation* (in the ordinary sense) is something *epistemic*, and not something in the world at all. But he believes there is another notion of causation, 'mechanical causation', which is in the world. (It has to do with energy flow; as Mackie describes it, it is hard to see either what it is, or that it could be spelled out without using counterfactuals, which would be fatal to Mackie's project of having a non-epistemic notion of causation.)

But Lewis, following Professor Robert Stalnaker, chooses to give *truth conditions* for contrary-to-fact conditionals. He postulates that there actually exist 'other possible worlds' (as in science fiction), and that there is a 'similarity metric' which determines how 'near' or how 'similar' any two possible worlds are (Lewis, 1973). A contrary-to-fact conditional, 'If X had happened, then Y would have happened', is true just in case Y is *actually* true in all the *nearest* 'parallel worlds' to the actual world in which X is actually true.

To me this smacks more of science fiction than of philosophy. But one thing is clear: a theory which requires an ontology of parallel worlds and a built-in 'similarity metric' certainly does not have a *materialist* ontology. More important, it does not have a *coherent* ontology: not only is the actual existence of parallel worlds a dotty idea, but the idea of an *intrinsic* similarity metric, a metric highly sensitive to what we regard as relevant conditions, or normal conditions, one which gives weight to what sorts of features *we* count as similarities and dissimilarities between states of affairs, is one which once again implies that the world is like a mind, or imbued with something very much like reason. And if *this* is true, then it must have a (suitably metaphysical) *explanation*. Objective idealism can hardly be a *little bit* true. ('It's all physics, except that there's this similarity metric' just doesn't make *sense*.)

ESSENCES AND OBJECTS

In this philosophical culture, the denial of intrinsic or 'essential' properties began with examples like the example of the thing whose shape is an 'essential' property under *one* description ('that statue') but not under a different description ('that piece of clay'). One philosopher who thinks a wholly wrong moral was drawn from this example is Saul Kripke.

According to Kripke, the statue and the piece of clay are two objects, not one. The fact that the piece of clay has a model property, namely the property 'being a thing which *could have been* spherical in shape', which the statue lacks (I assume this is not one of those contemporary statues) already proves the two objects cannot be identical, in Kripke's view.

Now, this sounds very strange at first hearing. If I put the statue on the scale, have I put *two objects* on the scale? If the piece of clay weighs 20 pounds and the statue weighs 20 pounds, why doesn't the scale read 40 and not 20 if both objects are on it right now? But what Kripke has in mind is not silly at all.

First of all, it also sounds strange to be told that a human being is not identical with the aggregation of the molecules in his body. Yet on a moment's reflection each of us is aware that he was not *that* aggregate of molecules a day ago. Seven years ago, precious few of those molecules were in my body. If after my death that exact set of molecules is assembled and placed in a chemical flask, it will be the same aggregation of molecules, but it won't be *me*. David Lewis (1976) has suggested that I and the aggregation of molecules are 'identical for a period of time' in somewhat the way that Highway 2 and Highway 16 can be 'identical for a stretch'; as he points out, 'identity for a time' is not strict logical identity. If A and B are identical in the strict sense, every property of A is a property of B; but it is not the case that every property of the aggregation of molecules is a property of *me*.

Just as we can recognize that I am not the same object as the aggregation of molecules in my body without denying that I *consist* of those molecules right now (the difference between the objects lies in the different statements that are true of them, not in their physical distinctness), so, one can agree with Kripke that the statue is not the same object as the piece of clay without denying that the piece of clay is the matter of the statue; once again the difference between the objects lies in the different statements that are true of them, not in their physical distinctness.

But now it begins to look as if objects, properly individuated, *do* have essences, do have *some* properties in a special way. Can Kripke's doctrine be of aid to materialism? (Kripke himself is quite averse to materialism, as is well known.)

A materialist whose ontology includes 'possible worlds' might introduce suitable intensional objects by identifying them with functions taking possible worlds as arguments and space–time regions in those worlds as values. Thus, the statue would be the function defined on each possible world Y in which the statue exists, whose value on Y is the space–time region occupied by the statue in Y. This would, indeed, make the 'statue' and the 'piece of clay' different 'objects' (different logical constructions) even if they occupy the same space–time region in the actual world, since there are other possible worlds in which they do not occupy the same space–time region.

But functions of this kind are standardly used in modern semantics to represent *concepts*. No one doubts that the *concept* 'that statue' is a different *concept* from the *concept* 'that piece of clay'; the question is whether there is some *individual* in the actual world to which one of these concepts *essentially* applies while the other only accidentally applies. The space–time region itself is *not* such an individual; and it is hard to see how a materialist is going to find one in *his* ontology.

Moreover, clever logical constructions are no answer to the philosophical difficulty. Doubtless one can come up with as many 'objects' as one wants given 'possible worlds' plus the resources of modern set theory; (the difficulty, indeed, is that one can come up with *too many*). Consider the metaphysical claim that my thoughts have some sort of intrinsic connection with external objects. If the events that take place in my brain are in a space–time region that has a set-theoretic connection with some abstract entity that involves certain external objects, then that same space–time region will have similar set-theoretic connections with some other abstract entities that involve some other external objects. To be sure, the materialist can say that my 'thoughts' *intrinsically* involve certain external objects by *identifying them* (the thoughts) with one abstract entity and not with another; but if this identification is supposed to be a feature of reality itself, then there must really *be* essences in the world in a sense which pure set theory can't hope to explicate.

The difficulty is that Kripke individuates objects *by their modal properties*, by what they (essentially) *could* and *could not* be. Kripke's ontology *presupposes* essentialism; it can not be used to ground it. And modal properties are not, on the face of it, part of the materialist's furniture of the world.

But, I will be reminded, I have myself spoken of 'essential properties' elsewhere (see Putnam, 1975*a*). I have said that there are possible worlds (possible *states* of the world, that is, not parallel worlds à la Lewis) in which some liquid other than H_2O has the taste of water (we might have different taste buds, for example), fills the lakes and rivers, etc., but no possible world in which *water* isn't H_2O. Once we have discovered what water is in the actual world, we have discovered its *nature*: is this not essentialism?

It *is* a sort of essentialism, but not a sort which can help the materialist. For what I have said is that it has long been our *intention* that a liquid should *count* as 'water' only if it has the same composition as

the paradigm examples of water (or as the majority of them). I claim that this was our intention even before we *knew* the ultimate composition of water. If I am right then, *given those referential intentions*, it was always impossible for a liquid other than H_2O to be water, even if it took empirical investigation to find it out. But the 'essence' of water in *this* sense is the product of our use of the word, the kinds of referential intentions we have: this sort of essence is not 'built into the world' in the way required by an *essentialist theory of reference itself* to get off the ground.

Similarly, Kripke has defended *his* essentialist theories by arguments which turn on speakers' referential intentions and practices; to date he has carefully refrained from trying to provide a metaphysical theory of reference (although he does seem to believe in mind-independent modal properties). I conclude that however one takes Kripke's theories (or mine); whether one takes them metaphysically, as theories of objective 'essences' which are somehow 'out there', or one takes them as theories of our referential practices and intentions, they are of no help to the materialist. On the metaphysical reading they are realist enough, but their realism is not of a materialist sort; on the purely semantical reading they *presuppose* the notion of reference, and cannot be used to support the metaphysical explanation of reference as intrinsic correspondence between thought and thing.

REFERENCE

Some metaphysical materialists might respond to what has been said by agreeing tht 'A causes B' does *not* describe a simple 'relation' between A and B. 'All you're saying is that causal statements *rest on* a distinction between background conditions and differentiating factors, and I agree that this distinction isn't built into the things themselves, but is a reflection of the way we think about the things', such a philosopher might say. But here he has used the words 'think about', i.e., he has appealed to the notion of *reference*.

The contemporary metaphysical materialist thinks about reference in the following way: the brain is a computer. Its computations involve *representations*. Some of these (perhaps all) are 'propositional': they resemble sentences in an internal *lingua mentis*. (They have been called 'sentence-analogs'.) Some of them could be sentences in a public language, as when we engage in interior monolog. A person refers to something when, for example, the person thinks 'the cat is on the mat' (the sentence-analog is 'subvocalized') and the entire organism-cum-environment situation is such that the words 'the cat' in the particular sentence-analog stand in a physical relation R (the relation of *reference*) to some cat and the words 'the mat' stand in the relation R to some mat.

But what is this relation R? And what on earth could make anyone think it is a *physical* relation?

Well, there is *one* way in which *no one*, to my knowledge, would try to define R, and that is by giving a list of all possible reference situations. It is useful, however, to consider why not. Suppose someone proposed to define reference (for some set of languages, including '*lingua mentis*') thus:

X refers to Y if and only if X is a (token) word or word-analog and Y is an object or event and the entire situation (including the organism that produced X and the environment that contains Y) is S_1 or S_2 or S_3 or . . . (infinite—possibly non-denumerably infinite—list of situations, described at the level of physics).

There are (at least) three things wrong with this.

First, besides the fact that the list would have to be infinite, such a list would not tell us what the situations S_1, S_2, . . . had in common. To define a physical property or relation by *listing* the situations in which it is found is not to say what it *is*. In fact, the materialists themselves object to *Tarski's* definition of reference on just this ground: that Tarski defines primitive reference (for a fixed language), by a list of cases, and, as Hartry Field (1972a, p. 363) writes,

Now, it would have been easy for a chemist, late in the last century, to have given a 'valence definition' of the following form:

(3) (E) (n) (E has valence $n \equiv E$ is potassium and n is $+1$, or . . . or E is sulphur and n is -2)

where in the blanks go a list of similar clauses, one for each element. But, though this is an extensionally correct definition of valence, it would not have been an acceptable reduction; and had it turned out that nothing else was possible—had all efforts to explain valence in terms of the structural properties of atoms proved futile—

scientists would have eventually had to decide either (a) to give up valence theory, or else (b) to replace the hypothesis of physicalism by another hypothesis (chemicalism?). It is part of scientific methodology to resist doing (b); and I also think it is part of scientific methodology to resist doing (a) as long as the notion of valence is serving the purposes for which it was designed (i.e., as long as it is proving useful in helping us characterize chemical compounds in terms of their valences). But the methodology is not to resist (a) and (b) by giving lists like (3); the methodology is to look for a real reduction. This is a methodology that has proved extremely fruitful in science, and I think we'd be crazy to give it up in linguistics. And I think we are giving up this fruitful methodology, unless we realize that we need to add theories of primitive reference to T_1 or T_2 if we are to establish the notion of truth as a physicalistically acceptable notion.

Secondly, it would be philosophically naive to think that such a list could answer any *philosophical* question about reference. For example, one could hold Quine's view, that there are definite *true* and *false* sentences in science, but *no* determinate reference relation (the true sentences have infinitely many models, and there is no such thing as *the* model, in Quine's view), and still accept the list. Quine would simply say that the terms used to describe the situations S_1, S_2, . . . etc. refer to different events in different models; thus the list, while correct in *each* admissible model, does not define a *determinate* reference relation (only a determinate reference relation *for each model*). Now Quine's view may be right, wrong, or meaningless; the question of the truth or falsity of metaphysical realism may be meaningful or meaningless (and if meaningful, may have a realist or a non-realist answer), but a list of cases (either this list or the one involved in the Tarskian truth definition referred to by Field), cannot speak to *this* issue. To think that it can is analogous to thinking (as G. E. Moore did) that one can refute Berkeley by holding up one's hand and saying 'This is a material object. Therefore matter exists.' This is, as Myles Burnyeat has put it, 'to philosophize as if Kant had never existed'. For better or worse, philosophy has gone second order.

Thirdly, the list is *too specific*. Reference is as 'abstract' as causation. In possible worlds which contain individual things or properties which are not physical (in the sense of 'physical': not definable in terms of the fundamental magnitudes of the physics of the actual world), we could still *refer*: we could refer to disembodied minds, or to an emergent non-material property of Goodness, or to all sorts of things, in the appropriate worlds. But the relevant situations could not, by hypothesis, be completely described in terms of the fundamental magnitudes of the physics of *our* world. A definition of reference from which it followed that we could not refer to a non-physical magnitude if there were one is just *wrong*.

I know of only one realist who has sketched a way of defining reference which meets these difficulties, and that is David Lewis (1974). Lewis proposes to treat reference as a *functional* property of the organism-cum-environment-situation.

Typical examples of functional properties come from the world of computers. Having a particular program, for example, is a functional (or in computer jargon a 'software' property) as opposed to an ordinary first-order physical property (a 'hardware' property). Functional properties are typically defined in batches; the properties or 'states' in a typical batch (say, the properties that are involved in a given computer program) are characterized by a certain *pattern*. Each property has specified cause and effect relations to the other properties in the pattern and to certain non-functional properties (the 'inputs' and 'outputs' of the programs).

Lewis' suggestion is that *reference* is a member of such a batch of properties: not functional properties of the organism, but functional properties of the organism-environment system. If this could be shown, it would answer the question of what all the various situations in which something refers to something else 'have in common': what they would have in common is something as abstract as a program, a scheme or formal pattern of cause-effect relationships. And if this could be shown, it would characterize reference in a way that makes it sufficiently abstract; the definition would not require any particular set of magnitudes to be the fundamental ones any more than the abstract description of a computer program does. Whether the second difficulty I noted would be met, I shall not attempt to judge.

The crucial point is that functional properties are defined *using the notions of cause and effect*. This is no problem for Lewis; Lewis believes he can define cause and effect using counterfactuals, and, as already mentioned, he gives truth conditions for counterfactuals in terms of a primitive notion of 'similarity of possible worlds'. Since he has a non-physical primitive in his system, he does not have to show that any of the notions he uses is physically definable. But the notion of 'similarity of possible worlds' is not one to which the materialist is entitled; and neither is he entitled to counterfactuals or to the notion of 'functional organization'.

As Charles Fried remarked in his Tanner Lectures, it is easy to *mistake* causality for a physical relation. *Act, smash, move*, etc. are causal verbs and describe events which are clearly physical ('Smashed', for example, conveys two kinds of information: the information that *momentum* was transferred from one thing to another, which is purely physical information, and the information that the *breaking* of the second thing was *caused* by the momentum transfer.) As Fried points out, the causal judgment may be quite complicated in cases when both objects were in motion before the collision. Once one has made the error of taking causality to be a physical relation, it is easy to think that functional properties are simply higher-order physical properties (an error I myself once committed), and then to think that reference (and just about anything else) may be a functional property and hence physical. But once one sees this is an error, there is no vestige of a reason that I know of to think reference is a physical relation.

If the materialist cannot *define* reference, he can, of course, just take it as *primitive*. But reference, like causality, is a flexible, interest-relative notion: what we count as *referring* to something depends on background knowledge and our willingness to be charitable in interpretation. To read a relation so deeply human and so pervasively intentional into the world and to call the resulting metaphysical picture satisfactory (never mind whether or not it is 'materialist') is absurd.

THE FAILURE OF NATURAL METAPHYSICS

As I've already pointed out, there are two traditional ways of attempting to overcome the obvious difficulties with a correspondence theory of truth. One way was to postulate a special mental power, an *intellektuelle Anschauung*, which gives the mind access to 'forms'. If the mind has direct access to the things in themselves, then there is no problem about how it can put them in correspondence with its 'signs'. The other way was to postulate a built-in structure of the world, a set of essences, and to say (what is certainly a dark saying) that this structure itself singles out *one* correspondence between signs and their objects. The two strategies were quite naturally related; if a philosopher believes in essences, he usually wants us to have epistemic access to them, and so he generally postulates an *intellektuelle Anschauung* to give us this access.

If all this is a failure, as Kant saw, where do we go from there? One direction, the only direction I myself see as making sense, might be a species of pragmatism (although the word 'pragmatism' has always been so ill-understood that one despairs of rescuing the term), 'internal' realism: a realism which recognizes a difference between '*p*' and 'I think that *p*', between being *right*, and merely thinking one is right without locating that objectivity in either transcendental correspondence or mere consensus. Nelson Goodman has done a wonderful job of 'selling' this point of view in *Ways of Worldmaking* (a book short enough to be read in an evening, and deep enough to be pondered for many). The other main direction—the one that does not make sense to me—is natural metaphysics, the tendency I have criticized here.

Goodman urges, shockingly, that we give up the notion of '*the* world'. Although he speaks of us as making *many* worlds, he does not mean that there are many worlds in the David Lewis (or science fiction) sense, but that rightness is relative to medium and message. We make many versions; the standards of rightness that determine what is right and what is wrong are corrigible, relative to task and technique, but not *subjective*. The question this tendency raises is whether a narrow path can indeed be found between the swamps of metaphysics and the quicksands of cultural relativism and historicism.

The approach to which I have devoted this paper is an approach which claims that there *is* a 'transcendental' reality in Kant's sense, one absolutely independent of our minds, that the regulative ideal of knowledge is to copy it or put our thoughts in 'corre-

spondence' with it, *but* (and this is what makes it 'natural' metaphysics) we need no *intellektuelle Anschauung* to do this: the 'scientific method' will do the job for us. 'Metaphysics within the bounds of science alone' might be its slogan.

I can sympathize with the urge behind this view (I would not criticize it if I did not feel its attraction). I am not inclined to scoff at the idea of a noumenal ground behind the dualities of experience, even if all attempts to talk about it lead to antinomies. Analytic philosophers have always tried to dismiss the transcendental as nonsense, but it does have an eerie way of reappearing. (For one thing, almost every philosopher makes statements which contradict his own explicit account of what can be justified or known; this even arises in formal logic, when one makes statements about 'all languages' which are barred by the prohibitions on self-reference. For another, almost everyone regards the statement that there is *no* mind-independent reality, that there are *just* the 'versions', or there is just the 'discourse', or whatever, as itself intensely paradoxical.) Because one cannot talk about the transcendent or even deny its existence without paradox, one's attitude to it must, perhaps, be the concern of religion rather than of rational philosophy.

The idea of a coherent theory of the noumena; consistent, systematic, and arrived at by 'the scientific method' seems to me to be chimerical. True, a metaphysician could say 'You have, perhaps, shown that *materialist* metaphysics is incoherent. If so, let us assume some primitive notions of an "intentional" kind, say "thinks about", or "explains", and construct a scientific theory of *these* relations.' But what reason is there to regard this as a reasonable program?

The whole history of science seems to accord badly with such dreams. Science as we know it has been anti-metaphysical from the seventeenth century on; and not just because of 'positivistic interpretations'. Newton was certainly no positivist; but he strongly rejected the idea that his theory of universal gravitation could or should be read as a description of metaphysically ultimate fact. ('*Hypotheses non fingo*' was a rejection of metaphysical 'hypotheses', not of scientific ones.)

And Newton was certainly right. Suppose we lived in a Newtonian world, and suppose we could say with confidence that Newton's theory of gravity and

Maxwell's theory of electromagnetism (referred to a privileged 'ether frame') were perfectly accurate. Even then, these theories admit of a bewildering variety of empirically equivalent formulations; formulations which agree on the equations while disagreeing precisely on their metaphysical interpretation. There are action-at-a-distance versions of *both* electromagnetism and gravity; there are versions of both in which an extended physical agent, the field, mediates the interactions between distant bodies; there are even *space-time* versions of *Newtonian* gravitational theory. Philosophers today argue about which of these would be 'right' in such a case; but I know of not a single first-rate physicist who takes an interest in such speculations.

The physics that has replaced Newton's has the same property. A theorist will say he is doing 'field theory' while his fingers are drawing Feynman diagrams, diagrams in which field interactions are depicted as exchanges of *particles* (calling the particles 'virtual' is, perhaps, a ghost of empiricist metaphysics). Even the statement that 'the electron we measure is not the bare electron of the theory, but the bare electron surrounded by a cloud of virtual *particles*' counts as a statement of *field* theory, if you please! What used to be the metaphysical question of atom or vortex has become a question of the choice of a notation!

Worse still, from the metaphysician's point of view, the most successful and most accurate physical theory of all time, quantum mechanics, has *no* 'realistic interpretation' that is acceptable to physicists. It is understood as a description of the world as *experienced by observers*; it does not even pretend to the kind of 'absoluteness' the metaphysician aims at (which is not to say that, given time and ingenuity, one could not come up with any number of empirical equivalents which *did* pretend to be observer independent; it is just that physicists refuse to take such efforts seriously).

There is, then, nothing in the history of science to suggest that it either aims at or should aim at one single *absolute* version of 'the world'. On the contrary, such an aim, which would require science itself to decide which of the empirically equivalent successful theories in any given context was 'really true', is contrary to the whole spirit of an enterprise whose strategy from the first has been to confine itself to claims with clear *empirical* significance. If metaphysics *is* ever revived as a culturally and humanly significant enterprise, it is far more likely to be along the lines of a Kurt Gödel or, perhaps, Saul Kripke—i.e., along the lines of those who *do* think, in spite of the history I cited, that we *do* have an *intellektuelle Anschauung*—than along the lines of natural metaphysics. But a successful revival along either line seems to be overwhelmingly unlikely.

STUDY QUESTIONS: PUTNAM, *WHY THERE ISN'T A READY-MADE WORLD*

1. What is metaphysical realism?
2. What is the difference between Russell and Moore's version of metaphysical realism and the version that is more popular today?
3. What is essence? How do some philosophers argue against essences?
4. According to Putnam, what is a major problem for a metaphysical realist position?
5. What does Putnam say about the modern mix of materialism and essentialism?
6. What are the two conclusions that Kant drew that few philosophers are willing to challenge today? Why does Putnam point these out?
7. What is the bold corollary that Kant drew that is challenged today?
8. Why does Putnam mention the idea that truth is assertibility under optimal conditions? What does that mean?
9. Materialism and scientism reflect a metaphysical impulse in two ways. What are they?
10. How does Putnam use his analysis of causation to argue against metaphysical realism?
11. What is the problem with the idea that one event can intrinsically explain another?
12. How does Putnam use the example of lighting a campfire?
13. How does Lewis analyze 'A causes B'? What is Putnam's objection to this analysis?

14. Why does Kripke assert that the statue and the piece of clay are two objects? What is the problem that Putnam sees with Kripke's suggestion?
15. At what point does Putnam turn the discussion to the nature of reference?
16. What are Putnam's objections to a physicalist theory of reference?
17. What is Lewis' view of reference?
18. What is the final conclusion that Putnam wishes to draw about reference? How does that relate to the theme of metaphysical realism?

Philosophical Bridges: Putnam's Influence

Despite the fact that later he repudiates the view, Putnam's early machine functionalism, the claim that mental states are computational, has had an important influence on the philosophy of mind. His were some of the first papers to defend a form of strong artificial intelligence, a view that has since gained some popularity.

In the philosophy of language, the causal theory of reference, first advocated by Saul Kripke, has also been seen as an important challenge to the more standard Fregean view of reference, which claims that the reference of a singular term is determined by its sense. Putnam's externalism, which we also mentioned in the Philosophical Overview, has also generated much controversy in the philosophy of mind.

Putnam's mild form of realism is an appealing view for many philosophers interested in this field. This is because it is a position that apparently escapes the problems of metaphysical realism, but at the same time, it avoids the problems of stronger forms of idealism. On the one hand, Putnam is a realist in the sense that he agrees that statements can be true or false independently of what we think about their truth. On the other hand, he is not a metaphysical realist because he denies that the world consists of absolutely mind-independent objects. John McDowell (*Mind and World*, 1994) advocates a similar kind of view.

BIBLIOGRAPHY

QUINE
Primary
From a Logical Point of View, Harvard University Press, 1953
Ontological Relativity, Columbia University Press, 1969
The Roots of Reference, Open Court, 1967
Ways of Paradox and Other Essays, Harvard University Press, 1976
Word and Object, MIT Press, 1960

Secondary
Barrett, R., and Gibson, R., *Perspectives on Quine*, Basil Blackwell, 1990
Gibson, Roger, *The Philosophy of W. V. O. Quine: An Expository Essay*, University Presses of Florida, 1982

Hookway, Christopher, *Language Experience and Reality*, Stanford University Press, 1988
Orenstein, Alex, *Willard Van Orman Quine*, Twayne, 1977

DAVIDSON
Primary
Essays on Actions and Events, Oxford University Press, 1980
Inquiries into Truth and Interpretation, Oxford University Press, 1984
Subjective, Intersubjective, Objective, Clarendon Press, 2001

Secondary

Evnine, Simone, *Donald Davidson*, Stanford University Press, 1991

Farrell, Frank, *Subjectivity, Realism and Post Modernism: The Recovery of the World*, Cambridge University Press, 1994

Malpas, J. E., *Donald Davidson and the Mirror of Meaning: Holism, Truth and Interpretation*, Cambridge University Press, 1992

Ramberg, Bjorn, *Donald Davidson's Philosophy of Language*, Basil Blackwell, 1989

KUHN
Primary

The Copernican Revolution, Harvard University Press, 1957

The Essential Tension, University of Chicago Press, 1977

The Structure of Scientific Revolutions, University of Chicago Press, 1962

Secondary

Gutting, G., ed., *Paradigms and Revolutions: Applications and Appraisals of Thomas Kuhn's Philosophy of Science*, University of Notre Dame Press, 1980

Horwich, P., ed., *World Changes: Thomas Kuhn and the Nature of Science*, MIT Press, 1993

Hoyningen-Huene, P., *Reconstructing Scientific Revolutions: Thomas Kuhn's Philosophy of Science*, trans. A. T. Levine, University of Chicago Press, 1993

GOODMAN
Primary

Fact Fiction and Forecast, Harvard University Press, 1954

The Structure of Appearances, Harvard University Press, 1951

Ways of World Making, Hackett, 1978

Secondary

Elgin, Catherine Z., *Philosophy of Nelson Goodman*, Garland Publishing, 1997

Gosselin, Mia, *Nominalism and Contemporary Nominalism: Ontological and Epistemological Implications of the Work of W. V. O. Quine and of N. Goodman*, Kluwer Academic, 1990

Hausman, Alan, and Wilson, Fred, *Carnap and Goodman: Two Formalists*, Nijhoff, 1967

Stalker, D. F., ed., *Grue? The New Riddle of Induction*, Open Court, 1994

RAWLS
Primary

Political Liberalism, Columbia University Press, 1993

A Theory of Justice, Harvard University Press, 1971

Secondary

Daniels, Norman, *Reading Rawls*, Oxford, 1975

Nozick, Robert, *Anarchy, State, and Utopia*, Oxford, 1978

Pogge, William, *Realizing Rawls*, Cornell University Press, 1989

Sandel, Michael, *Liberalism and the Limits of Justice*, Oxford, 1973

Kymlicka, Will, *Liberalism, Community & Culture*, Oxford, 1989

PUTNAM
Primary

Mathematics, Matter and Method, Cambridge University Press, 1979

Mind, Language and Reality, Cambridge University Press, 1975

Realism with a Human Face, Harvard University Press, 1990

Reason and Realism, Cambridge University Press, 1983

Secondary

Ben-Menahem, Yemina, *Hilary Putnam (Contemporary Philosophy in Focus)*, Cambridge University Press, 2005

Conant, James, and Zeglen, Urszula, *Hilary Putnam: Pragmatism and Realism*, Routledge, 2001

Norris, Christopher, *Hilary Putnam: Realism, Reason and the Uses of Uncertainty*, Manchester University Press, 2002

SECTION VI

◆ PHENOMENOLOGY AND EXISTENTIALISM ◆

 ## PROLOGUE

Twentieth-century continental philosophy begins with Husserl, who was the founder of phenomenology. Husserl's thought influenced Heidegger, who can be regarded as the originator of existentialism. Both phenomenology and existentialism are in different ways broadly both Kantian and Hegelian in spirit. However, as we shall see in section VII, continental philosophy in general has been influenced deeply by three nineteenth-century giants, Hegel, Marx, and Nietzsche. Hegel is influential primarily for his claim that all understanding must be historically situated. Marx is prominent for his analysis of power relations and for his critique of capitalism. Nietzsche is important for his critique of the Enlightenment conceptions of reason and truth, as well as for his rebellious spirit.

The term 'phenomenology' comes from the Greek word *phainomenon*, meaning appearance. Phenomenology is the study of experience as experience. The phenomenological method consists in a careful description of the essential natures of specific psychological phenomena. Husserl argued that experience has a certain structure, which permits it to have content, and, in so doing, he developed the phenomenological method as an alternative to the natural sciences. Toward the end of his life, Husserl applied the phenomenological method to the sciences themselves.

Phenomenology has had an important impact on continental philosophy. This is first because it constitutes a radical departure from the Cartesian and Empiricist view of experience as consisting of a collection of passively received ideas. Secondly, phenomenology is fundamentally opposed to the use of the methods of the natural sciences in the study of our experiential life. We should not impose scientific concepts on our experiential world. Thirdly, Husserl claims that consciousness has an inherent a priori structure. He employs a rich Kantian-like notion of the a priori and, thereby, rejects the Empiricist tradition that claims that all judgments are either analytic tautologies or else empirical and based on observation. In these three ways, phenomenology opposes logical positivism, which was a dominant trend in analytic philosophy up until the 1950s.

In his later work, *The Crisis of European Science and Transcendental Phenomenology* (1936), Husserl develops the idea of a historical life-world (Lebenswelt). The crisis arises because the modern natural sciences were founded on a quantitative view of nature that conceals the priority of perception and that results in a loss of meaning. Naturalism forgets the intentionality of consciousness. The aim of philosophy should be to restore the meaningfulness of the lived and historical life-world.

Heidegger

One of the more immediate impacts of phenomenology was its influence on Heidegger and existentialism. To answer the question 'What is Being?' Heidegger, in *Being and Time* (1927), developed the idea of fundamental ontology, which involves uncovering the mode of being that persons exhibit, called 'Dasein.' This mode of being consists in certain a priori existentials, among which the primary one is care. Care reveals itself both in Dasein's inauthentic and authentic modes of being. Inauthenticity is marked by Dasein's taking flight from its own being, or from the possibility to be itself and, in particular, from its own death. The structure of care also reveals the temporality of Dasein. It defines the very nature of past, present, and future.

Heidegger's project of fundamental ontology contradicts much traditional metaphysics, which attempts to define the nature of existence independently of human concerns. For Heidegger, the world must be characterized in terms of the existentials that comprise Dasein's being. Reality does not consist of the neutral objects as depicted by the sciences, which are only an abstraction from the character of everyday life.

After 1936, the emphasis of Heidegger's thought changed. Rather than trying to characterize Being through an existential analysis of Dasein's modes of being, he tries to depict Being itself directly. In various essays, he criticizes the representational, subject-object concept of knowledge and the calculating nature of Enlightenment rationality, which have characterized western philosophy since the time of Plato. He also condemns Nietzsche's notion of the will to power as part of this tradition. Drawing inspiration from the pre-Socratics, Heidegger contrasts the tradition of western metaphysics with poetic thinking and truth as 'letting be.'

Heidegger refused to be called an existentialist. In part, this was to distinguish his own work from that of the French existentialist Jean-Paul Sartre, which he inspired. In his *Letter on Humanism* (1947), Heidegger criticizes humanism and human-centered subjectivism on the basis that the idea of the subject, and its correlate the object, belong specifically to the modern period of philosophy. He tries to overcome this idea by showing how the history of philosophy is a manifestation and concealment of Being itself, rather than a result of the thought of particular philosophers about Being. The idea of the subject and humanism are part of the post-Platonic metaphysical tradition that conceals Being.

French Existentialism and Phenomenology

Heidegger's comments were directed in part toward Sartre's essay *Existentialism Is a Humanism* (1945) and his work *Being and Nothingness* (1943), which is the classic text of French existentialism. Sartre's companion, Simone de Beauvoir, was also a famous existentialist philosopher, and both were friends with the French phenomenologist Merleau-Ponty. After World War II, Sartre and Merleau-Ponty became Marxists and collaborated on a Marxist journal. In 1960, Sartre published his famous Marxist work, the *Critique of Dialectical Reason*.

Being and Nothingness has both ontological and ethical objectives. In terms of ontology, Sartre aims to respect the difference between consciousness and nonmental objects as modes of being, while rejecting a mind-matter substance dualism by distinguishing being-in-itself (consciousness) and being-for-itself, the nonconscious. He also distinguishes this duality from being-for-others. In terms of his existentialist ethics, Sartre describes the human condition in terms of freedom and the attempt to deny that freedom, or inauthentic bad faith. Existentialism is so called because it claims that any attempt to define human essence implies a denial of human freedom and, as such, exemplifies bad faith. For this reason, Sartre asserts that human existence precedes essence. Toward the end of *Being and Nothingness*, Sartre promised a full-scale ethical theory based on authenticity and freedom from bad faith. He composed *Notebooks for an Ethics*, which was published posthumously. At the time of his death, Sartre was working on an ethic based on we-consciousness, which remains incomplete and unpublished.

Simone de Beauvoir was concerned primarily with the social and ethical implications of existentialism, and especially with the oppression of women. Her book *The Ethics of Ambiguity* was published in 1947, and *The Second Sex* appeared in 1949. The latter is the pioneering work of twentieth-century feminism, which is largely responsible for placing questions related to sexual differences and feminism on the philosophical agenda. Her work was published only five years after French women were given the vote.

In his early life, Sartre's and de Beauvoir's friend Merleau-Ponty was interested primarily in psychology and perception. He studied the unpublished works of Husserl, which inspired his major book, the *Phenomenology of Perception* (1945), which is mostly famous for its phenomenology of the body. In brief, Merleau-Ponty extends and develops the phenomenological tradition initiated by Husserl. After the Second World War, Merleau-Ponty worked with Sartre and de Beauvoir on the left-wing journal, *Les Temps Modernes*. However, around 1952, Merleau-Ponty disagreed with Sartre concerning the role of the communist party and the Soviet Union, and there developed a split between the two, which began to heal shortly before the death of Merleau-Ponty in 1961.

EDMUND HUSSERL (1859–1938)

Biographical History

Edmund Husserl was born in Moravia, which today is in the Czech Republic. He began his academic life in mathematics at the Universities of Leipzig, Berlin, and Vienna, and he received his Ph.D. in Vienna in 1883. In 1884, he attended the lectures of the Austrian philosopher Franz Brentano (1838–1917). Profoundly impressed, Husserl decided to leave mathematics for philosophy. Later, he taught philosophy at Halle, Göttingen, and Freiburg, where he remained until his retirement in 1928. Toward the end of his life, the Nazis banned him from academic activities because of his Jewish roots.

Husserl's early writings were concerned with the nature of mathematics. His first book, *Philosophy of Arithmetic*, was published in 1891. His interests shifted, partly because of Frege's criticisms of his work, and Husserl developed the idea of phenomenology. His work *Ideas: General Introduction to Pure Phenomenology* was published in 1913. After his retirement, he wrote prolifically, but most of these works were published only after his death.

Philosophical Overview

Like Brentano, Husserl claimed that intentionality is the main defining feature of mental phenomena. Intentionality is 'the mark of the mental' that separates the study of the psychological from that of the physical sciences. As defined by Husserl, intentionality is the property of mental states such that they are about, or directed to, something in the world. For example, whenever we think, we must think about something, either some fact or an object. The same point applies to many mental states, such as wanting, believing, and perceiving; they are about something.

Such mental states have some puzzling characteristics. Contrast the following two features of perception. First, as Husserl's definition of intentionality indicates, intentional perceptual states are about objects in the world. We directly perceive objects in the world. For instance, we directly see trees, buildings, and other people, things that exist independently of our perception of them. Husserl rejects the Empiricist claim that we can only directly perceive our own ideas or private mental objects, and thereby he opposes the assertion that external objects exist behind a veil of perception, a thesis that implies Skepticism. The second feature of perception is that we can be subject to perceptual hallucinations. Additionally, we can think about flying horses and other things that do not exist. Yet, in such cases one must be seeing or thinking about something. Consequently, it seems that we may need the concept of nonexistent intentional objects to understand perception and thought. In other words, these points seem to imply that we do indeed perceive private mental objects after all, and that Husserl was mistaken to deny this.

How does Husserl avoid this problem? He tries to do so in three steps. First, he distinguishes the content of a perception from its object. In other words, intentional mental states have a meaning or a sense or content that, in his later writings, Husserl calls the 'noesis.' This should be distinguished from the object of a mental state, the actual entity in the world that the state is about or directed to, which Husserl calls the 'neoma.' Second, the meaning or content of a mental state permits it to be directed to something in the world. Moreover, the content determines what particular object the mental state is directed toward. Third, the content of a mental state is nothing over and above the way in which the real object is picked out; it is the way the object is presented. Consequently, this content is not an additional mental object. It would be a mistake to confuse the content of a mental state with its object, or noema.

IDEAS: GENERAL INTRODUCTION TO PURE PHENOMENOLOGY

In the selected sections of this book, Husserl describes pure phenomenology. The Introduction explains the structure and aims of the work. The basis of pure phenomenology is that the directedness of an intentional mental state depends on its content. Husserl explains that this assertion permits the idea that we can study mental acts without any ontological presuppositions concerning what exists. He calls this 'the bracketing of the natural standpoint.' This bracketing is the basis of Husserl's phenomenological method, which consists in directing the attention exclusively to the content of experience, rather than to the external object or to some matters of fact concerning experience. Phenomenology is the study of experience *as such*. Husserl's method, which he calls phenomenological or eidetic reduction, consists in bracketing experience, which means describing it in purely experiential terms without the natural or scientific presuppositions that usually surround experience.

Husserl explains that this method of studying consciousness is fundamentally different from the formal procedures of mathematics and the empirical methods of the natural sciences. The natural sciences take the philosophical question 'What makes experience and cognition possible?' for granted. They presuppose the phenomenological characterization of experience, and, therefore, they cannot undermine it, for instance, by explaining it in causal terms. Furthermore, the scientific method is inappropriate for understanding intentionality, which is the hallmark of the mental.

Through the application of his method, Husserl reveals a view of experience that is opposed fundamentally to the Cartesian and Empiricist traditions. Descartes, Locke, and Hume tend to treat experience as if it consisted in a collection of simple, atomic ideas that are passively received and immediately transparent to consciousness. In contrast, Husserl claims that experience has a complex, a priori internal structure, which makes the intentionality and self-reflection possible. This shows that experience is not a passively received set of simple atoms; it has a structure. At any moment, there are aspects of an experience that can go unnoticed. However, we can become aware of any single aspect of experience through active reflection, and, in this way, experience is not passive.

The bracketing of the natural standpoint requires us to rethink the distinction between experience and its object. We should not conceive of the object as something distinct in character from the possible perceptions of it. The noema is the object as presented to consciousness. The object should not be thought of as some entity that is beyond possible experience, which is a nonsensical idea. If cognition is given, then so is its object. However, this does not mean that the object is something essentially private. On the contrary, according to Husserl, objects are intersubjectively experienced; different persons can perceive the same object or noema.

In the phenomenal reduction, when we bracket our natural attitude toward objects, we exclude the incoherent idea of something transcendent that lies beyond the realm of possible cognition. For this reason, phenomenology requires a new conception of the distinction between the immanent and transcendental. Because there are no objects beyond possible experience, 'the transcendental' cannot signify such a realm. It indicates only the reflective stance that phenomenological analysis requires, as opposed to the natural attitude of empirical scientific enquiry.

INTRODUCTION

Pure Phenomenology, to which we are here seek-
41 ing the way, whose unique position in regard to all other sciences we wish to make clear, and to set forth as the most fundamental region of philosophy, is an essentially new science, which in virtue of its own governing peculiarity lies far removed from our ordinary thinking, and has not until our own day therefore shown an impulse to develop. It calls itself a science of "phenomena". Other sciences, long known to us, also treat of phenomena. Thus one hears psychology referred to as a science of psychical, and natural science as a science of physical "appearances" or phenomena.

Psychology is a science of experience. Keep-
43 ing to the customary sense of the word experi-
44 ence (*Erfahrung*), this has a twofold meaning:

1. Psychology is a science of *facts* (*Tat-sachen*), of "matters of fact"—in Hume's sense of the word.

2. Psychology is a science of *realities* (*Real-itäten*). The "phenomena" which it handles as psychological "phenomenology" are real events which as such, in so far as they have real exis-tence (*Dasein*), take their place with the real Subjects to which they belong in the one spatio-temporal world, the *omnitudo realitatis*.

As over against this psychological "phenom-enology", *pure or transcendental phenomenology will be established not as a science of facts, but as a science of essential Being* (as "*eidetic*" Science); a science which aims exclusively at establishing "knowledge of essences" (*Wesenserkenntnise*) and *absolutely no "facts"*. The corresponding Reduction which leads from the psychological phenomenon to the pure "essence", or, in respect of the judg-ing thought, from factual ("empirical") to "essen-tial" universality, is the *eidetic Reduction*.

In the second place, the phenomena of transcen-dental phenomenology will be characterized as non-real (irreal). Other reductions, the specifically transcendental, "purify" the psychological phe-nomena from that which lends them reality, and therewith a setting in the real "world". Our phe-nomenology should be a theory of essential Being, dealing not with real, but with transcendentally reduced phenomena.

What this all affirms when more closely considered will first become plain in the devel-opment that follow. In an anticipatory way it gives an outline sketch of the preliminary series of studies. I consider it necessary at this point to add only one remark: It will surprise the reader that in the two foregoing passages in italics, in place of the single division of sciences into real-istic and idealistic (or into empirical and *a priori*) which is universally adopted, two divi-sions are preferred, corresponding to the two pairs of opposites: Fact and Essence, Real and not-Real. The distinction conveyed by this two-fold opposition replacing that between real and ideal will find a thoroughgoing justification in the later course of our inquiries (as a matter of fact, in the Second Book). It will be shown that
45 the concept of reality requires a fundamental limitation in virtue of which a difference must be set up between real Being and individual (purely temporal) Being. The transition to the pure Essence provides on the one side a knowl-edge of the essential nature of the Real, on the other, in respect of the domain left over, knowl-edge of the essential nature of the non-real (*irreal*). It will transpire further that all transcen-dentally purified "experiences" are non-realities, and excluded from every connexion within the "real world". These same non-realities are studied by phenomenology, but not as singular particularities (*Einzelheiten*), rather in their "es-sential being". The extent, however, to which transcendental phenomena as singular *facta* are at all available for study, and the question of the relation which a factual study of such a kind may bear to the ideal of a Mataphysic, can be considered only in the concluding series of investigations.

In the *first* Book we shall treat not only of the general theory of the phenomenological Re-ductions which make the transcendentally puri-fied consciousness with its essential correlates perceptible (*sichtlich*) and accessible; we shall also seek to win definite ideas of the most general structures of this pure consciousness, and through their agency of the most general groups of prob-lems, directions of study and methods which per-tain to the new science.

In the *second* Book we make a thorough inquiry into certain specially important sets of problems the systematic formulation of which and solution under types is the precondition for bringing into real clearness the difficult rela-tions of phenomenology to the physical sciences of nature, to psychology, and to the sciences of the mind, and on another side also to the *a pri-ori* sciences as a collective whole. The phenom-enological sketches here traced in outline offer also the welcome means of considerably deep-ening the understanding of phenomenology reached in the *first* Book, and of winning from its immense circle of problems a far richer content of knowledge.

A *third* and concluding Book is dedicated to the Idea of Philosophy. The insight will be awakened that genuine philosophy, the idea of which 46 is to realize the idea of Absolute Knowledge, has its roots in pure phenomenology, and this in so earnest a sense that the systematically rigorous grounding and development of this first of all philosophies remains the perpetual precondition of all metaphysics and other philosophy "which would aspire to be a *science*".

Since phenomenology is here to be established as a science of Essential Being—as an *a priori*, or, as we also say, eidetic science—it will be useful to preface the labours devoted to phenomenology itself with a series of fundamental discussions upon Essence (*Wesen*) and the Science of Essential Being, and with a defence as against naturalism of the original and intrinsic authority of this Knowledge of Essence. . . .

FIRST SECTION

THE NATURE AND KNOWLEDGE OF ESSENTIAL BEING

Second Chapter

Naturalistic Misconstructions

. . . There is indeed an unavoidable and impor-
96 tant division to be drawn in the field of scientific inquiry. On the one side stand the *sciences of the dogmatic standpoint,* facing the facts and unconcerned about all problems of an epistemological or sceptical kind. They take their start from the primordial givenness of the facts they deal with (and in the testing of their ideas return always to these facts), and they ask what the nature of the immediately given facts may be, and what can be mediately inferred from the natural ground concerning these same facts and those of the domain as a whole. On the other side we have the rigorous inquiries of the epistemological, the *specifically philosophical standpoint.* They are concerned with the sceptical problems relating to the possibility of knowledge. Their object is finally

to solve the problem in principle and with the appropriate generality, and then, when applying the solutions thus obtained, to study their bearing on the critical task of determining the eventual meaning and value for knowledge of the results of the dogmatic sciences. *Having regard to the present situation,* and so long as a highly developed critique of knowledge that has attained to complete rigour and clearness is lacking, it is at any rate *right to fence off the field of dogmatic research from all "critical" forms of inquiry.* In other words, it seems right to us at present to see to it that epistemological (which as a rule are sceptical) prejudices upon whose validity as right or wrong philosophical science has to decide, but which do not necessarily concern the dogmatic worker, shall not obstruct the course of his inquiries. But it is precisely the way with scepticisms that they favour such unseasonable obstructions.

Herewith indeed we find indicated the special situation, to develop which the theory of knowledge is needed as a science having a direction of inquiry peculiar to itself. However self-contained the knowledge may be that is di-
97 rected towards pure fact and rests on insight, none the less, as the knowledge is bent reflectively back upon itself, the possibility of any type of knowledge being valid, including its intuitions and insights, appears beset with baffling obscurities, and with difficulties that are almost insoluble, more particularly with reference to the transcendence which the *objects* of knowledge claim to possess in relation to knowledge itself. On this very ground *scepticisms* arise which force their way in the face of all intuition, experience, and insight, and in the sequel might develop into factors *that obstruct the working of the practical sciences.* We get rid of these difficulties that concern the form of "*dogmatic*" natural *science* (a term, therefore, which should not express here any depreciation whatsover); *just through clearly grasping the most general principle of all method, that of the original right of all data,* and holding it vividly in mind, whilst we ignore the rich and varied problems relating to the possibility of the different kinds of knowledge and their respective correlatives.

SECOND SECTION

THE FUNDAMENTAL PHENOMENOLOGICAL OUTLOOK

First Chapter

The Thesis of the Natural Standpoint and Its Suspension

⁹⁹

§ 27. The World of the Natural Standpoint: I and My World About Me

Our first outlook upon life is that of natural human beings, imaging, judging, feeling, willing, *"from the natural standpoint".* Let us make clear to ourselves what this means in the form of simple mediations which we can best carry on in the first person.

I am aware of a world, spread out in space endlessly, and in time becoming and become, without end. I am aware of it, that means, first of all, I discover it immediately, intuitively, I experience it. . . .

As it is with the world in its ordered being as a spatial present—the aspect I have so far been considering—so likewise is it with the world in respect to its *ordered being in the succession of time.* . . . Moving freely within the moment of experience which brings what is present into my intuitional grasp, I can follow up these connexions of the reality which immediately surrounds me. I can shift my standpoint in space and time, look this way and that, turn temporally forwards and backwards; I can provide for myself constantly new and more or less clear and meaningful perceptions and representations, and images also more or less clear, in which I make intuitable to myself whatever can possibly exist really or supposedly

¹⁰³ in the steadfast order of space and time.

In this way, when consciously awake, I find myself at all times, and without my ever being able to change this, set in relation to a world which, through its constant changes remains one and ever the same. It is continually "present" for me, and I myself am a member of it. Therefore this world is not there for me as a mere *world of facts and affairs,* but, with the same immediacy, as a *world of values,* a *world of goods,* a *practical world.* Without further effort on my part I find

the things before me furnished not only with the qualities that befit their positive nature, but with value-characters such as beautiful or ugly, agreeable or disagreeable, pleasant or unpleasant, and so forth. . . .

§ 28. The "Cogito". My Natural World-about-me and the Ideal Worlds-about-me

It is then to this world, *the world in which I find myself and which is also my world-about-me,* that the complex forms of my manifold and shifting *spontaneities* of consciousness stand related: observing in the interests of research the bringing of meaning into conceptual form through description; comparing and distinguishing, collecting and counting, presupposing and inferring, the theorizing activity of consciousness, in short, in its different forms and stages.

All these, together with the sheer acts of
¹⁰⁴ the Ego, in which I become acquainted with the world as *immediately* given me, through spontaneous tendencies to turn towards it and to grasp it, are included under the one Cartesian expression: *Cogito.* In the natural urge of life I live continually in *this fundamental form of all "wakeful" living,* whether in addition I do or do not assert the *cogito,* and whether I am or am not "reflectively" concerned with the Ego and the *cogitare.* . . .

¹⁰⁵*§ 29. The "Other" Ego-subject and the Intersubjective Natural World-about-me*

Whatever holds good for me personally, also holds good, as I know, for all other men whom I find present in my world-about-me. Experiencing them as men, I understand and take them as Ego-subjects, units like myself, and related to their natural surroundings. But this in such wise that I apprehend the world-about-them and the world-about-me objectively as one and the same world, which differs in each case only through affecting consciousness differently. Each has his place whence he sees the things that are present, and each enjoys accordingly different appearances of the things. For each, again, the fields of perception and memory actually present are different, quite apart from the fact that even that which is here intersubjectively known in common is known in different ways, is differently apprehended, shows different grades of clearness, and so forth. Despite all this, we come to understandings with our neighbours, and set up in common an objective spatio-temporal fact-world as *the world about us that is there for us all, and to which we ourselves none the less belong.*

§ 30. *The General Thesis of the Natural Standpoint*

That which we have submitted towards the characterization of what is given to us from the natural standpoint, and thereby of the natural standpoint itself, was a piece of pure description *prior to all "theory".* In these studies we stand bodily aloof from all theories, and by 'theories' we here mean anticipatory ideas of every kind. . . .

107 ### § 31. *Radical Alteration of the Natural Thesis "Disconnexion", "Bracketing"*

Instead now of remaining at this standpoint, we propose to alter it radically. Our aim must be to convince ourselves of the possibility of this alteration on grounds of principle.

The General Thesis according to which the real world about me is at all times known not merely in a general way as something apprehended, but as a fact-world *that has its being out there,* does *not* consist of course *in an act proper,* in an articulated judgment *about* existence. It is and remains something all the time the standpoint is adopted, that is, it endures persistently during the whole course of our life of natural endeavour. . . .

The attempt to doubt everything has its place in the realm of our *perfect freedom.* We can 108 *attempt to doubt* anything and everything, however convinced we may be concerning what we doubt, even though the evidence which seals our assurance is completely adequate. . . .

It is likewise clear that the *attempt* to doubt any object of awareness in respect of its *being actually there necessarily conditions a certain suspension (Aufhebung) of the thesis;* and it is precisely this that interests us. It is not a transformation of the thesis into its antithesis, of positive into negative; it is also not a transformation into presumption, suggestion, indecision, doubt (in one or another sense of the

word); such shifting indeed is not at our free pleasure. *Rather is it something quite unique. We do not abandon the thesis we have adopted, we make no change in our conviction,* which remains in itself what it is so long as we do not introduce new motives of judgment, which we precisely refrain from doing. And yet the thesis undergoes a modification—whilst remaining in itself what it is, *we set it as it were "out of action", we "disconnect it", "bracket it".* It still remains there like the bracketed in the bracket, like the disconnected outside the connexional system. We can also say: The thesis is experience as lived *(Erlebnis), but we make "no use" of it,* and by that, of course, we do not indicate privation (as when we say of the ignorant that he makes no use of a certain thesis); in this case rather, as with all parallel expressions, we are 109 dealing with indicators that point to a definite but *unique form of consciousness,* which clamps on to the original simple thesis (whether it actually or even predicatively *posits* existence or not), and transvalues it in a quite peculiar way. *This transvaluing is a concern of our full freedom, and is opposed to all cognitive attitudes* that would set themselves up as co-ordinate with *the thesis,* and yet within the unity of "simultaneity" remain incompatible with it, as indeed it is in general with all attitudes whatsoever in the strict sense of the word. . . . In relation to *every* thesis and wholly uncoerced we can use this *peculiar, ἐποχή, a certain refraining from judgment which is compatible with the unshaken and unshakable because self-evidencing conviction of Truth.* The thesis is "put out of action", bracketed, it passes off into the modified status of a "bracketed thesis", and the judgment *simpliciter* into "bracketed judgment." . . .

§ 32 *The Phenomenological*

110 But our design is just to discover a new scientific domain, such as might be won precisely *through the method of bracketing,* though only through a definitely limited form of it.

The limiting consideration can be indicated in a word.

We put out of action the general thesis which belongs to the essence of the natural standpoint, we place in brackets whatever it includes respecting the nature of Being: *this entire natural world there-fore* which is continually "there for us", "present to our hand", and will ever remain there, is a "fact-world" of which we continue to be conscious, even though it pleases us to put it in brackets.

If I do this, as I am fully free to do, I do *not* then *deny* this "world", as though I were a soph-ist, *I do not doubt that it is there* as though I were a sceptic; but I use the "phenomenological" ἐποχή, which *completely bars* me *from using any judgment* 111 *that concerns spatio-temporal existence (Dasein).*

Thus *all sciences which relate to this natural world,* though they stand never so firm to me, though they fill me with wondering admiration, though I am far from any thought of objecting to them in the least degree, *I disconnect them all, I make absolutely no use of their standards, I do not appropriate a single one of the propositions that enter into their systems, even though their evidential value is perfect, I take none of them, no one of them serves me for a foundation*—so long, that is, as it is under-stood, in the way these sciences themselves understand it, as a truth *concerning the realities* of this world. *I may accept it only after I have placed it in the bracket.* That means: only in the modified consciousness of the judgment as it appears in dis-connexion, and *not as it figures within the science as its proposition, a proposition which claims to be valid and whose validity I recognize and make use of.* . . .

112 Consciousness and Natural Reality

§ 33. Intimation Concerning "Pure" or "Transcendental Consciousness" as Phenomenological Residuum

We have learnt to understand the meaning of the phenomenological ἐποχή, but we are still quite in the dark as to its serviceability. . . .

For what can remain over when the whole world is bracketed, including ourselves and all our thinking (cogitare)?

Since the reader already knows that the interest which governs these 'Mediations' con-cerns a new eidetic science, he will indeed at first expect the world as fact to succumb to the disconnexion. . . .

However, we do not take this path, nor does our goal lie in its direction. That goal we could also refer to as *the winning of a new region of Being,*

the distinctive character of which has not yet been defined, a region of *individual* Being, like every genuine region. We must leave the sequel to teach us what that more precisely means.

We proceed in the first instance by showing up simply and directly what we see; and since the Being to be thus shown up is neither more nor less than that which we refer to on essential grounds as "pure experiences (*Erlebnisse*)", "pure consciousness" with its pure "correlates of con-sciousness", and on the other side its "pure Ego", we observe that it is from *the Ego, the* conscious-ness, *the* experience as given to us from natural standpoint, that we take our start.

I, the real human being, am a real object like others in the natural world. I carry out *cogitat-iones,* "acts of consciousness" in both a narrower and a wider sense, and these acts, as belonging to this human subject, are events of the same natu-ral world. . . .

113 Now in its *widest connotation* the expression *"consciousness"* (then indeed less suited for its purpose) includes *all* experiences (*Erlebnisse*), and entrenched in the natural standpoint as we are even in our scientific thinking, grounded there in habits that are most firmly established since they have never misled us, we take all these data of psychological reflexion as real world-events, as the experiences (*Erlebnisse*) of animal beings. So natural is it to us to see them only in this light that, though acquainted already with the possibility of a change of standpoint, and on the search for the new domain of objects, we fail to notice that it is from out these centres of expe-rience (*Erlebnisse*) themselves that through the adoption of the new standpoint the new domain emerges. Connected with this is the fact that instead of keeping our eyes turned towards these centres of experience, we turned them away and sought the new objects in the ontological realms of arithmetic, geometry, and the like, whereby indeed nothing truly new was to be won.

Thus we fix our eyes steadily upon the sphere of Consciousness and study what it is that we find immanent in *it*. At first, without having yet carried out the phenomenological suspen-sions of the element of judgment, we subject this sphere of Consciousness in its essential nature to a systematic though in no sense exhaustive analysis. What we lack above all is a certain general insight into the essence of *consciousness in general*, and quite specially also of consciousness, so far as in and through its essential Being, the "natural" fact-world comes to be known. In these studies we go so far as is needed to furnish the full insight at which we have been aiming, to wit, *that Consciousness in itself has a being of its own which in its absolute uniqueness of nature remains unaffected by the phenomenological disconnexion. It therefore remains over as a "phenomenological residuum"*, as a region of Being which is in principle unique, and can become in fact the field of a new science—the science of Phenomenology.

Through this insight the "phenomenological" ἐποχή will for the first time deserve its 114 name; to exercise it in full consciousness of its import will turn out to be the necessary operation which *renders "pure" consciousness accessible to us, and subsequently the whole phenomenological region*. And thus we shall be able to understand why this region and the new science attached to it was fated to remain unknown. From the natural standpoint nothing can be seen except the natural world. So long as the possibility of the phenomenological standpoint was not grasped, and the method of relating the objectivities which emerge there-with to a primordial form of apprehension had not been devised, the phenomenological world must needs have remained unknown, and indeed barely divined at all. . . .

§ 34. *The Essence of Consciousness as Theme of Inquiry*

We limit still further the theme of our inquiry. Its 115 title ran: Consciousness, or more distinctly *Conscious experience (Erlebnis) in general*, to be taken in an extremely wide sense, about whose exact definition we are fortunately not concerned. . . .

As starting-point we take consciousness in a pregnant sense which suggests itself at once, most simply indicated through the Cartesian *cogito*, "I think". As is known, Descartes understood this in a sense so wide as to include every case of "I perceive, I remember, I fancy, I judge, feel, desire, will", and all experiences of the Ego that in any way resemble the foregoing, in all the countless fluctuations of their special patterns. . . .

We shall consider conscious experiences *in* 116 *the concrete fullness and entirety* with which they figure in their concrete context—the *stream of experience*—and to which they are closely attached through their own proper essence. It then becomes evident that every experience in the stream which our reflexion can lay hold on has *its own essence open to intuition*, a "content" which can be considered in its *singularity in and for itself*. We shall be concerned to grasp this individual content of the *cogitatio* in its *pure* singularity, and to describe it in its general features, excluding everything which is not to be found in the *cogitatio* as it is in itself. We must likewise describe the *unity of consciousness* which is demanded *by the intrinsic nature of the cogitationes*, and so necessarily demanded that they could not be without this unity.

§ 35. *The Cogito as "Act". The Modal Form of Marginal Actuality*

Let us start with an example. In front of me, in the dim light, lies this white paper. I see it, touch it. This perceptual seeing and touching of the paper as the full concrete experience *of the paper* that lies here as given in truth precisely with these qualities, precisely with this relative lack of clearness, with this imperfect definition, appearing to me from this particular angle—is a *cogitatio*, a conscious experience. The paper itself with its objective qualities, its extension in space, its objective position in regard to that spatial thing I call my body, is not *cogitatio*, but *cogitatum*, not perceptual experience, but something perceived. Now that which is perceived can itself very well be a conscious experience; but it is evident that 117 an object such as a material thing, this paper, for instance, as given in perceptual experience, is in principle other than an experience, a being of a completely different kind.

Before pursuing this point farther, let us amplify the illustration. In perception properly so-called, as an explicit awareness (*Gewahren*), I am turned towards the object, to the paper, for instance, I apprehend it as being this here and now. The apprehension is a singling out, every perceived object having a background in experience. Around and about the paper lie books, pencils, ink-well, and so forth, and these in a certain sense are also "perceived", perceptually there, in the "field of intuition"; but whilst I was turned towards the paper there was no turning in their direction, nor any apprehending of them, not even in a secondary sense. They appeared and yet were not singled out, were not posited on their own account. Every perception of a thing has such a zone of *background intuitions* (or background awarenesses, if "intuiting" already includes the state of being turned towards), and this also is a *"conscious experience"*, or more briefly a "consciousness *of*" all indeed that in point of fact lies in the co-perceived objective "background". We are not talking here of course of that which is to be found as an "objective" element in the objective space to which the background in question may belong, of all the things and thing-like events which a valid and progressive experience may establish there. What we say applies exclusively to that zone of consciousness which belongs to the model essence of a perception as "being turned towards an object", and further to that which belongs to the proper essence of this zone itself. . . .

§ 36. *Intentional Experience. Experience in General*

All experiences which have these essential prop-
119 erties in common are also called *"intentional experiences"* (acts in the *very wide sense* of the *Logical Studies*); in so far as they are a consciousness of something they are said to be *"intentionally related"* to this something.

We must, however, be quite clear on this point that *there is no question here of a relation between a psychological event—called experience (Erlebnis)—and some other real existent (Dasein)—called Object—or of a psychological connexion* obtaining between the one and the other *in objective reality.*
120 On the contrary, we are concerned with experiences in their essential purity, with *pure essences,* and with that which is *involved in* the essence "*a priori,*" in *unconditioned necessity.*

That an experience is the consciousness of something: a fiction, for instance, the fiction of this or that centaur; a perception, the perception of its "real" object; a judgment, the judgment concerning its subject-matter, and so forth, this does

not relate to the experimental fact as lived within the world, more specifically within some given psychological context, but to the pure essence grasped ideationally as pure idea. In the very essence of an experience lies determined not only *that,* but also *whereof* it is a consciousness, and in what determinate or indeterminate sense it is this. So too in the essence of consciousness as dormant lies included the variety of wakeful *cogitationes,* into which it can be differentiated through the modification we have already referred to as "the noticing of what was previously unnoticed".

Under *experiences* in the *widest sense* we understand whatever is to be found in the stream of experience, not only therefore intentional experiences, *cogitationes* actual and potential taken in their full concreteness, but all the real (*reellen*) phases to be found in this stream and in its concrete sections.

For it is easily seen that *not every real phase* of the concrete unity of an intentional experience has itself the *basic character of intentionality,* the property of being a "consciousness of something". This is the case, for instance, with all *sensory data,* which play so great a part in the perceptive intuitions of things. In the experience of the perception of this white paper, more closely in those components of it related to the paper's quality of whiteness, we discover through properly directed noticing the sensory datum "white". This "whiteness" is something that belongs inseparably to the essence of the concrete perception, as a *real (reelles)* concrete constitutive portion of it. As the content which presents the whiteness of the paper as it appears to us it is the *bearer of* an intentionality, but not itself a consciousness of something. . . .

§ 37. *The "Directedness" of the Pure Ego in the Cogito,*
121 *and the Noticing that Apprehends*

Though we are unable at this point to proceed farther with our descriptive analysis of intentional experiences in their essential nature, we would single out certain aspects as noteworthy in relation to further developments. If an intentional experience is actual, carried out, that is, after the manner of the *cogito,* the subject "directs" itself within it towards the intentional object. . . .

It should be noticed that *intentional* object of a consciousness (understood as the latter's full correlate) is by no means to be identified with *apprehended* object. We are accustomed without further thought to include the being apprehended in the concept of the object (of that generally which stands over against the subject), since in so far as we think of it and say something *about* it, we have made it into an object in the sense of something apprehended. . . .

122 The intentional object rather, that which is valued, enjoyed, beloved, hoped as such, the action as action, first becomes an apprehended object through a distinctively "*objectifying*" *turn of thought*. If one is turned towards some matter absorbed in appreciation, the apprehension of the matter is no doubt included in the total attitude; but it is not the *mere* matter in general, but the matter *valued* or the *value* which is (and the point will concern us more in detail later on) *the complete intentional correlate of the act of valuation*. Thus "*to be turned in appreciation* towards some matter" does not already imply "*having*" the value "*for object*" in the special sense of object apprehended, as indeed we must have the object if we are to predicate anything of it; and similarly in regard to all logical acts which are related to it.

Thus in acts like those of appreciation we have in *intentional object in a double sense*: we must distinguish between the "*subject matter*" *pure and simple* and the *full intentional object*, and corresponding to this, a *double intentio*, a twofold directedness. If we are directed towards some matter in an act of appreciation, the direction towards the matter in question is a noting and apprehending of it; but we are "directed"—only not in an apprehending way—also to the value. Not merely the *representing of the matter* in question, but also the *appreciating* which includes this representing, has the modus of actuality. . . .

In every act some mode of heeding (Achtsamkeit) 123 *holds sway. But wherever it is not the plain consciousness of a subject-matter, wherever some further "attitude towards" the subject-matter is grounded in*

such consciousness, *subject-matter and full intentional object* ("subject-matter" and "value", for instance), likewise *heeding the object and mentally scrutinizing it, separate out the one from the other*. . . .

§ 38. *Reflexions on Acts. Immanent and Transcendent Perceptions*

We add the following: Living in the *cogito* we have not got the *cogitatio* consciously before us as intentional object; but it can at any time become this: to its essence belongs in principle the possibility of a "*reflexive*" directing of the mental glance towards itself naturally in the form of a new *cogitatio* and by way of a simple apprehension. In other words, every *cogitatio* can become the object of a so-called "inner perception", and eventually the object of a *reflexive* valuation, an approval or disapproval, and so forth. . . .

We connect with the foregoing the distinc-
124 tion between *transcendent* and *immanent* perceptions and acts generally. We avoid talking about inner and outer perception as there are serious objections to this way of speaking. We give the following explanations:—

Under *acts immanently directed*, or, to put it more generally, under *intentional experiences immanently related*, we include those acts which are *essentially* so constituted *that their intentional objects, when these exist at all, belong to the same stream of experience as themselves*. We have an instance of this wherever an act is related to an act (a *cogitatio* to a *cogitatio*) of the same Ego, or likewise an act to a given sensible affect of the same Ego, and so forth. Consciousness and its object build up an individual unity purely set up through experiences.

Intentional experiences for which this does *not* hold good are *transcendently directed*, as, for instance, all acts directed towards essences, or towards the intentional experiences of other Egos with other experience-streams; likewise all acts directed upon things, upon realities generally, as we have still to show.

In the case of an immanently directed, or more briefly, *immanent* (the so-called "inner") *perception, perception and perceived essentially constitute an unmediated unity, that of a single concrete cogitatio*. The perceiving here so conceals its object in itself that it can be separated from it only through abstraction, and as something *essentially incapable of subsisting alone*. . . .

This type of *real (reellen) "self-containedness"* (in strictness a similitude only) is a *distinctive characteristic of immanent perception and of the mental attitudes founded upon it;* . . .

The perception of a thing not only does not contain in itself, in its real (*reellen*) constitution, the thing itself, it is also without *any essential unity with it*, its existence naturally presupposed. A *unity determined purely by the proper essence of the experiences themselves can be only the unity of the stream of experience*, or, which is the same thing, it is only with experiences that an experience can be bound into one whole of which the essence in its totality envelops these experiences' own essences and is grounded within them. This proposition will become still clearer in the sequel and its great significance will become apparent. . . .

§ 39. *Consciousness and Natural Reality. The View of the "Man in the Street"*

Individual consciousness is interwoven with the *natural world* in a *twofold* way: it is some *man's* consciousness, or that of some *man* or *beast*, and in a large number at least of its particularizations it is a consciousness of this world. *In respect now of this intimate attachment with the real world, what is meant by saying that consciousness has an essence "of its own"*, that with other consciousness it constitutes a self-contained *connexion determined purely through this, its own essence*, the connexion, namely, of the stream of consciousness? . . .

To what extent, in the first place, must the *material world* be fundamentally different in kind, *excluded from the experience's own essential nature?* . . .

§ 40. *"Primary" and "Secondary" Qualities. The Bodily Given Thing "Mere Appearance" of the "Physically True"*

If as a "man in the street" misled by sensibility I have indulged the inclination to spin out such thoughts as these, now, as "a man of science", I call to mind the familiar distinction between secondary and *primary* qualities, according to which the specific qualities of sense should be "merely subjective" and only the geometrico-physical qualities "objective.". . . So understood, the old Berkeleian objection would hold good, namely, that extension, this essential nucleus of corporeality and all primary qualities, is unthinkable apart from the secondary qualities. Rather *the whole essential content of the perceived thing*, all that is present in the body, with all its qualities and all that can ever be perceive, is *"mere appearance"*, and the *"true thing" is that of physical science*. When the latter defines the given thing exclusively through concepts such as atoms, ions, energies, and so forth, and in every case as space-filling processes whose sole *characteristica* are mathematical expressions, its reference is to *something that transcends the whole content of the thing as present to us in bodily form*. It cannot therefore mean even the thing as lying in natural sensible space; in other words, its physical space cannot be the space of the world of bodily perception: otherwise it would also fall under the Berkeleian objection.

The *"true Being"* would therefore be entirely and *fundamentally something that is defined otherwise than as that which is given in perception as corporeal reality*, which is given exclusively through its sensory determinations, among which must also be reckoned the sensori-spatial. *The thing as strictly experienced gives the mere "this"*, *an empty X which becomes the bearer of mathematical determinations, and of the corresponding mathematical formulæ, and exists not in perceptual space, but in an "objective space", of which the former is the mere "symbol", a Euclidean manifold of three dimensions that can be only symbolically represented.* . . .

§ 41. *The Real Nature of Perception and its Transcendent Object*

All this being presupposed, *what is it, we ask, that belongs to the concrete real nature (reellen Bestande) of the perception itself, as cogitatio?* Not the physical thing, as is obvious: radically transcendent as it is, transcendent over against the whole "world of appearance". . . .

It concerns us now to win a deeper insight
130 into *the relation of the transcendent to the Consciousness* that knows it, and to see how this mutual connexion, which has its own riddles, is to be understood.

We shut off the whole of physics and the whole domain of theoretical thought. We remain within the framework of plain intuition and the syntheses that belong to it, including perception. It is then evident that intuition and the intuited, perception and the thing perceived, though essentially related to each other, are in principle and of necessity *not really (reell) and essentially one and united.*

We start by taking an example. Keeping this table steadily in view as I go round it, changing my position in space all the time, I have continually the consciousness of the bodily presence out there of this one and self-same table, which in itself remains unchanged throughout. But the perception of the table is one that changes continuously, it is a continuum of changing perceptions. . . .

An empirical consciousness of a self-same thing
131 *that looks "all-round" its object, and in so doing is continually confirming the unity of its own nature, essentially and necessarily possesses a manifold system of continuous patterns of appearances and perspective variations, in and through which all objective phases of the bodily self-given which appear in perception manifest themselves perspectively in definite continua.* Every determinate feature has *its own* system of perspective variations; and for each of these features, as for the thing as a whole, the following holds good, namely, that it remains one and the same for the consciousness that in grasping it unites recollection and fresh perception synthetically together, despite interruption in the continuity of the course of actual perception. . . .

§ 42. *Being as Consciousness and Being as Reality.*
133 *Intrinsic Difference between the Modes of Tuition*

The studies we have just completed left us with the transcendence of the thing over against the perception of it, and as a further consequence, over against every consciousness generally which

refers to the thing; not merely in the sense that the thing as a real (*reelles*) constituent part of consciousness is as a matter of fact not to be found. . . . Thus a basic and essential difference arises between *Being as Experience* and *Being as Thing.* . . .

The inability to be perceived immanently, and therefore, generally, to find a place in the system of experience belongs in essence and "in principle" altogether to the thing as such, to every reality in that genuine sense which we
134 have still to fix and make clear. Thus the Thing itself, *simpliciter,* we call transcendent. In so doing we give voice to the most fundamental and pivotal difference between ways of being, that between *Consciousness* and *Reality.*

This opposition between immanence and transcendence, as our exposition has further brought out, is accompanied by a *fundamental difference in the mode of being given.* . . .

We perceive the Thing through the "perspective" manifestations of all its determinate qualities which in any given case are "real", and strictly "fall" within the perception. . . . If we
135 take the reference to ways of appearing to apply to ways of *experiencing* (it can also, as is clear from the description we have just given, bear a correlative ontic meaning), it comes to saying this, that it belongs to the essential nature of certain peculiarly constructed *types of experience,* or, more specifically, peculiarly constructed concrete perceptions, that the intentional element in them is known as a spatial thing; and that the ideal possibility of passing over into determinate, ordered, continuous perceptual patterns, which can always be continued, and are therefore never exhausted, belongs to their very essence. It lies then in the essential structure of these patterngroups that they establish the unity of a *singly intentional* consciousness: the consciousness of a *single* perceptual thing appearing with ever-increasing completeness, from endlessly new points of view, and with ever-richer determinations. On the other hand, a spatial thing is no other than an intentional unity, which, in principle, can be given only as the unity of such ways of appearing.

§ 43. Light on a Fundamental Error

It is thus a fundamental error to suppose that perception (and every other type of the intuition of things, each after its own manner) fails to come into contact with the thing itself. We are told that the thing in itself and in its itselfness is not given to us; . . . God, the Subject of absolutely perfect knowledge, and therefore also of every possible adequate perception, naturally possesses what to us finite beings is denied, the perception 136 of things is themselves.

But this view is nonsensical. It implies that there is no *essential difference* between transcendent and immanent, that in the postulated divine intuition a spatial thing is a real (*reelles*) constituent, and indeed an experience itself, a constituent of the stream of the divine consciousness and the divine experience. . . .

§ 44. The Merely Phenomenal Being of the 137 Transcendent, the Absolute Being of the Immanent

A certain *inadequacy* belongs, further, to the perception of things, and that too is an essential necessity. In principle a thing can be given only "in one of its aspects", and that not only means incompletely, in some sense or other imperfectly, but precisely that which presentation through perspectives prescribes. A thing is necessarily given in mere "*modes of appearing*", and the necessary factors in this case are *a nucleus of what is "really presented"*, an outlying zone of apprehension consisting of *marginal "co-data" of an accessory kind (uneigentlicher)*, and a more or less vague *indeterminacy*. And the meaning of this indeterminacy is once again foreshadowed by the general meaning of the thing perceived as such, or by the general and essential nature of this type of perception which we call thing-perception. . . .
138 *To remain for ever incomplete after this fashion is an ineradicable essential of the correlation Thing and Thing-perception.* . . .

We must note the following distinction also:
140 Even an experience (*Erlebnis*) is not, and never is, perceived in its completeness, it cannot be grasped adequately in its full unity. It is essentially something that flows, and staring from the present moment we can swim after it, our gaze

reflectively turned towards it, whilst the stretches we leave in our wake are lost to our perception. . . .

We now add the following case of contrast: It is of the essence of presentations to show gradual differences of relative clearness or dimness. . . .

Third Chapter

The Region of Pure Consciousness

§ 47. The Natural World as Correlate of Consciousness

147 . . . We must always bear in mind that *what things are* (the things about which alone we ever speak, and concerning whose being or non-being, so being or not so being, we can alone contend and reach rational decisions), *they are as things of experience.* . . .

This holds of every conceivable kind of tran-
148 scendence which might be treated as real or possible. *An object that has being in itself (an sich seiender) is never such as to be out of relation to consciousness and its Ego. The thing is thing of the world about me*, even the thing that is not seen and the really possible thing, not experienced, but experienceable or perhaps-experienceable. *Experienceability never betokens an empty logical possibility*, but one that has its *motive* in the system of experience. . . .

149 Motivations differ in respect of the contents which mark our apprehension of them or their own definition, being more or less richly organized, more or less restricted or vague in content according as they concern things already "known" or "wholly unknown" and "still undiscovered", or else, in regard to the seen thing, concern what we know or still ignore about it. Our exclusive concern is with the *essential configurations* of such systems which underlie pure eidetical research in all its possible developments. It is an essential requirement that what exists already *realiter*, but is not yet actually experienced, can come to be given, and that that then means that it belongs to the undetermined but *determinable* marginal field of my actual experience at the time being. . . .

§ 48. *Logical Possibility and Real Absurdity of a World Outside Our Own*

The hypothetical assumption of a Real Something outside this world is indeed a "logically" possible one, and there is clearly no formal contradiction in making it. But if we question the essential conditions of its validity, the kind of evidence (*Ausweisung*) demanded by its very meaning and the nature of the evidential generally as determined in principle through the thesis of a transcendent—however we may generalize correctly its essential nature—we perceive that the transcendent must needs be *experienceable*, and not merely by an Ego conjured into being as an empty logical possibility but by any *actual* Ego, as the demonstrable (*ausweisbare*) unity of its systematic experience. But we can see (we are indeed not yet far enough advanced here to be able to give detailed grounds for the view) that what is perceivable by *one* Ego must *in principle* be conceivable by *every* Ego. And though *as a matter of fact* it is not true that everyone stands or can stand in a relation of empathy of inward understanding with every other one as we ourselves, for instance, are unable to stand with the spirits that may frequent the remotest starry worlds, yet in point of principle there exist *essential possibilities for the setting up of an understanding*, possibilities, therefore, that worlds of experience sundered in point of fact may still be united together through actual empirical connexions into a single intersubjective world, the correlate of the unitary world of minds (of the universal extension of the human community). If we think this over, the logical possibility on formal grounds of realities outside the world, the *one* spatio-temporal world which is *fixed* through our *actual* experience is seen to be really nonsense. . . .

§ 49. *Absolute Conciousness as Residium After the Nullifying of the World*

. . . Let us now bring in the results we reached at the close of the last chapter; let us think of the possibility of non-Being which belongs essentially to every Thing-like transcendence: it is then evident *that the Being of consciousness*, of every stream of experience generally, *though it* would indeed be inevitably modified by a nullifying of the thing-world, would not be affected thereby in its own proper existence. Modified, certainly! For the nullifying of the world means, correlatively, just this, that in every stream of experience (the full stream, both ways endless, of the experiences of an Ego) certain ordered empirical connexions, and accordingly also systems of theorizing reason which take their bearings from these, would be excluded. But this does not involve the exclusion of other experiences and experiential systems. *Thus no real thing*, none that consciously presents and manifests itself through appearances, *is necessary for the Being of consciousness itself* (in the widest sense of the stream of experience).

Immanent Being is therefore without doubt absolute in this sense, that in principle nulla 're' indiget ad existendum.

On the other hand, the world of the transcendent "res" is related unreservedly to consciousness, not indeed to logical conceptions, but to what is actual.

That has already been made clear in a very general way in the analyses already carried out (in the foregoing paragraphs). What is transcendent is *given* through certain empirical connexions. . . .

Both immanent or absolute Being and transcendent Being are indeed "being" (*seiend*) and "object", and each has, moreover, its objective determining content; but it is evident that what then on either side goes by the name of object and objective determination bears the same name only when we speak in terms of the empty logical categories. Between the meanings of consciousness and reality yawns a veritable abyss. Here a Being which manifests itself perspectively, never giving itself absolutely, merely contingent and relative; there a necessary and absolute Being, fundamentally incapable of being given through appearance and perspective-patterns.

It us thus clear that in spite of all talk—well-grounded no doubt in the meaning intended—of a real Being of the *human Ego*, and its conscious experiences, *in* the world and of all that belongs thereto in any way in respect of "psychophysical connexions"—that in spite of all this, Consciousness, considered in its "*purity*", must be reckoned as *a self-contained system of Being*, as a system of

Absolute Being, into which nothing can penetrate, and from which nothing can escape; which has no spatio-temporal exterior, and can be inside no spatio-temporal system; which cannot experience causality from anything nor exert causality upon anything, it being presupposed that causality bears the normal sense of natural causality as a relation of dependence between realities.

On the other side, the whole *spatio-temporal world,* to which man and the human Ego claim to belong as subordinate singular realities, is *according to its own meaning mere intentional Being,* a Being, therefore, which has the merely secondary, relative sense of a Being *for* a consciousness. It is a Being which consciousness in its own experiences (*Erfahrungen*) posits, and is, in principle, intuitable and determinable only as the element common to the [harmoniously] motivated appearance-manifolds, but *over and beyond* this, is just nothing at all.

154 **§ 50. The Phenomenological Viewpoint and Pure Consciousness as the Field of Phenomenology**

Thus the meaning which "Being" bears in common speech is precisely inverted. The being which for us is first, is in itself second, i.e., it is what it is only in "relation" to the first. It is not as though a blind legal decree had ordained that the *ordo et connexio rerum* must direct itself according to the *ordo et connexio idearum.* Reality, that of the thing taken singly as also that of the whole world, essentially lacks independence. And in speaking of essence we adopt here our own rigorous use of the term. Reality is not in itself something absolute, binding itself to another only in a secondary way, it is, absolutely speaking, nothing at all, it has no "absolute essence" whatsoever, it has the essentiality of something which in principle is *only* intentional, *only* known, consciously presented as an appearance.

Now let us turn our thoughts back to the first chapter, to reflexious upon phenomenological reduction. It is now clear in point of fact that over against the natural theoretical standpoint, whose correlate is the world, a new standpoint must be available which in spite of the switching off of this psychophysical totality of nature waves

something over—the whole field of absolute consciousness. Thus, instead of living naïvely in experience (*Erfahrung*), and subjecting what we experience, transcendent nature, to theoretical inquiries, we perform the "phenomenological reduction". . . .

Let us make this clear to ourselves in detail. At the natural standpoint we simply *carry out* all the acts through which the world is there for us. We live naïvely unreflective in our perceiving and experiencing, in those thetic acts in which the unities of things appear to us, and not only appear but are given with the stamp of "presentness" and "reality". When we pursue natural science, we *carry out* reflexions ordered in accordance with the logic of experience, reflexions in which these realities, given and taken alike, are determined in terms of thought, in which also on the ground of such directly experienced and determined transcendences fresh inferences are drawn. At the phenomenological standpoint, acting on lines of general principle, we *tie up* the *performance* of all such cogitative theses, i.e., we "place in brackets" what has been carried our, "we do not associate these theses" with out new inquiries; instead of living *in* them and carrying *them* out, we carry out acts of *reflexion* directed towards them, and these we apprehend as the *absolute* Being which they are. We now live entirely in such acts of the second level, whose datum is the infinite field of absolute experiences— *the basic field of Phenomenology.* . . .

§ 52. Supplementary Remarks. The Physical Thing and
158 **the "Unknown Cause of Appearances"**

But we still need to add something by way of supplement. Our last reflexions bore chiefly on the thing of the sensory *imaginatio,* and we paid inadequate attention to the physical thing, for which the thing that appears to sense (what is given in perception) must functions as "mere appearance", much as though it were something "purely subjective". Meanwhile it follows from our previous studies that this mere subjectivity should not be confused (as it is so frequently) with an experiential subjectivity, as though the perceived things in their perceptual qualities were themselves experiences. . . .

It can be easily shown that, if the unknown cause we have assumed *exists (ist)* at all, it must be *in principle* perceptible and experienceable, if not by us, at least for other Egos who see better and farther than we do. We are not concerned here with any empty, psychological possibility, but with an essential possibility possessing content and validity. Further, we should need to show that the possible perception itself again, and with essential necessity, must be a perception through appearances, and that we have therefore fallen into an inevitable *regressus in infinitum.* Again, we should need to point out that an explanation of the perceptually given events through causal realities hypothetically assumed, through unknown entities of the nature of a thing (as, for instance, the explanation of certain planetary disturbances through the assumption of a still unknown new planet, Neptune), is something that differs in principle from explanation in the sense of a physical determination of experience things and through physical means of explanation after the style of atoms, ions, and the like. So too on similar lines much else could be discussed and developed. . . .

Returning then, let us take the position, easily tested, that in physical method the *perceived thing itself* is always and in principle *precisely the thing which the physicist studies and scientifically determines.*

This assertion appears to contradict the statements expressed on an earlier page, in which we sought to determine more closely the meaning of current phrases used by the physicists, and in particular the sense of the traditional separation between primary and secondary qualities. After excluding obvious misinterpretations, we said that "the thing we strictly experience" gives us "the mere this", an "empty *x*", which becomes the bearer of the exact physical determinations which do not themselves fall within experience properly-so-called. The "physically true thing" is thus "in principle differently determined" from that which is given "bodily" in perception itself. The latter displays purely sensory features which are precisely not physical.

None the less, the two expositions are compatible enough, and we do not need to challenge that interpretation of the physical viewpoint at all seriously. We have only to understand it correctly. On no account should we fall into the fundamentally perverse copy-and-sign-theories which, without taking the physical thing specially into account, we considered at an earlier stage and likewise disposed of in its most general form. An image or sign points to something that lies beyond it, which, could it but pass over into another form of presentation, into that of a dator intuition, might "itself" be apprehended. A sign and copy does not "announce" in its self the self that is signified (or copied). But the physical thing is nothing foreign to that which appears in a sensory body, but something that manifests itself in it and in it *alone* indeed in a primordial way, a way that is also *a priori* in that it rests on essential grounds which cannot be annulled. Moreover, even the sensory determining-content of the *x* which functions as bearer of the physical determinations does not clothe the latter in an alien dress that conceals them: rather it is only in so far as the *x* is the subject of the sensory determinations that it is also subject of the physical, which on its side *announces itself in* the sensory. In principle a thing, the precise thing of which the physicist speaks, can in accordance with what has been already set out in detail be given only sensorily, in sensory "ways of appearance", and it is the identical element which appears in the shifting continuity of these ways of appearance which the physicist in relation to all experienceable (thus perceived or perceivable) systems which can come under consideration as "conditioning circumstances", subjects to a causal analysis, to an inquiry into real necessary connexions. The thing which he observes, with which he experiments, which he sees continually, handles, places on the scales, "brings to the fusing-furnace", this and no other thing is the subject of physical predicates, since it is it that has the weight, mass, temperature, electrical resistance, and so forth. So too it is the perceived processes and connexions themselves which are defined through concepts such as force, acceleration, energy, atom, ion, and so forth. The thing that appears to sense, which has the sensory properties of shape, colour, smell, and taste, is therefore far from being a sign for *something else*, though to a certain extent a sign *for itself*.

Only so much can be said: The thing that appears with such and such sensory properties under the given phenomenal conditions is, *for the physicist*, who for such things generally, and in the form of relevant connexion between the appearances, has *already fixed the physical determination on general lines*, the sign and symbol for a wealth of causal properties of this same thing, which as such declare their presence in specific and familiar relations of dependence among appearances. What is there declared—even when revealed in intentional unities of conscious experiences—is clearly, in principle, transcendent.

It is clear from the foregoing that *even the higher transcendence of the physical thing does not imply any reaching out beyond the world for consciousness*, or, shall we say, for any Ego that functions as the subject of knowledge (singly or in the relation of empathy).

The situation as generally indicated is this, that physical thought builds itself up on the basis natural experience (*Erfahren*) (or of the natural theses, which it establishes). *Following the rational motives* which the connexions of experience suggest, it is compelled to adopt certain forms of apprehending its material, to construct such intentional systems as the reason of the case may require, and to utilize them for the *theoretical determination* of things as experienced through sense. Out of this springs up the opposition between the Thing of the plain sensory *imaginatio* and the Thing of the physical *intellectio*, and on 162 the latter side grow up all the ideal ontological through-constructions which express themselves in physical concepts, and derive their meaning as they should do exclusively from the method of natural science. . . .

§ 55. Conclusion. All Reality Exists through "The 168 Dispensing of Meaning". No "Subjective Idealism"

In a certain sense and with proper care in the use of words we may even say that *all real unities are "unities of meaning"*. Unities of meaning presuppose. . . .

a sense-giving consciousness, which, on its side, is absolute and not dependent in its turn on sense bestowed on it from another source. If the concept of reality is derived from *natural* realities, from the unities of possible experience, then "universe", "Nature as a whole", means just so much as the totality of realities; but to identify the same with the totality of *Being*, and therewith to make it absolute, is simply nonsense. An *absolute reality is just as valid as a round square*. Reality and world, here used, are just the titles for certain valid *unities of meaning*, namely, unities of "meaning" related to certain organizations of pure absolute consciousness which dispense meaning and show forth its validity in certain *essentially* fixed, specific ways.

If anyone objects, with reference to these discussions of ours, that they transform the whole world into subjective illusion and throw themselves into the arms of an "idealism such as Berkeley's", we can only make answer that he has not grasped the *meaning* of these discussions. We subtract just as little from the plenitude of the world's Being, from the totality of all realities, as we do from the plenary geometrical Being of a square when we deny (what in this case indeed can plainly be taken for granted) that it is round. 169 It is not that the real sensory world is "recast" or denied, but that an absurd interpretation of the same, which indeed contradicts its *own* mentally clarified meaning, is set aside. It springs from making the world absolute in a *philosophical* sense, which is wholly foreign to the way in which we naturally look out upon the world. This outlook is altogether natural, it pervades our unsophisticated action as we exhibit in practice the general thesis already described, it can therefore never be absurd. Absurdity first arises when one philosophizes and, in probing for ultimate information as to the meaning of the world, fails to notice that the whole being of the world consists in a certain "meaning" which presupposes absolute consciousness as the field from which the meaning is derived; and further, when in support of this attitude, one fails to notice that this field, *this existen-*

tial realm of absolute origins, is open to research on an intuitional basis, and contains an infinite wealth of insight-rooted knowledge of the highest scientific worth. It is true that we have not yet shown that this is so, it will first become clear to us in the course of our inquiries. . . .

What is essential for our purpose is to see upon evidence that the phenomenological reduction, as a means of disconnecting us from the natural standpoint and its general thesis, is possible, and that, when carried out, the absolute or pure transcendental consciousness is left over as residuum, to which it is then absurd to ascribe reality (*Realität*).

THIRD SECTION

PROCEDURE OF PURE PHENOMENOLOGY IN RESPECT OF METHODS AND PROBLEMS

Second Chapter

General Structures of Pure Consciousness

241 § 84 *Intentionality as the Main Phenomenological Theme*

We pass on now to a peculiarity distinctive of experiences, which we may definitely refer to as the general theme of "objectively" oriented phenomenology, namely, Intentionality. It is to this extent an essential peculiarity of the sphere of 242 experience in general, since all experiences in one way or another participate in intentionality, though we cannot in one and the same sense say of *every* experience that it has intentionality, as we can say for instance of every experience which enters as object into the focus of possible reflexion—be it even an abstract phase of experience—that it has a temporal character. It is intentionality which characterizes *consciousness* in the pregnant sense of the term, and justifies us in describing the whole stream of experience as at once a stream of consciousness and unity of *one* consciousness. . . .

We understood under Intentionality the unique peculiarity of experiences "to be the consciousness *of* something". It was in the explicit *cogito* that we first came across this wonderful property to which all metaphysical enigmas and riddles of the theoretical reason lead us eventu-

243 ally back: perceiving is the perceiving of something, maybe a thing; judging the judging of a certain matter; valuation, the valuing of a value; wish, the wish for the content wished, and so on.

Third Chapter

Noesis and Noema

257 § 88. *Real (Reelle) and Intentional Factors of Experience. The Noema*

If, as has been our custom inn the present meditations generally, we look out for distinctions of a very general kind, such as can be grasped at once on the very threshold of phenomenology, so to speak, and are determinative for all further methodical advance, we at once stumble across what, in respect of intentionality, is a quite fundamental distinction, namely, that between the *proper components* of the intentional experiences, and their *intentional correlates*, or the components of them. . . .

Thus on the one hand we have to distinguish the parts and phases which we find through a *real (reelle) analysis* of the experience in which we treat the experience as an object like any other, and question concerning its parts or the dependent phases which build it up on real (*reell*) lines. But on the other hand the intentional experience is the consciousness of something, and is so in the form its essence prescribes: as memory, for instance, or as judgment, or as will, and so forth: and so we can ask what can be said on essential lines concerning this "of something".

Every intentional experience, thanks to its noetic phase, is noetic, it is its essential nature to harbour in itself a "meaning" of some sort, it may be many meanings, and on the ground of this gift of meaning, and in harmony therewith, to develop further phases which through it become themselves "meaningful". Such noetic phases include, for instance, the directing of the glance of the pure Ego upon the object "intended" by it 258 in virtue of its gift of meaning, upon that which "it has in its mind as something meant." . . .

Corresponding at all points to the manifold data of the real (*reellen*) noetic content, there is a variety of data displayable in really pure (*wirklich reiner*) intuition, and in a correlative *"noematic content"*, or briefly *"noema"*—terms which we shall henceforth be continually using.

Perception, for instance, has its noema, and at the base of this its perceptual meaning, that is, the *perceived as such*. Similarly, the recollection, when it occurs, has as its own its *remembered as such* precisely as it is "meant" and "consciously known" in it; so again judging has as its own the *judged as such*, pleasure the pleasing as such, and so forth. We must everywhere take the noematic correlate, which (in a very extended meaning of the term) is here referred to as "meaning" (*Sinn*) *precisely* as it lies "immanent" in the experience of perception, of judgment, of liking, and so forth, i.e., *if we question in pure form this experience itself*, as we find it there presented to us.

We can make our meaning here full clear through the help of an illustrative analysis (which we propose to carry out in the light of pure intuition).

Let us suppose that we are looking with pleasure in a garden at a blossoming apple-tree, at the fresh young green of the lawn, and so forth. . . . From the natural standpoint the apple-259 tree is something that exists in the transcendent reality of space, and the perception as well as the pleasure a psychical state which we enjoy as real human beings. Between the one and the other real being (*Realen*), the real man or the real perception on the one hand, and the real apple-tree on the other, there subsist real relations. . . .

Let us now pass over to the phenomenological standpoint. The transcendent world enters its "bracket"; in respect of its real being we use the disconnecting ἐποχή. We now ask what there is to discover, on essential lines, in the nexus of noetic experiences of perception and pleasure-valuation. . . .

It may be that phenomenology has also something to say concerning hallucinations, illusions, and deceptive perceptions generally, and it has perhaps a great deal to say about them; but it is evident that here, in the part they play in the natural setting, they fall away before the phenomenological suspension. Here in regard to the perception, and also to any arbitrarily continued nexus of such perceptions (e.g., if we were to observe the blossoming tree *ambulando*), we have no such question to put as whether anything cor-260 responds to it in "the" real world. . . .

The tree has not forfeited the least shade of content from all the phases, qualities, characters *with which it appeared in this perception*, and "in" this pleasure proved "beautiful," "charming", and the like.

From our phenomenological standpoint we can and must put the question of essence: *What is the "perceived as such"? What essential phases does it harbour in itself in its capacity as noema?* We win the reply to our question as we wait, in pure surrender, on what is essentially *given*. We can than describe "that which appears as such" faithfully and in the light of perfect self-evidence. As just one other expression for this we have, "the describing of perception in its noematic aspect".

§ 89. *Noematic Statements and Statements Concerning Reality. The Noema in the Psychological Sphere*

It is clear that all *these* descriptive statements, though very similar in sound to statements concerning reality, have undergone a *radical* modification of meaning; . . .

"In" the reduced perception (in the phenomenologically pure experience) we find, as belonging to its essence indissolubly, the perceived as such, and under such titles as "material thing", "plant", "tree", "blossoming", and so forth. The *inverted commas* are clearly significant; they express that change of signature, the corresponding radical modification of the meaning of the words. The *tree plain and simple*, the thing in nature, is as different as it can be from this *perceived tree as such*, which as perceptual meaning belongs to the perception, and that inseparably. The tree plain and simple can burn away, resolve itself into its chemical elements, and so forth. But the meaning—the meaning of *this* perception, something that 261 belongs necessarily to its essence—cannot burn away; it has no chemical elements, no forces, no real properties.

Whatever in purely immanent and reduced form is peculiar to the experience, and cannot be thought away from it, as it is in itself, and in its eidetic setting passes *eo ipso* into the Eidos, is separated from all Nature and physics, and not less from all psychology by veritable abysses; and even this image, being naturalistic, is not strong enough to indicate the difference.

The perceptual meaning belongs of course *also* to the phenomenologically unreduced perception (to the perception in its psychological sense). Thus we can here clearly see at once how the phenomenological reduction can fulfill for the psychologist the methodically useful function of fixing the noematic meaning in sharp distinction from the object pure and simple, and of recognizing it as belonging inseparably to the psychological essence of the intentional experience, which would then be apprehended as real.

On both sides, whether the standpoint be psychological or phenomenological, we must assiduously see to it that the "perceived" as meaning includes nothing (thus nothing should be ascribed to it on the ground of "indirect information") that does not "really appear" in that which in the given case is the perceptual manifestation of the appearing reality, and precisely in the mode, the way of presentation in which we are aware of it in the actual perception. . . .

265 § 91. *Extension to the Farthest Reaches of Intentionality*

What has hitherto been more fully discussed with reference to perception really holds good of *all types of intentional experience*. In memory, after reduction, we find the remembered as such; in expectation, the expected as such; in imaginative fancy, the fancied as such.

"In" each of these experiences there "dwells" a noematic meaning, and however closely self-related, indeed, so far as a central nucleus is concerned, essentially self-same, the latter remains in different experiences, it differs in kind none the less when the experiences differ in kind; the common ground here is at least differently featured, and necessarily so. . . .

These are characters which we *find* as insep-
266 arable features *of* the perceived, fancied, remembered, etc., as such; *of the meaning of perception,*

the meaning of fancy, the meaning of memory, and as *necessarily belonging to these in correlation with the respective types of noetic experiences.*

Thus, where our interest lies in describing the intentional correlates faithfully and completely, we must never collect such data in a haphazard way, but group together characters that conform to certain essential laws, and fix their import with conceptual strictness.

We observe from this that within the *complete* noema (as we had in fact previously declared) we must separate out *as essentially different* certain *strata* which group themselves about a *central "nucleus,"* the sheer *"objective meaning",* that which in our examples was something that could be everywhere described in purely identical objective terms, because in the specifically different though parallel experiences there could be an identical element. . . .

§ 96. *Transition to the Chapters that Follow.*
279 *Concluding Remarks*

We have bestowed such great care, though on general lines, on working out the difference between noesis and noema (where by noesis we understand the concrete completely intentional experience as modified through the stressing of its noetic components) because the grasp and mastery of it is of the greatest consequence for phenomenology, is indeed quite decisive for its proper grounding. At first sight it appears to be concerning itself with what is obvious: every consciousness is the consciousness of something, and the modes of consciousness are very different. But on nearer approach we realized the great difficulties. They concern the understanding of the mode of being of the noema, the way in which it should "lie" in experience, and become "consciously known" there. They concern quite particularly the clear-cut separation between the real (*reeller*) portions of one's whole experience which belong to the experiencing itself, and those which belong to the noema, and should be attributed to it as its own. Also the correct articulation in parallel structures of noesis and noema, which follows on the separation between them, gives trouble enough. . . .

NOTES

[1]This term reads as 'epoché,' which literally means 'a cessation.' Husserl uses the term to refer to bracketing.

STUDY QUESTIONS: HUSSERL, *IDEAS*

1. What is phenomenology? What is pure phenomenology?
2. What is essential being? What does Husserl mean by the science of essential being?
3. What is phenomenological reduction?
4. What does he mean by eidetic science?
5. In what way does the world consist of not just facts but also values?
6. What is the role of the Cartesian *Cogito* in Husserl's method?
7. What does he mean by 'disconnexion' and 'bracketing'? What role do they play?
8. What is the 'natural standpoint'?
9. What is a bracketed judgment?
10. What is transcendental consciousness?
11. What does he mean by 'intentional experiences'?
12. What is the 'pure ego'? What does he mean by 'the directedness' of the pure ego?
13. What is the relationship between immanent and transcendent perceptions?
14. How does he distinguish 'being as consciousness' from 'being as reality'?
15. In what sense is immanent being absolute?
16. What is intentionality?
17. What does he mean by noesis and noema? How are these terms related? What is the significance?

Philosophical Bridges: Husserl's Influence

Husserl's influence on twentieth-century philosophy has been immense. Along with his teacher Brentano, he founded phenomenology, which has attracted many thinkers including the prominent Merleau-Ponty (1908–1961), and it has influenced many others. The most influential aspect of phenomenology is the method of describing carefully the essence of a psychological phenomenon on its own terms without presuppositions.

Husserl's most famous pupil, Heidegger, developed his own of variant of phenomenology called existential phenomenology. Husserl's phenomenology is the study of the essential structures of experience; existential phenomenology studies the a priori structures of our mode of being as they lived. While the phenomenological method of Husserl is to describe the essential nature of a specific experience, that of Heidegger is to give descriptions of the nature of our modes of being as they are lived.

Phenomenology was a major force in German philosophy until the 1930s, after which time it spread to France, where it touched, among many others, Sartre, de Beauvoir, and Merleau-Ponty, as well as Paul Ricoeur and Derrida. As a young man, Sartre went to Germany to study the thought of Husserl and Heidegger, and in his early writings, Sartre developed a theory of the imagination based on Husserl's phenomenology, as well as a phenomenological work on the emotions. Sartre calls his later work *Being and Nothingness* as 'an essay in phenomenological ontology.'

Merleau-Ponty's main early book, *The Phenomenology of Perception*, investigates the relations between the subject and its body and world. Insofar as it is concerned with perception, Merleau-Ponty's thinking is close to Husserl's except that the Frenchman stresses the importance of the phenomenology of bodily perception. Insofar as it is concerned with culture, Merleau-Ponty's thought draws inspiration from Husserl's later work on the life-world.

Paul Ricoeur was also influenced by phenomenology; he translated Husserl's *Ideas* into French and wrote a phenomenological study of the will (1960). Thereafter, Ricoeur moved increasingly toward hermeneutics. However, the philosophical hermeneutics of Ricoeur and Gadamer owes much to Gadamer's teacher Heidegger, whose thought, in turn, is indebted to Husserl. Like phenomenology, hermeneutical interpretation is a descriptive method that aims to characterize the meaning of an experience, practice, or sign. Hermeneutics is a continuation of the phenomenological tradition.

In the 1960s, Husserl's thought began to impact analytic philosophy. The kernel of Husserl's work is the idea of intentionality, which has become integral to almost all contemporary analytic thought regarding mental states. For example, although they have opposed views, the two analytic philosophers John Searle and Daniel Dennett are both very much concerned with the nature of intentionality. Searle, who wrote *Intentionality*, which draws heavily on the thought of Husserl, is a critic of strong artificial intelligence (AI). Dennett, who is the author of *The Intentional Stance*, supports strong AI, the view that all mental states are computational. Very roughly, the difference between them is that while Searle claims that brains have intrinsic intentionality (which computers do not), Dennett argues that all attributions of intentionality are only instrumentally justified. This discussion revolves around the nature of intentionality. In 1982, Hubert Dreyfus edited a book entitled *Husserl, Intentionality and Cognitive Science*.

Husserl's phenomenology has had some impact on the philosophy of the social sciences through the work of Alfred Schutz, while Max Scheler applied Husserl's methodology to the perception of value and religious experience.

In summary, much twentieth-century continental philosophy has its roots in Husserl's thought. For example, through its influence on Heidegger, we can trace its effect on the existentialism of Sartre and de Beauvoir, and also on the hermeneutic thought of Gadamer.

Martin Heidegger (1889–1976)

Biographical History

At the University of Freiburg, Martin Heidegger was the star pupil of Husserl, and his thought has important phenomenological strands. In 1923, Heidegger became professor at Marburg. Five years later, he succeeded Husserl as chair of philosophy at Freiburg, where he was elected rector of the university. His *Being and Time* was first published in German in 1927. By this time, Heidegger had developed a philosophical method quite different from Husserl's phenomenology.

Husserl was of Jewish descent, and when Heidegger joined the Nazi party in 1933, this sealed the rift between the two philosophers. The degree of Heidegger's involvement with Nazism, and its significance, has become a controversial topic. In any case, after World War II, Heidegger was banned from academic life until 1951 because of his Nazi sympathies. During this period, he lived in a hut in the Black Forest. He retired from teaching in 1959, and spent the last years of his life in seclusion.

Philosophical Overview

Heidegger's revolutionary approach to philosophy begins with his rejecting metaphysics as an investigation concerning what kinds of things exist, which is an ontic question. In contrast, his primary aim is to question what it means to be, which is an ontological question. This question has to be answered by characterizing different modes of Being and, in particular, the mode of Being that we ourselves possess. We are Dasein, or beings who can question the significance of Being. Heidegger says, 'Dasein is an entity for which, in its Being, that Being is an issue.' The meaning of our mode of being is constituted by the a priori existential characteristics of being Dasein, which are primarily to be in the world and to care. Such an investigation in 'fundamental ontology' will reveal the nature of our subjective concerns. According to Heidegger, this ontological investigation is more fundamental than the ontic one pursued in traditional metaphysics. This is because the ontic inquiry concerning what exists requires the ontological study of what existence means for Dasein.

The Existentials

Heidegger tries to uncover what it means to be by describing different ways of being, called existentials. He claims that there are two kinds of existentials: those that involve an everyday, inauthentic perspective, and those that are authentic, and take seriously the dimension of time. A mode of being is authentic when it involves Dasein's awareness of its own existence and meaning. The authentic/inauthentic distinction can be applied to all aspects of our lives. For example, there are authentic and inauthentic forms of talking, listening, and thinking. The existentials are a priori characteristics of Dasein's way of being; they are modes of living rather than merely necessary forms of thought, such as Kant's categories. These existentials are described briefly in the introduction to the reading, and they include being in the world, moods, understanding, and, most centrally, care.

The Primacy of Care

Care is the primary characteristic of Dasein as Dasein, and the other existentials involve care as part of their structure. The existential of moods shows the self in its actual state, which Heidegger calls facticity. The existential of understanding reveals what the self can be, which Heidegger calls existentiality. The existential of inauthenticity shows that the self is hiding from itself, which Heidegger calls fallness. All these three aspects of Dasein's way of being are different forms of caring. We care about the things ready at hand within the world; we care for the other beings around us; and we care in our anxiety, in our fleeing from ourselves, as well as in the possibility of an authentic existence.

To illustrate the primacy of care, Heidegger gives an analysis of angst, or anxiety or dread. Although Heidegger's analysis of angst or anxiety or dread is well-known, he could have described other kinds of mood to show the primacy of care. Angst is a turning away from the self, and, as such, it uncovers something about what it is a turning away from. It reveals care. This angst, or existential anxiety, is unlike fear in that it does not have a specific object. Fear is always directed toward something, but angst is not. It is a general feeling of dread that one has, especially at the prospect of death, or our own non-existence. Nevertheless, angst is not fear of death; it is rather a general feeling of not being at home in the world. It makes one confront oneself and one's possibilities, namely, either to be truly oneself or to lose oneself in inauthentic everyday life.

Time and Death

After characterizing the existentials, Heidegger needs to move from a study of the ways in which human beings exist, which is the existential analytic that comprises Part I of *Being and Time*, toward a study of what it means to be (the fundamental ontology that comprises Part II of *Being and Time*). The investigation must shift away from ways of being, and more directly toward what it means to be. Up to now, Heidegger has not emphasized the authentic ontological awareness that Dasein can have of itself as a being in time.

Each person dies his or her own death, which cannot be shared with another. Heidegger expresses this by affirming that death is one's 'ownmost.' This is an existential, a mode of being; it is part of what we are thrown into. In an inauthentic mode of existence, Dasein tries to escape and forget death.

Heidegger claims that an authentic awareness of death requires one to be conscious of it as the *possibility* of not-being, rather than just as the future event of dying. This is because the awareness of death as a possible state of not-being, as opposed to dying as a future event, focuses on our being-able-to-be, on our potential. This point ties death to authenticity, which requires full awareness of one's capacity and freedom to really be. For this reason, Heidegger stresses that authentic awareness of death must be consciousness of the possibility, of not-being. In this way, awareness of death as a possibility comprises consciousness of one's finitude.

Death is the future that can never arrive as an actuality. It can never become one's past, or a 'could have been.' Thus, it will never be an actuality for the individual. Death is the individual's own nonbeing. and in facing this one confronts the removal of all possibility. Nonetheless, by confronting death, the individual makes authentic being possible.

Furthermore, death also reveals the essentially temporal nature of our existence. For Dasein, to be is to be temporal. Heidegger analyzes the temporal nature of Dasein in terms of care. To have a future means to anticipate, that is, to look, or rather to care, forward. To have a past means to have come from something that one was and cared about. For the future and the past to have meaning, they must be essentially tied to Dasein's existence. In this way, the structure of time corresponds to that of care. The past reveals our thrownness—i.e., that we are, as it were, thrown into a world in which many factors are beyond our control; the future, the awareness of possibilities, and the present, the actual.

BEING AND TIME

The main aim of this selection from the first part of *Being and Time* is to uncover what it means to be by examining different modes of being, called existentials. In this introduction, we shall examine briefly the nature of these existentials, which are a priori characteristics of Dasein's mode of being.

A. *The first existential is Being-in-the-world. I find myself inescapably in the midst of a world that constitutes my surroundings and dwelling place; this world affects me and is meaningful to me. My primary relationship to things in this world is to use them; they are ready-to-hand as opposed to present-at-hand, or independent of any function, which is a derivative or secondary relationship and an abstraction. This is a point of importance for Heidegger. Often philosophers assume that the world is as science portrays it to be, and that we project our interests onto this neutral world. Heidegger offers a different analysis: our primary understanding of the world is and must be in* accordance with our normal concerns and cares. The world as it is described by theoretical physics, consisting of things present-at-hand, is an abstraction from this world of things ready-to-hand.

B. The second existential is Being-with. The self is inherently part of the world in which other persons live. Heidegger writes, 'The world of Dasein is a with-world. Being-in is being with Others. Their Being-in-Themselves within the world is Dasein-with.' There is no solipsistic or private Cartesian ego. On the contrary, I share the world with other Daseins, who also view objects in the world as ready-to-hand. To be Dasein is to be with other Daseins, who themselves are not pieces of equipment or mere instruments.

C. The third existential consists in moods, which are the way we find ourselves disposed to life a mood is the state in which one finds oneself. By 'mood,' Heidegger does not mean a passing emotional state, but rather a way of being attuned to the world. According to Heidegger, we are always in some mood or other. The idea of moods draws attention to two points about our general condition. First, it emphasizes to our 'thrownness.' Second, it stresses that what we encounter in the world matters to us. Moods constitute Dasein's awareness of his or her actual existence. For example, fear is one way to relate to a given part of the world, and it is one way in which the world becomes significant for us, i.e., as a threat. Fear is possible because my existence involves being concerned about what is.

D. Heidegger contrasts moods with another existential: understanding. Moods are various kinds of awareness of our actual condition. In contrast, our awareness of possible existence constitutes understanding. Understanding enables us to project the possibilities that comprise Dasein. The understanding of possibilities is fundamental to Heidegger's characterization of the human condition in three ways. First, it indicates that we are more than the actual. We are beings with possibilities and a future ahead of us. Second, we are essentially temporal beings, and, therefore, death is an essential feature of the human condition. Third, the potential of Dasein marks the difference between the authentic self and the inauthentic they-self. Heidegger writes, 'One lives inauthentically when one is unaware of the meaning of Being, and one is lost in the anonymous 'they': The 'they' prescribes one's state-of-mind, and determines what and how one sees.' Such a state is marked by an ambiguity in relation to oneself, idle talking or chatter with other people, and casual curiosity in relation to things. All three states display tranquil unconcern, or the passive and detached lack of care. The inauthentic state consists of being aware only of the actual, and not realizing that one's being also consists of possibilities. In particular, inauthenticity is marked by unawareness of one's nonexistence as a possibility. When Dasein is not aware of its own meaning, then it is not conscious of its finitude. It is important to note that the two most general features of the human condition are equally significant for Heidegger. On the one hand, there is actuality, or our being thrown into the world, and on the other hand, there is possibility, or the fact that our existence consists of more than we actually are at any time.

E. The last existential, care, is the most important of them all because it unifies the others, and, thus, it is the meaning of being Dasein in the most fundamental sense. There was a brief description of this in the Philosophical Overview.

INTRODUCTION

Our aim in the following treatise is to work out the question of the meaning of *being* and to do so concretely. Our provisional aim is the interpretation of *time* as the possible horizon for any understanding whatsoever of being.

From *Being and Time* by Martin Heidegger, translated by Joan Stambaugh, 1996.

I
The Necessity, Structure and Priority of the Question of Being

§2. *The Formal Structure of the Question of Being*

The question of the meaning of being must be *formulated*. If it is a—or even *the*—fundamental question, such questioning needs the suitable transparency. Thus we must briefly discuss what belongs to a question in general in order to be able to make clear that the question of being is an *eminent* one. . . .

As a seeking, questioning needs prior guidance from what it seeks. The meaning of being must therefore already be available to us in a certain way. We intimated that we are always already involved in an understanding of being. From this grows the explicit question of the meaning of being and the tendency toward its concept. We do not *know* what "being" means. But already when we ask, "What is being?" we stand in an understanding of the "is" without being able to determine conceptually what the "is" means. We do not even know the horizon upon which we are supposed to grasp and pin down the meaning. *This average and vague understanding of being is a fact.* . . .

What is *asked about* in the question to be elaborated is being, that which determines beings as beings, that in terms of which beings have always been understood no matter how they are discussed. The being of beings "is" itself not a being. . . .

Hence what is to be *ascertained*, the meaning of being, will require its own conceptualization, which again is essentially distinct from the concepts in which beings receive their determination of meaning. . . .

Regarding, understanding and grasping, choosing, and gaining access to, are constitutive attitudes of inquiry and are thus themselves modes of being of a particular being, of *the* being we inquirers ourselves in each case are. Thus to work out the question of being means to make a being—he who questions—transparent in its being. Asking this question, as a mode of *being* of a being, is itself essentially determined by what is asked about in it—being. This being which we ourselves in each case are and which includes inquiry among the possibilities of its being we formulate terminologically as Da-sein. The explicit and lucid formulation of the question of the meaning of being requires a prior suitable explication of being (Da-sein) with regard to its being. . . .

§3. *The Ontological Priority of the Question of Being*

. . . Being is always the being of a being. The totality of beings can, with respect to its various domains, become the field where particular areas of knowledge are exposed and delimited. These areas—for example, history, nature, space, life, human being, language, and so on—can in their turn become thematized as objects of scientific investigations. Scientific research demarcates and first establishes these areas of knowledge in a rough and ready fashion. The elaboration of the area in its fundamental structures is in a way already accomplished by prescientific experience and interpretation of the domain of being to which the area of knowledge is itself confined. . . .

Fundamental concepts are determinations in which the area of knowledge underlying all the thematic objects of a science attain an understanding that precedes and guides all positive investigation. Accordingly these concepts first receive their genuine evidence and "grounding" only in a correspondingly preliminary research into the area of knowledge itself. But since each of these areas arises from the domain of beings themselves, this preliminary research that creates the fundamental concepts amounts to nothing else than interpreting these beings in terms of the basic constitution of their being. This kind of investigation must precede the positive sciences—and it *can* do so. . . .

It is true that ontological inquiry is more original than the ontic inquiry of the positive sciences. But it remains naïve and opaque if its investigations into the being of beings leave the meaning of being in general undiscussed. And precisely the ontological task of a genealogy of the different possible ways of being (a genealogy which is not to be construed deductively) requires

a preliminary understanding of "what we really
11 mean by this expression 'being.'"

The question of being thus aims at an *a priori* condition of the possibility not only of the sciences which investigate beings of such and such a type—and are thereby already involved in an understanding of being; but it aims also at the condition of the possibility of the ontologies which precede the ontic sciences and found them. *All ontology, no matter how rich and tightly knit a system of categories it has at its disposal, remains fundamentally blind and perverts its innermost intent if it has not previously clarified the meaning of being sufficiently and grasped this clarification as its fundamental task.* . . .

4. The Ontic Priority of the Question of Being

Science in general can be defined as the totality of fundamentally coherent true propositions. This definition is not complete, nor does it get at the meaning of science. As ways in which human beings behave, sciences have this being's (the human being's) kind of being. We are defining this being terminologically as Da-sein. Scientific research is neither the sole nor the most immediate kind of being of this being that is possible. . . .

Da-sein is a being that does not simply occur among other beings. Rather it is ontically distinguished by the fact that in its being this being is concerned *about* its every being. Thus it is constitutive of the being of Da-sein to have, in its very
12 being, a relation of being to this being. And this in turn means that Da-sein understands itself in its being in some way and with some explicitness. It is proper to this being that it be disclosed to itself with and through its being. *Understanding of being is itself a determination of being of Da-sein.* The ontic distinction of Da-sein lies in the fact that it *is* ontological. . . .

We shall call the very being to which Da-sein can relate in one way or another, and somehow always does relate, existence [*Existenz*]. . . .

Da-sein always understands itself in terms of its existence, in terms of its possibility to be itself or not to be itself. Da-sein has either chosen these possibilities itself, stumbled upon them, or in each instance already grown up in them. Exis-

tence is decided only by each Da-sein itself in the manner of seizing upon or neglecting such possibilities. We come to terms with the question of existence always only through existence itself. We shall call *this* kind of understanding of itself
13 *existentiell* understanding. . . .

Sciences and disciplines are ways of being of Da-sein in which Da-sein also relates to beings that it need not itself be. But *being in a world* belongs essentially to Da-sein. Thus the understanding of being that belongs to Da-sein just as originally implies the understanding of something like "world" and the understanding of the being of beings accessible within the world. Ontologies which have beings unlike Da-sein as their theme are accordingly founded and motivated in the ontic structure of Da-sein itself. This structure includes in itself the determination of a pre-ontological understanding of being.

Thus *fundamental ontology,* from which alone all other ontologies can originate, must be sought in the *existential analysis of Da-sein.* . . .

If the interpretation of the meaning of being is to be become a task, Da-sein is not only the primary being to be interrogated; in ad-
15 dition to this it is the being that always already in its being is related to *what is sought* in this question. But then the question of being is nothing else than the radicalization of an essential tendency of being that belongs to Da-sein itself, namely, of the pre-ontological understanding of being.

II
The Double Task in Working Out the Question of Being: The Method of Investigation and Its Outline . . .

7. The Phenomenological Method of the Investigation

With the preliminary characterization of the the-
27 matic object of the investigation (the being of beings, or the meaning of being in general) its method would appear to be already prescribed. The task of ontology is to set in relief the being of beings and to explicate being itself. . . .

Since the term "ontology" is used in a formally broad sense for this investigation, the approach of clarifying its method by tracing the history of that method is automatically precluded. . . .

Phenomenology is the way of access to, and ₃₅ the demonstrative manner of determination of, what is to become the theme of ontology. *Ontology is possible only as phenomenology.* The phenomenological concept of phenomenon, as self-showing, means the being of beings—its meaning, modifications, and derivatives. This self-showing is nothing arbitrary, not is it something like an appearing. The being of beings can least of all be ₃₆ something "behind which" something else stands, something that "does not appear."

Essentially, nothing else stands "behind" the phenomena of phenomenology. Nevertheless, what is to become a phenomenon can be concealed. And precisely because phenomena are initially and for the most part *not* given phenomenology is needed. Being covered up is the counterconcept to "phenomenon." . . .

The way of encountering being and the ₃₇ structures of being in the mode of phenomenon must first be *wrested* from the objects of phenomenology. Thus the *point of departure* of the analysis, the *access* to the phenomenon, and *passage through* the prevalent coverings must secure their own method. The idea of an "originary" and "intuitive" grasp and explication of phenomena must be opposed to the naïveté of an accidental, "immediate," and unreflective "beholding."

As far as content goes, phenomenology is the science of the being of beings—ontology. In our elucidation of the tasks of ontology the necessity arose for a fundamental ontology which would have as its theme that being which is ontologically and ontically distinctive, namely, Da-sein. This must be done in such a way that our ontology confronts the cardinal problem, the question of the meaning of being in general. From the investigation itself we shall see that the methodological meaning of phenomenological description is *interpretation*. The *logos* of the phenomenological of Da-sein has the character *hermēneuein*, through which the proper meaning of being and the basic structures of the very being of Da-sein are *made known* to the understanding of being that belongs to Da-sein itself. Phenomenolgy of Da-sein is *hermeneutics* in the original signification of that word, which designates the work of interpretation. . . .

As the fundamental theme of philosophy being is not a genus of beings; yet it pertains to ₃₈ every being. Its "universality" must be sought in a higher sphere. Being and its structure transcend every being and every possible existent determination of a being. *Being is the transcendens pure and simple.* The transcendence of the being of Da-sein is a distinctive one since in it lies the possibility and necessity of the most radical *individuation.* Every disclosure of being as the *transcendens* is *transcendental* knowledge. *Phenomenological truth (disclosedness of being) is veritas transcendentalis.*

Ontology and phenomenology are not two different disciplines which among others belong to philosophy. Both terms characterize philosophy itself, its object and procedure. Philosophy is universal phenomenological ontology, taking its departure from the hermeneutic of Da-sein, which, as an analysis of *existence*, has fastened the end of the guideline of all philosophical inquiry at the point from which it *arises* and to which it *returns.* . . .

8. *The Outline of the Treatise*

The question of the meaning of being is the ₃₉ most universal and the emptiest. But at the same time the possibility inheres of its most acute individualization in each particular Da-sein. If we are to gain the fundamental concept of "being" and the perscription of the ontologically requisite conceptuality in all its necessary variations, we need a concrete guideline. The "special character" of the investigation does not belie the universality of the concept of being. For we may advance to being by way of a special interpretation of a particular being, Da-sein, in which the horizon for an understanding and a possible interpretation of being is to be won. But his being is in itself "historic," so that its most proper ontological illumination necessarily becomes a "historical" interpretation.

The elaboration of the question of being is a two-pronged task; our treatise therefore has two divisions.

Part One: The interpretation of Da-sein on the basis of temporality and the explication of time as the transcendental horizon of the question of being.

Part Two: Basic features of a phenomenological destructuring of the history of ontology on the guideline of the problem of temporality.

The first part consists of three divisions:

1. The preparatory fundamental analysis of Da-sein.
2. Da-sein and temporality.
3. Time and being.

PART ONE

THE INTERPRETATION OF DA-SEIN IN TERMS OF TEMPORALITY AND THE EXPLICATION OF TIME AS THE TRANSCENDENTAL HORIZON OF THE QUESTION OF BEING

Division One
The Preparatory Fundamental Analysis of Da-sein

What is primarily interrogated in the question of
41 the meaning of being is that being which has the character of Da-sein. In keeping with its uniqueness, the preparatory existential analytic of Da-sein itself needs a prefigurative exposition and delimitation from investigations which seem to run parallel (chapter I). Bearing in mind the point of departure of the investigation, we must analyze a fundamental structure of Da-sein: being-in-the-world (chapter II). This *"a priori"* of the interpretation of Da-sein is not a structure which is pieced together, but rather a structure which is primordially and constantly whole. It grants various perspectives on the factors which constitute it. These factors are to be kept constantly in view, bearing in mind the preceding whole of this structure. Thus, we have as the object of our analysis: the world in its worldliness (chapter III), being-in-the-world as being a self and being with others (chapter IV), being-in as such (chapter V). On the foundation of the analysis of this fundamental structure, a preliminary demonstration of the being of Da-sein is possible. Its existential meaning is *Care* (chapter VI). . . .

I
The Exposition of the Task of a Preparatory Analysis of Da-sein

9. *The Theme of the Analytic of Da-sein*

The being whose analysis our task is, is always we ourselves. The being of this being is always *mine.* In the being of this being it is related to its being. As the being of this being, it is entrusted to its
42 own being. It is being about which this being is concerned. From this characteristic of Da-sein two things follow:

1. The "essence" of this being lies in its to be. The whatness (*essentia*) of this being must be understood in terms of its being (*existentia*) insofar as one can speak of it at all. Here the ontological task is precisely to show that when we choose the word existence for the being of this being, this term does not and cannot have the ontological meaning of the traditional expression of *existentia.* Ontologically, *existentia* means *objective presence* [*Vorhandenheit*], a kind of being which is essentially inappropriate to characterize the being which has the character of Da-sein. We can avoid confusion by always using the interpretive expression *objective presence* [*Vorhandenheit*] for the term *existentia,* and by attributing existence as a determination of being only to Da-sein.

The "essence" of Da-sein lies in its existence. The characteristics to be found in this being are thus not objectively present "attributes" of an objectively present being which has such and such an "outward appearance," but rather possible ways for it to be, and only this. The thatness of this being is primarily being. Thus the term "Da-sein" which we use to designate this being does not express its what, as in the case of table, house, tree, but being.

2. The being which this being is concerned about in its being is always my own. Thus, Da-sein is never to be understood ontologically as a case and instance of a genus of beings as objectively present. To something objectively present its being is a matter of "indifference," more precisely, it "is" in such a way that its being can neither be indifferent nor non-indifferent to it. In accordance with the character of *always-being-my-own-being* [*Jemeinigkeit*], when we speak of

Da-sein, we must always use the *personal* pronoun along with whatever we say: "I am," "You are."

Da-sein is my own, to be always in this or that way. It has somehow always already decided in which way Da-sein is always my own. The being which is concerned in its being about its being is related to its being as its truest possibility. Da-sein *is* always its possibility. It does not "have" that possibility only as a mere attribute of something objectively present. And because Da-sein is always essentially its possibility, it *can* "choose" itself in its being, it can win itself, it can lose itself, or it can never and only "apparently" win itself. It can only have lost itself and it can only have not yet gained itself because it is essentially possible as authentic, that is, it belongs to itself. The two kinds of being of *authenticity* and *inauthenticity*—these expressions are terminologically chosen in the strictest sense of the word— are based on the fact that Da-sein is in general determined by always being-mine. But the inauthenticity of Da-sein does not signify a "lesser" being or a "lower" degree of being. Rather, inauthenticity can determine Da-sein even in its fullest concretion, when it is busy, excited, interested, and capable of pleasure.

The two characteristics of Da-sein sketched out—on the one hand, the priority of "*existentia*" over *essentia*, and then, always-being-mine— already show that an analytic of this being is confronted with a unique phenomenal region. This being does not and never has the kind of being of what is merely objectively present within the world. . . .

As a being, Da-sein always define itself in terms of a possibility which it *is* and somehow understands in its being. That is the formal meaning of the constitution of the existence of Da-sein. But for the *ontological* interpretation of this being, this means that the problematic of its being is to be developed out of the existentiality of its existence. However, this cannot mean that Da-sein is to be construed in terms of a concrete possible idea of existence. At the beginning of the analysis, Da-sein is precisely not to be interpreted in the differentiation of a particular existence; rather, to be uncovered in the indifferent way in which it is initially and for the most part. . . .

But the average everydayness of Da-sein must not be understood as a mere "aspect." In it, too, and even in the mode of inauthenticity, the structure of existentiality lies *a priori*. In it, too, Da-sein is concerned with a particular mode of its being to which it is related in the way of average everydayness, if only in the way of fleeing *from* it and of forgetting *it*. . . .

All explications arising from an analytic of Da-sein are gained with a view toward its structure of existence. Because these explications are defined in terms of existentiality, we shall call the characteristics of being of Da-sein *existentials*. They are to be sharply delimited from the determinations of being of those beings unlike Da-sein which we call *categories*. This expression is taken and retained in its primary ontological signification. . . .

Existentials and categories are the two fundamental possibilities of the characteristics of being. The being which corresponds to them requires different ways of primary interrogation. Beings are a *who* (existence) or else a *what* (objective presence in the broadest sense). It is only in terms of the clarified horizon of the question of being that we can treat the connection between the two modes of characteristics of being.

We intimated in the introduction that a task is furthered in the existential analytic of Da-sein, a task whose urgency is hardly less than that of the question of being itself: the exposition of *the a priori* which must be visible if the question "What is human being?" is to be discussed philosophically. The existential analytic of Da-sein is *prior* to any psychology, anthropology, and especially biology. By being delimited from these possible investigations of Da-sein, the theme of the analytic can become still more sharply defined. Its necessity can thus at the same time be demonstrated more incisively.

10. *How the Analytic of Da-sein is to be Distinguished from Anthropology, Psychology, and Biology*

After a theme for investigation has been initially outlined in positive terms, it is always important to show what is to be ruled out, although it can easily become unfruitful to discuss what is not going to happen. We must show that all previous questions and investigations which aim at Da-sein fail to see the real *philosophical* problem, regardless of their factual productivity. Thus, as long as they persist in this attitude, they may not claim to *be able* to accomplish what they are fundamentally striving for at all. In distinguishing existential analytic from anthropology, psychology, and biology, we shall confine ourselves to what is in principle the fundamental ontological question. Thus, our distinctions will be necessity inadequate for a "theory of science" simply because the scientific structure of the above-mentioned disciplines (not the "scientific attitude" of those who are working to further them) has today become completely questionable and needs new impulses which must arise from the ontological problematic. . . .

47 We choose Scheler's interpretation as an example, not only because it is accessible in print, but because he explicitly emphasizes the being of the person as such, and attempts to define it by defining the specific being of acts as opposed to everything "psychical." According to Scheler, the person can never be thought as a thing or a substance. Rather it is "the immediately co-experienced *unity* of ex-periencing—not just a thing merely thought behind and outside of what is immediately experienced." The person is not a thinglike substantial being. Furthermore, the being of the person cannot consist in being a subject of rational acts that have a certain lawfulness.

48 The person is not a thing, not a substance, not an object. Here Scheler emphasizes the same thing which Husserl is getting at when he requires for the unity of the person a constitution essentially different from that of things of nature. What Scheler says of the person, he applies to acts as well. "An act is never also an object, for it is the nature of the being of acts only to be experienced in the process itself and given in reflection." Acts are nonpsychical. Essentially the person exists only in carrying out intentional acts, and is thus essentially *not* an object. Every psychical objectification, and thus every comprehension of acts as something psychical, is identical with depersonalization. In any case, the person is given as the agent of intentional acts which are connected by the unity of a meaning.

Thus psychical being has nothing to do with being a person. Acts are carried out, the person carries them out. But what is the ontological meaning of "carrying out," how is the kind of being of the person to be defined in an ontologically positive way? But the critical question cannot stop at this. The question is about the being of the whole human being, whom one is accustomed to understand as a bodily-soul-like-spiritual unity. . . .

But in the question of the being of human being, this cannot be summarily calculated in terms of the kinds of being of body, soul, and spirit which have yet first to be defined. And even for an ontological attempt which is to proceed in this way, some idea of the being of the whole would have to be presupposed. . . .

On the other hand, Da-sein should never be defined ontologically by regarding it as life—(ontologically undetermined) and then as something else on top of that.

In suggesting that anthropology, psychology, and biology all fail to give an unequivocal and ontologically adequate answer to the question of the *kind of being* of this being that we ourselves are, no judgment is being made about the positive work of these disciplines. But, on the other hand, we must continually be conscious of the fact that these ontological foundations can never be disclosed by subsequent hypotheses derived from empirical material. Rather, they are always already "there" even when that empirical material is only *collected*. The fact that positivistic investigation does not see these foundations and considers them to be self-evident is no proof of the fact that they do not lie at the basis and are problematic in a more radical sense than any thesis of positivistic science can ever be. . . .

II
Being-in-the-World in General as the Fundamental Constitution of Da-sein

12. A Preliminary Sketch of Being-in-the-World in Terms of the Orientation toward Being-in as Such

In the preparatory discussions (section 9) we already profiled characteristics of being which are to provide us with a steady light for our further investigation, but which at the same time receive their structural concretion in this investigation. Da-sein is a being which is related understandingly in its being toward that being. In saying this we are calling attention to the formal concept of existence. Da-sein exists. Furthermore, Da-sein is the being which I myself always am. Mineness belongs to existing Da-sein as the condition of the possibility of authenticity and inauthenticity. Da-sein exists always in one of these modes, or else in the modal indifference to them.

These determinations of being of Da-sein, however, must now be seen and understood *a priori* as grounded upon that constitution of being which we call *being-in-the-world*. The correct point of departure of the analytic of Da-sein consists in the interpretation of this constitution.

The compound expression "being-in-the-world" indicates, in the very way we have coined it, that it stands for a *unified* phenomenon. This primary datum must be seen as a whole. But while being-in-the-world cannot be broken up into components that may be pieced together, this does not prevent it from having several constitutive structural factors. The phenomenal fact indicated by this expression actually gives as a threefold perspective. If we pursue it while keeping the whole phenomenon in mind from the outset we have the following:

1. *"In-the-world"*: In relation to this factor, we have the task of questioning the ontological structure of "world" and of defining the idea of *worldliness* as such (cf. chapter 3 of this division).

2. The *being* which always is in the way of being-in-the-world. In it we are looking for what we are questioning when we ask about the "who?". In our phenomenological demonstration we should be able to determine who is in the mode of average everydayness of Da-sein (cf. chapter 4 of this division).

3. *Being in* as such: The ontological constitution of in-ness itself is to be analyzed (cf. chapter 5 of this division). Any analysis of one of these constitutive factors involves the analysis of the others; that is, each time seeing the whole phenomenon. It is true that being-in-the-world is an *a priori* necessary constitu-

tion of Da-sein, but it is not at all sufficient to fully determine Da-sein's being. Before we thematically analyze the three phenomena indicated individually, we shall attempt to orient ourselves toward a characteristic of the third of these constitutive factors. . . .

In contrast, being-in designates a constitution of being of Dasein, and is an *existential*. But we cannot understand by this the objective presence of a material thing (the human body) "in" a being objectively present. Nor does the term being-in designate a spatial "in one another" of two things objectively present, any more than the world "in" primordially means a spatial relation of this kind. "In" stems from *innan-*, to live, *habitare*, to dwell. "An" means I am used to, familiar with, I take care of something. . . .

As an existential, "being with" the world never means anything like the being-objectively-present-together of things that occur. There is no such thing as the "being next to each other" of a being called "Da-sein" with another being called "world." It is true that, at times, we are accustomed to express linguistically the being together of two objectively present things in such a manner: "The table stands 'next to' the door," "The chair 'touches' the wall." Strictly speaking, we can never talk about "touching," not because in the last analysis we can always find a space between the chair and the wall by examining it more closely, but because in principle the chair can never touch the wall, even if the space between them amounted to nothing. The presupposition for this would be that the wall could be *encountered* "by" the chair. A being can only touch an objectively present being within the world if it fundamentally has the kind of being of being-in—only if with its Da-sein something like world is already discovered in terms of which beings can reveal themselves through touch and thus become accessible in their objective presence. Two beings which are objectively present within the world and are, moreover, *worldless* in themselves, can never "touch" each other, neither can *"be" "together with"* the other. . . .

Da-sein understands its ownmost being in the sense of a certain "factual objective presence."

56 And yet the "factuality" of the fact of one's own Da-sein is ontologically totally different from the factual occurrence of a kind of stone. The factuality of the fact Da-sein, as the way in which every Da-sein actually is, we call its *facticity*. The complicated structure of this determination of being it itself comprehensible *as a problem* only in the light of the existential fundamental constitutions of Da-sein which we have already worked out. The concept of facticity implies that an "innerworldly" being has being-in-the-world in such a way that it can understand itself as bond up in its "destiny" with the being of those beings which it encounters within its own world.

Initially it is only a matter of seeing the ontological distinction between being-in as an existential and the category of the "insideness" that things objectively present can have with regard to one another. If we define being-in in this way, we are not denying to Da-sein every kind of "spatiality." On the contrary. Da-sein itself has its own "being-in-space," which in its turn is possible only on *the basis of being-in-the-world in general*. . . .

With its facticity, the being-in-the-world of Da-sein is already dispersed in definite ways of being-in, perhaps even split up. The multiplicity of these kinds of being-in can be indicated by the following examples: to have to do with 57 something, to produce, order and take care of something, to use something, to give something up and let it get lost, to undertake, to accomplish, to find out, to ask about, to observe, to speak about, to determine. . . . These ways of being-in have the kind of being of *taking care of* which we shall characterize in greater detail. The *deficient* modes of omitting, neglecting, renouncing, resting, are also ways of taking care of something, in which the possibilities of taking care are kept to a "bare minimum." The term "taking care" has initially its prescientific meaning and can imply: carrying something out, settling something, "to straighten it out." The expression could also mean to take care of something in the sense of "getting it for oneself." Furthermore, we use the expression also in a characteristic turn of phrase: I will see to it or

take care that the enterprise fails. Here "to take care" amounts to apprehensiveness. In contrast to these prescientific ontic meanings, the expression "taking care" is used in this inquiry as an ontological term (an existential) to designate the being of a possible being-in-the-world. We do not choose this term because Da-sein is initially economical and "practical" to a large extent, but because the being of Da-sein itself is to be made visible as *care*. Again, this expression is to be understood as an ontological structure concept (compare chapter 6 of this division). The expression has nothing to do with "distress," "melancholy," or "the cares of life" which can be found ontically in every Da-sein. These—like their opposites, "carefreeness" and "gaiety"—are ontically possible only because Dasein, *ontologically* understood, is care. Because being-in-the-world belongs essentially to Da-sein, its being toward the world is essentially taking care. . . .

Both in Da-sein and for it, this constitution of being is always already somehow familiar. If it 59 is now to be recognized, the explicit *cognition* that this task implies takes *itself* (as a knowing of the world) as the exemplary relation of the "soul" to the world. The cognition of world (*noein*)—or addressing oneself to the "world" and discussing it (*logos*)—thus functions as the primary mode of being-in-the-world even though being-in-the world is not understood as such. But because this structure of being remains ontologically inaccessible, yet is ontically experienced as the "relation" between one being (world) and another (soul), and because being is initially understood by taking being as innerworldly beings for one's ontological support, one tries to conceive the relation between world and soul as grounded in these two beings and in the sense of their being; that is, as objective presence. Although it is experienced and known prephenomenologially, being-in-the-world is *invisible* if one interprets it in a way that is ontologically inadequate. One is just barely acquainted with this constitution of Da-sein only in the form given by an inadequate interpretation—and indeed, as something obvious. In this way it then becomes the "evident" point of departure for the problems of epistemology or a "metaphysics of knowledge." For what is more obvious than the fact that a "subject" is related to an "object" and the other way around? This "subject-object-relation" must be presupposed. But that is a presupposition which, although it is inviolate in its own facticity, is truly fatal, perhaps for that very reason, if its ontological necessity and especially its ontological meaning are left in obscurity.

Thus the phenomenon of being-in has for the most part been represented exclusively by a single examplar—knowing the world. This has not only been the case in epistemology; for even practical behavior has been understood as behavior which is *not* theoretical and "atheoretical." Because knowing has been given this priority, our understanding of its ownmost kind of being is led astray, and thus being-in-the-world must be delineated more precisely with reference to knowing the world, and must itself be made visible as an existential "modality" of being in. . . .

III
The Worldliness of the World

A. ANALYSIS OF ENVIRONMENTALITY AND WORLDLINESS IN GENERAL

67 *15. The Being of Beings Encountered in the Surrounding World*

The phenomenological exhibition of the being of beings encountered nearest to us can be accomplished under the guidance of the everyday being-in-the-world, which we also call *association in* the world *with* innerworldly beings. Associations are already dispersed in manifold ways of taking care of things. However, as we showed, the nearest kind of association is not mere perceptual cognition, but, rather, a handling, using, and taking care of things which has its own kind of "knowledge." . . .

This being is not the object of a theoretical "world"-cognition; it is what is used, produced, and so on. As a being thus encountered, it comes pre-thematically into view for a "knowing" which, as a phenomenological knowing, primarily looks toward being and on the basis of this thematization of being thematizes actual beings as well. . . .

Everyday Da-sein always already *is* in this way; for example, in opening the door, I use the doorknob. Gaining phenomenological access to the beings thus encountered consists rather in rejecting the interpretational tendencies crowding and accompanying us which cover over the phenomenon of "taking care" of things in general, 68 and thus even more so beings *as* they are encountered of their own accord *in* taking care. These insidious mistakes become clear when we ask: Which beings are to be our preliminary theme and established as a pre-phenomenal basis?

We answer: things. But perhaps we have already missed the pre-phenomenal basis we are looking for with this self-evident answer. For an unexpressed anticipatory ontological characterization is contained in addressing beings as "things" (*res*). An analysis which starts with such beings and goes on to inquire about being comes up with thingliness and reality. Ontological explication thus finds, as it proceeds, characteristics of being such as substantiality, materiality, extendedness, side-by-sideness. . . .

What we encounter as nearest to us, although we do not grasp it thematically, is the room, not as what is "between the four walls" in a 69 geometrical, spatial sense, but rather as material for living. On the basis of the latter we find "accomodations," and in accommodations the actual "individual" useful thing. A totality of useful things is always already discovered *before* the individual useful things. . . .

We shall call the useful thing's kind of being in which it reveals itself by itself *handiness*. It is only because useful things have *this* "being-in-themselves," and do not merely occur, that they are handy in the broadest sense and are at our disposal. . . .

Our association with useful things is subordinate to the manifold of references of the "in-order-to." . . .

As the *what-for* of the hammer, plane, and needle, the work to be produced has in its turn the kind of being of a useful thing. The shoe to 70 be produced is for wearing (footgear), the clock is made for telling time. . . .

71 The work produced refers not only to the what-for of its usability and the whereof of which it consists. The simple conditions of craft contain a reference to the wearer and user at the same time. . . .

Thus not only beings which are at hand are encountered in the work but also beings with the kind of being of Da-sein for whom what is produced becomes handy in its taking care. Here the world is encountered in which wearers and users live, a world which is at the same time our world. The work taken care of in each case is not only at hand in the domestic world of the workshop, but rather in the *public world*. . . .

The kind of being of these beings is "handiness." But it must not be understood as a mere characteristic of interpretation, as if such "aspects" were discursively forced upon "beings" which we initially encounter, as if an initially objectively present world-stuff were "subjectively colored" in this way. Such an interpretation overlooks the fact that in that case beings would have to be understood before-hand and discovered as purely objectively present, and would thus have priority and take the lead in the order of discovering and appropriating association with the "world." . . .

16. The Worldly Character of the Surrounding World Making Itself Known in Innerworldly Beings

. . . Modes of taking care belong to the everydayness of being-in-the-world, modes which let the beings taken care of be encountered in such a way that the worldly quality of innerworldly beings 73 appears. Beings nearest at hand can be met up with in taking care of things as unusable, as improperly adapted for their specific use. Tools turn out to be damaged, their material unsuitable. . . .

In associating with the world taken care of, what is unhandy can be encountered not only in the sense of something unusable or completely missing, but as something unhandy which is *not* missing at all and *not* unusable, but "gets in the way" of taking care of things. . . .

The modes of conspicuousness, obtrusive- 74 ness, and obstinacy have the function of bringing to the fore the character of objective presence in what is at hand. . . .

These still do not disguise themselves as mere things. Useful things become "things" in the sense of what one would like to throw away. But in this tendency to throw things away, what is at hand is still shown as being at hand in its unyielding objective presence. . . .

Handiness shows itself once again, and precisely in doing so the worldly character of what is at hand also shows itself, too. . . .

76 The foregoing analysis already makes it clear that the being-in-itself of innerworldly beings is ontologically comprehensible only on the basis of the phenomenon of world. . . .

Thus, it is something "in which" Da-sein as a being always already *was*, that to which it can always only come back whenever it explicitly moves toward something in some way.

According to our foregoing interpretation, being-in-the-world signifies the unthematic, circumspect absorption in the references constitutive for the handiness of the totality of useful things.

IV
Being-in-the-World as Being-with and Being a Self: The "They"

The analysis of the worldliness of the world continually brought the whole phenomenon of being-in-the-world into view without thereby delimiting all of its constitutive factors with the same phenomenal clarity as the phenomenon of world itself. The ontological interpretation of the world which discussed innerworldly things at hand came 114 first not only because Da-sein in its everydayness is in a world in general and remains a constant theme with regard to that world, but because it relates itself to the world in a predominant mode of being. Initially and for the most part, Da-sein is taken in by its world. This mode of being, being absorbed in the world, and thus being-in-which underlies it, essentially determine the phenomenon which we shall now pursue with the question: *Who* is it who is in the everydayness of Da-sein? All of the structures of being of Da-sein, thus also the phenomenon that answers to this question of who, are modes of its being. Their ontological characteristic is an existential one. . . .

By investigating in the direction of the phenomenon which allows us to answer the question of the who, we are led to structures of Da-sein which are equiprimordial with being-in-the-world: being-with and *Mitda-sein*. In this kind of being, the mode of everyday being a self is grounded whose explication makes visible what we might call the "subject" of everydayness, the *they*. This chapter on the "who" of average Da-sein thus has the following structure:

1. The approach to the existential question of the who of Da-sein (section 25).
2. The *Mitda-sein* of the others and everyday being-with (section 26). (3) Everyday being a self and the they (section 27).

25. The Approach to the Existential Question of the Who of Da-sein.

Da-sein is a being which I myself am, its being is in each case mine. . . . Ontologically, we understand it as what is always already and constantly objectively present in a closed region and for that region, as that which lies at its basis in an eminent sense, as the *subjectum*. As something self-same in manifold otherness, this subject has the character of the *self*. Even if one rejects a substantial soul, the thingliness of consciousness and the objectiv-
115 ity of the person, ontologically one still posits something whose being retains the meaning of objective presence, whether explicitly or not. Substantiality is the ontological clue for the determination of beings in terms of whom the question of the who is answered. Da-sein is tacitly conceived in advance as objective presence. In any case, the indeterminacy of its being always implies this meaning of being. However, objective presence is the mode of being of beings unlike Da-sein.

But, then, is the existential analytical an-
117 swer to the question of the who without any clues at all? By no means. . . .

If the "I" is an essential determination of Da-sein, it must be interpreted existentially. The question of the who can then be answered only by a phenomenal demonstration of a definite kind of being of Da-sein.

26. The Mitda-sein of the Others and Everyday Being-with

The answer to the question of the who of everyday Da-sein is to be won through the analysis of *the kind of being in which Da-sein, initially and*

for the most part, lives. Our investigation takes its orientation from being-in-the-world'

The "description" of the surrounding world nearest to us, for example, the work-world of the handworker, showed that together with the useful things found in work, others are "also encountered" for whom the "work" is to be done. . . . The world of Da-sein thus frees beings which are not only completely different form tools and things, but which themselves in accordance with their kind of being as *Da-sein* are themselves "in" the world as being-in-the-world in which they are at the same time encountered. These beings are neither ob-
118 jectively present nor at hand, but they *are like* the very Da-sein which frees them—*they are there, too, and there with it.* So, if one wanted to identify the world in general with innerworldly beings, one would have to say the "world" is also Da-sein.

But the characteristic of encountering the *others* is, after all, oriented toward one's *own* Da-sein.

"The others" does not mean everybody else but me—those from whom the I distinguishes itself. They are, rather, those from whom one mostly does *not* distinguish oneself, those among whom one is, too. This being-there-too with them does not have the ontological character of being objectively present "with" them within a world.

The world of Da-sein is a *with-world*. Being-in is *being-with* others. The innerworldly being-in-itself of others is *Mitda-sein*.

Da-sein understands itself, initially and for the most part, in terms of its world, and the *Mitda-sein* of others is frequently encountered from innerwoldly things at hand. But when the others become, so to speak, thematic in their Da-sein, they are not encountered as objectively present thing-persons, but we meet them "at work," that is, primarily in their being-in-the-world. Even when we see the other "just standing
120 around," he is never understood as a human-thing objectively present. "Standing around" is an existential mode of being, the lingering with everything and nothing which lacks heedfulness and circumspection. The other is encountered in his *Mitda-sein* in the world.

Being-with existentially determines Da-sein even when an other is not factically present and perceived. The being-along of Da-sein, too, is being-with in the world. The other can be *lacking* only *in* and *for* a being-with. Being-along is a deficient mode of being-with, its possibility is a proof for the latter. On the other hand, factical being alone is not changed by the fact that a second copy of a human being is "next to" me, or perhaps ten human beings. Even when these and still more are objectively present, Da-sein can be alone.

If *Mitda-sein* remains existentially constitutive for being-in-the-world, it must be interpreted, as must also circumspect association with the innerworldly things at hand which we characterized by way of anticipation as taking care of

121 things, in terms of the phenomenon of *care* which we used to designate the being of Da-sein in general. (Cf. chapter 6 of this division.) Taking care of things is a character of being which being-with cannot have as its own, although this kind of being is a *being toward* beings encountered in the world, as is taking care of things. The being to which Da-sein is related as being-with does not, however, have the kind of being of useful things at hand; it is itself Da-sein. This being is not taken care of, but is a matter of *concern*.

Being toward others is not only an autonomous irreducible relation of being, as being-with it already exists with the being of Da-sein.

125 Of course, it is indisputable that a lively mutual acquaintanceship on the basis of being-with often depends on how far one's own Da-sein has actually understood itself, but this means that it depends only upon how far one's essential being with others has made it transparent and not disguised itself. This is possible only if Da-sein as being-in-the world is always already with others. "Empathy" does not first constitute being-with, but is first possible on its basis, and is motivated by the prevailing modes of being-with in their inevitability.

27. *Everyday Being One's Self and the They*

The *ontologically* relevant result of the foregoing analysis of being-with is the insight that the "subject character" of one's own Da-sein and of the others is to be defined existentially, that is, in

126 terms of certain ways to be. In what is taken care of in the surrounding world, the others are encountered as what they are; they *are* what they do.

In taking care of the things which one has taken hold of, for, and against others, there is constant care as to the way one differs from them, . . .

Existentially expressed, being-with-one-another has the character of *distantiality*. The more inconspicuous this kind of being is to everyday Da-sein itself, all the more stubbornly and primordially does it work itself out.

But this distantiality which belongs to being-with is such that, as everyday being-with-one-another, Da-sein stands in *subservience* to the others. It itself *is* not; the others have taken its being away from it. The everyday possibilities of being of Da-sein are at the disposal of the whims of the others. These others are not *definite* others.

One belongs to the others oneself, and entrenches their power. "The others," whom one designates as such in order to cover over one's own essential belonging to them, are those who *are there* initially and for the most part in everyday being-with-one-another. The who is not this one and not that one, not oneself and not some and not the sum of them all. The "who" is the neuter, *the they*.

127 This being-with-one-another dissolves one's own Da-sein completely into the kind of being of "the others" in such a way that the others, as distinguishable and explicit, disappear more and more. In this inconspicuousness and unascertainability, the they unfolds its true dictatorship. We enjoy ourselves and have fun the way *they* enjoy themselves. We read, see, and judge literature and art the way *they* see and judge. But we also withdraw from the "great mass" the way *they* withdraw, we find "shocking" what *they* find shocking. The they, which is nothing definite and which all are, though not as a sum, prescribes the kind of being of everydayness.

The they has its own ways to be. The tendency of being-with which we called distantiality is based on the fact that being-with-one-another as such creates *averageness*. It is an existential character of the they. In its being, the they is essentially concerned with averageness. Thus, the they maintains itself factically in the averageness of what is proper, what is allowed, and what is not. Of what is granted success and what is not. This averageness, which prescribes what can and may be ventured, watches over every exception which thrusts itself to the fore. The care of averageness reveals, in turn, an essential tendency of Da-sein, which we call the *levelling down* of all possibilities of being.

Distantiality, averageness, and levelling down, as ways of being of the they, constitute what we know as "publicness."

In these characteristics of being which we have discussed—everyday being-among-one-another, distantiality, averageness, levelling down, publicness, disburdening of one's being, and accommodation—lies the initial "constancy" of 128 Da-sein. This constancy pertains not to the enduring objective presence of something, but to the kind of being of Da-sein as being-with. Existing in the modes we have mentioned, the self of one's own Da-sein and the self of the other have neither found nor lost themselves. One is in the manner of dependency and inauthenticity.

The they is an existential and belongs as a pri- 129 *mordial phenomenon to the positive constitution of Da-sein.*

The self of everyday Da-sein is the *they-self* which we distinguish from the *authentic self,* the self which has explicitly grasped itself. As the they-self, Da-sein is *dispersed* in the they and must first find itself. This dispersion characterizes the "subject" of the kind of being which we know as heedful absorption in the world nearest encountered. If *Da-sein* is familiar with itself as the they-self, this also means that the they prescribes the nearest interpretation of the world and of being-in-the-world. . . .

If Da-sein explicitly discovers the world and brings it near, if it discloses its authentic being to itself, this discovering of "world" and disclosing of Da-sein always comes about by clearing away coverings and obscurities, by breaking up the disguises with which Da-sein cuts itself off from itself.

V

Being-in as Such

28. The Task of a Thematic Analysis of Being-in

In the preparatory stage of the existential analytic of Da-sein we have for our leading theme this being's basic constitution, being-in-the-world. Our first aim is to bring into relief phe-131 nomenally the unitary primordial structure of the being of Da-sein by which its possibilities and ways "to be" are ontologically determined. Until now, the phenomenal characterization of being-in-the-world has been directed toward the structural moment of the world and has attempted to provide an answer to the question of the who of this being in its everydayness. But in first sketching out the tasks of a preparatory fundamental analysis of Da-sein we already provided an orientation to *being-in as such* and demonstrated it by the concrete mode of knowing the world.

Now, keeping in mind what has been achieved in the concrete analysis of world and who, we must turn our interpretation back to the phenomenon of being-in. By considering this more penetratingly, however, we shall not only get a new and more certain phenomenological view of the structural totality of being-in-the-world, but shall also pave the way to grasping the primordial being of Da-sein itself, care.

This chapter, which undertakes the explication of being-in as such, that is, of the being of the there, has two parts: (A) The existential constitution of the there. (B) The everyday being of 133 the there and the entanglement of Da-sein.

We see the two equiprimordially constitutive ways to be the there in *attunement* and *understanding.* For their analysis the necessary phenomenal confirmation can be gained by an interpretation of a concrete mode which is important for the following problematic. Attunement and understanding are equiprimordially determined by *discourse.*

Under part A (the existential constitution of the there) we shall treat Da-sein as attunement (section 29), fear as a mode of attunement (section 30), Da-sein as understanding (section 31), understanding and interpretation (section 32), statement as a derivative mode of interpretation (section 33), Da-sein, discourse, and language (section 34).

The analysis of the characteristics of the being of Da-sein is an existential one. This means that the characteristics are not properties of something objectively present, but essentially existential ways to be. Thus, their kind of being in everydayness must be brought out.

Under part B (the everyday being of the there and the entanglement of Da-sein), we shall analyze idle talk (section 35), curiosity (section 36), and ambiguity (section 37) as existential 134 modes of the everyday being of the there: we shall analyze them as corresponding to the constitutive phenomenon of discourse, the vision which lies in understanding, and the interpretation (meaning) belonging to that understanding. In these phenomena a fundamental kind of the being of the there becomes visible which we interpret as *entanglement*. This "entangling" shows a way of being moved which is existentially its own (section 38).

A. THE EXISTENTIAL CONSTITUTION OF THE THERE

29. *Da-sein as Attunement*

What we indicate *ontologically* with the term *attunement* is *ontically* what is most familiar and an everyday kind of thing: mood, being in a mood. Prior to all psychology of moods, a field which, moreover, still lies fallow, we must see this phenomenon as a fundamental existential and outline its structure. . . .

Mood makes manifest "how one is and is coming along." In this "how one is" being in a mood brings being to its "there."

That a Da-sein factically can, should, and must master its mood with knowledge and will may signify a priority of willing and cognition in certain possibilities of existing. But that must not 136 mislead us into ontologically denying mood as a primordial kind of being of Da-sein in which it is disclosed to itself *before* all cognition and willing and *beyond* their scope of disclosure. Moreover, we never master a mood by being free of a mood,

but always through a counter mood. The *first* essential ontological characteristic of attunement is: *Attunement discloses Da-sein in its thrownness, initially and for the most part in the mode of an evasive turning away.* . . .

Mood assails. It comes neither from "without" nor from "within" but rises from being-in-137 the-world itself as a mode of that being. But thus by negatively contrasting attunement with the reflective apprehension of the "inner," we arrive at a positive insight into its character of disclosure. *Mood has always already disclosed being-in-the-world as a whole and first makes possible directing oneself toward something.* . . .

It is a fundamental existential mode of being of the *equiprimordial disclosedness* of world, being-there-with, and existence because this disclosure itself is essentially being-in-the world.

Besides these two essential determinations of attunement just explicated, the disclosure of thrownness and the actual disclosure of the whole of being-in-the-world, we must notice a *third* which above all contributes to a more penetrating understanding of the worldliness of the world.

In attunement lies existentially a disclosive submission to world out of which things that matter to us can be encountered. Indeed, we must *ontologically* in principle leave the primary discovery of the world to "mere mood." Pure beholding, even if it penetrated into the innermost core of the being of something objectively present, would never be able to discover anything like what is threatening.

Attunement discloses Da-sein not only in its thrownness and dependence on the world already disclosed with its being, it is itself the existential kind of being in which it is continually surrendered to the "world" and lets itself be 139 concerned by it in such a way that it somehow evades its very self. The existential constitution of this evasion becomes clear in the phenomenon of entanglement.

Attunement is an existential, fundamental way in which Da-sein is its there. It not only characterizes Da-sein ontologically, but is at the same time of fundamental methodical significance for the existential analytic because of its disclosure. . . .

31. Da-sein as Understanding

Attunement is *one* of the existential structures in 143 which the being of the "there" dwells. Equiprimordially with it, *understanding* constitutes this being. Attunement always has its understanding, even if only by suppressing it. Understanding is always attuned. If we interpret understanding as a fundamental existential, we see that this phenomenon is conceived as a fundamental mode of the *being* of Da-sein. . . .

In understanding as an existential, the thing we are able to do is not a what, but being as existing. The mode of being of Da-sein as a potentiality of being lies existentially in understanding. Da-sein is not something objectively present which then has as an addition the ability to do something, but is rather primarily being-possible. Da-sein is always what it can be and how it is its possibility. The essential possibility of Da-sein concerns the ways of taking care of the "world" which we characterized, of concern for others and, always already present in all of this, the potentiality of being itself, for its own sake.

As an existential, possibility does not refer to a free-floating potentiality of being in the sense of the "liberty of indifference" (*libertas indifferentiae*). As essentially attuned, Da-sein has always already got itself into definite possibilities. As a potentiality for being which it *is*, it has let some go by; it constantly adopts the possi-
144 bilities of its being, grasps them, and goes astray. But this means that Da-sein is a being-possible entrusted to itself, *thrown possibility* throughout. Da-sein is the possibility of being free *for* its ownmost potentiality of being. Being-possible is transparent for it in various possible ways and degrees.

Understanding is the existential being of the ownmost potentiality of being of Da-sein in such a way that this being discloses in itself what its very being is about. The structure of this existential must be grasped more precisely.

Why does understanding always penetrate into possibilities according to all the essential dimensions of what can be disclosed to it? Because understanding in itself has the existential structure which we call *project*. It projects the being of Da-sein upon its for-the-sake-of-which just as primordially as upon significance as the 145 worldliness of its actual world. The project character of understanding constitutes being-in-the-world with regard to the disclosedness of its there as the there of a potentiality of being. Project is the existential constitution of being in the realm of factical potentiality of being. And, as thrown, Da-sein is thrown into the mode of being of projecting. Projecting has nothing to do with being related to a plan thought out, according to which Da-sein arranges its being, but, as Da-sein, it has always already projected itself and is, as long as it is, projecting. As long as it is, Da-sein always has understood itself and will understand itself in terms of possibilities.

Because of the kind of being which is constituted by the existential of projecting, Da-sein is constantly "more" than it actually is, if one wanted to and if one could register it as something objectively present in its content of being. But it is nevermore than it factically is because its potentiality of being belongs essentially to its facticity. But, as being-possible, Da-sein is also never less. It is existentially that which it is *not yet* in its potentiality of being.

As existentials, attunement and understanding characterize the primordial disclosedness of 148 being-in-the-world. In the mode of "being attuned" Da-sein "sees" possibilities in terms of which it is. In the projective disclosure of such possibilities, it is always already attuned. The project of its ownmost potentiality of being is delivered over to the fact of thrownness into the there.

32. Understanding and Interpretation

As understanding, Da-sein projects its being upon possibilities. This *being toward possibilities* that understands is itself a potentiality for being because of the way these disclosed possibilities come back to Da-sein. The project of understanding has its own possibility of development. We shall call the development of understanding *interpretation*. In interpretation understanding appropriates what it has understood in an understanding way.

In terms of the significance of what is disclosed in understanding the world, the being of taking care of what is at hand learns to understand what the relevance can be with what is actually encountered. Circumspection discovers, that is, the world which has already been understood is interpreted. What is at hand comes *explicitly* before sight that understands. All preparing, arranging, setting right, improving, rounding out, occur in such a way that things at hand for circumspection are interpreted in their in-order-to and are taken care of according to the interpretedness which has become visible. What has been circumspectly interpreted with regard to its in-order-to as such, what has been *explicitly* understood, has the structure of *something as something*.

What is disclosed in understanding, what is understood is always already accessible in such a way that in it its "as what" can be explicitly delineated. The "as" constitutes the structure of the explicitness of what is understood; it constitutes the interpretation. The circumspect, interpretive association with what is at hand in the surrounding world which "sees" this *as a table, a door, a car, a bridge* does not necessarily already have to analyze what is circumspectly interpreted in a particular *statement*.

But if any perception of useful things at hand always understands and interprets them, letting them be circumspectly encountered as something, does this not then mean that initially something merely objectively present is experienced which then is understood, *as a door, as a house*? That would be a misunderstanding of the specific disclosive function of interpretation. Interpretation does not, so to speak, throw a "significance" over what is nakedly objectively present and does not stick a value on it, but what is encountered in the world is always already in a relevance which is disclosed in the understanding of world, a relevance which is made explicit by interpretation.

Things at hand are always already understood in terms of a totality of relevance. This totality need not be explicitly grasped by a thematic interpretation. Even if it has undergone such an interpretation, it recedes again into an undifferentiated understanding. This is the very mode in which it is the essential foundation of everyday, circumspect interpretation. This is always based on a *fore-having*. As the appropriation of understanding in being that understands, the interpretation operates in being toward a totality of relevance which has already been understood. When something is understood but still veiled, it becomes unveiled by an act of appropriation and this is always done under the guidance of a perspective which fixes that with regard to which what has been understood is to be interpreted. The interpretation is grounded in a *foresight* that "approaches" what has been taken in fore-having with a definite interpretation in view. What is held in the fore-having and understood in a "fore-seeing" view becomes comprehensible through the interpretation. The interpretation can draw the conceptuality belonging to the beings to be interpreted from these themselves or else force them into concepts to which beings are opposed in accordance with their kind of being. The interpretation has always already decided, finally or provisionally, upon a definite conceptuality; it is grounded in a *fore-conception*.

The interpretation of something as something is essentially grounded in fore-having, fore-sight, and fore-conception. Interpretation is never a presuppositionless grasping of something previously given. When the particular concretion of the interpretation in the sense of exact text interpretation likes to appeal to what "is there," what is initially "there" is nothing else than the self-evident, undisputed prejudice of the interpreter, which is necessarily there in each point of departure of the interpretation as what is already "posited" with interpretation as such, that is, pre-given with fore-having, fore-sight, fore-conception. . . .

Meaning is that wherein the intelligibility of something maintains itself. What can be articulated in disclosure that understands we call meaning. The *concept of meaning* includes the formal framework of what necessarily belongs to what interpretation that understands articulates. *Meaning, structured by fore-having, fore-sight, and fore-conception, is the upon which of the project in terms of which something becomes intelligible as something.* Since understanding and interpretation constitute the existential constitution of 151 the being of the there, meaning must be understood as the formal, existential framework of the disclosedness belonging to understanding. Meaning is an existential of Da-sein, not a property which is attached to beings, which lies "behind" them or floats somewhere as a "realm between." Only Da-sein "has" meaning in that the disclosedness of being-in-the-world can be "fulfilled" through the beings discoverable in it. *Thus only Da-sein can be meaningful or meaningless.* This means that its own being and the beings disclosed with that being can be appropriated in understanding or they can be confined to incomprehensibility.

As the disclosedness of the there, understanding always concerns the whole of being-in-the-world. In every understanding of world, 152 existence is also understood, and vice versa. Furthermore, every interpretation operates within the fore-structure which we characterized. Every interpretation which is to contribute some understanding must already have understood what is to be interpreted. . . .

But if interpretation always already has to operate within what is understood and nurture itself from this, how should it then produce scientific results without going in a circle, especially when the presupposed understanding still operates in the common knowledge of human being and world? But according to the most elementary rules of logic, the *circle* is a *circulus vitiosus.* But the business of historical interpretation is thus banned *a priori* from the realm of exact knowledge. If the fact of the circle in understanding is not removed, historiography must be content with less strict possibilities of knowledge.

But to see a vitiosum *in this circle and to look* 153 *for ways to avoid it, even to "feel" that is an inevitable imperfection, is to misunderstand understanding from the ground up.* . . .

This circle of understanding is not a circle in which any random kind of knowledge operates, but it is rather the expression of the existential

fore-structure of Da-sein itself. The circle must not be degraded to a *vitiosum*, not even to a tolerated one. . . .

Because in accordance with its existential meaning, understanding is the potentiality for being of Da-sein itself, the ontological presuppositions of historiographical knowledge transcend in principle the idea of rigor of the most exact sciences. Mathematics is not more exact than historiographical, but only narrower with regard to the scope of the existential foundations relevant to it.

The "circle" in understanding belongs to the structure of meaning, and this phenomenon is rooted in the existential constitution of Da-sein, in interpretive understanding. Beings which, as being-in-the-world, are concerned about their being itself have an ontological structure of the circle.

167 ## B. THE EVERYDAY BEING OF THE THERE AND THE FALLING PREY OF DA-SEIN

In returning to the existential structures of the disclosedness of being-in-the-world, our interpretation has in a way lost sight of the everydayness of Da-sein. The analysis must again regain this phenomenal horizon that was our thematic point of departure. . . .

Things are so because one says so. Idle talk is constituted in this gossiping and passing the word along, a process by which its initial lack of grounds to stand on increases to complete 169 groundlessness. And this is not limited to vocal gossip, but spreads to what is written, as "scribbling." In this latter case, gossiping is based not so much on hearsay. It feeds on sporadic superficial reading: The average understanding of the reader will *never be able* to decide what has been drawn from primordial sources with a struggle, and how much is just gossip. Moreover, the average understanding will not even want such a distinction, will not have need of it, since, after all, it understands everything.

Idle talk is the possibility of understanding everything without any previous appropriation of the matter. . . .

The domination of the public way in which things have been interpreted has already decided upon even the possibilities of being attuned, that is, about the basic way in which Da-sein lets itself be affected by the world. The they prescribes that attunement, it determines what and how one "sees."

36. Curiosity

When curiosity has become free, it takes care to see not in order to understand what it sees, that is, to come to a being toward it, but *only* in order to see. It seeks novelty only to leap from it again to another novelty. The care of seeing is not concerned with comprehending and knowingly being in the truth, but with possibilities of abandoning itself to the world. Thus curiosity is characterized 172 by a specific *not-staying* with what is nearest. Consequently, it also does not seek the leisure of reflective staying, but rather restlessness and excitement from continual novelty and changing encounter. In not-staying, curiosity makes sure of the constant possibility of *distraction*. Curiosity has nothing to do with the contemplation that wonders at being, *thaumazein*, it has no interest in wondering to the point of not understanding. Rather, it makes sure of knowing, but just in order to have known.

Idle talk also controls the ways in which one may be curious. It says what one is to have read 173 and seen. The being everywhere and nowhere of curiosity is entrusted to idle task. These two everyday modes of being of discourse and sight are not only objectively present side by side in their uprooting tendency, but *one* way of being drags the *other* with it. Curiosity, for which nothing is closed off, and idle talk, for which there is nothing that is not understood, provide themselves (that is, the Da-sein existing in this way) with the guarantee of a supposedly genuine "lively life." But with this supposition a third phenomenon shows itself as characterizing the disclosedness of everyday Da-sein.

37. Ambiguity

When in everyday being with one another, we encounter things that are accessible to everybody and about which everybody can say everything, we can soon no longer decide what is disclosed in

genuine understanding and what is not. This ambiguity extends not only to the world, but likewise to being-with-one-another as such, even to the being of Da-sein toward itself.

Everything looks as if it were genuinely understood, grasped, and spoken whereas basically it is not, or it does not look that way, yet basically is. Ambiguity not only affects the way we avail ourselves of what is accessible for use and enjoyment, and the way we manage it, but it has already established itself in understanding as a potentiality for being, and in the way Da-sein projects itself and presents itself with possibilities. Not only does everyone know and talk about what is the case and what occurs, but everyone also already knows how to talk about what has to happen first, which is not yet the case, but "really" should be done. Everybody has always already guessed and felt beforehand what others also guess and feel.

38. Falling Prey and Thrownness

Idle talk, curiosity, and ambiguity characterize the way in which Da-sein is its "there," the disclosedness of being-in-the-world, in an everyday way. As existential determinations, these characteristics are not objectively present in Da-sein; they constitute its being. In them and in the connectedness of their being, a basic kind of the being of everydayness reveals itself, which we call the *entanglement* of Da-sein.

This term, which does not express any negative value judgment, means that Da-sein is initially and for the most part *together with* the "world" that it takes care of. This absorption in . . . mostly has the character of being lost in the publicness of the they. As an authentic potentiality for being a self, Da-sein has initially always already fallen away from itself and fallen prey to the "world." Falling prey to the "world" means being absorbed in being-with-one-another as it is guided by idle talk, curiosity, and ambiguity. What we called the inauthenticity of Da-sein may now be defined more precisely through the interpretation of falling prey. But inauthentic and unauthentic by no means signify "not really," as if Da-sein utterly lost its being in this kind of being. Inauthenticity does not mean anything like no-longer-being-in-the-world, but rather it constitutes precisely a distinctive kind of being-in-the-world which is completely taken in by the world and the *Mitda-sein* of the others in the they. Not-being-its-self functions as a *positive* possibility of beings which are absorbed in a world, essentially taking care of that world. This *nonbeing* must be conceived as the kind of being of Da-sein nearest to it and in which it mostly maintains itself.

Thus neither must the entanglement of Da-sein be interpreted as a "fall" from a purer and higher "primordial condition." Not only do we not have any experience of this ontically, but also no possibilities and guidelines of interpretation ontologically.

As factical being-in-the-world, Da-sein, falling prey, has already fallen *away from itself*; and it has not fallen prey to some being which it first runs into in the course of its being, or perhaps does not, but it has fallen prey to the *world* which itself belongs to its being. Falling prey is an existential determination of Da-sein itself, and says nothing about Da-sein as something objectively present, or about objectively present relations to beings from which it is "derived" or to beings with which it has subsequently gotten into a *commercium*.

The ontological-existential structure of falling prey would also be misunderstood if we wanted to attribute to it the meaning of a bad and deplorable ontic quality which could perhaps be removed in the advanced stages of human culture.

Idle talk discloses to Da-sein a being toward its world, to others and to itself—a being in which these are understood, but in a mode of groundless floating. Curiosity discloses each and every thing, but in such a way that being-in is everywhere and nowhere. Ambiguity conceals nothing from the understanding of Da-sein, but only in order to suppress being-in-the-world in this uprooted everywhere and nowhere.

With the ontological clarification of the kind of being of everyday being-in-the-world discernible in these phenomena, we first gain an existentially adequate determination of the fundamental constitution of Da-sein. What structure does the "movement" of falling prey show? . . .

Versatile curiosity and restlessly knowing it all masquerade as a universal understanding of Da-sein. But fundamentally it remains undetermined and unasked *what* is then really to be understood; nor has it been understood that understanding itself is a potentiality for being which must become *free* solely in one's *ownmost* Da-sein. When Da-sein, tranquillized and "understanding" everything, thus compares itself with everything, it drifts toward an alienation in which its ownmost potentiality for being-in-the-world is concealed. Entangled being-in-the-world is not only tempting and tranquillizing, it is at the same time *alienating*.

The leading question of this chapter pursued the being of the there. Its theme was the ontological constitution of the disclosedness essentially belonging to Da-sein. The being of disclosedness is constituted in attunement, understanding, and discourse. Its everyday mode of being is characterized by idle talk, curiosity, and ambiguity. These show the kind of movement of falling prey with the essential characteristics of temptation, tranquillization, alienation, and entanglement.

But with this analysis the totality of the existential constitution of Da-sein has been laid bare in its main features and the phenomenal basis has been obtained for a "comprehensive" interpretation of the being of Da-sein as care.

VI
Care as the Being of Da-sein

39. The Question of the Primordial Totality of the Structural Whole of Da-sein

Being-in-the-world is a structure that is primordial and constantly *whole*. In the previous chapters (division I, chapters II-V) this structure was clarified phenomenally as a whole and, always on this basis, in its constitutive moments. . . .

But this view must be held in readiness more freely and more securely when we now ask the question toward which the preparatory fundamental analysis of Da-sein was striving in general: *How is the totality of the structural whole that we pointed out to be determined existentially and ontologically?*

Being-in-the-world, to which being together with things at hand belongs just as primordially as being-with others, is always for the sake of itself. But the self is initially and for the most part inauthentic, the they-self.

Being-in-the-world is always already entangled. *The average everydayness of Da-sein* can thus be determined as *entangled-disclosed, thrown-projecting being-in-the world which is concerned with its ownmost potentiality in its being together with the "world" and in being-with with the others. . . .*

182   The ontological development of this fundamental existential phenomenon demands that we differentiate it from phenomena which at first might seem to be identified with care. Such phenomena are will, wisp, predilection, and urge. Care cannot be derived from them because they are themselves founded upon it.

Like any ontological analysis, the ontological interpretation of Da-sein as care, with whatever can be gained from the interpretation, is far removed from what is accessible to the pre-ontological understanding of being or even to our ontic acquaintance with beings. . . .

Thus we need a pre-ontological confirmation of the existential interpretation of Da-sein
183 as care. It lies in demonstrating that as soon as Da-sein expressed anything about itself, it has already interpreted itself as *care (cura)*, although only pre-ontologically.

The analytic of Da-sein which penetrates to the phenomenon of care is to prepare the way for the fundamental, ontological problematic, *the question of the meaning of being in general. . . .*

Because the ontological problematic has hitherto understood being primarily in the sense of objective presence ("reality," "world"-actuality), while the being of Da-sein remained ontologically undetermined, we need to discuss the ontological connection of care, worldliness, handiness, and objective presence (reality). That leads to a more exact determination of the concept of *reality* in the context of a discussion of the epistemological questions oriented toward this idea which have been raised by realism and idealism.

The conclusion of the preparatory funda-
184 mental analysis of Da-sein thus has as its theme the fundamental attunement of *Angst* as a distinctive disclosedness of Da-sein (section 40), the being of Da-sein as care (section 41), the confirmation of the existential interpretation of Da-sein as care in terms of the pre-ontological self-interpretation of Da-sein (section 42), Da-sein, worldliness, and reality (section 43), Da-sein, disclosedness, and truth (section 44).

40. The Fundamental Attunement of Angst as an Eminent Disclosedness of Da-sein

With the intention of penetrating to the being of the totality of the structural whole, we shall take our point of departure from the concrete analysis of entanglement carried out in the last chapter. The absorption of Da-sein in the they and in the "world" taken care of reveals something like a *flight* of Da-sein from itself as an authentic potentiality for being itself.

The falling prey of Da-sein to the they and
185 the world" taken care of, we called a "flight" from itself. But not every shrinking back from . . . , not every turning away from . . . is necessarily flight. Shrinking back from what fear discloses, from what is threatening, is founded upon fear and has the character of flight.

The turning away of falling prey is thus not a flight which is based on a fear of innerworldly beings. Any flight based on that kind of fear belongs still less to turning away, as turning away precisely *turns toward* innerworldly beings while
186 absorbing itself in them. *The turning away of falling prey is rather based on* Angst *which in turn first makes fear possible.*

In order to understand this talk about the entangled flight of Da-sein from itself, we must recall that being-in-the-world is the basic constitution of Da-sein. *That about which one has* Angst *is being-in-the-world as such.* How is what *Angst* is anxious about phenomenally differentiated from what fear is afraid of? What *Angst* is about is not an innerworldly being. Thus it essentially cannot be relevant. The threat does not have the character of a definite detrimentality which concerns what is threatened with a definite regard to a particular factical potentiality for being. What

Angst is about is completely indefinite. This indefiniteness not only leaves factically undecided which innerworldly being is threatening us, but also means that innerworldly beings in general are not "relevant." Nothing of that what is at hand and objectively present within the world, functions as what *Angst* is anxious about. . . .

In *Angst* we do not encounter this or that thing which, as threatening, could be relevant.

What oppresses us is not this or that, nor is it 187 everything objectively present together as a sum, but the *possibility* of things at hand in general, that is, the world itself. When *Angst* has quieted down, in our everyday way of talking we are accustomed to say "it was really nothing." This way of talking, indeed, gets at *what* it was ontically. Everyday discourse aims at taking care of things at hand and talking about them. That about which *Angst* is anxious is none of the innerworldly things at hand. But this "none of the things at hand," which is all that everyday, circumspect discourse understands, is not a total nothing. The nothing of handiness is based on the primordial "something," on the *world*

Being anxious discloses, primordially and directly, the world as world. It is not the case that initially we deliberately look away from innerworldly beings and think only of the world about which *Angst* arises, but *Angst* as a mode of attunement first discloses the *world as world*. . . .

It throws Da-sein back upon that for which it is anxious, its authentic potentiality-for-being-in-the-world. *Angst* individuates Da-sein to its ownmost being-in-the-world which, as understanding, projects itself essentially upon possibili188 ties. Thus along with that for which it is anxious, *Angst* discloses Da-sein as *being-possible*, and indeed as what can be individualized in individuation of its own accord.

Angst reveals in Da-sein its *being toward* its ownmost potentiality of being, that is, *being free for* the freedom of choosing and grasping itself. *Angst* brings Da-sein *before its being free for* . . . (*propensio in*), the authenticity of its being as possibility which it always already is. But at the same time, it is this being to which Da-sein as being-in-the-world is entrusted.

That *about which Angst* is anxious reveals itself as that *for which* it is anxious: being-in-the-world. . . .

We said earlier that attunement reveals "how one is." In *Angst* one has an "*uncanny*" feeling. Here the peculiar indefiniteness of that which Da-sein finds itself involved in with *Angst* initially finds expression: the nothing and nowhere. But uncanniness means at the same time not-being-at-home. . . .

Everyday familiarity collapses. Da-sein is in189 dividuated, but *as* being-in-the-world. Being-in enters the existential "mode" of *not-being-at-home*. . . .

Entangled flight *into* the being-at-home of publicness is flight *from* not-being-at-home, that is, from the uncanniness which lies in Da-sein as thrown, as being-in-the-world entrusted to itself in its being. This uncanniness constantly pursues Da-sein and threatens its everyday lostness in the they, although not explicitly. This threat can factically go along with complete security and self-sufficiency of the everyday way of taking care of things. *Angst* can arise in the most harmless situations.

It is true that it is the nature of every kind of attunement to disclose complete being-in-the-world in all its constitutive factors (world, 191 being-in, self). However, in *Angst* there lies the possibility of a distinctive disclosure, since *Angst* individualizes. This individualizing fetches Da-sein back from its falling prey and reveals to it authenticity and inauthenticity as possibilities of its being. The fundamental possibilities of Da-sein, which is always my own, show themselves in *Angst* as they are, undistorted by innerworldly beings to which Da-sein, initially and for the most part, clings.

41. *The Being of Da-sein as Care*

With the intention of grasping the totality of the structural whole ontologically, we must first ask whether the phenomenon of *Angst* and what is disclosed in it are able to give the whole of Da-sein in a way that is phenomenally equiprimordial. . . .

The total content of what lies in it can be enumerated. As attunement, being anxious is a way of being-in-the-world; that about which we have *Angst* is thrown being-in-the-world; that for which we have *Angst* is our potentiality-for-being-in-the-world. The complete phenomenon of *Angst* thus shows Da-sein as factical, existing being-in-the-world. The fundamental, ontological characteristics of this being are existentiality, facticity, and falling prey.

Da-sein is a being which is concerned in its being about that being. The "is concerned about . . ." has become clearer in the constitution of being of understanding as self-projective being toward its ownmost potentiality-for-being. This 192 potentiality is that for the sake of which any Da-sein is as it is. Da-sein has always already compared itself, in its being, with a possibility of itself. Being free *for* its ownmost potentiality-for-being, and thus for the possibility of authenticity and inauthenticity, shows itself in a primordial, elemental concretion in *Angst*. But ontologically, being toward one's ownmost potentiality-for-being means that Da-sein is always already *ahead* of itself in its being. Da-sein is always already "beyond itself," not as a way of behaving toward beings which it is *not*, but as being toward the potentiality-for-being which it itself is. This structure of being of the essential "being concerned about" we formulate as the *being-ahead-of-itself* of Da-sein.

The formal existential totality of the ontological structural whole of Da-sein must thus be formulated in the following structure: The being of Da-sein means being-ahead-of-oneself-already-in (the world) as being-together-with (innerworldly beings encountered). This being fills in the significance of the term *care*, which is used in a purely ontological and existential way. Any ontically intended tendency of being, such as worry or carefreeness, is ruled out.

Since being-in-the-world is essentially care, being-together-with things at hand could be 193 taken in our previous analyses as *taking care* of them, being with the *Mitda-sein* of others encountered within the world as *concern*. Being-together-with is taking care of things, because as a mode of being-in it is determined by its fundamental structure, care. Care not only characterizes existentiality, abstracted from facticity and falling prey,

but encompasses the unity of these determinations of being. Nor does care mean primarily and exclusively an isolated attitude of the ego toward itself. The expression "care for oneself," following the analogy of taking care and concern, would be a tautology. Care cannot mean a special attitude toward the self, because the self is already characterized ontologically as being-ahead-of-itself; but in this determination the other two structural moments of care, already-being-in . . . and being-together-with, are *also posited*.

As a primordial structural totality, care lies "before" every factical "attitude" and "position" of Da-sein, that is, it is always already *in* them as an existential *a priori*. . . .

The phenomenon of care in its totality is essentially something that cannot be split up; thus any attempts to derive it from special acts or drives such as willing and wishing or urge and 199 predilection, or of constructing it out of them, will be unsuccessful.

Willing and wishing are necessarily rooted ontologically in Da-sein as care, and are not simply ontologically undifferentiated experiences which occur in a "stream" that is completely indeterminate as to the meaning of its being. This is no less true for predilection and urge. They, too, are based upon care insofar as they are purely demonstrable in Da-sein in general. This does not exclude the fact that urge and predilection are ontologically constitutive even for beings which are only "alive." the basic ontological constitution of "living," however, is a problem in its own right and can be developed only reductively and privatively in terms of the ontology of Da-sein.

Care is ontologically "prior" to the phenomena we mentioned, which can, of course, always be adequately "described" within certain limits without the complete ontological horizon needing to be visible or even known as such.

42. Confirmation of the Existential Interpretation of Da-sein as Care in Terms of the Pre-ontological Self-interpretation of Da-sein

Our ontological interpretation of Da-sien has 200 brought the preontological self-interpretation of this being as "care" to the *existential concept* of care. The analytic of Da-sein does not aim, however, at an ontological basis for anthropology; it has a fundamental, ontological goal. This is the purpose that has inexplicitly determined the course of our considerations, our choice of phenomena, and the limits to which our analysis may penetrate. With regard to our leading question of the meaning of being and its development, our inquiry must now, however, *explicitly* secure what has been gained so far. But something like this cannot be attained by an external synopsis of what has been discussed. Rather, what could only be roughly indicated at the beginning of the existential analytic must be sharpened to a more penetrating understanding of the problem with the help of what we have gained.

STUDY QUESTIONS: HEIDEGGER, *BEING AND TIME*

1. What is the fundamental question?
2. What does Heidegger mean by 'the being of a being'? Is this, itself, a being? Why?
3. What does he mean by 'ontic priority'?
4. How does Heidegger define science? Does he think his definition is complete? Why?
5. What is Dasein?
6. What is the fundamental ontology? How must it be sought? How is it related to Dasein?
7. Why is ontology possible only as phenomenology? What does this mean? How does he make his case?
8. What is phenomenology?
9. What is the role of history?
10. What is the existential meaning of Dasein?
11. What is the essence of Dasein?
12. How is Dasein related to anthropology, biology, and psychology?
13. What is factual objective presence? How is it related to Dasein?
14. What does he mean by 'the worldliness of the world'?
15. What does he mean by 'handiness,' and what is its significance for his view?
16. What is the relationship between 'self,' 'world,' and 'they'?
17. What is the 'I'? How is it related to Dasein?
18. What is thrownness?
19. What is the relationship between Dasein and understanding?
20. How is interpretation defined in relation to the development of understanding?
21. What does he mean by 'entanglement'?
22. What is angst? What role does it play?

Philosophical Bridges: Heidegger's Influence

It is tempting to call Heidegger an existentialist, even though he refused the label, because Jean-Paul Sartre, who is an existentialist, inherits much from him. Sartre's project in *Being and Nothingness* is to characterize being through a series of phenomenological descriptions that focus on human lived experience by employing fundamental ontological categories such as being-for-itself and nothingness. This is clearly a Heidegger-inspired project.

At least three aspects of Heidegger's metaphysical thought have had a lasting impact and indicate how his ideas constitute a new direction in philosophy. First, there is the very nature of his project, which is to characterize our mode of being as it is lived in such a way as to disclose the meaning of our existence and finitude. Heidegger turned the attention of many philosophers toward the living of everyday life in a way that had not been done before.

Second, Heidegger's phenomenological descriptions are fundamentally at odds with much earlier traditional philosophy. For example, he stresses that we are thrown into a public world inhabited by other beings like us. In other words, he contends that the epistemological problems of Skepticism, solipsism, and other minds are misconceived.

Third, Heidegger argues that our primary understanding of the world must be as we encounter it, i.e., reflecting our concerns and cares. The world as it is described by theoretical physics is an abstraction from this world as we encounter it. This is a bold reversal of what most scientific thinkers claim.

Additionally, there are specific concepts in Heidegger's work that have been influential. For example, Sartre developed his notion of bad faith based on Heidegger's original idea of authenticity. Another central and influential idea introduced by Heidegger is the primacy of care. Recent virtue and feminist theories of ethics have also underlined the importance of care, though usually not deriving it directly from him.

Finally, Heidegger had a decisive influence on his pupil, Gadamer, who is considered one of the foremost exponents of hermeneutics, the interpretative study of texts and other systems of meaning. In *Being and Time*, Heidegger discusses the structure of interpretation and its relation to understanding and meaning. He contends that interpretation cannot be without presuppositions and that interpretation must be circular. Both ideas are central to Gadamer's hermeneutics. A hermeneutical circle is a nonvicious circle that occurs in interpretation. For example, to understand part of a text, one must interpret the whole. But to understand the whole, one must interpret the parts.

Jean-Paul Sartre (1905–1980)

Biographical History

French philosopher, playwright, and novelist Jean-Paul Sartre had an extraordinarily active intellectual life. Orphaned at a young age, Sartre was raised by his grandfather, in whose rich library he 'found my religion: nothing seemed to me more important than a book. I regarded the library as a temple.' He went on to study philosophy at the prestigious École Normale Supérieure and then at Berlin in Germany. He taught philosophy for a few years in France, but then resigned to pursue a full-time writing career. During World War II, Sartre joined the French Army but spent most of his time working on a novel and two plays. Captured by the Germans, he was a prisoner of war for eight months, during which time he wrote plays. He escaped using papers that the German officers had themselves forged for him. He returned to the French resistance and promptly resumed his writing, finishing two plays, *The Flies* and *No Exit*. The latter contains the famous line 'Hell is other people.' When Sartre's massive philosophical work, *Being and Nothingness*, appeared in 1943, it was instantly heralded as a new philosophical classic. By the war's end, he became the famous proponent of his atheistic brand of existentialism and a world-renowned leader of left-wing intellectuals. From 1946, Sartre developed his own understanding of Marxism, which culminated in his work *The Critique of Dialectical Reason* (1960). He was politically very active during this period, especially regarding the liberation of Algeria. In 1964, he won the Nobel Prize, but refused to accept it on the grounds that Alfred Nobel, who had made his fortune by inventing and selling dynamite, had profited from human suffering and that the prize was merely another political tool of the military-industrial complex. Toward the end of his life, Sartre wrote a three-volume work on Gustave Flaubert, entitled *The Family Idiot,* in which he studies how the novelist came to write as he did.

Philosophical Overview

In *Existentialism* (1957), Sartre explains the meaning of existentialism using his famous dictum 'Existence precedes essence.' This formula does not apply to most objects in the world. In the case of tables and chairs, essence precedes existence because such objects are created following a preconceived blueprint, which defines what they are essentially. In contrast, human existence has no blueprint and no designer because God does not exist, and so no antecedent idea of human nature exists, and there is no given purpose to life. In this way, there is no human essence that precedes human existence. Thus, it is an inevitable part of the human condition that we shape ourselves through our choices. We are each condemned to be free because we cannot ever do otherwise than choose who and what we are.

BEING AND NOTHINGNESS,
An Essay on Phenomenological Ontology

Being and Nothingness is a phenomenological description of being in increasingly concrete terms. It begins with an abstract characterization of the ontology of being, but soon moves to descriptions of human conduct and lived experience. Almost from the outset, Sartre distinguishes between two modes of being: that of conscious beings, 'being-for-itself,' and that of inert objects, 'being-in-itself.' This distinction is based on the fact that consciousness involves awareness of itself and thus it is 'being-for-itself.'

Sartre's description of this mode of being starts from the premise that consciousness is intentional because it is of something other than itself. Consciousness requires the ability to distinguish between itself and its object, which in turn requires the capacity to make negative judgments, or to conceive of what is not the case. In this sense, the essence of consciousness is nothingness. This power of negation is the basis of our freedom to imagine other possibilities, and of our freedom to act. Consequently, being conscious implies being free. Sartre calls the consciousness of one's own freedom 'anguish.' It is painful to recognize that nothing determines one's choices. For example, walking on a dangerous cliff path, one feels anguish because one knows that there is nothing to prevent one from throwing oneself over the side.

When we act in 'bad faith,' we try to pretend to ourselves that we are not free. For example, a café waiter tries to identify himself with his role in order to pretend that he has no choice with regard to his own actions. In this way, bad faith consists in the desire to become a passive object, and any attempt to attribute an essential nature to oneself constitutes an evasion of one's freedom. However, Sartre claims that it is possible to avoid bad faith and be authentic; we can achieve this by making our own individual choices, fully aware that nothing determines them for us. An individual must choose to defy the meaninglessness of life by deciding freely what to do and what to value.

Because God does not exist, no objective values are set for us, and there is no purpose to our existence. Furthermore, humans lack an essence; human existence precedes its essence. By this, Sartre does not mean that there are no universal truths about humans, such as the assertion that we need to eat. Rather, he means that there are no universally true statements concerning how humans should live. We are condemned to a radical freedom, which has no limit except that we cannot choose to be not free. This means that we must choose our own values. Nothing is given except the fact that nothing is given. We ourselves are fully and radically responsible for our lives.

Introduction

The Pursuit of Being

1. The Phenomenon

Modern thought has realized considerable progress by reducing the existent to the series of appearances which manifest it. Its aim was to overcome a certain number of dualisms which have embarrassed philosophy and to replace them by the monism of the phenomenon. Has the attempt been successful?

In the first place we certainly thus get rid of that dualism which in the existent opposes interior to exterior. There is no longer an exterior for the existent if one means by that a superficial covering which hides from sight the true nature of the object. And this true nature in turn, if it is to be the secret reality of the thing, which one can have a presentiment of or which one can suppose but can never reach because it is the "interior" of the object under consideration—this nature no longer exists. The appearances which manifest the existent are neither interior nor exterior; they are all equal, they all refer to other appearances, and none of them is privileged. Force, for example, is not a metaphysical conatus of an unknown kind which hides behind its effects . . . The appearance refers to the total series of appearances and not to a hidden reality which would drain to itself all the *being* of the existent. And the appearance for its part is not an inconsistent manifestation of this being. To the extent that men had believed in noumenal realities, they have presented appearance as a pure negative. It was "that which is not being"; it had no other being than that of illusion ^{xlvii} and error.

That is why we can equally well reject the dualism of appearance and essence. The appearance does not hide the essence, it reveals it; it *is* the essence. The essence of an existent is no longer a property sunk in the cavity of this existent; it the manifest law which presides over the succession of its appearances, it is the principle of the series.

Does this mean that by reducing the existent to its manifestations we have succeeded in overcoming *all* dualisms? It seems rather that we have converted them all into a new dualism: that of finite and infinite. Yet the existent in fact can not be reduced to a *finite* series of manifestations since each one of them is a relation to a subject constantly changing. Although an *object* may disclose itself only through a single *Abschattung*, the sole fact of there being a subject implies the possibility of multiplying the points of view *on* that *Abschattung*. This suffices to multiply to infinity the *Abschattung* under consideration. Furthermore if the series of appearances were finite, that would mean that the first appearances do not have the possibility of *reappearing*, which is absurd, or that they can be all given at once, which is still more absurd. Let us understand indeed that our theory of the phenomenon has replaced the *reality* of the thing by the *objectivity* of the phenomenon and that it had based this on an appeal to infinity.

This new opposition, the "finite and the infinite," or better, "the infinite in the finite," replaces the dualism of being and appearance. . . .

In thus replacing a variety of oppositions by a single dualism on which they all are based, have we gained or lost? This we shall soon see. . . .

Since there is nothing behind the appearance, and since it indicates only itself (and the total series of appearances), it can not be *supported* by any being other than its own. . . .

If the essence of the appearance is an "appearing" which is no longer opposed to any *being*, there arises a legitimate problem concerning the *being of this appearing*. It is this problem which will be our first concern and which will be the point of departure for our inquiry into being and nothingness.

II. The Phenomenon of Being and the Being of the Phenomenon

The appearance is not supported by any existent different from itself; it his its own *being*. The first being which we meet in our ontological inquiry is the being of the appearance. Is it itself an appearance? It seems so at first. The phenomenon is what manifests itself, and being manifests itself to all in some way, since we can speak of it and since we have a certain comprehension of it. Thus there must be for it a *phenomenon of being*, an appearance of being, capable of description as such. Being will be disclosed to us by some kind of immediate access—boredom, nausea, etc., and ontology will be the description of the phenomenon of being as it manifests itself; that is, without intermediary. However for any ontology we should raise a preliminary question: is the phenomenon of being thus achieved identical with the being of phenomena? In other words, is the being which discloses itself to me, which *appears* to me, of the same nature as the being of existents which appear to me? It seems that there is no difficulty. . . .

Li Let us consider further.

In a particular object one can always distinguish qualities like color, odor, etc. And proceeding from these, one can always determine an essence which they imply, as a sign implies its meaning. The totality "object-essence" makes an organized whole. The essence is not *in* the object; it is the meaning of the object, the principle of the series of appearances which disclose it. But being is neither one of the object's qualities, capable of being apprehended among others, nor a meaning of the object. . . .

The existent is a phenomenon; this means that it designates itself as an organized totality of qualities. It designates itself and not its being. Being is simply the condition of all revelation. It is being-for-revealing (*être-pour-dévoiler*) and not revealed being (*être dévoilé*).

If the being of phenomena is not resolved in a phenomenon of being and if nevertheless we can not say anything about being without considering this phenomenon of being, then the exact relation which unites the phenomenon of being to the being of the phenomenon must be established first of all. We can do this more easily if we will consider that the whole of the preceding remarks has been directly inspired by the revealing intuition of the phenomenon of being. By not considering being as the condition of revelation but rather being as an appearance which can be determined in concepts, we have understood first of all that knowledge can not by itself give an account of being; that is, the being of the phenomenon can not be reduced to the phenomenon of being. . . .

Lii What is implied by the preceding considerations is that the being of the phenomenon although coextensive with the phenomenon, can not be subject to the phenomenal condition—which is to exist only in so far as it reveals itself—and that consequently it surpasses the knowledge which we have of it and provides the basis for such knowledge.

Liii All consciousness, as Husserl has shown, is consciousness *of* something. This means that there is no consciousness which is not a *positing* of a transcendent object, or if you prefer, that consciousness has no "content." We must renounce those neutral "givens" which, according to the system of reference chosen, find their place either "in the world" or "in the psyche." A table is not *in* consciousness—not even in the capacity of a representation. A table is *in* space, beside the window, *etc.* The existence of the table in fact is a center of opacity for consciousness; it would require an infinite process to inventory the total contents of a thing. To introduce this opacity into consciousness would be to refer to infinity the inventory which it can make of itself, to make consciousness a thing. and to deny the cogito.

Liv However, the necessary and sufficient condition for a knowing consciousness to be knowledge *of* its object, is that it be consciousness of itself as being that knowledge. This is a necessary condition, for if my consciousness were not consciousness of being consciousness of the table, it would then be consciousness of that table without consciousness of being so. In other words, it would be a consciousness ignorant of itself, an unconscious—which is absurd. This is a sufficient condition, for my being conscious of being conscious of that table suffices in fact for me to be conscious of it. That is of course not sufficient to permit me to affirm that this table exists *in itself*—but rather that it exists *for me*.

Furthermore the reflecting consciousness posits the consciousness reflected-on, as its object. In the act of reflecting I pass judgment on the consciousness reflected-on; I am ashamed of it, I am proud of it, I will it, I deny it, etc. The immediate consciousness which I have of perceiving does not permit me either to judge or to will or to be ashamed. It does not *know* my perception, does not *posit* it; all that there is of intention in my actual consciousness is directed toward the outside, toward the world. In turn, this spontaneous consciousness of my perception is *constitutive* of my perceptive consciousness. In other words, every positional consciousness of an object is at the same time a non-positional consciousness of itself.

This self-consciousness we ought to consider not as a new consciousness, but as the *only mode of existence which is possible for a consciousness of something*. Just as an extended object is compelled to exist according to three dimensions, so an intention, a pleasure, a grief can exist only as immediate self-consciousness. If the intention is not a thing in consciousness, then the being of the intention can be only consciousness. . . .

Consciousness has nothing substantial, it is pure "appearance" in the sense that it exists only to the degree to which it appears. But it is precisely because consciousness is pure appearance, because it is total emptiness (since the entire world is outside it)—it is because of this identity of appearance and existence within it that it can be considered as the absolute.

IV. The Being of the Percipi

It seems that we have arrived at the goal of our inquiry. We have reduced things to the united totality of their appearances, and we have estab-

lished that these appearances lay claim to a being which is no longer itself appearance. The "*percipi*" referred us to a *percipiens*, the being of which has been revealed to us as consciousness. Thus we have attained the ontological foundation of knowledge, the first being to whom all other appearances appear, the absolute in relation to which every phenomenon is relative. . . .

Let us note first there is a being of the thing perceived—*as perceived*. Even if I wished to reduced this table to a synthesis of subjective impressions, I must at least remark that it reveals itself *qua table* through this synthesis, that it is the transcendent limit of the synthesis, the reason for it and its end. The table is before knowledge and can not be identified with the knowledge which we have of it; otherwise it would be consciousness—*i.e.*, pure immanence—and it would disappear as table. . . .

Now the mode of the *percipi* is the *passive*. If then the being of the phenomenon resides in its *percipi*, this being is passivity. Relativity and passivity—such are the characteristic structures of the *esse* in so far as this is reduced to the *percipi*. What is passivity? I am passive when I undergo a modification of which I am not the origin; that is, neither the source nor the creator. Thus my being supports a mode of being of which it is not the source.

V. The Ontological Proof

Being has not been given its due. We believed we had dispensed with granting transphenomenality to the being of the phenomenon because we had discovered the transphenomenality of the being of consciousness. We are going to see, on the contrary, that this very transphenomenality requires that of the being of the phenomenon. There is an "ontological proof" to be derived not from the reflective *cogito* but from the *pre-reflective* being of the *percipiens*. This we shall now try to demonstrate. . . .

As we have seen, consciousness is a real subjectivity and the impression is a subjective plenitude. But this subjectivity can not go out of itself to posit a transcendent object in such a way as to endow it with a plenitude of impressions. If then we wish at any price to make the being of the phenomenon depend on consciousness, the object must be distinguished from consciousness not by its *presence* but by its *absence*, not by its plenitude, but by its nothingness. If being belongs to consciousness, the object is not consciousness, not to the extent that it is another being, but that it is non-being. . . .

Lxiii   . . . Thus the being of the object is pure non-being. It is defined as a *lack*. It is that which escapes, that which by definition will never be given, that which offers itself only in fleeting and successive profiles.

Consciousness is consciousness *of* something. This means that transcendence is the constitutive structure of consciousness; that is, that consciousness is born *supported by* a being which is not itself. This is what we call the ontological proof.

. . . To say that consciousness is conscious-
Lxiv ness of something is to say that it must produce itself as a revealed-revelation of a being which is not it and which gives itself as already existing when consciousness reveals it.

Thus we have left pure appearance and have arrived at full being. Consciousness is a being whose existence posits its essence, and inversely it is consciousness of a being, whose essence implies its existence; that is, in which appearance lays claim to *being*. Being is everywhere. Certainly we could apply to consciousness the definition which Heidegger reserves for *Dasein* and say that it is a being such that in its being, its being is in question. But it would be necessary to complete the definition and formulate it more like this: *consciousness is a being such that in its being, its being is in question in so far as this being implies a being other than itself*.

We must understand that this being is no other than the transphenomenal being of phenomena and not a noumenal being which is hidden behind them. It is the being of this table, of this package of tobacco, of the lamp, more generally the being of the world which is implied by consciousness. It requires simply that the being of that which *appears* does not exist *only* in so far as it appears. The transphenomenal being of what exists *for* consciousness is itself in itself (*lui-même en soi*).

VI. Being-In-Itself

We can now form a few definite conclusions about the *phenomenon of being* which we have considered in order to make the preceding observations. Consciousness is the revealed-revelation of existents, and existents appear before consciousness on the foundation of their being. Nevertheless the primary characteristic of the being of an existent is never to reveal itself completely to consciousness. An existent can not be stripped of its being; being is the ever present foundation of the existent; it is everywhere in it and nowhere. There is no being which is not the being of a certain mode of being, none which can not be apprehended through the mode of being which manifests being and veils it at the same
Lxv time. Consciousness can always pass beyond the existent, not toward its being, but toward the *meaning of this being*.

. . . We must observe always:

1. That this elucidation of the meaning of being is valid only for the being of the phenomenon. Since the being of consciousness is radically different, its meaning will necessitate a particular elucidation, in terms of the revealed-revelation of another type of being, being-for-itself (*l'être-pour-soi*), which we shall define later and which is opposed to the being-in-itself (*l'être-en-soi*) of the phenomenon.

2. . . . In particular the preceding reflections have permitted us to distinguish two absolutely separated regions of being: the being of the *pre-reflective cogito* and the being of the phenomenon. But although the concept of being has this peculiarity of being divided into two regions without communication, we must nevertheless explain how these two regions can be placed under the same heading. That will necessitate the investigation of these two types of being, and it is evident that we can not truly grasp the meaning of either one until we can establish their true connection with the notion of being in general and the relations which unite them. We have indeed established by the examination of non-positional self-consciousness that the being
Lxvi of the phenomenon can on no account act upon consciousness. In this way we have ruled out a

realistic conception of the relations of the phenomenon with consciousness.

We have shown also by the examination of the spontaneity of the nonreflective cogito that consciousness can not get out of its subjectivity if the later has been initially given, and that consciousness can not act upon transcendent being nor without contradiction admit of the passive elements necessary in order to constitute a transcendent being arising from them. Thus we have ruled out the *idealist* solution of the problem. It appears that we have barred all doors and that we are now condemned to regard transcendent being and consciousness as two closed totalities without possible communication. It will be necessary to show that the problem allows a solution other than realism or idealism.

A certain number of characteristics can be fixed on immediately because for the most part they follow naturally from what we have just said. . . .

But if being is in itself, this means that it does Lxvii not refer to itself as self-consciousness does. It is this self. . . . In fact being is opaque to itself precisely because it is filled with itself. This can be better expressed by saying that *being is what it is*.

Being is. Being is in-itself. Being is what it is. Lxviii These are the three characteristics which the preliminary examination of the phenomenon of being allows us to assign to the being of phenomena. For the moment it is impossible to push our investigation further. This is not yet the examination of the *in-itself*—which is never anything but what it is—which will allow us to establish and to explain its relations with the for-itself. Thus we have left "appearances" and have been led pro- Lxix gressively to posit two types of being, the in-itself and the for-itself, concerning which we have as yet only superficial and incomplete information. A multitude of questions remain unanswered: What is the ultimate meaning of these two types of being? For what reasons do they both belong to *being* in general? What is the meaning of that being which includes within itself these two radically separated regions of being? If idealism and realism both fail to explain the relations which *in fact* unite these regions which *in theory* are with-

out communication, what other solution can we find for this problem? And how can the being of the phenomenon be transphenomenal?

It is to attempt to reply to these questions that I have written the present work.

PART ONE

THE PROBLEM OF NOTHINGNESS

₃Chapter One

The Origin of Negation

I. The Question

Once inquiry has led us to the heart of being. But we have been brought to an impasse since we have not been able to establish the connection between the two regions of being which we have discovered. No doubt this is because we have chosen an unfortunate approach.

In every question we stand before a being which we are questioning. Every question presupposes a being who questions and a being which is questioned. This is not the original relation of man to being-in-itself, but rather it stands within the limitations of this relation and takes it for granted. On the other hand, this being which we question, we question *about* something. That *about which* I question the being participates in the transcendence of being. I question being about its ways of being or about its being. From this point of view the question is a kind of expectation; I expect a reply from the being questioned. That is, on the basis of a pre-interrogative famil- ₅ iarity with being, I expect from this being a revelation of its being or of its way of being. The reply will be a "yes" or a "no." It is the existence of these two equally objective and contradictory possibilities which on principle distinguishes the question from affirmation or negation. . . .

There exists then for the questioner the permanent objective possibility of a negative reply. In relation to this possibility the questioner by the very fact that he is questioning, posits himself as in a state of indeterminations; he *does not know* whether the reply will be affirmative or negative. Thus the question is a bridge set up between two non-beings: the non-being of knowing in man, the possibility of non-being of being in transcendent being.

We set out upon our pursuit of being, and it seemed to us that the series of our questions had led us to the heart of being. But behold, at the moment when we thought we were arriving at the goal, a glance cast on the question itself has revealed to us suddenly that we are encompassed with nothingness. The permanent possibility of non-being, outside us and within, conditions our questions about being. Furthermore it is non-being which is going to limit the reply. What being *will be* must of necessity arise on the basis of what *it is not*. Whatever being is, it will allow this formulation: "Being is *that* and outside of that, *nothing.*"

Thus a new component of the real has just appeared to us—non-being. Our problem is thereby complicated, for we may no longer limit our inquiry to the relations of the human being to being in-itself, but must include also the relations of being with non-being and the relations of human non-being with transcendent-being. But let us consider further.

V. *The Origin of Nothingness*

It would be well at this point to cast a glance backward and to measure the road already covered. We raised first the question of being. Then examining this very question conceived as a type of human conduct, we questioned this in turn. We next had to recognize that no question could be asked, in particular not that of being, if negation did not exist. But this negation itself when inspected more closely referred us back to Nothingness as its origin and foundation. In order for negation to exist in the world and in order that we may consequently raise questions concerning Being, it is necessary that in some way Nothingness be given. We perceived then that Nothingness can be conceived neither *outside of* being, nor as a complementary, abstract notion, nor as an infinite milieu where being is suspended. Nothingness must be given at the heart of Being, in order for us to be able to apprehend that particular type of realities which we have called *négatités*. But this intra-mundane Nothingness cannot be produced by Being-in-itself; the notion of Being as full positivity does not contain Nothingness as one of its structures. We can not even say that Being excludes it. Being lacks all relation with it. Hence the question which is put to us now with a particular urgency: if Nothingness can be conceived neither outside of Being, nor in terms of Being, and if on the other hand, since it is non-being, it can not derive from itself the necessary force to "nihilate itself," *where does Nothingness come from?*

We shall be helped in our inquiry by a more complete examination of the conduct which served us as a point of departure. We must return to the question. We have seen, it may be recalled, that every question in essence posits the possibility of a negative reply. In a question we question a being about its being or its way of being. This way of being or this being is veiled; there always remains the possibility that it may unveil itself as a Nothingness. But from the very fact that we presume that an Existent can always be revealed as *nothing*, every question supposes that we realize a nihilating withdrawal in relation to the given, which becomes a simple *presentation*, fluctuation between being and Nothingness. . . .

Thus in posing a question, a certain negative element is introduced into the world. We see nothingness making the world irridescent, casting a shimmer over things. But at the same time the question emanates from a questioner who in order to motivate himself in his being as one who questions, disengages himself from being. This disengagement is then by definition a human process. Man presents himself at least in this instance as a being who causes Nothingness to arise in the world, inasmuch as he himself is affected with non-being to this end.

These remarks may serve as guiding thread as we examine the *négatités* of which we spoke earlier. There is no doubt at all that these are transcendent realities; distance, for example, is imposed on us as something which we have to take into account, which must be cleared with effort. However these realities are of a very peculiar nature; they all indicate immediately an essential relation of human reality to the world. They derive their origin from an act, an expectation, or a project of the human being; they all indicate an aspect of being as it appears to the human being who is engaged in the world. . . .

In order for the totality of being to order itself around us as instruments, in order for it to parcel itself into differentiated complexes which refer one to another and which can *be used*, it is necessary that negation rise up not as a thing among other things but as the rubric of a category which presides over the arrangement and the redistribution of great masses of being in things. Thus the rise of man in the midst of the being which "invests" him causes a world to be discovered. But the essential and primordial moment of this rise is the negation. Thus we have reached the first goal of this study. Man is the being through whom nothingness comes to the world. But this question immediately provokes another: What must man be in his being in order that through him nothingness may come to being?

Man's *relation* with being is that he can modify it. For man to put a particular existent out of circuit is to put himself out of circuit in relation to that existent. In this case he is not subject to it; he is out of reach; it can not act on him, for he has retired *beyond a nothingness*. Descartes following the Stoics has given a name to this possibility which human reality has to secrete a nothingness which isolates it—it is *freedom* But freedom here 25 is only a name. If we wish to penetrate further into the question, we must not be content with this reply and we ought to ask now, What is human freedom if through it nothingness comes into the world?

It is not yet possible to deal with the problem of freedom in all its fullness. In fact the steps which we have completed up to now show clearly that freedom is not a faculty of the human soul to be envisaged and described in isolation. What we have been trying to define is the being of man in so far as he conditions the appearance of nothingness, and this being has appeared to us as freedom. Thus freedom as the requisite condition for the nihilation of nothingness is not a *property* which belongs among others to the essence of the human being. We have already noticed furthermore that with man the relation of existence to

essence is not comparable to what it is for the things of the world. Human freedom precedes essence in man and makes it possible; the essence of the human being is suspended in his freedom. What we call freedom is impossible to distinguish from the *being* of "human reality." Man does not exist *first* in order to be free *subsequently*; there is no difference between the being of man and his *being-free*. This is not the time to make a frontal attack on a question which can be treated exhaustively only in the light of a rigorous elucidation of the human being. Here we are dealing with freedom in connection with the problem of nothingness and only to the extent that it conditions the appearance of nothingness. . . .

But we are not yet in a position to consider freedom as an inner structure of consciousness. We lack for the moment both instruments and technique to permit us to succeed in that enterprise. What interests us at present is a temporal operation since questioning is, like doubt, a kind of behavior; it assumes that the human being reposes first in the depths of being and then detaches himself from it by a nihilating withdrawal. Thus we are envisaging the condition of the nihilation as a relation to the self in the heart of a temporal process.

The room of someone absent, the books of 26 which he turned the pages, the objects which he touched are in themselves only *books*, *objects*; *i.e.*, full actualities. The very traces which he has left can be deciphered as traces of him only within a situation where he has been already posited as absent.

Now I have attempted to show elsewhere that if we posit the image *first* as a renascent perception, it is radically impossible to distinguish it *subsequently* from actual perceptions. The image must enclose in its very structure a nihilating thesis. It constitutes itself qua image while positing its object as existing *elsewhere* or *not existing*. It carries within it a double negation; first it is the nihilation of the world (since the world is not offering the imagined object as an actual object of perception), secondly the nihilation of the object of the image (it is posited as not actual), and finally by the same stroke it is the nihilation of itself (since it is not a concrete, full psychic process.)

Thus whatever may be the explanation
27 which we give of it, Pierre's absence, in order to be established or realized, requires a negative moment by which consciousness in the absence of all prior determination, constitutes itself as negation. If in terms of my perceptions of the room, I conceive of the former inhabitant who is no longer in the room, I am of necessity forced to produce an act of thought which no prior state can determine nor motivate, in short to effect in myself a break with being. And in so far as I continually use *négatités* to isolate and determine existents—*i.e.*, to think them—the succession of my "states of consciousness" is a perpetual separation of effect from cause, since every nihilating process must derive its source only from itself.

What separates prior from subsequent is
28 exactly *nothing*.

Thus the condition on which human reality can deny all or part of the world is that human reality carry nothingness within itself as the *nothing* which separates its present from all its past. But this is still not all, for the *nothing* envisaged would not yet have the sense of nothingness; a suspension of being which would remain unnamed, which would not be consciousness of suspending being would come from outside consciousness and by reintroducing opacity into the heart of this absolute lucidity, would have the effect of cutting it in two. Furthermore this nothing would by no means be negative. Nothingness, as we have seen above, is the ground of the negation because it conceals the negation within itself, because it is the negation as being. It is necessary then that conscious being constitute itself in relation to its past as separated from this past by a nothingness. It must necessarily be conscious of this cleavage in being, but not as a phenomenon which it experiences, rather as a structure of consciousness which it is. Freedom is the human being putting his past out of play by secreting his own nothingness. Let us understand indeed that this original necessity of being its own nothingness does not belong to consciousness intermittently and on the occasion of particular negations. This does not happen just at a particular moment in psychic life when negative or interrogative attitudes appear; consciousness continually experience itself as the nihilation of its past being. . . .

Does this consciousness exist? Behold a new
29 question has been raised here: if freedom is the being of consciousness, consciousness ought to exist a consciousness of freedom. What form does this consciousness of freedom assume? In freedom the human being *is* his own past (as also his own future) in the form of nihilation. If our analysis has not led us astray, there ought to exist for the human being, in so far as he is conscious of being, a certain mode of standing opposite his past and his future, as being both this past and this future and as not being them. We shall be able to furnish an immediate reply to this question; it is in anguish that man gets the consciousness of his freedom, or if you prefer, anguish is the mode of being of freedom as consciousness of being; it is in anguish that freedom is, in its being, in question for itself.

First we must acknowledge that Kierkegaard is right; anguish is distinguished from fear in that fear is fear of beings in the world whereas anguish is anguish before myself. Vertigo is anguish to the extent that I am afraid not of falling over the precipice, but of throwing myself over. A situation provokes fear if there is a possibility of my life being changed from without; my being provokes anguish to the extent that I distrust myself and my own reactions in that situation. The artillery preparation which precedes the attack can provoke fear in the soldier who undergoes the bombardment, but anguish is born in him when he tries to foresee the conduct with which he will face the bombardment, when he asks himself if he is going to be able to "hold up."

Now as we have seen, consciousness of being
31 is the being of consciousness. There is no question here of a contemplation which I could make after the event, of an horror already constituted; it is the very being of horror to appear to itself as "not being the cause" of the conduct it calls for. In short, to avoid fear, which reveals to me a transcendent future strictly determined, I take

refuge in reflection, but the latter has only an undetermined future to offer. This means that in establishing a certain conduct as a possibility and precisely because it is *my* possibility, I am aware that *nothing* can compel me to adopt that conduct. Yet I am indeed already there in the future; it is for the sake of that being which I will be there at the turning of the path that I now exert all my strength, and in this sense there is a already a relation between my future being and my present being. But a nothingness has slipped into the heart of this relation; I *am* not the self which I will be. First I am not that self because time separates me from it. Secondly, I am not

32 that self because what I am is not the foundation of what I will be. Finally I am not that self because no actual existent can determine strictly what I am going to be. Yet as I am already what I will be (otherwise I would not be interested in any one being more than another), *I am the self which I will be, in the mode of not being it.* It is through my horror that I am carried toward the future, and the horror nihilates itself in that it constitutes the future as possible. Anguish is precisely my consciousness of being my own future, in the mode of no-being.

The example which we have just analyzed has shown us what we could call "anguish in the face of the future." There exists another: anguish in the face of the past. It is that of the gambler who has freely and sincerely decided not to gamble any more and who when he approaches the gaming table, suddenly sees all his resolutions melt away. . . .

The earlier resolution of "not playing any-
33 more" is always *there*, and in the majority of cases the gambler when in the presence of the gaming table, turns toward it as if to ask it for help; for he does not wish to play, or rather having taken his resolution the day before, he thinks of himself still as not wishing to play anymore; he believes in the effectiveness of this resolution. But what he apprehends then in anguish is precisely the total inefficacy of the past resolution. It is there doubtless but fixed, ineffectual, surpassed by the very fact that I am conscious *of* it. The resolution is still *me* to the extent that I realize constantly my identity with myself across the temporal flux,

but it is no longer *me*—due to the fact that it has become an object *for* my consciousness. I am not subject to it, it fails in the mission which I have given it. The resolution is there still, I *am* it in the mode of not-being.

It would be in vain to object that the sole condition of this anguish is ignorance of the underlying psychological determinism. According to such a view my anxiety would come from lack of knowing the real and effective incentives which in the darkness of the unconscious determine my action. In reply we shall point out first that anguish has not appeared to us as a *proof* of human freedom; the latter was given to us as the necessary condition for the question. We wished only to show that there exists a specific consciousness of freedom, and we wished to show that this consciousness is anguish. This means that we wished to established anguish in its structure as consciousness of freedom.

This freedom which reveals itself to us in
34 anguish can be characterized by the existence of that *nothing* which insinuates itself between motives and act. It is not *because* I am free that my act is not subject to the determination of motives; on the contrary, the structure of motives as ineffective is the condition of my freedom. . . .

What we should note at present is that freedom, which manifests itself through anguish, is characterized by a constantly renewed obligation
35 to remake the *Self* which designates the free being. . . .

The gambler who must realize anew the synthetic apperception of a *situation* which would forbid him to play, must rediscover at the same time the *self* which can appreciate that situation, which "is an situation." This *self* with its a *priori* and historical content is the *essence* of man. Anguish as the manifestation of freedom in the face of self means that man is always separated by a nothingness from his essence. . . .

Man continually carries with him a prejudicative comprehension of his essence, but due to this very fact he is separated from it by a nothingness. Essence is all that human reality apprehends in itself as *having been*. It is here that anguish appears as an apprehension of self inasmuch as it exists in the perpetual mode of detachment from what is; better yet, in so far as it makes itself exist as such.

In anguish freedom is anguished before itself inasmuch as it is instigated and bound by nothing. . . . Anguish in fact is the recognition of a possibility as *my* possibility; that is, it is constituted when consciousness sees itself cut from its essence by nothingness or separated from the future by its very freedom. This means that a nihilating nothing removes form me all excuse 36 and that at the same time what I project as my future being is always nihilated and reduced to the rank of simple possibility because the future which I am remains out of my reach. But we ought to remark that in these various instances we have to do with a temporal form where I await myself in the future, where I "make an appointment with myself on the other side of that hour, of that day, or of that month." Anguish is the fear of not finding myself at that appointment, of no longer even wishing to bring myself there. . . .

Of course in every act of this kind, there remains the possibility of putting this act into question—in so far as it refers to more distant, more essential ends—as to its ultimate meanings and my essential possibilities. For example, the sentence which I write is the meaning of the letters which I trace, but the whole work which I wish to produce is the meaning of the sentence. And this work is a possibility in connection with which I can feel anguish; it is truly *my* possibility, 37 and I do not know whether I will continue it tomorrow; tomorrow in relation to it my freedom can exercise its nihilating power.

In order for my freedom to be anguished in connection with the book which I am wiring, this book must appear in its relation with me. . . .

It is necessary that in the very constitution of the book as my possibility, I apprehend my freedom as being the possible destroyer in the present and in the future of what I am.

Now at each instant we are thrust into the world and engaged there. . . .

The alarm which rings in the morning refers to the possibility of my going to work, which is *my* possibility. But to apprehend the summons of the alarm as a summons is to get up. Therefore 38 the very act of getting up is reassuring, for it eludes the question, "Is work *my* possibility?" Consequently it does not put me in a position to apprehend the possibility of quietism, of refusing to work, and finally the possibility of refusing the world and the possibility of death. In short, to the extent that I apprehend the meaning of the ringing, I am already up at its summons; this apprehension guarantees me against the anguished intuition that it is I who confer on the alarm clock its exigency—I and I alone.

In the same way, what we might call everyday morality is exclusive of ethical anguish. There is ethical anguish when I consider myself in my original relation to values. Values in actuality are demands which lay claim to a foundation. But this foundation can in no way be *being*, for every value which would base its ideal nature on its being would thereby cease event to be a value and would realize the heteronomy of my will. Value derives its being from its exigency and not its exigency from its being. . . .

It follows that my freedom is the unique foundation of values and that *nothing*, absolutely nothing, justifies me in adopting this or that particular value, this or that particular scale of values. As a being by whom values exist, I am unjustifiable. My freedom is anguished at being the foundation of values while itself without foundation. It is anguished in addition because values, due to the fact that they are essentially revealed to a freedom, can not disclose themselves without being at the same time "put into question," for the possibility of overturning the scale of values appears complementarily as *my* possibility. It is anguish before values which is the recognition of the ideality of values.

Ordinarily, however, my attitude with respect to values is eminently reassuring. In fact I am engaged in a world of values. . . .

Thus respectability acquires a being; it is not put into question. Values are sown on my path as thousands of little real demands, like the signs which order us to keep off the grass. . . .

39 We discover ourselves then in a world peopled with demands, in the heart of projects "in the course of realization." I write. I am going to

smoke. I have an appointment this evening with Pierre. I must not forget to reply to Simon. I do not have the right to conceal the truth any longer form Claude. All these trivial passive expectations of the real, all these commonplace, everyday values, derive their meaning from an original projection of myself which stands as my choice of myself in the world.

For the rest, there exist concretely alarm clocks, signboards, tax forms, policemen, so many guard rails against anguish. But as soon as the enterprise is held at a distance from me, as soon as I am referred to myself because I must await myself in the future, then I discover myself suddenly as the one who gives its meaning to the alarm clock, the one who by a signboard forbids himself to walk on a flower bed or on the lawn, the one from whom the boss's order borrows its urgency, the one who decides the interest of the book which he is writing, the one finally who makes the values exist in order to determine his action by their demands. I emerge alone and in anguish confronting the unique and original project which constitutes my being; all the barriers, all the guard rails collapse, nihilated by the consciousness of my freedom. I do not have nor can I have recourse to any value against the fact that it is I who sustain values in being. Nothing can ensure me against myself, cut off from the world and from my essence by this nothingness which I *am*. I have to realize the meaning of the world and of my essence; I make my decision concerning them—without justification and without excuse.

Anguish then is the reflective apprehension of freedom by itself. In this sense it is mediation, for although it is immediate consciousness of itself, it arises from the negation of the appeals of the world. It appears at the moment that I disengage myself from the world where I had been engaged. . . .

40 Everything takes place, in fact, as if our essential and immediate behavior with respect to anguish is flight. Psychological determinism, before being a theoretical conception, is first and attitude of excuse, or if you prefer, the basis of all attitudes of excuse. It is reflective conduct with respect to anguish; it asserts that there are within us antagonistic forces whose type of existence is comparable to that of things. It attempts to fill the void which encircles us, to re-establish the links between past and present, between present and future. . . . Is an anguish placed under judgment a disarmed anguish? Evidently not. However here a new phenomenon is born, a process of "distraction" in relation to anguish which, once again, supposes within it a nihilating power. . . .

But flight before anguish is not only an effort
42 at distraction before the future; it attempts also be disarm the past of its threat. What I attempt to flee here is my very transcendence in so far as it sustains and surpasses my essence. I assert that I am my essence in the mode of being of the in-itself. At the same time I always refuse to consider that essence a being historically constituted and as implying my action as a circle implies its properties. I apprehend it, or at least I try to apprehend it as the original beginning of my possible, and I do not admit at all that it has in itself a beginning. I assert then that an act is free when it exactly reflects my essence.

Such then is the totality of processes by
43 which we try to hide anguish from ourselves; we apprehend our particular possible by avoiding considering all other possibles, which we make the possibles of an undifferentiated Other. . . .

Thus we flee from anguish by attempting to apprehend ourselves form without as an Other or as *a thing*.

Do these various constructions succeed in stifling or hiding our anguish? It is certain that we can not overcome anguish, for we *are* anguish. . . .

We can hide an external object because it exists independently of us. For the same reason we can turn our look or our attention away from it. . . .

But if I *am* what I wish to veil, the question takes on quite another aspect. I can in fact wish "not to see" a certain aspect of my being only if I am acquainted with the aspect which I do not wish to see. This means that in my being I must indicate this aspect in order to be able to turn myself away from it; better yet, I must think of it constantly in order to take care not to think of it. In this connection it must be understood not only that I must of necessity perpetually carry within me what I wish to flee but also that I must aim at the object of my flight in order to flee it. This means that anguish, the intentional aim of anguish, and a flight from anguish toward reassuring myths must all be given in the unity of the same consciousness. In a word, I flee in order not to know, but I can not avoid knowing that I am fleeing; and the flight fro anguish is only a mode of becoming conscious of anguish. Thus anguish, properly speaking, can be neither hidden nor avoided.

We are now at the end of our first description.
44 The examination of the negation can not lead us farther. It has revealed to us the existence of a particular type of conduct: conduct in the face of non-being, which supposes a special transcendence needing separate study. We find ourselves then in the presence of two human ekstases: the ekstases which throws us into being-in-itself and the ekstases which engages us in non-being. It seems that our original problem, which concerned only the relations of man to being, is now considerably complicated. But in pushing our analysis of transcendence toward non-being to its conclusion, it is possible for us to get valuable information for the understanding of *all* transcendences. Furthermore the problem of nothingness can not be excluded from our inquiry. If man adopts any particular behavior in the face of being-in-itself— and our philosophical question is a type of such behavior—it is because he *is not* this being. We rediscover non-being as a condition of the transcendence toward being. We must then catch hold of the problem of nothingness and not let it go before its complete elucidation.

CHAPTER TWO

BAD FAITH

1. Bad Faith and Falsehood

47 The human being is not only the being by whom *négatités* are disclosed in the world; he is also the one who can take negative attitudes with respect to himself. In our Introduction we defined consciousness as "a being such that in its being, its being is in question in so far as this being implies

a being other than itself." But now that we have examined the meaning of "the question," we can at present also write the formula thus: "Consciousness is a being, the nature of which is to be conscious of the nothingness of its being."

Thus attitudes of negation toward the self permit us to raise a new question: What are we to say is the being of man who has the possibility of denying himself? But it is out of the question to discuss the attitude of "self-negation" in its universality. . . .

It is best to choose and to examine one attitude which is essential to human reality and which is such that consciousness instead of directing its negation outward turns it toward itself. This attitide, it seems to me, is *bad faith* (*mauvaise foi*).

Frequently this is identified with falsehood. We say indifferently of a person that he shows signs of bad faith or that he lies to himself. We shall willingly grant that bad faith is a lie to oneself, on condition that we distinguish the lie to oneself from lying in general. Lying is a negative attitude, we will agree to that. But this negation does not bear on consciousness itself; it aims only at the transcendent. The essence of the lie implies in fact that the liar actually is in complete possession of the truth which he is hiding. A man does not lie about what he is ignorant of; he does not lie when he spreads an error of which he himself is the dupe; he does not lie when he is mistaken. The ideal description of the liar would be a cynical consciousness, affirming truth within himself, denying it in his words, and denying that negation as such. . . .

The lie is also a normal phenomenon of
49 what Heidegger calls the "*Mitsein*." It presupposes my existence, the existence of the *Other*, my existence *for* the Other, and the existence of the Other *for* me. Thus there is no difficulty in holding that the liar must make the project of the lie in entire clarity and that he must possess a complete comprehension of the lie and of the truth which he is altering. It is sufficient that an overall opacity hide his intentions from the *Other*; it is sufficient that the Other can take the lie for truth. By the lie consciousness affirms that it exists by nature *as hidden from the Other*; it utilizes

for its own profit the ontological duality of myself and myself in the eyes of the Other.

The situation can not be the same for bad faith if this, as we have said, is indeed a lie to oneself. To be sure, the one who practices bad faith is hiding a displeasing truth or presenting as truth a pleasing untruth. Bad faith then has in appearance the structure of falsehood. Only what changes everything is the fact that in bad faith it is from myself that I am hiding the truth. Thus the duality of the deceiver and the deceived does not exist here. Bad faith on the contrary implies in essence the unity of a single consciousness. . . . It follows first that the one to whom the lie is told and the one who lies are one and the same person, which means that I must know in my capacity as deceiver the truth which is hidden from me in my capacity as the one deceived. Better yet I must know the truth very exactly *in order* to conceal it more carefully—and this not at two different moments, which at a pinch would allow us to reestablish a semblance of duality—but in the unitary structure of a single project. How then can the lie subsist if the duality which conditions it is suppressed?

To this difficulty is added another which is derived from the total translucency of consciousness. That which affects itself with bad faith must be conscious (of) its bad faith since the being of consciousness is consciousness of being. It appears then that I must be in good faith, at least to the extent that I am conscious of my bad faith. But then this whole psychic system is annihilated. We must agree in fact that if I deliberately and cynically attempt to lie to myself, I fail completely in this undertaking: . . .

Even though the existence of bad faith is very precarious, and though it belongs to the kind of psychic structures which we might call "metastable," it presents nonetheless an autonomous and durable form. It can even be the normal aspect of life for a very great number of people. A person can *live* in bad faith, which does not mean that he does not have abrupt awakenings to cynicism or to good faith, but which implies a constant and particular style of life. Our embarrassment then appears extreme

since we can neither reject nor comprehend bad faith. . . .

55 II. Patterns of Bad Faith

. . . We should examine more closely the patterns of bad faith and attempt a description of them. This description will permit us perhaps to fix more exactly the conditions for the possibility of bad faith; that is, to reply to the question we raised at the outset: "What must be the being of man if he is to be capable of bad faith?"

Take the example of a woman who has consented to go out with a particular man for the first time. She knows very well the intentions which the man who is speaking to her cherishes regarding her. She knows also that it will be necessary sooner or later for her to make a decision. But she does not want to realize the urgency; she concerns herself only with what is respectful and discreet in the attitude of her companion. She does not apprehend this conduct as an attempt to achieve what we call "the first approach;" that is, she does not want to see possibilities of temporal development which his conduct presents. . . .

But then suppose he takes her hand. This act of her companion risks changing the situation by calling for an immediate decision. To leave the hand there is to consent in herself to flirt, to engage herself. To withdraw it is to break the troubled and unstable harmony which gives the hour its charm. The aim is to postpone the moment of decision as long as possible. We know what happens next; the young woman leaves her hand there, but she *does not notice* that she is 56 leaving it. She does not notice because it happens by chance that she is at this moment all intellect. . . .

We shall say that this woman is in bad faith. But we see immediately that she uses various procedures in order to maintain herself in this bad faith. She has disarmed the actions of her companion by reducing them to being only what they are; that is, to existing in the mode of the in-itself. . . .

What unity do we find in these various aspects of bad faith? It is a certain art of forming contradictory concepts which unite in themselves both an idea and the negation of that idea. The basic concept which is thus engendered, utilizes the double property of the human being, who is at once a *facticity* and *a transcendence*. These two aspects of human reality are and ought to be capable of a valid coordination. But bad faith does not wish either to coordinate them nor to surmount them in a synthesis. Bad faith seeks to affirm their identity while preserving their differences. It must affirm facticity as *being* transcendence and transcendence as *being* facticity, in such a way that at the instant when a person apprehends the one, he can find himself abruptly faced with the other. . . .

57 We can see the use which bad faith can make of these judgments which all aim at establishing that I am not what I am. If I were only what I *am*, I could, for example, seriously consider an adverse criticism which someone makes of me, question myself scrupulously, and perhaps be compelled to recognize the truth in it. But thanks to transcendence, I am not subject to all that I am. I do not even have to discuss the justice of the reproach But the ambiguity necessary for bad faith comes form the fact that I affirm here that I *am* my transcendence in the mode of being of a thing. It is only thus, in fact, that I can feel that I escape all reproaches. It is in the sense that our young woman purifies the desire of anything humiliating by being willing to consider it only as pure transcendence, which she avoids even naming. But inversely "I Am Too Great for Myself," while showing our transcendence changed into facticity, is the source of an infinity of excuses for our failures or our weaknesses. Similarly the young coquette maintains transcendence to the extent that the respect, the esteem manifested by the actions of her admirer are already on the plane of the transcendent. But she arrests this transcendence, she glues it down with all the facticity of the present; respect is nothing other than respect, it is an arrested surpassing which no longer surpasses itself toward anything. But although this *metastable* concept of "transcendence-facticity" is one of the most basic instruments of bad faith, it is not the only one of its kind. We can equally well use another kind of duplicity derived from human reality which we

will express roughly by saying that its being-for-itself implies complementarily a being-for-others. Upon any one of my conducts it is always possible to converge two looks, mine and that of the Other. . . .

58 The equal dignity of being, possessed by my being-for-others and by my being-for-myself permits a perpetually disintegrating synthesis and a perpetual game of escape from the for-itself to the for-others and from the for-others to the for-itself. We have seen also the use which our young lady made of our being-in-the-midst-of-the-world—*i.e.*, of our inert presence as a passive object among other objects—in order to relieve herself suddenly from the functions of her being-in-the-world—that is, from the being which causes there to be world by projecting itself beyond the world toward its own possibilities. . . .

In all these concepts, which have only a transitive role in the reasoning and which are eliminated from the conclusion, (like hypochondriacs in the calculations of physicians), we find again the same structure. We have to deal with human reality as a being which is what it is not and which is not what it is. . . .

If man is what he is, bad faith is for ever impossible and candor ceases to be is ideal and becomes instead his being. But is man what he is? And more generally, how can he *be* what he is when he exists as consciousness of being? If candor or sincerity is a universal value, it is evident that the maxim "one must be what one 59 is" does not serve solely as a regulating principle for judgments and concepts by which I express what I am. It posits not merely an ideal of knowing but an ideal of *being*; it proposes for us an absolute equivalence of being with itself as a prototype of being. In this sense it is necessary that we *make ourselves* what we are. But what *are we* then if we have the constant obligation to make ourselves what we are, if our mode of being is having the obligation to be what we are?

Let us consider this waiter in the café. His movement is quick and forward, a little too precise, a little too rapid. He comes toward the patrons with a step a little too quick. He bends forward a little too eagerly; his voice, his eyes express an interest a little too solicitous for the order of the customer. Finally there he returns, trying to imitate in his walk the inflexible stiffness of some kind of automaton while carrying his tray with the recklessness of a tight-rope-walker by putting it in a perpetually unstable, perpetually broken equilibrium which he perpetually reestablishes by a light movement of the arm and hand. All his behavior seems to us a game. . . . But what is he playing? We need not watch long before we can explain it: he is playing *at being* a waiter in a café. There is nothing there to surprise us. The game is a kind of marking our and investigation. The child plays with his body in order to explore it, to take inventory of it; the waiter in the café plays with his condition in order to *realize* it. . . . There are indeed many precautions to imprison a man in what he is, as if we lived in perpetual fear that he might escape from it, that he might break away and suddenly elude his condition.

In a parallel situation, from within, the waiter in the café can not be immediately a café waiter in the sense that this inkwell is an inkwell, of the glass is a glass. It is by no means that he can not form reflective judgements or concepts concerning his condition. He knows 60 well what it "means:" the obligation of getting up at five o'clock, of sweeping the floor of the shop before the restaurant opens, of starting the coffee pot going, *etc.* He knows the rights which it allows: the right to the tips, the right to belong to a union, etc. . . .

Furthermore we are dealing with more than mere social positions; I am never any one of my attitudes, any one of my action. The good speaker is the one who *plays* at speaking, because he can not be *speaking*. The attentive pupil who wishes to be attentive, his eyes riveted on the teacher, his ears open wide, so exhausts himself in playing the attentive role that he ends up by no longer hearing anything. . . .

61 When Pierre lends at me, I know of course that he is looking at me. His eyes, things in the world, are fixed on my body, a thing in the world—that is the objective fact of which I can say: it *is*. But it is also a fact *in the world*. . . .

62 My reactions, to the extent that I project myself toward the Other, are no longer for myself but are rather mere *presentations;* they await being constituted as graceful or uncouth, sincere or insincere, etc., by an apprehension which is always beyond my efforts to provoke, an apprehension which will be provoked by my efforts only if of itself it lends them force (that is, only in so far as it causes itself to be provoked from the outside), *which is its own mediator with the transcendent.* Thus the objective fact of the being-in-itself of the consciousness of the Other is posited in order to disappear in negativity and in freedom: consciousness of the Other is as not-being; its being-in-itself " here and now" is not-to-be.

Consciousness of the Other is what it is not. . . .

Under these conditions what can be the significance of the ideal of sincerity except as a task impossible to achieve, of which the very meaning is in contradiction with the structure of my consciousness. To be sincere, we said, is to be what one is. That supposes that I am not originally what I am. . . . But we definitely establish that the original structure of "not being what one is" renders impossible in advance all movement toward being in itself or "being what one is." And this impossibility is not hidden from consciousness; on the contrary, it is the very stuff of consciousness; it is the embarrassing constraint which we constantly experience; it is our very incapacity to recognize ourselves, to constitute ourselves as being what we are. It is this necessity which means that, as soon as we posit ourselves as a certain being, by a legitimate judgment, based on inner experience or correctly deduced from a *priori* or empirical premises, then by that very positing we surpass this being—and that not toward another being by toward emptiness, toward *nothing*.

How then can we blame another for not being sincere or rejoice in our own sincerity since 63 this sincerity appears to us at the same time to be impossible? . . .

What then is sincerity except precisely a phenomenon of bad faith? Have we not shown indeed that in bad faith human reality is constituted as a being which is what it is not and which 65 is not what it is? . . .

Thus the essential structure of sincerity does not differ from that of bad faith since the sincere man constitutes himself as what he is *in order not to be it*. This explains the truth recognized by all that one can fall into bad faith through being
66 sincere. . . .

Bad faith is possible only because sincerity is conscious of missing its goal inevitably, due to its
67 very nature. . . .

Thus in order for bad faith to be possible, sincerity itself must be in bad faith. The condition of the possibility for bad faith is that human reality, in its most immediate being, in the intrastructure of the pre-reflective *cogito*, must be what it is not and not be what it is. . . .

III. The "Faith" of Bad Faith

70 In bad faith there is no cynical lie nor knowing preparation for deceitful concepts. But the first act of bad faith is to flee what it can not flee, to flee what it is. The very project of flight reveals to bad faith an inner disintegration in the heart of being, and it is this disintegration which bad faith wishes to be. In truth, the two immediate attitudes which we can take in the face of our being are conditioned by the very nature of this being and its immediate relation with the in-itself. Good faith seeks to flee the inner disintegration of my being in the direction of the in-itself which it should be and is not. Bad faith seeks to flee the in-itself by mean of the inner disintegration of my being. But it denies this very disintegration as it denies that it is itself bad faith. Bad faith seeks by means of "not-being-what-one-is" to escape from the in-itself which I am not in the mode of being what one is not. It denies itself as bad faith and aims at the in it-self which I am not in the mode of "not-being-what-one-is-not." If bad faith is possible, it is because it is an immediate, permanent threat to every project of the human being; it is because consciousness conceals in its being a permanent risk of bad faith. The origin of this risk is the fact that the nature of consciousness simultaneously is to be what it is not and not to be what it is. In the light of these remarks we can now approach the onto-

logical study of consciousness, not as the totality of the human being, but as the instantaneous nucleus of this being. . . .

431 **PART FOUR**

HAVING, DOING, AND BEING

"Having," "doing," and "being" are the cardinal categories of human reality. Under them are subsumed all types of human conduct, *Knowing*, for example, is a modality of *having*. These categories are not without connection with one another, and several writers have emphasized these ties. . . . Is the supreme value of human activity a *doing* or a *being*? And whichever solution we adopt, what is to become of *having*? Ontology should be able to inform us concerning this problem; moreover it is one of ontology's essential tasks if the for-itself is the being which is defined by *action*. Therefore we must not bring this work to a close without giving a broad outline for the study of action in general and of the essential relations of *doing*, of *being*, and of *having*.

Chapter One

433 **Being and Doing: Freedom**

I. Freedom: The First Condition of Action

It is strange that philosophers have been able to argue endlessly about determinism and free-will, to cite examples in favor of one or the other thesis without ever attempting first to make explicit the structures contained in the very idea of *action*. The concept of an act contains, in fact, numerous subordinate notions which we shall have to organize and arrange in a hierarchy: to act is to modify the *shape* of the world; it is to arrange means in view of an end; it is to produce an organized instrumental complex such that by a series of concatenations and connections the modification effected on one of the links causes modifications throughout the whole series and finally produces an anticipated result. But this is not what is important for us here. We should observe first that an action is on principle *intentional*. The careless smoker who has through negligence causes the explosion of a powder magazine has not *acted*. On the other hand the worker who is charged with dynamiting a quarry and who obeys the given orders has acted when he has produced the expected explosion; he knew what he was doing or, if you prefer, he intentionally realized a conscious project.

This does not mean, of course, that one must foresee all the consequences of his act. The emperor Constantine when he established himself at Byzantium, did not foresee that he would create a center of Greek culture and language, the appearance of which would ultimately provoke a schism in the Christian Church and which would contribute to weakening the Roman Empire. Yet he performed an act just in so far as he realized his project of creating a new residence for emperors in the Orient. Equating the result with the intention is here sufficient for us to be able to speak of action. But if this is the case, we establish that the action necessarily implies as its condition the recognition of a "desideratum;" that is, of an objective lack or again of a *négatité*.

434 This means that from the moment of the first conception of the act, consciousness has been able to withdraw itself from the full world of which it is consciousness and to leave the level of being in order frankly to approach that of non-being. Consciousness in so far as it is considered exclusively in its being, is perpetually referred from being to being and can not find in being any motive for revealing non-being. . . .

How can anyone fail to see that all these considerations are *negative;* that is, that they aim at what is not, not at what is. To say that sixty per cent of the anticipated taxes have been collected can pass, if need be for a positive appreciation of the situation *such as it is*. . . .

435 Two important consequences result. (1) No factual state whatever it may be (the political and economic structure of society, the psychological "state," *etc.*) is capable by itself of motivating any act whatsoever. For an act is a projection of the for-itself toward what is not, and what is can in no way determine by itself what is not. (2) No factual state can determine consciousness to

436 apprehend it as a *négatité* or as a lack. . . .

Under no circumstances can the past in any way by itself produce *an act*; that is, the positing of an end which turns back upon itself so as to illuminate it. This what Hegel caught sight of when he wrote that "the mind is the negative," although he seems not to have remembered this when he came to presenting his own theory of action and of freedom. In fact as soon as one attributes to consciousness this negative power with respect to the world and itself, as soon as the nihilation forms an integral part of the *positing* of an end, we must recognize that the indispensable and fundamental condition of all action is the freedom of the acting being.

438 We cannot, however, stop with these superficial considerations; if the fundamental condition of the act is freedom, we must attempt to describe this freedom more precisely. But at the start we encounter a great difficulty. Ordinarily, to describe something is a process of making explied by aiming at the structures of a particular essence. Now freedom has no essence. It is not subject to any logical necessity; we must say of it what Heidegger said of the *Dasein* in general: "In it existence precedes and commands essence." Freedom makes itself an act, and we ordinarily attain it across the act which it organizes with the causes, motives, and end which the act

439 implies. . . . I am indeed an existent who *learns* his freedom through his acts, but I am also an existent whose individual and unique existence temporalizes itself as freedom. As such I am necessarily a consciousness (of) freedom since nothing exists in consciousness except as the non-thetic consciousness of existing. Thus my freedom is perpetually in question in my being; it is not a quality added on or a *property* of my nature. It is very exactly the stuff of my being; and as in my being, my being is in question, I must necessarily possess a certain comprehension of freedom. It is this comprehension which we intend at present to make explicit.

In our attempt to reach to the heart of freedom we may be helped by the few observations which we have made on the subject in the course of this work and which we must summarize her. In the first chapter we established the fact that if negation comes into the world through human-reality, the latter must be a being who can realize a nihilating rupture with the world and with himself; and we established that the permanent possibility of this rupture is the same as freedom. But on the other hand, we stated that this permanent possibility of nihilating what I am in the form of "having-been" implies for man a particular type of existence. We were able then to determine by means of analyses like that of bad faith that human reality is its own nothingness. For the for-itself, to be is to nihilate the in-itself which it is. Under these conditions freedom can be nothing other than this nihilation. It is through this that the for-itself escapes its being as its essence; it is through this that the for-itself is always something other than what can be *said* of it. For in the final analysis the For-itself is the one which escapes this very denomination, the one which is already beyond the name which is given to it, beyond the property which is recognized in it. To say that the for-itself has to be what it is, to say that it is what it is not while not being what it is, to say that in it existence precedes and conditions essence or inversely according to Hegel, that for it "Wesen ist was gewesen ist"—all this is to say one and the same thing: to be aware that man is free. Indeed by the sole fact that I am conscious of the causes which inspire my action, these causes are already transcendent objects for my consciousness; they are outside. In vain shall I seek to catch hold of them; I escape them by my very existence. I am condemned to exist forever beyond my essence, beyond the causes and motives of my act. I am condemned to be free. This means that no limits to my freedom can be found except freedom itself or, if you prefer, that we are not free to cease being free. To the extent that the for-itself wishes to hide its own nothingness from itself and to incorporate 440 the in-itself as its true mode of being, it is trying also to hide its freedom from itself. . . .

Man is free because he is not himself but presence to himself. The being which is what it is can not be free. Freedom is precisely the nothingness which *is made-to-be* at the heart of man and which forces human-reality to *make itself* instead of *to be*. As we have seen, for human reality, to be is to *choose oneself*; nothing comes to it either from the outside or from within which it can *receive or accept*.

Without any help whatsoever, it is entirely 441 abandoned to the intolerable necessity of making itself be—down to the slightest detail. Thus freedom is not a being; it is *the being* of man—*i.e.*, his nothingness of being. If we start by conceiving of man as a plenum, it is absurd to try to find in him afterwards moments or psychic regions in which he would be free. As well look for emptiness in a container which one has filled beforehand up to the brim! Man can not be sometimes slave and sometimes free; he is wholly and forever free or he is not free at all.

But these observations are still not our primary concern. They have only a negative bearing. The study of the will should, on the contrary, enable us to advance further in our understanding of freedom. And this is why the fact which strikes us first is that if the will is to be autonomous, then it is impossible for us to consider it as a *given* psychic fact; that is, in-itself. It can not belong to the category defined by the psychologist as "states of consciousness." Here as everywhere else we assert that the state of consciousness is a pure idol of a positive psychology. If the will is to be freedom, then it is of necessity negativity and the power of nihilation. . . .

But this is not all: the will, far from being 443 the unique or at least the privileged manifestation of freedom, actually—like every event of the for-itself—must presuppose the foundation of an original freedom in order to be able to constitute itself as will. The will in fact is posited as a reflective decision in relation to certain ends. But it does not create these ends. It is rather a mode of being in relation to them: it decrees that the pursuit of these ends will be reflective and deliberative. Passion can posit the same ends. . . .

Human reality can not receive its ends, as we have seen, either from outside or from a so-called inner "nature." It chooses them and by this very choice confers upon them a transcendent existence as the external limit of its projects. From this point of view—and if it is understood that the existence of the *Dasein* precedes and commands its essence—human reality in and through its very upsurge decides to define its own being by its ends. It is therefore the positing of my ultimate ends which characterizes my being and which is identical with the sudden thrust of the freedom which is mine. And this thrust is an *existence*; it has nothing to do with an 444 essence or with a property of a being which would be engendered conjointly with an idea.

Thus since freedom is identical with my existence, it is the foundation of ends which I shall attempt to attain either by the will or by passionate efforts.

If these ends are already posited, then what remains to be decided at each moment is the way in which I shall conduct myself with respect to them; in other words, the attitude which I shall assume. Shall I act by volition or by passion? Who can decide except me? In fact, if we admit that circumstances decide for me (for example, I can act by volition when faced with a minor danger but if the peril increases, I shall fall into passion), we thereby suppress all freedom. It would indeed be absurd to declare that the will is autonomous when it appears but that external circumstances strictly determine the moment of its appearance.

557 **Chapter Two**

Doing and Having

I. Existential Psychoanalysis

If it is true that human reality—as we have attempted to establish—identifies and defines itself by the ends which it pursues, then a study and classification of these ends becomes indispensable. In the preceding chapter we have considered the For-itself only from then point of view of its free project, which is the impulse by which it thrusts itself toward its end. We should now question this end itself, for it *forms a part* of absolute subjectivity and is, in fact, its transcendent, objective limit. This is what empirical psychology has hinted at by admitting that a particular man is defined by his desires. Here, however, we must be on our guard against two

errors. First, the empirical psychologist, while defining man by his desires, remains the victim of the illusion of substance. He views desire as being *in* man by virtue of being "contained" by his consciousness, and he believes that the meaning of the desire is inherent in the desire itself. Thus he avoids everything which could evoke the idea of transcendence. But if I desire a house or a glass of water or a woman's body, how could this body, this glass, this piece of property reside in my desire, and how can my desire be anything but the consciousness of these objects as desirable? Let us beware then of considering these desires as little psychic entities dwelling in consciousness; they are consciousness itself in its original projective, transcendent structure, for consciousness is on principle consciousness *of* something.

The other error, which fundamentally is closely connected with the first, consists in considering psychological research as terminated as soon as the investigator has reached the concrete ensemble of empirical desires. Thus a man would be defined by the bundle of drives or tendencies which empirical observation could establish. Naturally the psychologist will not always limit himself to making up the *sum* of these tendencies; he will want to bring to light their relationships, their agreements and harmonies; he will try to present the ensemble of desires as a syn-558 thetic organization in which each desires acts on the others and influences them. . . .

The problem poses itself in approximately 563 these terms: If we admit that the person is a totality, we can not hope to reconstruct him by an addition or by an organization of the diverse tendencies which we have empirically discovered in him. On the contrary, in each inclination, in each tendency the person expresses himself completely, although from a different angle, a little as Spinoza's substance expresses itself completely in each of its attributes. But if this is so, we should discover in each tendency, in each attitude of the subject, a meaning which transcends it. A jealousy of a particular date in which a subject historicizes himself in relation to a certain woman, signifies for the one who knows how to interpret it, the total relation to the world by which the subject constitutes himself as a self. In other words this *empirical* attitude is by itself the expression of the "choice of an intelligible character." There is no mystery about this. We no longer have to do with an intelligible pattern which can be present in our thought only, while we apprehend and conceptualize the unique pattern of the subject's empirical existence. If the empirical attitude signifies the choice of the intelligible character, it is because it is itself this choice. Indeed the distinguishing characteristic of the intelligible choice, as we shall see later, is that it can exist only as the transcendent meaning of each concrete, empirical choice. It is by no 564 means first effected in some unconscious or on the noumenal level to be *subsequently* expressed in a particular observable attitude; there is not even an *ontological* pre-eminence over the empirical choice, but it is on principle that which must always detach itself from the empirical choice as its *beyond* and the infinity of its transcendence. Thus if I am rowing on the river, I am nothing— either here or in any other world—save this concrete project of rowing. But this project itself inasmuch as it is the totality of my being, expresses my original choice in particular circumstances; it is nothing other than the choice of myself as a totality in these circumstances. That is why a special method must aim at detaching the fundamental meaning which the project admits and which can be only the individual secret of the subject's being-in-the-world. It is then rather by a *comparison* of the various empirical drives of a subject that we try to discover and disengage the fundamental project which is common to them all—and not by a simple summation or reconstruction of these tendencies; each drive or tendency is the entire person.

There is naturally an infinity of possible projects as there is an infinity of possible human beings. Nevertheless, if we are to recognize certain common characteristics among them and if we are going to attempt to classify them in larger categories, it is best first to undertake individual investigations in the cases which we can study more easily. In our research, we will be guided by this principle: to stop only in the presence of evident irreducibility; that is, never to believe that we have reached the initial project until the projected end appears as *the very being* of the subject under consideration.

Thus we can advance to further but have 565 encountered the self-evident irreducible when we have reached the *project of being;* for obviously it is impossible to advance further than *being,* and there is no difference between the project of being, possibility, value, on the one hand, and *being,* on the other. Fundamentally man is *the desire to be,* and the existence of this desire is *not* to be established by an empirical induction; it is the result of an *a priori* description of the being of the for-itself, since desire is a lack and since the for-itself is the being which is to itself its own lack of being. The original project which is expressed in each of our expirically observable tendencies is then the *project of being;* or, if you prefer, each empirical tendency exists with the original project of being, in a relation of expression and symbolic satisfaction just as conscious drives, with Freud, exist in relation to the complex and to the original libido. Moreover the desire to be by no means exists *first* in order to cause itself to be expressed subsequently by desires *a posteriori.* There is nothing outside of the symbolic expression which it finds in concrete desires. There is not first a single desire of being, then a thousand particular feelings, but the desire to be exists and manifests itself only in and through jealousy, greed, love of art, cowardice, courage, and a thousand contingent, empirical expressions which always cause human reality to appear to us only as *manifested* by *a particular man,* by a specific person.

As for the being which is the object of this desire, we know a *priori* what this is. The for-itself is the being which is to itself its own lack of being. The being which the for-itself lacks is the in-itself. The for-itself arises as the nihilation of the in-itself and this nihilation is defined as the project toward the in-itself. Between the nihilated in-itself and the projected in-itself the for-itself is nothingness. Thus the end and the goal of the nihilation which I am is the in-itself. Thus 566 human reality is the desire of being-in-itself. . . .

567 Freedom is precisely the being which makes itself a lack of being. But since desire, as we have established, is identical with lack of being, freedom can arise only as being which makes itself a desire of being; that is, as the project-for-itself of being in-itself for-itself. Here we have arrived at an abstract structure which can by no means be considered as the nature or essence of freedom. Freedom is existence, and in it existence pre-
568 cedes essence. The upsurge of freedom is immediate and concrete and is not to be distinguished from its choice; that is, from the person himself. But the structure under consideration can be called the *truth* of freedom, that is, it is the human meaning of freedom.

It should be possible to establish the human truth of the person, as we have attempted to do by an ontological phenomenology. The catalogue of empirical desires ought to be made the object of appropriate psychological investigation, observation and induction and, as needed, experience can server to draw up this list. They will indicate to the philosopher the comprehensible relations which can unite to each other various desires and various patterns of behaviors, and will bring to light certain concrete connections between the subject of experience and "situations" experientially defined (which at bottom originate only from limitations applied in the name of positivity to the fundamental situation of the subject in the world). But in establishing and classifying fundamental desires of *individual persons* neither of these methods is appropriate. Actually there can be no question of determining *a priori* and ontologically what appears in all the unpredictability of a free act. This is why we shall limit ourselves here to indicating very summarily the possibilities of such a quest and its perspectives. The very fact that we can subject any man whatsoever to such an investigation—that is what belongs to human reality in general. Or, if you prefer, this is what can be established by an ontology. But the inquiry itself and its results are on principle wholly outside the possibilities on an ontology.

On the other hand, pure, simple empirical description can only give us catalogues and put us in the presence of pseudo-irreducibles (the desire to write, to swim, a taste for adventure, jealousy, etc.). It is not enough in fact to draw up a list of behavior patterns, of drives and inclinations, it is necessary also to *decipher* them; that is, it is necessary to know how to *question* them. This research can be conducted only according to the rules of a specific method. It is this method which we call existential psychoanalysis.

The *principle* of this psychoanalysis is that man is a totality and not a collection. Consequently he expresses himself as a whole in even his most insignificant and his most superficial behavior. In other words there is not a taste, a mannerism, or an human act which is not *revealing*.

The *goal* of psychoanalysis is to *decipher* the empirical behavior patterns of man; that is to bring out in the open the revelations which each one of them contains and to fix them conceptually.

Its *point of departure* is *experience*; its pillar of support is the fundamental, pre-ontological comprehension which man has of the human person. Although the majority of people can well ignore the indication contained in a gesture, a word, a sign and can look with scorn on the revelation which they carry, each human individual never-
569 theless possesses *a priori* the *meaning* of the revelatory value of these manifestations and is capable of deciphering them, at least if he is aided and guided by a helping hand. Here as elsewhere, truth is not encountered by chance; it does not belong to a domain where one must seek it without ever having any presentiment of its location, as one can go to look for the source of the Nile or of the Niger. It belongs *a priori* to human comprehension and the essential task is an hermeneutic; that is, a deciphering, a determination, and a conceptualization.

Its *method* is comparative. Since each example of human conduct symbolizes in its own manner the fundamental choice which must be brought to light, and since at the same time each one disguises this choice under its occasional character and is historical opportunity, only the comparison of these acts of conduct can effect the emergence of the unique revelation which they all express in a different way. The first outline of this method has been furnished for us by the psychoanalysis of Freud and his disciples. For this reason it will be profitable here to indicate more specifically the points where existential psychoanalysis will be inspired by psychoanalysis proper and those where it will radically differ from it.

Both kinds of psychoanalysis consider all objectively discernible manifestations of "psychic life" as symbols maintaining symbolic relations to the fundamental, total structures which constitute the individual person. Both consider that there are no primary givens such as hereditary dispositions, character, *etc*. Existential psychoanalysis recognizes nothing *before* the original upsurge of human freedom; empirical psychoanalysis holds that the original affectivity of the individual is virgin wax *before* its history. The libido is nothing besides its concrete fixations, save for a permanent possibility of fixing anything whatsoever upon anything whatsoever. Both consider the human being as a perpetual, searching, historization. Rather than uncovering static, constant givens they discover the meaning, orientation, and adventures of this history. Due to this fact both consider man in the world and do not imagine that one can question the being of a man without taking into account all his situation. Psychological investigations aim at reconstituting the life of the subject from birth to the moment of the cure; they utilize all the objective documentation which they can find; letters, witnesses, intimate diaries, "social" information of every kind. What they aim at restoring is less a pure psychic even than a twofold structure: the crucial event of infancy and the psychic crystallization around this event. Here again we have to do with a situation. Each "historical" fact from this point of view will be considered at once as a *factor* of the psychic evolution and as a *symbol* of that evolution. For it is nothing in itself. It operates only according to the way in which it is taken and this very manner of taking it expresses symbolically the internal disposition of the individual.

Empirical psychoanalysis and existential psychoanalysis both search within an existing situation for a fundamental attitude which can

not be expressed by simple, logical definitions because it is prior to all logic, and which requires reconstruction according to the laws of specific syntheses. Empirical psychoanalysis seeks to determine the *complex*, the very name of which indicates the polyvalence of all the meanings which are referred back to it. Existential psychoanalysis seeks to determine the *original choice*. This original choice operating in the face of the world and being a choice of position in the world is total like the complex; it is prior to logic like the complex. It is this which decides the attitude of the person when confronted with logic and principles; therefore there can be no possibility of questioning it in conformance to logic. It brings together in a prelogical synthesis the totality of the existent, and as such it is the center of reference for an infinity of polyvalent meanings.

Both our psychoanalyses refuse to admit that the subject is in a privileged position to proceed in these inquiries concerning himself. They equally insist on a strictly objective method, using as documentary evidence the data of reflection as well as the testimony of others. Of course the subject can undertake a psychoanalytic investigation of himself. But in this case he must renounce at the outset all benefit stemming from his peculiar position and must question himself exactly as if he were someone else. Empirical psychoanalysis in fact is based on the hypothesis of the existence of an unconscious psyche, which on principle escapes the intuition of the subject. Existential psychoanalysis rejects the hypothesis of the unconscious; it makes the psychic act coextensive with consciousness. But if the fundamental project is fully experienced by the subject and hence wholly conscious, that certainly does not mean that it must by the same token be *known* by him; quite the contrary.

At this point the similarity between the two kinds of psychoanalysis ceases. They differ fundamentally in that empirical psychoanalysis has decided upon its own irreducible instead of allowing this to make itself known in a self-evident intuition. The libido or the will to power in actuality constitutes a psycho-biological residue which is not clear in itself and which does not appear to us as *being beforehand* the irreducible limit of the investigation. Finally it is experience which establishes that the foundation of complexes is this libido or this will to power; and these results of empirical inquiry are perfectly contingent, they are not convincing. Nothing prevents our conceiving *a priori* of a "human reality" which would not be expressed by the will to power, for which the libido would not constitute the original, undifferentiated project.

On the other hand, the choice to which existential psychoanalysis will lead us, precisely because it is a choice, accounts for its original contingency, for the contingency of the choice 572 is the reverse side of its freedom. Furthermore, inasmuch as it is established on the *lack of being*, conceived as a fundamental characteristic of being, it receives its legitimacy *as a choice*, and we know that we do not have to push further. Each result then will be at once fully contingent and legitimately irreducible. Moreover it will always remain *particular*; that is, we will not achieve as the ultimate goal of our investigation and the foundation of all behavior an abstract, general term libido for example, which would be differentiated and made concrete first in complexes and then in detailed acts of conduct, due to the action of external facts and the history of the subject. On the contrary, it will be a choice which remains unique and which is from the start absolute concreteness.

The fact that the ultimate term of this existential inquiry must be a *choice*, distinguishes even better the psychoanalysis for which we have outlined the method and principal features. It thereby abandons the supposition that the environment acts mechanically on the subject under consideration. The environment can act on the subject only to the exact extent that he comprehends it; that is, transforms it into a situation. Hence no objective description of this environment could be of any use to us.

Precisely because the goal of the inquiry must 573 be to discover a *choice* and not a *state*, the investigator must recall on every occasion that his object is not a datum buried in the darkness of the uncon-

scious but a free, conscious determination—which is not even resident in consciousness, but which is one with this consciousness itself. Empirical psychoanalysis, to the extent that its method is better than its principles, is often in sight of an existential discovery, but it always stops part way. When it thus approaches the fundamental choice, the resistance of the subject collapses suddenly and he recognizes the images of himself which is presented to his as if he were seeing himself in a mirror. This involuntary testimony of the subject is precious for the psychoanalyst; he sees there the sign that he has reached his goal; he can pass on from the investigation proper to the cure.

This comparison allows us to understand 574 better what an existential psychoanalysis must be if it is entitled to exist. It is a method destined to bring to light, in a strictly objective form, the subjective choice by which each living person makes himself a person; that is, makes known to himself what he is. Since what the method seeks is a *choice of being* at the same time as a *being*, it must reduce particular behavior patterns to fundamental relations—not of sexuality or of the will to power, but *of being*—which are expressed in this behavior. It is then guided from the start toward a comprehension of being and must not assign itself any other goal than to discover being and the mode of being of the being confronting this being. It is forbidden to stop before attaining this goal. . . .

575 At most we can find the foreshadowing of it in certain particularly successful biographies. We hope to be able to attempt elsewhere two examples in relation to Flaubert and Dostoevsky. But it matters little to us whether it now exist; then important thing is that it is possible.

CONCLUSION

617 *I. In-Itself and For-Itself: Metaphysical Implications*

We are finally in a position to form conclusions. Already in the Introduction we discovered consciousness as an appeal to being, and we showed that the *cogito* refers immediately to a being-in-itself which is the *object* of consciousness. But after our description of the In-itself and the For-itself, it appeared to us difficult to establish a bond between them, and we feared that we might fall into an insurmountable dualism. This dualism threatened us again in another way. In fact to the extent that it can be said of the For-itself that it *is*, we found ourselves confronting two radically distinct modes of being: that of the For-itself which has to be what it is—*i.e.,* which is what it is not and which is not what it is—and that of the In-itself which is what it is. We asked then if the discovery of these tow types of being had resulted in establishing an hiatus which would divide Being (as a general category belonging to all existents) into two incommunicable regions, in each one of which the notion of Being must be taken in an original and unique sense.

Our research has enabled us to answer the first of these questions: the For-itself and the In-itself are reunited by a synthetic connection which is nothing other than the For-itself itself. The For-itself, in fact, is nothing buy the pure nihilation of the In-itself; it is like a hole of being at the heart of Being. . . . The For-itself is like a tiny nihilation which has its origin at the heart of Being; and this nihilation is sufficient to cause a total upheaval to *happen* to the In-itself. This upheaval is the world. The for-itself has no reality save that of being the nihilation of being. Its sole qualification comes to it from the fact that it is the nihilation of an individual and particular In-itself and not of a being in general. The For-itself is not nothingness in general but a particular privation; it constitutes itself as the privation of *this being.* Therefore we have no business asking about the way in which the for-itself can be united with the in-itself since the for-itself is in no way an autonomous substance. As a nihilation *it is made-to-be* by the in-itself; as an internal negation it must by means of the in-itself make known to itself what it is not and consequently what it has to be. If the *cogito* necessarily leads outside the self, if consciousness is a slippery slope on which one cannot take one's stand without immediately finding oneself tipped outside onto being-in-itself, this is because consciousness does not have by itself any sufficiency of being as an absolute subjectivity; from the start it refers to the thing.

For consciousness there is no being except for this precise obligation to be a revealing intuition of something. . . .

. . . To be other than being is to be self-consciousness in the unity of the temporalizing ekstates. Indeed what can the otherness be if not that game of musical chairs played by the reflected and the reflecting which we described as at the heart of the for-itself? For the only way in which the other can exist as other is to be consciousness (of) being other. Otherness is, in fact, an internal negation, and only a consciousness can be constituted as in internal negation. Every other conception of otherness will amount to positing it as an in-itself—that is, establishing between it and being an external relation which would necessitate the presence of a witness so as to establish that the other is other than the in-itself. However the other can not be other without emanating from being; in this respect it is relative to the in-itself. But neither can it be other without *making itself other*; otherwise its otherness would become a given and therefore a *being* capable of being considered in-itself. In so far as it is relative to the in-itself, the other is affected with facticity; in so far as it makes itself, it is an absolute. This is what we pointed out when we said that the for-itself is not the foundation of its being-as-nothingness-of-being but that it perpetually founds its nothingness-of-being. Thus the for-itself is an absolute *Unselbständig*, what we have called a non-substantial absolute. Its reality is purely *interrogative*. If it can posit questions this is because it is itself always *in question*; its being is never *given* but *interrogated* since it is always separated from itself by the nothingness of otherness. The for-itself is always in suspense because its being is a perpetual reprieve. If it could ever join with its being, then the otherness would by the same stroke disappear and along with it possibles, knowledge, the world. Thus the *ontological* problem of knowledge is resolved by the affirmation of the ontological primacy of the in-itself over the for-itself.

620 Ontology furnishes us two pieces of information which server as the basis for metaphysiscs.

Thus ontology teaches us two things: (1) *If* then in-itself were to found itself, it could attempt to do so only by making itself consciousness; that is, the concept of *causa sui* includes within it that of presence to self—*i.e.*, the nihilating decompression of being; (2) Consciousness is *in fact* a project of founding itself; that is, of attaining to the dignity of the in-itself foritself or in-itself-as-self-cause. But we can not derive anything further from this. Nothing allows us to affirm on the ontological level that the nihilation of the in-itself in for-itself has for its meaning—from the start and at very heart of the in-itself—the project of being its own self cause. Quite the contrary. Ontology here comes up against a profound contradiction since it is 621 through the for-itself that the possibility of a foundation comes to the world. In order to be a project of founding itself, the in-itself would of necessity have to be originally a presence to itself—*i.e.*, would have to be already consciousness. Ontology will therefore limit itself to declaring that *everything takes place as if* the initself in a project to found itself gave itself the modification of the for-itself.

It remains for us to consider the second problem which we formulated in our Introduction: If the in-itself and the for-itself are two modalities of *being*, is there not an hiatus at the very core of the idea of being? And is its comprehension not severed into two incommunicable parts by the very fact that its extension is constituted by two radically heterogenous classes? What is there in common between the being which is what it is, and the being which is what it is not and which is not what it is? What can help us here, however, is the conclusion of our preceding inquiry. We have just shown in fact that the in-itself and the for-itself are not juxtaposed. Quite the contrary, the for-itself without the in-itself is a kind of abstraction; it could not exist any more than a color could exist without form or a sound without pitch and without timbre. A consciousness which would be consciousness *of* nothing would be an absolute nothing. But if consciousness is bound to the in-itself by an *internal* relation, doesn't this mean that it is articulated with the in-itself so as to constitute a totality, and is it not this totality which would be given the name *being* or reality? Doubtless the for-itself is a nihilation, but as a nihilation it *is*; and it is in *a priori* unity with the in-itself.'

625 *II. Ethical Implications*

Ontology itself can not formulate ethical precepts. It is concerned solely with what is, and we can not possibly derive imperatives from ontology's indicatives. It does, however, allows us to catch a glimpse of what sort of ethics will assume its responsibilities when confronted 626 with a *human reality in situation*. Ontology has revealed to us, in fact, the origin and the nature of *value*; we have seen that value is the *lack* in relation to which the for-itself determines its being as *a lack*. By the very fact that the foritself *exists*, as we have seen, value arises to haunt its being for-itself. It follows that the various tasks of the for-itself can be made the object of an existential psychoanalysis, for they all aim at producing the missing synthesis of consciousness and being in the form of value or self-cause. Thus existential psychoanalysis is *moral description*, for it releases to us the ethical meaning of various human projects. It indicates to us the necessity of abandoning the psychology of interest along with any utilitarian interpretation of human conduct—by revealing to us the *ideal* meaning of all human attitudes. These meanings are beyond egoism and altruism, beyond also any behavior which is called *disinterested*. Man makes himself man in order to be God, and selfness considered from this point of view can appear to be an egoism; but precisely because there is no common measure between human reality and the self-cause which it wants to be, one could just as well say that man loses himself in order that the self-cause may exist. We will consider then that all human existence is a passion, the famous *self-interest* being only one way freely chosen among others to realize this passion.

But the principal result of existential psychoanalysis must be to make us repudiate the *spirit of seriousness*. The spirit of seriousness has two characteristics: it considers values as transcendent givens independent of human subjectivity, and it transfers the quality of "desirable" from the ontological structure of things of their simple material constitution. For the spirit of seriousness, for example, *bread* is desirable because it is *necessary* to live (a value written in an intelligible heaven) and because bread *is* nourishing. The result of the serious attitude, which as we know rules the world, is to cause the symbolic values of things to be drunk in by their empirical idiosyncrasy as ink by a blotter; it puts forward the opacity of the desired object and posits it in itself as a desirable irreducible. Thus we are already on the moral plane but concurrently on that of bad faith, for it is an ethics which is ashamed of itself and does not dare speak its name. It has obscured all its goals in order to free itself from anguish. Man pursues being blindly by hiding from himself the free project which is this pursuit. He makes himself such that he is *waited for* by all tasks placed along his way. Objects are mute demands, and he is nothing in himself but the passive obedience to these demands.

Existential psychoanalysis is going to reveal to man the real goal of his pursuit, which is being as a synthetic fusion of the in-itself with the for-itself; existential psychoanalysis is going to acquaint man with his passion. In truth there are many men who have practiced this psychoanalysis on themselves and who have not waited to learn its principles in order to make use of them as a means of deliverance and salvation. Many men, in fact, know that the goal of their pursuit is being; and to the extent that they posses this knowledge, they refrain from appropriating things for their own sake and try to realize the symbolic appropriation of their being in itself. . . .

But ontology and existential psychoanalysis (or the spontaneous and empirical application which men have always made of these disciplines) must reveal to the moral agent that he is the *being by whom values exist*. It is then that his freedom will become conscious of itself and will reveal itself in anguish as the unique source of value and the nothingness by which the *world* exists.

STUDY QUESTIONS: SARTRE, *BEING AND NOTHINGNESS*

1. Why can we reject the dualism of appearance and reality? What replaces it, and why?
2. What is Sartre's point about the table? At page liii? And at page lix?
3. Why does Sartre call consciousness 'total emptiness'?
4. What does Sartre mean by 'being-in-itself'?
5. What does Sartre say about the nature of consciousness?
6. What is 'being-for-itself'?
7. Why are 'non-being' and 'nothingness' important? How does nothingness arise, according to Sartre?
8. 'Human freedom precedes essence in man and makes it possible.' Explain what Sartre means by this.
9. What form does consciousness of freedom assume, according to Sartre?
10. How does Sartre distinguish anguish from fear? What is anguish?
11. How does Sartre use the examples of the book he is writing and the alarm clock that rings?
12. How does anguish relate to nothingness?
13. What is bad faith? Is it the same as self-deception?
14. What is consciousness?
15. What does he mean by 'self-negation'?
16. What does he mean by the Other?

17. Of what does bad faith seek to affirm the identity while preserving the differences?
18. When is bad faith impossible?
19. What is the example of the waiter in the café intended to show?
20. How are sincerity and bad faith related?
21. What makes bad faith possible?
22. Does bad faith involve conscious, cynical lying? Does it involve knowing preparation for deceit?
23. What is the ontological study of consciousness?
24. 'To the extent that the for-itself wishes to hide its own nothingness from itself and to incorporate the in-itself as its true mode of being, it is trying also to hide its freedom from itself.' Please explain what Sartre means by this.
25. Sartre says that in each inclination, the person expresses himself completely. What point is he making? What is he denying?
26. What is the original project of a person? How does Sartre try to establish this claim?
27. What is the principle of existential psychoanalysis? What is its goal? What is its point of departure? Its method?
28. What are the differences between existential and empirical psychoanalysis?
29. What are Sartre's main metaphysical conclusions? Given that there are two modes of being, why is there no hiatus at the core of being?
30. What are Sartre's main ethical conclusions? What is the real goal of a person's pursuit that existential psychoanalysis will reveal?

Philosophical Bridges: Sartre's Influence

Sartre's existentialism has had a very wide appeal. It has introduced into popular western culture key existentialist ideas, such as the concepts of bad faith, authenticity, and anguish, as well as the existentialist conception of freedom. This popularity is in part because Sartre married literature and philosophy in a way that very few other thinkers have been able to. In doing so, he opened up new directions and questions for philosophical thought, such as 'What are the relations between literature and philosophy?' The philosophy of literature owes much to Sartre. Furthermore, the art of thinking about philosophical issues in a literary way was also a relatively new style of doing philosophy prior to Sartre. Additionally, although Sartre was by no means the first novelist to introduce existentialist themes into literature, he did so in a more philosophically explicit way than any other author had before.

One of the most influential of Sartre's ideas is that an ethical philosophy centered on authenticity. Sartre intended to write a systematic work expounding such a moral theory, but he never did. Nevertheless, *Being and Nothingness* and his posthumous *Notebooks for an Ethics* (1983) outline many of the elements of such a theory. Many more recent writers have taken on this theme.

Toward the end of *Being and Nothingness*, Sartre explains existential psychoanalysis as a new approach to the field. His ideas were taken up, developed, and put into practice by Rollo May in the United States and R. D. Laing in the UK, among others. In brief, existentialist psychotherapy stresses that a person is defined by the choices that he or she makes. We live inauthentically when we deny that what we are is a result of our choices, for example by blaming external circumstances. By coming to realize this, we thereby recover responsibility for ourselves and allow ourselves to actively choose. The biographies that Sartre wrote are oriented in this direction.

In summary, as well as introducing existentialism to the public and in addition to his influence on literature and psychoanalysis, Sartre inspired a whole generation of French thinkers such as Merleau-Ponty, Albert Camus, Emmanuel Levinas and Simone de Beauvoir.

SIMONE DE BEAUVOIR (1908–1986)

Biographical History

During her active intellectual life, Simone de Beauvoir wrote sociological and cultural essays, novels, and a famous autobiography, as well as philosophical works. She studied philosophy at the Sorbonne and École Normale Supérieure. After reading Husserl in the 1930s, she published her first novel, *She Came to Stay*, in 1943. Her first major philosophical work was *The Ethics of Ambiguity* (1947). Her most famous work, *The Second Sex*, appeared in 1949. However, de Beauvoir is also well known for her four volumes of autobiography, *Memoirs of a Dutiful Daughter* (1958), *The Prime of Life* (1960), *Force of Circumstance* (1963), and *All Said and Done* (1972). In 1970, de Beauvoir wrote *Old Age*, an investigation of the social construction of old age. In 1981, she published her last book, *Adieux: A Farewell to Sartre*.

Philosophical Overview

The Second Sex documents the oppression of women through a study of history, myths, and literature, as well as through an examination of women's lives today, their different social roles, and their typical life histories.

De Beauvoir argues against any attempt to differentiate between the sexes in terms of some essential qualities because any essentialist definition will imply a denial of the freedom of the individual. This does not mean that there are no biological differences between the sexes. It means that the social meaning of such differences is not predetermined and that, therefore, these differences do not amount to essential identities that differentiate women from men. Any attempt to define an individual in terms of some essential qualities would imply a limit on that person's freedom. In this way, her work is an existentialist ethic as applied to women.

However, de Beauvoir's work also stresses that freedom depends on social and political conditions; in contrast, Sartre saw freedom as ontological. Furthermore, de Beauvoir emphasizes the importance of interpersonal relationships in the construction of a person's identity in a way that Sartre does not. In particular, women are objectified as the Other by their socially constructed roles, which limits their capacity to be free. In contrast, men are identified as the subject. Because women are identified with their gender, their social roles tend to condemn them to be considered as objects and as the second sex. This stress on interpersonal relationships marks an important difference of emphasis between de Beauvoir and Sartre. In *Being and Nothingness*, Sartre tends to regard the person as an autonomous individual. In contrast, de Beauvoir stresses that women's freedom is already socially compromised by their social roles. For this reason, she claims, 'One is not born a woman, one becomes one.'

THE SECOND SEX

We have selected the conclusion of de Beauvoir's classic work in which she describes and records many of the different facets of the oppression of women. The conclusion is directed toward answering whether fraternity between the sexes is possible and toward understanding what it might consist in. After analyzing from various angles the ways in which men dominate women, de Beauvoir reaches the conclusion that 'justice can never be done in the midst of injustice.' She asserts that there are situations that are incapable of a satisfactory solution because they are determined by unsatisfactory conditions. In other words, the whole social context needs to be changed for women to be treated equally. Complete economic and social equality will bring about 'inner metamorphosis.'

De Beauvoir replies to critics who claim that such changes are impossible. She does so by arguing that woman is a social product and not a natural state. Woman is determined by the way in which 'her body and relation to the world are modified through the action of others.' She also responds to the objection that such equality would be undesirable: would such equality destroy the relationships between men and women? In reply, she points out that, under conditions of equality, men and women would have relationships that are fraternal rather than oppressive.

CONCLUSION

No, woman is not our brother; through indolence and depravity we have made of her a being apart, unknown, having no weapon other than her sex, which not only means constant strife but is moreover an unfair weapon of the eternal little slave's mistrust— adoring or hating, but never our frank companion, a being set apart as if in *esprit de corps* and freemasonry.

Many men would still subscribe to these words of Laforgue; many think that there will always be "strife and dispute," as Montaigne put it, and that fraternity will never be possible. The fact is that today neither men nor women are satisfied with each other. But the question is to know whether there is an original curse that condemns them to rend each other or whether the conflicts in which they are opposed merely mark a transitional moment in human history.

We have seen that in spite of legends no physiological destiny imposes an eternal hostility upon Male and Female as such; even the famous praying mantis devours her male only for want of other food and for the good of the species: it is to this, the species, that all individuals are subordinated, from the top to the bottom of the scale of animal life. Moreover, humanity is something more than a mere species: it is a historical development; it is to be defined by the manner in which it deals with its natural, fixed characteristics, its *facticité*. Indeed, even with the most extreme bad faith in the world, it is impossible to demonstrate the existence of a rivalry between the human male and female of a truly physiological nature. Further, their hostility may be allocated rather to that intermediate terrain between biology and psychology: psychoanalysis. Woman, we are told, envies man his penis and wishes to castrate him; but the childish desire for the penis is important in the life of the adult woman only if she feels her femininity as a mutilation; and then it is as a symbol of all the privileges of manhood that she wishes to appropriate the male organ. We may readily agree that her dream of castration has this symbolic significance: she wishes, it is thought, to deprive the male of his transcendence.

But her desire, as we have seen, is much more ambiguous: she wishes, in a contradictory fashion, to *have* this transcendence, which is to suppose that she at once respects it and denies it, that she intends at once to throw herself into it and keep it within herself. This is to say that the drama does not unfold on a sexual level; further, sexuality has never seemed to us to define a destiny, to furnish in itself the key to human behavior, but to express the totality of a situation that it only helps to define. The battle of the sexes is not immediately implied in the anatomy of man and woman. The truth is that when one evokes it, one takes for granted that in the timeless realm of Ideas a battle is being waged between those vague essences the Eternal Feminine and the Eternal Masculine; and one neglects the fact that this titanic combat assumes on earth two totally different forms, corresponding with two different moments of history.

The woman who is shut up in immanence endeavors to hold man in that prison also; thus the prison will be confused with the world, and woman will no longer suffer from being confined there: mother, wife, sweetheart are the jailers. Society, being codified by man, decrees that woman is inferior: she can do away with this inferiority only by destroying the male's superiority. She sets about mutilating, dominating man, she contradicts him, she denies his truth and his values. But in doing this she is only defending herself; it was neither a changeless essence nor a mistaken choice that doomed her to immanence, to inferiority. They were imposed upon her. All oppression creates a state of war. And this is no exception. The existent who is regarded as inessential cannot fail to demand the re-establishment of her sovereignty.

Today the combat takes a different shape; instead of wishing to put man in a prison, woman endeavors to escape from one; she no longer seeks to drag him into the realms of immanence but to emerge, herself, into the light of transcendence. Now the attitude of the males creates a new conflict: it is with a bad grace that the man lets her go. He is very well pleased to remain the sovereign subject, the absolute superior, the essential being; he refuses to accept his companion as an equal in any concrete way. She replies to his lack of confidence in her by assuming an aggressive attitude. It is no longer a question of a war between individuals each shut up in his or her sphere: a caste claiming its rights goes over the top and it is resisted by the privileged caste. Here two transcendences are

face to face; instead of displaying mutual recognition, each free being wishes to dominate the other.

This difference of attitude is manifest on the sexual plane as on the spiritual plane. The "feminine" woman in making herself prey tries to reduce man, also, to her carnal passivity; she occupies herself in catching him in her trap, in enchaining him by means of the desire she arouses in him in submissively making herself a thing. The emancipated woman, on the contrary, wants to be active, a taker, and refuses the passivity man means to impose on her. Thus Elise and her emulators deny the values of the activities of virile type; they put the flesh above the spirit, contingence above liberty, their routine wisdom above creative audacity. But the "modern" woman accepts masculine values: she prides herself on thinking, taking action, working, creating, on the same terms as men; instead of seeking to disparage them, she declares herself their equal.

In so far as she express herself in definite action, this claim is legitimate, and male insolence must then bear the blame. But in men's defense it must be said that women are wont to confuse the issue. A Mabel Dodge Luhan intended to subjugate D. H. Lawrence by her feminine charms so as to dominate him spiritually thereafter; many women, in order to show by their successes their equivalence to men, try to secure male support by sexual means; they play on both sides, demanding old-fashioned respect and modern esteem, banking on their old magic and their new rights. It is understandable that a man becomes irritated and puts himself on the defensive; but he is also double-dealing when he requires woman to play the game fairly while he denies them the indispensable trump cards through distrust and hostility. Indeed, the struggle cannot be clearly drawn between them, since woman is opaque in her very being; she stands before man not as a subject but as an object paradoxically endued with subjectivity; she takes herself simultaneously as *self* and as *other*, a contradiction that entails baffling consequences. When she makes weapons at once of her weakness and of her strength, it is not a matter of designing calculation: she seeks salvation spontaneously in the way that has been imposed on her, that of passivity, at the same time when she is actively demanding her sovereignty; and no doubt this procedure is unfair tactics, but it is dictated to her by the ambiguous situation assigned her. Man, however, becomes indignant when he treats her as a free and independent being and then realizes that she is still a trap for him; if he gratifies and satisfies her in her posture as prey, he finds her claims to autonomy irritating; whatever he does, he feels tricked and she feels wronged.

The quarrel will go on as long as men and women fail to recognize each other as peers; that is to say, as long as femininity is perpetuated as such. Which sex is the more eager to maintain it? Woman, who is being emancipated from it, wishes none the less to retain its privileges; and man, in that case, wants her to assume its limitations. "It is easier to accuse one sex than to excuse the other," says Montaigne. It is vain to apportion praise and blame. The truth is that if the vicious circle is so hard to break, it is because the two sexes are each the victim at once of the other and of itself. Between two adversaries confronting each other in their pure liberty, an agreement could be easily reached: the more so as the war profits neither. But the complexity of the whole affair derives from the fact that each camp is giving aid and comfort to the enemy; woman is pursuing a dream of submission, man a dream of identification. Want of authenticity does not pay: each blames the other for the unhappiness he or she has incurred in yielding to the temptations of the easy way; what man and woman loathe in each other is the shattering frustration of each one's own bad faith and baseness.

We have seen why men enslaved women in the first place; the devaluation of femininity has been a necessary step in human evolution, but it might have led to collaboration between the two sexes; oppression is to be explained by the tendency of the existent to flee from himself by means of identification with the other, whom he oppresses to that end. In each individual man that tendency exists today; and the vast majority yield to it. The husband wants to find himself in his wife, the lover in his mistress, in the form of a stone image; he is seeking in her the myth of his virility, of his sovereignty, of his immediate reality. "My husband never goes to the movies," says his wife, and the dubious masculine opinion is graved in the marble of eternity. But he is himself the slave of his double: what an effort to build up an image in which he is always in danger! In spite of everything his success in this depends upon the capricious freedom of women: he must constantly try to keep this propitious to him. Man is concerned with the effort to appear male, important, superior; he pretends so as to get pretense in return; he, too, is aggressive, uneasy; he feels hostility for women because he is afraid of them, he is afraid of them because he is afraid of the personage, the image, with which he identifies himself. What time and strength he squanders in liquidating, sublimating, transferring complexes, in talking about women, in seducing them, in fearing them! He would be liberated himself in their liberation. But this is precisely what he dreads. And so he obstinately persists in the mystifications intended to keep woman in her chains.

That she is being tricked, many men have realized. "What a misfortune to be a woman! And yet the misfortune, when one is a woman, is at bottom not to comprehend that it is one," says Kirkegaard. For a long time there have been efforts to disguise this misfortune. . . .

To forbid her working, to keep her at home, is to defend her against herself and to assure her happiness. We have seen what poetic veils are thrown over her monotonous burdens of housekeeping and maternity: in exchange for her liberty she has received the false treasures of her "femininity." Balzac illustrates this maneuver very well in counseling man to treat her as a slave while persuading her that she is a queen. Less cynical, many men try to convince themselves that she is really privileged. . . .

Free from troublesome burdens and cares, she obviously has "the better part." But it is disturbing that with an obstinate perversity—connected no doubt with original sin—down through the centuries and in all countries, the people who have the better part are always crying to their benefactors: "It is too much! I will be satisfied with yours!" But the munificent capitalists, the generous colonists, the superb males, stick to their guns: "Keep the better part, hold on to it!"

It must be admitted that the males find in woman more complicity than the oppressor usually finds in the oppressed. And in bad faith they take authorization from this to declare that she has *desired* the destiny they have imposed on her. We have seen that all the main features of her training combine to bar her from the roads of revolt and adventure. Society in general—beginning with her respected parents—lies to her by praising the lofty values of love, devotion, the gift of herself, and then concealing from her the fact that neither lover nor husband nor yet her children will be inclined to accept the burdensome charge of all that. She cheerfully believes these lies because they invite her to follow the easy slope: in this others commit their worst crime against her; throughout her life from childhood on, they damage and corrupt her by designating as her true vocation this submission, which is the temptation of every existent in the anxiety of liberty. If a child is taught idleness by being amused all day along and never being led to study, or shown its usefulness, it will hardly be said, when he grows up, that he chose to be incapable and ignorant; yet this is how woman is brought up, without ever being impressed with the necessity of taking charge of her own existence. So she readily lets herself come to count on the protection, love, assistance, and supervision of others, she lets herself be fascinated with the hope of self-realization without *doing* anything. She does wrong in yielding to the temptation; but man is in no position to blame her, since he has led her into the temptation. When conflict arises between them, each will hold the other responsible for the situation; she will reproach him with having made her what she is: "No one taught me to reason or to earn my own living"; he will reproach her with having accepted the consequences: "You don't know anything, you are an incompetent," and so on. Each sex thinks it can justify itself by taking the offensive; but the wrongs done by one do not make the other innocent.

The innumerable conflicts that set men and women against one another come from the fact that neither is prepared to assume all the consequences of this situation which the one has offered and the other accepted. The doubtful concept of "equality in inequality," which the one uses to mask his despotism and the other to mask her cowardice, does not stand the test of experience: in their exchanges, woman appeals to the theoretical equality she has been guaranteed, and man the concrete inequality that exists.

The result is that in every association on endless debate goes on concerning the ambiguous meaning of the words *give* and *take*: she complains of giving her all, he protests that she takes his all. Woman has to learn that exchanges—it is a fundamental law of political economy—are based on the value the merchandise offered has for the buyer, and not for the seller: she has been deceived in being persuaded that her worth is priceless. The truth is that for man she is an amusement, a pleasure, company, an inessential boon; he is for her the meaning, the justification of her existence. The exchange, therefore, is not of two items of equal value.

This inequality will be especially brought out in the fact that the time they spend together—which fallaciously seems to be the same time—does not have the same value for both partners. During the evening the lover spends with his mistress he could be doing something of advantage to his career, seeing friends, cultivating business relationships, seeking recreation; for a man normally integrated in society, time is a positive value: money, reputation, pleasure. For the idle, bored woman, on the contrary, it is a burden she wishes to get rid of; when she succeeds in killing time, it is a benefit to her: the man's presence is pure profit. In a liaison what most clearly interests the man, in many cases, is the sexual benefit he gets from it: if need be, he can be content to spend no more time with his mistress than is required for the sexual act; but—with exceptions—what she, on her part, wants is to kill all the excess time she has no her hands; and—like the storekeeper who will not sell potatoes unless the customer will take turnips also—she will not yield her body unless her lover will take hours of conversation and "going out" into the bargain. A balance is reached if, on the whole, the cost does not seem too high to the man, and this depends, of course, on the strength of his desire and the importance he gives to what is to be sacrificed. . . .

As a rule he consents to assume the burden because he knows very well that he is on the privileged side, he has a bad conscience; and if he is of reasonable good will he tries to compensate for the inequality by being generous. He prides himself on his compassion, however, and at the first clash he treats the woman as ungrateful and thinks, with some irritation: "I'm too good to her." She feels she is behaving like a beggar when she is convinced of the high value of her gifts, and that humiliates her. . . .

Once again it is useless to apportion blame and excuses: justice can never be done in the midst of injustice. A colonial administrator has no possibility of acting rightly toward the natives, nor a general toward his soldiers; the only solution is to be neither colonist nor military chief; but a man could not prevent himself from being a man. So there he is, culpable in spite of himself and laboring under the effects of a fault he did not himself commit; and here she is, victim and shrew in spite of herself. . . .

In daily life we meet with an abundance of these cases which are incapable of satisfactory solution because they are determined by unsatisfactory conditions. A man who is compelled to go on materially and morally supporting a woman whom he no longer loves feels he is victimized; but if he abandons without resources the woman who has pledged her whole life to him, she will be quite as unjustly victimized The evil originates not in the perversity of individuals—and bad faith first appears when each blames the other—it originates rather in a situation against which all individual action is powerless. Women are "clinging," they are a dead weight, and they suffer for it; the point is that their situation is like that of a parasite sucking out the living strength of another organism. Let them be provided with living strength of their own, let them have the means to attack the world and wrest from it their own subsistence, and their dependence will be abolished—that of man also. There is no doubt that both men and women will profit greatly from the new situation.

A world where men and women would be equal is easy to visualize, for that precisely is what the Soviet Revolution *promised:* women raised and trained exactly like men were to work under the same conditions and for the same wages. Erotic liberty was to be recognized by custom, but the sexual act was not to be considered a "service" to be paid for; woman was to be *obliged* to provide herself with other ways of earning a living; marriage was to be based on a free agreement that the spouses could break at will; maternity was to be voluntary, which meant that contraception and abortion were to be authorized and that, on the other hand, all mothers and their children were to have exactly the same rights, in or out of marriage; pregnancy leaves were to be paid for by the State, which would assume charge of the children, signifying not that they would be *taken away* from their parents, but that they would not be *abandoned* to them.

But is it enough to change laws, institutions, customs, public opinion, and the whole social context, for men and women to become truly equal? "Women will always be women," say the skeptics. Other seers prophesy that in casting off their femininity they will not succeed in changing themselves into men and they will become monsters. This would be to admit that the women of today is a creation of nature; it must be repeated once more that in human society nothing is natural and that woman, like much else, is a product elaborated by civilization. The intervention of others in her destiny is fundamental: if this action took a different direction, it would produce a quite different result. Woman is determined not by her hormones or by mysterious instincts, but by the manner in which her body and her relation to the world are modified through the action of others than herself. The abyss that separates the adolescent boy and girl has been deliberately opened out between them since earliest childhood; later on, woman could not be other than what she *was made*, and that past was bound to shadow her for life. If we appreciate its influence, we see clearly that her destiny is not predetermined for all eternity.

We must not believe, certainly, that a change in woman's economic condition alone is enough to transform her, though this factor has been and remains the basic factor in her evolution; but until it has brought about the moral, social, cultural, and other consequences that it promises and requires, the new woman cannot appear. At this moment they have been realized nowhere, in Russia no more than in France or the United States; and this explains why the woman of today is torn between the past and the future. She appears most often as a "true woman" disguised as a man, and she feels herself as ill at ease in her flesh as in her masculine garb. She must shed her old skin and cut her own new clothes. This she could do only through a social evolution.

If the little girl were brought up from the first with the same demands and rewards, the same severity and the same freedom, as her brothers, taking part in the same studies, the same games, promised the same future, surrounded with women and men who seemed to her undoubted equals, the meanings of the castration complex and of the Œdipus complex would be profoundly modified. Assuming on the same basis as the father the material and moral responsibility of the couple, the mother would enjoy the same lasting prestige; the child would perceive around her an androgynous world and not a masculine world. Were the emotionally more attracted to her father—which is not even sure—her love for him would be tinged with a will to emulation and not a feeling of powerlessness; she would not be oriented toward passivity. Authorized to test her powers in work and sports, competing actively with the boys, she would not find the absence of the penis—compensated by the promise of a child—enough to give rise to an inferiority complex; correlatively, the boy would not have a superiority complex if it were not instilled into him and if he looked up to women with as much respect as to men. The little girl would not seek sterile compensation in narcissism and dreaming, she would not take her fate for granted; she would be interested in what she was *doing*, she would throw herself without reserve into undertakings.

Woman is the victim of no mysterious fatality; the peculiarities that identify her as specifically a woman get their importance from the significance placed upon them. They can be surmounted, in the future, when they are regarded in new perspectives. Thus, as we have seen, through her erotic experience woman feels—and often detests—the domination of the male; but this is no reason to conclude that her ovaries condemn her to live forever on her knees. Virile aggressiveness seems like a lordly privilege only within a system that in its entirety conspires to affirm masculine sovereignty; and woman *feels* herself profoundly passive in the sexual act only because she already *thinks* of herself as such.

As a matter of fact, man, like woman, is flesh, therefore passive, the plaything of his hormones and of the species, the restless prey of his desires. And she, like him, in the midst of the carnal fever, is a consenting, a voluntary gift, an activity; they live out in their several fashions that strange ambiguity of existence made body. In those combats where they think they confront one another, it is really against the self that each one struggles, projecting into the partner that part of the self which is repudiated; instead of living out the ambiguities of their situation, each tries to make the other bear the abjection and tries to reserve the honor for the self. If, however, both should assume the ambiguity with a clear-sighted modesty, correlative of an authentic pride, they would see each other as equals and would live out their erotic drama in amity. The fact that we are human beings is infinitely more important than all the peculiarities that distinguish human beings from one another; it is never the given that confers superiorities: "virtue," as the ancients called it, is defined at the level of "that which depends on us." In both sexes is played out the same drama of the flesh and the spirit, of finitude and transcendence; both are gnawed away by time and laid in wait for by death, they have the same essential need for one another; and they can gain from their liberty the same glory. If they were to taste it, they would no longer be tempted to dispute fallacious privileges, and fraternity between them could then come into existence.

I shall be told that all this is utopian fancy, because woman cannot be "made over" unless society has first made her really the equal of man. Conservatives have never failed in such circumstances to refer to that vicious circle; history, however, does not revolve. If a caste is kept in a state of inferiority, no doubt it remains inferior; but liberty can break the circle. Let the Negroes vote and they become worthy of having the vote: let woman be given responsibilities and she is able to assume them. The fact is that oppressors cannot be expected to make a move of gratuitous generosity; but at one time the revolt of the oppressed, at another time even the very evolution of the privileged caste itself, creates new situations; thus men have been led, in their own interest, to give partial emancipation to women: it remains only for women to continue their ascent, and the successes they are obtaining are an encouragement for them to do so. It seems almost certain that sooner or later they will arrive at complete economic and social equality, which will bring about an inner metamorphosis.

However this may be, there will be some to object that if such a world is possible it is not desirable. When woman is "the same" as her male, life will lose its salt and spice. This argument, also, has lost its novelty: those interested in perpetuating present conditions are always in tears about the marvelous past that is about to disappear, without having so much as a smile for the young future. . . .

There is no denying that feminine dependence, inferiority, woe, give women their special character; assuredly woman's autonomy, if it spares men many troubles, will also deny them many conveniences; assuredly there are certain forms of the sexual adventure which will be lost in the world of tomorrow. But this does not mean that love, happiness, poetry, dream, will be banished from it.

Let us not forget that our lack of imagination always depopulates the future; for us it is only an abstraction; each one of us secretly deplores the absence there of the one who was himself. But the humanity of tomorrow will be living in its flesh and in its conscious liberty; that time will be its present and it will in turn prefer it. New relations of flesh and sentiment of which we have no conception will arise between the sexes; already, indeed, there have appeared between men and women friendships, rivalries, complicities, comradeships—chaste or sensual—which past centuries could not have conceived. To mention one point, nothing could seem to me more debatable than the opinion that dooms the new world to uniformity and hence to boredom. I fail to see that this present world is free from boredom or that liberty ever creates uniformity.

To begin with, there will always be certain differences between man and woman; her eroticism, and therefore her sexual world, have a special form of their own and therefore cannot fail to engender a sensuality, a sensitivity, of a special nature. This means that her relations to her own body, to that of the male, to the child, will never be identical with those the male bears to his own body, to that of the female, and to the child; those who make much of "equality in difference" could not with good grace refuse to grant me the possible existence of differences in equality. Then again, it is institutions that create uniformity. Young and pretty, the slaves of the harem are always the same in the sultan's embrace:

Christianity gave eroticism its savor of sin and legend when it endowed the human female with a soul; if society restores her sovereign individuality to woman, it will not thereby destroy the power of love's embrace to move the heart.

It is nonsense to assert that revelry, vice, ecstasy, passion, would become impossible if man and woman were equal in concrete matters; the contradictions that put the flesh in opposition to the spirit, the instant to time, the swoon of immanence to the challenge of transcendence, the absolute of pleasure to the nothingness of forgetting, will never be resolved; in sexuality will always be materialized the tension, the anguish, the joy, the frustration, and the triumph of existence. To emancipate woman is to refuse to confine her to the relations she bears to man, not to deny them to her; let her have her independent existence and she will continue none the less to exist for him *also*: mutually recognizing each other as subject, each will yet remain for the other an *other*. The reciprocity of their relations will not do away with the miracles—desire, possession, love, dream, adventure—worked by the division of human beings into two separate categories; and the words that move us—giving, conquering, uniting—will not lose their meaning. On the contrary, when we abolish the slavery of half of humanity, together with the whole system of hypocrisy that it implies, then the "division" of humanity will reveal its genuine significance and the human couple will find its true form. "The direct, natural, necessary relation of human creatures is the *relation of man to woman*," Marx has said. "The nature of this relation determines to what point man himself is to be considered as a *generic being*, as mankind; the relation of man to woman is the most natural relation of human being to human being. By it is shown, therefore, to what point the *natural* behavior of man has become *human* or to what point the *human* being has become his *natural* being, to what point his *human nature* has become his *nature*."

The case could not be better stated. It is for man to establish the reign of liberty in the midst of the world of the given. To gain the supreme victory, it is necessary, for one thing, that by and through their natural differentiation men and women unequivocally affirm their brotherhood.

STUDY QUESTIONS: DE BEAUVOIR, *THE SECOND SEX*

1. What is de Beauvoir's view of the Laforgue quote?
2. Does she believe in physiological destiny?
3. What is her view of psychoanalysis?
4. What are the 'Eternal Feminine' and the 'Eternal Masculine,' and what role do these play?
5. What does all oppression create?
6. What does she mean by 'transcendence'? How is it connected to sexuality?
7. By what action, according to de Beauvoir, does the male feel tricked and the woman wronged?
8. Why did men enslave women?
9. Why are men afraid of women, according to her?
10. What is her view of 'femininity'?
11. How does she view blame and excuses?
12. What use does she make of the Oedipus complex?
13. What is her view of Christianity? Of communism? Of political and religious institutions in general?
14. What is her view of Marx?

Philosophical Bridges: de Beauvoir's Influence

De Beauvoir's thesis that women are treated as 'the Other' by men has provided a vocabulary for expressing the nature of oppression that has been taken up by many feminist writers, including Luce Irigaray. The idea is that being male is assumed as the norm for humanity, and women become treated as 'the Other.'

De Beauvoir makes a fundamental distinction that has become vital to later discussions of sexual oppression and differences. She differentiates the biological differences from their social meaning. 'One is not born a woman, one becomes one.' De Beauvoir thereby stresses that a person's identity is social constituted, and this is another idea that has become very important in later discussions of the nature of sexual, racial, and other forms of oppression. Furthermore, de Beauvoir initiated discussion of the nature of sexual equality: how can sexual equality be understood in a way that respects gender differences?

Although de Beauvoir emphasizes the importance of social factors, she does so within a general existentialist framework. This means that she elucidates the notion of subjugation in terms of a person being treated as an object in a way that denies her personhood. This analysis takes feminism beyond the assertion that women have had unequal opportunities to participate in society's wealth and other goods. Simone de Beauvoir is the first in a tradition of French feminist thinkers, which includes Luce Irigaray, Julia Kristeva, Michèle Le Doeuff, and Hélène Cixous.

De Beauvoir has inspired feminist and other thinkers not only for the content of her thought but also for the integrity with which she expressed it. De Beauvoir had a distinctive way of doing existentialist philosophy, which is both social and personal. *The Second Sex* covers all aspects of the social status and identity of women to show how oppression is reinforced. In a similar spirit, de Beauvoir's *Old Age* (1970) studies the social construction of aging. Moreover, her autobiographical volumes and her book regarding her mother's death (*A Very Easy Death*, 1964) can be seen as very personal existential studies.

The extent of Simone de Beauvoir's influence on Sartre is a contentious point. De Beauvoir's philosophical novel, *She Came to Stay* (1943), was written before *Being and Nothingness*, and her ideas about human relationships expressed in that novel had an important influence on Sartre's thinking, though the extent of that influence is disputed. However, after the end of World War II, Sartre regarded his earlier work *Being and Nothingness* as too individualistic because it emphasized inadequately the social dimension of human existence and freedom. De Beauvoir certainly influenced this deep change in Sartre's philosophy.

MAURICE MERLEAU-PONTY (1908–1961)

Biographical History

Maurice Merleau-Ponty studied philosophy with his fellow students Sartre and de Beauvoir at the École Normale Supérieure. In 1949, he was appointed chair in child psychology and pedagogy at the Sorbonne. In 1952, he was given the philosophy chair at the College de France. Although he was inspired deeply by Husserl and Heidegger, Merleau-Ponty was also influenced by the thought of Hegel and Marx. Furthermore, Merleau-Ponty had extensive knowledge of Gestalt and child developmental psychology, as well as behavioral and brain studies. His early books are *The Structure of Behavior* (1942) and *The Phenomenology of Perception* (1945), which was his major work. After the end of World War II, Merleau-Ponty worked in collaboration with Sartre on the journal *Les Temps Modernes*. He produced several essays on communism, which are collected in the book *Humanism and Terror* (1947). Around 1952, he began distancing himself from Marxism and from Sartre, and his book *Adventures of the Dialectic*, published in 1955, contains a critique of his earlier views and those of Sartre.

Philosophical Overview

We can divide Merleau-Ponty's thinking roughly into four stages. In the first period, his main concern was phenomenological psychology, especially the areas of behavior and perception. Both *The Structure of Behavior* (1942) and *The Phenomenology of Perception* (1945) belong to this period. The first is an attempt to distinguish his own phenomenological view from the dominant psychological theories of the time, such as John B. Watson's behaviorism, psychoanalytic theory, and Kurt Koffka's gestalt theory. The second is described below.

In the second stage, Merleau-Ponty was influenced by Ferdinand de Saussure's structural theory of signs outlined in the *Course in General Linguistics,* which is explained briefly in the Prologue to the next section. This led Merleau-Ponty to try to integrate phenomenology and structuralism through the idea of the structures of the experience of signs. It also led to a widening of his interests: he became more interested in aesthetics, politics, and history. His work *Sense and Nonsense* (1948) belongs to this period.

Third, in his book *The Prose of the World* (published posthumously), Merleau-Ponty develops the concept of indirect language, which is a not fully verbalized language of expression and which was a major concern of his throughout the 1950s.

Fourth, at the time of his death, Merleau-Ponty was working on a manuscript, since published as *The Visible and the Invisible*, in which he elaborates the notion of visibility first developed in the article 'Eye and Mind' (1960). In this article, Merleau-Ponty contrasts the painter Paul Cézanne's landscapes with his later portraits and explains in what ways this shift made seeing more visible to Cézanne. Merleau-Ponty uses this as an analogy to show the limitations of the standard approaches to philosophy, which through intellectualization distance what should be visible.

THE PHENOMENOLOGY OF PERCEPTION

The selections from Merleau-Ponty's early work *The Phenomenology of Perception* investigate the relations between the subject and its body and world, with a special emphasis on perception and cultural experience. The book also contains sections on spatiality, sexuality, expression, speech and literature, history, and Sartre's conception of freedom.

Primacy of Perception

Although Husserl was a major source of inspiration for Merleau-Ponty, he argues that Husserl's phenomenological reduction or bracketing is too idealist and individualistic. It does not stress sufficiently the reality of objects and of other people. According to Merleau-Ponty, phenomenology is an attempt to describe the world as it is experienced and lived. This involves a rejection of the Empiricist thesis that perception consists of sensations. The idea of discrete sensations cannot explain the essential intentionality, structure, and meaningfulness of perception.

The World

Like Husserl and Heidegger, Merleau-Ponty denies the claim that the scientific description of the world is fundamental. Scientific causal explanations of perception already take for granted the primacy and meaningfulness of perception. The world as experienced and lived in is meaningful, and the descriptions provided by science are only an abstraction from this life-world. However, this does not mean that we should adopt an idealist analysis of objects. Objects cannot be reduced to individual experience or consciousness. Therefore, Merleau-Ponty tries to avoid the dichotomy between scientific realism on the one hand and idealism on the other.

The Body

A central theme of much of Merleau-Ponty's thought is the need for phenomenology to take into account the bodily nature of our existence. Scientific theories tend to treat the body mechanistically as if it were just another object. According to Merleau-Ponty, the body is the subject of experience, which engages with the world, and, in this way, the meaning of the body is that it is the condition that allows the subject to have a world at all. Merleau-Ponty explicates the notion of embodiment, which replaces mind-body dualism, by showing how sexuality is part of our being-in-the-world, how spatiality must be understood primarily as our way of moving around in the world, and how bodily movement is already a form of expression as well as a condition of language.

Other Persons

For Merleau-Ponty, an important challenge facing phenomenology is to explain the relationship between the individual's perceptual world and other persons, thereby avoiding the individualism that he perceives as part of Husserl's and Sartre's philosophies. We perceive directly other people as embodied living beings. However, the primary contact with others is via language, because of which other perspectives can enter into the individual's phenomenological field, and through which we share a common world. Merleau-Ponty provides increasingly rich descriptions of this encounter with other people by analyzing literature, art, history, and politics. Finally, he challenges Sartre's notion of individualistic autonomy by arguing that autonomy is a mode of engagement with the world.

vii PREFACE

What is phenomenology? It may seem strange that this question has still to be asked half a century after the first works of Husserl. The fact remains that it has by no means been answered. Phenomenology is the study of essences; and according to it, all problems amount to finding definitions of essences: the essence of perception, or the essence of consciousness, for example. But phenomenology is also a philosophy which puts essences back into existence, and does not expect to arrive at an understanding of man and the world from any starting point other than that of their 'facticity'. It is a transcendental philosophy which places in abeyance the assertions arising out of the natural attitude, the better to understand them; but it is also a philosophy for which the world is always 'already there' before reflection begins—as an inalienable presence; and all its efforts are concentrated upon re-achieving a direct and primitive contact with the world, and endowing that contact with a philosophical status. It is the search for a philosophy which shall be a 'rigorous science', but it also offers an account of space, time and the world as we 'live' them. It tries to give a direct description of our experience as it is, without taking account of its psychological origin and the causal explanations which the scientist, the historian or the sociologist may be able to provide. Yet Husserl in his last works mentions a 'genetic phenomenology', and even a 'constructive phenomenology'. . . .

The reader pressed for time will be inclined to give up the idea of covering a doctrine which says everything, and will wonder whether a philosophy which cannot define its scope deserves all the discussion which has gone on around it, and whether he is not faced rather by a myth or a viii fashion. . . .

We shall find in ourselves, and nowhere else, the unity and true meaning of phenomenology. It is less a question of counting up quotations than of determining and expressing in concrete form this *phenomenology for ourselves* which has given a number of present day readers the impression, on reading Husserl or Heidegger, not so much of encountering a new philosophy as of recognizing what they had been waiting for. Phenomenology is accessible only through a phenomenological method. Let us, therefore, try systematically to bring together the celebrated phenomenological themes as they have grown spontaneously together in life. Perhaps we shall then understand why phenomenology has for so long remained at an initial stage, as a problem to be solved and a hope to be realized.

It is a matter of describing, not of explaining or analysing. Husserl's first directive to phenomenology, in its early stages, to be a 'descriptive psychology', or to return to the 'things themselves', is from the start a foreswearing of science. I am not he outcome or the meeting-point of numerous casual agencies which determine my bodily or psychological make-up. I cannot conceive myself as nothing but a bit of the world, a mere object of biological, psychological or sociological investigation. I cannot shut myself up within the realm of science. All my knowledge of the world, even my scientific knowledge, is gained from my own particular point of view, or from some experience of the world without which the symbols of science would be meaningless. The whole universe of science is built upon the world as directly

From *Phenomenology of Perception* by Maurice Merleau-Ponty, translated by Colin Smith. Reprinted by permission of Taylor & Francis and Editions Gallimard.

experienced, and if we want to subject science itself to rigorous scrutiny and arrive at a precise assessment of its meaning and scope, we must begin by reawakening the basic experience of the world of which science is the second-order expression. Science has not and never will have, by its nature, the same significance *qua* form of being as the world which we perceive, for the simple reason that it is a rationale or explanation of that world. I am, not a 'living creature' nor even a 'man', nor again even 'a consciousness' endowed with all the characteristics which zoology, social anatomy or inductive psychology recognize in these various products of the natural or historical process—I am the absolute source, my existence does not stem from my antecedents, from my physical and social environment; instead it moves out towards them and sustains them, for I alone bring into being for myself (and therefore into being in the only sense that the world can have for me) the tradition which I elect to carry on, or the horizon whose distance from me would be abolished—since that distance is not one of its properties—if I were not there to scan it with my gaze. Scientific points of view, according to which my existence is a moment of the world's, are always both naïve and at the same time dishonest, because they take for granted, without explicitly mentioning it, the other point of view, namely that of consciousness, through which from the outset a world forms itself round me and begins to exist for me. To return to things themselves is to return to that world which precedes knowledge, of which knowledge always *speaks*, and in relation to which every scientific schematization is an abstract and derivative sign-language, as it geography in relation to the countryside in which we have learnt beforehand what a forest, a prairie or a river is.

This move is absolutely distinct from the idealist return to consciousness, and the demand for a pure description excludes equally the procedure of analytical reflection on the one hand, and that of scientific explanation on the other. Descartes and particularly Kant *detached* the subject, or consciousness, by showing that I could not possibly apprehend anything as existing unless I first of all experienced myself as existing in the act of apprehending it. They presented consciousness, the absolute certainty of my existence for myself, as the condition of there being anything at all; and the act of relating as the basis of relatedness. It is true that the act of relating is nothing if divorced from the spectacle of the world in which relations are found; the unity of consciousness in Kant is achieved simultaneously with that of the world. . . .

Analytical reflection starts from our experience of the world and goes back to the subject as to a condition of possibility distinct from that experience, reveling the all-embracing synthesis as that without which there would be no world. To this extent it ceases to remain part of our experience and offers, in place of an account, a reconstruction. It is understandable, in view of this, that Husserl, having accused Kant of adopting a 'faculty psychologism', should have urged, in place of a noetic analysis which bases the world on the synthesizing activity of the subject, his own *'noematic reflection'* which remains within the object and, instead of begetting it, brings to light its fundamental unity.

The world is there before any possible analysis of mine, and it would be artificial to make it the outcome of a series of syntheses which link, in the first place sensations, then aspects of the object corresponding to different perspectives, when both are nothing but products of analysis, with no sort of prior reality. . . .

Thus reflection is carried off by itself and installs itself in an impregnable subjectivity, as yet untouched by being and time. But this is very ingenuous, or at least it is an incomplete form of reflection which loses sight of its own beginning. When I begin to reflect my reflection bears upon an unreflective experience; moreover my reflection cannot be unaware of itself as an event, and so it appears to itself in the light of a truly creative act, of a changed structure of consciousness, and yet it has to recognize, as having priority over its own operations, the world which is given to the subject because the subject is given to himself. The real has to be described, not constructed or formed. . . . If the reality of my perception were based solely on the intrinsic coherence of 'representations', it ought to be for ever hesitant and, being wrapped up in my conjectures on probabilities, I ought to be ceaselessly taking apart misleading syntheses, and reinstating in reality stray phenomena which I had excluded in the first place. But this does not happen. The real is a closely woven fabric. It does not await our judgment before incorporating the most surprising phenomena, or before rejecting the most plausible figments of our imagination. Perception is not a science of the world, it is not even an act, a deliberate taking up of a position; it is the background from which all acts stand out, and is presupposed by them. The world is not an object such that I have in my possession the law of its making; it is the natural setting of, and field for, all my thoughts and all my explicit perceptions. Truth does not 'inhabit' only 'the inner man', or more accurately, there is no inner man, man is in the world, and only in the world does he know himself. When I return to myself from an excursion into the realm of dogmatic common sense or of science, I find, not a source of intrinsic truth, but a subject destined to the world.

xi

All of which reveals the true meaning of the famous phenomenological reduction. There is probably no question over which Husserl spent more time—or to which he more often returned, since the 'problematic of reduction' occupies an important place in his unpublished work. For a long time, and even in recent texts, the reduction is presented as the return to a transcendental consciousness before which the world is spread out and completely transparent, quickened through and through by a series of apperceptions which it is the philosopher's task to reconstitute on the basis of their outcome. Thus my sensation or redness is *perceived as* the manifestation of a certain redness experienced, this in turn as the manifestation of a red surface, which is the manifestation of a piece of red cardboard, and this finally is the manifestation or outline of a red thing, namely this book. We are to understand, then, that it is the apprehension of a certain *hylè*, as indicating a phenomenon of a higher degree, the *Sinngebung*, or active meaning-giving operation which may be said to define conscious-

ness, so that the world is nothing but 'world-as-meaning', and the phenomenological reduction is idealistic, in the sense that there is here a transcendental idealism which treats the world as an indivisible unity of value shared by Peter and Paul, in which their perspectives blend. 'Peter's consciousness' and 'Paul's consciousness' are in communication, the perception of the world 'by Peter' is not Peter's doing any more than its perception 'by Paul' is Paul's doing; in each case it is the doing of pre-personal forms of consciousness, whose communication raises no problem, since it is demanded by the very definition of consciousness, meaning or truth. In so far as I am a consciousness, that is, in so far as something has meaning for me, I am neither here nor there, neither Peter nor Paul; I am in no way distinguishable from an 'other' consciousness, since we are immediately in touch with the world and since the world is, by definition, unique, being the system in which all truths cohere. A logically consistent transcendental idealism ride the world of its opacity and its transcendence. The world is precisely that thing of which we form a representation, not as men or as empirical subjects, but in so far as we are all one light and participate in the One without destroying its unity. Analytical reflection knows nothing of the problem of other minds, or of that of the world, because it insists that with the first glimmer of consciousness there appears in me theoretically the power of reaching some universal truth, and that the other person, being equally without thisness, location or body, the Alter and the Ego are one and the same in the true world which is the unifier of minds. There is no difficulty in understanding how *I* can conceive the Other, because the I and consequently the Other are not conceived as part of the woven stuff of phenomena; they have validity rather than existence. . . .

xii

For Husserl, on the contrary, it is well known that there is a problem of other people, and the *alter ego* is a paradox. . . .

Hitherto the *Cogito* depreciated the perception of others, teaching me as it did that the I is accessible only to itself, since it defined *me* as the thought which I have of myself, and which clearly I am alone in having, at least in this ultimate sense. For the 'other' to be more than an empty word, it is necessary that my existence should never be reduced to my bare awareness of existing, but that it should take in also the awareness that *one* may have of it, and thus include my incarnation in some nature and the possibility, at least, of a historical situation. The *Cogito* must reveal me in a situation, and it is on this condition alone that transcendental subjectivity can, as Husserl puts it, *be* an intersubjectivity. As a meditating Ego, I can clearly distinguish from myself the world and things, since I certainly do not exist in the way in which things exist. I must even set aside from myself my body understood as a thing among things, as a collection of physico-chemical processes. But even if the *cogitatio,* which I thus discover, is without location in objective time and space, it is not without place in the phenomenological world. The world, which I distinguished from myself as the totality of things or of processes linked by causal relationships, I rediscover 'in me' as the permanent horizon of all my *cogitationes* and as a dimension in relation to which I am constantly situating myself. The true *Cogito* does not define the subject's existence in terms of the thought he has of existing, and furthermore does not convert the indubitability of the world into the indubitability of thought about the world, nor finally does it replace the world itself by the world as meaning. On the contrary it recognizes my thought itself as an inalienable fact, and does away with any kind of idealism in revealing me as 'being-in-the-world'. . . .

The best formulation of the reduction is probably that given by Eugen Fink, Husserl's assistant, when he spoke of 'wonder' in the face of the world. Reflection does not withdraw from the world towards the unity of consciousness as the world's basis; it steps back to watch the forms of transcendence fly up like sparks from a fire; it slackens the intentional threads which attach us to the world and thus brings them to our notice; it alone is consciousness of the world because it reveals that world as strange and paradoxical. . . .

All the misunderstandings with his interpreters, with the existentialist 'dissidents' and finally with himself, have arisen from the fact that in order to see the world and grasp it as paradoxical, we must break with our familiar acceptance of it and, also, from the fact that from this break we can learn nothing but the unmotivated upsurge of the world. The most important lesson which the reduction teaches us is the impossibility of a complete reduction. This is why Husserl is constantly re-examining the possibility of the reduction. If we were absolute mind, the reduction would present no problem. But since, on the contrary, we are in the world, since indeed our reflections are carried out in the temporal flux on to which we are trying to seize (since they *sich einströmen,* as Husserl says), there is no thought which embraces all our thought. The philosopher, as the unpublished works declare, is a perpetual beginner, which means that he takes for granted nothing that men, learned or otherwise, believe they know. It means also that philosophy itself must not take itself for granted, in so far as it may have managed to say something true; that it is an ever-renewed experiment in making its own beginning; that it consists wholly in the description of this beginning, and finally, that radical reflection amounts to a consciousness of its own dependence on an unreflective life which is its initial situation, unchanging, given once and for all. Far from being, as has been thought, a procedure of idealistic philosophy, phenomenological reduction belongs to existential philosophy: Heidegger's 'being-in-the-world' appears only against the background of the phenomenological reduction.

A misunderstanding of a similar kind confuses the notion of the 'essences' in Husserl. Every reduction, says Husserl, as well as being transcendental is necessarily eidetic. That means that we cannot subject our perception of the world to philosophical scrutiny without ceasing to be identified with that act of positing the world, with that interest in it which delimits us, without drawing back from our commitment which is itself thus made to appear as a spectacle, without passing from the *fact* of our existence to its *nature,* from the Dasein to the Wesen. But it is clear that the essence is here not the end, but a means, that our effective involvement in the world is precisely what has to be understood and made amenable to conceptualization, for it is what polarizes all our conceptual particularizations. . . .

xv   Husserl's essences are destined to bring back all the living relationships of experience, as the fisherman's net draws up from the depths of the ocean quivering fish and seaweed. . . .

In the silence of primary consciousness can be seen appearing not only what words mean, but also what things mean: the core of primary meaning round which the acts of naming and expression take shape.

Seeking the essence of consciousness will therefore not consist in developing the *Wortbe-deutung* of consciousness and escaping from existence into the universe of things said; it will consist in rediscovering my actual presence to myself, the fact of my consciousness which is in the last resort what the word and the concept of consciousness mean. Looking for the world's essence is not looking for what it is as an idea once it has been reduced to a theme of discourse; it is looking for what it is as a fact for us, before any thematization. Sensationalism 'reduces' the world by nothing that after all we never experience anything but states of ourselves. Transcendental idealism too 'reduces' the world since, in so far as it guarantees the world, it does so by regarding it as thought or consciousness of the world, and as the mere correlative of our knowl-

xvi edge, with the result that it becomes immanent in consciousness and the aseity of things is thereby done away with. The eidetic reduction is, on the other hand, the determination to bring the world to light as it is before any falling back on ourselves has occurred, it is the ambition to make reflection emulate the unreflective life of consciousness. I aim at and perceive a world. If I said, as do the sensationalists, that we have here only 'states of consciousness', and if I tried to distinguish my perceptions from my dreams with the aid of 'criteria', I should overlook the phenomenon of the world. . . .

To seek the essence of perception is to declare that perception is, not presumed true, but defined as access to truth. So, if I now wanted, according to idealistic principles, to base this *de facto* self-evident truth, this irresistible belief, on some absolute self-evident truth, that is, on the absolute clarity which my thoughts have for me; if I tried to find in myself a creative thought which bodied forth the framework of the world or illumined it through and through, I should once more prove unfaithful to my experience of the world, and should be looking for what it is. The self-evidence of perception is not adequate though or apodeictic self-evidence. The world is not what I think, but what I live through. I am

xviii open to the world, I have no doubt that I am in communication with it, but I do not possess it; it is inexhaustible. 'There is a world', or rather: 'There is the world'; I can never completely account for this ever-reiterated assertion in my life. This facticity of the world is what constitutes the *Weltlichkeit der Welt,* what causes the world to be the world. . . .

We can now consider the notion of intentionality, too often cited as the main discovery of phenomenology, whereas it is understandable only through the reduction. "All consciousness is consciousness of something'; there is nothing new in that. . . .

It is not a matter of duplicating human consciousness with some absolute thought which, from outside, is imagined as assigning to it its aims. It is a question of recognizing consciousness itself as a project of the world, meant for a world which it neither embraces nor possesses, but towards which it is perpetually directed—and the

xviii world as this pre-objective individual whose imperious unity decrees what knowledge shall take as its goal. This is why Husserl distinguishes between intentionality of act, which is that of our judgements and of those occasions when we voluntarily take up a position—the only intentionality discussed in the *Critique of Pure Reason*—and operative intentionality (*fungierende Intentionalität*), or that which produces the natural and antepredicative unity of the world and of our life, being apparent in our desires, our evaluations and in the landscape we see, more clearly than in objective knowledge, and furnishing the text which our knowledge tries to translate into precise language. Our relationship to the world, as it is untiringly enunciated within us, is not a thing which can be any further clarified by analysis; philosophy can only place it once more before our eyes and present it for our ratification. . . .

Should the starting-point for the understanding of history be ideology, or politics, or religion, or economics? Should we try to understand a doctrine from its overt content, or from the psychological make-up and the biography of its author? We must seek an understanding from all these angles simultaneously, everything has meaning, and we shall find this same structure of being underlying all relationship. All these views are true provided that they are not isolated, that we delve deeply into history and reach the unique core of existential meaning which emerges in each perspective. It is true, as Marx says, that history does not walk on its head, but it is also true that it does not think with its feet. Or one should say rather that it is neither its 'head' not its 'feet' that we have to worry about, but its body. All economic and psychological explanations of a doctrine are true, since the thinker never thinks from any starting-point but the one constituted by what he is. Reflection even on a doctrine will be complete only of it succeeds in linking up with the doctrine's history and the extraneous explanations of it, and in putting back the causes and meaning of the doctrine in an existential structure. There is, as Husserl says, a 'genesis of meaning' (*Sinngenesis*), which alone, in the last resort, teaches us what the doctrine 'means.' Like understanding, criticism must be pursued at all levels, and naturally, it will be insufficient, for the refutation of a doctrine, to relate it to some accidental event in the author's life: its significance goes beyond, and there is no pure accident in existence or in coexistence, since both absorb random events and transmute them into the rational.

Finally, as it is indivisible in the present history is equally so in its sequences. Considered in the light of its fundamental dimensions, all periods of history appear as manifestations of a single existence, or as episodes in a single drama—without our knowing whether it has an ending. Because we are in the world, we are *condemned to meaning,* and we cannot do or say anything without its acquiring a name in history.

Probably the chief gain from phenomenology is to have united extreme subjectivism and extreme objectivism in its notion of the world or of rationality. Rationality is precisely proportioned to the experiences in which it is disclosed. To say that there exists rationality is to say that perspectives blend, perceptions confirm each other, a meaning emerges. But it should not be set in a realm apart, transposed into absolute Spirit, or into a world in the realist sense. The phenomenological world is not pure being, but the sense which is revealed where the paths of my various experiences intersect, and also where my own and other people's intersect and engage each other like gears. It is thus inseparable from subjectivity and intersubjectivity, which find their unity when I either take up my past experiences in those of the present, or other people's in my own. For the first time the philosopher's thinking is sufficiently conscious not to anticipate itself and endow its own results with reified form in the world. The philosopher tries to conceive the world, others and himself and their interrelations. But the meditating Ego, the 'impartial spectator' (*uninteressierter Zuschauer*) do not rediscover an already given rationality, they 'establish themselves', and establish it, by an act of initiative which has no guarantee in being, its justification resting entirely on the effective power which it confers on us of taking our own history upon ourselves.

The phenomenological world is not the bringing to explicit expression of a per-existing being, but the laying down of being. Philosophy is not the reflection of a pre-existing truth, but, like art, the act of bringing truth into being. One may well ask how this creation is *possible,* and if it does not recapture in things a pre-existing Reason. The answer is that the only pre-existent Logos is the world itself, and that the philosophy which brings it into visible existence does not begin by being *possible*; it is actual or real like the world of which it is a part, and no explanatory hypothesis is clearer than the act whereby we take up this unfinished world in an effort to complete and conceive it. Rationality is not a *problem*. There is behind it no unknown quantity which has to be determined by deduction, or, beginning with it, demonstrated inductively. We witness every minute the miracle of related experiences, and yet nobody knows better than we do how this miracle is worked, for we are ourselves this network of relationships. The world and reason are not problematical. We may say, if we wish, that they are mysterious, but their mystery defines them: there can be no question of dispelling it by some 'solution', it is on the hither side of all solutions. True philosophy consists in relearning to look at the world, and in this sense a historical account can give meaning to the world quite as 'deeply' as a philosophical treatise. We take our fate in our hands, we become responsible for our history through reflection, but equally by a decision on which we stake our life, and in both cases what is involved is a violent act which is validated by being performed.

Phenomenology, as a disclosure of the world, rests on itself, or rather provides its own xxi foundation. All cognitions are sustained by a 'ground' of postulates and finally by our communication with the world as primary embodiment of rationality. Philosophy, as radical reflection, dispenses in principle with this resource. As, however, it too is in history, it too exploits the world and constituted reason. It must therefore put to itself the question which it puts to all branches of knowledge, and so duplicate itself infinitely, being, as Husserl says, a dialogue or infinite meditation, and, in so far as it remains faithful to its intention, never knowing where it is going. The unfinished nature of phenomenology and the inchoative atmosphere which has surrounded it are not to be taken as a sign of failure, they were inevitable because phenomenology's task was to reveal the mystery of the world and of reason. If phenomenology was a movement before becoming a doctrine or a philosophical system, this was attributable neither to accident, nor to fraudulent intent. It is as painstaking as the works of Balzac, Proust, Valéry or Cézanne—by reason of the same kind of attentiveness and wonder, the same demand for awareness, the same will to seize the meaning of the world or of history as that meaning comes into being. In this way it merges into the general effort of modern thought.

INTRODUCTION

TRADITIONAL PREJUDICES AND THE RETURN TO PHENOMENA

I

3 **The 'Sensation' as a Unit of Experience**

At the outset of the study of perception, we find in language the notion of sensation, which seems immediate and obvious: I have a sensation of redness, of blueness, of hot or cold. It will, however, be seen that nothing could in fact be more confused, and that because they accepted it readily, traditional analyses missed the phenomenon of perception. . . .

Pure sensation will be the experience of an undifferentiated, instantaneous, dotlike impact. . . .

Let us imagine a white patch on a homogeneous background. All the points in the patch have a certain 'function' in common, that of 4 forming themselves into a 'shape'. The colour of the shape is more intense, and as it were more resistant than that of the background; the edges of the white patch 'belong' to it, and are not part of the background although they adjoin it: the patch appears to be placed on the background and does not break it up. Each part arouses the expectation of more than it contains, and this elementary perception is therefore already charged with a *meaning*. . . .

The perceptual 'something' is always in the middle of something else, it always forms part of a 'field'. A really homogeneous area offering *nothing to be* cannot be given to *any perception*. The structure of actual perception alone can teach us what perception is. The pure impression is, therefore, not only undiscoverable, but also imperceptible and so inconceivable as an instant of perception. If it is introduced, it is because instead of attending to the experience of perception, we overlook it in favor of the object perceived. A visual field is not made up of the limited views. But an object seen is made up of bits of matter, and spatial points are external to each other. An isolated datum of perception is inconceivable, at least if we do the mental experiment of attempting to perceive such a thing. But in the world there are either isolated objects or a physical void.

I shall therefore give up any attempt to define sensation as pure impression. Rather, to see is to have colours or lights, to hear is to have sounds, to sense (*sentir*) is to have qualities. To know what sense-experience is, then, is it not enough to have seen a red or to have heard an A? But red and green are not sensations, they are the sensed (*sensibles*), and quality is not an element of consciousness, but a property of the object. Instead of providing a simple means of delimiting sensations, if we consider it in the experience itself which evinces it, the quality is as rich and mysterious as the object, or indeed the whole spectacle, perceived. . . .

There are two ways of being mistaken about 5 quality: one is to make it into an element of consciousness, when in fact it is an object *for* consciousness, to treat is as an incommunicable impression, whereas it always has a meaning; the other is to think that this meaning and this object at the level of quality, are fully developed and determinate. The second error, like the first, springs from our prejudice about the world. . . . We ought, then, to perceive a segment of the world precisely delimited, surrounded by a zone of blackness, packed full of qualities with no interval between them, held together by definite relationships of size similar to those lying on the retina. The fact is that experience offers nothing like this, and we shall never, using the world as our starting-point, understand what a *field of vision* is. Even if it is possible to trace out a perimeter of vision by gradually approaching the centre of the lateral stimuli, the results of such measurement vary from one moment to another, and one never manages to determine the instant when a stimulus once seen is seen no longer. The region 6 surrounding the visual field is not easy to describe,

but what is certain is that it is neither black nor grey. There occurs here an *indeterminate vision*, a *vision of something or other*, and, to take the extreme case, what is behind my back is not without some element of visual presence. . . .

Psychologists have for a long time taken great care to overlook these phenomena. In the world taken in itself everything is determined. There are many unclear sights, as for example a landscape on a misty day, but then we always say that no real landscape is in itself unclear. It is so only for us. The object, psychologists would assert, is never ambiguous, but becomes so only through our inattention. . . .

We must recognize the indeterminate as a positive phenomenon. It is in this atmosphere that quality arises. Its meaning is an equivocal meaning; we are concerned with an expressive value rather than with logical signification. The determinate quality by which empiricism tried to define sensation is an object, not an element, of consciousness, indeed it is the very lately developed object of scientific consciousness. For these two reasons, it conceals rather than reveals subjectivity.

The two definitions of sensation which we have just tried out were only apparently direct. We have seen that they were based on the object perceived. In this they were in agreement with common sense, which also identifies the sensible by the objective conditions which govern it. The visible is what is seized upon *with* the eyes, the sensible is what is seized on *by* the senses. Let us 7 follow up the idea of sensation on this basis, and see what becomes of this 'by' and this 'with', and the notion of sense-organ, in the first-order thinking constituted by science. . . .

The objective world being given, it is assumed that it passes on to the sense-organs messages which must be registered, then deciphered in such a way as to reproduce in us the original text. Hence we have in principle a point-by-point correspondence and constant connection between the stimulus and the elementary perception. But this 'constancy hypothesis' conflicts with the data of consciousness, and the very psychologists who accept it recognize its purely theoretical character. For example, the intensity of a sound under certain circumstances lowers its pitch; the addition of auxiliary lines makes two 8 figures unequal which are objectively equal; a coloured area appears to be the same colour over the whole of its surface, whereas the chromatic thresholds of the different parts of the retina ought to make it red in one place, orange somewhere else, and in certain cases colourless. . . .

The law of constancy cannot avail itself, against the testimony of consciousness, of any crucial experiment in which it is not already implied, and wherever we believe that we are establishing it, it is already presupposed. If we turn back to the phenomena, they show us that the apprehension of a quality, just as that of size, is bound up with a whole perceptual context, and that the stimuli no longer furnish us with the indirect means we were seeking of isolating a 13 layer of immediate impressions.

2

'Association' and the 'Projection of Memories'

Once introduced, the notion of sensation distorts any analysis of perception. Already a 'figure' on a 'background' contains, as we have seen, much more than the qualities presented at a given time. It has an 'outline', which does not 'belong' to the background and which 'stands out' from it; it is 'stable' and offers a 'compact' area of colour, the background on the other hand having no bounds, being of indefinite colouring and 'running on' under the figure. The different parts of the whole—for example, the portions of the figure nearest to the background—possess, then, besides a colour and qualities, a particulars *significance*. The question is, what makes up this significance, what do the words 'edge' and 'outline' mean, what happens when a collection of qualities is *apprehended* as a figure on a background? But once sensation is introduced as an element of knowledge, we are left no leeway in our reply. A being capable of sense-experience (*sentir*)—in the sense of coinciding absolutely with an impression or a quality—could have no other mode of knowing. That a quality, an area of red should signify something, that it should be, for example, seen as

a patch on a background, means that the red is not this warm colour which I feel and live in and lose myself in, but that it announces something else which it does not include, that it exercises a cognitive function, and that its parts together make up a whole to which each is related without leaving its place. Henceforth the red is no longer merely there, it represents something for me, and what it represents is not possessed as a 'real part' of my perception, but only aimed at as an 'intentional part'. . . .

If we admit 'sensation' in the classical sense, 14 the meaning of that which is sensed can be found only in further sensations, actual or virtual. Seeing a figure can be only simultaneously experiencing all the atomic sensations which go to form it. Each one remains for ever what it is, a blind contact, an impression, while the whole collection of these becomes 'vision,' and forms a picture before us because we learn to pass quickly from one impression to another. A shape is nothing but a sum of limited views, and the consciousness of a shape is a collective entity. The sensible elements of which it is made up cannot lose the opacity which defines them as sensory given, and open themselves to some intrinsic connection, to some law of conformation governing them all.

Knowledge thus appears as a system of sub- 15 stitutions in which one impression announces others without ever justifying the announcement, in which words lead one to expect sensations as evening leads one to expect night. The significance of the percept is nothing but a cluster of images which begin to reappear without reason. The simplest images or sensations are, in the last analysis, all that there is to understand in words, concepts being a complicated way of designating them, and as they are themselves inexpressible impressions, understanding is a fraud or an illusion. Knowledge never has any hold on objects, which bring each other about, while the mind acts as a calculating machine, which has no idea why its results are true. Sensation admits of no philosophy other than that of nominalism, that is, the reduction of meaning to the misinterpretation of vague resemblance or to the meaninglessness of association by contiguity.

Now the sensation and images which are supposed to be the beginning and the end of all knowledge never make their appearance anywhere other than within a horizon of meaning, and the significance of the percept, far from resulting from an association, is in fact presupposed in all association, whether it concerns the conspectus of a figure before one, or the recollection of former experiences. Our perceptual field is made up of 'things' and 'spaces between things'. The parts of a thing are not bound together by a merely external association arising from their interrelatedness observed while the object is in movement. For in the first place I see, as things, groupings which I have never seen in movement; houses, the sun, mountains, for example.

19 From this can be judged the worth of accepted formulas about 'the rôle of memories in perception'. Even outside empiricism there is talk of 'the contributions of memory'. People go on saying that 'to perceive is to remember'. It is shown that in the reading of a book the speed of the eye leaves gaps in the retinal impressions, *therefore* the sense-data must be filled out by a projection of memories. A landscape or newspaper seen upside down are said to represent our original view of them, or normal view of them being now natural by reason of what is added to it by memory. 'Because of the unaccustomed arrangement of impressions the influence of psychic causes can no longer be felt. It is not asked why differently arranged impressions make the newspaper unreadable or the landscape unrecognizable. The answer is: because in order to fill out perception, memories need to have been made possible by the physiognomic character of the data. Before any contribution by memory, what is seen must at the present moment so organize itself as to present a picture to me in which I can recognize my former experiences. Thus the appeal to memory presupposes what it is supposed to explain: the patterning of data, the imposition of meaning on a chaos of sense-data. No sooner is the recollection of memories made possible than it becomes superfluous, since the work it is being asked to do is already done. . . .

21 It finally is conceded that memories do not by themselves project themselves upon sensations, but that consciousness compares them with the present data, retaining only those which accord with them, then one is admitting an original text which carries its meaning within itself, and setting it over against that of memories: this original text is perception itself. In short, it is a mistake to think that with the 'projection of memories' we are bringing into perception some mental activity, and that we have taken up a position opposed to that of empiricism. The theory is no more than a consequence, a tardy and ineffective correction of empiricism, accepting its postulates, sharing the same difficulties and, like empiricism, concealing phenomena instead of elucidating them.

The postulate, as always, consists in *deducing* the given from what happens to be furnished by the sense organs. For example, in the illusion of proofreaders, the elements actually seen are reconstituted according to the eye movements, the speed of reading and the time needed for the retinal impression. Then, by subtracting these theoretical data from total perception, the 'recollected elements' are obtained which, in turn, are treated as mental entities. Perception is built up with states of consciousness as a house is built with bricks, and a mental chemistry is invoked which fuses these materials into a compact whole. Like all empiricist theories, this one describes only blind processes which could never be the equivalent of knowledge, because there is, in this mass of sensations and memories, *nobody who sees*, nobody who can appreciate the falling into line of datum and recollection, and, on the other hand, no solid object protected by a meaning against the teeming horde of memories. We must then discard this postulate which obscures the whole question. The cleavage between given and remembered, arrived at by way of objective causes, is arbitrary. When we come back to phenomena we find, as a basic layer of experience, a whole already pregnant with an irreducible meaning: not sensations with gaps between them, into 22 which memories may be supposed to slip, but the features, the layout of a landscape or a word, in spontaneous accord with the intentions of the moment, as with earlier experience. . . .

To perceive is not to experience a host of impressions accompanied by memories capable of clinching them; it is to see, standing forth from a cluster of data, an immanent significance without which no appeal to memory is possible. To remember is not to bring into the focus of consciousness a self-subsistent picture of the past; it is to thrust deeply into the horizon of the past and take apart step by step the interlocked perspectives until the experiences which it epitomizes are as if relived in their temporal setting. To perceive is not to remember.

The relationships 'figure' and 'background', 'thing' and 'not-thing', and the horizon of the past appear, then, to be structures of consciousness irreducible to the qualities which appear in them. Empiricism will always retain the expedient of treating this *a priori* as if it were the product of some mental chemistry. The empiricist will concede that every object is presented against a background which is not an object, the present lying between two horizons of absence, past and future. But, he will go on, these significations are derivative. The 'figure' and the 'background', the 'thing' and its 'surrounding', the 'present' and the 'past', are words which summarize the experience of a spatio-temporal perspective, which in the end comes down to the elimination either of memory or of the marginal impressions. . . .

23   The adoption of this new way of looking at things, which reverses the relative positions of the clear and the obscure, must be undertaken by each one for himself, whereupon it will be seen to be justified by the abundance of phenomena which it elucidates. Before its discovery, these phenomena were inaccessible, yet to the description given of them empiricism can always retort that it *does not understand*. . . .

But though the phenomenal field may indeed by a new world, it is never totally overlooked by natural thought, being present as its horizon, and the empiricist doctrine itself is an attempt to analyse consciousness. By way of guarding against myths it is, then, desirable to point out everything that is made incomprehensible by empiricist constructions and all the basic phenomena which they conceal. They hide from us in the first place 'the cultural world' or 'human world' in which nevertheless almost our whole life is led. For most of us, Nature is no more than a vague and remote entity, overlaid by cities, roads, houses and above all by the presence of other people. Now, for empiricism, 'cultural' objects and faces owe their distinctive form, their magic power, to transference and projection of memory, so that only by accident has the human world any meaning. There is nothing in the appearance of a landscape, an object or a body whereby it is predestined to look 'gay' or 'sad', 'lively' or 'dreary', 'elegant' or 'coarse'. Once more seeking a definition of what we perceive through the physical and chemical properties of the stimuli which may act upon our sensory apparatus, empiricism excludes from perception the anger or the pain which I nevertheless read

24 in a fact, the religion whose essence I seize in some hesitation or reticence, the city whose temper I recognize in the attitude of a policeman or the style of a public building. There can no longer be any *objective spirit*: mental life withdraws into isolated consciousnesses devoted solely to introspection, instead of extending, as it apparently does in fact, over human space which is made up by those with whom I argue or live, filling my place of work or the abode of my happiness. Joy and sadness, vivacity and obtuseness are data of introspection, and when we invest landscapes or other people with these states, it is because we have observed in ourselves the coincidence between these internal perceptions and the external signs associated with them by the accidents of our constitution. Perception thus impoverished becomes purely a matter of knowledge, a progressive noting down of qualities and of their most habitual distribution, and the perceiving subject approaches the world as the scientist approaches his experiments. If on the other hand we admit that all these 'projections', all these 'associations', all these 'transferences' are based on some intrinsic characteristic of the object, the 'human world' ceases to be a metaphor and becomes once more what it really is, the seat and as it were the *homeland* of our thoughts. The perceiving subject ceases to be an 'acosmic' thinking subject, and action, feeling and will remain to be explored as original ways of positing

an object, since 'an object looks attractive or repulsive before it looks black or blue, circular or square'.

But not only does empiricism distort experience by making the cultural world an illusion, when in fact it is in it that our existence finds its sustenance. The natural world is also falsified, and for the same reasons. What we object to in empiricism is not its having taken this as its primary theme of analysis. For it is quite true that every cultural object refers back to a natural background against which it appears and which may, moreover, be confused and remote. Our perception senses how near is the canvas underneath the picture, or the crumbling cement under the building, or the tiring actor under the character. But the nature about which empiricism talks is a collection of stimuli and qualities, and it is ridiculous to pretend that nature thus conceived is, even in intention merely, the primary object of our perception: it does in fact follow the experience of cultural objects, or rather it is one of them. We shall, therefore, have to rediscover the natural world too, and its mode of existence, which is not to be confused with that of the scientific object.

52 **4**

The Phenomenal Field

It will now be seen in what direction the following chapters will carry their inquiry. 'Sense experience' has become once more a question for us. Empiricism had emptied it of all mystery by bringing it down to the possession of a quality. This had been possible only at the price of moving far from the ordinary acceptation of the word. Between sense experience and knowing, common experience establishes a difference which is not that between the quality and the concept. This rich notion of sense experience is still to be found in Romantic usage, for example in Herder. . . .

Vision is already inhabited by a meaning (*sens*) which gives it a function in the spectacle of the world and in our existence. The pure *quale* would be given to us only if the world were a spectacle and one's own body a mechanism with which some impartial mind made itself acquainted. Sense experience, on the other hand,

invests the quality with vital value, grasping it first in its meaning for us, for that heavy mass which is our body, whence it comes about that it always involves a reference to the body. The problem is to understand these strange relationships which are woven between the parts of the landscape, or between it and me as incarnate subject, and through which an object perceived can concentrate in itself a whole scene or become the *imago* of a whole segment of life. Sense experience is that vital communication with the world which makes it present as a famil-
54 iar setting of our life. . . .

Science has first been merely the sequel or amplification of the process which constitutes perceived things. Just as the thing is the invariant of all sensory fields and of all individual perceptual fields, so the scientific concept is the means of fixing and objectifying phenomena. Science defined a theoretical state of bodies not subject to the action of any force, and *ipso facto* defined force, reconstituting with the aid of these ideal components the processes actually observed. It established statistically the chemical properties of pure bodies, deducing from these those of empirical bodies, and seeming thus to hold the plan of creation or in any case to have found a reason immanent in the world. . . .

The living body, under these circumstances,
55 could not escape the determinations which alone made the object into an object and without which it would have had no place in the system of experience. The value predicates which the reflecting judgment confers upon it had to be sustained, in being, by a foundation of physico-chemical properties. In ordinary experience we find a fittingness and a meaningful relationship between the gesture, the smile and the tone of a speaker. But this reciprocal relationship of expression which presents the human body as the outward manifestation of a certain manner of being-in-the-world, had, for mechanistic physiology, to be resolved into a series of causal relations. . . .

The impelling intentions of the living creature were converted into objective movements: to the will only an instantaneous fiat was allowed, the execution of the being entirely given over to a nervous mechanism. Sense experience, thus detached from the affective and motor functions, became the mere reception of a quality, and physiologists thought they could follow, from the point of reception to the nervous centres, the projection of the external world in the living body. The latter, thus transformed, ceased to be my body, the visible expression of a concrete Ego, and became one object among all others. Conversely, the body of another person could not appear to me as encasing another Ego. It was merely a machine, and the perception of the other could not really be *of the other,* since it resulted from an inference and therefore placed behind the automation no more than a consciousness in general, a transcendent cause and not an inhabitant of his movements. . . .

Thus, while the living body became an exte-
56 rior without interior, subjectivity became an interior without exterior, an impartial spectator. The naturalism of science and the spiritualism of the universal constituting subject, to which reflection on science led, had this in common, that they levelled out experience: in face of the constituting I, the empirical selves are objects. The empirical Self is a hybrid notion, a mixture of in-itself and for-itself, to which reflective philosophy could give no status. In so far as it has a concrete content it is inserted in the system of experience and is therefore not a subject; in so far as it *is* a subject, it is empty and resolves itself into the transcendental subject.

Now this philosophy is collapsing before our eyes. The natural object was the first to disappear and physics has itself recognized the limits of its categories by demanding a recasting and blending of the pure concepts which it had adopted. For its part the organism presents physico-chemical analysis not with the practical difficulties of a complex object, but with the theoretical difficulty of a meaningful being. In more general terms the idea of a universe of thought or a universe of values, in which all thinking lives come into contact and are reconciled, is called into question. Nature is *not* in itself geometrical and it appears so only to a careful observer who contents himself with macrocosmic data. Human society is *not* a community of reasonable minds, and only in fortunate countries where a biologi-

cal and economic balance has locally and temporarily been struck has such a conception of it been possible. . . .

57 We shall no longer hold that perception is incipient science, but conversely that classical science is a form of perception which loses sight of its origins and believes itself complete. The first philosophical act would appear to be to return to the world of actual experience which is prior to the objective world, since it is in it that we shall be able to grasp the theoretical basis no less than the limits of that objective world, restore to things their concrete physiognomy, to organisms their individual ways of dealing with the world, and to subjectivity its inherence in history. Our task will be, moreover, to rediscover phenomena, the layer of living experience through which other people and things are first given to us, the system 'Self-others-things' as it comes into being; to reawaken perception and foil its trick of allowing us to forget it as a fact and as perception in the interest of the object which it presents to us and of the rational tradition to which it gives rise.

This phenomenal field is not an 'inner world', the 'phenomenon' is not a 'state of consciousness', or a 'mental fact', and the experience of phenomena is not an act of introspection or an intuition in Bergson's sense. . . .

The return to the 'immediate data of consciousness' became therefore a hopeless enterprise since the philosophical scrutiny was trying to *be* what it could not, in principle, *see.* The difficulty was not only to destroy the prejudice of the exterior, as all philosophies urge the beginner to do, or to describe the mind in a language made for representing things. It was much more fundamental, since interiority, defined by the impression, by its nature evaded every attempt to express it. . . .

The immediate was therefore a lonely, blind and mute life. The return to the phenomenal presents none of these peculiarities. . . .

More generally it is the very notion of the immediate which is transformed: henceforth the
58 immediate is no longer the impression, the object which is one with the subject, but the meaning, the structure, the spontaneous arrangement of

parts. My own 'mental life' is given to me in precisely the same way, since the criticism of the constancy hypothesis teaches me to recognize the articulation and melodic unity of my behaviour as original data of inner experience, and since introspection, when brought down to its positive content, consists equally in making the immanent meaning of any behaviour explicit. Thus what we discover by going beyond the prejudice of the objective world is not an occult inner world. Nor is this world of living experience completely closed to naïve consciousness, as is Bergson's interiority.

59 If, as we see, phenomenological psychology is distinguished in all its characteristics from introspective psychology, it is because it is different in basic principle. Introspective psychology detected, on the perimeter of the physical world, a zone of consciousness in which physical concepts are no longer valid, but the psychologist still believed consciousness to be no more than a sector of being, and he decided to explore this sector as the physicist explores his. He tried to describe the givens of consciousness but without putting into question the absolute existence of the world surrounding it. In company with the scientist and common sense, he presupposed the objective world as the logical framework of all his descriptions, and as the setting of his thought. He was unaware that this presupposition dominated the meaning given to the word 'being', forcing it to bring consciousness into existence under the name of 'psychic fact', and thus diverting it from a true grasp of consciousness or from truly immediate experience, and stultifying the many precautions taken to avoid distorting the 'interior'. This is what happened to empiricism when it replaced the physical world by a world of inner events.

Psychological reflection, once begun, then, outruns itself through its own momentum. . . .

60 It can no longer be a question of describing the world of living experience which it carries within itself like some opaque datum, it has to be constituted. The process of making explicit, which had laid bare the 'lived-through' world which is prior to the objective one, is put into operation upon the 'lived-through' world itself,

thus revealing, prior to the phenomenal field, the transcendental field. The system 'self-others-world' is in its turn taken as an object of analysis and it is now a matter of awakening the thoughts which constitute other people, myself as individual subject and the world as a pole of my perception. This new 'reduction' would then recognize only one true subject, the thinking Ego. . . .

Such is the ordinary perspective of a transcendental philosophy, and also, to all appearances at least, the programme of a transcendental phenomenology. Now the phenomenal field as we have revealed it in this chapter, places a fundamental difficulty in the way of any attempt to make experience directly and totally explicit. . . .

61 If then we want reflection to maintain, in the object on which it bears, its descriptive character,stics, and thoroughly to understand that object, we must not consider it is a mere return to a universal reason and see it as anticipated in unreflective experience, we must regard it as a creative operation which itself participates in the facticity of that experience. That is why phenomenology, alone of all philosophies, talks about a transcendental *field*. This word indicates that reflection never holds, arrayed and objectified before its gaze, the whole world and the plurality of monads, and that its view is never other than partial and of limited power. It is also why phenomenology is phenomenology, that is, a study of the *advent* of being to consciousness, instead of presuming its possibility as given in advance. . . .

62 The mistake of reflective philosophies is to believe that the thinking subject can absorb into its thinking or appropriate without remainder the object of its thought, that our being can be brought down to our knowledge. As thinking subject we are never the unreflective subject that we seek to know; but neither can we become wholly consciousness, or make ourselves into the transcendental consciousness. If we were consciousness, we would have to have before us the world, our history and perceived objects in their uniqueness as systems of transparent relationships. . . .

A philosophy becomes transcendental, or radical, not by taking its place in absolute consciousness without mentioning the ways by which this is reached, but by considering itself as a problem; not by postulating a knowledge rendered totally explicit, but by recognizing as the fundamental philosophic problem this *presumption* on reason's part.

That is why we had to begin our examination of perception with psychological considerations. If we had not done so, we would not have understood the whole meaning of the transcendental problem, since we would not, starting from the natural attitude, have methodically followed the procedures which lead to it. We had to frequent the phenomenal field and become acquainted, through psychological descriptions, with the subject to phenomena, if we were to avoid placing ourselves from the start, as does reflexive philosophy, in a transcendental dimension assumed to be eternally given, thus bypassing the full problem of constitution.

PART ONE

THE BODY

EXPERIENCE AND OBJECTIVE THOUGHT. THE PROBLEM OF THE BODY

Obsessed with being, and forgetful of the perspectivism of my experience, I henceforth treat it as an object and deduce it from a relationship between objects. I regard my body, which is my point of view upon the world, as one of the objects of that world. My recent awareness of my gaze as a means of knowledge I now repress, and treat my eyes as bits of matter. They then take their place in the same objective space in which I trying to situate the external object and I believe that I am producing the perceived perspective by the projection of the objects on my retina. . . .

In the same way, finally, if the objects which surround the house or which are found in it remained what they are in perceptual experience, that is, acts of seeing conditioned by a certain perspective, the house would not be posited as an autonomous being. Thus the positing of one single object, in the full sense, demands the compositive bringing into being of all these experiences in one act of manifold creation. Therein it exceeds perceptual experience and the synthesis of horizons—as the notion of a *universe*, that is to say, a completed and explicit totality, in which the relationships are those of reciprocal determination, exceeds that of a *world*, or an open and indefinite multiplicity of relationships which are of reciprocal implication.[1] I detach myself from my experience and pass to the *idea*. Like the object, the idea purports to be the same for everybody, valid in all times and places and the individuation of an object in an objective point of time and space finally appears as the expression of a universal positing power.[2] I am no longer concerned with my body, nor with time, nor with the world, as I experience them in ante- predicative knowledge, in the inner communion that I have with them. I now refer to my body only as an idea, to the universe as idea, to the idea of space and the idea of time.

The whole life of consciousness is characterized by the tendency to posit objects, since it is consciousness, that is to say self-knowledge, only is so far as it takes hold of itself and draws itself together in an identifiable object. And yet the absolute positing of a single object is the death of consciousness, since it congeals the whole of existence, as a crystal placed in a solution suddenly crystallizes it.

We cannot remain in this dilemma of having to fail to understand either the subject or object. We must discover the origin of the object at the very centre of our experience; we must describe the emergence of being and we must understand how, paradoxically, there is *for us* an *in-itself*. In order not to prejudge the issue, we shall take objective thought on its own terms not ask it any questions which it does not ask itself. If we are led to rediscover experience behind it, this shift of ground will be attributable only to the difficulties which objective thought itself raises. Let us consider it then at work in the constitution of our body as object, since this is a crucial moment in the genesis of the objective world. It will be seen that one's own body evades, even within science itself, the treatment to which it is intended to subject it. And since the genesis of the objective body is only a moment in the constitution of the object the body, by withdrawing from the objective world, will carry with it the intentional threads liking it to its surrounding and finally reveal to us the perceiving subject as the perceived world.

3

The Spatiality of One's Own Body and Motility

146 . . . The body is our general medium for having a world. Sometimes it is restricted to the actions necessary for the conservation of life, and accordingly it posits around us a biological world; at other times, elaborating upon these primary actions and moving from their literal to a figurative meaning, it manifests through them a core of new significance: this is true of motor habits such as dancing. Sometimes, finally, the meaning aimed at cannot be achieved by the body's natural means; it must than build itself an instrument, and it projects thereby around itself a cultural world. At all levels it performs the same function which is to endow the instantaneous expressions of spontaneity with 'a little renewable action and independent existence.' Habit is merely a form of this fundamental power. We say that the body has understood and habit has been cultivated when it has absorbed a new meaning, and assimilated a fresh core of significance.

To sum up, what we have discovered thorough the study of motility, is a new meaning of the word 'meaning'. The great strength of intellectualist psychology and idealist philosophy comes from their having no difficulty in showing 147 that perception and thought have an intrinsic significance and cannot be explained in terms of the external association of fortuitously agglomerated contents. The *Cogito* was the coming to self-awareness of this inner core. But all meaning was *ipso facto* conceived as an act of thought, as the work of a pure *I*, and although rationalism easily refuted empiricism, it was itself unable to account for the variety of experience, for the ele-

ment of senselessness in it, for the contingency of contents. Bodily experience forces us to acknowledge an imposition of meaning which is not the work of a universal constituting consciousness, a meaning which clings to certain contents. My body is that meaningful core which behaves like a general function, and which nevertheless exists, and is susceptible to disease. In it we learn to know that union of essence and existence which we shall find again in perception generally, and which we shall then have to describe more fully.

6

The Body as Expression and Speech

We have become accustomed, through the influence of the Cartesian tradition, to disengage from the object: the reflective attitude simultaneously purifies the common notions of body and soul by defining the body as the sum of its parts with no interior, and the soul as a being wholly present to itself without distance. These definitions make matters perfectly clear both within and outside ourselves: we have the transparency of an object with no secret recesses, the transparency of a subject which is nothing but what it thinks it is. The object is an object through and through, and consciousness a consciousness through and through. There are two senses, and two only, of the word 'exist': one exists as a thing or else one exists as a consciousness. The experience of our own body, on the other hand, reveals to us an ambiguous mode of existing. If I try to think of it as a cluster of third person processes—'sight', 'motility', 'sexuality'—I observe that these 'functions' cannot be interrelated, and related to the external world, by causal connections, they are all obscurely drawn together and mutually implied in a unique drama. Therefore the body is not an object. For the same reason, my awareness of it is not a thought, that is to say, I cannot take it to pieces and reform it to make a clear idea. Its unity is always implicit and vague. It is always something other than what it is, always sexuality and at the same time freedom, rooted in nature at the very moment when it is transformed by cultural influences, never hermetically sealed and never left behind. Whether it is a question of another's body or my own, I have no means of knowing the human body other than that of living it, which means taking up on my own account the drama which is being played out in it, and losing myself in it. I am my body, at least wholly to the extent that I possess experience, and yet at the same time my body is as it were a 'natural' subject, a provisional sketch of my total being. Thus experience of one's own runs counter to the reflective procedure which detaches subject and object from each other, and which gives us only the thought about the body, or the body as an idea, and not the experience of the body or the body in reality.

PART TWO

THE WORLD AS PERCEIVED

THE THEORY OF THE BODY IS ALREADY
203   A THEORY OF PERCEPTION

Our own body is in the world as the heart is in the organism: it keeps the visible spectacle constantly alive, it breathes life into it and sustains it inwardly, and with it forms a system. When I walk round my flat, the various aspects in which it presents itself to me could not possibly appear as views of one and the same thing if I did not know that each of them represents the flat seen from one spot or another, and if I were unaware of my own movements, and of my body as retaining its identity through the stages of those movements. . . .

I feel the substance of my body escaping from me through my head and overrunning the boundaries of my objective body. It is in his own body that the patient feels the approach of this
206 Other whom he has never seen with his eyes, as the normal person is aware, through a certain burning feeling in the nape of the neck, the someone is watching him from behind. Conversely, a certain form of external experience implies and produces a certain consciousness of one's own body. Many patients speak of a 'sixth sense' which seems to produce third hallucinations. Stratton's subject, whose visual filed has been objectively inverted, at first sees everything upside down; on the third day of the experiment, when things are beginning to regain their upright position, he is filled with 'the strange impression of looking at the fire out of the back of his head'. This is because there is an immediate equivalence between the orientation of the visual field and the awareness of one's own body as the potentiality of that field, so that any upheaval experimentally brought about can appear indifferently either as the inversion of phenomenal objects or as a redistribution of sensory functions in the body. If a subject focuses for long-distance vision, he has a double image of his own finger as indeed of all objects near to him. If he is touched or pricked, he is aware of being touched or pricked in two places. Diplopia is thus extended into a bodily duplication. Every external perception is immediately synonymous with a certain perception of my body, just as every perception of my body is made explicit in the language of external perception. If, then, as we have seen to be the case, the body is not a transparent object, and is not presented to us in virtue of the law of its consti-
207 tution, as the circle is to the geometer, if it is an expressive unity which we can learn to know only by actively taking it up, this structure will be passed on to the sensible world. The theory of the body schema is, implicitly, a theory of perception. We have relearned to feel our body: we have found underneath the objective and detached knowledge of the body that other knowledge which we have of it in virtue of its always being with us and of the fact that we are our body. In the same way we shall need to reawaken our experience of the world as it appears to us in so far as we are in the world through our body, and in so far as we perceive the world with our body. But by thus remaking contact with the body and with the world, we shall also rediscover ourself, since, perceiving as we do with our body, the body is a natural self and, as it were, the subject of perception.

STUDY QUESTIONS: MERLEAU-PONTY, *THE PHENOMENOLOGY OF PERCEPTION*

1. How does Merleau-Ponty explain the idea that phenomenology is a descriptive psychology?
2. Why does Merleau-Ponty assert, 'I am not a "living creature"'?
3. How does Merleau-Ponty distinguish his descriptive psychology from analytical reflection? Why is this difference important?
4. Why is there no difficulty for Merleau-Ponty in conceiving the Other?
5. What are Merleau-Ponty's views on Husserl's reduction?
6. What does Merleau-Ponty say about the world?
7. What does Merleau-Ponty say about the attempt to define sensation in terms of pure impressions?
8. What is the first mistake regarding qualities?
9. Why is the indeterminate important for sensation?
10. How does Merleau-Ponty criticize the view that perception consists of sensations?
11. Does Merleau-Ponty agree with the statement that memory projections play a vital role in perception?
12. Empiricism distorts experience by making the cultural world an illusion. What does this claim mean, and how would Merleau-Ponty support it?
13. How is the living body important for our understanding of perception, according to Merleau-Ponty?
14. Why is the return to the 'immediate data of consciousness' a hopeless enterprise?
15. How is phenomenological psychology different from introspective psychology?
16. Why is the experience of our own body important?

Philosophical Bridges: Merleau-Ponty's Influence

The influence of Merleau-Ponty has at least two aspects. First, he has been influential as a phenomenologist who continued and extended the tradition initiated by Husserl. In this regard, Merleau-Ponty's emphasis on the public and social nature of our knowledge of objects and other persons has made phenomenology seem more palatable than the works of Husserl, which are often difficult to understand on these crucial points and sometimes seem individualistic and idealistic. This does not address whether or not Merleau-Ponty provides an accurate interpretation of Husserl's thought. However, by applying the phenomenological method to cultural phenomena and by picking up Husserl's later notion of the life-world, Merleau-Ponty anticipates many of the hermeneutical ideas developed in detail by Gadamer.

Furthermore, several thinkers have taken up Merleau-Ponty's insistence that we should treat the living body seriously in our thinking about perception and human existence more generally. For example, this point has been used in critical discussions of strong artificial intelligence. The notion of gendered embodiment has been important in some feminist thought. Second, Merleau-Ponty's later works have been influential especially in the areas of literary and art theory for the concepts of indirect language and visibility.

BIBLIOGRAPHY

GENERAL

Critchley, S., and Schroeder, W., *A Companion to Continental Philosophy*, Blackwell, 1998

D'Amico, *Contemporary Continental Philosophy*, Westview Press, 1999

Kearney, Richard, *Continental Philosophy in the 20th Century*, Routledge, 1994

Matthews, Eric, *Twentieth Century French Philosophy*, Oxford University Press, 1996

HUSSERL
Primary

Cartesian Meditations, trans. D. Cairns, Nijhoff, 1970

The Crisis of European Sciences and Transcendental Philosophy, trans. D. Carr, Northwestern University Press, 1970

The Idea of Phenomenology, trans. W. Alston and G. Nakhnikian, Nijhoff, 1970.

Ideas: General Introduction to Pure Phenomenology, trans. Boyce Gibson, Allen and Unwin, 1952

Ideas Pertaining to a Pure Phenomenology and to a Phenomenological Philosophy, Book I, trans. F. Kersten, Nijhoff, 1983

Secondary

Bell, D., *Husserl*, Routledge, 1990

Bernet, R., Kern, I., and Marbach, E., *An Introduction to Husserlian Phenomenology*, Northwestern University Press, 1993

Dreyfus, H., and Hall, H., eds., *Husserl, Intentionality and Cognitive Science*, MIT Press, 1982

Smith, B., and Smith, D., eds., *The Cambridge Companion to Husserl*, Cambridge University Press, 1995

Ströker, Elizabeth, *Husserl's Transcendent Phenomenology*, Stanford University Press, 1993

HEIDEGGER
Primary

Basic Writings, ed. D. F. Krell, Harper and Row, 1992

Being and Time, trans. Joan Stambaugh, State University of New York Press, 1996

History of the Concept of Time, trans. T. Kisiel, Indiana University Press, 1985

An Introduction to Metaphysics, trans. R. Manheim, Yale University Press, 1959

The Question Concerning Technology and Other Essays, trans. W. Lovitt, Harper and Row, 1977

Secondary

Dreyfuss, Hubert, *Being in the World: A Commentary on Heidegger's Being and Time*, MIT Press, 1991

Gelven, Michael, *A Commentary on Heidegger's Being and Time*, Northern Illinois University Press, 1989

Guignon, Charles, *The Cambridge Companion to Heidegger*, Cambridge University Press, 1993

Marx, Werner, *Heidegger and the Tradition*, trans. T. Kisiel, Northwestern University Press, 1971

Poeggler, Otto, *Heidegger's Path of Thinking*, trans. D. Margurshuk and S. Barber, Humanities Press, 1987

SARTRE
Primary

Being and Nothingness, trans. Hazel Barnes, Philosophical Library, 1948

Between Existentialism and Marxism, trans. J. Matthews, New Left Books, 1974

Critique of Dialectical Reason, Vol. 1, trans. A. Sheridan Smith, New Left Books, 1976

Notebook for an Ethics, trans. D. Pellhauer, University of Chicago Press, 1992

Secondary

Catalona, J., *A Commentary on Sartre's 'Being and Nothingness,'* Harper & Row, 1974

Caws, Peter, *Sartre*, Routledge, 1979

Cooper, David, *Existentialism: A Reconstruction*, Blackwell, 1990

Danto, Arthur C., *Jean-Paul Sartre*, Viking Press, 1975

Detmer, D., *Freedom as Value: A Critique of the Ethical Theory of Jean-Paul Sartre*, Open Court, 1988

Howells, Christina, *The Cambridge Companion to Sartre*, Cambridge University Press, 1992

Warnock, Mary, *The Philosophy of Sartre*, Hutchinson, 1965

DE BEAUVOIR
Primary

The Ethics of Ambiguity, trans. Bernard Frechtman, Citadel Press, 1970

The Second Sex, trans. H. M. Parshley, Alfred A. Knopf, 1952

Secondary

Barnes, Hazel, *The Literature of Possibility: A Study of Humanistic Existentialism*, Tavistock, 1959

Bergoffen, Debra, *Gendered Phenomenologies, Erotic Generosities: The Philosophy of Simone de Beauvoir*, State University of New York Press, 1996

Fulbrook, Edward, and Fulbrook, Kate, *Beauvoir: A Critical Introduction*, Polity Press, 1997

Hatcher, Donald, *Understanding the Second Sex*, Peter Lang, 1984

MERLEAU-PONTY

Primary

Phenomenology of Perception, trans. Colin Smith, Routledge, 1962

The Prose of the World, trans. John O'Neill, Northwestern University Press, 1973

Sense and Non-sense, trans. Hubert Dreyfus and Patricia Dreyfus, Northwestern University Press, 1964

The Structure of Behavior, trans. Alden Fisher, Beacon Press, 1963

The Visible and the Invisible, trans. A. Lingis, Northwestern University Press, 1968

Secondary

Johnson, Galen, and Smith, Michael, eds., *Ontology and Alterity in Merleau-Ponty*, Northwestern University Press, 1990

Langer, Monica M., *Merleau Ponty's Phenomenology of Perception: A Guide and Commentary*, Florida State University Press, 1989

Madison, G. B., *The Phenomenology of Merleau-Ponty*, Ohio University Press, 1982

Schmidt, James, *Maurice Merleau-Ponty: Between Phenomenology and Structuralism*, St. Martin's, 1985

VII

✦ HERMENEUTICS AND ✦
POST-MODERNISM

 PROLOGUE

After World War II, continental philosophy is principally marked by four factors. First, there is the emergence of hermeneutics as a continuation and extension of the phenomenological tradition. Second, there is also a renewed interest in Marx, and the work of critical theory. Third, there is the advent of structuralism as an intellectual force, especially in France in the 1950's and 1960's. Finally, there is a renewed interest in Nietzsche, again especially in France after 1960. To put it in simple terms, the first two factors led to the work of Habermas, and the second two led to the development of the post-structuralist and post-modern thought of Foucault and Derrida. However, as we shall see, this is a simplistic classification because there is considerable interaction and interplay between these four factors.

Hermeneutics

The German thinker Wilhelm Dilthey (1833–1911) argued that interpretation was the hallmark of the human as opposed to the natural sciences, which explain natural phenomena causally. Dilthey conceived interpretation as a kind of empathetic understanding of others. The more contemporary hermeneutics advanced by Gadamer attempts to combine some aspects of Dilthey's notion of interpretation with the insights of the phenomenological and Heideggerian traditions. Gadamer argues that interpretation should not be regarded as a psychological and subjective act, as Dilthey supposed. It is rather an ontological process that happens to us because we are situated within a historical tradition. This idea is influenced by Heidegger's explication of the existential called understanding, which consists in making latent meanings explicit. Hermeneutics can be contrasted with the structuralist movement, which attempts to understand texts and systems of signs without any reference to the subjectivity of the author and reader, and which tends to portray language non-historically, without essential reference to tradition.

Critical Theory and Habermas

To understand the work of Habermas, we need some background. Marx's complete writings were published only after the end of World War II, and they contained his early works, which generally were unknown beforehand. Marx's early Paris manuscripts show the important influence of Kant and Hegel on his thought, and reveal a more philosophical approach than the economic materialism and determinism of his published later works. For example, in the early period, Marx writes about the nature of alienation, historical explanation and the relationship between theory and practice.

Through the works of the political philosopher Georg Lukacs, Marxism became an important intellectual force in Western Europe. Sartre became a vocal Marxist after 1950, though not a communist. Indeed, in general, this new Western form of Marxism should be distinguished from the official party line of the Soviet Union, which can be considered as a form of state dictatorship. In particular, Western Marxism was an important influence because of the idea that social awareness and explanation cannot be non-historical. Any philosophy and ideology has to be understood in its historical context.

Furthermore, after World War II, there was a renewed interest in the Critical Theory movement, which is sometimes called the Frankfurt School. The Frankfurt School emerged initially in the 1930's under the guidance of the philosopher Max Horkheimer (1895–1973), as a new inter-disciplinary approach to the social sciences. The other central figures in this movement were Theodore Adorno, Herbert Marcuse and Erich Fromm. The Frankfurt School tried to develop a conception of the social sciences, which was opposed to positivism, and according to which the social sciences should not limit themselves to just describing and understanding social phenomena in their historical context. The social sciences should also provide a critical evaluation of social ideology and the mass-produced culture of capitalism. Marx claimed that capitalism treats labor merely as a means to production and, thereby, it leads to alienation. Critical Theory extends this critique by arguing that, by treating human beings purely instrumentally, capitalism threatens democratic values. Furthermore, 20th century capitalism involves consumers being manipulated by advertising and popular mass-culture into having more and more desires, or false needs.

However, from the beginning, Critical Theory was dogged by a philosophical problem, the gap between theory and practice or, in other words, between description and evaluation. How can an evaluative critique be valid? This problem was especially acute for the Critical Theorists because, in the *Dialectic of Enlightenment* (1947), Horkheimer and Adorno criticized the enlightenment notion of reason, drawing inspiration from Nietzsche. They saw the instrumental rationality of science and technology as a basic cause of capitalism's ills. Therefore, they faced the thorny problem of how a critique of rationality could be rationally based. Thinkers in this tradition responded differently to this challenge. In brief, Marcuse argued that the problem could be solved by appeal to a Freudian view of human nature, and Adorno claimed that the solution lay in developing our aesthetic sensibility.

The philosophy of Habermas can be seen as an attempt to rethink this whole problem and provide a philosophical foundation for the Frankfurt School tradition, thereby rescuing it from later postmodernism. He tries to rescue Critical Theory by shifting the focus from the subject to communication. In brief, Habermas argues that certain values are inherent within and presupposed by the very act of communication. He develops his insight into a theory called 'Discourse Ethics.' Analysis of communication leads Habermas towards a new participatory view of democracy but, at the same time, it allows for an immanent critique of capitalist ideology. In this way, Habermas aims also to reject post-structuralism.

Structuralism and Beyond

In 1916, the theoretical work of the Swiss linguist Ferdinand de Saussure, *Course in General Linguistics,* was published posthumously. Saussure invented semiology, the general science of signs, according to which all signs consist of both a signifier and the signified. For example, the signifier would be the word 'tree,' and the signified would be the concept 'tree.' A sign is determined by the differences between it and all the other signs in a whole language or system of signs. Furthermore, this system of signs is both social and structured.

Saussure's work inspired the anthropologist Claude Lévi-Strauss to found structuralism, a new approach to the social sciences, which consists in applying Saussure's linguistics to the study of societies. Lévi-Strauss argues that the social sciences should follow the successful example of linguistics by seeking rules that exhibit meaningful order and syntactical structure in social practices, which are to be viewed as a system of signs. Anthropology should be looking for structural features that are common to all societies. Both in anthropology and linguistics, we need structural abstract models that make observed facts intelligible.

Lévi-Strauss' approach to the social sciences has two general theoretical features. First, it tries to explain social phenomena in a way that transcends the characterizations a society would give of itself. He argues that, in this way, the social sciences can become more scientific. Second, Lévi-Strauss explicitly rejects individualistic psychological explanations of social phenomena. He claims to dissolve the self. Structuralism treats the concept of the self as part of social system of signs. In this way, as a social science, structuralism opposes both a strict division between the natural and the social sciences as well as historical relativism, without being positivistic.

At the same time, structuralism has important philosophical implications. First, the idea that language is a structured holistic system of social signs rejects the alternative view that language is a transparent representation of an objective reality. In particular, in so doing, it means to provide an antidote to the absolute Cartesian notion of the self, and rejects the idea of the knowing subject inherent in phenomenology. The notion of the self is a social construct, and the meaning of signs does not depend on the subject. During the 1960's and 1970's, structuralism became a very popular intellectual movement in France. It inspired Lacan to employ a similar approach to the unconscious and its manifestations, and thereby to invent structural psychoanalysis. To some extent, we can understand the work of recent French philosophers, such as Lyotard, Foucault and Derrida, as an extension of, and a reaction to, some elements of structuralism and, for this reason, they are often called post-structuralists.

The Revival of Nietzsche

This reaction against structuralism was caused in part by a renewed interest in Nietzsche. Later French thinkers, such Foucault, embrace the historicism inherent in Hegel, Marx and Nietzsche's concept of genealogy. In other words, they accept the claim that no philosophical position can be understood independently of its historical context and, in this way, they reject the non-historical aspects of structuralism.

However, at the same time, they tend to follow the perspectivism and anti-rationalism of Nietzsche. In the 1930's, the French thinker George Bataille produced various works on Nietzsche. In 1947, the German Critical Theorists, Horkheimer and Adorno, wrote the *Dialectic of Enlightenment,* a critique of the enlightenment conception of reason, based on many of Nietzsche's insights. Finally, in 1962, the Frenchman Gilles Deleuze published an influential book, *Nietzsche and Philosophy.* Because of this Nietzschian influence, later French thinkers, such as Foucault, reject Hegel's and Marx's idea of a single grand narrative that can make sense out of history. Similarly, they also criticize the Enlightenment and Kantian idea of the interpretation of history as the progress of reason. Furthermore, Foucault, in particular, adopts and extends Nietzsche's conception of power. Like the Frankfurt School, these later French thinkers are critical of the modern and Enlightenment notion of reason. However, unlike Habermas, they do not try to reconstruct a more pragmatic and social conception of rationality. Because of this, they are sometimes called postmodern thinkers.

Hans Georg Gadamer (1900–2002)

Biographical History

Hans Georg Gadamer studied his doctoral thesis on Plato under the supervision of Heidegger, and spent most of his academic life at the University of Heidelberg in Germany. He retired in 1968. His work *Truth and Method* was first published in 1960.

Philosophical Overview

Hermeneutics is the part of philosophy most directly concerned with interpretation. It is a relatively recent development, which has arisen in part because literary theorists, art critics, legal thinkers, social scientists, and historical scholars have realized that their work involves a shared set of problems, as well as a common approach. Hermeneutics has its roots in the works of Dilthey and phenomenology, as well as that of Heidegger, who characterized his own work as hermeneutical phenomenology. Habermas also works with a broadly hermeneutical approach. Another important recent exponent of hermeneutics is Paul Ricoeur.

Truth and Method formulates the basic principles of hermeneutics, which are described below, and applies them to the fields of art, history, and language. Gadamer's main aims are to avoid both historical relativism and the reductionism inherent in formalistic and scientific approaches to language. Therefore, interpretation must be constrained by truth, without adhering to a rigid method.

The hermeneutical approach has four main characteristics. First, it applies to things that have some kind of intentionality, even derivatively. Consequently, for example, there can be interpretation and a hermeneutics of people's behavior, social practices, texts, paintings, animal behavior, legal precedents, and historical traditions. However, there is no hermeneutics of atoms, weather patterns, or galaxies, unless there were a reason for treating these systems as intentional.

Second, interpretation is usually contrasted with causal explanation. In part, hermeneutics originated as a response to the logical positivist idea that the methodology of the natural sciences could be imported into the social sciences. In the natural sciences, we typically explain an event by citing its causes, which would include some causal laws. However, the hermeneutic tradition denies that this causal methodology of the natural sciences can be extended into social studies because, in the social sciences, we are concerned with actions as actions, and with intentional states as such, actions which have content or meaning. The point of interpretation is to understand the content or meaning of these states and of actions, and this hermeneutical process does not involve citing lawlike causes. For example, interpreting a religious ritual requires understanding its meaning for the people engaged in it from their point of view, and not in explaining the ritual causally, for example, in terms of its potential survival value.

Third, interpretation is essentially holistic. For example, to understand a ceremony requires comprehending a host of concepts that the people concerned employ, which in turn requires understanding other social practices of the group. There is a web of interrelated meanings that need to be understood. This point manifests itself in the famous hermeneutical circle, according to which interpretation involves a circle: to understand the parts of a text or practice, one needs to grasp the meaning of the whole, which requires understanding the parts. However, this is not a vicious circle. It reveals how understanding involves correcting one in light of the other. Habermas expresses the point as follows: 'We can decipher parts of a text only if we anticipate an understanding, however diffuse, of the whole; and conversely, we can correct this anticipation only to the extent that we explicate individual parts.'

Fourth, Gadamer's hermeneutical approach stresses that interpretation is inherently historical. Whenever one seeks to understand anything, one must employ concepts, ideas, and presuppositions that are part of one's own historical tradition. Because of its inherent historical nature, the interpretation of a text cannot consist merely in reconstructing the intentions of the author. Gadamer says that the meaning of a text goes beyond its author because the project of interpreting a text is one of making the best overall sense of it in the present historical context. Gadamer points out that 'a hermeneutical consciousness exists only under specific historical conditions.' For example, according to this view, knowing the intentions of the framers of the Constitution of the United States is not necessary or sufficient for understanding the meaning of the document itself; interpreting the meaning of the text must involve understanding its significance in our context, today.

TRUTH AND METHOD

Gadamer's strategy is to show how interpretation functions in the arts, and from there, to examine its workings in the human sciences, and finally its relation to language. His book *Truth and Method* is structured around these three parts.

The central problem his work addresses can be seen in the following contrast. On the one hand, there is no such thing as presupposition-free interpretation. All interpretation must start from the set of concepts and meanings of the interpreter, which Heidegger calls 'the fore-structure.' However, on the other hand, interpretation consists in entering into the point of view of another or into a text that has presuppositions different from one's own. When one characterizes the content of someone's intentional mental state, one must do so in terms of his or her point of view. When one tries to understand a text, one cannot simply impose one's own ideas on it; one needs to interpret it correctly. One aims at truth.

How do we reconcile these two points? Gadamer claims that we can reconcile the two points through the self-reflective nature of interpretation. To understand something requires us to examine critically the fore-structures or presuppositions of our own interpretation in light of the uncovered meanings inherent in what is being interpreted. In other words, we should place our presuppositions into a critical dialogue with the text that is being read. In this way, our own understanding changes through the process of interpretation. Gadamer says; 'The important thing is to be aware of one's own bias, so that the text can present itself in all its otherness and thus assert its own truth against one's own fore-meaning' (Gadamer, 269). Viewed in this fashion, the cultural and historical presuppositions one brings to an interpretation cannot be regarded as an obstacle to understanding. They are a necessary part of it. Interpretation cannot be prejudice free. However, interpretation must be both open and critical in order for it to be enriching and self-reflective. In this sense, it is akin to entering into a dialogue with a text.

   Gadamer stresses that the process of interpretation must be deeply self-reflective because it must be constrained by truth. A reading of a text ought to be true, or not erroneous. This requirement necessitates the element of self-reflection, as opposed to some rigid predefined method. However, this point does not mean that there is necessarily only one correct way to understand a text, but it does rule out the idea that it is merely a matter of opinion. There is such a thing as misunderstanding or misinterpretation. Because of this, interpretation is a dialectical process; one must be willing to have one's initial assumptions negated by the meaning of a text. In this way, there can be truth without method.

INTRODUCTION

These studies are concerned with the problem of hermeneutics. The phenomenon of understanding and of the correct interpretation of what has been understood is not a problem specific to the methodology of the human sciences alone. There has long been a theological and a legal hermeneutics, which were not so much theoretical as corollary and ancillary to the practical activity of the judge or clergyman who had completed his theoretical training. Even from its historical beginnings, the problem of hermeneutics goes beyond the limits of the concept of method as set by modern science. The understanding and the interpretation of texts is not merely a concern of science, but obviously belongs to human experience of the world in general. The hermeneutic phenomenon is basically not a problem of method at all. It is not concerned with a method of understanding by means of which texts are subjected to scientific investigation like all other objects of experience. It is not concerned primarily with amassing verified knowledge, such as would satisfy the methodological ideal of science—yet it too is concerned with knowledge and with truth. In understanding tradition not only are texts understood, but insights are acquired and truths known. But what kind of knowledge and what kind of truth?

   Given the dominance of modern science in the philosophical elucidation and justification of the concept of knowledge and the concept of truth, this question does not appear legitimate. Yet it is unavoidable, even within the sciences. The phenomenon of understanding not only pervades all human relations to the world. It also has an independent validity within science, and it resists any attempt to reinterpret it in terms of scientific method. The following investigations start with the resistance in modern science itself to the universal claim of scientific method. They are concerned to seek the experience of truth that transcends the domain of scientific method wherever that experience is to be found, and to inquire into its legitimacy. Hence the human sciences are connected to modes of experience that lie outside science: with the experiences of philosophy, of art, and of history itself. These are all modes of experience in which a truth is communicated that cannot be verified by the methodological means proper to science.

   Contemporary philosophy is well aware of this. But it is quite a different question how far the truth claim of such modes of experience outside science can be philosophically legitimated. The current interest in the hermeneutic phenomenon rests, I think, on the fact that only a deeper investigation of the phenomenon of understanding can provide this legitimation. This conviction is strongly supported by the importance that contemporary philosophy attaches to the history of philosophy. In regard to the historical tradition of philosophy, understanding occurs to us as a superior experience enabling us easily to see through the illusion of historical method characteristic of research in the history of philosophy. It is part of the elementary experience of philosophy that when we try to understand the classics of philosophical thought, they of themselves make a claim to truth that the consciousness of later times can neither reject nor transcend. The naive self-esteem of the present moment may rebel against the idea that philosophical consciousness admits the possibility that one's own philosophical insight may be inferior to that of Plato or Aristotle, Leibniz, Kant, or Hegel. One might think it a weakness that contemporary philosophy tries to interpret and assimilate its classical heritage with this acknowledgment of its own weakness. But it is undoubtedly a far greater weakness for philosophical thinking not to face such self-examination but to play at being Faust. It is clear that in understanding the texts of these great thinkers, a truth is known that could not be attained in any other way, even if this contradicts the yardstick of research and progress by which science measures itself.

The same thing is true of the experience of art. Here the scholarly research pursued by the "science of art" is aware from the start that it can neither replace nor surpass the experience of art. The fact that through a work of art a truth is experienced that we cannot attain in any other way constitutes the philosophic importance of art, which asserts itself against all attempts to rationalize it away. Hence, together with the experience of philosophy, the experience of art is the most insistent admonition to scientific consciousness to acknowledge its own limits.

Hence the following investigation starts with a critique of aesthetic consciousness in order to defend the experience of truth that comes to us through the work of art against the aesthetic theory that lets itself be restricted to a scientific conception of truth. But the book does not rest content with justifying the truth of art; instead, it tries to develop from this starting point a conception of knowledge and of truth that corresponds to the whole of our hermeneutic experience. Just

as in the experience of art we are concerned with truths that go essentially beyond the range of methodical knowledge, so the same thing is true of the whole of the human sciences: in them our historical tradition in all its forms is certainly made the *object* of investigation, but at the same time *truth comes to speech in it*. Fundamentally, the experience of historical tradition reaches far beyond those aspects of it that can be objectively investigated. It is true or untrue not only in the sense concerning which historical criticism decides, but always mediates truth in which one must *try to share*.

Hence these studies on hermeneutics, which start from the experience of art and of historical tradition, try to present the hermeneutic phenomenon in its full extent. It is a question of recognizing in it an experience of truth that not only needs to be justified philosophically, but which is itself a way of doing philosophy. The hermeneutics developed here is not, therefore, a methodology of the human sciences, but an attempt to understand what the human sciences truly are, beyond their methodological self-consciousness, and what connects them with the totality of our experience of world. If we make understanding the object of our reflection, the aim is not an art or technique of understanding, such as traditional literary and theological hermeneutics sought to be. Such an art or technique would fail to recognize that, in view of the truth that speaks to us from tradition, a formal technique would arrogate to itself a false superiority. Even though in the following I shall demonstrate how much there is of *event* effective in all *understanding,* and how little the traditions in which we stand are weakened by modern historical consciousness, it is not my intention to make prescriptions for the sciences or the conduct of life, but to try to correct false thinking about what they are.

I hope in this way to reinforce an insight that is threatened with oblivion in our swiftly changing age. Things that change force themselves on our attention far more than those that remain the same. That is a general law of our intellectual life. Hence the perspectives that result from the experience of historical change are always in danger of being exaggerated because they forget what persists unseen. In modern life, our historical consciousness is constantly overstimulated. As a consequence—though, as I hope to show, it is a pernicious short circuit—some react to this overestimation of historical change by invoking the eternal orders of nature and appealing to human nature to legitimize the idea of natural law. It is not only that historical tradition and the natural order of life constitute the unity of the world in which we live as men; the way we experience one another, the way we experience historical traditions, the way we experience the natural givenness of our existence and of our world, constitute a truly hermeneutic universe, in which we are not imprisoned, as if behind insurmountable barriers, but to which we are opened.

A reflection on what truth is in the human sciences must not try to reflect itself out of the tradition whose binding force it has recognized. Hence in its own work it must endeavor to acquire as much historical self-transparency as possible. In its concern to understand the universe of understanding better than seems possible under the modern scientific notion of cognition, it has to try to establish a new relation to the concepts which it uses. It must be aware of the fact that its own understanding and interpretation are not constructions based on principles, but the furthering of an event that goes far back. Hence it will not be able to use its concepts unquestioningly, but will have to take over whatever features of the original meaning of its concepts have come down to it.

The philosophical endeavor of our day differs from the classical tradition of philosophy in that it is not a direct and unbroken continuation of it. Despite its connection with its historical origin, philosophy today is well aware of the historical distance between it and its classical models. This is especially to be found in its changed attitude to the concept. However important and fundamental were the transformations that took place with the Latinization of Greek concepts and the translation of Latin conceptual language into the modern languages, the emergence of historical consciousness over the last few centuries is a much more radical

rupture. Since then, the continuity of the Western philosophical tradition has been effective only in a fragmentary way. We have lost that naive innocence with which traditional concepts were made to serve one's own thinking. Since that time, the attitude of science towards these concepts has become strangely detached, whether it takes them up in a scholarly, not to say self-consciously archaizing way, or treats them as tools. Neither of these truly satisfies the hermeneutic experience. The conceptual world in which philosophizing develops has already captivated us in the same way that the language in which we live conditions us. If thought is to be conscientious, it must become aware of these anterior influences. A new critical consciousness must now accompany all responsible philosophizing which takes the habits of thought and language built up in the individual in his communication with his environment and places them before the forum of the historical tradition to which we all belong.

The following investigation tries to meet this demand by linking as closely as possible an inquiry into the history of concepts with the substantive exposition of its theme. That conscientiousness of phenomenological description which Husserl has made a duty for us all; the breadth of the historical horizon in which Dilthey has placed all philosophizing; and, not least, the penetration of both these influences by the impulse received from Heidegger, indicate the standard by which the writer desires to be measured, and which, despite all imperfection in the execution, he would like to see applied without reservation.

PART I: THE QUESTION OF TRUTH AS IT EMERGES IN THE EXPERIENCE OF ART

I

Transcending the Aesthetic Dimension

1. The Significance of the Humanist Tradition for the Human Sciences

(A) The Problem of Method

The logical self-reflection that accompanied the development of the human sciences in the nineteenth century is wholly governed by the model of the natural sciences. A glance at the history of the word Geisteswissenschaft shows this, although only in its plural form does this word acquire the meaning familiar to us. The human sciences (Geisteswissenschaften) so obviously understand themselves by analogy to the natural sciences that the idealistic echo implied in the idea of Geist ("spirit") and of a science of Geist fades into the background.

But the specific problem that the human sciences present to thought is that one has not rightly grasped their nature if one measures them by the yardstick of a progressive knowledge of regularity. The experience of the socio-historical world cannot be raised to a science by the inductive procedure of the natural sciences. Whatever "science" may mean here, and even if all historical knowledge includes the application of experiential universals to the particular object of investigation, historical research does not endeavor to grasp the concrete phenomenon as an instance of a universal rule. The individual case does not serve only to confirm a law from which practical predictions can be made. Its ideal is rather to understand the phenomenon itself in its unique and historical concreteness. However much experiential universals are involved, the aim is not to confirm and extend these universalized experiences in order to attain knowledge of a law—e.g., how men, peoples, and states evolve—but to understand how this man, this people, or this state is what it has become or, more generally, how it happened that it is so.

What kind of knowledge is it that understands that something is so because it understands that it has come about so? What does "science" mean here? Even if one acknowledges that the ideal of this knowledge is fundamentally different in kind and intention from the natural sciences, one will still be tempted to describe the human sciences in a merely negative way as the "inexact sciences."

But in fact the human sciences are a long way from regarding themselves as simply inferior to the natural sciences. Instead, possessed of the intellectual heritage of German classicism, they carried forward the proud awareness that they were the true representatives of humanism. The period of German classicism had not only brought about a renewal of literature and aesthetic criticism, which overcame the outmoded baroque ideal of taste and of Enlightenment rationalism; it had also given the idea of humanity, and the ideal of enlightened reason, a fundamentally new content. More than anyone, Herder transcended the perfectionism of the Enlightenment with his new ideal of "cultivating the human" (Bildung zum Menschen) and thus prepared the ground for the growth of the historical sciences in the nineteenth century. The *concept of self-formation, education, or cultivation* (Bildung), which became supremely important at the time, was perhaps the greatest idea of the eighteenth century, and it is this concept which is the atmosphere breathed by the human sciences of the nineteenth century, even if they are unable to offer any epistemological justification for it.

3. *Retrieving the Question of Artistic Truth*

97 The pantheon of art is not a timeless present that presents itself to a pure aesthetic consciousness, but the act of a mind and spirit that has collected and gathered itself historically. Our experience of the aesthetic too is a mode of self-understanding. Self-understanding always occurs through understanding something other than the self, and includes the unity and integrity of the other. Since we meet the artwork in the world and encounter a world in the individual artwork, the work of art is not some alien universe into which we are magically transported for a time. Rather, we learn to understand ourselves in and through it, and this means that we sublate (aufheben) the discontinuity and atomism of isolated experiences in the continuity of our own existence. For this reason, we must adopt a standpoint in relation to art and the beautiful that does not pretend to immediacy but corresponds to the historical nature of the human condition. The appeal to immediacy, to the instantaneous flash of genius, to the significance

of "experiences" (Erlebnisse), cannot withstand the claim of human existence to continuity and unity of self-understanding. The binding quality of the experience (Erfahrung) of art must not be disintegrated by aesthetic consciousness.

This negative insight, positively expressed, is that art is knowledge and experiencing an artwork means sharing in that knowledge.

This raises the question of how one can do justice to the truth of aesthetic experience (Erfahrung) and overcome the radical subjectivization of the aesthetic that began with Kant's *Critique of Aesthetic Judgment*. We have shown that it was a methodological abstraction corresponding to a quite particular transcendental task of laying foundations which led Kant to relate aesthetic judgment entirely to the condition of the subject. If, however, this aesthetic abstraction was subsequently understood as a content and was changed into the demand that art be understood "purely aesthetically," we can now see how this demand for abstraction ran into indissoluble contradiction with the true experience of art.

Is there to be no knowledge in art? Does not the experience of art contain a claim to truth which is certainly different from that of science, but just as certainly is not inferior to it? And is not the task of aesthetics precisely to ground the fact that the experience (Erfahrung) of art is a mode of knowledge of a unique kind, certainly different from that sensory knowledge which provides science with the ultimate data from which it constructs the knowledge of nature, and certainly different from all moral rational knowledge, and indeed from all conceptual knowledge—but still knowledge, i.e., conveying truth?

This can hardly be recognized if, with Kant, one measures the truth of knowledge by the scientific concept of knowledge and the scientific concept of reality. It is necessary to take the concept of experience (Erfahrung) more broadly than Kant did, so that the experience of the work of art can be understood as experience. For this we can appeal to Hegel's admirable lectures on aesthetics. Here the truth that lies in every artistic experience is recognized and at the same time mediated with historical consciousness. Hence

aesthetics becomes a history of worldviews—i.e., a history of truth, as it is manifested in the mirror of art. It is also a fundamental recognition of the task that I formulated thus: to legitimate the knowledge of truth that occurs in the experience of art itself.

The familiar concept of worldview—which first appears in Hegel in the *Phenomenology of Mind* as a term for Kant's and Fichte's postulatory amplification of the basic moral experience into a moral world order—acquires its special stamp only in aesthetics. It is the multiplicity and the possible change of worldviews that has given the concept of worldview its familiar 98 ring. . . . Hegel's philosophy at the same time disavows the way of truth it has recognized in the experience of art. If we want to justify art as a way of truth in its own right, then we must fully 99 realize what truth means here. It is in the human sciences as a whole that an answer to this question must be found. For they seek not to surpass but to understand the variety of experiences—whether of aesthetic, historical, religious, or political consciousness—but that means they expect to find truth in them. We will have to go into the relationship between Hegel and the self-understanding of the human sciences represented by the "historical school" and also into the way the two differ about what makes it possible to understand aright what truth means in the human sciences. At any rate, we will not be able to do justice to the problem of art from the point of view of aesthetic consciousness but only within this wider framework.

We made only one step in this direction in seeking to correct the self-interpretation of aesthetic consciousness and in retrieving the question of the truth of art, to which the aesthetic experience bears witness. Thus our concern is to view the experience of art in such a way that it is understood as experience (Erfahrung). The experience of art should not be falsified by being turned into a possession of aesthetic culture, thus neutralizing its special claim. We will see that this involves a far-reaching hermeneutical consequence, for *all encounter with the language of art is an encounter with an unfinished event and is itself part of this event*. This is what must be emphasized against aesthetic consciousness and its neutralization of the question of truth.

100 In order to do justice to the experience (Erfahrung) of art we began with a critique of aesthetic consciousness. The experience of art acknowledges that it cannot present the full truth of what it experiences in terms of definitive knowledge. There is no absolute progress and no final exhaustion of what lies in a work of art. The experience of art knows this of itself. At the same time we cannot simply accept what aesthetic consciousness considers its experience to be. For as we saw, it ultimately considers its experience to be the discontinuity of experiences (Erlebnisse). But we have found this conclusion unacceptable.

We do not ask the experience of art to tell us how it conceives of itself, then, but what it truly is and what its truth is, even if it does not know what it is and cannot say what it knows— just as Heidegger has asked what metaphysics is, by contrast to what it thinks itself to be. In the experience of art we see a genuine experience (Erfahrung) induced by the work, which does not leave him who has it unchanged, and we inquire into the mode of being of what is experienced in this way. So we hope to better understand what kind of truth it is that encounters us there.

We will see that this opens up the dimension in which, in the "understanding" practiced by the human sciences, the question of truth is raised in a new way.

If we want to know what truth is in the field of the human sciences, we will have to ask the philosophical question of the whole procedure of the human sciences in the same way that Heidegger asked it of metaphysics and we have asked it of aesthetic consciousness. But we shall not be able simply to accept the human sciences' own understanding of themselves, but must ask what their mode of understanding in truth is. The question of the truth of art in particular can serve to prepare the way for this more wide-ranging question, because the experience of the work of art includes understanding, and thus itself represents a hermeneutical phenomenon—but not at all in the sense of a scientific method. Rather,

understanding belongs to the encounter with the work of art itself, and so this belonging can be illuminated only on the basis of the *mode of being of the work of art itself*.

II
The Ontology of the Work of Art and Its Hermeneutic Significance

2. Aesthetic and Hermeneutic Consequences

161 Literary art can be understood only from the ontology of the work of art, and not from the aesthetic experiences that occur in the course of the reading. Like a public reading or performance, being read belongs to literature by its nature. They are stages of what is generally called "reproduction" but which in fact is the *original* mode of being of all performing arts, and that mode of being has proved exemplary for defining the mode of being of all art.

But this has a further consequence. The concept of literature is not unrelated to the reader. Literature does not exist as the dead remnant of an alienated being, left over for a later time as simultaneous with its experiential reality. Literature is a function of being intellectually preserved and handed down, and therefore brings its hidden history into every age. Beginning with the establishment of the canon of classical literature by the Alexandrian philologists, copying and preserving the "classics" is a living cultural tradition that does not simply preserve what exists but acknowledges it as a model and passes it on as an example to be followed. Through all changes of taste, the effective grandeur that we call "classical literature" remains a model for all later writers, up to the time of the ambiguous "battle of the ancients and moderns," and beyond.

162 The qualitative distinction accorded a work by the fact that it belongs to world literature places the phenomenon of literature in a new perspective. Even though only literature that has value of its own as art is declared to belong to world literature, the concept of literature is far wider than that of the literary work of art. All written texts share in the mode of being of literature— not only religious, legal, economic, public and private texts of all kinds, but also scholarly writ-

ings that edit and interpret these texts: namely the human sciences as a whole. Moreover, all scholarly research takes the form of literature insofar as it is essentially bound to language. Literature in the broadest sense is bounded only by what can be said, for everything that can be said can be written.

We may ask ourselves, then, whether what we have discovered about the mode of being of art still applies to literature in this broad sense. Must we confine the normative sense of literature which we elaborated above to literary works that can be considered works of art, and must we say that they alone share in the ontological valence of art? Do the other forms of literature have no share in it?

Or is there no such sharp division here? There are works of scholarship whose literary merit has caused them to be considered works of art and part of world literature. This is clear from the point of view of aesthetic consciousness, inasmuch as the latter does not consider the significance of such works' contents but only the quality of their form as important. But since our criticism of aesthetic consciousness has shown the limited validity of that point of view, this principle dividing literary art from other written texts becomes dubious for us. We have seen that aesthetic consciousness is unable to grasp the essential truth even of literary art. For literary art has in common with all other texts the fact that it speaks to us in terms of the significance of its contents. Our understanding is not specifically concerned with its formal achievement as a work of art but with what it says to us.

The difference between a literary work of art and any other text is not so fundamental. It is true that there is a difference between the language of poetry and the language of prose, and again between the language of poetic prose and that of "scientific" or "scholarly" prose. These differences can certainly also be considered from the point of view of literary form. But the essential difference between these various "languages" obviously lies elsewhere: namely in the distinction between the claims to truth that each makes. All written works have a profound community in that language is what makes the contents meaningful. In this light, when texts are

understood by, say, a historian, that is not so very different from their being experienced as art. And it is not mere chance that the concept of literature embraces not only works of literary art but everything passed down in writing.

At any rate, it is not by chance that literature is the place where art and science merge. The mode of being of a text has something unique and incomparable about it. It presents a specific problem of translation to the understanding. Nothing is so strange, and at the same time so demanding, as the written word. Not even meeting speakers of a foreign language can be compared with this strangeness, since the language of gesture and of sound is always in part immediately intelligible. The written word and what partakes of it—literature—is the intelligibility of mind transferred to the most alien medium. Nothing is so purely the trace of the mind as writing, but nothing is so dependent on the understanding mind either. In deciphering and interpreting it, a miracle takes place: the transformation of something alien and dead into total contemporaneity and familiarity. This is like nothing else that comes down to us from the past. The remnants of past life—what is left of buildings, tools, the contents of graves—are weather-beaten by the storms of time that have swept over them, whereas a written tradition, once deciphered and read, is to such an extent pure mind that it speaks to us as if in the present. That is why the capacity to read, to understand what is written, is like a secret art, even a magic that frees and binds us. In it time and space seem to be superseded. People who can read what has been handed down in writing produce and achieve the sheer presence of the past.

Hence we can see that in our context, despite all aesthetic distinctions, the concept of literature is as broad as possible. Just as we were able to show that the being of the work of art is play and that it must be perceived by the spectator in order to be actualized (vollendet), so also it is universally true of texts that only in the process of understanding them is the dead trace of meaning transformed back into living meaning. We must ask whether what we found to be true of the experience of art is also true of texts as a whole, including those that are not works of art. We saw that the work of art is actualized only when it is "presented," and we were drawn to the conclusion that all literary works of art are actualized only when they are read. Is this true also of the understanding of any text? Is the meaning of all texts actualized only when they are understood? In other words, does being understood belong (gehört) to the meaning of a text just as being heard (Zu-Gehör-Bringen) belongs to the meaning of music? Can we still talk of understanding if we are as free with the meaning of the text as the performing artist with his score?

(D) Reconstruction and Integration as Hermeneutic Tasks

The classical discipline concerned with the art of understanding texts is hermeneutics. If my argument is correct, however, the real problem of hermeneutics is quite different from what one might expect. It points in the same direction in which my criticism of aesthetic consciousness has moved the problem of aesthetics. In fact, hermeneutics would then have to be understood in so comprehensive a sense as to embrace the whole sphere of art and its complex of questions. Every work of art, not only literature, must be understood like any other text that requires understanding, and this kind of understanding has to be acquired. This gives hermeneutical consciousness a comprehensiveness that surpasses even that of aesthetic consciousness. *Aesthetics has to be absorbed into hermeneutics.* This statement not only reveals the breadth of the problem but is substantially accurate. Conversely, hermeneutics must be so determined as a whole that it does justice to the experience of art. Understanding must be conceived as a part
165 of the event in which meaning occurs, the event in which the meaning of all statements—those of art and all other kinds of tradition—is formed and actualized.

In the nineteenth century, the hermeneutics that was once merely ancillary to theology and philology was developed into a system and made the basis of all the human sciences. It wholly transcended its original pragmatic purpose of making it possible, or easier, to understand writ-

ten texts. It is not only the written tradition that is estranged and in need of new and more vital assimilation; everything that is no longer immediately situated in a world—that is, all tradition, whether art or the other spiritual creations of the past: law, religion, philosophy, and so forth—is estranged from its original meaning and depends on the unlocking and mediating spirit that we, like the Greeks, name after Hermes: the messenger of the gods. It is to the *rise of historical consciousness* that hermeneutics owes its centrality within the human sciences. But we may ask whether the whole extent of the problem that hermeneutics poses can be adequately grasped on the basis of the premises of historical consciousness.

PART II: THE EXTENSION OF THE QUESTION OF TRUTH TO UNDERSTANDING IN THE HUMAN SCIENCES

II

Elements of a Theory of Hermeneutic Experience

1. The Elevation of the Historicity of Understanding to the Status of a Hermeneutic Principle

(A) The Hermeneutic Circle and the Problem of Prejudices

(I) HEIDEGGER'S DISCLOSURE OF THE FORE-STRUCTURE OF UNDERSTANDING

265 Heidegger entered into the problems of historical hermeneutics and critique only in order to explicate the fore-structure of understanding for the purposes of ontology. Our question, by contrast, is how hermeneutics, once freed from the ontological obstructions of the scientific concept of objectivity, can do justice to the historicity of understanding. Hermeneutics has traditionally understood itself as an art or technique. . . .

What Heidegger is working out here is not
266 primarily a prescription for the practice of understanding, but a description of the way interpretive understanding is achieved. The point of Heidegger's hermeneutical reflection is not so much to prove that there is a circle as to show

that this circle possesses an ontologically positive significance. The description as such will be obvious to every interpreter who knows what he is about. All correct interpretation must be on guard against arbitrary fancies and the limitations imposed by imperceptible habits of thought, and it must direct its gaze "on the things themselves" (which, in the case of the literary critic, are meaningful texts, which themselves are again concerned with objects). For the interpreter to let himself be guided by the things themselves is obviously not a matter of a single, "conscientious" decision, but is "the first, last, and constant task." For it is necessary to keep one's gaze fixed on the thing throughout all the constant distractions that originate in the interpreter himself. A person who is trying to understand a text is always projecting. He projects a meaning for the text as a whole as soon as some initial meaning emerges in the text. Again, the initial meaning emerges only because he is reading the text with particular expectations in regard to a certain meaning. Working out this fore-projection, which is constantly revised in terms of what emerges as he penetrates into the meaning, is understanding what is there.

This description is, of course, a rough abbreviation of the whole. The process that Heidegger describes is that every revision of the fore-projection is capable of projecting before itself a new projection of meaning; rival projects can emerge side by side until it becomes clearer what the unity of meaning is; interpretation begins with fore-conceptions that are replaced by more suitable ones. This constant process of new projection constitutes the movement of understanding and interpretation. A person who is trying to understand is exposed to distraction from fore-meanings that are not borne out by the things themselves. Working out appropriate projections, anticipatory in nature, to be confirmed "by the things" themselves, is the constant task of understanding. The only "objectivity" here is the confirmation of a fore-meaning in its being worked out. Indeed, what characterizes the arbitrariness of inappropriate fore-meanings if not that they come to nothing in being worked out? But understanding realizes its full potential only when the

fore-meanings that it begins with are not arbitrary. Thus it is quite right for the interpreter not to approach the text directly, relying solely on the fore-meaning already available to him, but rather explicitly to examine the legitimacy—i.e., the origin and validity—of the fore-meanings dwelling within him.

This basic requirement must be seen as the radicalization of a procedure that we in fact exercise whenever we understand anything. Every text presents the task of not simply leaving our own linguistic usage unexamined—or in the case of a foreign language the usage that we are familiar with from writers or from daily intercourse. Rather, we regard our task as deriving our understanding of the text from the linguistic usage of the time or of the author. The question is, of course, how this general requirement can be fulfilled. Especially in the field of semantics we are confronted with the problem that our own use of language is unconscious. How do we discover that there is a difference between our own customary usage and that of the text?

I think we must say that generally we do so in the experience of being pulled up short by the text. Either it does not yield any meaning at all or its meaning is not compatible with what we had expected. This is what brings us up short and alerts us to a possible difference in usage. Someone who speaks the same language as I do uses the words in the sense familiar to me—this is a general presupposition that can be questioned only in particular cases. The same thing is true in the case of a foreign language: we all think we have a standard knowledge of it and assume this standard usage when we are reading a text.

What is true of fore-meanings that stem from usage, however, is equally true of the fore-meanings concerning content with which we read texts, and which make up our fore-understanding. Here too we may ask how we can break the spell of our own fore-meanings. There can, of course, be a general expectation that what the text says will fit perfectly with my own meanings and expectations. But what another person tells me, whether in conversation, letter, book, or whatever, is generally supposed to be his own and not my opinion; and this is what I am to take note of without necessarily having to share it. Yet this presupposition is not something that makes understanding easier, but harder, since the fore-meanings that determine my own understanding can go entirely unnoticed. If they give rise to misunderstandings, how can our misunderstandings of a text be perceived at all if there is nothing to contradict them? How can a text be protected against misunderstanding from the start?

If we examine the situation more closely, however, we find that meanings cannot be understood in an arbitrary way. Just as we cannot continually misunderstand the use of a word without its affecting the meaning of the whole, so we cannot stick blindly to our own fore-meaning about the thing if we want to understand the meaning of another. Of course this does not mean that when we listen to someone or read a book we must forget all our fore-meanings concerning the content and all our own ideas. All that is asked is that we remain open to the meaning of the other person or text. But this openness always includes our situating the other meaning in relation to the whole of our own meanings or ourselves in relation to it. Now, the fact is that meanings represent a fluid multiplicity of possibilities (in comparison to the agreement presented by a language and a vocabulary), but within this multiplicity of what can be thought—i.e., of what a reader can find meaningful and hence expect to find—not everything is possible; and if a person fails to hear what the other person is really saying, he will not be able to fit what he has misunderstood into the range of his own various expectations of meaning. Thus there is a criterion here also. *The hermeneutical task becomes of itself a questioning of things* and is always in part so defined. This places hermeneutical work on a firm basis. A person trying to understand something will not resign himself from the start to relying on his own accidental fore-meanings, ignoring as consistently and stubbornly as possible the actual meaning of the text until the latter becomes so persistently audible that it breaks through what the interpreter imagines it to be. Rather, a person trying to understand a text is prepared for it to tell him something. That is why a hermeneutically trained consciousness must be,

from the start, sensitive to the text's alterity. But this kind of sensitivity involves neither "neutrality" with respect to content nor the extinction of one's self, but the foregrounding and appropriation of one's own fore-meanings and prejudices. The important thing is to be aware of one's own bias, so that the text can present itself in all its otherness and thus assert its own truth against one's own fore-meanings.

The recognition that all understanding inevitably involves some prejudice gives the hermeneutical problem its real thrust. In light of this insight it appears that *historicism, despite its critique of rationalism and of natural law philosophy, is based on the modern Enlightenment and unwittingly shares its prejudices*. And there is one prejudice of the Enlightenment that defines its essence: the fundamental prejudice of the Enlightenment is the prejudice against prejudice itself, which denies tradition its power.

The history of ideas shows that not until the Enlightenment does *the concept of prejudice* acquire the negative connotation familiar today. Actually "prejudice" means a judgment that is rendered before all the elements that determine a situation have been finally examined. In German legal terminology a "prejudice" is a provisional legal verdict before the final verdict is reached. For someone involved in a legal dispute, this kind of judgment against him affects his chances adversely. Accordingly, the French *préjudice*, as well as the Latin *praejudicium*, means simply "adverse effect," "disadvantage," "harm." But this negative sense is only derivative. The negative consequence depends precisely on the positive validity, the value of the provisional decision as a prejudgment, like that of any precedent.

Thus "prejudice" certainly does not necessarily mean a false judgment, but part of the idea is that it can have either a positive or a negative value. This is clearly due to the influence of the Latin *praejudicium*. There are such things as *préjugés légitimes*. This seems a long way from our current use of the word. The German *Vorurteil*, like the English "prejudice" and even more than the French *préjugé*, seems to have been limited in its meaning by the Enlightenment critique of religion simply to the sense of an "unfounded judgment." The only thing that

271 gives a judgment dignity is its having a basis, a methodological justification (and not the fact that it may actually be correct). For the Enlightenment the absence of such a basis does not mean that there might be other kinds of certainty, but rather that the judgment has no foundation in the things themselves—i.e., that it is "unfounded." This conclusion follows only in the spirit of rationalism. It is the reason for discrediting prejudices and the reason scientific knowledge claims to exclude them completely.

In adopting this principle, modern science is following the rule of Cartesian doubt, accepting nothing as certain that can in any way be doubted, and adopting the idea of method that follows from this rule. In our introductory observations we have already pointed out how difficult it is to harmonize the historical knowledge that helps to shape our historical consciousness with this ideal and how difficult it is, for that reason, to comprehend its true nature on the basis of the modern conception of method. This is the place to turn those negative statements into positive ones. The concept of "prejudice" is where we can start.

B. Prejudices as Conditions of Understanding

293 Heidegger's description and existential grounding of the hermeneutic circle constitute a decisive turning point. Nineteenth-century hermeneutic theory often discussed the circular structure of understanding, but always within the framework of a formal relation between part and whole—or its subjective reflex, the intuitive anticipation of the whole and its subsequent articulation in the parts. According to this theory, the circular movement of understanding runs backward and forward along the text, and ceases when the text is perfectly understood. This view of understanding came to its logical culmination in Schleiermacher's theory of the divinatory act, by means of which one places oneself entirely within the writer's mind and from there resolves all that is strange and alien about the text. In contrast to this approach, Heidegger describes the circle in such a way that the understanding of the text

remains permanently determined by the anticipatory movement of fore-understanding. The circle of whole and part is not dissolved in perfect understanding but, on the contrary, is most fully realized.

The circle, then, is not formal in nature. It is neither subjective nor objective, but describes understanding as the interplay of the movement of tradition and the movement of the interpreter. The anticipation of meaning that governs our understanding of a text is not an act of subjectivity, but proceeds from the commonality that binds us to the tradition. But this commonality is constantly being formed in our relation to tradition. Tradition is not simply a permanent precondition; rather, we produce it ourselves inasmuch as we understand, participate in the evolution of tradition, and hence further determine it ourselves. Thus the circle of understanding is not a "methodological" circle, but describes an element of the ontological structure of understanding.

The circle, which is fundamental to all understanding, has a further hermeneutic implication which I call the "fore-conception of completeness." But this, too, is obviously a formal

294 condition of all understanding. It states that only what really constitutes a unity of meaning is intelligible. So when we read a text we always assume its completeness, and only when this assumption proves mistaken—i.e., the text is not intelligible—do we begin to suspect the text and try to discover how it can be remedied. The rules of such textual criticism can be left aside, for the important thing to note is that applying them properly depends on understanding the content.

The fore-conception of completeness that guides all our understanding is, then, always determined by the specific content. Not only does the reader assume an immanent unity of meaning, but his understanding is likewise guided by the constant transcendent expectations of meaning that proceed from the relation to the truth of what is being said. Just as the recipient of a letter understands the news that it contains and first sees things with the eyes of the person who wrote the letter—i.e., considers what he writes as true, and is not trying to understand the writer's peculiar opinions as such—so also do we understand traditionary texts on the basis of expectations of meaning drawn from our own prior relation to the subject matter. And just as we believe the news reported by a correspondent because he was present or is better informed, so too are we fundamentally open to the possibility that the writer of a transmitted text is better informed than we are, with our prior opinion. It is only when the attempt to accept what is said as true fails that we try to "understand" the text, psychologically or historically, as another's opinion. The prejudice of completeness, then, implies not only this formal element—that a text should completely express its meaning—but also that what it says should be the complete truth.

Here again we see that understanding means, primarily, to understand the content of what is said, and only secondarily to isolate and understand another's meaning as such. Hence the most basic of all hermeneutic preconditions remains one's own fore-understanding, which comes from being concerned with the same subject. This is what determines what can be realized as unified meaning and thus determines how the fore-conception of completeness is applied.

295 Thus the meaning of "belonging"—i.e., the element of tradition in our historical-hermeneutical activity—is fulfilled in the commonality of fundamental, enabling prejudices. Hermeneutics must start from the position that a person seeking to understand something has a bond to the subject matter that comes into language through the traditionary text and has, or acquires, a connection with the tradition from which the text speaks. On the other hand, hermeneutical consciousness is aware that its bond to this subject matter does not consist in some self-evident, unquestioned unanimity, as is the case with the unbroken stream of tradition. Hermeneutic work is based on a polarity of familiarity and strangeness; but this polarity is not to be regarded psychologically, with Schleiermacher, as the range that covers the mystery of individuality, but truly hermeneutically—i.e., in regard to what has been said: the language in which the text addresses us, the story that it tells us. Here too there is a tension. It is in the play between the tra-

ditionary text's strangeness and familiarity to us, between being a historically intended, distanciated object and belonging to a tradition. *The true locus of hermeneutics is this in-between.*

Given the intermediate position in which hermeneutics operates, it follows that its work is not to develop a procedure of understanding, but to clarify the conditions in which understanding takes place. But these conditions do not amount to a "procedure" or method which the interpreter must of himself bring to bear on the text; rather, they must be given. The prejudices and fore-meanings that occupy the interpreter's consciousness are not at his free disposal. He cannot separate in advance the productive prejudices that enable understanding from the prejudices that hinder it and lead to misunderstandings.

296 Rather, this separation must take place in the process of understanding itself, and hence hermeneutics must ask how that happens. But that means it must foreground what has remained entirely peripheral in previous hermeneutics: temporal distance and its significance for understanding.

This point can be clarified by comparing it with the hermeneutic theory of romanticism. We recall that the latter conceived of understanding as the reproduction of an original production. Hence it was possible to say that one should be able to understand an author better than he understood himself.

That subsequent understanding is superior to the original production and hence can be described as superior understanding does not depend so much on the conscious realization that places the interpreter on the same level as the author (as Schleiermacher said) but instead denotes an insuperable difference between the interpreter and the author that is created by historical distance. Every age has to understand a transmitted text in its own way, for the text belongs to the whole tradition whose content interests the age and in which it seeks to understand itself. The real meaning of a text, as it speaks to the interpreter, does not depend on the contingencies of the author and his original audience. It certainly is not identical with

them, for it is always co-determined also by the historical situation of the interpreter and hence by the totality of the objective course of history. A writer like Chladenius, who does not yet view understanding in terms of history, is saying the same thing in a naive, ingenuous way when he says that an author does not need to know the real meaning of what he has written; and hence the interpreter can, and must, often understand more than he. But this is of fundamental importance. Not just occasionally but always, the meaning of a text goes beyond its author. That is why understanding is not merely a reproductive but always a productive activity as well. Perhaps it is not correct to refer to this productive element in understanding as "better understanding." For this phrase is, as we have shown, a principle of criticism taken from the Enlightenment and revised on the basis of the aesthetics of genius. Understanding is not, in fact, understanding better, either in the sense of superior knowledge of the subject because of clearer ideas or in the sense of fundamental superiority of conscious over unconscious production. It is enough to say
297 that we understand in a *different* way, *if we understand at all*.

Such a conception of understanding breaks right through the circle drawn by romantic hermeneutics. Since we are now concerned not with individuality and what it thinks but with the truth of what is said, a text is not understood as a mere expression of life but is taken seriously in its claim to truth. That this is what is meant by "understanding" was once self-evident (we need only recall Chladenius). . . .
332 We can, then, distinguish what is truly common to all forms of hermeneutics: the meaning to be understood is concretized and fully realized only in interpretation, but the interpretive activity considers itself wholly bound by the meaning of the text. Neither jurist nor theologian regards the work of application as making free with the text.
358 Hermeneutical experience is concerned with *tradition*. This is what is to be experienced. But tradition is not simply a process that experience

teaches us to know and govern; it is *language*—i.e., it expresses itself like a Thou. A Thou is not an object; it relates itself to us. It would be wrong to think that this means that what is experienced in tradition is to be taken as the opinion of another person, a Thou. Rather, I maintain that the understanding of tradition does not take the traditionary text as an expression of another person's life, but as meaning that is detached from the person who means it, from an I or a Thou. Still, the relationship to the Thou and the meaning of experience implicit in that relation must be capable of teaching us something about hermeneutical experience. For tradition is a genuine partner in dialogue, and we belong to it, as does the I with a Thou.

It is clear that the *experience of the Thou* must be special because the Thou is not an object but is in relationship with us. For this reason the elements we have emphasized in the structure of experience will undergo a change. Since here the object of experience is a person, this kind of experience is a moral phenomenon—as is the knowledge acquired through experience, the understanding of the other person. Let us therefore consider the change that occurs in the structure of experience when it is experience of the Thou and when it is hermeneutical experience.

There is a kind of experience of the Thou that tries to discover typical behavior in one's fellowmen and can make predictions about others on the basis of experience. We call this a knowledge of human nature. We understand the other person in the same way that we understand any other typical event in our experiential field—i.e., he is predictable. His behavior is as much a means to our end as any other means. From the moral point of view this orientation toward the Thou is purely self-regarding and contradicts the moral definition of man. As we know, in interpreting the categorical imperative Kant said, inter alia, that the other should never be used as a means but always as an end in himself.

If we relate this form of the I-Thou relation—the kind of understanding of the Thou that constitutes knowledge of human nature—to the hermeneutical problem, the equivalent is naive faith in method and in the objectivity that can be attained through it. Someone who understands tradition in this way makes it an object— i.e., he confronts it in a free and uninvolved way—and by methodically excluding everything subjective, he discovers what it contains. We saw that he thereby detaches himself from the continuing effect of the tradition in which he himself has his historical reality. It is the method of the social sciences, following the methodological ideas of the eighteenth century and their programatic formulation by Hume, ideas that are a clichéd version of scientific method. But this covers only part of the actual procedure of the human sciences, and even that is schematically reduced, since it recognizes only what is typical and regular in behavior. It flattens out the nature of hermeneutical experience in precisely the same way as we have seen in the teleological interpretation of the concept of induction since Aristotle.

A second way in which the Thou is experienced and understood is that the Thou is acknowledged as a person, but despite this acknowledgment the understanding of the Thou is still a form of self-relatedness. Such self-regard derives from the dialectical appearance that the dialectic of the I-Thou relation brings with it. This relation is not immediate but reflective. To every claim there is a counterclaim. This is why it is possible for each of the partners in the relationship reflectively to outdo the other. One claims to know the other's claim from his point of view and even to understand the other better than the other understands himself. In this way the Thou loses the immediacy with which it makes its claim. It is understood, but this means it is co-opted and preempted reflectively from the standpoint of the other person. Because it is a mutual relationship, it helps to constitute the reality of the I-Thou relationship itself. The inner historicity of all the relations in the lives of men consists in the fact that there is a constant struggle for mutual recognition. This can have very varied degrees of tension, to the point of the complete domination of one person by the other. But even the most extreme forms of mastery and slavery are a genuine dialectical relationship of the kind that Hegel has elaborated.

The experience of the Thou attained here is more adequate than what we have called the knowledge of human nature, which merely seeks to calculate how the other person will behave. It is an illusion to see another person as a tool that can be absolutely known and used. Even a slave still has a will to power that turns against his master, as Nietzsche rightly said. But the dialectic of reciprocity that governs all I-Thou relationships is inevitably hidden from the consciousness of the individual. The servant who tyrannizes his master by serving him does not believe that he is serving his own aims by doing so. In fact, his own self-consciousness consists precisely in withdrawing from the dialectic of this reciprocity, in reflecting himself out of his relation to the other and so becoming unreachable by him. By understanding the other, by claiming to know him, one robs his claims of their legitimacy. In particular, the dialectic of charitable or welfare work operates in this way, penetrating all relationships between men as a reflective form of the effort to dominate. The claim to understand the other person in advance functions to keep the other person's claim at a distance. We are familiar with this from the teacher-pupil relationship, an authoritative form of welfare work. In these reflective forms the dialectic of the I-Thou relation becomes more clearly defined.

In the hermeneutical sphere the parallel to this experience of the Thou is what we generally call *historical consciousness*. Historical consciousness knows about the otherness of the other, about the past in its otherness, just as the understanding of the Thou knows the Thou as a person. In the otherness of the past it seeks not the instantiation of a general law but something historically unique. . . .

A person who believes he is free of prejudices, relying on the objectivity of his procedures and denying that he is himself conditioned by historical circumstances, experiences the power of the prejudices that unconsciously dominate him as a vis a tergo. A person who does not admit that he is dominated by prejudices will fail to see what manifests itself by their light. It is like the relation between I and Thou. A person who reflects himself out of the mutuality of such a relation changes this relationship and destroys its moral bond. *A person who reflects himself out of a living relationship to tradition destroys the true meaning of this tradition in exactly the same way.* In seeking to understand tradition historical con-

361 sciousness must not rely on the critical method with which it approaches its sources, as if this preserved it from mixing in its own judgments and prejudices. It must, in fact, think within its own historicity. To be situated within a tradition does not limit the freedom of knowledge but makes it possible.

Knowing and recognizing this constitutes the third, and highest, type of hermeneutical experience: the openness to tradition characteristic of historically effected consciousness. It too has a real analogue in the I's experience of the Thou. In human relations the important thing is, as we have seen, to experience the Thou truly as a Thou—i.e., not to overlook his claim but to let him really say something to us. Here is where openness belongs. But ultimately this openness does not exist only for the person who speaks; rather, anyone who listens is fundamentally open. Without such openness to one another there is no genuine human bond. Belonging together always also means being able to listen to one another. When two people understand each other, this does not mean that one person "understands" the other. Similarly, "to hear and obey someone" (auf jemanden hören) does not mean simply that we do blindly what the other desires. We call such a person slavish (hörig). Openness to the other, then, involves recognizing that I myself must accept some things that are against me, even though no one else forces me to do so.

This is the parallel to the hermeneutical experience. I must allow tradition's claim to validity, not in the sense of simply acknowledging the past in its otherness, but in such a way that it has something to say to me. This too calls for a fundamental sort of openness. Someone who is open to tradition in this way sees that historical consciousness is not really open at all, but rather, when it reads its texts "historically," it has always thoroughly smoothed them out

beforehand, so that the criteria of the historian's own knowledge can never be called into question by tradition. Recall the naive mode of comparison that the historical approach generally engages in. The 25th "Lyceum Fragment" by Friedrich Schlegel reads: "The two basic principles of so-called historical criticism are the postulate of the commonplace and the axiom of familiarity. The postulate of the commonplace is that everything that is really great, good, and beautiful is improbable, for it is extraordinary or at least suspicious. The axiom of familiarity is that things must always have been just as they are for us, for things are naturally like this." By contrast, historically effected consciousness rises above such naive comparisons and assimilations by letting itself experience tradition and by

362 keeping itself open to the truth claim encountered in it. The hermeneutical consciousness culminates not in methodological sureness of itself, but in the same readiness for experience that distinguishes the experienced man from the man captivated by dogma. As we can now say more exactly in terms of the concept of experience, this readiness is what distinguishes historically effected consciousness.

(II) THE LOGIC OF QUESTION AND ANSWER

369 Thus we return to the conclusion that the hermeneutic phenomenon too implies the primacy of dialogue and the structure of question and answer. That a historical text is made the object of interpretation means that it puts a question to the interpreter.

370   Thus interpretation always involves a relation to the question that is asked of the interpreter. To understand a text means to understand this question. But this takes place, as we showed, by our attaining the hermeneutical horizon. We now recognize this as the *horizon of the question* within which the sense of the text is determined.

Thus a person who wants to understand must question what lies behind what is said. He must understand it as an answer to a question. If we go back *behind* what is said, then we inevitably ask questions *beyond* what is said. We understand the sense of the text only by acquiring the horizon of the question—a horizon that, as such, necessarily includes other possible answers. Thus the meaning of a sentence is relative to the question to which it is a reply, but that implies that its meaning necessarily exceeds what is said in it. As these considerations show, then, the logic of the human sciences is a logic of the question. . . .

373 Historical tradition can be understood only as something always in the process of being defined by the course of events. Similarly, the philologist dealing with poetic or philosophical texts knows that they are inexhaustible. In both cases it is the course of events that brings out new aspects of meaning in historical material. By being re-actualized in understanding, texts are drawn into a genuine course of events in exactly the same way as are events themselves. This is what we described as the history of effect as an element in hermeneutical experience. Every actualization in understanding can be regarded as a historical potential of what is understood. It is part of the historical finitude of our being that we are aware that others after us will understand in a different way. And yet it is equally indubitable that it remains the same work whose fullness of meaning is realized in the changing process of understanding, just as it is the same history whose meaning is constantly in the process of being defined. The hermeneutical reduction to the author's meaning is just as inappropriate as the reduction of historical events to the intentions of their protagonists.

However, we cannot take the reconstruction of the question to which a given text is an answer simply as an achievement of historical method. The most important thing is the question that the text puts to us, our being perplexed by the traditionary word, so that understanding it must 374 already include the task of the historical self-mediation between the present and tradition. Thus the relation of question and answer is, in fact, reversed. The voice that speaks to us from the past—whether text, work, trace—itself poses a question and places our meaning in openness. In order to answer the question put to us, we the interrogated must ourselves begin to ask questions. We must attempt to reconstruct the ques-

tion to which the traditionary text is the answer. But we will be unable to do so without going beyond the historical horizon it presents us. Reconstructing the question to which the text is presumed to be the answer itself takes place within a process of questioning through which we try to answer the question that the text asks us. A reconstructed question can never stand within its original horizon: for the historical horizon that circumscribed the reconstruction is not a truly comprehensive one. It is, rather, included within the horizon that embraces us as the questioners who have been encountered by the traditionary word.

Hence it is a hermeneutical necessity always to go beyond mere reconstruction. We cannot avoid thinking about what the author accepted unquestioningly and hence did not consider, and bringing it into the openness of the question. This is not to open the door to arbitrariness in interpretation but to reveal what always takes place. Understanding the word of tradition always requires that the reconstructed question be set within the openness of its questionableness— i.e., that it merge with the question that tradition is for us. If the "historical" question emerges by itself, this means that it no longer arises as a question. It results from the cessation of understanding—a detour in which we get stuck. Part of real understanding, however, is that we regain the concepts of a historical past in such a way that they also include our own comprehension of them. Above I called this "the fusion of horizons." With Collingwood, we can say that we understand only when we understand the question to which something is the answer, but the intention of what is understood in this way does not remain foregrounded against our own intention. Rather, reconstructing the question to which the meaning of a text is understood as an answer merges with our own questioning. For the text must be understood as an answer to a real question.

The close relation between questioning and understanding is what gives the hermeneutic experience its true dimension. However much a person trying to understand may leave open the truth of what is said, however much he may dis- 375 miss the immediate meaning of the object and consider its deeper significance instead, and take the latter not as true but merely as meaningful, so that the possibility of its truth remains unsettled, this is the real and fundamental nature of a question: namely to make things indeterminate. Questions always bring out the undetermined possibilities of a thing. That is why we cannot understand the questionableness of something without asking real questions, though we can understand a meaning without meaning it. *To understand the questionableness of something is already to be questioning.* There can be no tentative or potential attitude to questioning, for questioning is not the positing but the testing of possibilities. Here the nature of questioning indicates what is demonstrated by the actual operation of the Platonic dialogue. A person who thinks must ask himself questions. Even when a person says that such and such a question might arise, this is already a real questioning that simply masks itself, out of either caution or politeness.

This is the reason why understanding is always more than merely re-creating someone else's meaning. Questioning opens up possibilities of meaning, and thus what is meaningful passes into one's own thinking on the subject. Only in an inauthentic sense can we talk about understanding questions that one does not pose oneself—e.g., questions that are outdated or empty. We understand how certain questions came to be asked in particular historical circumstances. Understanding such questions means, then, understanding the particular presuppositions whose demise makes such questions "dead." An example is perpetual motion. The horizon of meaning of such questions is only apparently still open. They are no longer understood as questions. For what we understand, in such cases, is precisely that there is no question.

To understand a question means to ask it. To understand meaning is to understand it as the answer to a question.

377 The dialectic of question and answer disclosed in the structure of hermeneutical experience now permits us to state more exactly what kind of consciousness historically effected consciousness is. For the dialectic of question and answer that we demonstrated makes understand-

ing appear to be a reciprocal relationship of the same kind as conversation. It is true that a text does not speak to us in the same way as does a Thou. We who are attempting to understand must ourselves make it speak. But we found that this kind of understanding, "making the text speak," is not an arbitrary procedure that we undertake on our own initiative but that, as a question, it is related to the answer that is expected in the text. Anticipating an answer itself presupposes that the questioner is part of the tradition and regards himself as addressed by it. This is the truth of historically effected consciousness. It is the historically experienced conscious-
378 ness that, by renouncing the chimera of perfect enlightenment, is open to the experience of history. We described its realization as the fusion of the horizons of understanding, which is what mediates between the text and its interpreter.

The guiding idea of the following discussion is *that the fusion of horizons that takes place in understanding is actually the achievement of language.* Admittedly, what language is belongs among the most mysterious questions that man ponders. Language is so uncannily near our thinking, and when it functions it is so little an object, that it seems to conceal its own being from us. In our analysis of the thinking of the human sciences, however, we came so close to this universal mystery of language that is prior to everything else, that we can entrust ourselves to what we are investigating to guide us safely in the quest. In other words we are endeavoring to approach the mystery of language from the conversation that we ourselves are.

When we try to examine the hermeneutical phenomenon through the model of conversation between two persons, the chief thing that these apparently so different situations—understanding a text and reaching an understanding in a conversation—have in common is that both are concerned with a subject matter that is placed before them. Just as each interlocutor is trying to reach agreement on some subject with his partner, so also the interpreter is trying to understand what the text is saying. This understanding of the subject matter must take the form of language. It is not that the understanding is subsequently put into words; rather, the way understanding occurs—whether in the case of a text or a dialogue with another person who raises an issue with us—is the coming-into-language of the thing itself. Thus we will first consider the structure of dialogue proper, in order to specify the character of that other form of dialogue that is the understanding of texts. Whereas up to now we have framed the constitutive significance of the *question* for the hermeneutical phenomenon in terms of conversation, we must now demonstrate the linguisticality of dialogue, which is the basis of the question, as an element of hermeneutics.

Our first point is that the language in which something comes to speak is not a possession at the disposal of one or the other of the interlocutors. Every conversation presupposes a common language, or better, creates a common language. Something is placed in the center, as the Greeks say, which the partners in dialogue both share, and concerning which they can exchange ideas with one another. Hence reaching an understanding on the subject matter of a conversation necessarily means that a common language must first be worked out in the conversation. This is
379 not an external matter of simply adjusting our tools; nor is it even right to say that the partners adapt themselves to one another but, rather, in a successful conversation they both come under the influence of the truth of the object and are thus bound to one another in a new community. To reach an understanding in a dialogue is not merely a matter of putting oneself forward and successfully asserting one's own point of view, but being transformed into a communion in which we do not remain what we were.

PART III

THE ONTOLOGICAL SHIFT OF HERMENEUTICS GUIDED BY LANGUAGE

> *Everything presupposed in hermeneutics is but language.*
>
> F. Schleiermacher

1. Language as the Medium of Hermeneutic Experience

383 We say that we "conduct" a conversation, but the more genuine a conversation is, the less its con-

duct lies within the will of either partner. Thus a genuine conversation is never the one that we wanted to conduct. Rather, it is generally more correct to say that we fall into conversation, or even that we become involved in it. The way one word follows another, with the conversation taking its own twists and reaching its own conclusion, may well be conducted in some way, but the partners conversing are far less the leaders of it than the led. No one knows in advance what will "come out" of a conversation. Understanding or its failure is like an event that happens to us. Thus we can say that something was a good conversation or that it was ill fated. All this shows that a conversation has a spirit of its own, and that the language in which it is conducted bears its own truth within it—i.e., that it allows something to "emerge" which henceforth exists.

In our analysis of romantic hermeneutics we have already seen that understanding is not based on transposing oneself into another person, on one person's immediate participation with another. To understand what a person says is, as we saw, to come to an understanding about the subject matter, not to get inside another person and relive his experiences (Erlebnisse). We emphasized that the experi-
384 ence (Erfahrung) of meaning that takes place in understanding always includes application. Now we are to note *that this whole process is verbal*. It is not for nothing that the special problematic of understanding and the attempt to master it as an art—the concern of hermeneutics—belongs traditionally to the sphere of grammar and rhetoric. Language is the medium in which substantive understanding and agreement take place between two people.

In situations where coming to an understanding is disrupted or impeded, we first become conscious of the conditions of all understanding. Thus the verbal process whereby a conversation in two different languages is made possible through translation is especially informative. Here the translator must translate the meaning to be understood into the context in which the other speaker lives. This does not, of course, mean that he is at liberty to falsify the meaning of what the other person says. Rather, the meaning must be preserved, but since it must be understood within a new language world, it must establish its validity within it in a new way. Thus every translation is at the same time an interpretation. We can even say that the translation is the culmination of the interpretation that the translator has made of the words given him.

The example of translation, then, makes us aware that language as the medium of understanding must be consciously created by an explicit mediation. This kind of explicit process is undoubtedly not the norm in a conversation. Nor is translation the norm in the way we approach a foreign language. Rather, having to rely on translation is tantamount to two people giving up their independent authority. Where a translation is necessary, the gap between the spirit of the original words and that of their reproduction must be taken into account. It is a gap that can never be completely closed. But in these cases understanding does not really take place between the partners of the conversation, but between the interpreters, who can really have an encounter in a common world of understanding. (It is well known that nothing is more difficult than a dialogue in two different languages in which one person speaks one and the other person the other, each understanding the other's language but not speaking it. As if impelled by a higher force, one of the languages always tries to establish itself over the other as the medium of understanding.)

Where there is understanding, there is not translation but speech. To understand a foreign language means that we do not need to translate it into our own. When we really master a lan-
385 guage, then no translation is necessary—in fact, any translation seems impossible. Understanding how to speak is not yet of itself real understanding and does not involve an interpretive process; it is an accomplishment of life. For you understand a language by living in it—a statement that is true, as we know, not only of living but dead languages as well. Thus the hermeneutical problem concerns not the correct mastery of language but coming to a proper understanding about the subject matter, which takes place in the medium of language. Every language can be learned so

perfectly that using it no longer means translating from or into one's native tongue, but thinking in the foreign language. Mastering the language is a necessary precondition for coming to an understanding in a conversation. Every conversation obviously presupposes that the two speakers speak the same language. Only when two people can make themselves understood through language by talking together can the problem of understanding and agreement even be raised. Having to depend on an interpreter's translation is an extreme case that doubles the hermeneutical process, namely the conversation: there is one conversation between the interpreter and the other, and a second between the interpreter and oneself.

Conversation is a process of coming to an understanding. Thus it belongs to every true conversation that each person opens himself to the other, truly accepts his point of view as valid and transposes himself into the other to such an extent that he understands not the particular individual but what he says. What is to be grasped is the substantive rightness of his opinion, so that we can be at one with each other on the subject. Thus we do not relate the other's opinion to him but to our own opinions and views. Where a person is concerned with the other as individuality—e.g., in a therapeutic conversation or the interrogation of a man accused of a crime—this is not really a situation in which two people are trying to come to an understanding.

Everything we have said characterizing the situation of two people coming to an understanding in conversation has a genuine application to hermeneutics, which is concerned with *understanding texts*. Let us again start by considering the extreme case of translation from a foreign language. Here no one can doubt that the translation of a text, however much the translator may have dwelt with and empathized with his author, cannot be simply a re-awakening of the original
386 process in the writer's mind; rather, it is necessarily a re-creation of the text guided by the way the translator understands what it says. No one can doubt that what we are dealing with here is interpretation, and not simply reproduction. A new light falls on the text from the other language

and for the reader of it. The requirement that a translation be faithful cannot remove the fundamental gulf between the two languages. However faithful we try to be, we have to make difficult decisions. In our translation if we want to emphasize a feature of the original that is important to us, then we can do so only by playing down or entirely suppressing other features. But this is precisely the activity that we call interpretation. Translation, like all interpretation, is a highlighting. A translator must understand that highlighting is part of his task.

389 The essential relation between language and understanding is seen primarily in the fact that the essence of tradition is to exist in the medium of language, so that the preferred *object* of interpretation is a verbal one.

(A) Language as Determination of the Hermeneutic Object

The fact that tradition is essentially verbal in character has consequences for hermeneutics. The understanding of verbal tradition retains special priority over all other tradition. Linguistic tradition may have less perceptual immediacy than monuments of plastic art. Its lack of immediacy, however, is not a defect; rather, this apparent lack, the abstract alienness of all "texts," uniquely expresses the fact that everything in language belongs to the process of understanding. Linguistic tradition is tradition in the proper sense of the word—i.e., something handed down. It is not just something left over, to be investigated and interpreted as a remnant of the past. What has come 390 down to us by way of verbal tradition is not left over but given to us, told us—whether through direct retelling, in which myth, legend, and custom have their life, or through written tradition, whose signs are, as it were, immediately clear to every reader who can read them.

The full hermeneutical significance of the fact that tradition is essentially verbal becomes clear in the case of a *written* tradition. The detachability of language from speaking derives from the fact that it can be written. In the form of writing, all tradition is contemporaneous with each present time. Moreover, it involves a unique co-existence of past and present, insofar

as present consciousness has the possibility of a free access to everything handed down in writing. No longer dependent on retelling, which mediates past knowledge with the present, understanding consciousness acquires—through its immediate access to literary tradition—a genuine opportunity to change and widen its horizon, and thus enrich its world by a whole new and deeper dimension. The appropriation of literary tradition even surpasses the experience connected with the adventure of traveling and being immersed in the world of a foreign language. At every moment the reader who studies a foreign language and literature retains the possibility of free movement back to himself, and thus is at once both here and there.

A written tradition is not a fragment of a past world, but has already raised itself beyond this into the sphere of the meaning that it expresses. The ideality of the word is what raises everything linguistic beyond the finitude and transience that characterize other remnants of past existence. It is not this document, as a piece of the past, that is the bearer of tradition but the continuity of memory. Through it tradition becomes part of our own world, and thus what it communicates can be stated immediately. Where we have a written tradition, we are not just told a particular thing; a past humanity itself becomes present to us in its general relation to the world. That is why our understanding remains curiously unsure and fragmentary when we have no written tradition of a culture but only dumb monuments, and we do not call this information about the past "history." Texts, on the other hand, always express a whole. Meaningless strokes that seem strange and incomprehensible prove suddenly intelligible in every detail when they can be interpreted as writing—so much so that even the arbitrariness of a corrupt text can be corrected if the context as a whole is understood.

Thus written texts present the real hermeneutical task. Writing is self-alienation. Overcoming it, reading the text, is thus the highest task of understanding. Even the pure signs of an inscription can be seen properly and articulated correctly only if the text can be transformed back 391 into language. As we have said, however, this transformation always establishes a relationship to what is meant, to the subject matter being discussed. Here the process of understanding moves entirely in a sphere of meaning mediated by the verbal tradition. Thus in the case of an inscription the hermeneutical task starts only after it has been deciphered (presumably correctly). Only in an extended sense do non-literary monuments present a hermeneutical task, for they cannot be understood of themselves. What they mean is a question of their interpretation, not of deciphering and understanding the wording of a text.

392 Writing has the methodological advantage of presenting the hermeneutical problem in all its purity, detached from everything psychological. However, what is from our point of view and for our purpose a methodological advantage is at the same time the expression of a specific weakness that is even more characteristic of writing than of speaking. The task of understanding is presented with particular clarity when we recognize the weakness of all writing. We need only recall what Plato said, namely that the specific weakness of writing was that no one could come to the aid of the written word if it falls victim to misunderstanding, intentional or unintentional.

394 Everything written is, in fact, the paradigmatic object of hermeneutics. What we found in the extreme case of a foreign language and in the problems of translation is confirmed here by the autonomy of reading: understanding is not 395 a psychic transposition. The horizon of understanding cannot be limited either by what the writer originally had in mind or by the horizon of the person to whom the text was originally addressed. . . . What is fixed in writing has detached itself from the contingency of its origin and its author and made itself free for new relationships. Normative concepts such as the author's meaning or the original reader's understanding in fact represent only an empty space that is filled from time to time in understanding.

(B) Language as Determination of the Hermeneutic Act

This brings us to the second aspect of the relationship between language and understanding. Not only is the special object of understanding, namely tradition, of a verbal nature; understanding itself has a fundamental connection with language. We started from the proposition that understanding is already interpretation because it creates the hermeneutical horizon within which the meaning of a text comes into force. But in order to be able to express a text's meaning and subject matter, we must translate it into our own language. However, this involves relating it to the whole complex of possible meanings in which we linguistically move. We have already investigated the logical structure of this in relation to the special place of the *question* as a hermeneutical phenomenon. In now considering the verbal nature of all understanding, we are expressing from another angle what we already saw in considering the dialectic of question and answer.

Here we are emphasizing a dimension that is generally ignored by the dominant conception that the historical sciences have of themselves. For the historian usually chooses concepts to describe the historical particularity of his objects without expressly reflecting on their origin and justification. He simply follows his interest in the material and takes no account of the fact that the scriptive concepts he chooses can be highly detrimental to his proper purpose if they assimilate what is historically different to what is familiar and thus, despite all impartiality, subordinate the alien being of the object to his own preconceptions. Thus, despite his scientific method, he behaves just like everyone else—as a child of his time who is unquestioningly dominated by the concepts and prejudices of his own age.

Insofar as the historian does not admit this naivete to himself, he fails to reach the level of reflection that the subject matter demands. But his naivete becomes truly abysmal when he starts to become aware of the problems it raises and so demands that in understanding history one must leave one's own concepts aside and think only in the concepts of the epoch one is trying to understand. This demand, which sounds like a logical implementation of historical consciousness is, as will be clear to every thoughtful reader, a naive illusion. The naivete of this claim does not consist in the fact that it goes unfulfilled because the interpreter does not sufficiently attain the ideal of leaving himself aside. This would still mean that it was a legitimate ideal, and one should strive to reach it as far as possible. But what the legitimate demand of the historical consciousness—to understand a period in terms of its own concepts—really means is something quite different. The call to leave aside the concepts of the present does not mean a naive transposition into the past. It is, rather, an essentially relative demand that has meaning only in relation to one's concepts. Historical consciousness fails to understand its own nature if, in order to understand, it seeks to exclude what alone makes understanding possible. *To think historically* means, in fact, *to perform the transposition that the concepts of the past undergo when we try to think in them*. To think historically always involves mediating between those ideas and one's own thinking. To try to escape from one's own concepts in interpretation is not only impossible but manifestly absurd. To interpret means precisely to bring one's own preconceptions into play so that the text's meaning can really be made to speak for us.

In our analysis of the hermeneutical process we saw that to acquire a horizon of interpretation requires a fusion of horizons. This is now confirmed by the verbal aspect of interpretation. The text is made to speak through interpretation. But no text and no book speaks if it does not speak a language that reaches the other person. Thus interpretation must find the right language if it really wants to make the text speak. There cannot, therefore, be any single interpretation that is correct "in itself," precisely because every interpretation is concerned with the text itself. The historical life of a tradition depends on being constantly assimilated and interpreted. An interpretation that was correct in itself would be a foolish ideal that mistook the nature of tradition. Every interpretation has to adapt itself to the hermeneutical situation to which it belongs.

Being bound by a situation does not mean that the claim to correctness that every interpretation must make is dissolved into the subjective or the occasional. We must not here abandon the insights of the romantics, who purified the problem of hermeneutics from all its occasional elements. Interpretation is not something

pedagogical for us either; it is the act of understanding itself, which is realized—not just for the one for whom one is interpreting but also for the interpreter himself—in the explicitness of verbal interpretation. Thanks to the verbal nature of all interpretation, every interpretation includes the possibility of a relationship with others. There can be no speaking that does not bind the speaker and the person spoken to. This is true of the hermeneutic process as well. But this relationship does not determine the interpretative process of understanding—as if interpreting were a conscious adaptation to a pedagogical situation; rather, this process is simply *the concretion of the meaning itself*. Let us recall our emphasis on the element of application, which had completely disappeared from hermeneutics. We saw that to understand a text always means to apply it to ourselves and to know that, even if it must always be understood in different ways, it is still the same text presenting itself to us in these different ways. That this does not in the least relativize the claim to truth of every interpretation is seen from the fact that all interpretation is essentially verbal. The verbal explicitness that understanding achieves through interpretation does not create a second sense apart from that which is understood and interpreted. The interpretive concepts are not, as such, thematic in understanding. Rather, it is their nature to disappear behind what they bring to speech in interpretation. Paradoxically, an interpretation is right when it is capable of disappearing in this way. And yet at the same time it must be expressed as something that is supposed to disappear. The possibility of understanding is dependent on the possibility of this kind of mediating interpretation.

398

This is also true in those cases when there is immediate understanding and no explicit interpretation is undertaken. For in these cases too interpretation must be possible. But this means that interpretation is contained potentially within the understanding process. It simply makes the understanding explicit. Thus interpretation is not a means through which understanding is achieved; rather, it enters into the content of what is understood. Let us recall that this means not only that the sense of the text can be realized as a unity but that the subject matter of which the text speaks is also expressed. The interpretation places the object, as it were, on the scales of words. There are a few characteristic variations on this general statement that indirectly confirm it. When we are concerned with understanding and interpreting verbal texts, interpretation in the medium of language itself shows what understanding always is: assimilating what is said to the point that it becomes one's own. Verbal interpretation is the form of all interpretation, even when what is to be interpreted is not linguistic in nature—i.e., is not a text but a statue or a musical composition. We must not let ourselves be confused by forms of interpretation that are not verbal but in fact presuppose language. It is possible to demonstrate something by means of contrast—e.g., by placing two pictures alongside each other or reading two poems one after the other, so that one is interpreted by the other. In these cases demonstration seems to obviate verbal interpretation. But in fact this kind of demonstration is a modification of verbal interpretation. In such demonstration we have the reflection of interpretation, and the demonstration is used as a visual shortcut. Demonstration is interpretation in much the same sense as is a translation that embodies an interpretation, or the correct reading aloud of a text that has already decided the questions of interpretation, because one can only read aloud what one has understood. Understanding and interpretation are indissolubly bound together.

399

We must rightly understand the fundamental priority of language asserted here. Indeed, language often seems ill suited to express what we feel. In the face of the overwhelming presence of works of art, the task of expressing in words what they say to us seems like an infinite and hopeless undertaking. The fact that our desire and capacity to understand always go beyond any statement that we can make seems like a critique of language. But this does not alter the fundamental priority of language. The possibilities of our knowledge seem to be far more individual than the possibilities of expression offered by language. Faced with the socially motivated tendency toward uniformity with which language forces

401

understanding into particular schematic forms which hem us in, our desire for knowledge tries to escape from these schematizations and predecisions. However, the critical superiority which we claim over language pertains not to the conventions of verbal expression but to the conventions of meaning that have become sedimented in language. Thus that superiority says nothing against the essential connection between understanding and language. In fact it confirms this connection. For all critique that rises above the schematism of our statements in order to understand finds its expression in the form of language. Hence language always forestalls any objection to its jurisdiction. Its universality keeps pace with the universality of reason. Hermeneutical consciousness only participates in what constitutes the general relation between language and reason. If all understanding stands in a necessary relation of equivalence to its possible interpretation, and if there are basically no bounds set to understanding, then the verbal form in which this understanding is interpreted must contain within it an infinite dimension that transcends all bounds. Language is the language of reason itself.

One says this, and then one hesitates. For this makes language so close to reason—which means, to the things it names—that one may ask why there should be different languages at all, since all seem to have the same proximity to reason and to objects. When a person lives in a language, he is filled with the sense of the unsurpassable appropriateness of the words he uses for the subject matter he is talking about. It seems impossible that other words in other languages could name the things equally well. The suitable word always seems to be one's own and unique, just as the thing referred to is always unique. The agony of translation consists ultimately in the fact that the original words seem to be inseparable from the things they refer to, so that to make a text intelligible one often has to give an interpretive paraphrase of it rather than translate it. The more sensitively our historical consciousness reacts, the more it seems to be aware of the untranslatability of the unfamiliar. But this makes the intimate unity of word and thing a hermeneutical scandal. How can we possibly understand

402

anything written in a foreign language if we are thus imprisoned in our own?

It is necessary to see the speciousness of this argument. In actual fact the sensitivity of our historical consciousness tells us the opposite. The work of understanding and interpretation always remains meaningful. This shows the superior universality with which reason rises above the limitations of any given language. The hermeneutical experience is the corrective by means of which the thinking reason escapes the prison of language, and it is itself verbally constituted. . . .

403 It is obvious that an instrumentalist theory of signs which sees words and concepts as handy tools has missed the point of the hermeneutical phenomenon. If we stick to what takes place in speech and, above all, in every dialogue with tradition carried on by the human sciences, we cannot fail to see that here concepts are constantly in the process of being formed. This does not mean that the interpreter is using new or unusual words. But the capacity to use familiar words is not based on an act of logical subsumption, through which a particular is placed under a universal concept. Let us remember, rather, that understanding always includes an element of application and thus produces an ongoing process of concept formation. We must consider this now if we want to liberate the verbal nature of understanding from the presuppositions of philosophy of language. The interpreter does not use words and concepts like a craftsman who picks up his tools and then puts them away. Rather, we must recognize that all understanding is interwoven with concepts and reject any theory that does not accept the intimate unity of word and subject matter.

Language is not just one of man's posses-
433 sions in the world; rather, on it depends the fact that man has a *world* at all. The world as world exists for man as for no other creature that is in the world. But this world is verbal in nature. This is the real heart of Humboldt's assertion (which he intended quite differently) that languages are worldviews. By this Humboldt means that language maintains a kind of independent life vis-à-vis the individual member of a linguis-

tic community; and as he grows into it, it introduces him to a particular orientation and relationship to the world as well. But the ground of this statement is more important, namely that language has no independent life apart from the world that comes to language within it. Not only is the world world only insofar as it comes into language, but language, too, has its real being only in the fact that the world is presented in it. Thus, that language is originarily human means at the same time that man's being-in-the-world is primordially linguistic.

From the relation of language to world fol-
445 lows its unique *factualness* (Sachlichkeit). It is matters of fact (Sachverhalte) that come into language. That a thing behaves (eine Sache verhalt sich) in various ways permits one to recognize its independent otherness, which presupposes a real distance between the speaker and the thing. That something can foreground itself as a genuine matter of fact and become the content of an assertion that others can understand depends on this distance. In the structure of a matter of fact that foregrounds itself, there is always a negative aspect as well. To be this and not that constitutes the determinacy of all beings. Fundamentally, therefore, there are also negative matters of fact. This is the aspect of language that Greek philosophy conceived for the first time.

By pursuing the natural experience of the world in its linguistic form, it conceives the world as being. Whatever it conceives as existent emerges as logos, as an expressible matter of fact, from the surrounding whole that constitutes the world-horizon of language. What is thus conceived of as existing is not really the *object* of statements, but it "comes to language in statements." It thereby acquires its truth, its being evident in human thought. Thus Greek ontology is based on the factualness of language, in that it conceives the essence of language in terms of statements.

On the other hand, however, it must be emphasized that language has its true being only in dialogue, in *coming to an understanding*. This is not to be understood as if that were the purpose of language. Coming to an understanding is not a mere action, a purposeful activity, a setting up of signs through which I transmit my will to others. Coming to an understanding as such, rather, does not need any tools, in the proper sense of the word. It is a life process in which a community of life is lived out. To that extent, coming to an understanding through human conversation is no different from the understanding that occurs between animals. But human language must be thought of as a special and unique life process since, in linguistic communication, "world" is disclosed. Reaching an understanding in language places a subject matter before those communicating like a disputed object set between them. Thus the world is the common ground, trodden by none and recognized by all, uniting all who talk to one another. All kinds of human community are kinds of linguistic community: even more, they form language. For language is by nature the language of conversation; it fully realizes itself only in the process of coming to an understanding. That is why it is not a mere means in that process.

For this reason invented systems of artificial communication are never languages. For artificial languages, such as secret languages or systems of mathematical symbols, have no basis in a community of language or life; they are introduced and applied only as means and tools of communication. For this reason they always presuppose a prior agreement, which is that of language. It is well known that the consensus by which an artificial language is introduced necessarily belongs to another language. In a real community of language, on the other hand, we do not first decide to agree but are always already in agreement, as Aristotle showed. The object of understanding is not the verbal means of understanding as such but rather the world that presents itself to us in common life and that embraces everything about which understanding can be reached. Agreeing about a language is not the paradigmatic case but rather a special case—agreeing about an instrument, a system of signs, that does not have its being in dialogue but serves rather to convey information. The fact that human experience of the world is verbal in nature broadens the horizon of our analysis of hermeneutical experience. What we saw in the case of translation and the possibility of communication across the frontiers of our own languages is confirmed: the verbal world in which we live is not a barrier that prevents knowledge of being-in-itself but fundamentally embraces everything in which our insight can be enlarged and deepened. It is true that those who are brought up in a particular linguistic and cultural tradition see the world in a different way from those who belong to other traditions. It is true that the historical "worlds" that succeed one another in the course of history are different from one another and from the world of today; but in whatever tradition we consider it, it is always a human—i.e., verbally constituted—world that presents itself to us. As verbally constituted, every such world is of itself always open to every possible insight and hence to every expansion of its own world picture, and is accordingly available to others.

This is of fundamental importance, for it makes the expression "*world in itself*" problematical. The criterion for the continuing expansion of our own world picture is not given by a "world in itself" that lies beyond all language. Rather, the infinite perfectibility of the human experience of the world means that, whatever language we use, we never succeed in seeing anything but an ever more extended aspect, a "view" of the world. Those views of the world are not relative in the sense that one could oppose them to the "world in itself," as if the right view from some possible position outside the human, linguistic world could discover it in its being-in-itself. No one doubts that the world can exist without man and perhaps will do so. This is part of the meaning in which every human, linguistically constituted view of the world lives. In every worldview the existence of the world-in-itself is intended. It is the whole to which linguistically schematized experience refers. The multiplicity of these worldviews does not involve any relativization of the "world." Rather, what the world is is not different from the views in which it presents itself. The relationship is the same in the perception of things.

Seen phenomenologically, the "thing-in-itself" is, as Husserl has shown, nothing but the continuity with which the various perceptual perspectives on objects shade into one another. . . .

448 In the same way as with perception we can speak of the "linguistic shadings" that the world undergoes in different language-worlds. But there remains a characteristic difference: every "shading" of the object of perception is exclusively distinct from every other, and each helps co-constitute the "thing-in-itself" as the continuum of these nuances—whereas, in the case of the shadings of verbal worldviews, each one potentially contains every other one within it—i.e., each worldview can be extended into every other. It can understand and comprehend, from within itself, the "view" of the world presented in another language.

Thus, we hold, the fact that our experience of the world is bound to language does not imply an exclusiveness of perspectives. If, by entering foreign language-worlds, we overcome the prejudices and limitations of our previous experience of the world, this does not mean that we leave and negate our own world. Like travelers we return home with new experiences. Even if we emigrate and never return, we still can never wholly forget. Even if, as people who know about history, we are fundamentally aware that all human thought about the world is historically conditioned, and thus are aware that our own thought is conditioned too, we still have not assumed an unconditional standpoint. In particular it is no objection to affirming that we are thus fundamentally conditioned to say that this affirmation is intended to be absolutely and unconditionally true, and therefore cannot be applied to itself without contradiction. The consciousness of being conditioned does not supersede our conditionedness. It is one of the prejudices of reflective philosophy that it understands matters that are not at all on the same logical level as standing in propositional relationships. Thus the reflective argument is out of place here. For we are not dealing with relationships between judgments which have to be kept free from contradictions but with life relationships. Our verbal experience of the world has the capacity to embrace the most varied relationships of life.

We have, then, a confirmation of what we 450 stated above, namely that in language the world itself presents itself. Verbal experience of the world is "absolute." It transcends all the relative ways being is posited because it embraces all being-in-itself, in whatever relationships (relativities) it appears. Our verbal experience of the world is prior to everything that is recognized and addressed as existing. *That language and world are related in a fundamental way does not mean, then, that world becomes the object of language.* Rather, the object of knowledge and statements is always already enclosed within the world horizon of language. That human experience of the world is verbal does not imply that a world-in-itself is being objectified.

The world of objects that science knows, and from which it derives its own objectivity, is one of the relativities embraced by language's relation to the world. In it the concept of "being-in-itself" acquires the character of a *determination of the will*. What exists in itself is independent of one's own willing and imagining. But in being known in its being-in-itself, it is put at one's disposal in the sense that one can reckon with it—i.e., use it for one's own purposes.

But is it really the case that this world is a 451 world of being-in-itself where all relativity to Dasein has been surpassed and where knowledge can be called an absolute science? Is not the very concept of an "absolute object" a contradiction in terms? Neither the biological nor the physical 452 universe can, in fact, deny its concrete existential relativity. In this, physics and biology have the same ontological horizon, which it is impossible for them, as science, to transcend. They know what is, and this means, as Kant has shown, as it is given in space and time and is an object of experience. This even defines the progressive knowledge that science aims for. The world of physics cannot seek to be the whole of what exists. For even a world equation that contained everything, so that the observer of the system would also be included in the equations, would still assume the existence of a physicist who, as the calculator, would not be an object calculated. A physics that calculated itself and was its own calculation would be self-contradictory. The same thing is true of biology, which investigates the environments of all living things, including, therefore, the human environment. What is known in it certainly also embraces the being of the scientist, for he too is a living creature and a man. But from this it in no way follows that biological science is a mere product of life and only has meaning as such. Rather, biology studies what exists in exactly the same way as does physics; it is not itself what it studies. The being-in-itself toward which research, whether in physics or biology, is directed is relative to the way being is posited in its manner of inquiry. There is not the slightest reason, beyond this, to admit science's metaphysical claim to know being-in-itself. Each science, as a science, has in advance projected a field of objects such that to know them is to govern them.

We find quite another situation when we consider man's relationship to the world as a whole, as it is expressed in language. The world that appears in language and is constituted by it does not have, in the same sense, being-in-itself, and is not relative in the same sense as the object of the natural sciences. It is not being-in-itself, insofar as it is not characterized by objectivity and can never be given in experience as the comprehensive whole that it is. But as the world that it is, it is not relative to a particular language either. For to live in a linguistic world, as one does as a member of a linguistic community, does not mean that one is placed in an environment as animals are. We cannot see a linguistic world from above in this way, for there is no point of view outside the experience of the world in language from which it could become an object. Physics does not provide this point of view, because the world—i.e., the totality of what exists, is not the object of its research and calculation. Nor does comparative linguistics, which studies the structure of languages, have any non-linguistic point of view from which we could know the in-itself quality of what exists and for which the various forms of the linguistic experi-

453 ence of the world could be reconstructed, as a schematized selection, from what exists in itself—in a way analogous to animal habitats, the principles of whose structure we study. Rather,

every language has a direct relationship to the infinity of beings. To have language involves a mode of being that is quite different from the way animals are confined to their habitat. By learning foreign languages men do not alter their relationship to the world, like an aquatic animal that becomes a land animal; rather, while preserving their own relationship to the world, they extend and enrich it by the world of the foreign language. Whoever has language "has" the world.

If we keep this in mind, we will no longer confuse the factualness (Sachlichkeit) of language with the *objectivity (Objektivität) of science*. The distance involved in a linguistic relationship to the world does not, as such, produce the objectivity that the natural sciences achieve by eliminating the subjective elements of the cognitive process. The distance and the factualness of language, of course, are also genuine achievements and do not just happen automatically. We know how putting an experience into words helps us cope with it. It is as if its threatening, even annihilating, immediacy is pushed into the background, brought into proportion, made communicable, and hence dealt with. Such coping with experience, however, is obviously something different from the way science works on it, objectivizing it and making it available for whatever purposes it likes. Once a scientist has discovered the law of a natural process, he has it in his power. No such thing is possible in the natural experience of the world expressed in language. Using language by no means involves making things available and calculable. It is not just that the statement or judgment is merely one particular form among the many other linguistic orientations—they themselves remain bound up with man's life orientation. Consequently, objectivizing science regards the linguisticality of the natural experience of the world as a source of prejudices. With its methods of precise mathematical measurement the new science, as we learn from the example of Bacon, had to make room for its own constructs by directly opposing the prejudice of language and its naive teleology.

Thus there is undoubtedly no understanding

490 that is free of all prejudices, however much the will of our knowledge must be directed toward

escaping their thrall. Throughout our investigation it has emerged that the certainty achieved by using scientific methods does not suffice to ⁴⁹¹ guarantee truth. This especially applies to the human sciences, but it does not mean that they are less scientific; on the contrary, it justifies the claim to special humane significance that they have always made. The fact that in such knowledge the knower's own being comes into play certainly shows the limits of method, but not of science. Rather, what the tool of method does not achieve must—and really can—be achieved by a discipline of questioning and inquiring, a discipline that guarantees truth.

STUDY QUESTIONS: GADAMER, *TRUTH AND METHOD*

1. What is the problem of hermeneutics?
2. According to Gadamer, in what sense are 'the human sciences' sciences? In what sense are they not?
3. How does art contain a claim to truth? What does 'truth' mean in this context?
4. How does Gadamer understand literature?
5. Why does Gadamer say that the understanding of texts by a historian is not so very different from the experience of art?
6. 'Aesthetics has to be absorbed into hermeneutics.' What does Gadamer mean, and how does he support that claim?
7. In what way is interpretation a form of projection?
8. Why is prejudice necessary for interpretation? What is prejudice? What implications does this point have for the nature of interpretation?
9. What is the hermeneutical circle of part and whole? What importance does it have?
10. How is the connection of tradition important for the interpretation of a text?
11. How is the idea that a text expresses the truth important for Gadamer's understanding of interpretation?
12. How is historical consciousness important in hermeneutics?
13. What is the hermeneutic priority of the question?
14. What is the main point that Gadamer makes in relation to translation?
15. Gadamer says that tradition is linguistic in character. What does this mean, and why is it important?
16. In what ways is language not just one of man's possessions? Why is this point so important?
17. How would Gadamer react to the claim that language is primarily a tool for communication?
18. How does Gadamer support his thesis 'The world of physics cannot seek to be the whole of what exists'?
19. How does Gadamer contrast the world as known through the natural sciences and the world as it appears in language?
20. What replaces method?

Philosophical Bridges: Gadamer's Influence

Gadamer's philosophical hermeneutics has had an important impact in part because it elucidates the practice of many different disciplines, such as history, social interpretation, legal theory, and literary theory. For example, in the philosophy of law, Dworkin argues for a theory of legal interpretation that is influenced by Gadamer's hermeneutics (in *Law's Empire*). It has influenced many social anthropologists, such as Clifford Geertz, who argues that the understanding of cultural practices should be hermeneutic.

In general terms, Gadamer's hermeneutical theory has served as a meeting point for thinkers who deny that the methods of the natural science can be extended into the social sciences. The theory not only contains an explanation of why such methods cannot be extended into the human sciences but also provides an alternative account of what the social sciences are doing.

Philosophical hermeneutics has also been influential in its emphasis on the claim that understanding is never culturally and historically neutral. In this way, Gadamer's approach has appealed to thinkers who have rejected foundationalism and the search for certainty, as well as to those who are skeptical of objectively neutral and absolute knowledge. For example, Rorty's *Philosophy and the Mirror of Nature* contains a discussion of hermeneutics, contrasting it with traditionally conceived epistemology on these points.

Gadamer's philosophy has also been influential because it takes the phenomenological tradition of Husserl and Heidegger in a new direction. Paul Ricoeur has taken up the hermeneutical torch and has argued that understanding anything human must take the form of a narrative. Additionally, Gadamer himself has argued that philosophical hermeneutics implies certain values of communicative rationality and solidarity. In this way, Habermas also continues in the same tradition.

JÜRGEN HABERMAS (1929–)

Biographical History

Jürgen Habermas completed his doctoral thesis on Schelling at the University of Bonn in 1954. Early in his career his philosophy was Heideggerian, but from 1956 to 1959, he studied with Theodore Adorno at the Frankfurt Institute for Social Research. After teaching at the Universities of Heidelberg and Frankfurt, he was appointed director of the Max Planck Institute in 1971. In 1984, he returned to the University of Frankfurt, where he serves as the Distinguished Professor of Philosophy.

Philosophical Overview

In the Prologue, we sketched very briefly the program of the Frankfurt School. One of Habermas' main aims is to ground Critical Theory in a new overall account of rationality, in part by drawing on elements of the phenomenological and hermeneutical traditions, but mainly through an analysis of communication.

In his early work, *Knowledge and Human Interests* (1969), Habermas traces the historical development of the critique of knowledge from Kant to positivism and Freud in order to reveal the human interests latent in three kinds of knowledge. His aim is to free the relevant notions of rationality from the misconceptions of interest-neutral positivism. Regarding the knowledge of the natural sciences, we have a technical interest in predicting and controlling natural and objectified processes. With the hermeneutical or interpretative knowledge of the social and cultural sciences, there is a practical interest in understanding each other. Concerning the critical aspect of the social sciences, our interest is in emancipation from domination, which amounts to an ideal of social arrangements based on undistorted and open communication.

However, even the pursuit of knowledge in the natural sciences is a social enterprise conducted in a community, which assumes a lack of ideological constraints. For this reason, the possibility of scientific inquiry presupposes the critical interest in emancipation. Thus, Habermas argues that the interest in freedom from the domination of Critical Theory is primary.

In his later works, *The Theory of Communicative Action* (1981), *Moral Consciousness and Communicative Action* (1983), and *The Philosophical Discourse of Modernity* (1985), Habermas extends this analysis with a view to replacing a means-ends approach to rationality with a communicative conception of rationality. In effect, Habermas claims that there are various norms inherent in communicative actions, more specifically those that pertain to sincerity, truth, and rightness. Concerning the last, Habermas' discourse ethics attempts to ground the notion of justice understood as rational acceptability in the norms that are implicit in the communicative acts concerning conflicts of interest. This is the main focus of the book *Moral Consciousness and Communicative Action*, which we have selected for this volume.

In one of his other works from around the same period, *The Theory of Communicative Action*, Habermas argues that this discourse ethic needs to be supplemented with a theory of individual moral development and of social evolution. He outlines an account of moral development, similar to recent child developmental theories, based on the concept of communicative competence. On similar lines, he also outlines a theory of social development or evolution based on the idea of a rationalized life-world, derived from Husserl's later works.

Habermas employs his analysis of the norms of communication to develop a political theory that is compatible with the pluralism of modern society. For example, in *Between Facts and Norms* (1992), he applies the conception of justification to democracy by appealing to the idea of generally accepted reasons. Underlying this analysis is his claim that the processes required for the creation of social communicative structures have a different logic than those needed for the formation of productive structures. Democracy appeals to different norms than capitalism. Thus, democratic institutions are ways to counteract the invasion of individuals' life-worlds by bureaucratic and monetary systems.

MORAL CONSCIOUSNESS AND COMMUNICATIVE ACTION

This book was published in 1983. Habermas begins the work with a theory of universal pragmatics, an account of communication in natural languages. The basic idea is that communicative competence includes more than just the phonetic, syntactic, and semantic abilities that permit us to produce and understand grammatical sentences. It also includes a pragmatic ability to understand how particular utterances in their context relate to experience of the speaker and the outer world, as well as to socially shared normative expectations. In particular, this pragmatic ability involves recognizing the validity of utterances. For instance, in relation to the speaker's intentions and feelings, utterances can be assessed for their sincerity. In relation to the external world, they can be judged for their truth. In relation to the social world, they can be appraised in terms of their moral rightness.

Such validity claims can be criticized and disputed, but such criticisms will themselves appeal to certain social norms, which are inherent in the communicative act itself.

For example, we try to settle factual disputes by appeal to a process of argumentation and justification and, thereby, to a conception of truth understood as the rational acceptability of assertions in ideal conditions, which Habermas calls an ideal speech situation. In effect, the relevant notion of normative validity (i.e., truth) becomes one of rational acceptability that is tied to the relevant communicative and argumentative processes in ideal conditions. This is a discourse theory of truth.

Habermas' main aim is to use this kind of analysis to construct a theory of discourse ethics that illuminates the notion of justice. The basic idea is much the same as before. We try to settle disputes concerning conflicts of interest by appealing to a process of argumentation and, thereby, to a concept of justice understood as rational acceptability. The relevant norm (i.e., justice) is the idea of rational acceptability, which is inherent in the communicative processes of settling a dispute. In the case of justice, the relevant processes concern conflicts of interest, and the relevant notion of validity is that of universalizability. In order to be valid, moral norms must be universalizable. In ideal conditions, the norms must be able to satisfy all the participants. In other words, the consequences of the general application of such norms must be acceptable ideally to everyone involved.

This introduces the notion of reciprocity into practical discourse. Each participant must take into account the perspectives and interests of the other persons involved. This is required for the adjudication of the conflict of interests to be fair, and this is how Habermas interprets the notion of the common good. Furthermore, each participant in a practical discourse is free to reject the reasons offered by another in favor of accepting some moral norm. This is Habermas' reading of the notion of respect for the individual, or autonomy. At the same time, each individual must be willing to submit his or her interests to public critique with the aim of reaching consensus. This is how Habermas understands the concept of solidarity.

RECONSTRUCTION AND INTERPRETATION IN THE SOCIAL SCIENCES

Introduction

Let me begin with a personal reminiscence. When in 1967 I argued for the first time that the social sciences should not abandon the hermeneutic dimension of research and that any attempt to suppress the problem of interpretation would entail serious distortions, I was concerned with two basic types of objections. The first was the insistence that hermeneutics is not a matter of methodology at all. Hans-Georg Gadamer pointed out that the problem of interpretation arises in nonscientific contexts: in everyday life, in history, art, and literature, and more generally in the way we handle what has been passed down to us in the form of traditions. The task of philosophical hermeneutics, then, according to Gadamer, is to shed light on ordinary processes of understanding, not on systematic investigations or procedures for collecting and analyzing data. Gadamer conceives of "method" as something that is opposed to "truth"; truth is attained only through the skilled and prudent practice of understanding or interpretation. On this view, hermeneutics as an activity is at best an art but never a method; as far as science is concerned, hermeneutics is a subversive force that undermines all systematic approaches.

The second type of objection originated with representatives of mainstream social science, and it complemented the first type. It holds that the problem of interpretation lies in the mystification of interpretation and that there are no general problems of

From *Moral Consciousness and Communicative Action* by Jurgen Habermas, translated by C. Lenhardt and S. Nicholsen, 1980. Reprinted by permission of The MIT Press as publisher.

interpretation but only particular ones, for whose solution standard research techniques are adequate. If we operationalize our theoretical terms carefully and test for the validity and reliability of our research instruments, we can be safe from uncontrolled factors which might otherwise infiltrate our inquiry, factors stemming from the unanalyzed and unwieldy complexity of ordinary language and everyday life.

In the debate of the midsixties, hermeneutics was either inflated into a philosophical substitute for Heideggerian ontology or trivialized as a problem resulting from difficulties in measurement. This constellation has changed markedly since then Today the main arguments of philosophical hermeneutics have been for the most part accepted, albeit not as a philosophical doctrine but rather as a research paradigm *within* the social sciences, notably anthropology, sociology, and social psychology. Paul Rabinow and William Sullivan have christened this the "interpretive turn." . . .

Two Modes of Language Use

Let me begin by clarifying what I mean by hermeneutics. Any meaningful expression—be it an utterance, verbal or nonverbal, or an artefact of any kind, such as a tool, an institution, or a written document—can be identified from a double perspective, both as an observable event and as an understandable objectification of meaning. We can describe, explain, or predict a noise equivalent to the sounds of a spoken sentence without having the slightest idea what this utterance means. To grasp (and state) its meaning, one has to participate in some (actual or imagined) communicative action in the course of which the sentence in question is used in such a way that it is intelligible to speakers, hearers, and bystanders belonging to the same speech community. . . .

In one mode of language use, *one says what is or is not the case*. In the other, *one says something to someone else in a way that allows him to understand what is being said*. Only the second mode of language use is internally or conceptually tied up with the conditions of communication. Saying how things stand does not necessarily depend on any kind of real or imagined communication; one does not need to *make* a statement, that is, perform a speech act. Instead, one may say *p* to oneself, or simply think that *p*. In contrast, understanding what is said to one requires partici-

pation in communicative action. There must be a speech situation (or at least one must be imagined) in which a speaker, in communicating *with* a hearer *about* something, gives expression to what *he* means. . . .

Hermeneutics watches language at work, so to speak, language as it is used by participants to reach a common *understanding* or a shared *view*. The visual metaphor of an observer *who looks on*, however, should not obscure the fact that language in its performative use is embedded in relationships that are more complicated than the simple *about* relationship (and the kind of intentions correlated with it). . . .

Viewed from this perspective, language serves three functions: (a) that of reproducing culture and keeping traditions alive (this is the perspective from which Gadamer developed his philosophical hermeneutics), (b) that of social integration or the coordination of the plans of different actors in social interaction (my theory of communicative action was developed from this perspective), and (c) that of socialization or the cultural interpretation of needs (this was the perspective from which G. H. Mead developed his social psychology).

The cognitive, noncommunicative use of language, then, calls for an analysis of the relationship between a sentence and a particular state of affairs that uses concepts of corresponding intentions, propositional attitudes, direction of fit, and conditions of satisfaction. The communicative use of language, in contrast, poses the problem of the connection between this *about* relation and the two other relations (being an expression *of* something and sharing something *with* someone). . . .

Interpretation and the Objectivity of Understanding

If we compare the third-person attitude of someone who simply says how things stand (this is the attitude of the scientist, for example) with the performative attitude of someone who tries to understand what is said to him (this is the attitude of the interpreter, for example), the implications of the hermeneutic dimension of research for methodology become clear. Let me touch on three of the more important implications of hermeneutic procedures.

First, interpreters relinquish the superiority that observers have by virtue of their privileged position, in that they themselves are drawn, at least potentially, into negotiations about the meaning and validity of utterances. By taking part in communicative action, they accept in principle the same status as those whose utterances they are trying to understand. No longer immune to the affirmative or negative positions taken by experimental subjects or lay persons, interpreters give themselves over to a process of reciprocal critique. Within a process of reaching understanding, actual or potential, it is impossible to decide a priori who is to learn from whom.

Second, in assuming a performative attitude, the interpreter not only relinquishes a position of superiority vis-à-vis his object domain; he also has to grapple with the problem of the context dependency of his interpretation. He cannot be sure in advance that he and his experimental subjects operate on the basis of the same background assumptions and practices. The interpreter's own global preunderstanding of the hermeneutic situation can be examined piece by piece but cannot be put into question as a whole.

Third, just as problematic as the interpreter's disengagement in questions of validity and the decontextualization of interpretations of such questions is the fact that everyday language extends to nondescriptive utterances and noncognitive claims to validity. In everyday life we agree (or disagree) more frequently about the rightness of actions and norms, the appropriateness of evaluations and standards, and the authenticity or sincerity of self-presentations than about the truth of propositions. That is why the knowledge we use when we say something to someone extends beyond strictly propositional or truth-related knowledge. To understand what is said to him, the interpreter has to command knowledge that is based on *additional* claims to validity. A correct interpretation, therefore, is not true in the sense in which a proposition that reflects an existing state of affairs is true. It would be better to say that a correct interpretation fits, suits, or explicates the meaning of the *interpretandum*, that which the interpreter is to understand.

These are the three implications of the fact that understanding what is said requires *participation* and not merely *observation*. . . .

In short, every science that accepts the inclusion of objectivations of meaning in its object domain has to take into account the methodological implications of the interpreter's *participant role*. The interpreter does not have to give meaning to the things he observes; rather, he has to explicate the given meaning of objectivations that can be understood only from within the context of communication processes. These implications threaten the very context independence and value neutrality that seem necessary to the *objectivity* of theoretical knowledge. . . .

The Rationality Presupposed in Interpretation

. . . The paradigm case for hermeneutics is the interpretation of a traditional text. While the interpreter initially seems to have understood what the author is saying, he subsequently comes to the confusing realization that he has not adequately understood the text, that is, not so well that he could answer the author's questions if he had to. The interpreter takes this to be a sign that he is still putting the text in a context other than the one in which it was in fact embedded. Next he tries to understand why the author—in the tacit belief that certain states of affairs obtain, that certain values and norms are valid, and that certain experiences can be attributed to certain subjects—makes the assertions he does, observes or violates the conventions he does, and expresses the intentions, dispositions, feelings, and other such things he does. But only to the extent to which the interpreter also grasps the *reasons* why the author's utterances seemed rational to the author himself does he understand what the author meant.

The interpreter, then, understands the meaning of a text only insofar as he understands *why* the author felt justified in putting forth certain propositions as being true, in recognizing certain values and norms as being right, and in expressing certain experiences (or attributing them to others) as being authentic. . . .

Interpreters cannot understand the semantic content of a text if they do not make themselves aware of the reasons the author could have brought forth in his own time and place if required to do so.

For reasons to be sound and for them to be merely considered sound are not the same thing, whether we are dealing with reasons for asserting facts, for recommending norms and values, or for expressing desires and feelings. That is why the interpreter cannot simply look at and understand such reasons without at least implicitly passing judgment on them *as* reasons, that is, without taking a positive or negative position on them. The interpreter may leave some claims to validity open and may decide, unlike the author, to consider some questions unanswered, to leave them as open problems. But reasons can be *understood* only insofar as they are taken seriously as reasons and *evaluated*. . . .

There is a sense in which any interpretation is a *rational* interpretation. In the act of understanding, which entails an evaluation of reasons as well, the interpreter cannot avoid appealing to standards of rationality and hence to standards that he himself considers binding on all parties, including the author and his contemporaries (to the extent to which they could and would have participated in the communication that the interpreter is now resuming). While such a (normally implicit) appeal to presumably universal standards of rationality may, to a certain extent, be inescapable for the dedicated interpreter who is bent on understanding, this by no means proves that those standards are truly rational. . . .

Insofar as rational reconstructions explicate the conditions for the validity of utterances, they also explain deviant cases, and through this indirect legislative authority they acquire a *critical* function as well. Insofar as they extend the differentiations between individual claims to validity beyond traditional boundaries, they can even establish new analytic standards and thus assume a *constructive* role. And insofar as we succeed in analyzing very general conditions of validity, rational reconstructions can claim to be describing universals and thus to represent a *theoretical* knowledge capable of competing with other such knowledge. At this level, weak *transcendental* arguments make their appearance, arguments aimed at demonstrating that the presuppositions of relevant practices are inescapable, that is, that they cannot be cast aside. . . .

DISCOURSE ETHICS: NOTES ON A PROGRAM OF PHILOSOPHICAL JUSTIFICATION

In his recent book *After Virtue*, Alasdair MacIntyre argues that the Enlightenment's project of establishing a secularized morality free of metaphysical and religious assumptions has failed. He accepts as the incontestable outcome of the Enlightenment what Max Horkheimer once pointed out with critical

intent, the idea that an instrumental reason restricted to purposive rationality must let its ends be determined by blind emotional attitudes and arbitrary decisions: "Reason is calculative; it can assess truths of fact and mathematical relations but nothing more. In the realm of practice it can speak only of means. About ends it must be silent." Since Kant this conclusion has been opposed by cognitivist moral philosophies that maintain that in one sense or another practical questions admit of truth. . . .

I would like to support my assessment of the current state of the debate in ethics by presenting my own program of philosophical justification. In so doing, I will address other cognitivist approaches only in passing.

I Preliminary Remarks

1 On the phenomenology of the moral

The comments by MacIntyre cited above are reminiscent of a critique of instrumental reason directed against certain one-sided conceptions characteristic of the modern understanding of the world, notably its stubborn tendency to narrow down to the cognitive-instrumental domain the domain of questions that can be decided on the basis of reasons. Moral-practical questions of the form What ought I to do? are considered not amenable to rational debate unless they can be answered in terms of purposive rationality. This pathology of modern consciousness calls for an explanation in terms of *social theory*. . . .

P. F. Strawson's well-known essay "Freedom and Resentment" points in this direction. It develops a linguistic phenomenology of ethical consciousness whose purpose is maieutically to open the eyes of the empiricist in his role as moral skeptic to his own everyday oral intuitions.

Strawson begins by examining an emotional response which in its obstrusiveness is well suited to convince even the most diehard skeptic that moral experience has real content. That response is the indignation we feel in the face of personal insults. . . .

Resentment is an expression, albeit a relatively powerless one, of moral condemnation. . . .

2

Strawson's remarks are important for methodological reasons as well. The moral philosopher must take up a vantage point from which he can perceive moral phenomena *as* moral phenomena. Strawson shows how different moral feelings are linked to each other internally. The personal responses of the injured party can be compensated for by excuses, as we saw. The aggrieved party, for his part, can forgive an injustice he has suffered. To the feelings of the insulted person corresponds the gratitude felt by someone who is the recipient of a good deed. To the condemnation of a wrong corresponds the admiration we feel for a good act. Our feelings of indifference, contempt, malevolence, satisfaction, recognition, encouragement, consolation, etc., have innumerable nuances. Among them the feelings of guilt and obligation are of course crucial. In trying to explain this web of emotional attitudes and feelings with the tools of linguistic analysis, Strawson is interested primarily in the fact that all these emotions are embedded in a practice of everyday life that is accessible to us only in a performative attitude. This gives the web of moral feelings a certain *ineluctability*: we cannot retract at will our commitment to a lifeworld whose members we are. In comparison, the objectivating attitude toward moral phenomena, which we must first have perceived from a participant's perspective, is secondary. . . .

At this point Strawson draws together the diverse strands of his argument. The only way to avoid misconstruing what it means to justify a mode of action in moral-practical terms, he insists, is to maintain our focus on the web of moral feelings that is embedded in the communicative practice of everyday life and to situate properly the question What ought I to do? "Inside the general structure or web of human attitudes and feelings of which I have been speaking, there is endless room for modification, redirection, criticism, and justification. But questions of justification are internal to the structure or relate to modifications internal to it. The existence of the general framework of attitudes itself is something we are given with the fact of human society. As a whole, it neither calls for, nor permits, an *external* 'rational' justification."

Strawson's phenomenology of the moral is relevant because it shows that the world of moral phenomena can be grasped only in the performative attitude of participants in interaction, that resentment and personal emotional responses in general point to suprapersonal standards for judging norms

and commands, and that the moral-practical justification of a mode of action aims at an aspect *different* from the feeling-neutral assessment of means-ends relations, even when such assessment is made from the point of view of the general welfare. It is no coincidence that Strawson analyzes feelings. Feelings seem to have a similar function for the moral justification of action as sense perceptions have for the theoretical justification of facts.

II The Principle of Universalization as a Rule of Argumentation

The propaedeutic comments I have just made were meant to defend the cognitivist approach in ethics against the metaethical diversionary tactics of value skepticism and to lay the groundwork for answering the question of in what sense and in what way moral commands and norms can be justified. In the substantive portion of my reflections (section 3) I will begin by reviewing the role played by normative validity claims in the practice of daily life in order to explain how the deontological claim connected with commands and norms is distinguished from the assertoric claim. I will argue that there are compelling reasons for recasting moral theory in the form of an analysis of moral argumentation. In section 4 I will introduce the principle of universalization (U) as a bridging principle that makes agreement in moral argumentation possible. The version of the principle that I will give excludes any monological application of this rule for argumentation. Finally, in section 5 I will take up certain ideas of Ernst Tugendhat and show that moral justifications are dependent on argumentation actually being carried out, not for pragmatic reasons of an equalization of power, but for internal reasons, namely that real argument makes moral insight possible.

3 Assertoric and normative claims to validity in communicative action

The attempt to ground ethics in the form of a logic of moral argumentation has no chance of success unless we can identify a special type of validity claim connected with commands and norms and can identify it on the level on which moral dilemmas initially emerge: within the horizon of the lifeworld, where Strawson had to look for moral phenomena when he marshalled the evidence of ordinary language against the skeptic. . . .

I call interactions *communicative* when the participants coordinate their plans of action consensually, with the agreement reached at any point being evaluated in terms of the intersubjective recognition of validity claims. In cases where agreement is reached through explicit linguistic processes, the actors make three different claims to validity in their speech acts as they come to an agreement with one another about something. Those claims are claims to truth, claims to rightness, and claims to truthfulness, according to whether the speaker refers to something in the objective world (as the totality of existing states of affairs), to something in the shared social world (as the totality of the legitimately regulated interpersonal relationships of a social group), or to something in his own subjective world (as the totality of experiences to which one has privileged access). Further, I distinguish between communicative and strategic action. Whereas in strategic action one actor seeks to *influence* the behavior of another by means of the threat of sanctions or the prospect of gratification in order to *cause* the interaction to continue as the first actor desires, in communicative action one actor seeks *rationally* to *motivate* another by relying on the illocutionary binding/bonding effect (*Bindungseffekt*) of the offer contained in his speech act.

The fact that a speaker can rationally motivate a hearer to accept such an offer is due not to the validity of what he says but to the speaker's guarantee that he will, if necessary, make efforts to redeem the claim that the hearer has accepted. It is this guarantee that effects the coordination between speaker and hearer. In the case of claims to truth or rightness, the speaker can redeem his guarantee discursively, that is, by adducing reasons; in the case of claims to truthfulness he does so through consistent behavior. (A person can convince someone that he means what he says only through his actions, not by giving reasons.) As soon as the hearer accepts the guarantee offered by the speaker, obligations are assumed that have consequences for the interaction, obligations that are contained in the meaning of what was said. In the case of orders and directives, for instance, the obligations to act hold primarily for the hearer, in the case of promises and announcements, they hold for the speaker, in the case of agreements and contracts, they are symmetrical, holding for both parties,

and in the case of substantive normative recommendations and warnings, they hold asymmetrically for both parties.

Unlike these regulative speech acts, the meaning of a constative speech act gives rise to obligations only insofar as the speaker and the hearer agree to base their actions on situational definitions that do not contradict the propositions they accept as true at any given point. Obligations to act flow directly from the meaning of an expressive speech act in that the speaker specifies what it is that his behavior does not contradict and will not contradict in the future. Owing to the fact that communication oriented to reaching understanding has a validity basis, a speaker can persuade a hearer to accept a speech-act offer by guaranteeing that he will redeem a criticizable validity claim. In so doing, he creates a binding/bonding effect between speaker and hearer that makes the continuation of their interaction possible.

The two *discursively redeemable* claims to validity that are of particular interest to us, claims to propositional truth and claims to normative rightness, play their roles as coordinators of action in different ways. A number of asymmetries between them suggest that they occupy different "positions" in the community.

On the face of it, *assertoric statements* used in *constative speech acts* appear to be related to *facts* as *normative statements* used in *regulative speech acts* are related to *legitimately ordered interpersonal relations*. The *truth* of propositions seems to signify the *existence* of states of affairs in much the same way as the *rightness* of actions signifies the *observance* of norms. . . .

In theoretical discourse the gap between particular observations and general hypotheses is bridged by some canon or other of induction. An analogous bridging principle is needed for practical discourse. Accordingly, all studies of the logic of moral argumentation end up having to introduce a moral principle as a rule of argumentation that has a function equivalent to the principle of induction in the discourse of the empirical sciences.

Interestingly enough, in trying to identify such a moral principle, philosophers of diverse backgrounds always come up with principles whose basic idea is the same. *All* variants of cognitivist ethics take their bearings from the basic intuition contained in Kant's categorical imperative. What I am concerned with here is not the diversity of Kantian formulations but their underlying idea, which is designed to take into account the impersonal or general character of valid universal commands. The moral principle is so conceived as to exclude as invalid any norm that could not meet with the qualified assent of all who are or might be affected by it. This bridging principle, which makes consensus possible, ensures that only those norms are accepted as valid that express a *general will*. As Kant noted time and again, moral norms must be suitable for expression as "universal laws." The categorical imperative can be understood as a principle that requires the universalizability of *modes of action* and *maxims*, or of the *interests* furthered by them (that is, those embodied in the norms of action). Kant wants to eliminate as invalid all those norms that "contradict" this requirement. . . .

The principle of universalization is by no means exhausted by the requirement that moral norms must take the *form* of unconditionally universal "ought" statements. The *grammatical form* of normative statements alone, which does not permit such sentences to refer to or be addressed to particular groups or individuals, is not a sufficient condition for valid moral commands, for we could give such universal form to commands that are plainly immoral. What is more in some respects the requirement of formal universality may well be too restrictive; it may make sense to submit nonmoral norms of action (whose range of jurisdiction is socially and spatiotemporally limited) to a practical discourse (restricted in this case to those affected and hence relative), and to test them for generalizability. . . .

Kurt Baier and Bernard Gert come closer to this meaning of the principle of universalization when they argue that valid moral norms must be generally teachable and publicly defendable. . . .

The intuition expressed in the idea of the generalizability of maxims intends something more than this, namely, that valid norms must *deserve* recognition by *all* concerned. It is not sufficient, therefore, for *one person* to test whether he can will the adoption of a contested norm after considering the consequences and the side effects that would occur if all persons followed that norm or whether every other person in an identical position could will the adoption

of such a norm. In both cases the process of judging is relative to the vantage point and perspective of *some* and not *all* concerned. True impartiality pertains only to that standpoint from which one can generalize precisely those norms that can count on universal assent because they perceptibly embody an interest common to all affected. It is these norms that deserve intersubjective recognition. Thus the impartiality of judgment is expressed in a principle that constrains *all* affected to adopt the perspectives of *all others* in the balancing of interests. . . .

Thus every valid norm has to fulfill the following condition:

> (U) *All* affected can accept the consequences and the side effects its *general* observance can be anticipated to have for the satisfaction of *everyone's* interests (and these consequences are preferred to those of known alternative possibilities for regulation).

We should not mistake this principle of universalization (U) for the following principle, which already contains the distinctive idea of an ethics of discourse.

> (D) Only those norms can claim to be valid that meet (or could meet) with the approval of all affected in their capacity *as participants in a practical discourse*.

This principle of discourse ethics (D), to which I will return after offering my justification for (U), already *presupposes* that we *can* justify our choice of a norm. At this point in my argument, that presupposition is what is at issue. I have introduced (U) as a rule of argumentation that makes agreement in practical discourses possible whenever matters of concern to all are open to regulation in the equal interest of everyone. Once this bridging principle has been justified, we will be able to make the transition to discourse ethics. I have formulated (U) in a way that precludes a monological application of the principle. First, (U) regulates only argumentation among a plurality of participants; second, it suggests the perspective of real-life argumentation, in which all affected are admitted as participants. . . .

If we keep in mind the action-coordinating function that normative validity claims play in the communicative practice of everyday life, we see why the problems to be resolved in moral argumentation cannot be handled monologically but require a cooperative effort. By entering into a process of moral argumentation, the participants continue their communicative action in a reflexive attitude with the aim of restoring a consensus that has been disrupted. Moral argumentation thus serves to settle conflicts of action by consensual means. Conflicts in the domain of norm-guided interactions can be traced directly to some disruption of a normative consensus. Repairing a disrupted consensus can mean one of two things: restoring intersubjective recognition of a validity claim after it has become controversial or assuring intersubjective recognition for a new validity claim that is a substitute for the old one. Agreement of this kind expresses a *common will*. If moral argumentation is to produce this kind of agreement, however, it is not enough for the individual to reflect on whether he can assent to a norm. It is not even enough for each individual to reflect in this way and then to register his vote. What is needed is a "real" process of argumentation in which the individuals concerned cooperate. Only an intersubjective process of reaching understanding can produce an agreement that is reflexive in nature; only it can give the participants the knowledge that they have collectively become convinced of something.

From this viewpoint, the categorical imperative needs to be reformulated as follows: "Rather than ascribing as valid to all others any maxim that I can will to be a universal law, I must submit my maxim to all others for purposes of discursively testing its claim to universality. The emphasis shifts from what each can will without contradiction to be a general law, to what all can will in agreement to be a universal norm." This version of the universality principle does in fact entail the idea of a cooperative process of argumentation. For one thing, nothing better prevents others from perspectivally distorting one's own interests than actual participation. It is in this pragmatic sense that the individual is the last court of appeal for judging what is in his best interest. On the other hand, the descriptive terms in which each individual perceives his interests must be open to criticism by others. Needs and wants are interpreted in the light of cultural values. Since cultural values are always components of intersubjectively shared traditions, the revision of the values used to interpret needs and wants cannot be a matter for individuals to handle monologically.

5 Argumentation versus participation

Discourse ethics, then, stands or falls with two assumptions: (a) that normative claims to validity have cognitive meaning and can be treated *like* claims to truth and (b) that the justification of norms and commands requires that a real discourse be carried out and thus cannot occur in a strictly monological form, i.e., in the form of a hypothetical process of argumentation occurring in the individual mind. . . .

III Discourse Ethics and Its Bases in Action Theory

With the introduction of the principle of universalization, the first step in the justification of a discourse ethics has been accomplished. We can review the systematic content of the argument in the form of an imaginary debate between an advocate of ethical cognitivism and an advocate of moral skepticism.

The opening round was a matter of opening the die-hard skeptic's eyes to the domain of *moral phenomena*. In the second round the issue was whether practical questions *admit of truth*. We saw that as an ethical subjectivist the skeptic could score some points against the ethical objectivist. The cognitivist could salvage his position by asserting that for normative statements a claim to validity is only *analogous to a truth claim*. The third round opened with the skeptic's realistic observation that it is often impossible to reach a consensus on questions of moral principle, despite the best intentions of all concerned. Faced with a *pluralism of ultimate value orientations*, which seems to support the skeptic's position, the cognitivist has to try to demonstrate the existence of a bridging principle that makes consensus possible. A moral principle having been proposed, the question of cultural relativism occupies the next round of the argumentation. The skeptic voices the objection that (U) represents a hasty generalization of moral intuitions peculiar to our own Western culture, a challenge to which the cognitivist will respond with a *transcendental justification* of his moral principle. In round 5 the skeptic brings in further objections to the strategy of transcendental justification, and the cognitivist meets them with a more cautious version of Apel's argument.

In the sixth round, in the face of this promising justification of a discourse ethics, the skeptic can take refuge in a *refusal to enter into discourse*. But as we will see, by doing so he has maneuvered himself into a hopeless position. The theme of the seventh and last round of the debate is the skeptic's revival of the objections to ethical formalism that Hegel brought up in his criticism of Kant. On this issue the astute cognitivist will not hesitate to meet the well-considered reservations of his opponent halfway.

The external form of my presentation does not coincide precisely with the ideal course of the seven-round debate I have just sketched. To counter the deeply ingrained reductionist concept of rationality characteristic of empiricism and the reinterpretation of basic moral experiences that corresponds to it, I stressed (in section 1) the web of moral feelings and attitudes that is interwoven with the practice of everyday life. I turned next (in section 2) to metaethical arguments denying that practical questions admit of truth. These proved to be irrelevant because we abandoned the false identification of normative and assertoric claims to validity and showed (in section 3) that propositional truth and normative rightness play different pragmatic roles in everyday communication. The skeptic was not impressed by this argument and restated his doubts that even the specific claims to validity associated with commands and norms could be justified. This objection fails if one adopts the principle of universalization (introduced in section 4) and can demonstrate (as in section 5) that this moral principle is a rule of argumentation comparable to the principle of induction and is not a principle of participation in disguise.

This is where the debate stands now. Next the skeptic will demand a justification for this bridging principle. . . .

6 Is a justification of the moral principles necessary and possible?

The demand for a justification of the moral principle is hardly unreasonable when one recalls that Kant's categorical imperative, as well as the many variations of the universalization principle put forward by ethical cognitivists following in his footsteps, expresses a moral intuition whose scope is questionable. Certainly only such norms of action as embody generalizable interests correspond to *our* conceptions of justice. But this "moral point of view" might be only the expression of the particular moral ideas of our Western culture. . . .

In view of the anthropological data available we cannot but concede that the moral code expounded by Kantian moral theories is indeed only one among many:

There are, then, grounds for suspecting that the claim to universality raised by ethical cognitivists on behalf of the moral principle they happen to favor is based on an ethnocentric fallacy. Cognitivists cannot evade the skeptic's demand that it be justified. . . .

I am not dramatizing the situation when I say that faced with the demand for a justification of the universal validity of the principle of universalization, cognitivists are in trouble. The skeptic feels emboldened to recast his *doubts* about the possibility of justifying a universalist morality as an *assertion* that it is impossible to justify such a morality. Hans Albert took this tack with his *Treatise on Critical Reason* by applying to practical philosophy Popper's model of critical testing, which was developed for the philosophy of science and intended to take the place of traditional foundationalist and justificationist models. The attempt to justify moral principles with universal validity, according to Albert, ensnares the cognitivist in a "Münchhausen trilemma" in which he must choose between three equally unacceptable alternatives: putting up with an infinite regress, arbitrarily breaking off the chain of deduction, and making a circular argument. The status of this trilemma, however, is problematic. It arises only if one presupposes a *semantic concept of justification* that is oriented to a deductive relationship between statements and based solely on the concept of logical inference. This deductive concept of justification is obviously too narrow for the exposition of the pragmatic relations between argumentative speech acts. Principles of induction and universalization are introduced as rules of argumentation for the sole purpose of bridging the logical gap in *nondeductive* relations. Accordingly, these bridging principles are not susceptible to deductive justification, which is the only form of justification allowed by the Münchhausen trilemma.

Carrying on this line of argument, Karl-Otto Apel has subjected fallibilism to an illuminating metacritique and refuted the objection to the Münchhausen trilemma. . . .

He revives the transcendental mode of justification using the tools of a pragmatics of language. One of the key elements of Apel's transcendental-pragmatic line of argumentation is the notion of a *performative contradiction*. . . .

Apel illustrates the significance of performative contradictions for understanding the classical arguments of the philosophy of consciousness. . . .

The speaker raises a truth claim for the following proposition:

a. I do not exist (here and now).

At the same time, by uttering statement (a), he ineluctably makes an existential assumption, the propositional content of which may be expressed,

b. I exist (here and now),

where the personal pronoun in both statements refers to one and the same person.

Similarly, Apel uncovers a performative contradiction in the objection raised by the "consistent fallibilist," who in his role as ethical skeptic denies the possibility of grounding moral principles and presents the above-mentioned trilemma. Apel characterizes the argument as follows: The proponent asserts the universal validity of the principle of universalization. He is contradicted by an opponent relying on the Münchhausen trilemma. On the basis of this trilemma the opponent concludes that attempts to ground the universal validity of principles are meaningless. This the opponent calls the principle of fallibilism. But the opponent will have involved himself in a performative contradiction if the proponent can show that in making his argument, he has to make assumptions that are inevitable in *any* argumentation game aiming at critical examination and that the propositional content of those assumptions contradicts the principle of fallibilism. This is in fact the case, since in putting forward his objection, the opponent necessarily assumes the validity of at least those logical rules that are irreplaceable if we are to understand his argument as a refutation. In taking part in the process of reasoning, even the consistent fallibilist has already accepted as valid a minimum number of unavoidable rules of criticism. Yet this state of affairs is incompatible with the principle of fallibilism. . . .

Apel turns this form of performative refutation of the skeptic into a mode of justification, which he describes as follows: "If, on the one hand, a presupposition cannot be challenged in argumentation without actual performative self-contradiction, and if, on the other hand, it cannot be deductively grounded without formal-logical petitio principii, then it belongs to those transcendental-pragmatic presuppositions of argumentation that one must always (already) have accepted, if the language game of argumentation is to be meaningful."

Thus the necessary justification of the proposed moral principle could take the following form: every argumentation, regardless of the context in which it occurs, rests on pragmatic presuppositions from whose propositional content the principle of universalism (U) can be derived.

7 The structure and status of the transcendental-pragmatic argument

Having established that a transcendental-pragmatic justification of the moral principle is in fact possible, I will now present the argument itself. I will begin in section 1 by enumerating certain conditions that all transcendental-pragmatic arguments must satisfy. I will then use these criteria to assess two of the best known proposals of this kind, namely those of R. S. Peters and K. O. Apel. In section 2 I will present a version of the transcendental-pragmatic argument that can stand up to the familiar objections against it. Finally, in section 3 I will show that this justification of discourse ethics cannot have the status of an ultimate justification and why there is no need to claim this status for it.

Following Collingwood, a type of philosophical analysis has gained credence in England that corresponds quite closely to the procedure Apel terms "transcendental pragmatics." . . .

The purpose of such arguments is to prove that certain discourses entail inescapable presuppositions; moral principles have to be derivable from the propositional content of such presuppositions. . . .

One cannot demonstrate a transfer of this kind as Apel and Peters try to do, namely by deriving basic ethical norms *directly* from the presuppositions of argumentation. Basic norms of law and morality fall outside the jurisdiction of moral theory; they must be viewed as substantive principles to be justified in practical discourses. Since historical circumstances change, every epoch sheds its own light upon fundamental moral-practical ideas. Nevertheless, in such practical discourses we always already make use of substantive normative rules of argumentation. It is *these rules* alone that transcendental pragmatics is in a position to derive.

2

We must return to the justification of the principle of universalization. We are now in a position to specify the role that the transcendental-pragmatic argument can play in this process. Its function is to help to show that the principle of universalization, which acts as a rule of argumentation, is implied by the presuppositions of argumentation in general. This requirement is met if the following can be shown:

> Every person who accepts the universal and necessary communicative presuppositions of argumentative speech and who knows what it means to justify a norm of action implicitly presupposes as valid the principle of universalization, whether in the form I gave it above or in an equivalent form.

It makes sense to distinguish three levels of presuppositions of argumentation along the lines suggested by Aristotle: those at the logical level of products, those at the dialectical level of procedures, and those at the rhetorical level of processes. . . .

For the logical-semantic level, the following rules can serve as *examples:*

(1.1) No speaker may contradict himself.
(1.2) Every speaker who applies predicate F to object A must be prepared to apply F to all other objects resembling A in all relevant aspects.
(1.3) Different speakers may not use the same expression with different meanings.

The presuppositions of argumentation at this level are logical and semantic rules that have no ethical content. They are not a suitable point of departure for a transcendental-pragmatic argument.

In *procedural* terms, arguments are processes of reaching understanding that are ordered in such a way that proponents and opponents, having assumed a hypothetical attitude and being relieved of the

pressures of action and experience, can test validity claims that have become problematic. At this level are located the pragmatic presuppositions of a special form of interaction, namely everything necessary for a search for truth organized in the form of a competition. . . .

Again I cite a few examples from Alexy's catalog of rules:

(2.1) Every speaker may assert only what he really believes.
(2.2) A person who disputes a proposition or norm not under discussion must provide a reason for wanting to do so.

Some of these rules obviously have an ethical import. At this level what comes to the fore are presuppositions common both to discourses and to action oriented to reaching understanding as such, e.g., presuppositions about relations of mutual recognition. . . .

Finally, in *process* terms, argumentative speech is a process of communication that, in light of its goal of reaching a rationally motivated agreement, must satisfy improbable conditions. In argumentative speech we see the structures of a speech situation immune to repression and inequality in a particular way: it presents itself as a form of communication that adequately approximates ideal conditions. . . .

The presupposition of something like an "unrestricted communication community," an idea that Apel developed following Peirce and Mead, can be demonstrated through systematic analysis of performative contradictions. Participants in argumentation cannot avoid the presupposition that, owning to certain characteristics that require formal description, the structure of their communication rules out all external or internal coercion other than the force of the better argument and thereby also neutralizes all motives other than that of the cooperative search for truth.

Following my analysis, R. Alexy has suggested the following rules of discourse for this level:

(3.1) Every subject with the competence to speak and act is allowed to take part in a discourse.
(3.2) **a.** Everyone is allowed to question any assertion whatever.

b. Everyone is allowed to introduce any assertion whatever into the discourse.

c. Everyone is allowed to express his attitudes, desires, and needs.

(3.3) No speaker may be prevented, by internal or external coercion, from exercising his rights as laid down in (3.1) and (3.2).

A few explanations are in order here. Rule (3.1) defines the set of potential participants. It includes all subjects without exception who have the capacity to take part in argumentation. Rule (3.2) guarantees all participants equal opportunity to contribute to the argumentation and to put forth their own arguments. Rule (3.3) sets down conditions under which the rights to universal access and to equal participation can be enjoyed equally by all, that is, without the possibility of repression, be it ever so subtle or covert.

If these considerations are to amount to more than a definition favoring an ideal form of communication and thus prejudging everything else, we must show that these rules of discourse are not mere *conventions*; rather, they are inescapable presuppositions.

The presuppositions themselves are identified by convincing a person who contests the hypothetical reconstructions offered that he is caught up in performative contradictions. . . .

Here I will content myself with discussing a few examples, indicating what such an analysis might actually look like.

The statement

(1) Using good reasons, I finally convinced H that p can be read as someone's report on the outcome of a discourse. In this discourse the speaker, by using reasons, motivated the hearer to accept the truth claim connected with the assertion that p, that is, to consider p true. Central to the meaning of the word "convince" is the idea that a subject other than the speaker adopts a view on the basis of good reasons. This is why the statement

(2) Using lies, I finally convinced H that p is nonsensical. It can be revised to

(3) Using lies, I finally talked H into believing that p.

I can refer someone to a dictionary to look up the meaning of the verb "to convince." But that will not explain *why* statement (2) is a semantic paradox that can be resolved by statement (3). To explain that, I can start with the internal connection between the expressions "to convince someone of something" and "to come to a reasoned agreement about something." In the *final* analysis, convictions rest on a consensus that has been attained discursively. Now statement (2) implies that H has formed his conviction under conditions that simply do not permit the formation of convictions. Such conditions contradict the pragmatic presuppositions of argumentation as such (in this case rule (2.1)). This presupposition holds not only for particular instances but inevitably for every process of argumentation. I can prove this by making a proponent who defends the truth of statement (2) aware that he thereby gets himself into a performative contradiction. For as soon as he cites a reason for the truth of (2), he enters a process of argumentation and has thereby accepted the presupposition, among others, that he can never *convince* an opponent of something by resorting to lies; at most, he can talk him into believing something to be true. But then the content of the assertion to be justified contradicts one of the presuppositions the proponent must operate with if his statement is to be regarded as a justification. . . .

If after these cursory remarks we accept the rules tentatively set down by Alex (pending a more detailed analysis), we have at our disposal, in conjunction with a weak idea of normative justification (i.e., one that does not prejudge the matter), premises that are strong enough for the derivation of the universalization principle (U).

If every person entering a process of argumentation must, among other things, make presuppositions whose content can be expressed in rules (3.1) to (3.3) and if we understand what it means to discuss hypothetically whether norms of action ought to be adopted, then everyone who seriously tries to *discursively* redeem normative claims to validity intuitively accepts procedural conditions that amount to implicitly acknowledging (U). It follows from the aforementioned rules of discourse that a contested norm cannot meet with the consent of the participants in a practical discourse unless (U) holds, that is. . . .

Unless all affected can *freely* accept the consequences and the side effects that the *general* observance of a controversial norm can be expected to have for the satisfaction of the interests of *each individual.*

But once it has been shown that (U) can be grounded upon the presuppositions of argumentation through a transcendental-pragmatic derivation, discourse ethics itself can be formulated in terms of the principle of discourse ethics (D), which stipulates,

Only those norms can claim to be valid that meet (or could meet) with the approval of all affected in their capacity as participants in a practical discourse.

The justification of discourse ethics outlined here avoids confusions in the use of the term "moral principle." The only moral principle here is the universalization principle (U), which is conceived as a rule of argumentation and is part of the logic of practical discourses. (U) must be carefully distinguished from the following:

- Substantive principles or basic norms, which can only be the *subject matter* of moral argumentation
- The normative content of the presuppositions of argumentation, which can be expressed in terms of rules, as in (3.1) to (3.3)
- The principle of discourse ethics (D), which stipulates the basic idea of a moral theory but does not form part of a logic of argumentation

Previous attempts to ground discourse ethics were flawed because they tended to collapse *rules, contents, presuppositions* of argumentation and in addition confused all of these with moral principles in the sense of principles of philosophical ethics. (D) is the assertion that the philosopher as moral theorist ultimately seeks to justify. The program of justification I have outlined in this essay describes what I regard as the most-promising *road* to that goal. This road is the transcendental-pragmatic justification of a rule of argumentation with normative content. . . .

3

F. Kambartel has characterized the transcendental-pragmatic justification of discourse ethics as a procedure whereby a proponent tries to convince an opponent "who asks for justification of a rational principle put forth by someone else that his intention in asking the question, rightly understood, already involves an acceptance of that same principle." . . .

Demonstrating the existence of performative contradictions helps to identify the rules necessary for any argumentation game to work; if one is to argue at all, there are no substitutes. The fact that there are *no alternatives* to these rules of argumentation is what is being proved; the rules themselves are not being *justified.* True, the participants must have accepted them as a "fact of reason" in setting out to argue. But this kind of argument cannot accomplish a transcendental deduction in the Kantian sense. . . .

My programmatic justification of discourse ethics requires all of the following:

1. A definition of a universalization principle that functions as a rule of argumentation
2. The identification of pragmatic presuppositions of argumentation that are inescapable and have a normative content
3. The explicit statement of that normative content (e.g., in the form of discourse rules)
4. Proof that a relation of material implication holds between steps (3) and (1) in connection with the idea of the justification of norms

Step (2) in the analysis, for which the search for performative contradictions provides a guide, relies upon a maieutic method that serves

2a. to make the skeptic who presents an objection aware of presuppositions he knows intuitively,
2b. to cast this pretheoretical knowledge in an explicit form that will enable the skeptic to recognize his intuitions in this description,
2c. to corroborate, though counterexamples, the proponent's assertion that there are no alternatives to the presuppositions he has made explicit.

Substeps (2b) and (2c) contain unmistakable hypothetical elements. The description we employ to pass from knowing how to knowing that is a hypothetical reconstruction that can provide only a more or less correct rendering of intuitions. It needs maieutic confirmation. Similarly, the assertion that there is no alternative to a given presupposition, that it is one of the inescapable (i.e., necessary and general) presuppositions, has the status of an assumption. Like a lawlike hypothesis (*Gesetzeshypothese*), it must be checked against individual cases. . . .

No harm is done, however, if we deny that the transcendental-pragmatic justification constitutes an ultimate justification. Rather, discourse ethics then takes its place among the reconstructive sciences concerned with the rational bases of knowing, speaking, and acting. If we cease striving for the foundationalism of traditional transcendental philosophy, we acquire new corroborative possibilities for discourse ethics. In competition with other ethical approaches, it can be used to describe empirically existing moral and legal ideas. It can be built into theories of the development of moral and legal consciousness at both the sociocultural and the ontogenetic levels and in this way can be made susceptible to indirect corroboration.

STUDY QUESTIONS: HABERMAS, MORAL CONSCIOUSNESS AND COMMUNICATIVE ACTION

1. Is hermeneutics, according to Habermas, a matter of methodology?
2. What is his view of Gadamer? Does he agree with Gadamer's view of philosophical hermeneutics?
3. What are the two modes of language use that he distinguishes?
4. How are language and hermeneutics related?
5. What is 'objectivity of understanding'?
6. What is the paradigm case for hermeneutics? Why?
7. How does an interpreter become aware of the semantic content of a text?
8. What is his view of MacIntyre? Kant? Strawson?
9. What is the principle of universalization? How is it used, and what is its importance?
10. When are interactions *communicative*? What does he mean by this, and why is it important?
11. What is the importance of Kant's categorical imperative for Habermas' view?
12. What is the condition that every evaluative norm must fulfill?
13. What is the role of action theory?
14. What are the objections to ethical formalism that Hegel brought against Kant? What is Habermas' view of this?
15. What is 'transcendental pragmatics,' and what is Habermas' view of it?

Philosophical Bridges: Habermas' Influence

In post–Cold War western philosophy, one of the major remaining expressions of a broadly Marxist approach to political theory is Habermas' reconstruction of the Frankfurt School's notion of social critique. Habermas aims to legitimize a Marx-inspired critique of capitalism through a theory that at the same time provides a model of participatory democracy. Habermas' theory captures well the political climate of some European countries after the fall of the Berlin Wall. In part, this explains why the theory has been so influential.

Furthermore, Habermas legitimizes his critique not in terms of a Marxist theory of history but rather on the basis of a theory of rationality rooted in a theory of communication. In other words, he separates aspects of a left-wing critique of capitalism from Marxism's dialectical materialist theory of history.

Habermas' influence is also due to the fact that he defends politically the Enlightenment ideal of emancipation in a way that permits at the same time a radical criticism of the modern notion of instrumental rationality. He critiques modernity without rejecting it. In this manner, Habermas presents an intermediary position that lies between the political theories that accept the modern tradition, such as those of Nozick and Rawls, and the radical postmodern theories that try to reject modernism, such as those of Foucault and Derrida.

Another influential aspect of Habermas' project is that he argues for the compatibility of science and morality. He distinguishes between the natural sciences, the social sciences, and morality by attempting to show how each appeals to and requires a different kind of intersubjectively valid set of norms. In each case, he defends the norms in question.

Habermas is widely regarded as the leading German philosopher of today. There are two other factors that explain this. First, his theory is very wide ranging. For instance, it covers the relationship between the natural sciences, the social sciences, and morality, but it also is rooted in a theory of language. It is concerned with political ideology but also with psychology. Second, in keeping with the spirit of his own theory of communication, Habermas takes great care to respond to critics and to locate his views within a wider philosophical conversation.

Michel Foucault (1926–1984)

Biographical History

Born in Poitiers, France, Michel Foucault studied philosophy and psychology at the École Normale Supérieure, working for a time with Merleau-Ponty. Around 1948, he formed a friendship with the Marxist Louis Althusser, but one of his main sources of philosophical inspiration was Nietzsche. He wrote his master's thesis on Hegel, and completed his doctoral dissertation on madness in the classical period in 1960. Foucault was influenced by historians of culture and science, who stress that no idea can be understood outside of its historical context. When, in 1969, he was elected chair at the College de France, he chose the title 'Professor of the History of Systems of Thought.' During the 1970s, he was very active politically, helping to form a group to support prisoners and participating in protests on behalf of marginalized groups. In 1983, he took a post at the University of California, Berkeley, but died the following year of AIDS.

Philosophical Overview

One of the unifying themes of Foucault's diverse corpus is the aim of showing how concepts and practices that might be taken as necessities are in fact historically contingent. No idea can be understood outside of its historical context. Foucault applies this claim to the concept of human nature, which arose out of the historical conditions of the Enlightenment. This is why he says, 'Man is an invention of recent date. And perhaps one nearing its end.' The work of Foucault eschews universal generalizations, but rather seeks to study specific discourses and their limitations in their historical context. Indeed, he argues, through his historical studies, that there are no universals to human experience.

Early Works: Archeology

Foucault's early works included *Madness and Civilization* (1961), which was his doctoral dissertation, and *The Birth of a Clinic* (1963). In these influential works, Foucault documents the history of the way madness has been perceived in western culture. For example,

384 Section Seven / Hermeneutics and Post-modernism

madness was treated as an illness requiring confinement only after the creation of a centralizing state. In earlier periods, mad people were permitted to roam freely, and madness was not hidden; there was no real distinction between reason and unreason, as there is today. Foucault's study is a critical history of the origins of psychiatry and an account of the political circumstances that led to changes in our perception of madness.

One of the main philosophical ambitions of these early works is to reveal how the concept of madness, like claims to knowledge in general, are a function of political practices and concerns, within a established network of power, which is historically situated. Thereby, Foucault aims to undermine the rationalist and positivist idea of inquiry as a politically neutral search for universal truth and, at the same time, to uncover the power structures of society. However, this project does not constitute a rejection of the notion of truth. Rather, what passes as truth, and the relevant criteria for establishing truth, are never independent of both political forces and historical context.

In *The Order of Things* (1966) and *The Archeology of Knowledge* (1969), Foucault turns to the history of epistemology. In the first of these works, he studies the modern period, from roughly 1600 to 1800, with the aim of showing how discontinuities in the development of thought are caused when the structural *episteme* of a period is eclipsed and new ways of describing emerge suddenly. For example, at the end of the eighteenth century, in medicine, the language of anatomy replaced that of humors. An *episteme* is roughly the common and structural knowledge assumptions of a historical period. For example, the concept of the individual ('man') emerges in the Enlightenment, which makes possible the human sciences of the nineteenth century. These *epistemes* are to be revealed by a process that Foucault calls archeology. The idea of archeology, which requires digging out the unconscious rules that govern the knowledge claims of a period, should be contrasted with the phenomenological method, which requires returning to the nonstructuralist notion of the subject.

In *The Archeology of Knowledge*, Foucault aims to advance the idea of archeology by contrasting it with other approaches to the history of ideas. He does so with the notion of a discourse or discourse practice. Discourses are formed by the regularities within systems of speech and between such systems as well as historical practices, all of which are governed by certain formation rules that may be transformed historically. Examples of discourses are the religious discourse regarding sexual behavior that involves confession, the mercantile discourse on wealth and the clinical language of modern psychiatry.

Middle Period: Genealogy

During the 1970's, Foucault employs the wider Nietzschian concept of genealogy, rather than the less politically oriented notion of archeology. Genealogy involves revealing historically how knowledge claims are linked to centralizing power structures in a society. According to Foucault, this wider concept explains how the unconscious rules that govern a discourse come to be accepted. It makes the exercise of power more explicitly central to the historical study of systems of thought. The relationship between the exercise of power and knowledge becomes internal; Foucault argues, 'All knowledge claims presuppose and constitute power relations.' He examines the ways in which different forms of inquiry, as a means for producing truth, function, at the same time, as mechanisms for exercising power. Consider, for example, how measurement, investigation, examination, inquisition, rationality, and confession function as both.

It is important to note that Foucault tries to document power relations and the strategies for the exercise of power, rather than attempt to evaluate them. One group exercises power over another by modifying its 'field of possible actions.' The exercise of power is an inescapable feature of all societies, and, hence, liberation from all power relations is not an ideal. Furthermore, not all power relations are bad. The aim of genealogy is to reveal how power is exercised and to show how the techniques of power are particular to specific historical conditions that may change. The application of this new approach is shown in the work *Discipline and Punish* (1975), in which Foucault narrates the birth of the modern prison as an instrument of social control. This work inspired left-wing activism in France directed to the closing of maximum-security prisons.

Foucault claims that, during the nineteenth century, power relations became more intense as a result of industrialization and population growth. The result is an increase in the use of certain techniques for managing large groups of people, which Foucault calls 'normalization.' This technique involves describing and measuring people according to certain developmental norms and treating variation from the norms as deviancy, subject to the control of punishment.

Later Works: Techniques of the Self

Foucault's last works were two of the planned four volumes of the *History of Sexuality: The Use of Pleasure* and *The Care of the Self*. The first volume was published in 1976 and the second in 1984, the same month that he died of AIDS. Although Foucault studies how our understanding of sexuality changed with the political control of sexual relations, these later works also introduce two new dimensions to his thought. First, he examines how particular power techniques, such as training and discipline, can turn individuals into different kinds of subjects. Second, he observes the ways in which different techniques of the self enable individuals to reflect on and transform themselves, especially in relation to differing conceptions of the moral subject. Foucault conceives of ethics as the relationship of the self to the self within different kinds of moral life. For example, there are historically different conceptions of the goal of being an ethical person, of the ethical work required to reach that goal, and of the ways in which the self relates to moral obligations as modes of subjugation.

TRUTH AND POWER

This piece is an interview that Foucault gave with Alesandro Fontana and Pasquale Pasquino, which was published in 1980 in the book *Power and Knowledge*. First, Foucault describes the background to his work on criminality, which led him to isolate the notion of relations of power, which had emerged in his previous books *Madness and Civilization* and *The Order of Things*. He also describes how power can be exercised in institutions that normally fall outside the field of political analysis, such as mental and penal institutions and psychiatric methods. Foucault calls the required form of investigation 'genealogy' because it is a form of history that does not involve appeal to the subject. He also explains why the characterization of power as repressive is one-sided; it fails to show how relations of power can produce, for instance, pleasure, knowledge, and forms of discourse. Finally, Foucault discusses the role of the intellectual in political struggles, which leads him to examine the power relations that produce truth. Foucault claims that the political problems of intellectuals should be framed not in terms of 'science' and 'ideology' but rather 'truth' and 'power.'

Interviewers: Alessandro Fontana, Pasquale Pasquino

INTERVIEWERS: Could you briefly outline the route which led you from your work on madness in the Classical age to the study of criminality and delinquency? . . .

FOUCAULT: When I was studying during the early 1950s, one of the great problems that arose was that of the political status of science and the ideological functions which it could serve. . . .

These can all be summed up in two words: power and knowledge. I believe I wrote *Madness and Civilisation* to some extent within the horizon of these questions. For me, it was a matter of saying this: if, concerning a science like theoretical physics or organic chemistry, one poses the problem of its relations with the political and economic structures of society, isn't one posing an excessively complicated question? Doesn't this set the threshold of possible explanations impossibly high? But on the other hand, if one takes a form of knowledge (*savoir*) like psychiatry, won't the question be much easier to resolve, since the epistemological profile of psychiatry is a low one and psychiatric practice is linked with a whole range of institutions; economic requirements and political issues of social regulation? Couldn't the interweaving of effects of power and knowledge be grasped with greater certainty in the case of a science as 'dubious' as psychiatry? It was this same question which I wanted to pose concerning medicine in *The Birth of the Clinic:* medicine certainly has a much more solid scientific armature than psychiatry, but it too is profoundly enmeshed in social structures. What rather threw me at the time was the fact that the question I was posing totally failed to interest those to whom I addressed it. They regarded it as a problem which was politically unimportant and epistemologically vulgar.

INTERVIEWERS: . . . What do you think today about this concept of discontinuity, on the basis of which you have been all too rapidly and readily labelled as a 'structuralist' historian? . . .

FOUCAULT: This business about discontinuity has always rather bewildered me. In the new edition of the *Petit Larousse* it says: 'Foucault: a philosopher who founds his theory of history on discontinuity'. That leaves me flabbergasted. No doubt I didn't make myself sufficiently clear in *The Order of Things*, though I said a good deal there about this question. It seemed to me that in certain empirical forms of knowledge like biology, political economy, psychiatry, medicine etc., the rhythm of transformation doesn't follow the smooth, continuist schemas of development which are normally accepted. The great biological image of a progressive maturation of science still underpins a good many historical analyses; it does not seem to me to be pertinent to history. In a science like medicine, for example, up to the end of the eighteenth century one has a certain type of discourse whose gradual transformation, within a period of twenty-five or thirty years, broke not only with the 'true' propositions which it had hitherto been possible to formulate but also, more profoundly, with the ways of speaking and seeing, the whole ensemble of practices which served as supports for medical knowledge. These are not simply new discoveries, there is a whole new 'régime' in discourse and forms of knowledge. And all this happens in the space of a few years. This is something which is undeniable, once one has looked at the texts with sufficient attention. My problem was not at all to say, '*Voilà*, long live discontinuity, we are in the discontinuous and a good thing too', but to pose the question, 'How is it that at certain moments and in certain orders of knowledge, there are these sudden take-offs, these hastenings of evolution, these transformations which fail to correspond to the calm, continuist image that is normally accredited?' But the important thing here is not that such changes can be rapid and extensive, or rather it is that this extent and rapidity are only the sign of something else: a modification in the rules of formation of statements which are accepted as scientifically true. Thus it is not a change of content (refutation of old errors, recovery of old truths), nor is it a change of theoretical form (renewal of a paradigm, modification of systematic ensembles). It is a question of what *governs* statements, and the way in which they *govern* each other so as to constitute a set of propositions which are scientifically acceptable, and hence capable of being verified or falsified by scientific procedures. In short, there is a problem of the régime, the politics of the scientific statement. At this level it's not so much a matter of knowing what external power imposes itself on science, as of what effects of power circulate among scientific statements, what constitutes, as it were, their internal régime of power, and how and why at certain moments that régime undergoes a global modification.

It was these different régimes that I tried to identify and describe in *The Order of Things*, all the while making it clear that I wasn't trying for the moment to explain them, and that it would be necessary to try and do this in a subsequent work. But what was lacking here was this problem of the 'discursive régime', of the effects of power peculiar to the play of statements. I confused this too much with systematicity, theoretical form, or something like a paradigm. This same central problem of power, which at that time I had not yet properly isolated, emerges in two very different aspects at the point of junction of *Madness and Civilisation* and *The Order of Things*. . . .

INTERVIEWERS: This question of power that you have addressed to discourse naturally has particular effects and implications in relation to methodology and contemporary historical researches. Could you briefly situate within your work this question you have posed—if indeed it's true that you have posed it?

FOUCAULT: I don't think I was the first to pose the question. On the contrary, I'm struck by the difficulty I had in formulating it. When I think back now, I ask myself what else it was that I was talking about, in *Madness and Civilisation* or *The Birth of the Clinic*, but power? Yet I'm perfectly aware that I scarcely ever used the word and never had such a field of analyses at my disposal. I can say that this was an incapacity linked undoubtedly with the political situation we found ourselves in. It is hard to see where, either on the Right or the Left, this problem of power could then have been posed. On the Right, it was posed only in terms of constitution, sovereignty, etc., that is, in juridical terms; on the Marxist side, it was posed only in terms of the State apparatus. The way power was exercised—concretely and in detail—with its specificity, its techniques and tactics, was something that no one attempted to ascertain; they contented themselves with denouncing it in a polemical and global fashion as it existed among the 'others', in the adversary camp. Where Soviet socialist power was in question, its opponents called it totalitarianism; power in Western capitalism was denounced by the Marxists as class domination; but the mechanics of power in themselves were never analysed. This task could only begin after 1968, that is to say on the basis of daily struggles at grass roots level, among those whose fight was located in the fine meshes of the web of power. This was where the concrete nature of power became visible, along with the prospect that these analyses of power would prove fruitful in accounting for all that had hitherto remained outside the field of political analysis. To put it very simply, psychiatric internment, the mental normalisation of individuals, and penal institutions have no doubt a fairly limited importance if one is only looking for their economic significance. On the other hand, they are undoubtedly essential to the general functioning of the wheels of power. So long as the posing of the question of power was kept subordinate to the economic instance and the system of interests which this served, there was a tendency to regard these problems as of small importance.

INTERVIEWERS: So a certain kind of Marxism and a certain kind of phenomenology constituted an objective obstacle to the formulation of this problematic?

FOUCAULT: Yes, if you like, to the extent that it's true that, in our student days, people of my generation were brought up on these two forms of analysis, one in terms of the constituent subject, the other in terms of the economic in the last instance, ideology and the play of superstructures and infrastructures.

INTERVIEWERS: Still within this methodological context, how would you situate the genealogical approach? As a questioning of the conditions of possibility, modalities and constitution of the 'objects' and domains you have successively analysed, what makes it necessary?

FOUCAULT: I wanted to see how these problems of constitution could be resolved within a historical framework, instead of referring them back to a constituent object (madness, criminality or whatever). But this historical contextualisation needed to be something more than the simple relativisation of the phenomenological subject. I don't believe the problem can be solved by historicising the subject as posited by the phenomenologists, fabricating a subject that evolves through the course of history. One has to dispense with the constituent subject, to get rid of the subject itself, that's to say, to arrive at an analysis which can account for the constitution of the subject within a historical framework. And this is what I would call genealogy, that is, a form of history which can account for the constitution of knowledges, discourses, domains of objects etc., without having to make reference to a subject which is either transcendental in relation to the field of events or runs in its empty sameness throughout the course of history.

INTERVIEWERS: Marxist phenomenology and a certain kind of Marxism have clearly acted as a screen and an obstacle; there are two further concepts which continue today to act as a screen and an obstacle, ideology on the one hand and repression on the other. . . .

Could you perhaps use this occasion to specify more explicitly your thoughts on these matters?

FOUCAULT: The notion of ideology appears to me to be difficult to make use of, for three reasons. The first is that, like it or not, it always stands in virtual opposition to something else which is supposed to count as truth. Now I believe that the problem does not consist in drawing the line between that in a discourse which falls under the category of scientificity or truth, and that which comes under some other category, but in seeing historically how effects of truth are produced within discourses which in themselves are neither true nor false. The second drawback is that the concept of ideol-

ogy refers, I think necessarily, to something of the order of a subject. Thirdly, ideology stands in a secondary position relative to something which functions as its infrastructure, as its material, economic determinant, etc. For these three reasons, I think that this is a notion that cannot be used without circumspection.

The notion of repression is a more insidious one, or at all events I myself have had much more trouble in freeing myself of it, in so far as it does indeed appear to correspond so well with a whole range of phenomena which belong among the effects of power. When I wrote *Madness and Civilisation,* I made at least an implicit use of this notion of repression. I think indeed that I was positing the existence of a sort of living, voluble and anxious madness which the mechanisms of power and psychiatry were supposed to have come to repress and reduce to silence. But it seems to me now that the notion of repression is quite inadequate for capturing what is precisely the productive aspect of power. In defining the effects of power as repression, one adopts a purely juridical conception of such power, one identifies power with a law which says no, power is taken above all as carrying the force of a prohibition. Now I believe that this is a wholly negative, narrow, skeletal conception of power, one which has been curiously widespread. If power were never anything but repressive, if it never did anything but to say no, do you really think one would be brought to obey it? What makes power hold good, what makes it accepted, is simply the fact that it doesn't only weigh on us as a force that says no, but that it traverses and produces things, it induces pleasure, forms knowledge, produces discourse. It needs to be considered as a productive network which runs through the whole social body, much more than as a negative instance whose function is repression. In *Discipline and Punish* what I wanted to show was how, from the seventeenth and eighteenth centuries onwards, there was a veritable technological take-off in the productivity of power. Not only did the monarchies of the Classical period develop great state apparatuses (the army, the police and fiscal administration), but above all there was established at this period what one might call a new 'economy' of power, that is to say procedures which allowed the effects of power to circulate in a manner at once continuous, uninterrupted, adapted and 'individualised' throughout the entire social body. These new techniques are both much more efficient and much less wasteful (less costly economically, less risky in their results, less open to loopholes and resistances) than the techniques previously employed which were based on a mixture of more or less forced tolerances (from recognised privileges to endemic criminality) and costly ostentation (spectacular and discontinuous interventions of power, the most violent form of which was the 'exemplary', because exceptional, punishment).

INTERVIEWERS: Repression is a concept used above all in relation to sexuality. It was held that bourgeois society represses sexuality, stifles sexual desire, and so forth.

FOUCAULT: It is customary to say that bourgeois society repressed infantile sexuality to the point where it refused even to speak of it or acknowledge its existence. It was necessary to wait until Freud for the discovery at last to be made that children have a sexuality. Now if you read all the books on pedagogy and child medicine—all the manuals for parents that were published in the eighteenth century—you find that children's sex is spoken of constantly and in every possible context. One might argue that the purpose of these discourses was precisely to prevent children from having a sexuality. But their *effect* was to din it into parents' heads that their children's sex constituted a fundamental problem in terms of their parental educational responsibilities, and to din it into children's heads that their relationship with their own body and their own sex was to be a fundamental problem as far as *they* were concerned; and this had the consequence of sexually exciting the bodies of children while at the same time fixing the parental gaze and vigilance on the peril of infantile sexuality. The result was a sexualising of the infantile body, a sexualising of the bodily relationship between parent and child, a sexualising of the familial domain. 'Sexuality' is far more of a positive product of power than power was ever repression of sexuality. I believe that it is precisely these positive mechanisms that need to be investigated, and here

one must free oneself of the juridical schematism of all previous characterisations of the nature of power. Hence a historical problem arises, namely that of discovering why the West has insisted for so long on seeing the power it exercises as juridical and negative rather than as technical and positive.

I wonder if this isn't bound up with the institution of monarchy. This developed during the Middle Ages against the backdrop of the previously endemic struggles between feudal power agencies. The monarchy presented itself as a referee, a power capable of putting an end to war, violence and pillage and saying no to these struggles and private feuds. It made itself acceptable by allocating itself a juridical and negative function, albeit, one whose limits it naturally began at once to overstep. Sovereign, law and prohibition formed a system of representation of power which was extended during the subsequent era by the theories of right: political theory has never ceased to be obsessed with the person of the sovereign. Such theories still continue today to busy themselves with the problem of sovereignty. What we need, however, is a political philosophy that isn't erected around the problem of sovereignty, nor therefore around the problems of law and prohibition. We need to cut off the King's head: in political theory that has still to be done.

To pose the problem in terms of the State means to continue posing it in terms of sovereign and sovereignty, that is to say in terms of law. If one describes all these phenomena of power as dependant on the State apparatus, this means grasping them as essentially repressive: the Army as a power of death, police and justice as punitive instances, etc. I don't want to say that the State isn't important; what I want to say is that relations of power, and hence the analysis that must be made of them, necessarily extend beyond the limits of the State. In two senses: first of all because the State, for all the omnipotence of its apparatuses, is far from being able to occupy the whole field of actual power relations, and further because the State can only operate on the basis of other, already existing power relations. The State is superstructural in relation to a whole series of power networks that invest the body, sexuality, the family, kinship, knowledge, technology and so forth.

INTERVIEWERS: Even if you are only perhaps at the beginning of your researches here, could you say how you see the nature of the relationships (if any) which are engendered between these different bodies: the molar body of the population and the micro-bodies of individuals? . . .

FOUCAULT: I believe one must keep in view the fact that along with all the fundamental technical inventions and discoveries of the seventeenth and eighteenth centuries, a new technology of the exercise of power also emerged which was probably even more important than the constitutional reforms and new forms of government established at the end of the eighteenth century. In the camp of the Left, one often hears people saying that power is that which abstracts, which negates the body, represses, suppresses, and so forth. I would say instead that what I find most striking about these new technologies of power introduced since the seventeenth and eighteenth centuries is their concrete and precise character, their grasp of a multiple and differentiated reality. In feudal societies power functioned essentially through signs and levies. Signs of loyalty to the feudal lords, rituals, ceremonies and so forth, and levies in the form of taxes, pillage, hunting, war etc. In the seventeenth and eighteenth centuries a form of power comes into being that begins to exercise itself through social production and social service. It becomes a matter of obtaining productive service from individuals in their concrete lives. And in consequence, a real and effective 'incorporation' of power was necessary, in the sense that power had to be able to gain access to the bodies of individuals, to their acts, attitudes and modes of everyday behaviour. Hence the significance of methods like school discipline, which succeeded in making children's bodies the object of highly complex systems of manipulation and conditioning. But at the same time, these new techniques of power needed to grapple with the phenomena of population, in short to undertake the administration, control and direction of the accumulation of men (the economic system that promotes the accumulation of capital and the system of power that ordains the accumulation of men are, from the seventeenth century on, correlated and inseparable phenomena): hence there arise the problems of demography, public health, hygiene, housing conditions, longevity and fertility. And I believe that the political significance of the problem of sex is due to the fact that sex is located at the point of intersection of the discipline of the body and the control of the population.

INTERVIEWERS: Finally, a question you have been asked before: the work you do, these preoccupations of yours, the results you arrive at, what use can one finally make of all this in everyday political struggles? . . . What does this imply about the role of intellectuals?

FOUCAULT: For a long period, the 'left' intellectual spoke and was acknowledged the right of speaking in the capacity of master of truth and justice.[1] He was heard, or purported to make himself heard, as the spokesman of the universal. To be an intellectual meant something like being the consciousness/conscience of us all. I think we have here an idea transposed from Marxism, from a faded Marxism indeed. Just as the proletariat, by the necessity of its historical situation, is the bearer of the universal (but its immediate, unreflected bearer, barely conscious of itself as such), so the intellectual, through his moral, theoretical and political choice, aspires to be the bearer of this universality in its conscious, elaborated form. The intellectual is thus taken as the clear, individual figure of a universality whose obscure, collective form is embodied in the proletariat.

Some years have now passed since the intellectual was called upon to play this role. A new mode of the 'connection between theory and practice' has been established. Intellectuals have got used to working, not in the modality of the 'universal', the 'exemplary', the 'just-and-true-for-all', but within specific sectors, at the precise points where their own conditions of life or work situate them (housing, the hospital, the asylum, the laboratory, the university, family and sexual relations). This has undoubtedly given them a much more immediate and concrete awareness of struggles. And they have met here with problems which are specific, 'non-universal', and often different from those of the proletariat or the masses. And yet I believe intellectuals have actually been drawn closer to the proletariat and the masses, for two reasons. Firstly, because it has been a question of real, material, everyday struggles, and secondly because they have often been confronted, albeit in a different form, by the same adversary as the proletariat, namely the multinational corporations, the judicial and police apparatuses, the property speculators, etc. This is what I would call the 'specific' intellectual as opposed to the 'universal' intellectual.

This new configuration has a further political significance. It makes it possible, if not to integrate, at least to rearticulate categories which were previously kept separate. The intellectual *par excellence* used to be the writer: as a universal consciousness, a free subject, he was counter-posed to those intellectuals who were merely *competent instances* in the service of the State or Capital—technicians, magistrates, teachers.

Magistrates and psychiatrists, doctors and social workers, laboratory technicians and sociologists have become able to participate, both within their own fields and through mutual exchange and support, in a global process of politicisation of intellectuals. This process explains how, even as the writer tends to disappear as a figurehead, the university and the academic emerge, if not as principal elements, at least as 'exchangers', privileged points of intersection. If the universities and education have become politically ultrasensitive areas, this is no doubt the reason why. And what is called the crisis of the universities should not be interpreted as a loss of power, but on the contrary as a multiplication and re-inforcement of their power-effects as centres in a polymorphous ensemble of intellectuals who virtually all pass through and relate themselves to the academic system.

It is possible to suppose that the 'universal' intellectual, as he functioned in the nineteenth and early twentieth centuries was in fact derived from a quite specific historical figure: the man of justice, the man of law, who counterposes to power, despotism and the abuses and arrogance of wealth the universality of justice and the equity of an ideal law. The great political struggles of the eighteenth century were fought over law, right, the constitution, the just in reason and law, that which can and must apply universally. What we call today 'the intellectual' (I mean the intellectual in the political, not the sociological sense of the word, in

other words the person who utilises his knowledge, his competence and his relation to truth in the field of political struggles) was, I think, an offspring of the jurist, or at any rate of the man who invoked the universality of a just law, if necessary against the legal professions themselves (Voltaire, in France, is the prototype of such intellectuals). The 'universal' intellectual derives from the jurist or notable, and finds his fullest manifestation in the writer, the bearer of values and significations in which all can recognise themselves. The 'specific' intellectual derives from quite another figure, not the jurist or notable, but the savant or expert.

It seems to me that we are now at a point where the function of the specific intellectual needs to be reconsidered. Reconsidered but not abandoned, despite the nostalgia of some for the great 'universal' intellectuals and the desire for a new philosophy, a new world-view. Suffice it to consider the important results which have been achieved in psychiatry: they prove that these local, specific struggles haven't been a mistake and haven't led to a dead end. One may even say that the role of the specific intellectual must become more and more important in proportion to the political responsibilities which he is obliged willy-nilly to accept, as a nuclear scientist, computer expert, pharmacologist, etc. It would be a dangerous error to discount him politically in his specific relation to a local form of power, either on the grounds that this is a specialist matter which doesn't concern the masses (which is doubly wrong: they are already aware of it, and in any case implicated in it), or that the specific intellectual serves the interests of State or Capital (which is true, but at the same time shows the strategic position he occupies), or, again, on the grounds that he propagates a scientific ideology (which isn't always true, and is anyway certainly a secondary matter compared with the fundamental point: the effects proper to true discourses).

The important thing here, I believe, is that truth isn't outside power, or lacking in power: contrary to a myth whose history and functions would repay further study, truth isn't the reward of free spirits, the child of protracted solitude, nor the privilege of those who have succeeded in liberating themselves. Truth is a thing of this world: it is produced only by virtue of multiple forms of constraint. And it induces regular effects of power. Each society has its régime of truth, its 'general politics' of truth: that is, the types of discourse which it accepts and makes function as true; the mechanisms and instances which enable one to distinguish true and false statements, the means by which each is sanctioned; the techniques and procedures accorded value in the acquisition of truth; the status of those who are charged with saying what counts as true.

In societies like ours, the 'political economy' of truth is characterised by five important traits. 'Truth' is centred on the form of scientific discourse and the institutions which produce it; it is subject to constant economic and political incitement (the demand for truth, as much for economic production as for political power); it is the object, under diverse forms, of immense diffusion and consumption (circulating through apparatuses of education and information whose extent is relatively broad in the social body, not withstanding certain strict limitations); it is produced and transmitted under the control, dominant if not exclusive, of a few great political and economic apparatuses (university, army, writing, media); lastly, it is the issue of a whole political debate and social confrontation ('ideological' struggles).

It seems to me that what must now be taken into account in the intellectual is not the 'bearer of universal values'. Rather, it's the person occupying a specific position—but whose specificity is linked, in a society like ours, to the general functioning of an apparatus of truth. In other words, the intellectual has a three-fold specificity: that of his class position (whether as petty-bourgeois in the service of capitalism or 'organic' intellectual of the proletariat); that of his conditions of life and work, linked to his condition as an intellectual (his field of research, his place in a laboratory, the political and economic demands to which he submits or against which he rebels, in the university, the hospital, etc.); lastly, the specificity of the politics of truth in our societies. And it's with this last factor that his position can take on a general significance and that his local, specific struggle can

have effects and implications which are not simply professional or sectoral. The intellectual can operate and struggle at the general level of that régime of truth which is so essential to the structure and functioning of our society. There is a battle 'for truth', or at least 'around truth'—it being understood once again that by truth I do not mean 'the ensemble of truths which are to be discovered and accepted', but rather 'the ensemble of rules according to which the true and the false are separated and specific effects of power attached to the true', it being understood also that it's not a matter of a battle 'on behalf' of the truth, but of a battle about the status of truth and the economic and political role it plays. It is necessary to think of the political problems of intellectuals not in terms of 'science' and 'ideology', but in terms of 'truth' and 'power'. And thus the question of the professionalisation of intellectuals and the division between intellectual and manual labour can be envisaged in a new way.

All this must seem very confused and uncertain. Uncertain indeed, and what I am saying here is above all to be taken as a hypothesis. In order for it to be a little less confused, however, I would like to put forward a few 'propositions'—not firm assertions, but simply suggestions to be further tested and evaluated.

'Truth' is to be understood as a system of ordered procedures for the production, regulation, distribution, circulation and operation of statements.

'Truth' is linked in a circular relation with systems of power which produce and sustain it, and to effects of power which it induces and which extend it. A 'régime' of truth.

This régime is not merely ideological or superstructural; it was a condition of the formation and development of capitalism. And it's this same régime which, subject to certain modifications, operates in the socialist countries (I leave open here the question of China, about which I know little).

The essential political problem for the intellectual is not to criticise the ideological contents supposedly linked to science, or to ensure that his own scientific practice is accompanied by a correct ideology, but that of ascertaining the possibility of constituting a new politics of truth. The problem is not changing people's consciousnesses—or what's in their heads—but the political, economic, institutional régime of the production of truth.

It's not a matter of emancipating truth from every system of power (which would be a chimera, for truth is already power) but of detaching the power of truth from the forms of hegemony, social, economic and cultural, within which it operates at the present time.

The political question, to sum up, is not error, illusion, alienated consciousness or ideology; it is truth itself. Hence the importance of Nietzsche.

STUDY QUESTIONS: FOUCAULT, *TRUTH AND POWER*

1. How are power and knowledge related, according to Foucault? How was this important to his own development?
2. What is the nineteenth-century sense of the term 'science,' and how has it changed in the twentieth century, according to Foucault?
3. What role does the concept of 'discontinuity' play, in his view?
4. What is his view of Marx and 'Marxist phenomenology'?
5. What does 'historicising the subject' mean and involve? What is the subject?
6. What is his view of human sexuality? How does it relate to philosophy? What role does it play in his overall view?
7. How are repression and sexuality related?
8. How, in his view, are power and sexuality related?
9. What is his view of war?
10. How does he view school discipline?
11. What does he mean by the 'political economy' of truth?
12. What is the 'politics' of truth?
13. Why does Foucault think that Nietzsche is so important?

TECHNOLOGIES OF THE SELF

In this work, Foucault explains his concept of the technologies of the self, which are means of changing or transforming oneself with or without the help of others for the sake of achieving some goal such as happiness or perfection. He examines various Stoic technologies of the self, such as self-examination, remembering, and the interpretation of dreams. These he compares to various early Christian techniques, such as confession, obedience, and contemplation.

I

Technologies of the Self

When I began to study the rules, duties, and prohibitions of sexuality, the interdictions and restrictions associated with it, I was concerned not simply with the acts that were permitted and forbidden but with the feelings represented, the thoughts, the desires one might experience, the inclination to seek within the self any hidden feeling, any movement of the soul, any desire disguised under illusory forms. There is a very significant difference between interdictions

From "Technologies of the Self" from *Ethics, Subjectivity and Truth* by Michel Foucault, edited by Paul Rabinow, 1997.

about sexuality and other forms of interdiction. Unlike other interdictions, sexual interdictions are constantly connected with the obligation to tell the truth about oneself.

Two facts may be raised against me: first, that confession played an important part in penal and religious institutions for all offenses, not only in sex. But the task of analyzing one's sexual desire is always more important than analyzing any other kind of sin.

I am also aware of the second objection: that sexual behavior more than any other was submitted to very strict rules of secrecy, decency, and modesty so that sexuality is related in a strange and complex way both to verbal prohibition and to the obligation to tell the truth, of hiding what one does and of deciphering who one is.

The association of a prohibition and a strong injunction to speak is a constant feature of our culture. The theme of the renunciation of the flesh was linked to the confession of the monk to the abbot, to the monk confiding to the abbot everything that was on his mind.

I conceived of a rather odd project: not the study of the evolution of sexual behavior but of the historical study of the link between the obligation to tell the truth and the prohibitions weighing on sexuality. I asked: How had the subject been compelled to decipher himself in regard to what was forbidden? It is a question that interrogates the relation between asceticism and truth.

Max Weber posed the question: If one wants to behave rationally and regulate one's action according to true principles, what part of one's self should one renounce? What is the ascetic price of reason? To what kind of asceticism should one submit? I posed the opposite question: How have certain kinds of interdictions required the price of certain kinds of knowledge about oneself? What must one know about oneself in order to be willing to renounce anything?

Thus, I arrived at the hermeneutics of technologies of the self in pagan and early Christian practice. I encountered certain difficulties in this study because these practices are not well known. First, Christianity has always been more interested in the history of its beliefs than in the history of real practices. Second, such a hermeneutics was never organized into a body of doctrine like textual hermeneutics. Third, the

hermeneutics of the self has been confused with theologies of the soul—concupiscence, sin, and the fall from grace. Fourth, a hermeneutics of the self has been diffused across Western culture through numerous channels and integrated with various types of attitudes and experience, so that it is difficult to isolate and separate it from our own spontaneous experiences.

Context of Study

My objective for more than twenty-five years has been to sketch out a history of the different ways in our culture that humans develop knowledge about themselves: economics, biology, psychiatry, medicine, and penology. The main point is not to accept this knowledge at face value but to analyze these so-called sciences as very specific "truth games" related to specific techniques that human beings use to understand themselves.

As a context, we must understand that there are four major types of these "technologies," each a matrix of practical reason: (1) technologies of production, which permit us to produce, transform, or manipulate things; (2) technologies of sign systems, which permit us to use signs, meanings, symbols, or signification; (3) technologies of power, which determine the conduct of individuals and submit them to certain ends or domination, an objectivizing of the subject; (4) technologies of the self, which permit individuals to effect by their own means, or with the help of others, a certain number of operations on their own bodies and souls, thoughts, conduct, and way of being, so as to transform themselves in order to attain a certain state of happiness, purity, wisdom, perfection, or immortality.

These four types of technologies hardly ever function separately, although each one of them is associated with a certain type of domination. Each implies certain modes of training and modification of individuals, not only in the obvious sense of acquiring certain skills but also in the sense of acquiring certain attitudes. I wanted to show both their specific nature and their constant interaction. For instance, the relation between manipulating things and domination appears clearly in Karl Marx's *Capital*, where every technique of production requires modification of individual conduct—not only skills but also attitudes.

Usually, the first two technologies are used in the study of the sciences and linguistics. It is the last two, the technologies of domination and self, which have most kept my attention. I have attempted a history of the organization of knowledge with respect to both domination and the self. For example, I studied madness not in terms of the criteria of formal sciences but to show what type of management of individuals inside and outside of asylums was made possible by this strange discourse. This encounter between the technologies of domination of others and those of the self I call "governmentality."

Perhaps I've insisted too much on the technology of domination and power. I am more and more interested in the interaction between oneself and others, and in the technologies of individual domination, in the mode of action that an individual exercises upon himself by means of the technologies of the self.

The Development of Technologies of the Self

I wish to sketch out the evolution of the hermeneutics of the self in two different contexts that are historically contiguous: (1) Greco-Roman philosophy in the first two centuries A.D. of the early Roman Empire, and (2) Christian spirituality and the monastic principles developed in the fourth and fifth centuries of the late Roman Empire.

Moreover, I wish to take up the subject not only in theory but in relation to a set of practices in late antiquity. Among the Greeks, these practices took the form of a precept: *epimeleisthai sautou*, "to take care of yourself," to take "care of the self," "to be concerned, to take care of yourself."

The precept of the "care of the self" [*souci de soi*] was, for the Greeks, one of the main principles of cities, one of the main rules for social and personal conduct and for the art of life. For us now, this notion is rather obscure and faded. When one is asked "What is the most important moral principle in ancient philosophy?" the immediate answer is not "Take care of oneself" but the Delphic principle, *gnōthi seauton* ("Know yourself").

Without doubt, our philosophical tradition has overemphasized the latter and forgotten the former. The Delphic principle was not an abstract one concerning life; it was technical advice, a rule to be observed for the consultation of the oracle. "Know yourself" meant "Do not suppose yourself to be a god." Other commentators suggest that it meant "Be aware of what you really ask when you come to consult the oracle."

In Greek and Roman texts, the injunction of having to know oneself was always associated with the other principle of the care of the self, and it was that need to care for oneself that brought the Delphic maxim into operation. It is implicit in all Greek and Roman culture and has been explicit since Plato's *Alcibiades I*.

Summary

There are several reasons why "Know yourself" has obscured "Take care of yourself." First, there has been a profound transformation in the moral principles of Western society. We find it difficult to base rigorous morality and austere principles on the precept that we should give more care to ourselves than to anything else in the world. We are more inclined to see taking care of ourselves as an immorality, as a means of escape from all possible rules. We inherit the tradition of Christian morality which makes self-renunciation the condition for salvation. To know oneself was, paradoxically, a means of self-renunciation.

We also inherit a secular tradition that sees in external law the basis for morality. How then can respect for the self be the basis for morality? We are the inheritors of a social morality that seeks the rules for acceptable behavior in relations with others. Since the sixteenth century, criticism of established morality has been undertaken in the name of the importance of recognizing and knowing the self. Therefore, it is difficult to see the care of the self as compatible with morality. "Know thyself" has obscured "Take care of yourself" because our morality, a morality of asceticism, insists that the self is that which one can reject.

The second reason is that, in theoretical philosophy from Descartes to Husserl, knowledge of the self (the thinking subject) takes on an ever-increasing importance as the first step in the theory of knowledge.

To summarize: There has been an inversion in the hierarchy of the two principles of antiquity, "Take care of yourself" and "Know yourself." In Greco-Roman culture, knowledge of oneself appeared as the consequence of the care of the self. In the modern world, knowledge of oneself constitutes the fundamental principle.

III

In my discussion of Plato's *Alcibiades*, I have isolated three major themes: (1) the relation between care of the self and care for the political life; (2) the relation between the care of the self and defective education; and (3) the relation between the care of the self and knowing oneself. Whereas we saw in the *Alcibiades* the close relation between "Take care of yourself" and "Know yourself," taking care of yourself eventually was absorbed in knowing yourself.

We can see these three themes in Plato, also in the Hellenistic period, and four to five centuries later in Seneca, Plutarch, Epictetus, and the like. If the problems are the same, the solutions and themes are quite different and, in some cases, the opposite of the Platonic meanings.

First, to be concerned with self in the Hellenistic and Roman periods is not exclusively a preparation for political life. Care of the self has become a universal principle. One must leave politics to take better care of the self.

Second, the concern with oneself is not just obligatory for young people concerned with their education; it is a way of living for everybody throughout their lives.

Third, even if self-knowledge plays an important role in the care of the self, it involves other relationships as well.

IV

I have spoken of three Stoic technologies of the self: letters to friends and disclosure of self; examination of self and conscience, including a review of what was done, of what should have been done, and comparison of the two. Now I want to consider the third Stoic technique, *askēsis*, not a disclosure of the secret self but a remembering.

For Plato, one must discover the truth that is within one. For the Stoics, truth is not in oneself but in the *logoi*, the teachings of the masters. One memorizes what one has heard, converting the statement one hears into rules of conduct. The subjectivation of truth is the aim of these techniques. During the imperial period, one could not assimilate ethical principles without a theoretical framework such as science, as for example in Lucretius's *De Rerum natura*. There are structural questions underlying the practice of the examination of the self every night. I want to underscore the fact that in Stoicism it is not the deciphering of the self, not the means to disclose secrecy, which is important; it is the memory of what one has done and what one has had to do.

In Christianity, asceticism always refers to a certain renunciation of the self and of reality because most of the time the self is a part of that reality that must be renounced in order to gain access to another level of reality. This move to attain the renunciation of the self distinguishes Christian asceticism.

In the philosophical tradition inaugurated by Stoicism, *askēsis* means not renunciation but the progressive consideration of self, or mastery over oneself, obtained not through the renunciation of reality but through the acquisition and assimilation of truth. It has as its final aim not preparation for another reality but access to the reality of this world. The Greek word for this is *paraskeuazō* ("to get prepared"). It is a set of practices by which one can acquire, assimilate, and transform truth into a permanent principle of action. *Alētheia* becomes *ēthos*. It is a process of the intensification of subjectivity.

What are the principal features of *askēsis*? They include exercises in which the subject puts himself in a situation in which he can verify whether he can confront events and use the discourses with which he is armed. It is a question of testing the preparation. Is this truth assimilated enough to become ethics so that we can behave as we must when an event presents itself?

In addition to letters, examination, and *askēsis*, we must now evoke a fourth technique in the examination of the self, the interpretation of dreams. It was to have an important destiny in the nineteenth century, but it occupied a relatively marginal position in the ancient world. Philosophers had an ambivalent attitude toward the interpretation of dreams. Most Stoics are critical and skeptical about such interpretation; but there is still the popular and general practice of it. There were experts who were able to interpret dreams, including Pythagoras and some of the Stoics, and some experts who wrote books to teach people to interpret their own dreams. There were huge amounts of literature on how to do it, but the only surviving dream manual is *The Interpretation of Dreams* by Artemidorus (second century A.D.). Dream interpretation was important because, in antiquity, the meaning of a dream was an announcement of a future event.

V

I wish to examine the scheme of one of the main techniques of the self in early Christianity and what it was as a truth game. To do so, I must look at the transition from pagan to Christian culture, in which it is possible to see clear-cut continuities and discontinuities.

Christianity belongs to the salvation religions. It is one of those religions which is supposed to lead the individual from one reality to another, from death to life, from time to eternity. In order to achieve that, Christianity imposed a set of conditions and rules of behavior for a certain transformation of the self.

Christianity is not only a salvation religion, it is a confessional religion; it imposes very strict obligations of truth, dogma, and canon, more so than do the pagan religions. Truth obligations to believe this or that were and are still very numerous. The duty to accept a set of obligations, to hold certain books as permanent truth, to accept authoritarian decisions in matters of truth, not only to believe certain things but to show that one believes, and to accept institutional authority are all characteristic of Christianity.

Christianity requires another form of truth obligation different from faith. Each person has the duty to know who he is, that is, to try to know what is happening inside him, to acknowledge faults, to recognize temptations, to locate desires; and everyone is obliged to disclose these things either to God or to others in the community and, hence, to bear public or private witness against oneself. The truth obligations of faith and the self are linked together. This link permits a purification of the soul impossible without self-knowledge.

The difference between the Stoic and Christian traditions is that in the Stoic tradition examination of self, judgment, and discipline show the way to self-knowledge by superimposing truth about self through memory, that is, by memorizing the rules. In exomologesis, the penitent superimposes truth about self by violent rupture and dissociation. It is important to emphasize that this exomologesis is not verbal. It is symbolic, ritual, and theatrical.

VI

During the fourth century, we find a very different technology for the disclosure of the self, *exagoreusis*, much less famous than exomologesis but more important. This one is reminiscent of the verbalizing exercises in relation to a teacher-master of the pagan philosophical schools. We can see the transfer of several Stoic techniques of the self to Christian spiritual techniques.

At least one example of self-examination, proposed by Chrysostom, was exactly the same form and the same administrative character as that described by Seneca in *De Ira*. In the morning, we must take account of our expenses, and in the evening we must ask ourselves to render account of our conduct of ourselves, to examine what is to our advantage and what is prejudicial against us, with prayers instead of indiscreet words. That is exactly the Senecan style of self-examination. It is also important to note that this self-examination is rare in Christian literature.

The well-developed and elaborated practice of the self-examination in monastic Christianity is different from the Senecan self-examination and very different from Chrysostom and from exomologesis. This new kind of practice must be understood from the viewpoint of two principles of Christian spirituality: obedience and contemplation.

In Seneca, the relationship of the disciple with the master was important, but it was instrumental and professional. It was founded on the capacity of the master to lead the disciple to a happy and autonomous life through good advice. The relationship would end when the disciple gained access to that life.

For a long series of reasons, obedience has a very different character in monastic life. It differs from the Greco-Roman type of relation to the master in the sense that obedience is not based just upon a need for self-improvement but must bear on all aspects of a monk's life. There is no element in the life of the monk which may escape from this fundamental and permanent relation of total obedience to the master. Cassian repeats an old principle from the oriental tradition: "Everything the monk does without permission of his master constitutes a theft." Here, obedience is complete control of behavior by the master, not a final autonomous state. It is a sacrifice of the self, of the subject's own will. This is the new technology of the self.

The monk must have the permission of his director to do anything, even die. Everything he does without permission is stealing; there is not a single moment when the monk can be autonomous. Even when he becomes a director himself, he must retain the spirit of obedience. He must keep the spirit of obedience as a permanent sacrifice of the complete control of behavior by the master. The self must constitute itself through obedience.

The second feature of monastic life is that contemplation is considered the supreme good. It is the obligation of the monk to turn his thoughts continuously to that point which is God and to make sure that his heart is pure enough to see God. The goal is permanent contemplation of God.

This new technology of the self, which developed from obedience and contemplation in the monastery, presents some peculiar characteristics. Cassian gives a rather clear exposition of this technology of the self, a principle of self-examination which he borrowed from the Syrian and Egyptian monastic traditions.

The scrutiny of conscience consists of trying to immobilize consciousness, to eliminate movements of the spirit which divert one from God. That means we must examine any thought that presents itself to consciousness to see the relation between act and thought, truth and reality, to see if there is anything in this thought which will move our spirit, provoke our desire, turn our spirit away from God. The scrutiny is based on the idea of a secret concupiscence.

There are three major types of self-examination: (1) self-examination with respect to thoughts in correspondence to reality (Cartesian); (2) self-examination

with respect to the way our thoughts relate to rules (Senecan); (3) the examination of self with respect to the relation between the hidden thought and an inner impurity. At this moment begins the Christian hermeneutics of the self with its deciphering of inner thoughts. It implies that there is something hidden in ourselves and that we are always in a self-illusion that hides the secret.

In conclusion, in the Christianity of the first centuries, there are two main forms of disclosing self, of showing the truth about oneself. The first is exomologesis, or a dramatic expression of the situation of the penitent as sinner which makes manifest his status as sinner. The second is what was called in the spiritual literature exagoreusis. This is an analytical and continual verbalization of thoughts carried on in the relation of complete obedience to someone else; this relation is modeled on the renunciation of one's own will and of one's own self.

There is a great difference between exomologesis and exagoreusis; yet we have to underscore the fact that there is one important element in common: you cannot disclose without renouncing. In exomologesis, the sinner must "kill" himself through ascetic macerations. Whether through martyrdom or through obedience to a master, disclosure of self is the renunciation of one's own self. In exagoreusis, on the other hand, you show that, in permanently verbalizing your thoughts and permanently obeying the master, you are renouncing your will and yourself. This practice continues from the beginning of Christianity to the seventeenth century. The inauguration of penance in the thirteenth century is an important step in its rise.

This theme of self-renunciation is very important. Throughout Christianity there is a correlation between disclosure of the self, dramatic or verbalized, and the renunciation of self. My hypothesis, from looking at these two techniques, is that it is the second one, verbalization, that becomes the more important. From the eighteenth century to the present, the techniques of verbalization have been reinserted in a different context by the so-called human sciences in order to use them without renunciation of the self but to constitute, positively, a new self. To use these techniques without renouncing oneself constitutes a decisive break.

STUDY QUESTIONS: FOUCAULT, *TECHNOLOGIES OF THE SELF*

1. How did Foucault arrive at the question of the hermeneutics of the technologies of the self in pagan and early Christian practice?
2. What are the four major types of technologies?
3. According to Foucault, what are the two most important principles in ancient philosophy? Which one is usually emphasized? Which one would Foucault stress, and why?
4. According to Foucault, what are the three Stoic technologies of the self?
5. What is the main Stoic technique for mastery over oneself?
6. What are the main differences and discontinuities between the Stoic and early Christian technologies of the self?
7. What are the main characteristics of monastic life?
8. What are 'exomologesis' and 'exagoreusis'?

Philosophical Bridges: Foucault's Influence

In their different ways, Foucault and Derrida have contributed much to the attempt to usher the postmodern age into philosophy. In this regard, Foucault's writings have had an important influence on contemporary thought in at least four ways. First, his work on knowledge and power has drawn attention to the way knowledge claims can reflect power relations. He examines how claims to knowledge reveal the centralizing power structures in a society and how different forms of inquiry function as mechanisms for exercising power. Other writers have extended this overall approach in order to reveal how social practices oppress and marginalize minority groups.

Second, Foucault challenges the ideas that current philosophical theories present ahistorical necessities and that they can operate in a historical vacuum. This challenge has influenced the philosophical climate. Many thinkers are more aware of the way in which their own theories are historically and culturally located and contingent. There is also perhaps greater suspicion of grand political theories, such as Marxism, conservatism, and liberalism. Foucault himself eschews such theories for the more modest task of documenting how power relations function in particular historical contexts.

Third, in general, as a result of his work, many philosophers are more historically conscious in the sense that they would accept that understanding a theory requires one to see how it functioned in the social context of the time. Furthermore, Foucault's rejection of the Enlightenment notion of a universal history, a single narrative that describes the cultural development of humankind, has encouraged philosophers to look at the specifics of each period.

Fourth, because of the above points, Foucault's work has been seen as presenting a forceful challenge to the idea of the objectivity of knowledge, where 'objectivity' means roughly independent of any cultural and historical perspective. Furthermore, it has undermined the idea that inquiry can be a politically neutral and value-free search for universal truth. In this way, Foucault has been regarded as a figurehead for the view that the notion of objectivity should be replaced by the idea of an irreducible variety of perspectives within changing social systems, with no overarching single perspective that encompasses and explains this multitude.

In general, following Foucault, postmodern thinkers tend to regard with suspicion general theories that lay a claim to universal truth, and instead emphasize the historical nature of particular claims and their changing relation to the social context. In this regard, Foucault's influence extends beyond philosophy. His general approach to the nature of understanding has impacted political theorists and sociologists.

JACQUES DERRIDA (1930–)

Biographical History

Born in Algeria, Jacques Derrida became interested in philosophy through reading Sartre. In 1949, he went to the École Normale Supérieure, where he became interested in Husserl and, later, structuralism and the work of Foucault. His thesis and first book was on Husserl's geometry (1962). In 1967, Derrida published three major works: *Of Grammatology*, *Writing and Difference*, and *Speech and Phenomena*. These form the basis for a subsequent huge output. He has written over 40 books, which include *Dissemination*, *Margins of Philosophy*, and *Positions*, which were published in 1972. His other works include *The Post Card*, *Writing and Difference*, *Glas*, *The Truth in Painting*, *Spurs*, and *Memoirs of the Blind*. Derrida's deconstructivist approach has become popular as a style of literary criticism partly because of the influence of the American literary theorist Paul de Man.

Philosophical Overview

The Metaphysics of Presence

According to Derrida, the history of western philosophy is dominated by the metaphysics of presence, which understands being as a presence, such as the Empiricist idea of sense data, a given in experience that is supposed to legitimize claims to truth. By deconstructing such a metaphysic, one reveals how it is built using supposedly fundamental distinctions that are really problematic constructs open to question. In this way, deconstruction attempts to show how the metaphysics of presence lacks the ultimate grounds that it seeks, such as a priori concepts and sense data.

Derrida claims that such metaphysical systems employ binary, oppositional structures, such as mind/body, true/false, presence/absence, male/female, reason/emotion, literal/metaphorical, sign/signifier, rational/irrational, and theory/practice. Such structures are dogmatically and violently hierarchical because they always assume that one of the pair is dominant. For instance, meaning is prior to its linguistic expression, and literal meaning is superior to metaphor. In part, deconstruction is a way of revealing, disturbing, and undermining such violent binaries.

Writing and Speech

One of the binaries that Derrida first deconstructed is that of speech and writing. The western tradition privileges speech over writing, which is considered merely as a mechanical extension of speech. Writing is considered as a graphic signifier of speech, which is itself a phonic signifier of an idealized signified. Derrida questions this oppositional privileging, which carries with it a host of other positions regarding, for instance, truth, sexual difference, and death. For example, the western tradition is suspicious of writing because texts invite repeatedly different readings that cannot be paternally corrected by the author. Texts cannot control their reading. Furthermore, speech encourages the idea that language has a single meaning, given to it by the speaker of an utterance. This is why thinking is usually conceived of as a form of inner speech. In this way, privileging speech over writing reinforces the metaphysics of presence. For this reason, Derrida focuses on texts rather than spoken discourse, in sharp contrast to, for example, Habermas.

Derrida rejects logocentricism, the claim that interpretation will tend to converge on a single reading or meaning of a text that simply waits to be discovered. This does not mean that all readings are equally valuable. Nor does it imply abandoning the idea that readings of a text require evidence, but it does mean that no single reading can claim to be exhaustive. Texts do not read themselves, and there can be no single official interpretation of a text, for example, the one that coincides with the author's intentions, which in any case can be identified only by reading the text.

Deconstruction

Derrida puts these ideas into practice through deconstruction, which is the process of reading a text in a way that involves highlighting those aspects of it that contradict its dominant readings. However, Derrida does not claim to deconstruct texts actively; rather, he reveals or discloses the metaphysics of presence and opposition that is inevitably part of any text. Deconstruction is not demolition. The process of deconstruction involves carefully picking out the blind spots of a text that reveal its shadow texts or subtexts, which dislocate its dominant reading by undoing the oppositional hierarchies that it depends on. What does this undoing consist in? Sometimes, in showing how the hierarchy is reversed within the text itself, thereby revealing its hidden contradictions and, sometimes, in showing how the relevant binaries can become blurred and nuanced. Sometimes, it consists in showing how they depend on a particular kind of opposition to the exclusion of others. The general aim of deconstruction is to open up texts in order to undermine the metaphysics of presence and logocentricism.

Derrida often concentrates on texts that form part of the philosophical tradition, thereby undercutting the vision that the tradition has of itself. According to Derrida, this process subverts not only the history of philosophy, but also the practice of traditional philosophy itself, which relies on the metaphysics of presence. This reliance is due to the fact that meaning and identity are always generated on the basis of differences. Language works through a movement among differences, which always requires the absent. Therefore, there are no present self-identical concepts or meanings, but rather a moving system of relations between signs, each defined by what it is not, or by the absent. To elucidate this point, Derrida employs the idea of a trace, which is a signifier whose meaning is never present but depends on its interconnections in an ever-changing web of signifiers.

Transcendental Signified and Identity

In the philosophical tradition, the idea of a present is due to the belief that there is a transcendental signified beyond a system of signs, such as the subject, the world, facts, God, or matter. According to Derrida, the transcendental signified is never realized. It is always deferred. This is because there is nothing beyond the interplay of signs through their differences; there is no transcendental signified, and, for this reason, Derrida says that there is nothing outside of a text and, in this sense, the world must be considered as a text.

All of this means that the hard identities of meaning that traditional philosophy requires are never achieved. In fact, we can easily fall into the trap of thinking of difference in binary opposition to identity, and vice versa. In other words, Derrida's view of identity must be applied also to 'identity.' Derrida uses the word '*différance*' partly to circumvent the identity/difference binary. Furthermore, his term carries the suggestion of the French word '*differer*,' which means to defer or to put off. The self-identity of meaning and the transcendental signified are always deferred, never achieved. '*Différance*' is the interplay between differing and deferring.

This view has implications for the notion of the self. There is no self-identical concept of the self, which would amount to a transcendental signified. As in structuralism, 'the self' is a sign within a system of signs.

To return to the beginning, the metaphysics of presence is based on the idea of self-identity and especially the self-identity of meaning. This is why Derrida says, 'It deconstructs itself.' By showing how language requires a movement of *différance*, deconstruction reveals how the apparently self-identical deconstructs itself.

Comparisons

Finally, and very briefly, let us examine how Derrida's thought differs from that of some other recent continental thinkers. Husserl takes the present moment of consciousness as the locus of all meaning. In contrast, Derrida adopts the structuralist view that all meaning depends on a system of signs that cannot be understood in terms of the intentions of an individual subject. There is no self beyond a system of signs. Furthermore, the present moment of experience is constituted by its relations to the apparently absent immediate past and future, through memory and anticipation. The undivided present of consciousness is a constantly deferred illusion. These points constitute the prelude to Derrida's deconstruction of consciousness. According to Derrida, Heidegger's fundamental ontology is a logocentric project of revealing *the* meaning of Being. Finally, whereas Derrida agrees with the structuralist critique of subjectivity that makes it prior to any system of signs, he also criticizes structuralism for treating a system of signs as essentially closed and static. This, he thinks, is equivalent to seeking a transcendental ground for meaning, which is always deferred and never attained.

POSITIONS

This selection consists of three interviews, which were published in 1981 as part of the book *Positions*. This is a relatively accessible book, which, at the same time, provides a flavor of the ways in which Derrida likes to play with words and ideas.

In the first interview, which is called 'Implications', Derrida explains his use of '*différance*,' and his views on writing. The second interview is with the well-known French feminist philosopher Julia Kristeva, and it is called 'Semiology and Grammatology.' In this interview, Derrida explains how Saussure's semiotics has had a double role: serving both as a criticism of traditional metaphysics and, at the same time, reinforcing such metaphysics. Derrida also explains how and why many thinkers exclude writing from linguistics and that the antidote is to produce a new concept of writing, which is *différance*, or *gram*. Remember that Derrida tries to undermine the assumption that words have a relatively static and self-identical meaning. These are never achieved, always deferred. Furthermore, signs function through a continuous interplay of differences. '*Différance*' is a play on 'defer' and 'differ.' This concept transforms semiology into grammatology.

In the third interview, Derrida provides an overview or a 'traveler's impressions' of some aspects of his project, as well as a brief reply to some of the misunderstandings of his work. First, Derrida characterizes the peculiar role that '*différance*' plays in his thinking. However, Derrida is concerned to block any attempt to elevate '*différance*' into a master-concept. It would be self-defeating to treat '*différance*' as a self-identical concept or as a sign with transcendental signifier. For this reason, Derrida distinguishes his work from the ideas of Hegel, whose dialectic tries to resolve the conflict between binary opposites through the creation of a third term (thesis and antithesis lead to a synthesis). Derrida contrasts his '*différance*' with Hegel's notion of difference, which presupposes self-presence or self-identity.

Later in the piece, Derrida affirms that he has tried to 'systematize a deconstructive critique against the authority of meaning, as the transcendental signified,' and explains this project in relation to the dismantling of logocentrism, which is the assumption that the interpretation of a text will converge on a single meaning that waits to be discovered. 'Phonocentric' means privileging speech over writing. He discusses logocentrism and phonocentrism in relation to Saussure and Plato's opposition between philosophy and myth.

Derrida moves on to indicate some features of his critique of Heidegger's search for the true and authentic etymology of words. Derrida briefly points out some of the ways in which Heidegger's work assumes a metaphysics of presence, which Derrida questions. Finally, Derrida indicates how a metaphysical conception of history reinforces the kinds of philosophical views that he challenges.

IMPLICATIONS

INTERVIEW WITH HENRI RONCE

DERRIDA: I try to keep myself at the *limit* of philosophical discourse. I say limit and not death, for I do not at all believe in what today is so easily called the death of philosophy (nor, moreover, in the simple death of whatever—the book, man, or god, especially since, as we all know, what is dead wields a very specific power). Thus, the limit on the basis of which philosophy became possible, defined itself as the *epistēmē*, functioning within a system of fundamental constraints, conceptual oppositions outside of which philosophy becomes impracticable. In my readings, I try therefore, by means of a necessarily double gesture. . . .

RONSE: You say in your Freud that one writes with two hands. . . .

DERRIDA: Yes, by means of this double play, marked in certain decisive places by an erasure which allows what it obliterates to be read, violently inscribing within the text that which attempted to govern it from without, I try to respect as rigorously as possible the internal, regulated play of philosophemes or epistimemes by making them slide—without mistreating them—to the point of their nonpertinence, their exhaustion, their closure. To "deconstruct" philosophy, thus, would be to think—in the most faithful, interior way—the structured genealogy of philosophy's concepts, but at the same time to determine—from a certain exterior that is unqualifiable or unnameable by philosophy—what this history has been able to dissimulate or forbid, making itself into a history

From *Positions* by Jacques Derrida, translated by Alan Bass. Reprinted by permission of The University of Chicago Press as publisher.

by means of this somewhere motivated repression. By means of this simultaneously faithful and violent circulation between the inside and the outside of philosophy—that is of the West—there is produced a certain textual work that gives great pleasure. That is, a writing interested in itself which also enables us to read philosophemes—and consequently all the texts of our culture—as kinds of symptoms (a word which I suspect, of course, as I explain elsewhere) of something that *could not be presented* in the history of philosophy, and which, moreover, is *nowhere present*, since all of this concerns putting into question the major determination of the meaning of Being as *presence*, the determination in which Heidegger recognized the destiny of philosophy.

Ronse: In your essays at least two meanings of the word "writing" are discernible: the accepted meaning, which opposes (phonetic) writing to the speech that it allegedly represents (but you show that there is no purely phonetic writing), and a more radical meaning that determines writing in general, before any tie to what glossematics calls an "expressive substance"; this more radical meaning would be the common root of writing and speech.

The treatment accorded to writing in the accepted sense serves as a revelatory index of the repression to which archi-writing is subject. An inevitable repression whose necessity, forms, and laws are to be investigated. This (archi-) writing is linked to a chain of other names: archi-trace, reserve, articulation, *brisure*, supplement, and *différance*. Much has been said above about the *a* of *différance*. What does it signify?

Derrida: I do not know if it *signifies* at all—perhaps something like the production of what metaphysics calls the sign (signified/signifier). You have noticed that this *a* is written or read, but cannot be heard. And first off I insist upon the fact that any discourse—for example, ours, at this moment—on this alteration, this graphic and grammatical aggression, implies an irreducible reference to the mute intervention of a written sign. The present participle of the verb *différer*, on which this noun is modeled, ties together a configuration of con-

cepts I hold to be systematic and irreducible, each one of which intervenes, or rather is accentuated, at a decisive moment of the work. *First, différance* refers to the (active *and* passive) movement that consists in deferring by means of delay, delegation, reprieve, referral, detour, postponement, reserving. In this sense, *différance* is not preceded by the originary and indivisible unity of a present possibility that I could reserve, like an expenditure that I would put off calculatedly or for reasons of economy. What defers presence, on the contrary, is the very basis on which presence is announced or desired in what represents it, its sign, its trace. . . .

Ronse: From this point of view *différance* is an economical question?

Derrida: I would even say that it is *the* economical concept, and since there is no economy without *différance*, it is the most general structure of economy, given that one understands by economy something other than the classical economy of metaphysics, or the classical metaphysics of economy. *Second*, the movement of *différance*, as that which produces different things, that which differentiates, is the common root of all the oppositional concepts that mark our language, such as, to take only a few examples, sensible/intelligible, intuition/signification, nature/culture, etc. As a common root, *différance* is also the element of the *same* (to be distinguished from the identical) in which these oppositions are announced. *Third, différance* is also the production, if it can still be put this way, of these differences, of the diacriticity that the linguistics generated by Saussure, and all the structural sciences modeled upon it, have recalled is the condition for any signification and any structure. These differences—and, for example, the taxonomical science which they may occasion—are the effects of *différance*; they are neither inscribed in the heavens, nor in the brain, which does not mean that they are produced by the activity of some speaking subject. From this point of view, the concept of *différance* is neither simply structuralist, nor simply geneticist, such an alternative itself being an "effect" of *différance*. I would even say, but perhaps we will come to this later, that it is not simply a concept. . . .

This is why it has never been a question of opposing a graphocentrism to a logocentrism, nor, in general, any center to any other center. *Of Grammatology* is not a defense and illustration of grammatology. And even less a rehabilitation of what has always been called writing. It is not a question of returning to writing its rights, its superiority or its dignity. Plato said of writing that it was an orphan or a bastard, as opposed to speech, the legitimate and high-born son of the "father of logos." At the moment when one attempts to interrogate this family scene, and to investigate all the investments, ethical and otherwise, of this entire history, nothing would be more ridiculously mystifying than such an ethical or axiological reversal, returning a prerogative or some elder's right to writing. I believe that I have explained myself clearly on this subject. *Of Grammatology* is the title of a question: a question about the necessity of a science of writing, about the conditions that would make it possible, about the critical work that would have to open its field and resolve the epistemological obstacles; but it is also a question about the limits of this science. And these limits, on which I have insisted no less, are also those of the classical notion of science, whose projects, concepts, and norms are fundamentally and systematically tied to metaphysics.

SEMIOLOGY AND GRAMMATOLOGY

INTERVIEW WITH JULIA KRISTEVA

KRISTEVA: Semiology today is constructed on the model of the sign and its correlates: *communication* and *structure*. What are the "logocentric" and ethnocentric limits of these models, and how are they incapable of serving as the basis for a notation attempting to escape metaphysics?

DERRIDA: All gestures here are necessarily equivocal. And supposing, which I do not believe, that someday it will be possible *simply* to escape metaphysics, the concept of the sign will have marked, in this sense, a simultaneous impediment and progress. For if the sign, by its root and its implications, is in all its aspects metaphysical, if it is in systematic solidarity with stoic and medieval theology, the work and the displacement to which it has been submitted—and of which it also, curiously, is the instrument—have had *delimiting* effects. For this work and displacement have permitted the critique of how the concept of the sign belongs to metaphysics, which represents a simultaneous *marking* and *loosening* of the limits of the system in which this concept was born and began to serve, and thereby also represents, to a certain extent, an uprooting of the sign from its own soil. This work must be conducted as far as possible, but at a certain point one inevitably encounters "the logocentric and ethnocentric limits" of such a model. At this point, perhaps, the concept is to be abandoned. But this point is very difficult to determine, and is never pure. All the heuristic and critical resources of the concept of the sign have to be exhausted, and exhausted equally in all domains and contexts. Now, it is inevitable that not only inequalities of development (which will always occur), but also the necessity of certain contexts, will render strategically indispensable the recourse to a model known elsewhere, and even at the most novel points of investigation, to function as an obstacle.

To take only one example, one could show that a semiology of the Saussurian type has had a double role. *On the one hand*, an absolutely decisive critical role:

1. It has marked, against the tradition, that the signified is inseparable from the signifier, that the signified and signifier are the two sides of one and the same production. Saussure even purposely refused to have this opposition or this "two-sided unity" conform to the relationship between soul and body, as had always been done. "This two-sided unity has often been compared to the unity of the human person, composed of a body and a soul. The comparison is hardly satisfactory." (*Cours de linguistique générale*, p. 145)

2. By emphasizing the *differential* and *formal* characteristics of semiological functioning, by showing that it "is impossible for sound, the material element, itself to belong to language" and that "in its essence it [the linguistic signifier] is not at all phonic" (p. 164); by desubstantializing both the signified content and the "expressive substance"—which therefore is no longer in a privileged or exclusive way phonic—by making linguistics a division of general semiology (p. 33), Saussure powerfully contributed to turning against the metaphysical tradition the concept of the sign that he borrowed from it.

And yet Saussure could not not confirm this tradition in the extent to which he continued to use the concept of the sign. No more than any other, this concept cannot be employed in both an absolutely novel and an absolutely conventional way. One necessarily assumes, in a noncritical way, at least some of the implications inscribed in its system. There is at least one moment at which Saussure must renounce drawing all the conclusions from the critical work he has undertaken, and that is the not fortuitous moment when he resigns himself to using the word "sign," lacking anything better. After having justified the introduction of the words "signified" and "signifier," Saussure writes: "As for *sign*, if we retain it, it is because we find nothing else to replace it, everyday language suggesting no other" (pp. 99–100). And, in effect, it is difficult to see how one could evacuate the *sign* when one has begun by proposing the opposition signified/signifier.

Now, "everyday language" is not innocent or neutral. It is the language of Western metaphysics, and it carries with it not only a considerable number of presuppositions of all types, but also presuppositions inseparable from metaphysics, which, although little attended to, are knotted into a system. This is why *on the other hand*:

1. The maintenance of the rigorous distinction—an essential and juridical distinction—between the *signans* and the *signatum*, the equation of the *signatum* and the concept (p. 99), inherently leaves open the possibility of thinking a *concept signified in and of itself*, a concept simply present for thought, independent of a relationship to language, that is of a relationship to a system of signifiers. By leaving open this possibility—and it is inherent even in the opposition signifier/signified, that is in the sign—Saussure contradicts the critical acquisitions of which we were just speaking. He accedes to the classical exigency of what I have proposed to call a "transcendental signified," which in and of itself, in its essence, would refer to no signifier, would exceed the chain of signs, and would no longer itself function as a signifier. On the contrary, though, from the moment that one questions the possibility of such a transcendental signified, and that one recognizes that every signified is also in the position of a signifier, the distinction between signified and signifier becomes problematical at its root. Of course this is an operation that must be undertaken with prudence for: (a) it must pass through the difficult deconstruction of the entire history of metaphysics which imposed, and never will cease to impose upon semiological science in its entirety this fundamental quest for a "transcendental signified" and a concept independent of language; this quest not being imposed from without by something like "philosophy," but rather by everything that links our language, our culture, our "system of thought" to the history and system of metaphysics; (b) nor is it a question of confusing at every level, and in all simplicity, the signifier and the signified. That this opposition or difference cannot be radical or absolute does not prevent it from functioning, and even from being indispensable within certain limits—very wide limits. For example, no translation would be possible without it. In effect, the theme of a transcendental signified took shape within the horizon of an absolutely pure, transparent, and unequivocal translatability. In the limits to which it is possible, or at least *appears* possible, translation practices the difference between signified and signifier. But if this difference is never pure, no more so is translation, and for the notion of translation we would have to substitute a notion of *transformation:* a regulated transformation of one language by another, of one text by another. We will never have, and in fact have never had, to do with some "transport" of pure signified from one language to another, or within one and the same language, that the signifying instrument would leave virgin and untouched.

2. Although he recognized the necessity of putting the phonic substance between brackets ("What is essential in language, we shall see, is foreign to the phonic character of the linguistic sign" [p. 21]. "In its essence it [the linguistic signifier] is not at all phonic" [p. 164]), Saussure, for essential, and essentially metaphysical, reasons had to privilege speech, everything that links the sign to *phonē.* He also speaks of the "natural link" between thought and voice, meaning and sound (p. 46). He even speaks of "thought-sound" (p. 156). I have attempted elsewhere to show what is traditional in such a gesture, and to what necessities it submits. In any event, it winds up contradicting the most interesting critical motive of the *Course,* making of linguistics the regulatory model, the "pattern" for a general semiology of which it was to be, by all rights and theoretically, only a part. The theme of the arbitrary, thus, is turned away from its most fruitful paths (formulization) toward a hierarchizing teleology: "Thus it can be said that entirely arbitrary signs realize better than any others the ideal of the semiological process; this is why language, the most complex and most widespread of the systems of expression, is also the most characteristic one of them all; in this sense linguistics can become the *general pattern for all semiology,* even though language is only a particular system" (p. 101). One finds exactly the same gesture and the same concepts in Hegel. The contradiction between these two moments of the *Course* is also marked by Saussure's recognizing elsewhere that "it is not spoken language that is natural to man, but the faculty of constituting a language, that is a system of distinct signs . . . ," that is, the possibility of the *code* and of *articu-lation,* independent of any substance, for example, phonic substance.

3. The concept of the sign (signifier/signified) carries within itself the necessity of privileging the phonic substance and of setting up linguistics as the "pattern" for semiology. *Phonē,* in effect, is the signifying substance *given to consciousness* as that which is most intimately tied to the thought of the signified concept. From this point of view, the voice is consciousness itself. When I speak, not only am I conscious of being present for what I think, but I am conscious also of keeping as close as possible to my thought, or to the "concept," a signifier that does not fall into the world, a signifier that I hear as soon as I emit it, that seems do depend upon my pure and free spontaneity, requiring the use of no instrument, no accessory, no force taken from the world. Not only do the signifier and the signified seem to unite, but also, in this confusion, the signifier seems to erase itself or to become transparent, in order to allow the concept to present itself as what it is, referring to nothing other than its presence. The exteriority of the signifier seems reduced. Naturally this experience is a lure, but a lure whose necessity has organized an entire structure, or an entire epoch; and on the grounds of this epoch a semiology has been constituted whose concepts and fundamental presuppositions are quite precisely discernible from Plato to Husserl, passing through Aristotle, Rousseau, Hegel, etc.

4. To reduce the exteriority of the signifier is to exclude everything in semiotic practice that is not psychic. Now, only the privilege accorded to the phonetic and linguistic sign can authorize Saussure's proposition according to which the "linguistic sign is therefore a two-sided *psychic* entity" (p. 99). Supposing that this proposition has a rigorous sense in and of itself, it is difficult to see how it could be extended to every sign, be it phonetic-linguistic or not. It is difficult to see therefore, except, precisely, by making of the phonetic sign the "pattern" for all signs, how general semiology can be inscribed in a psychology. However, this is what Saussure does: "One can thus conceive of a science that would study the life of signs at the heart of social life; it would form a part of social psychology, and consequently of general psychology; we will name it semiology (from the Greek *sēmeion,* 'sign'). It would teach what signs consist of, what laws regulate them. Since it does not yet exist, one cannot say what it will be; but it has a

right to exist, its place is determined in advance. Linguistics is only a part of this general science, the laws that semiology will discover will be applicable to linguistics, and the latter will find itself attached to a well defined domain in the set of human facts. It is for the psychologist to determine the exact place of semiology" (p. 33).

Kristeva: What is the *gram* as a "new structure of nonpresence"? What is *writing* as *différance*? What rupture do these concepts introduce in relation to the key concepts of semiology—the (phonetic) *sign* and *structure*? How does the notion of *text* replace, in grammatology, the linguistic and semiological notion of what is *enounced*?

Derrida: The reduction of writing—as the reduction of the exteriority of the signifier—was part and parcel of phonologism and logocentrism. We know how Saussure, according to the traditional operation that was also Plato's, Aristotle's, Rousseau's, Hegel's, Husserl's, etc., excludes writing from the field of linguistics—from language and speech—as a phenomenon of exterior representation, both useless and dangerous: "The linguistic object is not defined by the combination of the written word and the spoken word, the latter alone constituting this object" (p. 45); "writing is foreign to the internal system [of language]" (p. 44); "writing veils our view of language: it does not clothe language, but travesties it" (p. 51). The tie of writing to language is "superficial," "factitious." It is "bizarre" that writing, which should only be an "image," "usurps the principal role" and that "the natural relationship is inversed" (p. 47). Writing is a "trap," its action is "vicious" and "tyrannical," its misdeeds are monstrosities, "teratological cases," "linguistics should put them under observation in a special compartment" (p. 54), etc. Naturally, this representativist conception of writing ("Language and writing are two distinct sign systems; the unique *raison d'être* of the second is to *represent* the first" [p. 45]) is linked to the practice of phonetic-alphabetic writing, to which Saussure realized his study is "limited" (p. 48). In effect, alphabetical writing seems to present speech, and at the same time to erase itself before speech. Actually, it could be shown, as I have attempted to do, that there is no purely phonetic writing, and

that phonologism is less a consequence of the practice of the alphabet in a given culture than a certain ethical or axiological *experience* of this practice. Writing *should* erase itself before the plenitude of living speech, perfectly represented in the transparence of its notation, immediately present for the subject who speaks it, and for the subject who receives its meanings, content, value.

Now, if one ceases to limit oneself to the model of phonetic writing, which we privilege only by ethnocentrism, and if we draw all the consequences from the fact that there is no purely phonetic writing (by reason of the necessary spacing of signs, punctuation, intervals, the differences indispensable for the function of graphemes, etc.), then the entire phonologist or logocentrist logic becomes problematical. Its range of legitimacy becomes narrow and superficial. This delimitation, however, is indispensable if one wants to be able to account, with some coherence, for the principle of difference, such as Saussure himself recalls it. This principle compels us not only not to privilege one substance—here the phonic, so called temporal, substance—while excluding another—for example, the graphic, so called spatial, substance—but even to consider every process of signification as a formal play of differences. That is, of traces.

Why traces? And by what right do we reintroduce grammatics at the moment when we seem to have neutralized every substance, be it phonic, graphic, or otherwise? Of course it is not a question of resorting to the same concept of writing and of simply inverting the dissymmetry that now has become problematical. It is a question, rather, of producing a new concept of writing. This concept can be called *gram* or *différance*. The play of differences supposes, in effect, syntheses and referrals which forbid at any moment, or in any sense, that a simple element be *present* in and of itself, referring only to itself. Whether in the order of spoken or written discourse, no element can function as a sign without referring to another element which itself is not simply present. This interweaving results in each "element"—phoneme or grapheme—being constituted on the basis of the trace within it of the other elements of the chain or system. This interweaving, this textile, is the *text* produced only in the transformation of another text. Nothing, neither among the elements nor within the system, is anywhere ever simply present or absent. There are only, everywhere, differences and traces of traces. The gram, then, is the most general concept of semiology—which thus becomes grammatology—and it covers not only the field of writing in the restricted sense, but also the field of linguistics. The advantage of this concept—provided that it be surrounded by a certain interpretive context, for no more than any other conceptual element it does not signify, or suffice, by itself—is that in principle it neutralizes the phonologistic propensity of the "sign," and *in fact counterbalances* it by liberating the entire scientific field of the "graphic substance" (history and systems of writing beyond the bounds of the West) whose interest is not minimal, but which so far has been left in the shadows of neglect.

The gram as *différance*, then, is a structure and a movement no longer conceivable on the basis of the opposition presence/absence. *Différance* is the systematic play of differences, of the traces of differences, of the *spacing* by means of which elements are related to each other. This spacing is the simultaneously active and passive (the *a* of *différance* indicates this indecision as concerns activity and passivity, that which cannot be governed by or distributed between the terms of this opposition) production of the intervals without which the "full" terms would not signify, would not function. It is also the becoming-space of the spoken chain—which has been called temporal or linear; a becoming-space which makes possible both writing and every correspondence between speech and writing, every passage from one to the other.

The activity or productivity connoted by the *a* of *différance* refers to the generative movement in the play of differences. The latter are neither fallen from the sky nor inscribed once and for all in a closed system, a static structure that a synchronic and taxonomic operation could exhaust. Differences are the effects of transformations, and from this vantage the theme of *différance* is incompatible with the static, synchronic, taxonomic, ahistoric motifs in the concept of *structure*. But it goes without saying that this motif is not the only

one that defines structure, and that the production of differences, *différance*; is not a structural: it produces systematic and regulated transformations which are able, at a certain point, to leave room for a structural science. The concept of *différance* even develops the most legitimate principled exigencies of "structuralism."

Language, and in general every semiotic code—which Saussure defines as "classifications"—are therefore effects, but their cause is not a subject, a substance, or a being somewhere present and outside the movement of *différance*. Since there is no presence before and outside semiological *différance*, one can extend to the system of signs in general what Saussure says of language: "Language is necessary for speech to be intelligible and to produce all its effects; but speech is necessary for language to be established; historically, the fact of speech always comes first." There is a circle here, for if one rigorously distinguishes language and speech, code and message, schema and usage, etc., and if one wishes to do justice to the two postulates thus enunciated, one does not know where to begin, nor how something can begin in general, be it language or speech. Therefore, one has to admit, before any dissociation of language and speech, code and message, etc. (and everything that goes along with such a dissociation), a systematic production of differences, the *production* of a system of differences—a *différance*—within whose effects one eventually, by abstraction and according to determined motivations, will be able to demarcate a linguistics of language and a linguistics of speech, etc.

Nothing—no present and in-*different* being—thus precedes *différance* and spacing. There is no subject who is agent, author, and master of *différance*, who eventually and empirically would be overtaken by *différance*. Subjectivity—like objectivity—is an effect of *différance*, an effect inscribed in a system of *différance*. This is why the *a* of *différance* also recalls that spacing is temporization, the detour and postponement by means of which intuition, perception, consummation—in a word, the relationship to the present, the reference to a present reality, to a *being*—are always *deferred*. Deferred by virtue of the very principle of difference which holds that an element functions and signifies, takes on or conveys meaning, only by referring to another past or future element in an economy of traces. This economic aspect of *différance*, which brings into play a certain not conscious calculation in a field of forces, is inseparable from the more narrowly semiotic aspect of *différance*. It confirms that the subject, and first of all the conscious and speaking subject, depends upon the system of differences and the movement of *différance*, that the subject is constituted only in being divided from itself, in becoming space, in temporizing, in deferral; and it confirms that, as Saussure said, "language [which consists only of differences] is not a function of the speaking subject." At the point at which the concept of *différance*, and the chain attached to it, intervenes, all the conceptual oppositions of metaphysics (signifier/signified; sensible/intelligible; writing/speech; passivity/activity; etc.)—to the extent that they ultimately refer to the presence of something present (for example, in the form of the identity of the subject who is present for all his operations, present beneath every accident or event, self-present in its "living speech," in its enunciations, in the present objects and acts of its language, etc.)—become nonpertinent. They all amount, at one moment or another, to a subordination of the movement of *différance* in favor of the presence of a value or a *meaning* supposedly antecedent to *différance*, more original than it, exceeding and governing it in the last analysis. This is still the presence of what we called above the "transcendental signified."

KRISTEVA: The putting into question of the sign being a putting into question of scientificity, to what extent is or is not grammatology a "science"? Do you consider certain semiotic works close to the grammatological project, and if so, which ones?

DERRIDA: Grammatology must deconstruct everything that ties the concept and norms of scientificity to ontotheology, logocentrism, phonologism. This is an immense and interminable work that must ceaselessly avoid letting the transgression of the classical project of science fall back into a prescientific empiricism. This supposes a kind of *double register* in grammatological practice: it must simultaneously go beyond metaphysical positivism and scientism, and accentuate whatever in the effective work of science contributes to freeing it of the metaphysical bonds that have borne on its definition and its movement since its beginnings. Grammatology must pursue and consolidate whatever, in scientific practice, has always already begun to exceed the logocentric closure. This is why there is no simple answer to the question of whether grammatology is a "science." In a word, I would say that it *inscribes* and *delimits* science; it must freely and rigorously make the norms of science function in its own writing; once again, it *marks* and at the same time *loosens* the limit which closes classical scientificity.

For the same reason, there is no *scientific* semiotic work that does not serve grammatology. And it will always be possible to turn against the metaphysical presuppositions of a semiotic discourse the grammatological motifs which science produces in semiotics. It is on the basis of the formalist and differential motif present in Saussure's *Cours* that the psychologism, phonologism and exclusion of writing that are no less present in it can be criticized. Similarly, in Hjelmslev's glossematics, if one drew all the consequences of the critique of Saussure's psychologism, the neutralization of expressive substances—and therefore of phonologism—the "structuralism," "immanentism," the critique of metaphysics, the thematics of play, etc., then one would be able to exclude an entire metaphysical conceptuality that is naively utilized (the couple expression/content in the tradition of the couple signifier/signified; the opposition form/substance applied to each of the two preceding terms; the "empirical principle," etc.). One can say *a priori* that in every proposition or in every system of semiotic research—and you could cite the most current examples better than I—metaphysical presuppositions coexist with critical motifs. And this by the simple fact that up to a certain point they inhabit the same language. Doubtless, grammatology is less another science, a new discipline charged with a new content or new domain, than the vigilant practice of this textual division.

POSITIONS

INTERVIEW WITH JEAN-LOUIS HOUDEBINE AND GUY SCARPETTA

HOUDEBINE: To open this interview, perhaps we could . . . take off from the "word" or "concept" of *différance* "which is . . . literally neither a word nor a concept": . . .

DERRIDA: The motif of *différance,* when marked by a silent *a,* in effect plays neither the role of a "concept," nor simply of a "word." I have tried to demonstrate this. This does not prevent it from producing conceptual effects and verbal or nominal concretions. Which, moreover—although this is not immediately noticeable—are simultaneously imprinted and fractured by the corner of this "letter," by the incessant work of its strange "logic." The "sheaf" which you recall is a historic and systematic crossroads; and it is above all the structural impossibility of limiting this network, of putting an edge on its weave, of tracing a margin that would not be a new mark. Since it cannot be elevated into a master-word or a master-concept, since it blocks every relationship to theology, *différance* finds itself enmeshed in the work that pulls it through a chain of other "concepts," other "words," other textual configurations. Perhaps later I will have occasion to indicate why such other "words" or "concepts" later or simultaneously imposed themselves; and why room had to be left for their insistence (for example, *gram, reserve, incision, trace, spacing, blank—sens blanc, sang blanc, sans blanc, cent blancs, semblant— supplement, pharmakon, margin-mark-march,* etc.). By definition the list has no taxonomical closure, and even less does it constitute a lexicon. First, because these are not *atoms,* but rather focal points of economic condensation, sites of passage necessary for a very large number of marks, slightly more effervescent crucibles. Further, their effects do not simply turn back on themselves by means of an auto-affection without opening. Rather they spread out in a chain over the practical and theoretical entirely of a text, and each time in a different way.

What interested me then, that I am attempting to pursue along other lines now, was, at the same time as a "general economy," a kind of *general strategy of deconstruction.* The latter is to avoid both simply *neutralizing* the binary oppositions of metaphysics and simply *residing* within the closed field of these oppositions, thereby confirming it.

Therefore we must proceed using a double gesture, according to a unity that is both systematic and in and of itself divided, a double writing, that is, a writing that is in and of itself multiple, what I called, in *"La double séance,"* a double science. On the other hand, we must traverse a phase of *overturning.* To do justice to this necessity is to recognize that is a classical philosophical opposition we are not dealing with the peaceful coexistence of a *vis-à-vis,* but rather with a violent hierarchy. One of the two terms governs the other (axiologically, logically, etc.), or has the upper hand. To deconstruct the opposition, first of all, is to overturn the hierarchy at a given moment. To overlook this phase of overturning is to forget the conflictual and subordinating structure of opposition. Therefore one might proceed too quickly to a *neutralization* that *in practice* would leave the previous field untouched, lea-ving one no hold on the previous opposition, thereby preventing any means of *intervening* in the field effectively. We know what always have been the *practical* (particularly *political*) effects of *immediately* jumping *beyond* oppositions, and of protests in the simple form of *neither* this *nor* that. When I say that this phase is necessary, the word *phase* is perhaps not the most rigorous one. It is not a question of a chronological phase, a given moment, or a page that one day simply will be turned, in order to go on to other things. The necessity of this phase is structural; it is the necessity of an interminable analysis: the hierarchy of dual oppositions always reestablishes itself. Unlike those authors whose death does not await their demise, the time for overturning is never a dead letter.

That being said—and on the other hand— to remain in this phase is still to operate on the terrain of and from within the deconstructed system. By means of this double, and precisely stratified, dislodged and dislodging, writing, we must also mark the interval between inversion, which brings low that what was high, and the irruptive emergence of a new "concept," a concept that can no longer be, and never could be, included in the previous regime. If this interval, this biface or biphase, can be inscribed only in a bifurcated writing (and this holds first of all for a new concept of writing, that *simultaneously* provokes the overturning of the hierarchy speech/writing, and the entire system attached to it, *and* releases the dissonance of a writing within speech, thereby disorganizing the entire inherited order and invading the entire field), then it can only be marked in what I would call a *grouped* textual field: in the last analysis it is impossible to *point* it out, for a unilinear text, or a punctual *position*, an operation signed by a single author, are all by definition incapable of practicing this interval.

Henceforth, in order better to mark this interval (*La dissémination*, the text that bears this title, since you have asked me about it, is a systematic and playful exploration of the interval—"écart," *carré, carrure, carte, charte, quatre*, etc.) it has been necessary to analyze, to set to work, *within* the text of the history of philosophy, as well as *within* the so-called literary text (for example, Malarmé), certain marks, shall we say (I mentioned certain ones just now, these are many others), that *by analogy* (I underline) I have called undecidables, that is, unities of simulacrum, "false" verbal properties (nominal or semantic) that can no longer be included within philosophical (binary) opposition, but which, however, inhabit philosophical opposition, resisting and disorganizing it, *without ever* constituting a third term, without ever leaving room for a solution in the form of speculative dialectics (the *pharmakon* is neither remedy nor poison, neither good nor evil, neither the inside nor the outside, neither speech nor writing; the *supplement* is neither a plus nor a minus, neither an outside nor the complement of an inside, neither accident nor essence, etc.; the *hymen* is neither confusion nor distinction, neither identity nor difference, neither consummation nor virginity, neither the veil nor unveiling, neither the inside nor the outside, etc.; the *gram* is neither a signifier nor a signified, neither a sign nor a thing, neither a presence nor an absence, neither a position nor a negation, etc.; *spacing* is neither space nor time; the *incision* is neither the incised integrity of a beginning, or of a simple cutting into, nor simple secondarity. Neither/nor, that is, *simultaneously* either *or*; the mark is also the *marginal* limit, the *march*, etc.). In fact, I attempt to bring the critical operation to bear against the unceasing re-appropriation of this work of the simulacrum by a dialectics of the Hegelian type (which even idealizes and "semantizes" the value of *work*), for Hegelian idealism consists precisely of a *relève* of the binary oppositions of classical idealism, a resolution of contradiction into a third term that comes in order to *aufheben*, to deny while raising up, while idealizing, while sublimating into an anamnesic interiority (*Errinnerung*), while *interning* difference in a self-presence.

Since it is still a question of elucidating the relationship to Hegal—a difficult labor, which for the most part remains before us, and which in a certain way is interminable, at least if one wishes to execute it rigorously and minutely—I have attempted to distinguish *différance* (whose *a* marks, among other things, its productive and conflictual characteristics) from Hegelian difference, and have done so precisely at the point at which Hegel, in the greater *Logic*, determines difference as contradiction only in order to resolve it, to interiorize it, to life it up (according to the syllogistic process of speculative dialectics) into the self-presence of an onto-theological or onto-teleological synthesis.... Since this conflictuality of *différance*—which can be called contradiction only if one demarcates it by means of a long work on Hegel's concept of contradiction—can never be totally resolved, it marks its effects in what I call the text in general, in a text which is not reduced to a book or a library, and which can never be governed by a referent in the classical sense, that is, by a thing or by a transcendental signified that would regulate its movement. You can well see that it is not because I wish to appease or reconciliate that I prefer to employ the mark "*différance*" rather then refer to the system of difference-and-contradiction. . . .

In the last analysis *dissemination* means nothing, and cannot be reassembled into a definition. I will not attempt to do so here, and I prefer to refer to the work of the texts. If dissemination, seminal *différance*, cannot be summarized into an exact conceptual tenor, it is because the force and form of its disruption *explode* the semantic horizon. . . . Dissemination, on the contrary, although producing a nonfinite number of semantic effects, can be led back neither to a present of simple origin . . . nor to an eschatological presence. It marks an irreducible and *generative* multiplicity. The supplement and the turbulence of a certain lack fracture the limit of the text, forbidding an exhaustive and closed formalization of it, or at least a saturating taxonomy of its themes, its signified, its meaning.

Here, of course, we are *playing* on the fortuitous resemblance, the purely simulated common parentage of *seme* and *semen*. There is no communication of meaning between them. And yet, by means of this floating, purely exterior collusion, accident produces a kind of semantic mirage: the deviance of meaning, its reflection-effect in writing, sets something off.

I have attempted not to formalize this motivic regime of the surplus (and the) lack in the neutrality of a critical discourse (I have said why an exhaustive formalization in the classical sense is impossible; "*La double séance*" is a deconstructive "critique" of the notion of "criticism"), but rather to rewrite it, to inscribed and *relaunch* its schemes. In "*La dissémination*" and "*La double séance*" (these two texts are inseparable) it is a question of remarking a nerve, a fold, an angle that interrupts totalization: in a certain place, a place of well-determined form, no series of semantic valences can any longer be closed or reassembled. Not that it opens onto an inexhaustible wealth of meanings or the transcendence of a semantic excess. By means of this angle, this fold, this doubled fold of an undecidable, a mark marks both the marked and the mark, the re-marked site of the mark. The writing which, at this moment, re-marks itself

(something completely other than a representation of itself) can no longer be counted on the list of themes (it is not a theme, and can in no case become one); it must be subtracted from (hollow) and added to (relief) the list. The hollow is the relief, but the lack and the surplus can never be stabilized in the plenitude of a form or an equation, in the stationary correspondence of a symmetry or a homology. . . .

This work always has this theoretical result among others: a criticism concerned only with content. . . . can no more measure itself against *certain* texts (or rather the structure of certain textual *scenes*) than can a purely formalist criticism which would be interested only in the code, the pure play of signifiers, the technical manipulation of a text-object, thereby overlooking the genetic effects or the ("historical," if you will) inscription of the text read *and* of the new text this criticism itself writes. These two insufficiencies are rigorously complementary. They cannot be defined without a deconstruction of classical rhetoric and its implicit philosophy: I began this deconstruction in "*La double séance*" and have attempted to systematize it in "*La mythologie blanche*." The critique of formalist structuralism was undertaken from the first texts of *Writing and Difference*. . . . It is now quite some time, permit me to recall, since I risked the following sentence, that is, that I *wrote* it, for the silent work of italics and quotation marks should not be subtracted from it, as happens too often (for instead of investigating only the content of thoughts, it is also necessary to analyze the way in which texts are *made*): "*In a certain way, 'thought' means nothing.*" "Thought" (quotation marks: the words "thought" and what is called "thought") means nothing: it is the substantified void of a highly derivative ideality, the effect of a *différance* of forces, the illusory autonomy of a discourse or a consciousness whose hypostasis is to be deconstructed, whose "causality" is to be analyzed, etc. First. Secondly, the sentence can be read thus: if there is thought—and there is, and it is just as suspect, for analogous critical reasons, to contest the authority of all "thought"—then whatever will continue to be called thought, and which, for example, will designate the deconstruction of logocentrism, means nothing, for in the last analysis it no longer derives from "meaning." Wherever it operates, *"thought" means nothing*. . . .

Must I recall that from the first texts I published, I have attempted to systematize a deconstructive critique precisely against the authority of meaning, as the *transcendental signified* or as *telos*, in other words history determined in the last analysis as the history of meaning, history in its logocentric, metaphysical, idealist (I will come back to these words in a moment) representation, even up to the complex marks it has left in Heidegger's discourse. I can be reproached for being insistent, even monotonous, but it is difficult for me to see how a concept of history as the "history of meaning" can be attributed to me. Truthfully, at the root of the misunderstanding might be the following: I am constituted as the proprietor of what I analyze, to wit, a metaphysical concept of history as ideal, teleological history, etc. As this concept is much more generally extended than is usually believed, and certainly far beyond the philosophies labeled "idealist," I am very wary of the concept of history; and the marks of this wariness, which doubtless we will have occasion to come back to, may have provoked the misunderstandings of a first reading. . . .

Don't you see, what has seemed necessary and urgent to me, in the historical situation which is our own, is a general determination of the condition for the emergence and the limits of philosophy, of metaphysics, of everything that carries it on and that it carries on. In *Of Grammatology* I simultaneously proposed everything that can be reassembled under the rubric of *logocentrism*—and I cannot pursue this any further here—along with the project of *deconstruction*. Here, there is a powerful historical and systematic unity that must be determined first if one is not to take dross for gold every time that an emergence, rupture, break mutation, etc. is allegedly delineated. Logocentrism is *also*, fundamentally, an idealism. It is the matrix of idealism. Idealism is its more direct representation, the most constantly dominant force. And the dismantling of logocentrism is

simultaneously—*a fortiori*—a deconstitution of idealism or spiritualism in all their variants. Really, it is not a question of "erasing" the "struggle" against idealism. Now of course, logocentrism is a wider concept than idealism, for which it serves as a kind of overflowing foundation. And a wider concept than phonocentrism, too. It constitutes a system of predicates, certain of which can always be found in the philosophies that *call themselves* nonidealist, that is, antiidealist. The handing of the concept of logocentrism, therefore, is delicate and sometimes troubling. . . .

Nor have I ever said that "Saussure's project," in its principle or in its entirety, was "logocentrist" or "phonocentrist."

The work of my reading does not take this form. (When I try to decipher a text I do not constantly ask myself if I will finish by answering *yes* or *no*, as happens in France at determined periods of history, and generally on Sunday.) Saussure's text, like any other, is not homogeneous. Yes, I did analyze a "logocentrist" and "phonocentrist" layer of it (which had not been demarcated, and whose bearing is considerable), but I did so in order to show immediately that it was in contradiction to Saussure's scientific project, such as it may be read and such as I took it into account. I cannot demonstrate this again here.

I have never, directly or indirectly, as is alleged for reasons that remain to be analyzed, identified writing with myth. Here I understand the concept of writing as I have attempted to determine it. Inversely, I sometimes have been interested in the gesture by means of which philosophy excluded writing from its field, or form the field of scientific rationality, in order to keep it in an exterior that *sometimes* took the form of *myth*. This is the operation that I investigated, particularly in *"La pharmacie de Platon,"* which demanded new ways, and could proceed neither along the lines of *mythology*, of course, nor the *philosophical* concept of science. In particular, the issue is to deconstruct practically the *philosophical* opposition between philosophy and myth, between *logos* and *mythos*. Practically, I insist, this can only be done textually, along the lines of an *other* writing, with all the implied risks. And I fear that these risks will grow greater still.

Abasement, the abasement of writing: evidently it is not a question—which would be contradictory to the entire context—of raising up writing from what I, myself, considered to be its abasement. Abasement is precisely the *representation* of writing, of its situation *in* the philosophical hierarchy (high/low). Here, too, what I denounce is attributed to me, as if one were in less of a hurry to criticize or to discuss me, than first to put oneself in my place in order to do so. It is a question, therefore, as concerns this value of abasement or fall, of what philosophy (and everything that is part of its system) thought it was doing, intended to do, by operating form the vantage of life present to itself in its logos, of ontological or original plenitude: which is precisely what the deconstructing operation has defined itself against. And the notion of "fall," which is thoroughly complementary to the notion of "origin," was a constant target, in *Of Grammatology* and elsewhere. Consequently I have never incorporated the theme of a prelapsarian writing that would have fallen, through I know now what original sin, into the debased and degraded field of history. On the contrary. Since this is too evident for anyone who wishes to begin to read, I will not insist, and go on the relationship with Heidegger.

I do maintain, as you recalled in your question, that Heidegger's text is extremely important to me, and that it constitutes a novel, irreversible advance all of whose critical resources we are far from having exploited.

That being said—and apart from the fact that for all kinds of reasons, and, I believe, in numerous ways, what I write does not, shall we say, *resemble* a text of Heideggerean filiation (I cannot analyze this in detail here)—I have marked quite explicitly, in *all* the essays I have published, as can be verified, a *departure* from the Heideggerean problematic. This departure is related particularly to the concepts of *origin* and *fall* of which we were just speaking. And, among other places, I have analyzed it as concerns time, "the transcendental horizon of the question of Being," in *Being and Time,* that is, at a strategically decisive point. This departure also, and correlatively, intervenes as concerns the value *proper* (propriety, propriate, appropriation, the entire family of *Eigentlichkeit, Eigen, Ereignis*) which is perhaps the most continuous and most difficult thread of Heidegger's thought. (I will take this occasion of specify, in passing, that I have also explicitly criticized this value of propriety and of original authenticity, and that I even, if it can be put thus, started there. This fanatacism or monotony might be startling, but I cannot seriously be made to say the opposite: "Grammatology, the general science of the 'archi-trace,' presents itself as an explicating thought of the myth of origins. It is a search not for 'historical origins,' but for the *original,* the true, the *authentic etymon* always already present which obscures it." [E. Roudinesco, p. 223.] Here, misunderstanding takes on grandiose proportions.) Wherever the values of propriety, of a proper meaning, of proximity to the self, of etymology, etc. imposed themselves in relation to the body, consciousness, language, writing, etc., I have attempted to analyze the metaphysical desire and presuppositions that were at work. This can already be ascertained in "*La parole soufflée*" (1965; in *Writing and Difference*), but also everywhere else. "*La mythologie blanche*" systematizes the critique of etymologism in philosophy and rhetoric. Naturally, to come back to Heidegger, doubtless the most decisive and most difficult point is that of meaning, the present and presence. In "*Ousia and Grammē*" I proposed a very schematic problematic, or rather a kind of grid, for reading Heidegger's texts from this point of view. This entails an immense labor, and things will never be simple. Since in the course of an interview like this one I can only formulate, shall we say, a traveler's impressions, I sometimes have the feeling that the Heideggerean problematic is the most "profound" and "powerful" defense of what I attempt to put into question under the rubric of the *thought of presence.* . . .

DERRIDA: What we must be wary of, I repeat, is the *metaphysical* concept of history. This is the concept of history as the history of meaning, as we were just saying a moment ago: the history of meaning developing itself, producing itself, fulfilling itself. And doing so linearly, as you recall: in a straight or circular line. This is why, moreover, the "closure of metaphysics" cannot have the form of a *line*, that is, the form in which philosophy recognizes it, in which philosophy recognizes itself. The closure of metaphysics, above all, is not a circle surrounding a homogeneous field, a field homogeneous with itself on its inside, whose outside then would be homogeneous also. The limit has the form of always different faults, of fissures whose mark or scar is borne by all the texts of philosophy.

The metaphysical character of the concept of history is not only linked to linearity, but to an entire *system* of implications (teleology, eschatology, elevating and interiorizing accumulation of meaning, a certain type of traditionality, a certain concept of continuity, of truth, etc.). Therefore it is not an accidental predicate which could be removed by a kind of local ablation, without a general displacement of the organization, without setting the entire system to work. It has happened that I have spoken very quickly of a "metaphysical concept." But I have never believed that there were *metaphysical* concepts *in and of themselves*. No concept is by itself, and consequently in and of itself, metaphysical, outside all the textual work in which it is inscribed. This explains why, although I have formulated many reservations about the "metaphysical" concept of history, I very *often* use the word "history" in order to reinscribe its force and in order to produce another concept or conceptual chain of "history": in effect a "monumental, stratified, contradictory" history; a history that also implies a new logic of *repetition* and the *trace*, for it is difficult to see how there could be history without it. . . .

To ask another kind of question: on the basis of what minimal semantic kernel will these heterogeneous, irreducible histories still be named "histories"? How can the minimum that they must have in common be determined if the common noun history is to be conferred in a way that is not purely conventional or purely con-

fused? It is here that the question of the system of essential predicates that I mentioned above is reintroduced. Socrates asks what science is. He is answered: there is this science, and then that one, and yet again that one. Socrates insists on having an impoverished answer which, cutting short empirical enumeration, would tell him about the scientificity of science, and why all these different sciences are called *science*. But in asking about the historicity of history, about what permits us to call "histories" these histories irreducible to the reality of a general history, the issue is precisely not to return to a question of the Socratic type. The issue is rather to show that the risk of metaphysical reappropriation is ineluctable, that it happens very fast, as soon as the question of the concept and of meaning, or of the essentiality that necessarily regulates the risk, is asked. As soon as the question of the historicity of history is asked—and how can it be avoided if one is manipulating a plural or heterogeneous concept of history?—one is impelled to respond with a definition of essence, of quiddity, to reconstitute a system of essential predicates, and one is also led to refurbish the semantic grounds of the philosophical tradition. A philosophical tradition that always, finally, amounts to an inclusion of historicity on an ontological grounds, precisely. Henceforth, we must not only ask what is the "essence" of history, the historicity of history, but what is the "history" of "essence" in general? And if one wishes to mark a break between some "new concept of history" and the question of the essence of history (as with the concept that the essence regulates), the question, of the history of essence and the history of the concept, finally the history of the meaning of Being, you have a measure of the work which remains to be done.

That being said, the concept of history, no more than any other, cannot be subject to a simple and instantaneous mutation, the striking of a name from the vocabulary. We must elaborate a strategy of the textual work which at every instant borrows an old word from philosophy in order immediately to demarcate it. This is what I was alluding to just now in speaking of a double gesture or double stratification. We must first *overturn* the traditional concept of history, but at the same time mark the *interval*, take care that by virtue of the overturning, and by the simple fact of conceptualization, that the interval not be *reappropriated*. Certainly a new conceptualization is to be produced, but it must take into account the fact that conceptualization itself, and by itself alone, can reintroduce what one wants to "criticize." This is why this work cannot be purely "theoretical" or "conceptual" or "discursive," I mean cannot be the work of a discourse entirely regulated by essence, meaning, truth, consciousness, ideality, etc. What I call *text* is also that which "practically" inscribes and overflows the limits of such a discourse. *There is* such a general text everywhere that (that is, everywhere) this discourse and its order (essence, sense, truth, meaning, consciousness, ideality, etc.) are *overflowed*, that is, everywhere that their authority is put back into the position of a *mark* in a chain that this authority intrinsically and illusorily believes it wishes to, and does in fact, govern. This general text is not limited, of course, as will (or would) be quickly understood, to writings on the page. The writing of this text, moreover, has the exterior limit only of a certain *re-mark*. Writing on the page, and then "literature," are determined types of this re-mark. They must be investigated in their specificity, and in a new way, if you will, in the specificity of their "history," and in their articulation with the other "historical" fields of the text in general.

This is why, briefly, I so often use the word "history," but so often too with the quotation marks and precautions that may have led to the attribution to me of (I am going to abuse this expression, which will lead me to prefer another: "good style") a "rejection of history."

STUDY QUESTIONS: DERRIDA, *POSITIONS*

1. Why are Derrida's readings a double gesture?
2. What is it to deconstruct philosophy?
3. What does Derrida mean by '*différance*'?
4. What did Plato say about writing? How does Derrida reply?
5. In what ways is Saussure's semiology critical of traditional metaphysics?
6. In what ways does Saussure's semiology contradict such a critique of metaphysics?
7. How did Saussure privilege speech?
8. How does Derrida propose to overcome the problematic conception of writing?
9. Derrida says that there is no presence before and outside of semiological *différance*. What does he this mean? How does support this claim?
10. Derrida says that nothing precedes *différance* and spacing. In particular, what is he excluding? How does he support this conclusion?
11. What is grammatology?
12. What must grammatology deconstruct?
13. In the third interview, how does Derrida answer the question of whether *différance* is a concept? What is the significance of this question?
14. What does Derrida mean by deconstruction?
15. What does he mean by double science?
16. What is his view to Hegel and Hegelian idealism? How does he contrast Hegelian idealism from classical idealism?
17. What does he mean by dissemination?
18. What is his view of structuralism? How is his view different?

19. What does 'thought' mean?
20. Does he see Saussure's project as logocentrist? Why? What is the significance of this?
21. What is abasement? How is it relevant to the activity of writing? Reading?
22. Is he sympathetic or unsympathetic to the metaphysical concept of history? Why?
23. How, and why, does Derrida 'reject' history?

Philosophical Bridges: Derrida's Influence

Like Foucault, Derrida is regarded as a pioneer of postmodern thought, whose work has influenced the philosophical climate in the western world by trying to undercut some basic assumptions of modern philosophy. His work is influential primarily because it challenges modern conceptions of truth by rejecting the idea of correspondence with reality. Because words only have meaning in relation to other signs, Derrida denies the claim that a sign has a self-identical and stable meaning and also the thesis that signs can refer to a reality that exists beyond all language. As a consequence, the idea of objectivity understood in representational terms is to be abandoned as relying on a transcendental signified. This challenge has been seen as having two especially significant implications:

> First, it seems to provide a radical critique of the absolute Cartesian notion of the self and of the Enlightenment idea of the autonomous individual. Derrida argues that such notions would amount to a transcendental signified and that there is no self-identical concept of the self beyond a play of signs. This has generated support for the thesis that the self is a social and linguistic construction.
>
> Second, it denies the naturalist and realist idea of real essences in the natural world, as well as the allied notion of human nature. This has been taken by some thinkers to imply that science does not give us knowledge of how the world really is beyond the signs of the sciences; in that way, it is one perspective among many.

Derrida's conception of binary opposites has also been influential because it has been seen as illuminating the nature of oppression or domination. Derrida claims that philosophical theories work by positing a binary, such as reason versus emotion or mind versus body, and by implicitly assuming that one of the pair is dominant. For example, Luce Irigaray's radical feminism argues that in the binary 'male versus female,' male has been conceived as dominant. Irigaray claims that, in western philosophy, the subject has always been conceived of as masculine, women are regarded as inferior men or as objects, and philosophy has concentrated on the problems and concerns of men. In this way, the language and culture of our society deny women their identity as subjects. Irigaray employs a version of Derrida's deconstruction to reveal and subvert the male dominance of philosophy.

Like Foucault, Derrida has had considerable influence outside of philosophy. He is regarded as a central figure in postmodern literary criticism whose notion of deconstructive readings has introduced a new way of approaching texts.

BIBLIOGRAPHY

GENERAL
Gutting, Gary, *French Philosophy in the Twentieth Century*, Cambridge University Press, 2000

GADAMER
Primary
Philosophical Hermeneutics, University of California Press, 1977, translated by D. Linge
Truth and Method, Crossroad, 1989, translated by J. Weinsheimer and D. Marshall
Literature and Philosophy in Dialogue, trans. Robert Paslick, State University of New York Press, 1994

Secondary
Michelffelder, Diane and Palmer, Richard (eds), *Dialogue and Deconstruction: The Gadamer-Derrida Encounter*, SUNY Press, 1995
Grondin, Jean, *The Sources of Hermeneutics*, SUNY Press, 1995
Warnke, Georgia, *Gadamer: Hermeneutics, Tradition and Reason*, Stanford University Press, 1987

HABERMAS
Primary
Knowledge and Human Interests, Beacon, 1971, translated by J. Shapiro
Legitimation Crisis, Beacon, 1975, translated by T. McCarthy
Theory and Practice, Beacon, 1973, translated by J. Viertel
The Theory of Communicative Action (two vols.), Beacon, 1984, translated by T. McCarthy
Moral Consciousness and Communicative Action, MIT Press, 1990, translated by C. Lenhardt and S. Nicholsen
Between Facts and Norms: Contributions to a Discourse Theory of Law and Democracy, MIT Press, 1996, W. Rehg

Secondary
Cooke, M, *Language and Reason: A Study of Harbermas' Pragmatics*, MIT Press, 1994
Bernstein, Richard (ed), *Habermas and Modernity*, MIT Press, 1985

Ingram, David, *Habermas and the Dialectic of Reason*, Yale University Press, 1987
McCarthy, Thomas, *The Critical Theory of Jürgen Habermas*, MIT Press, 1978
White, Stephen, *The Cambridge Companion to Habermas*, Cambridge University Press, 1995

FOUCAULT
Primary
Madness and Civilization, Pantheon, 1965, translated by R. Howard
The Birth of a Clinic: An Archeology of Medical Perception, Pantheon Books, translated by A. Sheridan Smith
The Archeology of Knowledge, Pantheon Books, 1972, translated by A. Sheridan Smith
The Order of Things: An Archeology of the Human Sciences, Vintage Books, 1973
The Care of Self: The History of Sexuality, vol. 3, trans. R. Hurley, Pantheon, 1986
The Foucault Reader, Pantheon, 1984, ed. P. Rabinow

Secondary
Cousins, Mark, and Hussain, Athar, *Michel Foucault*, St. Martin's Press, 1984
Dreyfus, H., and Rabinow, Paul, *Michel Foucault: Beyond Structuralism and Hermeneutics*, University of Chicago Press, 1982
Gutting, G., *The Cambridge Companion to Foucault*, Cambridge University Press, 1994
Macey, David, *The Lives of Michel Foucault*, Hutchinson, 1993

DERRIDA
Primary
Of Grammatology, trans. G. C. Spivak, Johns Hopkins University Press, 1967
Writing and Difference, trans. Alan Bass, University of Chicago Press, 1967
Dissemination, trans. Barbara Johnson, University of Chicago Press, 1972
Speech and Phenomena and Other Essays on Husserl's Theory of Signs, Northwestern University Press, 1973

Secondary

Bennington, Geoffrey, and Derrida, Jacques, *Jacques Derrida*, University of Chicago Press, 1993

Gasche, Rodolphe, *The Tain of the Mirror*, Harvard University Press, 1986

Norris, Christopher, *Derrida*, Harvard University Press, 1987

RECENT NORTH AMERICAN PHILOSOPHY

PROLOGUE

As we mentioned in the General Introduction, one aspect of philosophy in the late twentieth century is an increased cross-fertilization between the two traditions of analytic and continental philosophy. For instance, Habermas is very conversant with both types of philosophy and weaves together strands from both. Increasingly, North American philosophers are familiar with both traditions, even if they specialize in aspects of only one. Although there still exist substantial differences in style, aim, and content between most so-called analytic and continental philosophers, nevertheless this symbiosis is a significant feature of some recent philosophy. Richard Rorty and Charles Taylor are well-known representatives of this trend. Neither can be classified as analytic or continental.

It is an oversimplification to speak of two traditions, when there exist such fundamental differences between Gadamer, Habermas, and Derrida, as well as between Quine, Kuhn, and Putnam. Likewise, there are important differences between Taylor and Rorty, despite the similarities between them. Both reject representational theories of knowledge (the thesis that knowledge represents the world) and think that this rejection has important political and social implications. One major difference is that Rorty has been more influenced by the pragmatism of Dewey than has Taylor. Another is that whereas Rorty also draws inspiration from the work of Derrida and postmodern thinking, Taylor is influenced more directly by the hermeneutic tradition. Additionally, Rorty and Taylor draw very different political conclusions from their respective analyses.

RICHARD RORTY (1931–)

Biographical History

Richard Rorty, who was born in New York City, studied at the University of Chicago, receiving his B.A. in 1949 and his M.A. in 1952. His M.A. thesis was on Whitehead and was supervised by Charles Hartshorne. He studied at Yale for his Ph.D., which he received in 1956 with a dissertation entitled 'The Concept of Potentiality.' From 1961 to 1982, he taught at Princeton University, after which he was professor of humanities at the University of Virginia. He is currently professor of comparative literature at Stanford University. His first major work was *Philosophy and the Mirror of Nature* (1979), a critique of the thesis that language and mental states mirror or represent nature. Since then, Rorty's publications, such as *Contingency, Irony and Solidarity*, have made him a well-known exponent of a combination of pragmatism, postmodernism, and liberalism.

Philosophical Overview

Rorty's central philosophical thesis is antirepresentationalism, which means that the whole idea that mental states and language represent reality is mistaken. This means that there is no viable metaphysical distinction between appearance and reality, and no true description of how the world is. Consequently, the idea or hope that the sciences might provide such a true description is forlorn.

Rorty rejects anything but a minimal theory of truth. In other words, he eschews any attempt to explain the concept of truth beyond saying how the word 'true' functions, which is as follows: 'The sentence "S" is true if and only if S.' In particular, of course, he argues against the correspondence theory of truth, which claims that a sentence or belief is true if and only if it corresponds to the facts. This, however, does not mean that truth is a subjective invention.

Rorty tries to replace representationalism with a form of pragmatism, according to which having knowledge is a question of 'acquiring habits of action for coping with reality.' Our links with the rest of the world are causal and not epistemological. Nevertheless, he gives an account of how beliefs can be justified, which he calls epistemological behaviorism. To justify a belief is to cite other beliefs, which do not need any justification in the context, in such a way that satisfies the standards implicit in the relevant societal justificatory practices. Culturally, there will be certain beliefs that are taken as a cultural given, and different cultures may take different judgments as a given. Nevertheless, Rorty claims that any belief is open to revision if it does not cohere with the other beliefs that the person has. Rorty's holist view negates the thesis that knowledge must have foundations.

In brief, Rorty is not a relativist concerning truth because he denies any theory of truth. He is a relativist about justification because he holds that justification is relative to *our* practices. This view he calls 'ethnocentrism.' This implies that most of our cherished values and practices cannot be justified without circularity. Our ethnocentric perspective cannot be privileged as truer than any other. An ironist is someone who recognizes this situation. In this regard and also insofar as Rorty is against all representation theories and eschews the notion of truth, we might compare his claims with the postmodern views of Derrida. In this way, his thought belongs to a Nietzschian tradition. Politically, Rorty espouses a form of liberalism.

SOLIDARITY OR OBJECTIVITY?

Rorty's idea is that there are two fundamentally different ways of making sense of our lives. With the idea of solidarity, we do so in terms of participating in a community; and with 'objectivity,' we do so in terms of an immediate relation to a nonhuman reality. He distinguishes realists and pragmatists in terms of the primacy of objectivity or solidarity. Realists try to ground solidarity in objectivity, and pragmatists explain objectivity in terms of solidarity. For pragmatists, the desire for objectivity is the desire for the widest possible intersubjective agreement. Rorty distinguishes pragmatism from forms of relativism and argues that recent philosophers such as Davidson and Putnam come close to accepting the form of pragmatism that he (Rorty) advocates.

There are two principal ways in which reflective human beings try, by placing their lives in a larger context, to give sense to those lives. The first is by telling the story of their contribution to a community. This community may be the actual historical one in which they live, or another actual one, distant in time or place, or a quite imaginary one, consisting perhaps of a dozen heroes and heroines selected from history or fiction or both. The second way is to describe themselves as standing in immediate relation to a nonhuman reality. This relation is immediate in the sense that it does not derive from a relation between such a reality and their tribe, or their nation, or their imagined band of comrades. I shall say that stories of the former kind exemplify the desire for solidarity, and that stories of the latter kind exemplify the desire for objectivity. Insofar as a person is seeking solidarity, she does not ask about the relation between the practices of the chosen community and something outside that community. Insofar as she seeks objectivity, she distances herself from the actual persons around her not by thinking of herself as a member of some other real or imaginary group, but rather by attaching herself to something which can be described without reference to any particular human beings.

The tradition in Western culture which centers around the notion of the search for Truth, a tradition which runs form the Greek philosophers through the Enlightenment, is the clearest example of the attempt to find a sense in one's existence by turning away from solidarity to objectivity. The idea of Truth as something to be pursued for its own sake, not because it will be good for oneself, or for one's real or imaginary community, is the central theme of this tradition. It was perhaps the growing awareness by the Greeks of the sheer diversity of human communities which stimulated the emergence of this ideal. A fear of parochialism, of being confined within the horizons of the group into which one happens to be born, a need to see it with the eyes of a stranger, helps produce the skeptical and ironic tone characteristic of Euripides and Socrates. Herodotus' willingness to take the barbarians seriously enough to describe their customs in detail may have been a necessary prelude to Plato's claim that the way to transcend skepticism is to envisage a common goal of humanity—a goal set by human nature rather than by Greek culture. The combination of Socratic alienation and Platonic hope give rise to the idea of the intellectual as someone who is in touch with the nature of things, not by way of the opinions of his community, but in a more immediate way.

Plato developed the idea of such an intellectual by means of distinctions between knowledge and opinion, and between appearance and reality. Such distinctions conspire to produce the idea that

"Solidarity or Objectivity?" from *Objectivity, Relativism and Truth* by Richard Rorty, Cambridge University Press, 1991.

rational inquiry should make visible a realm to which nonintellectuals have little access, and of whose very existence they may be doubtful. In the Enlightenment, this notion became concrete in the adoption of the Newtonian physical scientist as a model of the intellectual. To most thinkers of the eighteenth century, it seemed clear that the access to Nature which physical science had provided should now be followed by the establishment of social, political, and economic institutions which were in accordance with Nature. Ever since, liberal social thought has centered around social reform as made possible by objective knowledge of what human beings are like—not knowledge of what Greeks or Frenchmen or Chinese are like, but of humanity as such. We are the heirs of this objectivist tradition, which centers around the assumption that we must step outside our community long enough to examine it in the light of something which transcends it, namely, that which it has in common with every other actual and possible human community. This tradition dreams of an ultimate community which will have transcended the distinction between the natural and the social, which will exhibit a solidarity which is not parochial because it is the expression of an ahistorical human nature. Much of the rhetoric of contemporary intellectual life takes for granted that the goal of scientific inquiry into man is to understand "underlying structures," or "culturally invariant factors," or "biologically determined patterns."

Those who wish to ground solidarity in objectivity—call them "realists"—have to construe truth as correspondence to reality. So they must construct a metaphysics which has room for a special relation between beliefs and objects which will differentiate true from false beliefs. They also must argue that there are procedures of justification of belief which are natural and not merely local. So they must construct an epistemology which has room for a kind of justification which is not merely social but natural, springing from human nature itself, and made possible by a link between that part of nature and the rest of nature. On their view, the various procedures which are thought of as providing rational justification by one or another culture may or may not really *be* rational. For to be truly rational, procedures

of justification *must* lead to the truth, to correspondence to reality, to the intrinsic nature of things.

By contrast, those who wish to reduce objectivity to solidarity—call them "pragmatists"—do not require either a metaphysics or an epistemology. They view truth as, in William James' phrase, what is good for *us* to believe. So they do not need an account of a relation between beliefs and objects called "correspondence," nor an account of human cognitive abilities which ensures that our species is capable of entering into that relation. They see the gap between truth and justification not as something to be bridged by isolating a natural and transcultural cultural sort of rationality which can be used to criticize certain cultures and praise others, but simply as the gap between the actual good and the possible better. From a pragmatist point of view, to say that what is rational for us now to believe may not be *true*, is simply to say that somebody may come up with a better idea. It is to say that there is always room for improved belief, since new evidence, or new hypotheses, or a whole new vocabulary, may come along. For pragmatists, the desire for objectivity is not the desire to escape the limitations of one's community, but simply the desire for as much intersubjective agreement as possible, the desire to extend the reference of "us" as far as we can. Insofar as pragmatist make a distinction between knowledge and opinion, it is simply the distinction between topics on which such agreement is relatively easy to get and topics on which agreement is relatively hard to get.

"Relativism" is the traditional epithet applied to pragmatism by realist. Three different views are commonly referred to by this name. The first is the view that every belief is as good as every other. The second is the view that "true" is an equivocal term, having as many meanings as there are procedures of justification. The third is the view that there is nothing to be said about either truth or rationality apart from descriptions of the familiar procedures of justification which a given society—*ours*—uses in one or another area of inquiry. The pragmatist holds the ethnocentric third view. But he does not hold the self-refuting first view, nor the eccentric second view. He thinks that his views are better than the realists', but he does not think that his views correspond to the nature of things. He thinks that the very flexibility of the word "true"—the fact that it is merely an expression of commendation—insures its univocity. The term "true", on his account, means the same in all cultures, just as equally flexible terms like "here," "there," "good," "bad," "you," and "me," mean the same in all cultures. But the identity of meaning is, of course, compatible with diversity of reference, and with diversity of procedures for assigning the terms. So he feels free to use the term "true" as a general term of commendation in the same way as his realist opponent does—and in particular to use it to commend his own view.

However, it is not clear why "relativist" should be thought an appropriate term for the ethnocentric third view, the one which the pragmatist *does* hold. For the pragmatist is not holding a positive theory which says that something is relative to something else. He is, instead, making the purely *negative* point that we should drop the traditional distinction between knowledge and opinion, construed as the distinction between truth as correspondence to reality and truth as a commendatory term for well-justified beliefs. The reason that the realist calls this negative claim "relativistic' is that he cannot believe that anybody would seriously deny that truth has an intrinsic nature. So when the pragmatist says that there is nothing to be said about truth save that each of us will commend as true those beliefs which he or she finds good to believe, the realist is inclined to interpret this as one more positive theory about the nature of truth: a theory according to which truth is simply the contemporary opinion of a chosen individual or group. Such a theory would, of course, be self-refuting. But the pragmatist does not have a theory of truth, much less a relativistic one. As a partisan of solidarity, his account of the value of cooperative human inquiry has only an ethical base, not an epistemological or metaphysical one. Not having *any* epistemology, *a fortiori* he does not have a relativistic one.

The question of whether truth or rationality has an intrinsic nature, of whether we ought to have a positive theory about either topic, is just the question of whether our self-description ought to be constructed around a relation to human nature or around a relation to a particular collection of human beings, whether we should desire objectivity or solidarity. It is

hard to see how one could choose between these alternatives by looking more deeply into the nature of knowledge, or of man, or of nature. Indeed, the proposal that this issue might be so settled begs the question in favor of the realist, for it presupposes that knowledge, man, and nature *have* real essences which are relevant to the problem at hand. For the pragmatist, by contrast, "knowledge" is, like "truth," simply a compliment paid to the beliefs which we think so well justified that, for the moment, further justification is not needed. An inquiry into the nature of knowledge can, on his view, only be a sociohistorical account of how various people have tried to reach agreement on what to believe.

The view which I am calling "pragmatism" is almost, but not quite, the same as what Hilary Putnam, in his recent *Reason, Truth, and History,* calls "the internalist conception of philosophy." Putnam defines such a conception as one which give up the attempt at a God's eye view of things, the attempt at contact with the nonhuman which I have been calling "the desire for objectivity." Unfortunately, he accompanies his defense of the antirealist views I am recommending with a polemic against a lot of the other people who hold these views—e.g., Kuhn, Feyerabend, Foucault, and myself. We are criticized as "relativists." Putnam presents "internalism" as a happy *via media* between realism and relativism. He speaks of "the plethora of relativistic doctrines being marketed today" and in particular of "the French philosophers" as holding "some fancy mixture of cultural relativism and 'structuralism.'" But when it comes to criticizing these doctrines all that Putnam finds to attack is the so-called "incommensurability thesis": vis., "terms used in another culture cannot be equated in meaning of reference with any terms or expression *we* posses." He sensibly agrees with Donald Davidson in remarking that this thesis is self-refuting. Criticism of this thesis, however, is destructive of, at most, some incautious passages in some early writings by Feyerabend. Once this thesis is brushed aside, it is hard to see how Putnam himself differs from most of those he criticizes.

Putnam accepts the Davidsonian point that, as he puts it, "the whole justification of an interpretative scheme . . . is that it renders the behavior of others at least minimally reasonable by *our* lights." It would seem natural to go on from this to say that we cannot get outside the range of those lights, that we cannot stand on neutral ground illuminated only by the natural light of reason, But Putnam draws back from this conclusion. He does so because he construes the claim that we cannot do so as the claim that the range of our thought is restricted by what he calls "institutionalized norms," publicly available criteria for settling all arguments, including philosophical arguments. He rightly says that there are no such criteria, arguing that the suggestion that there are is as self-refuting as the "incommensurability thesis." He is, I think, entirely right in saying that the notion that philosophy is or should become such an application of explicit criteria contradicts the very idea of philosophy. One can gloss Putnam's point by saying that "philosophy" is precisely what a culture becomes capable of when it ceases to define itself in terms of explicit rules, and becomes sufficiently leisured and civilized to rely on inarticulate know-how, to substitute *phronesis* for codification, and conversation with foreigners for conquest of them.

But to say that we cannot refer every question to explicit criteria institutionalized by our society does not speak to the point which the people whom Putnam calls "relativists" are making. One reason these people are pragmatists is precisely that they share Putnam's distrust of the positivistic idea that rationality is a matter of applying criteria.

Such a distrust is common, for example, to Kuhn, Mary Hesse, Wittgenstein, Michael Polanyi, and Michael Oakeshott. Only someone who did think of rationality in this way would dream of suggesting that "true" means something different in different societies. For only such a person could imagine that there was anything to pick out to which one might make "true" relative. Only if one shares the logical positivists' idea that we all carry around things called "rules of language" which regulate what we say when, will one suggest that there is no way to break out of one's culture.

In the most original and powerful section of his book, Putnam argues that the notion that "rationality . . . is defined by the local cultural norms" is merely the demonic counterpart of positivism. It is, as he says, "a scientistic theory inspired by anthropology as positivism was a scientific theory inspired

by the exact sciences." By "scientism" Putnam means the notion that rationality consists in the application of criteria. Suppose we drop this notion, and accept Putnam's own Quinean picture of inquiry as the continual reweaving of a web of beliefs rather than as the application of criteria to cases. Then the notion of "local cultural norms" will lose its offensively parochial overtones. For now to say that we must work by our own lights, that we must be ethnocentric, is merely to say that beliefs suggested by another culture must be tested by trying to weave them together with beliefs we already have. It is a consequence of this holistic view of knowledge, a view *shared* by Putnam and those he criticizes as "relativists," that alternative cultures are not to be thought of on the model of alternative geometries. Alternative geometries are irreconcilable because they have axiomatic structures, and contradictory axioms. They are *designed* to be irreconcilable. Cultures are not so designed, and do not have axiomatic structures. To say that they have "institutionalized norms" is only to say, with Foucault, that knowledge is never separable from power—that one is likely to suffer if one does not hold certain beliefs at certain times and places. But such institutional backups for beliefs take the form of bureaucrats and policemen, not of "rules of language" and "criteria of rationality." To think otherwise is the Cartesian fallacy of seeing axioms where there are only shared habits, of viewing statements which summarize such practices as if they reported constraints enforcing such practices. Part of the force of Quine's and Davidson's attack on the distinction between the conceptual and the empirical is that the distinction between different cultures does not differ in kind from the distinction between different theories held by members of a single culture. The Tasmanian aborigines and the British colonists had trouble communicating, but this trouble was different only in extent from the difficulties in communication experienced by Gladstone and Disraeli. The trouble in all such cases is just the difficulty of explaining why other people disagree with us, of reweaving our beliefs so as to fit the fact of disagreement together with the other beliefs we hold. The same Quinean arguments which dispose of the positivists' distinction between analytic and synthetic truth dispose of the anthropologists' distinction between the intercultural and the intracultural.

On this holistic account of cultural norms, however, we do not need the notion of a universal transcultural rationality which Putnam invokes against those whom he calls "relativists." Just before the end of his book, Putnam says that once we drop the notion of a God's-eye point of view we realize that:

> we can only hope to produce a more rational conception of rationality or a better conception of morality if we operate from within our tradition (with its echoes of the Greek agora, of Newton, and so on, in the case of rationality, and with its echoes of scripture, of the philosophers, of the democratic revolutions, and so on . . . in the case of morality.) We are invited to engage in a truly human dialogue.

With this I entirely agree, and so, I take it, would Kuhn, Hesse, and most of the other so-called "relativists"— perhaps even Foucault. But Putnam then goes on to pose a further question:

> Does this dialogue have an ideal terminus? Is there a true conception of rationality, an ideal morality, even if all we ever have are our conceptions of these?

I do not see the point of this question. Putnam suggests that a negative answer—the view that "there is only the dialogue"—is just another form of self-refuting relativism. But, once again, I do not see how a claim that something does not exist can be construed as a claim that something is relative to something else. In the final sentence of his book, Putnam says that "The very fact that we speak of our different conceptions as different conceptions of rationality posits a Grenzbegriff, a limit-concept of ideal truth." But what is such a posit supposed to do, except to say that from God's point of view the human race is heading in the right direction? Surely Putnam's "internalism" should forbid him to say anything like that. To say that we think we're heading in the right direction is just to say, with Kuhn, that we can, by hindsight, tell the story of the past as a story of progress. To say that we still have a long way to go, that our present views should not be cast in bronze, is too platitudinous to require support by positing limit-concepts. So it is hard to see what difference is made by the difference

between saying "there is only the dialogue" and saying "there is also that to which the dialogue converges."

I would suggest that Putnam here, at the end of the day, slides back into the scientism he rightly condemns in others. For the root of scientism, defined as the view that rationality is a matter of applying criteria, is the desire for objectivity, the hope that what Putnam calls "human flourishing" has a transhistorical nature. I think that Feyerabend is right in suggesting that until we discard the metaphor of inquiry, and human activity generally, as converging rather than proliferating, as becoming more unified rather than more diverse, we shall never be free of the motives which once led us to posit gods. Positing Grenzbegriffe seems merely a way of telling ourselves that a nonexistent God would, if he did exist, be pleased with us. If we could ever be moved solely by the desire for solidarity, setting aside the desire for objectivity altogether, then we should think of human progress as making it possible for human beings to do more interesting things and be more interesting people, not as heading towards a place which has somehow been prepared for humanity in advance. Our self-image would employ images of making rather than finding, the images used by the Romantics to praise poets rather than the images used by the Greeks to praise mathematicians. Feyerabend seems to me right in trying to develop such a self-image for us, but his project seems misdescribed, by himself as well as by his critics, as "relativism."

Those who follow Feyerabend in this direction are often thought of as necessarily enemies of the Enlightenment, as joining in the chorus which claims that the traditional self-descriptions of the Western democracies are bankrupt, that they somehow have been shown to be "inadequate" or "self-deceptive." Part of the instinctive resistance to attempts by Marxists, Sartreans, Oakeshottians, Gadamerians and Foucauldians to reduce objectivity to solidarity is the fear that our traditional liberal habits and hopes will not survive the reduction. Such feelings are evident, for example, in Habermas' criticism of Gadamer's position as relativistic and potentially repressive, in the suspicion that Heidegger's attacks on realism are somehow linked to his Nazism, in the hunch that Marxist attempts to interpret values as class interests are usually just apologies for Leninist takeovers, and in the suggestion that Oakeshott's skepticism about rationalism in politics is merely an apology for the status quo.

I think that putting the issue in such moral and political terms, rather than in epistemological or metaphilosophical terms, makes clearer what is at stake. For now the question is not about how to define words like "truth" or "rationality" or "knowledge" or "philosophy," but about what self-image our society should have of itself. The ritual invocation of the "need to avoid relativism" is most comprehensible as an expression of the need to preserve certain habits of contemporary European life. These are the habits nurtured by the Enlightenment, and justified by it in terms of an appeal of Reason, conceived as a transcultural human ability to correspond to reality, a faculty whose possession and use is demonstrated by obedience to explicit criteria. So the real question about relativism is whether these same habits of intellectual, social, and political life can be justified by a conception of rationality as criterionless muddling through, and by a pragmatist conception of truth.

I think that the answer to this question is that the pragmatist cannot justify these habits without circularity, but then neither can the realist. The pragmatists' justification of toleration, free inquiry, and the quest for undistorted communication can only take the form of a comparison between societies which exemplify these habits and those which do not, leading up to the suggestion that nobody who was experienced both would prefer the latter. It is exemplified by Winston Churchill's defense of democracy as the worst form of government imaginable, except for all the others which have been tried so far. Such justification is not by reference to a criterion, but by reference to various detailed practical advantages. It is circular only in that the terms of praise used to describe liberal societies will be drawn from the vocabulary of the liberal societies themselves. Such praise has to be in *some* vocabulary, after all, and the terms of praise current in primitive or theocratic or totalitarian societies will not produce the desired result. So the pragmatist admits that he has no ahistorical standpoint from which to endorse the habits of modern democracies he wishes to praise. These consequences are just what partisans of solidarity expect. But among partisans of objectivity they give

rise, once again, to ears of the dilemma formed by ethnocentrism on the one hand and relativism on the other. Either we attach a special privilege to our own community, or we pretend an impossible tolerance for every other group.

I have been arguing that we pragmatists should grasp the ethnocentric horn of this dilemma. We should say that we must, in practice, privilege our own group, even though there can be no noncircular justification for doing so. We must insist that the face that nothing is immune from criticism does not mean that we have a duty to justify everything. We Western liberal intellectuals should accept the fact that we have to start from where we are, and that this means that there are lots of views which we simply cannot take seriously. To use Neurath's familiar analogy, we can *understand* the revolutionary's suggestion that a sailable boat can't be made out of the planks which make up ours, and that we must simply abandon ship. But we cannot take his suggestion seriously. We cannot take it as a rule for action, so it is not a live option. For some people, to be sure, the option *is* live. These are the people who have always hoped to become a New Being, who have hoped to be converted rather than persuaded. But we—the liberal Rawlsian searches for consensus, the heirs of Socrates, the people who wish to link their days dialectically each to each—cannot do so. Our community—the community of the liberal intellectuals of the secular modern West—wants to be able to give a *post factum* account of any change of view. We want to be able, so to speak, to justify ourselves to our earlier selves. This preference is not built into us by human nature. It is just the way *we* live now.

This lonely provincialism, this admission that we are just the historical moment that we are, not the representatives of something ahistorical, is what makes traditional Kantian liberals like Rawls draw back from pragmatism. "Relativism," by contrast, is merely a red herring. The realist is, once again, projecting his own habits of thought upon the pragmatist when he charges him with relativism. For the realist thinks that the whole point of philosophical thought is to detach oneself from any particular community and look down at it from a more universal standpoint. When he hears the pragmatist repudiating the desire for such a standpoint he cannot quite believe it. He thinks that everyone, deep down inside, *must* want such detachment. So he attributes to the pragmatist a perverse from of his own attempted detachment, and sees him as an ironic, sneering aesthete who refuse to take the choice between communities seriously, a mere "relativist." But the pragmatist dominated by the desire for solidarity, can only be criticized for taking his own community *too* seriously. He can only be criticized for ethnocentrism, not for relativism. To be ethnocentric is to divide the human race into the people to whom one must justify one's beliefs and the others. The first group—one's *ethnos*—comprises those who share enough of one's beliefs to make fruitful conversation possible. In this sense, everybody is ethnocentric when engaged in actual debate, no matter now much realist rhetoric about objectivity he produces in his study.

What is disturbing about the pragmatist's picture is not that it is relativistic but that it takes away two sorts of metaphysical comfort to which our intellectual tradition has become accustomed. One is the thought that membership in our biological species carries with it certain "rights," a notion which does not seem to make sense unless the biological similarities entail the possession of something nonbiological, something which links our species to a nonhuman reality and thus gives the species moral dignity. This picture of rights as biologically transmitted is so basic to the political discourse of the Western democracies that we are troubled by any suggestion that "human nature" is not a useful moral concept. The second comfort is provided by the thought that our community cannot wholly die. The picture of a common human nature oriented towards correspondence to reality as it is in itself comforts us with the thought that even if our civilization is destroyed, even if all memory of our political or intellectual or artistic community is erased, the race is fated to recapture the virtues and the insights and the achievements which were the glory of that community. The notion of human nature as an inner structure which leads all members of the species to converge to the same point, to recognize the same theories, virtues, and works of art as worthy of honor, assures us that even if the Persians had won, the arts and sciences of the Greeks would sooner or later have appeared elsewhere. It assures that even if the Orwellian bureaucrats of ter-

ror rule for a thousand years the achievements of the Western democracies will someday be duplicated by our remote descendants. It assures us that "man will prevail," that something reasonably like *our* world-view, *our* virtues, *our* art, will bob up again whenever human beings are left alone to cultivate their inner natures. The comfort of the realist picture is the comfort of saying not simply that there is a place prepared for our race in our advance, but also that we now know quite a bit about what the place looks like. The inevitable ethnocentrism to which we are all condemned is thus as much a part of the realist's comfortable view as of the pragmatist's uncomfortable one.

The pragmatist gives up the first sort of comfort because he thinks that so say that certain people have certain rights is merely to say that we should treat them in certain ways. It is not to give a *reason* for treating them in those ways. As to the second sort of comfort, he suspects that the hope that something resembling *us* will inherit the earth is impossible to eradicate, as impossible as eradicating the hope of surviving our individual deaths through some satisfying transfiguration. But he does not want to turn this hope into a theory of the nature of man. He wants solidarity to be our *only* comfort, and to be seen not to require metaphysical support.

My suggestion that the desire for objectivity is in part a disguised form of the fear of the death of our community echoes Nietzsche's charge that the philosophical tradition which stems from Plato is an attempt to avoid facing up to contingency, to escape from time and chance. Nietzsche thought that realism was to be condemned not only by arguments from its theoretical incoherence, the sort of argument we find in Putnam and Davidson, but also on practical, pragmatic, grounds. Nietzsche thought that the test of human character was the ability to live with the thought that there was not convergence. He wanted us to be able to think of truth as:

> a mobile army of metaphors, metonyms, and anthromorphisms—in short a sum of human relations, which have been enhanced, transposed, and embellished poetically and rhetorically and which after long use seem firm, canonical, and obligatory to a people.

Nietzsche hoped that eventually there might be human beings who could and did think of truth in

430 ◆ SECTION EIGHT / RECENT NORTH AMERICAN PHILOSOPHY

this way, but who still liked themselves, who saw themselves as *good* people for whom solidarity was *enough*.

I think that pragmatism's attack on the various structure-content distinctions which buttress the realist's notion of objectivity can best be seen as an attempt to let us think of truth in this Nietzschean way, as entirely a matter of solidarity. That is why I think we need to say, despite Putnam, that "there is only the dialogue," only *us*, and to throw out the last residues of the notion of "transcultural rationality." But this should not lead us to repudiate, as Nietzsche sometimes did, the elements in our movable host which embody the ideas of Socratic conversation, Christian fellowship, and Enlightenment science. Nietzsche ran together his diagnosis of philosophical realism as an expression of fear and resentment with his own resentful idiosyncratic idealizations of silence, solitude, and violence. Post-Nietzschean thinkers like Adorno and Heidegger and Foucault have run together Nietzsche's criticisms of the metaphysical tradition on the one hand with his criticisms of bourgeois civility, of Christian love, and of the nineteenth century's hope that science would make the world a better place to live, on the other. I do not think that there is any interesting connection between these two sets of criticisms. Pragmatism seems to me, as I have said, a philosophy of solidarity rather than of despair. From this point of view, Socrates' turn away from the gods, Christianity's turn from an Omnipotent Creator to the man who suffered on the Cross, and the Baconian turn from science as contemplation of eternal truth to science as instrument of social progress, can be seen as so many preparations for the act of social faith which is suggested by a Nietzschean view of truth.

The best argument we partisans of solidarity have against the realistic partisans of objectivity is Nietzsche's argument that the traditional Western metaphysico-epistemological way of firming up our habits simply isn't working anymore. It isn't doing its job. It has become as transparent a device as the postulation of deities who turn out, by a happy coincidence, to have chosen *us* as their people. So the pragmatist suggestion that we substitute a "merely" ethical foundation for our sense of community—or, better, that we think of our sense of community as

having no foundation except shared hope and the trust created by such sharing—is put forward on no practical grounds. It is *not* put forward as a corollary of a metaphysical claim that the objects in the world contain no intrinsically action-guiding properties, nor of an epistemological claim that we lack a faculty of moral sense, nor of a semantic claim that truth is reducible to justification. It is a suggestion about how we might think of ourselves in order to avoid the kind of resentful belatedness—characteristic of the bad side of Nietzsche—which now characterizes much of high culture. This resentment arises from the realization, which I referred to at the beginning of this chapter, that the Enlightenment's search for objectivity has often gone sour.

The rhetoric of scientific objectivity, pressed too hard and taken too seriously, has led us to people like B. F. Skinner on the one hand and people like Althusser on the other—two equally pointless fantasies, both produced by the attempt to be "scientific" about our moral and political lives. Reaction against scientism led to attacks on natural science as a sort of false god. But there is nothing wrong with science, there is only something wrong with the attempt to divinize it, the attempt characteristic of realistic philosophy. This reaction has also led to attacks on liberal social thought of the type common to Mill and Dewey and Rawls as a mere ideological superstructure, one which obscures the realities of our situation and represses attempts to change that situation. But there is nothing wrong with liberal democracy, nor with the philosophers who have tried to enlarge its scope. There is only something wrong with the attempt to see their efforts as failures to achieve something which they were not trying to achieve—a demonstration of the "objective" superiority of our way of life over all other alternatives. There is, in short, nothing wrong with the hopes of the Enlightenment, the hopes which created the Western democracies. The value of the ideals of the Enlightenment is, for us pragmatists, just the value of some of the institutions and practices which they have created. In this essay I have sought to distinguish these institutions and practices from the philosophical justifications for them provided by partisans of objectivity, and to suggest an alternative justification.

STUDY QUESTIONS: RORTY, *SOLIDARITY OR OBJECTIVITY?*

1. What is the difference between objectivity and solidarity?
2. What is a realist? What is a pragmatist? How do pragmatists characterize objectivity? How would a realist characterize objectivity?
3. What are the three types of relativism that Rorty distinguishes? Which of these does the pragmatist hold?
4. According to Rorty, in what ways are his views similar to Putnam's?
5. What are the misgivings that some philosophers, such as Habermas, have of the attempt to reduce objectivity to solidarity? How does Rorty diagnose the problem?
6. What is Rorty's suggested solution to this problem of how to justify tolerance and free inquiry?
7. According to Rorty, what makes traditional Kantian liberals such as Rawls withdraw from pragmatism? What is Rorty's answer to that?
8. What is ethnocentrism?
9. What are the two metaphysical comforts that pragmatism removes?
10. What does Rorty say about transcultural rationality? What does he distinguish it from?
11. According to Rorty, what is the best argument against traditional western epistemology and metaphysics?
12. 'There is . . . nothing wrong with the hopes of the Enlightenment.' How would Rorty justify that claim?

Philosophical Bridges: Rorty's Influence

Rorty's way of blending some aspects of Dewey's pragmatism with some elements of postmodern thought is part of his appeal. Perhaps, the most influential aspect of Rorty's philosophy is his rejection of traditional modern views, i.e., his antifoundationalism, his antirepresentationalism, and his anti-essentialism. Among these, perhaps the most influential are his criticism of representational views of meaning, and the allied Nietzschian claim that no cultural perspective is privileged. Rorty is among the few recent philosophers whose name is wellknown outside of philosophical circles.

CHARLES TAYLOR (1931–)

Biographical History

Charles Taylor studied for a B.A. in history at McGill University, Canada, and for a B.A. degree in philosophy, politics and economics at Oxford University, England. In 1961, he took his D.Phil. at Oxford, where he was later appointed the Chicele Professor of Moral Philosophy. He is professor of political science and philosophy at McGill University. Taylor's first book was *The Explanation of Behaviour* (1967), followed by *Hegel* (1975). Two volumes of his philosophical papers were published in 1985. Perhaps his two best-known works are *Sources of the Self* (1989) and *The Ethics of Authenticity* (1991).

Philosophical Overview

One root of Taylor's philosophy is outlined in his first work, *The Explanation of Behaviour*, which was an extended argument against behaviorism. Purely causal theories in the social sciences cannot explain intentional action, which requires an understanding of ends. Another root is his constitutive view of language. Linguistic activity involves essentially the construction of objects that have significance to an agent. This view of meaning has several implications. First, it implies a rejection of the sharp distinction between knowing subject and the known object, which underlies much traditional epistemology. Second, it shows that a person is inescapably a participant in a linguistic community and forms the basis of Taylor's communitarianism, as well as his rejection of individualism.

In *Sources of the Self*, Taylor contends that human agency requires frameworks of strong evaluation such as the Platonic conception of reason or Romantic views of self-expression. In other words, these frameworks, and the commitments they require, are part of what constitutes us as agents. One major aim of the book is to reveal how modern conceptions of the self have been constructed and have shifted.

In his work *The Ethics of Authenticity*, Taylor argues that the search for self-fulfillment is defeated by the modern notion of the self, which is atomistic, alienated, and punctual. A punctual conception views the self in terms of the ability to control rationally the world and the nonrational parts of itself. In this way, it is disengaged from itself as well as from nature, and views both instrumentally. Modernity is marked by an over emphasis on instrumental thinking and individualism, and an underevaluation of intrinsic values and the community.

Taylor's political philosophy is broadly communitarian. He distinguishes the ontological and advocacy aspects of communitarianism. According to the ontological aspect, social phenomena cannot be reduced to the aggregate behavior of individuals, and society cannot be regarded as a social contract amongst individuals. On the contrary, our individuality depends on the social. Taylor argues that what counts as good for a person has an irreducible social nature. Concerning the advocacy aspect, Taylor critiques the idea of negative freedom, which identifies freedom with the absence of interference, on the grounds that it does not recognize qualitative differences between desires, which any viable conception of freedom must.

OVERCOMING EPISTEMOLOGY

Taylor characterizes epistemology as the claim that knowledge is a correct representation of an independent reality. He claims that this view has three important implications: it implies a conception of the self as disengaged, punctual, and atomistic. In other words, in order to assess critically some of the most important assumptions of modernity, we need to critique epistemology. Taylor then shows how Heidegger and Merleau-Ponty, as well as Hegel and Wittgenstein, undermine epistemology through argumentation based on the conditions of intentionality, and he traces some of the implications of these critiques for morality.

Taylor shows how some writers, who reject the epistemological tradition, would dispute this critical evaluation of epistemology based on the conditions of intentionality. For instance, Foucault and Derrida, who favor a Nietzschian conception of the self as self-making, offer a different set of criticisms of epistemology. In a different vein, Habermas agrees with the general critique of epistemology offered in terms of the conditions of intentionality but nevertheless tries to defend a formal notion of reason.

Epistemology, once the pride of modern philosophy, seems in a bad way these days. Fifty years ago, during the heyday of logical empiricism, which was not only a powerful movement in philosophy but also immensely influential in social science, it seemed as though the very center of philosophy was its theory of knowledge. That was clearly philosophy's main contribution to a scientific culture. Science went ahead and gathered knowledge; philosophical reflection concerned the validity of claims to knowledge. The preeminence of epistemology explains a phenomenon like Karl Popper. On the strength of his reputation as a theorist of scientific knowledge, he could obtain a hearing for his intemperate views about famous philosophers of the tradition, which bore a rather distant relation to the truth. It is reminiscent of a parallel phenomenon in the arts, whereby the political opinions of a great performer or writer are often listened to with an attention and respect that their intrinsic worth hardly commands.

Of course, all this was only true of the Anglo-Saxon world. On the Continent the challenge to the epistemological tradition was already in full swing. Heidegger and Merleau-Ponty had a wide influence. It would be too simple to say that this skeptical stance has now spread to the English-speaking world. Rather it seems true to say that epistemology has come under more intensive critical scrutiny in both cultures. In France, the generation of structuralists and poststructuralists was if anything even more alienated from this whole manner of thinking than Merleau-Ponty had been. In England and America, the arguments of both generations of continental thinkers have begun to have an impact. The publication of Richard Rorty's influential *Philosophy and the Mirror of Nature*

(1979) helped both to crystallize and to accelerate a trend toward the repudiation of the whole epistemological enterprise.

In some circles it is becoming a new orthodoxy that the whole enterprise from Descartes, though Locke and Kant, and pursued by various nineteenth- and twentieth-century succession movements, was a mistake. What is becoming less and less clear, however, is what exactly it means to overcome the epistemological standpoint or to repudiate the enterprise. Just what is one trying to deny?

Rorty's book seems to offer a clear and plausible answer. The heart of the old epistemology was the belief in a *foundational* enterprise. What the positive sciences needed to complete them, on this view, was a rigorous discipline that could check the credentials of all truth claims. An alleged science could be valid only if its findings met this test; otherwise it rested on sand. Epistemology would ultimately make clear just what made knowledge claims valid, and what ultimate degree of validity they could lay claim to. (One could, of course, come up with a rather pessimistic, skeptical answer to the latter question. Epistemology was not necessarily a rationalist enterprise. Indeed, its last great defenders were and are empiricists.)

In practice, epistemologists took their cue from what they identified as the successful science of their day, all the way from Descartes's infatuation with mathematics to the contemporary vogue for reduction to physics. But the actual foundational science was not itself supposed to be dependent on any of the empirical sciences, and this obviously on pain of a circularity that would sacrifice its foundational character. Arguments about the source of valid knowledge claims were not supposed to be empirical.

From *After Philosophy: End or Transformation?* by Kenneth Baynes, James Bohman, and Thomas McCarthy, 1987. Reprinted by permission of The MIT Press as publisher.

If we follow this description, then it is clear what overcoming epistemology has to mean. It will mean abandoning foundationalism. On this view, Quine would figure among the prominent leaders of this new philosophical turn, since he proposes to "naturalize" epistemology, that is, deprive it of its a priori status and consider it as one science among others, one of many mutually interacting departments of our picture of the world. And so Rorty does seem to consider him, albeit with some reservations.

But there is a wider conception of the epistemological tradition, from whose viewpoint this last would be a rather grotesque judgment. This is the interpretation that focuses not so much on foundationalism as on the understanding of knowledge that made it possible. If I had to sum up this understanding in a single formula, it would be that knowledge is to be seen as correct representation of an independent reality. In its original form, it saw knowledge as the inner depiction of an outer reality.

The reason why some thinkers prefer to focus on this interpretation, rather than merely on the foundationalist ambitions that are ultimately (as Quine has shown) detachable from it, is that it is bound up with very influential and often not fully articulated notions about science and about the nature of human agency. Through these it connects with certain central moral and spiritual ideas of the modern age. If one's aim is, in challenging the primacy of epistemology, to challenge these ideas as well, then one has to take it up in this wider—or deeper—focus, and not simply show the vanity of the foundational enterprise.

I would like now to trace some of these connections. One of them is evident: the link between the representational conception and the new, mechanistic science of the seventeenth century. This is, in fact, twofold. On one side, the mechanization of the world picture undermined the previously dominant understanding of knowledge and thus paved the way for the modern view. The most important traditional view was Aristotle's, according to which when we come to know something, the mind (*nous*) becomes one with the object of thought. Of course this is not to say that they become materially the same thing; rather, mind and object are informed by the same *eidos*. Here was a

conception quite different from the representational model, even though some of the things Aristotle said could be construed as supporting the latter. The basic bent of Aristotle's model could much better be described as participational: being informed by the same *eidos*, the mind participates in the being of the known object, rather than simply depicting it.

But this theory totally depends on the philosophy of Forms. Once we no longer explain the way things are in terms of the species that inform them, this conception of knowledge is untenable and rapidly becomes almost unintelligible. We have great difficulty in understanding it today. The representation view can then appear as the only available alternative.

This is the negative connection between mechanism and modern epistemology. The positive one obtrudes as soon as we attempt to explain our knowing activity itself in mechanistic terms. The key to this is obviously perception, and if we see it as another process in a mechanistic universe, we have to construe it as involving as a crucial component the passive reception of impression from the external world. Knowledge then hangs on a certain relation holding between what is "out there" and certain inner states that this external reality causes in us. This construal, valid for Locke, applies just as much to the latest artificial-intelligence models of thinking. It is one of the mainsprings of the epistemological tradition.

The epistemological construal is, then, an understanding of knowledge that fits well with modern mechanistic science. This is one of its great strengths, and certainly it contributes to the present vogue of computer-based models of the mind. But that's not all this construal has going for it. It is in fact heavily overdetermined. For the representational view was also powered by the new ideals of science, and new conceptions of the excellence of thought, that arose at the same time.

This connection was central to Descartes's philosophy. It was one of his leading ideas that science, or real knowledge, doest not simply consist of a congruence between ideas in the mind and the reality outside. If the object of my musings happens to coincide with real events in the world, this doesn't give me *knowledge* of them. The congruence has to come about through a reliable method, generating well-founded confidence. Science requires certainty, and this can only be based on that undeniable clarity Descartes called *évidence*. "Toute science est une connaissance certaine et évidente," runs the opening sentence of the second rule in *Rules for the Direction of the Mind*.

Now certainty is something the mind has to generate for itself. It requires a reflexive turn, where instead of simply trusting the opinions you have acquired through your upbringing, you examine their foundation, which is ultimately to be found in your own mind. Of course, the theme that the sage has to turn away from merely current opinion, and make a more rigorous examination that leads him to science, is a very old one, going back at least to Socrates and Plato. But what is different with Descartes is the reflexive nature of this turn. The seeker after science is not directed away from shifting and uncertain opinion towards the order of the unchanging, as with Plato, but rather within, to the contents of his own mind. These have to be carefully distinguished both from external reality and from their illusory localizations in the body, so that then the correct issue of science, that is, of certainty, can be posed—the issue of the correspondence of idea to reality, which Descartes raises and then disposes of through the supposition of the *malin génie* and the proof of his negation, the veracious God.

The confidence that underlines this whole operation is that certainty is something we can generate for ourselves, by ordering our thoughts correctly—according to clear and distinct connections. This confidence is in a sense independent of the positive outcome of Descartes's argument to the existence of a veracious God, the guarantor of our science. The very fact of reflexive clarity is bound to improve our epistemic position, as long as knowledge is understood representationally. Even if we couldn't prove that the *malin génie* doesn't exist, Descartes would still be in a better position than the rest of us unreflecting minds, because he would have measured the full degree of uncertainty that hangs over all our beliefs about the world, and clearly separated out our undeniable belief in ourselves.

Descartes is thus the originator of the modern notion that certainty is the child of reflexive clarity, or the examination of our own ideas in abstraction from what they "represent," which has exercised such a powerful influence on western culture, way beyond those who share his confidence in the power of argument to prove strong these about external reality. Locke and Hume follow in the same path, although Hume goes about as far in the direction of skepticism as any modern has. Still, it remains true for Hume that we purge ourselves of our false confidence in our too-hasty extrapolations by focusing attention on their origin in our ideas. It is *there* that we see, for instance, that our beliefs in causation are based on nothing more than constant conjunction, that the self is nothing but a bundle of impressions, and so on.

This reflexive turn, which first took form in the seventeenth- and eighteenth-century "way of ideas," is indissolubly linked to modern representational epistemology. One might say it presupposes this construal of knowledge. If Plato or Aristotle were right, the road to certainty couldn't be inward—indeed, the very notion of certainty would be different: defined more in terms of the kinds of being that admit of it, rather than by the ordering of our thoughts. But I believe there is also a motivational connection in the other direction: the ideal of self-given certainty is a strong incentive to construe knowledge in such a way that our thought about the real can be distinguished from its objects and examined on its own. And this incentive has long outlived the original way of ideas. Even in an age when we no longer want to talk of Lockean "ideas" or of "sense data," where the representational view is reconstrued in terms of linguistic representations or bodily states (and these are perhaps not genuine alternatives), there is still a strong draw toward distinguishing and mapping the *formal* operations of our thinking. In certain circles is would seem that an almost boundless confidence is placed in the defining of formal relations as a way of achieving clarity and certainty about our thinking, be it in the (mis)application of rational choice theory to ethical problems or in the great popularity computer models of the mind.

The latter is an excellent example of what I called the "overdetermination" of the epistemological construal. The plausibility of the computer as a model of thinking comes partly from the fact that it is a machine, hence living "proof" that materialism can accommodate explanations in terms of intelligent performance; but partly too it comes from the widespread faith that our intelligent performances are ultimately to be understood in terms of formal operations. The computer, it has been said, is a "syntactic engine." A controversy rages over precisely this point. The most perspicuous critics of the runaway enthusiasm with the computer model, such as Hubert Dreyfus, tirelessly point out how implausible it is to understand certain of our intelligent performances in terms of a formal calculus, including our most common everyday actions, such as making our way around rooms, streets, and gardens or picking up and manipulating the objects we use. But the great difficulties that computer simulations have encountered in this area don't seem to have dimmed the enthusiasm of real believers in the model. It is as though they had been vouchsafed some revelation a priori that it *must* all be done by formal calculi. Now this revelation, I submit, comes from the depths of our modern culture and the epistemological model anchored in it, whose strength is based not just on its affinity to mechanistic science but also on its congruence to the powerful ideal of reflective, self-given certainty.

For this has to be understood as something like a moral ideal. The power of this ideal can be sensed in the following passage from Husserl's *Cartesian Meditations* (1929), all the more significant in that Husserl had already broken with some of the main theses of the epistemological tradition. He asks in the first meditation whether the "hopelessness" of the current philosophical predicament doesn't spring from our having abandoned Descartes's original emphasis on self-responsibility:

> Should the supposedly exaggerated demand for a finally possible and disengaged philosophy of presuppositionlessness or impartiality not, on the contrary, belong rather to a philosophy that in the deepest sense shapes itself in real autonomy out of finally self-produced evidences and, so, is thereby absolutely self-responsible?

The ideal of self-responsibility is foundational to modern culture. It emerges not only in our picture of the growth of modern science through the heroism of the great scientists, standing against the opinion of his age on the basis of his own self-responsible certainty—Copernicus, Galileo (he wobbled a bit before the Holy Office, but who can blame him?), Darwin, Freud. It is also closely linked to the modern ideal of freedom as self-autonomy, as the passage from Husserl implies. To be free in the modern sense is to be self-responsible, to rely on your own judgment, to find your purpose in yourself.

And so the epistemological tradition is also intricated in a certain notion of freedom, and the dignity attaching to us in virtue of this. The theory of knowledge partly draws its strength from this connection. But, reciprocally, the ideal of freedom has also drawn strength from its sensed connection with the construal of knowledge seemingly favored by modern science. From this point of view it is fateful that this notion of freedom has been interpreted as involving certain key theses about the nature of the human agent; we might call them anthropological beliefs. Whether these are in fact inseparable from the modern aspiration to autonomy is an open question, and a very important one, to which I will return briefly later. But the three connected notions I want to mention here are closely connected historically with the epistemological construal.

The first is the picture of the subject as ideally disengaged, that is, as free and rational to the extent that he has fully distinguished himself from the natural and social worlds, so that his identity is no longer to be defined in terms of what likes outside him in these worlds. The second, which flows from this, is a punctual view of the self, ideally ready as free and rational to treat these words—and even some of the features of his own character—instrumentally, as subject to change and reorganizing in order the better to secure the welfare of himself and others. The third is the social consequence of the first two: an atomistic construal of society as constituted by, or ultimately to be explained in terms of, individual purposes.

The first notion emerges originally in classical dualism, where the subject withdraws even from his own body, which he is able to look on as an object; but it continues beyond the demise of dualism in the contemporary demand for a neutral, objectifying science of human life and action. The second originates in the ideals of the government and reform of the self that have such an important place in the seventeenth century and of which Locke develops an influential version; it continues today in the tremendous force that instrumental reason and engineering models have in our social policy, medicine, psychiatry, politics, and so on. The third notion takes shape in social-contract theories of the seventeenth century, but continues not only in their contemporary successors but also in many of the assumptions of contemporary liberalism and mainstream social science.

We don't need to unpack these ideas any further to see that the epistemological tradition is connected with some of the most important moral and spiritual ideas of our civilization—and also with some of the most controversial and questionable. To challenge them is sooner or later to run up against the force of this tradition, which stands with them in a complex relation of mutual support. Overcoming or criticizing these ideas involves coming to grips with epistemology. But this means taking it in what I identified as its broad focus, the whole representational construal of knowledge, not just as the faith in foundationalism.

When we turn to the classic critiques of epistemology, we find that they have, in fact, mostly been attuned to this interpenetration of the scientific and the moral. Hegel, in his celebrated attack on this tradition in the introduction to the *Phenomenology of Spirit*, speaks of a "fear of error" that "reveals itself rather as fear of the truth." He goes on to show how this stance is bound up with a certain aspiration to individuality and separatedness, refusing what he sees as the "truth" of subject-object identity. Heidegger notoriously treats the rise of the modern epistemological standpoint as a stage in the development of a stance of domination to the world, which culminates in contemporary technological society. Merleau-Ponty draws more explicitly political connections and clarifies the alternative notion of freedom that arises from the critique of empiricism and intellectualism. The moral consequences of the devastating critique of epistemology in the later Wittgenstein are less evident, since he was strongly averse to making this kind of this explicit. But those who followed him have shown a certain affinity for the critique of disengagement, instrumental reason, and atomism.

It is safe to say that all these critics were largely motivated by a dislike of the moral and spiritual con-

sequences of epistemology and by a strong affinity for some alternative. Indeed, the connection between the scientific and the moral is generally made more evident in their work than in that of mainstream supporters of the epistemological standpoint. But an important feature of all these critiques is that they establish a new moral outlook *through* overturning the modern conception of knowledge. They don't simply register their dissidence from the anthropological beliefs associated with this conception, but show the foundations of these beliefs to be unsound, based as they are in an untenable construal of knowledge.

All four of the men I have mentioned—whom I take to be the most important critics of epistemology, the authors of the most influential forms of critique—offer new construals of knowledge. Moreover, in spite of the great differences, all four share a basic form of argument, which finds its origins in Kant and which one might call "the argument from transcendental conditions."

By this I mean something like the following. We argue the inadequacy of the epistemological construal, and the necessity of a new conception, from what we show to be the indispensable conditions of there being anything like experience or awareness of the world in the first place. Just how to characterize this reality, whose conditions we are defining, can itself be a problem, of course. Kant speaks of it simply as "experience"; but Heidegger, with his concern to get beyond subjectivistic formulations, ends up talking about the "clearing" (*Lichtung*). Where the Kantian expression focuses on the mind of the subject and the conditions of having what we can call experience, the Heideggerian formulation points us toward another facet of the same phenomenon, the fact that anything can *appear* or come to light at all. This requires that there be a being *to* whom it appears, *for* whom it is an object; it requires a knower, in some sense. But the *Lichtung* formulation focuses us on the fact (which we are meant to come to perceive as astonishing) that the knower-known complex *is* at all, rather than taking the knower for granted as "subject" and examining what makes it possible to have any knowledge or experience of a world.

For all this extremely important shift in the center of gravity of what we take as the starting point, there is a continuity between Kant and Heidegger,

Wittgenstein, or Merleau-Ponty. They all start from the intuition that this central phenomenon of experience, or the clearing, is not made intelligible on the epistemological construal, in either its empiricist or rationalist variants. That construal offers an account of stages of the knower consisting of an ultimately incoherent amalgam of two features: (a) these states (the ideas) are self-enclosed, in the sense that they can be accurately identified and described in abstraction from the "outside" world (this is, of course, essential to the whole rationalist thrust of reflexive testing of the grounds of knowledge); and (b) they nevertheless point toward and represent things in that outside world.

The incoherence of this combination may be hidden from us by the existence of things that seem to have feature (a), such as certain sensations, and even of states that seem to combine (a) and (b), such as stable illusions. But what clearly emerges from the whole argument of the last two centuries is that the condition of states of ourselves having (b) is that they cannot satisfy (a). This already began to be evident with classical empiricism in its uncertain shuffling between two definitions of the "idea" or "impression": on one reading, it was simply a content of the mind, an inner quasi-object, and it called for an object-description; on another, it had to be a claim about how things stood, and it could only be captured in a *that*-clause.

Feature (b) is what later came to be called in the Brentano-Husserl tradition "intentionality": our ideas are essentially *of* or *about* something. Here is another way of characterizing the central condition of experience or the clearing. What Kant calls transcendental conditions are conditions of intentionality, and the lines of argument that descend from Kant can be seen as exploring what these have to be.

Kant already showed that the atomistic understanding of knowledge that Hume espoused was untenable in the light of these conditions. If our states were to count as experience of an objective reality, they had to be bound together to form a coherent whole, or bound together by rules, as Kant conceived it. However much this formulation may be challenged, the incoherence of the Humean picture, which made the basis of all knowledge the reception of raw, atomic, uninterpreted data, was brilliantly demon-

strated. How did Kant show this? He established in fact an argument form that has been used by his successors even since. It can be seen as a kind of appeal to intuition. In the case of this particular refutation of Hume (which is, I believe, the main theme of the transcendental deduction in the first edition of the *Critique of Pure Reason*), he makes us aware, first, that we wouldn't have what we recognize as experience at all unless it were construable as of an object (I take this as a kind of proto-thesis of intentionality), and second, that their being of an object entails a certain relatedness among our "representations." Without this, Kant says, "it would be possible for appearances to crowd in upon the soul and yet to be such as would never allow of experience." Our perceptions "would not then belong to any experience, consequently would be without an object, merely a blind play of representations, less even than a dream."

I think this kind of appeal to intuition is better understood as an appeal to what I want to call our "agent's knowledge." As subjects effectively engaged in the activities of getting to perceive and know the world, we are capable of identifying certain conditions without which our activity would fall apart into incoherence. The philosophical achievement is to define the issues properly. Once this is done, as Kant does so brilliantly in relation to Humean empiricism, we find there is only one rational answer. Plainly we couldn't have experience of the world at all if we had to start with a swirl of uninterpreted data. Indeed, there would be no "data," because even this minimal description depends on our distinguishing what is given by some objective source from what we merely supply ourselves.

Now the four authors I mention push this argument form further, and explore conditions of intentionality that require a more fundamental break with the epistemological tradition. In particular, they push it far enough to undermine the anthropological beliefs I described earlier: beliefs in the disengaged subject, the punctual self, and atomism.

The arguments of Heidegger and Merleau-Ponty put paid to the first view. Heidegger, for instance, shows—especially in his celebrated analysis of being-in-the-world—that the condition of our forming disengaged representations of reality is that we must be already engaged in coping with our world, dealing with the things in it, at grips with them. Disengaged description is a special possibility, realizable only intermittently, of a being (*Dasein*) who is always "in" the world in another way, as an agent engaged in realizing a certain form of life. That is what we are about "first and mostly" (*zunächst und zumeist*).

The tremendous contribution of Heidegger, like that of Kant, consists in having focused the issue properly. Once this is done, we can't deny the picture that emerges. Even in our theoretical stance to the world, we are agents. Even to find out about the world and formulate disinterested pictures, we have to come to grips with it, experiment, set ourselves to observe, control conditions. But in all this, which forms the indispensable basis of theory, we are engaged as agents coping with things. It is clear that we couldn't form disinterested representations any other way.

But once we take this point, then the entire epistemological position is undermined. Obviously foundationalism goes, since our representations of things—the kinds of objects we pick out as whole, enduring entities—are grounded in the way we deal with those things. These dealings are largely inarticulate, and the project of articulating them fully is an essentially incoherent one, just because any articulative project would itself rely on a background or horizon of nonexplicit engagement with the world.

But the argument here cuts deeper. Foundationalism is undermined because you can't go on digging under our ordinary representations to uncover further, more basic representations. What you get underlying our representations of the world—the kinds of things we formulate, for instance, in declarative sentences—is not further representation but rather a certain grasp of the world that we have as agents in it. This shows the whole epistemological construal of knowledge to be mistaken. It doesn't just consist of inner pictures of outer reality, but grounds in something quite other. And in this "foundation," the crucial move of the epistemological construal—distinguishing states of the subject (our "ideas") from features of the external world—can't be effected. We can draw a neat line between my *picture* of an object and that object, but not between my *dealing* with the object and that object. It may make sense to ask us to focus on what we *believe* about something, say a football, even in the absence of that thing; but when it

comes to *playing* football, the corresponding suggestion would be absurd. The actions involved in the game can't be done without the object; they include the object. Take it away and we have something quite different—people miming a game on the stage, perhaps. The notion that our understanding of the world is grounded in our dealings with it is equivalent to the thesis that this understanding is not ultimately based on representations at all, in the sense of depictions that are separately identifiable from what they are of.

Heidegger's reflections take us entirely outside the epistemological construal. Our reflections on the conditions of intentionality show that these include our being "first and mostly" agents in the world. But this also ruins the conception of the agent as one whose ideal could be total disengagement. This turns out to be an impossibility, one that it would be destructive to attempt. We can't turn the background against which we think into an object for us. The task of reason has to be conceived quite differently: as that of articulating the background, "disclosing" what it involves. This may open the way to detaching ourselves from or altering part of what has constituted it—may, indeed, make such alteration irresistible; but only through our unquestioning reliance on the rest.

And just as the notion of the agent underpinning the ideal of disengagement is rendered impossible, so is the punctual notion of the self. Heidegger and Merleau-Ponty both show how the inescapability of the background involves an understanding of the depth of the agent, but they do so by exploring the conditions of intentionality in complementary directions. Heidegger shows how *Dasein's* world is defined by the related purposes of a certain way of life shared with others. Merleau-Ponty shows how our agency is essentially embodied and how this lived body is the locus of directions of action and desire that we never fully grasp or control by personal decision.

This critique also puts in question the third anthropological belief I singled out above, atomism. I have just mentioned how Heidegger's notion of *Dasein's* way of life is essentially that of a collectivity. A general feature of paradigm-setting critiques is that they strongly reject this third view and show instead the priority of society as the locus of the individual's identify. But crucially this point is made through an exploration of the role of language. The new theory of language that arises at the end of the eighteenth century, most notably in the work of Herder and Humboldt, not only gives a new account of how language is essential to human thought, but also places the capacity to speak not simply in the individual but primarily in the speech community. This totally upsets the outlook of the mainstream epistemological tradition. Now arguments to this effect have formed part of the refutation of the atomism that has proceeded through an overturning of standard modern epistemology.

Important examples of arguments of this kind are Hegel's in the first chapter of the *Phenomenology of Spirit,* against the position he defines as "sensible certainly," where he shows both the indispensability of language and its holistic character; and Wittgenstein's famous demonstrations of the uselessness of "ostensive definitions," where he makes plain the crucial role played by language in identifying the object and the impossibility of a purely private language. Both are, I believe, excellent examples of arguments that explore the conditions of internationality and show their conclusions to be inescapable.

It is evident that these arguments give us a quite different notion of what it is to overcome epistemology from those that merely eschew foundationalism. We can measure the full gulf comparing any of the four—Heidegger, perhaps, or Merleau-Ponty—with the Quine of "Epistemology Naturalized." It is plain that the essential elements of the epistemological construal have remained standing in Quine, and not surprisingly therefore the central anthropological beliefs of the tradition. Disengagement emerges in his "taste for desert landscapes"; the punctual self in his behaviorism; and atomism in his particular brand of political conservatism. In face of difference of this magnitude, a question arises concerning what it means to "overcome epistemology."

A picture has been emerging here of what this ought to be—a tendentious one, I freely admit. It accepts the wider or deeper definition of the task: overcoming the distorted anthropological beliefs through a critique and correction of the construal of knowl-

edge that is interwoven with them and has done so much to give them undeserved credit. Otherwise put: through a clarification of the conditions of intentionality, we come to a better understanding of what we are as knowing agents—and hence also as language beings—and thereby gain insight into some of the crucial anthropological questions that underpin our moral and spiritual beliefs.

For all its radical break with the tradition, this kind of philosophy would in one respect by in continuity with it. It would be carrying further the demand for self-clarity about our nature as knowing agents, by adopting a better and more critically defensible notion of what this entails. Instead of searching for an impossible foundational justification of knowledge or hoping to achieve total reflexive clarity about the bases of our beliefs, we would now conceive this self-understanding as awareness about the limits and conditions of our knowing, an awareness that would help us to overcome the illusions of disengagement and atomic individuality that are constantly being generated by a civilization founded on mobility and instrumental reason.

We could understand this as carrying the project of modern reason, even of "self-responsible" reason, further by giving it a new meaning. This is how Husserl conceived the critical project in his last great lectures on the "crisis of European science," given in Vienna in 1935. Husserl thinks of us as struggling to realize a fundamental task, that of the "europäischen Geist," whose goal is to achieve the fullness of reflexive clarity. We should see ourselves as philosopher-functionaries ("Funktionäre der neuzeitlichen philosophischen Menschheit"). The first foundation (*Urstiftung*) of the European tradition points to a final foundation (*Endstiftung*), and only in the latter is the former fully revealed:

> Only through the final establishment can the unified directedness of all philosophies and philosophers open up. From here elucidation can be attained which enables us to understand past thinkers in a way that they could never have understood themselves.

Husserl's hope here sounds ridiculously overstated, which may have something to do with his having failed to push through his critique of foundationalism to the end. Overstatement has played an important role, as we will see, in casting discredit on the task as I have outlined it. But if we purge Husserl's formulation of the prospect of a "final foundation" where absolute apodicticity would at last be won, if we concentrate merely on the gain for reason in coming to understand what is illusory in the modern epistemological project and in articulating the insights about us that flow from this, then the claim to have taken the modern project of reason a little farther, and to have understood our forbears a little better than they understood themselves, is not so unbelievable.

What reflection in this direction would entail is already fairly well known. It involves, first, conceiving reason differently, as including—alongside the familiar forms of the Enlightenment—a new department, whose excellence consists in our being able to articulate the background of our lives perspicuously. We can use the word "disclosure" for this, following Heidegger. And along with this goes a conception of critical reasoning, of especial relevance for moral thinking, that focuses on the nature of transitions in our thought, of which "immanent critique" is only the best-known example.

In moral thought, what emerges from this critique is a rejection of moralities based purely on instrumental reason, such as utilitarianism; and also critical distance from those based on a punctual notion of the self, such as the various derivations of Kant. The critique of John Rawls's theory by Michael Sandel, in the name of a less "thin" theory of the agent, is an excellent example of this. In social theory, the result is a rejection of atomist theories, of reductive causal theories (such as "vulgar" Marxism or sociobiology), and of theories that cannot accommodate intersubjective meaning. Social science is seen as being closer to historiography of a certain kind. In politics, the antiatomist thrust of the critique makes it hostile to certain forms of contemporary conservatism, but also to radical doctrines of nonsituated freedom. I believe there is a natural affinity between this critique, with its stress on situated freedom and the roots of our identity in community, on the one hand, and the civic humanist tradition on the other, as the works of a number of writers, from Humboldt to Arendt, testify.

It might seem now as though everything should run on smoothly, toward a set of anthropological conclusions with a certain moral-political hue. But in fact all this is hotly contested, not just by those who wish to defend the epistemological tradition, which would be understandable, but by those who consider themselves its critics. Foremost among these are a range of thinkers who have defined themselves in relation to a certain reading of Nietzsche. The most interesting and considerable of them, in my opinion, is Foucault. In keeping with the themes of this chapter, we can perhaps get most directly to the basis of their dissent if we go to the moral or spiritual outlook they wish to defend. In the case of Foucault this became relatively clear at the end of his life. He rejected the concept of punctual self, which could take an instrumental stance toward its life and character—this is indeed what arises out of the practices and "truths" of this disciplinary society he painted in such repellent color (whatever protestation of neutrality accompanied the depiction.) But he couldn't accept the rival notion of a deep or authentic self that arises out of the critical traditions of Hegel and, in another way, Heidegger or Merleau-Ponty. This seemed to him another prison. He rejected both in favor of a Nietzschean notion of the self as potentially self-making, the self as a work of art, a central conception of an "aesthetics of existence."

Something analogous, but on a much more frivolous level, seems to animate some of the poststructuralists thinkers—Derrida, for instance. Paradoxically, for all the talk of the "end of subjectivity," one of the strong attractions of this kind of position is precisely the license it offers to subjectivity, unfettered by anything in the nature of a correct interpretation or an irrecusable meaning of either life or text, to effect its own transformations, to invent meanings. Self-making is again primary.

Nietzsche's insights into the way in which language imposes order an our world, into theory as a kind of violence, were crucial to all view of this kind. It offers an alternative to the kind of possible critique of epistemology in which we discover something deeper and more valid about ourselves in carrying it through—the kind I have been describing. Instead it attacks the very aspiration to truth, as this is usually understood. All epistemic orders are imposed, and the epistemological construal is just another one of those orders. It has no claim to ultimate correctness, not because it has been shown inadequate by an exploration of the conditions of intentionality, but because all such claims are bogus. They mistake an act of power for a revelation of truth. Husserl's *Urstiftung* takes on a quite different and more sinister air.

Clearly this is the critique of epistemology that is most compatible with the spiritual stance of self-making. It makes the will primary in a radical way, whereas the critique through conditions of intentionality purports to show us more of what we really are like—to show us, as it were, something of our deep or authentic nature as selves. So those who take the Nietzschean road are naturally very reluctant to understand the critique as a *gain* in reason. They would rather deny that reason can have anything to do with our choices of what to be.

This is not to say that they propose the end of epistemology as a radical break. Just as the critique through conditions of intentionality represents a kind of continuity-through-transformation in the tradition of self-critical reason, so the Nietzschean refusal represents a continuity-through-transformation of another facet of the modern identity—the primacy of the will. This played an important role in the rise of modern science and its associated epistemological standpoint; in a sense, a voluntaristic anthropology, with its roots in a voluntaristic theology, prepared the ground over centuries for the seventeenth-century revolution, most notably in the form of nominalism. It is a crucial point of division among moderns, what we think of primacy of the will. This is one of the issues at stake between these two conceptions of what it means to overcome the epistemological tradition.

Although this represents perhaps the most dramatic opposition among critics of epistemology, it is far from exhausting the field. Hebermas, for instance, has staked out a position equivalent to neither. Against the neo-Nietzscheans, he would strongly defend the tradition of critical reason, but he has his own grounds for distrusting Heideggerian disclosure and wants instead to hold on to a formal understanding of reason and, in consequence, a procedural ethic, although purged of the monological errors of earlier variants. He has drawn heavily on the critique of epistemology in the four authors mentioned above, but fears for the fate of a truly universal and critical ethic if one were to go all the way with this critique.

How do we adjudicate this kind of dispute? How do we decide what it really means to overcome epistemology? I can't hope to decide the issue here, only to make a claim as to how it should be settled. In order to define this better, I want to return to the most dramatic dispute, that between the neo-Nietzscheans and the defenders of critical reason.

It seems to me that, whoever, is ultimately right, the dispute has to be fought on the terrain of the latter. The Nietzschean position also stands and falls with a certain construal of knowledge: that it is relative to various ultimately imposed "regimes of truth," to use Foucault's expression. This has to show itself to be superior construal to that which emerges from the exploration of the condition of intentionality. Does it?

Certainly the Nietzschean conception has brought important insights: no construal is quite innocent, something is always suppressed; and what is more, some interlocutors are always advantaged relative to others, for any language. But the issue is whether this settles the matter of truth between construals. Does it mean that there can be no talk of epistemic gain in passing from one construal to another? That there is such a gain is the claim of those exploring the conditions of intentionality. This claim doesn't stand and fall with a naive, angelic conception of philosophical construals as utterly uninvolved with power. Where is the argument that will show the more radical Nietzchean claim to be true and the thesis of critical reason untenable?

I regret to say that one hears very little serious argument in this domain. Neo-Nietzscheans seem to think that they are dispensed from it since it is already evident or, alternatively, that they are debarred from engaging in it on pain of compromising their position. Derrida and his followers seem to belong to the first category. The main weight of argument is carried here by an utterly caricatural view of the alternative as involving a belief in a kind of total self-transparent clarity, which would make even Hegel blush. The rhetoric deployed around this has the effect of obscuring the possibility that there might be a third alternative to the two rather dotty ones on offer; and as long as you go along with this, the Derridian view seems to win as the least mad, albeit by a hair.

Others try to argue on behalf of Foucault that he couldn't enter the argument concerning construals of knowledge without abandoning his Nietzschean position, that there is nothing to *argue* between them. True enough, but then the issue whether there is something to argue itself demands some kind of support. Something can surely be said about that. Indeed, much *has* been said, by Nietzsche for one, and some also by Foucault—in talking for instance of "regimes of truth"; the question is whether it is really persuasive or involves a lot of slippery slides and evasion.

In short, the arguments for not arguing seriously are uniformly bad. And in fact Foucault did on one occasion make a serious attempt to engage with the exploration of the conditions of intentionality, and that was in the latter part (chapter 9) of *The Order of Things*, where he talks about the invention of Man and the "transcendental-empirical double." This was admittedly prior to his last, much more centrally

Nietzschean phase, but it can be seen as preparing the ground for this, as indeed Dreyfus and Rabinow see it.

The arguments here seem to me much more to build on the Heideggerian and Merleau-Pontyan critique against Kant rather than to challenge this critique. And the arguments, if valid, would have the consequence that nothing coherent could be said at all about the conditions of intentionality. I can't see how this could fail to undercut the Nietzschean view as well. In *The Order of Things* Foucault takes refuge in a species of structuralism, which is meant to avoid this question altogether. But he abandons it soon afterwards, and we are left uncertain where the argument is meant to take us. In general among neo-Nietzscheans, however, an atmosphere reigns in which this issue is felt as already settled. We are exhorted by Lyotard not to take metanarratives seriously any more, but the argument for this seems to rely on caricature.

If I am right, the issue is far from settled. And yet at stake in this struggle over the corpse of epistemology are some of the most important spiritual issues of our time. The question, what it is to overcome epistemology, turns out to be of more than just historical interest.

STUDY QUESTIONS: TAYLOR, *OVERCOMING EPISTEMOLOGY*

1. According to Taylor, what is the epistemological tradition?
2. Descartes is the originator of which notion? Historically, why is this important?
3. In the modern sense, to be free is to be what? How does this view of freedom relate to epistemology?
4. What are the three connected notions that Taylor mentions? For what purpose does he mention them? What is the punctual view of the self?
5. Who are the four authors that Taylor mentions as the most important critics of epistemology? What form of argument do they share?
6. What is the important point that Heidegger's notion of 'clearing' points toward? Why is it important?
7. What do the views of Heidegger and Merleau-Ponty 'put paid to'? More positively, what does this show us? Why does this undermine foundationalism?
8. According to Taylor, how do the views of Heidegger and Merleau-Ponty undercut the notion of the punctual self? What undermines the idea of atomism?
9. Why does Taylor compare Heidegger and Quine? What are the differences he points to?
10. Why does Taylor contend that overcoming epistemology requires clarification of the conditions of intentionality? What insights do we hope to gain from such a clarification?
11. What does Taylor mean by 'disclosure' and 'immanent critique'? Why are they important?
12. According to Taylor, what emerges from this critique in terms of morality?
13. How does Taylor portray the differences between Foucault's conception of the self and Heidegger's?

14. How does Taylor characterize the 'Nietzschian road'? What are the main differences between it and the path that he is advocating?
15. What points does Taylor make about Habermas?
16. What are the main conclusions of his article?

Philosophical Bridges: Taylor's Influence

Three aspects of Taylor's work have been especially influential. First, his idea that the self is historically constructed has had an impact among some philosophers. Second, there is his critique of modernity. *The Ethics of Authenticity* was published originally in Canada with the title *The Malaises of Modernity*. Finally, there is his work on multiculturalism and the politics of recognition. Taylor argues that the valuing of cultural differences contradicts the modern idea of universal respect that ignores differences. Within a liberal tradition, the claims of different cultural perspectives to be recognized as of equal worth require some form of relativism. In other words, the individualism of liberal thought is inadequate for dealing with issues of multiculturalism, which require the idea of communicative interaction and engagement within a community.

Philosophical Bridges: The Influence of Twentieth-Century Philosophers

The influence of twentieth-century philosophy lies perhaps in the fact that it covers a wealth of different themes and contains a great diversity of views and approaches, even more than any earlier period. Philosophy has bloomed. First, in the last decades of the century, the analytic and continental traditions have influenced each other more directly. Whereas earlier continental philosophy tended to concern itself with existential life and death issues, analytic philosophers were disposed to focus on detailed questions related to the analysis of linguistic meaning and the epistemology of the sciences. There is now much more cross-fertilization and overlap between these two traditions, as well as the emergence of new feminist and cross-cultural approaches.

Second, philosophy has begun to interact more energetically with other disciplines in interesting and potentially fruitful ways. For instance, consider Habermas' work within the philosophy of the social sciences, Kuhn's explanations in the history of the natural sciences, Rawls' political theory, and Derrida's work in literary theory. These are only a tiny sample of philosophy's interactions with other disciplines in the twentieth-century.

Third, while some philosophy became rather technical in the twentieth century, philosophers have also addressed many issues of practical everyday concern. In this regard, we might consider the works of Heidegger and Sartre, as well as the expanding fields of applied ethics and the philosophy of law.

Fourth, toward the end of the century, philosophers have become engaged increasingly in sociopolitical concerns. For instance, there is the flourishing field of feminist philosophy. There are many philosophers writing in the area of ecology, as well as those concerned with technology. There are philosophers concerned with race, diversity, and cross-cultural comparisons, as well as those working in the areas of poverty and development.

BIBLIOGRAPHY

RORTY

Primary

Consequences of Pragmatism, University of Minnesota Press, 1982

Contingency, Irony and Solidarity, Cambridge University Press, 1988

Objectivity, Relativism and Truth, Cambridge University Press, 1991

Philosophy and Social Hope, Penguin, 2000

Philosophy and the Mirror of Nature, Princeton University Press, 1979

Truth and Progress, Cambridge University Press, 1998

Secondary

Brandom, Robert, ed., *Rorty and His Critics*, Blackwell, 2000

Malachowski, Alan, ed., *Reading Rorty*, Blackwell, 1990

Nielson, Kai, *After the Demise of the Tradition: Rorty, Critical Theory, and the Fate of Philosophy*, Westview Press, 1991

Saatkamp, H. R., ed., *Rorty and Pragmatism: The Philosopher Responds to His Critics*, Vanderbilt University Press, 1995

TAYLOR

Primary

The Ethics of Authenticity, Harvard University Press, 1991

Multiculturalism: Examining the Politics of Recognition, Princeton University Press, 1994

Philosophical Arguments, Harvard University Press, 1995

Philosophical Papers (I and II), Cambridge University Press, 1985

Sources of the Self, Harvard University Press, 1989

Secondary

Abbey, Ruth, *Charles Taylor: Philosophy Now*, Princeton University Press, 2000

Tully, J., and Weinstock, D., *Philosophy in an Age of Pluralism: The Philosophy of Charles Taylor in Question*, Cambridge University Press, 1994

◆ SOURCES ◆

SECTION I: LOGICAL ATOMISM

Page 8: Russell, Bertrand, 'Descriptions,' in *Introduction to Mathematical Philosophy*, MacMillan, 1938, 167–80 (complete).

Page 17: Wittgenstein, Ludwig, *Tractatus Logicus Philosophicus*, from D. Kolak, *Wittgenstein's Tractatus*, Mayfield, 1998, selections from Preface and Propositions:

1, 1.1, 1.11, 1.12, 1.13; 1.2, 1.21;

2, 2.01–2.0122, 2.01231, 2.0124, 2.013–2.0272; 2.03–2.063, **2.1,** 2.11–2.19, **2.2,** 2.22–2.225

3, 3.001–3.02, 3.03–3.032, 3.04, **3.1,** 3.11–3.144, **3.2,** 3.201–3.21, 3.22–3.24, 3.25–3.263 **3.3,** 3.31, 3.318–3.321, 3.323–3.325, 3.33, 3.332–3.334, **3.4, 3.5**

4, 4.001–4.011, 4.02–4.023, 4.024–4.03, 4.04–4.041, 4.05–4.06, **4.1,** 4.11–4.114, 4.1213, 4.125, **4.2,** 4.21–4.2211, 4.23–4.241, 4.25–4.26, **4.3,** 4.31, **4.4,** 4.41, 4.46–4.462, **4.5,** 4.51,

5, 5.01, **5.1,** 5.101, 5.12, 5.13–5.1362, 5.14–5.143, 5.152, **5.2,** 5.21–5.23, 5.24, 5.25, **5.3,** 5.31, 5.32, **5.4,** 5.41–5.42, 5.45, 5.452, 5.46, 5.47, 5.471–5.4711, 5.473–5.4732, **5.5,** 5.501–5.51, 5.52, 5.53–5.5301, 5.54–5.5422, **5.5, 5.6,** 5.61–5,641

6, 6.001–6.031, **6.1,** 6.11, 6.12, 6.124, 6.127, **6.2,** 6.21–6.22, 6.23, 6.24–6.241, **6.3,** 6.31–6.36, 6.362–6.375, **6.4,** 6.41–6.4312, 6.432–6.45, **6.5,** 6.51–6.54, and **7.**

SECTION II: PRAGMATISM

Page 40: Dewey, John, *The Quest for Certainty*, Capricorn Books, 1960, selections from ch. 10, 'The Construction of the Good,' selections from 254–86.

SECTION III: LOGICAL POSITIVISM

Page 55: Carnap, Rudolf:

1. With Hahn and Neurath, *The Scientific Conception of the World: The Vienna Circle*, from Neurath, *Empiricism and Sociology*, Dordrecht Kluwer Publishers, 1973, 299–318.

2. *The Logical Structure of the World*, University of California Press, 1967, trans. Rolf George, selections from 5–10,

11–15, 19–21, 28–30, 31–32, 37–41, 191–94, 195–200, and 201–13.

Page 88: Ayer, A. J., 'The Elimination of Metaphysics,' from *Language, Truth and Logic*, Dover, 1952, selections from ch. 1, p. 33–45.

SECTION IV: ORDINARY LANGUAGE PHILOSOPHY

Page 98: Wittgenstein, Ludwig, *Philosophical Investigations*, Blackwell, 1958, trans. E. Anscombe, selections from Preface; paragraphs 1–3, 5, 6, 8, 11, 13–15, 17, 18, 19, 23, 28, 38, 43, 65–67, 84, 85, 87, 88, 90, 98, 99, 102, 103, 109, 115, 116, 119, 123–28, 149–51, 185–88, 198, 199, 201, 202, 206, 214–19, 224, 225, 231–45, 248, 249, 250, 252, 253, 255–61, 265, 266, 269, 271, 274, 275, 278, 279, 292, 293, 295–98, 304–9, 311, 353, 381, 384, 412, 414–16, 431, 432, 445, 464, 485, 580, 593, and 599.

Page 117: Ryle, Gilbert, 'Descartes Myth,' from *Concept of Mind*, Hutchinson, 1949, ch. 1 (complete).

SECTION V: ANALYTIC PHILOSOPHY

Page 125: Quine, W. V. O.:

1. 'Two Dogmas of Empiricism,' from *From a Logical Point of View*, Harvard University Press, 1953 (complete).

2. 'Reasons for the Indeterminacy of Translation,' from *Journal of Philosophy*, 67, no. 6 (1970): 178–83 (complete).

Page 147: Goodman, Nelson, 'Grue and Bleen,' from *Fact, Fiction and Forecast*, Bobbs-Merrill, 1965.

Page 157: Kuhn, Thomas, *The Structure of Scientific Revolutions*, University of Chicago Press, 1970, selections from chs. 9 and 10.

Page 170: Davidson, Donald:

1. 'Truth and Meaning,' from *Inquiries into Truth and Interpretation*, Oxford University Press, 1984, ch. 2, 17–36 (complete).

2. 'Mental Events,' from *Essays on Actions and Events*, Oxford University Press, 1980, ch. 11, 'Mental Events' (complete).

Page 193: Rawls, John, *A Theory of Justice*, Oxford University Press, 1971, selections from sections 1, 3, 4, 11, 24, and 46 (selections from pages 3–5, 11–14, 15–16, 17–21, 60–62, 63–65, 136–39, 302–3).

Page 206: Putnam, Hilary, 'Why There Isn't a Ready Made World' in *Realism and Reason*, vol. 3 of *Philosophical Papers*, 205–28.

SECTION VI: PHENOMENOLOGY AND EXISTENTIALISM

Page 225: Husserl, Edmund, *Ideas: General Introduction to Pure Phenomenology*, George Allen and Unwin, New York, trans. W. Boyce Gibson, 1952, selections from 41, 43–46, 96–97, 101–4, 105, 107–11, 112, 114, 115–17, 119–23, 123–25, 126, 128–31, 133–35, 136–37, 138, 140, 147, 148, 149–53, 154–55, 158–62, 168–70, 241–43, 257–61, 265–66, and 279.

Page 247: Heidegger, Martin:
Being and Time, State University of New York Press, 1996, trans. Joan Stambaugh, selections from xix, 3–12, 23–24, 31–35, 37, 38, 39–47, 49–53, 55, 62–69, 71, 107–8, 110–14, 117–21, 123, 125, 126–31, 134–36, 138–44, 156, 158–59, 161–62, 164–66, 169–81, 183, and 186.

Page 274: Sartre, Jean-Paul, *Being and Nothingness: An Essay on Phenomenological Ontology*, trans. Hazel Barnes, Philosophical Library, 1956. Selections from Introduction and 3–6, 21–29, 31–33, 34–44, 47–50, 55–67, 70, 431, 433–36, 438–41, 442–44, 557–58, 563–66, 567–70, 571–75, 617–19, 620–21, and 625–27.

Page 303: De Beauvoir, Simone, *The Second Sex*, Alfred A. Knopf, 1952 (trans. H. M. Parshley), Conclusion (selections).

Page 312: Merleau-Ponty, Maurice, *Phenomenology of Perception*, Routledge, 1996 (trans. Colin Smith) selections from Preface and 3–8, 13–15, 19, 21–24, 52–53, 54–55, 56–58, 59–63, 70–72, 146–47, 198–99, 203, and 206.

SECTION VII: HERMENEUTICS AND POSTMODERNISM

Page 337: Gadamer, Hans Georg, *Truth and Method*, translation rev. J. Weinsheimer and D. Marshall, Continuum Press, 1989, selections from Introduction (xxi–xxv) and 3–5, 9, 97–100, 161–65, 265–71, 293–97, 332, 358–62, 369–70, 373–75, 377–79, 383–86, 389–92, 395–99, 401–3, 433, 445–48, 450–53, 490–91.

Page 367: Habermas, Jürgen, *Moral Consciousness and Communicative Action*, trans. C. Lenhardt and S. Nicholsen, MIT Press, 1990, selections from 21–32, 43–45, 47, 50, 57–60, 62–68, 76–83, 86–98.

Page 383: Foucault, Michel:
1. *Power and Knowledge*, selections from 109–10, 112–13, 115–22, 124–28, 130–33, Pantheon Books, 1980.
2. Technologies of the Self, from *Ethics, Subjectivity and Truth*, New Press, ed. P. Rabinow, 1997, 223–49 (selections).

Page 400: Derrida, Jacques, *Positions*, University of Chicago Press, 1981, trans. Alan Bass, selections from 6–9, 12–13, 17–23, 24–29, 35–36, 39–44, 46–47, 49–51, 52–55, 56–57, and 58–60.

SECTION VIII: RECENT NORTH AMERICAN THINKERS

Page 422: Rorty, Richard, 'Solidarity or Objectivity?' *Objectivity, Relativism and Truth*, Cambridge University Press, 1991, 21–34.

Page 431: Taylor, Charles, 'Overcoming Epistemology,' *Philosophical Arguments*, Harvard University Press, 1995, 1–19.